SLAVE THI
THE ROMAN

Roman comedy evolved early in the war-torn 200s BCE. Troupes of lower-class and slave actors traveled through a militarized landscape full of displaced persons and the newly enslaved; together, the actors made comedy to address mixed-class, hybrid, multilingual audiences. Surveying the extant fragments of early comedy and the whole of the Plautine corpus, where slaves are central figures, this book is grounded in the history of slavery and integrates theories of resistant speech, humor, and performance. Part I shows how actors joked about what people feared – natal alienation, beatings, sexual abuse, hard labor, hunger, poverty – and how street-theater forms confronted debt, violence, and war loss. Part II catalogues the onstage expression of what people desired: revenge, honor, free will, legal personhood, family, marriage, sex, food, free speech; a way home, through memory; and manumission, or escape – all complicated by the actors' maleness. Comedy starts with anger.

AMY RICHLIN is Professor of Classics at the University of California, Los Angeles. She is a path-breaking historian of Roman sexuality. From the time of her first book, *The Garden of Priapus: Sexuality and Aggression in Roman Humor* (1983), she has searched for the subcultures of muted groups and outgroups outside the literary canon. An outspoken feminist, she edited *Pornography and Representation in Greece and Rome* (1992) and co-edited *Feminist Theory and the Classics* (1993); her essays on Roman women's history are collected in *Arguments with Silence* (2014). Since 2000, she has been working on Roman comedy, and addressed the need to teach about ancient Orientalism in *Rome and the Mysterious Orient: Three Plays by Plautus* (2005). *Slave Theater in the Roman Republic: Plautus and Popular Comedy* advances her endeavor to find the forgotten, bringing slave voices back to history.

SLAVE THEATER IN THE ROMAN REPUBLIC

Plautus and Popular Comedy

AMY RICHLIN

University of California, Los Angeles

CAMBRIDGE
UNIVERSITY PRESS

CAMBRIDGE
UNIVERSITY PRESS

University Printing House, Cambridge CB2 8BS, United Kingdom

One Liberty Plaza, 20th Floor, New York, NY 10006, USA

477 Williamstown Road, Port Melbourne, VIC 3207, Australia

314-321, 3rd Floor, Plot 3, Splendor Forum, Jasola District Centre, New Delhi - 110025, India

79 Anson Road, #06-04/06, Singapore 079906

Cambridge University Press is part of the University of Cambridge.

It furthers the University's mission by disseminating knowledge in the pursuit of education, learning and research at the highest international levels of excellence.

www.cambridge.org
Information on this title: www.cambridge.org/9781316606438
DOI: 10.1017/9781316585467

First published 2017
First paperback edition 2019

A catalogue record for this publication is available from the British Library

Library of Congress Cataloging in Publication data
Names: Richlin, Amy, 1951– author.
Title: Slave theater in the Roman Republic : Plautus and popular comedy / Amy Richlin.
Description: New York : Cambridge University Press, 2017.
Identifiers: LCCN 2017037837 | ISBN 9781107152311 (hardback)
Subjects: LCSH: Theater – Rome – History. | Latin drama (Comedy) – History and criticism. |
Actors – Rome. | Th eater and society – Rome – History. |
Slavery – Rome – Social conditions. | Civilization, Classical.
Classification: LCC PA6073 .D86 2016 | DDC 792.0937090/14–dc23
LC record available at https://lccn.loc.gov/2017037837

ISBN 978-1-107-15231-1 Hardback
ISBN 978-1-316-60643-8 Paperback

For Sandra Joshel

Contents

Tables

x

Preface

I wrote this book with a photograph of Eduard Fraenkel in front of me, a photograph that used to sit on the desk of my teacher, Gordon Williams, who was Fraenkel's friend. I thought of them as I worked; I wrote for them, a book they are not here to see. Apart from urging me to work harder, they reminded me daily of the vast wealth of earlier scholarship on the *palliata*. The Plautine corpus is a universe; every detail of it opens up questions examined by a long genealogy of scholars. A book that took all their remarks into account would be many times the length of this one, already long enough, but I am truly sorry for the omissions. Readers should note that the text itself upon which my arguments are based is a porous one; a century-old collection of actors' notes and performance transcripts assembled by scholars in the first century BCE has fascinated scholars ever since, so that our understanding today depends on two thousand years of scholarship, most of which is now in remote storage, but which still calls out to engage in the ongoing conversation. My goal is to understand what happened between actors and audiences in Latium in the 200s BCE, and in that pursuit I have had much help. It is a pleasure now to give due thanks.

First, to Lon Grabowski, who had to live with this all these years: for countless trips to the movies, for conversations about everything from Bugs Bunny to bread riots, and for a laugh so great it makes actors play to him.

To the readers for the press, for their manifold generosity: their time, their erudition, their tact, their thoroughness (it was clear that they read with the Latin text open beside them). Special thanks to the third reader, who, unpersuaded by the book's main argument, still fully supported publication while providing a detailed list of points of contention. This is a model few could live up to; I believe there is something about the spirit of Plautus that evokes a generous spirit in those who study him.

Hence many thanks to the generous community of scholars working on Roman comedy, especially Dorota Dutsch, C. W. Marshall, Timothy

Moore, Niall Slater, and above all Sharon James, whose own book was nearing completion simultaneously and whose lively emails sparked lively ideas. My thanks and love to Mary-Kay Gamel, David Konstan, and James Tatum, for whose help and support I have had occasion to be grateful many times over the years. Kathleen McCarthy has been ever gracious in the face of opposing argument, as has Peter G. McC. Brown, who very kindly sent me the text of his 2013 Glasgow conference paper.

Rebecca Langlands, luckily for me, spent two terms at UCLA in 2014–15 as Palevsky Visiting Professor, and I learned much from her about political culture and popular memory; she was good enough to send me early drafts of her forthcoming book on Roman exemplarity. Alex Dressler likewise sent me his essay on Plautus, property, and aesthetics, which appeared just in time for too-brief mention here, a token of some red-letter comic conversations.

Several eminent historians took the time to help with bibliography and advice, particularly John Bodel, Tim Cornell, Arthur Eckstein, Peter Garnsey, and Brent Shaw: giving directions, as it were, to a stranger in town, a most friendly deed. Jessica Clark shared her experience in the fields of Roman political culture and military history; Peter Holliday shared his expertise in the public art of the mid-Republic; David Lewis and Kostas Vlassopoulos both sent me copies of illuminating work in progress on ancient slavery and the writing of its history. I owe a special debt to Keith Bradley, who was a reader for the 2014 *Classical Antiquity* article that laid out this book's main argument and whose influence pervades the bibliography and, I hope, the argumentation.

Several experts read chapters and provided detailed comments: Timothy Moore read chapter 3 and saved me from numerous errors; Marilyn Skinner read chapter 5 with her usual acumen and care; Matthew Leigh read chapter 7 with insightful erudition, as always. I cannot thank him enough for his constant support and exchange of ideas throughout this project, not only as a reader for the *CA* article but back at least to 2006.

My UCLA colleagues provided essential consultation and support: Sander Goldberg, who read the first draft in 2009 with salutary stringency; Mario Telò, who shared his own work in progress on Plautus; and most of all Brent Vine, who read chapter 6 and answered endless questions. All points linguistic in this book depend on his tutelage; associated errors are obviously mine. I am thankful to the university for a sabbatical in the fall of 2015; UCLA also provided two excellent research assistants, Grace Gillies and Kristie Keller, who checked chapter 1, the whole bibliography, and the timeline (Appendix 1). Since I kept adding bibliography until the manuscript was torn from my grip, I doubtless imported more errors, despite their best efforts: may they someday have assistants as good as they were. The students in several UCLA courses on comedy taught me a lot about what is funny and why, particularly Grace Gillies, with her love of the low, and Hans Bork, with his love of language – now both doctoral candidates: may they finish their dissertations and go on to glory.

Thanks to Dan-el Padilla Peralta for letting me read work in progress, and to my former students Caroline Cheung, Henry Gruber, and Katie Tardio, for help in understanding the historical significance of the distribution of pottery; also to my fellow panelists at the 2016 SCS meeting – Page duBois, Matthew Leigh, Ellen O'Gorman, William Owens, Dan-el Padilla Peralta – as well as to Peter Rose for trenchant comment from the audience and subsequent comments on chapter 1.

My old friend Thomas Fedorek helped me find Dr. Olivier Pansiéri when all academic channels failed. My heartfelt thanks to Dr. Pansiéri for writing to me about his father, who died, as he says, too young.

It took some doing to produce this book, and I am grateful to Gabe Moss for the map of the Trerus Valley, to Rachel Kamins for formatting the timeline, and to Michael Sharp and the team at Cambridge University Press for ever-ready help. Copy-editor Jane Robson made many tidy improvements. Special thanks to the peerless Jodi Haraldson for formatting and merging the manuscript in the autumn of 2016, a bad time for us all.

Thanks to fellow participants at the 2009 Langford Conference in Tallahassee: C. W. Marshall, Kathleen McCarthy, Timothy Moore, Niall Slater, John Starks, and especially Kenneth Reckford for his warm hospitality and his belief in the project. Thanks to fellow participants at the 2013 Glasgow conference on "Popular Comedy" organized by Costas Panayotakis and Ian Ruffell: a galvanizing experience. Thanks to Stavros Frangoulidis and Stephen Harrison for inviting me to the Eighth Trends in Classics conference in 2014 at Thessaloniki, and to Lawrence Tritle for including me in the 2013 conference on "The Many Faces of War" at Loyola, where I had the chance to speak with Peter Meineck and the poet Michael Casey. Thanks as well to Stephen Harrison and Sebastian Matzner for the invitation to participate in the "Complex Inferiorities" conference at Corpus Christi College, Oxford, in 2014, where I had the benefit of Ellen O'Gorman's comments on the levels of abjection in the plays.

This work has been presented on several continents and I am grateful to the audiences at all of them: at the American Philological Association Annual Meeting in 2011 (Timothy Moore's landmark seminar on the audience of the *palliata*), Boston University, Claremont Graduate

University, St Anne's College, Oxford, the Society for Classical Studies Annual Meeting in 2015 (panel on "The Other Side of Victory," organized by Jessica Clark), Stanford University (the great "Cargo Culture" conference in 2014), SUNY Buffalo, UNESP (Assis, Brazil, with special thanks to the members of my *minicurso*), University of British Columbia, University of California at Davis, University of California at Santa Barbara, University of North Carolina at Chapel Hill (the 2012 NEH Institute run by Sharon James and Timothy Moore), and the University of Southern California. I was honored by invitations to present this work in the Agnes Kirsopp Lake Michels Lecture at Bryn Mawr College in 2006; the Gail A. Burnett Lecture in Classics at San Diego State University in 2006; the Frank M. Snowden Lecture at Howard College in 2014; the Brackenridge Distinguished Visiting Lecture at the University of Texas at San Antonio in 2014; the Lauritsen Lecture in History at the University of Minnesota in 2015; and a keynote lecture to the Classical Association meeting at Edinburgh in 2016. All these audiences asked questions that made me think.

Most of all, I learned from working closely with Plautus' words onstage, first as directed by Mary-Kay Gamel and performed by the casts of three productions of my translation of *Persa* in 2004–5; under the direction of Meryl Friedman in the 2007 Getty Villa production of my translation of *Rudens*; and in the 2016 performance of *Mostellaria* at the Getty Villa by the *commedia*-inspired Troubadour Theater Company. Special thanks to Shelby Brown, and to Ralph Flores not only for the invitation to consult but for sharing his great sense of theater with my 2015 class on ancient comedy.

This book is dedicated to Sandra Joshel, whose lifetime of work on Roman slavery has been an inspiration and a direct influence on me since we first team-taught Mythology in the spring of 1978, at Rutgers: a mythic friendship, and one that continues to make me think and laugh. She read the 2009 draft and commented on every page, and like a true friend told me that stringency was in order; she urged me always to think about Roman slavery in its own terms and times. Her own work, as will be seen, shaped this book's very structure, and so I offer it to her, a tribute to her knowledge, her wisdom, and her dedication to history from below.

Stillwell Point, California
July 2009–July 2017

Acknowledgments

Cover image: Statuette of a seated comic actor. Unknown artist; Greek (South Italian; Apulia?), 325–275 B.C. Terracotta; 4.5 × 1.75 × 2.5 inches. J. Paul Getty Museum 96.AD.164. Digital image courtesy of the Getty's Open Content Program.

Thanks to the editors and to Walter de Gruyter GmbH for permission to reprint selections from Amy Richlin, "The Kings of Comedy," in *Roman Drama and its Contexts*, ed. Stavros Frangoulidis, Stephen J. Harrison, and Gesine Manuwald, Trends in Classics – Supplementary Volumes 34: 67–95 (2016).

Thanks to the University of California Press for permission to reprint selections from Amy Richlin, "Talking to Slaves in the Plautine Audience" in *Classical Antiquity* 33.1 (April 2014), 175–226. © 2014 by the Regents of the University of California. Published by the University of California Press.

Thanks to the University of Minnesota Press for permission to reprint selections from the translation of "Oleana" by Theodore Blegen and Martin B. Ruud, *Norwegian Emigrant Songs and Ballads* (University of Minnesota Press, 1936), pp. 192–8, © 1936 by the University of Minnesota. Copyright renewed 1964 by Theodore C. Blegen.

Thanks to the University of Wisconsin Press for permission to reprint a revised and expanded version of "Slave-Woman Drag," which appeared on pp. 37–67 of: Dorota Dutsch, Sharon James, and David Konstan (eds), *Women in Roman Republican Drama*. © 2015 by the Board of Regents of the University of Wisconsin System. Reprinted courtesy of the University of Wisconsin Press.

Note to Readers

For the convenience of general readers, the text used throughout is the Oxford Classical Text edited by W. M. Lindsay, or occasionally the Loeb text edited by Wolfgang de Melo (2011a, b, c, 2012, 2013), both readily available. The discussion of textual problems is kept to a minimum, but readers should bear in mind that the text we have is imperfect and that arguments based on any single word must be checked against commentaries and critical editions. I follow de Melo in numbering the fragments as in the edition of Salvator Monda (2004), which differs somewhat from Lindsay's numbering. References to Eduard Fraenkel's *Plautine Elements in Plautus* are to "Fraenkel 2007," as this useful and widely available volume is a combined translation of the text of *Plautinisches im Plautus* (1922) and the addenda of *Elementi Plautini in Plauto* (1960), so for "Fraenkel 2007" read "Fraenkel 2007[1922 + 1960]." Translations throughout are my own except as otherwise noted.

Appendix 1 is a timeline that lays out the lifespans of the comic playwrights alongside the major wars and incidents of mass enslavement through which they lived. It is hoped that historians of theater will look at the wars, that military historians will look at the playwrights, and that literary historians will take notice of the incidents of mass enslavement.

For the convenience of readers who might come to this book from fields other than Roman comedy, Appendix 2 has a list of all Plautus' extant plays with brief plot summaries geared to this book's focus, and, from Livius Andronicus, Naevius, Plautus, Ennius, and Caecilius Statius, the names of comedies with extant fragments (Caecilius Statius probably was not writing before the 190s at the earliest, however).

In addition, chapter 2 includes lists of the names of female prostitutes and boy slaves (table 2.1) and adult male slaves (table 2.2) in Plautus' plays, which will, I hope, help the reader overwhelmed by names.

CHAPTER I

History and Theory

Prologue

It is generally held by historians of slavery that Roman slaves left little to express their feelings and ideas about their experience. The main goal of this book is to suggest that they left quite a bit, and that historians can find in the remains of the *palliata* much that testifies to the experience of the bottom layers of central Italian society in the 200s BCE, not only in Rome but in other Latin-speaking cities and towns. Within the *framework* of the plays, which, as the prologue speakers sometimes tell the audience, derives from the Greek plays known as *Nea*, the *fabric* of the plays is Italian, and low. However, "low" itself is complicated. In what follows, the reader must bear in mind that slavery was a civil status, not a social class, and that, as a status, in Rome at this time, it was fluid; slaves were not a caste, whatever philosophers may have said about natural slaves; slavery, then, was a lived process. At the same time, Rome had, in the census, a clearly defined class system that ranked male citizens according to property and thereby slotted them into voting classes and military ranks; the plays also class people according to the kind of labor they do. A "Roman audience," then, included not only slaves but freed slaves, alongside other free persons, from poor to wealthy; people who self-identified across status lines by neighborhood or trade. Slaves and the free poor onstage overlap.[1] Moreover, in this period all people, of any social class, were vulnerable to enslavement or might have lost kin to enslavement. Each audience member existed at the intersection of relationships: ascendants and descendants, neighbors,

---

[1] On the fluid nature of slavery in Rome in this period, see Taylor 2013[1960]: 132–49; on slavery as a "logical or juridical" class but not a social class, Finley 1998[1980]: 145; on slavery as process, Stewart 2012: 48–79, esp. at 78–9. On the census, see Brunt 1971a: 15–16; on class as relational, see Rose 2012: 36; on distinctions made onstage between skilled and unskilled labor, and between labor and begging, see chapter 2. For a detailed historical argument on the issues in this chapter, see Richlin 2014b: 202–19.

employers, owners, former owners, slaves and freed, and sexual partners of all kinds, both paid and unpaid. As this book will make evident, "owner" and "slave" are relational terms, and "owner" does not imply "upper-class," or even "free," although "rich owner" does. Modern readers must work to realize that slavery structured all these relationships; we live after abolition, but they did not. As comedies do, the *palliata* put the audience's world onstage. It was popular comedy in the literal sense that it showed the world of the *populus*, not restricted to Roman citizens, and with a decided emphasis on life at the bottom of the heap, which is where freed slaves tended to wind up in Rome in the 200s. Things had changed in Italy by the time Terence came on the scene in the 160s, after Pydna, so this book goes only to the death of Plautus in 184, an event, so his epitaph claims, that caused Comedy herself to grieve.[2]

"Slave Theater in the Roman Republic": this book, then, has a tendentious title. More accurately, it should be called "The *Palliata* from 300 to 184 BCE as the Performance Art of Urban Slaves, Displaced Persons, and the Free Poor in Central Italy." Even "Plautus and Popular Comedy" is problematic: Plautus holds center stage here only because we have twenty complete plays ascribed to him, while, as John Wright showed, the writers of the early *palliata* are indistinguishable in terms of content, style, and language; the *palliata* was shaped by oral performance forms and by improvisation by the whole troupe, so that any given extant play cannot accurately be ascribed to a single author. The dates: despite the widely accepted start date of 240 BCE (first public performance of a play by Livius Andronicus), this genre must have been developing for some decades before that date, and kept on adapting; nor were plays performed only once, so material in any given extant play cannot be assigned to a single date of performance. The location: it is an accident due to later events that the plays we have were preserved as Roman, by later Romans, rather than as belonging to, say, Praeneste, or to Latium in general, for Latin was not the exclusive property of Rome. The personnel: we do not know for sure who was under the

---

[2] On the shared life of slaves, freed slaves, and the working poor, see Finley 1998[1980]: 149, 170–1 (for earlier and later periods); evidence in Richlin 2014b: 206–10. Birth and death dates for Plautus are insecure, based on Cicero's claim that Plautus died in the year 184 BCE (*Brut.* 60), and that he lived to be an old man (*Sen.* 50); the epitaph comes from Gellius 1.24.3, attributed to Varro *De poetis*, who thought it was genuine. On the tenuous nature of all data on writers in this period, see further below. Many have perceived a marked difference in kind between the early writers of the *palliata* and Terence; this was a main part of John Wright's argument (1974). For a sample opinion, see Slater 1985: 169: "Such a belles-lettrist was Terence. His plays show the marks of his lack of practical theatre experience. He evidently thought little of the native Italian traditions, and used elements of them only grudgingly in his plays."

masks, or even that there were masks. Of all these points, the most secure is that at least some of the actors were slaves, as evidenced by jokes in the plays about actors' status. It was, then, of great importance to historians of slavery when C. W. Marshall clarified the part played by group improvisation in the formation of the text: hence "slave theater."[3] Actors, of course, are performers, not witnesses at a tribunal, and they told their stories in the form of jokes, a mode of communication with rules of its own. But performance is a joint creation of actors and audience, and in the *palliata* the actors – themselves from the bottom layers of society – gave the people what they wanted and joked about a life that was familiar to all present. As the slave/god Mercurius says in *Amphitruo*, kings are for tragedy, slaves are for comedy: high and low, in life and onstage. In a century racked by war throughout the Mediterranean, mass enslavements and city sackings filled the landscape with people who had lost everything.[4]

If we could see that landscape from space and then zoom in on a road in central Italy around 260 BCE, we might see a team of men walking alongside a cart pulled by a donkey. The men are short and wiry; they look tough, even the two youngest ones, who are only about fifteen. They are not only tough but thin, because their world has been at war for their whole lives and they hardly ever get enough to eat. Their bodies are marked with scars, and one has been tattooed across his face, souvenir of an old failed escape. Two of them are singing; they sing very well, and somebody riding in the cart starts to play along with them on a *tibia*, an instrument like two oboes played together. This is a *grex* of comic actors, walking along the via Latina through Latium, because they have just put on a show at the market day at Anagnia and are heading south to Frusino to put on a show at the market day there. Four of them grew up speaking Greek – one came from Sicily, one came from southern Italy, one came from a city in northern Greece, one came from Alexandria. One of them grew up speaking Umbrian in the hinterlands of Ariminum, a new *colonia* on the northern Adriatic coast. Two of them grew up speaking Oscan in small towns in

---

[3] On the stylistic unity of the *palliata*: Wright 1974. On indigenous oral performance: essays in Benz, Stärk, and Vogt-Spira 1995; Lefèvre 2014 (a summary); Wallochny 1992; Marshall 2006: 263–6 for a critique and overview. On improvisation by the troupe working together: Marshall 2006: 268–79. On the evidence for old formulae in the comic fragments of Livius Andronicus: Richlin 2017b: 186–8. On the presentation of the plays: Goldberg 1998. On masks: Marshall 2006: 126–58. The acting troupe as *grex*: *As.* 3, *Cas.* 22, *Ps.* 1335, cf. *Cist.* 731–3 on a *grex venalium*; jokes on actors' slave status, *Am.* 26–31, *Cas.* 84–6, *Cist.* 784–5. See Marshall 2006: 84 on the "network of economic ties" laid out in *As.* 1–3, and further below.

[4] For a survey of mass enslavements in this period, see Volkmann 1990, supplemented for Rome's actions in Italy in the 290s by Harris 1979: 59 n. 4, and see Appendix 1 below.

the far south. One of them, the one with the red hair, grew up speaking a Celtic language, because he comes from the far north, in the Po Valley, and nobody else in the group can speak his language. One of them grew up speaking Punic, because his mother came from Carthage. Two of them grew up speaking Latin, which is the language they are all speaking now, as they talk and tell jokes and rehearse. Of these eleven, six grew up bilingual, through mixed parentage or enslavement.[5] Most of them are either slaves or freed slaves, and the five slaves belong to their fellow actors; all of them either were raised as performers or were made so at an early age. The group leader bought the two boys at a market a few years ago because they could both carry a tune, and one of them was an acrobat. The leader has sex with the pretty one when he wants to.

All along the way they meet up with groups of people on the road; a lot of them are refugees, because their town has been sacked or their land has been appropriated, and they have to find a new home. Some of these people have been allowed to leave their homes just with what they can carry. A lot of them are on their way to Rome, which is the biggest city nearby, and they have relatives there. The actors know that in all the towns they come to there will be people in the audience like these, who have been violently displaced by the wars and by what goes along with war in the world they all know: the enslavement of captives after an army sacks a town – sometimes only the women and children, who have to watch when the men are killed; the rape of these captives by soldiers; the poverty or shame that can make a woman abandon a child who is then picked up and enslaved; the kidnapping and human trafficking that thrive when the world is at war. Comedians have often remarked that comedy starts with anger, which is a way of saying that comedy springs from history, from lived experience; this book sees how that is so in the *palliata*.

Biographies of ancient writers are generally viewed with suspicion, but some more than others, and some aspects more than others. For example, there is no evidence outside the ancient biographical tradition and authors' self-statements, now also rarely trusted, on the social status of the writers of the *palliata*, but scholars generally agree that their status, as the lives say,

---

[5] On the advantages of donkey-carts over ox-carts in transport, see Adams 2012: 230. On interactions among languages in Italy during the Republic, see Langslow 2012, although, like many surveys, his treats the entire Republic synoptically, which obscures historical shifts important to the present argument. On the size of the troupe, see Marshall 2006: 94–120; he estimates a maximum size of nine, and I have added a *tibicen* and an apprentice/stagehand/stage manager. On the *tibia* and *tibicines*, see Moore 2012: 26–63.

was low.[6] Yet Plautus' biography, which appears in Aulus Gellius by way of Varro, is often dismissed. Here it is (Gell. 3.3.14):

> *Saturionem* et *Addictum* et tertiam quandam, cuius nunc mihi nomen non suppetit, in pistrino eum scripsisse Varro et plerique alii memoriae tradiderunt, cum pecunia omni, quam in operis artificum scaenicorum pepererat, in mercatibus perdita inops Romam redisset et ob quaerundum victum ad circumagendas molas, quae trusatiles appellantur, operam pistori locasset.

> Varro says, and many others have handed down the story, that he wrote *Fatso* and *Wage Slave* and a third play, the name of which now escapes me, in a mill. He had lost in trading ventures all the money that he had made in jobs related to the theater, and had returned to Rome, penniless, and in order to make enough money to eat he had hired out his labor to a miller, for turning the mill (the kind they call a push-mill).

Folkloric this story may be – Gellius says as much, in the words *plerique alii memoriae tradiderunt* – but folklore has a significance of its own, and the elements in the story link the *palliata* with the world of the 200s BCE. The two plays Plautus writes in the mill have significant titles: *Saturio*, the name of the hungry man in *Persa*, a name always evoking the dream of enough food; *Addictus*, the word for a person who has been adjudged to his creditor to pay off his debt (see chapter 3). Both plays have extant fragments. Gellius goes on to recount that Naevius, too, is said to have written two plays in dire circumstances – in his case, when he was in prison for insulting the *principes civitatis* "in the fashion of the Greek poets," that is, by name (3.3.15). (This story is sometimes held to be incredible, but plenty of books have been written in prison: *Mein Kampf*, 1923; Gramsci's *Prison Notebooks*, 1929–35; *Letter from Birmingham Jail*, 1963; *Soul on Ice*, 1965: political, if not funny.[7]) Like many characters in the plays, Plautus is involved in trade; he has lost his money, becoming *inops* – destitute; he

---

[6] Representative is Manuwald 2011: 90–2, who says the dramatic poets were "of low social status … slaves, freedmen or free foreigners." Gruen 1996b: 87–91, claiming these poets gained high status by proximity to the Greek theatrical guilds, has been influential among historians, but is wrong on this point; see Le Guen 2014: 370–3 (no Dionysiac *tekhnitai* in the western Mediterranean in this period).

[7] Opinions vary as to whether to believe the stories about Naevius and political critique: Beta 2014 (yes); Boyle 2006: 53–5 (cautiously); Fantham 2005: 219–20, 222 (focuses on Naevius' "advocacy of speaking out"); Goldberg 2005: 162, 165, 169 (yes, but not related to drama); Gruen 1996a: 92–106 (no); Gunderson 2015: 50–1 (as a thought experiment); Moore 1998: 62, 73 ("almost certainly"); Williams 1982: 4–5 (entirely); Wiseman 1998: 39 (yes, against Gruen); cf. Kruschwitz 2013, who includes Naevius among those who fostered the political dimensions of Roman theater and interactions with the audience. Boyle rightly observes (55), "What is not speculation is that Naevius … made the implicit imbrication of politics and drama overt." Well attested in the fragments, both comic and tragic.

has been working in *operis artificum*, both words tainted with the idea of manual labor for pay; he has indeed hired himself out for pay; and to a miller, to work in a mill, one of the paradigmatic slave punishments. In fact it is partly the consonance of the life with the work that has caused critics to doubt it, perhaps illogically. More damningly, Friedrich Leo in 1912 pointed out the resemblances between the lives of all the early Latin poets and biographical traditions about contemporary Greek philosophers. Like Plautus in the mill, the Stoic Cleanthes is said to have worked at night not only for a gardener but for a woman flour-dealer, for whom he used to grind the barley-groats; Menedemus, along with his best friend Asclepiades, is said to have worked at night in a mill, although both later rose to fame as colleagues in the Eretrian school of philosophy. Leo concludes, "Die Geschichte von Plautus ist nichts als eine Variante dieser von niemandem geglaubten Anekdoten" (1912: 76, "The story of Plautus is nothing but a variant of these anecdotes, which are believed by no one"). Varro, he argues, is not reliable. But what is most fascinating about Leo's comparison is that the comic writers, as well as the jokes that circulate under their names, are part of the circulation of cultural cargo in the Hellenistic Mediterranean, as in the story of Stratonicus (below) – who (in one version) is said to have been killed by the same king who threatened Menedemus.[8] Just barely a part, though, and only in Latin. In Leo's view, most of the dates, most of the stories about Plautus and his fellow comedians are too poorly attested, indeed too contradictorily attested, to be believed; in which case, on the timeline in Appendix 1, all data on writers must bear an asterisk. Still, the dates must be approximately right, nor are clichés *ipso facto* false. These little-known men, along with unknown others, were vying for the *palma* mentioned in the plays as the prize for the *artifex* – the playwright: *omnes illacrimabiles*, for, in Latium, there was

---

[8] Leo on the lives of Livius, Naevius, Plautus, and Terence: 1912: 63–86. On Leo's rationalizing approach and its sources, see Pansiéri 1997: 98; Pansiéri goes on to examine each element in the life to see if it is historically plausible (99–146), concluding that "l'insignifiance, la sécheresse même de ces anecdotes … sont des gages de crédibilité" (146). On Cleanthes (331–232 BCE), Diogenes Laertius 7.168–69; on Menedemus (345/4–261/0) and Asclepiades, Diogenes Laertius 2.125 (a builder, a poor man, a scene-painter) and 2.129–30 (trouble with Nicocreon king of Cyprus), and Athenaeus 4.168b (the mill). The two Greek stories are marked by similar structural elements, and the version in Athenaeus leads with the formula ἱστόρησαν [X and Y] ἄλλοι τε πλείους; compare Gellius *Varro et plerique alii memoriae tradiderunt*. On the other hand, both the Greek stories are embedded in much larger anecdotal-patchwork biographies, while for Plautus and the rest there are just these isolated bits. For ways of reading "floating" stories like these, see Langlands 2016; on anecdotes about comedians, see Richlin 2016.

no list of prizewinners.[9] As with actors (below), the very lack of evidence attests to the writers' low status.

There is nothing in Plautus' biography that is any more improbable than what is said about Livius or Caecilius Statius or Terence; a life story like this is about what you would expect for someone in the theater in the 200s BCE. In a time before either authorship or acting acquired prestige in Italy, authors acted alongside actors in their plays. As for the story that Plautus was an Umbrian from Sarsina, which comes from Pompeius Festus (274L): like the origins of the other playwrights, it seems too random to have been invented. Terence, we hear, was highly paid for his work; Ennius had a patron; nothing like that for Plautus, who chose as his identity for all time the most clownish of stage names (see chapter 2).

* * *

This book about low theater is divided into two parts: "What Was Given" (chapters 2–3) and "What Was Desired" (chapters 4–8). Part I starts from Paul Willis's idea that social agents begin from "what was given" – the hand they have been dealt – and form their identity in reaction. Plautus' characters are often assumed to be static, their identity a legacy from Greek New Comedy. The character-types in the plays were already classified in antiquity, and thus have often been treated by modern scholars as a set of cardboard cut-outs that persist from fourth-century Athens into the late Republic; this is facilitated by a tendency to lump together everything from Menander to Terence as "New Comedy." A survey of the most common *experiences* in the early *palliata*, however, shows something both lively and local: a preoccupation with the bodily sufferings of slaves and the free poor through beatings, sexual exploitation, and hunger (chapter 2). A chief example: the character of the Greek *parasitos*, the comic hanger-on, zooms in on hunger as his defining trait as he translates himself into the *parasitus*. In addition, the characteristic *language* of the plays, tied to traditional Italian oral forms by Eckard Lefèvre and the scholars of the Freiburg school, fills them with a kind of speech that audience members knew from lower-class street performance: cheering, verbal dueling, cries for help, the charivari, and the peculiarly Italian form of dunning known as *flagitatio*, strongly associated in the plays with debt (chapter 3). In the

---

[9] Cf. *Am.* 69–70, *sive qui ambissent palmam <his> histrionibus/ seu quoiquam artifici*; *Poen.* 37, *ne palma detur quoiquam artifici iniuria*; and (fig.) *Trin.* 706, *facile palmam habes ... vicit tua comoedia*, with discussion at Moore 1998: 86. See Manuwald 2011: 88, who focuses on "single actors," with some later sources.

chaos of the 200s in the Mediterranean, debt was pervasive, and was often the cause of popular unrest. Roman slaves could buy their way out of slavery, if they practiced the top-down virtue of being *frugi*, as the plays often remark; they do so with irony, for one of the constitutive elements of being a slave, even more so than for the poor, was limited access to money, and this need haunts the plays.

Part II shows how, in reaction to what was given, the plays express the desires of people at the bottom: not only do the powerless say what it is they want, but they also talk about how the powerless can say what they are not allowed to say. As social practices like corporal punishment marked off slave from free, so the plays work to make slaves whole, and claim honor for those who by definition had none. Slaves onstage elevate themselves at the expense of owners (chapter 4); they engage in various kinds of double speech, often self-consciously, pointing to the general nature of the plays themselves as double speech (chapter 6); they engage the audience in the memory of home and family in the time before enslavement (chapter 7); they wish for freedom, sometimes in the practical form of manumission (much more common onstage than is generally stated), sometimes in the form of fantastical escape (chapter 8). They act out the experience of slave-women as well as of male slaves, although the experience of actual women is emphatically at a remove; the actors, as men in drag, convey a complex set of gendered desires among slaves and owners, boys and adult males, appealing in different ways to different audience members (chapter 5). Interaction with the audience, as in many forms of comedy, is central to the *palliata*; in Althusserian terms, "*the plays interpellate the audience segmentally and intermittently.* That is, different lines of the play address different audience members in their various social roles, thereby reinforcing those roles, and not all audience members are being addressed at any one time."[10] Comedy is a prime method by which people form their identities; in the mass trauma of ongoing war, those thrown to the bottom needed to be addressed, and their roles needed to be "reinforced," not in Althusser's closed sense, but in a way that gave them a voice. In the 200s, this is what the *palliata* did.[11]

---

[10] Richlin 2005: 2–3; cf. Moore 1998: 1–4 and *passim*, Revermann 2006: 38 on "sequentiality," Richlin 2013a: 352–3 (a clarification). Cf. Rebecca Langlands's concepts of "serial multivalency" and "simultaneous multivalency" (forthcoming).

[11] The term *palliata*, short for *comoedia palliata*, is earliest attested by the antiquarian Varro in the first century BCE (*Gram.* 306), but is often used by modern scholars, as I will do here. It denotes comedies acted in Greek dress – the *pallium*. The prologue speakers just call what they are performing *comoediae*, a Latinized Greek word, thus perfectly self-reflexive.

Models of the *Palliata*

Eduard Fraenkel's 1922 *Plautinisches im Plautus* is the foundation of all subsequent understanding of the *palliata* as the product of its own time and place. Fraenkel was arguing with the then standard reading of the plays, in particular as fostered by his teacher, Friedrich Leo, which held that they were translations of the *Nea* into Latin, as indeed the plays claim to be, and are, in a way; Leo's goal was to reconstruct as much as he could of those lost Greek originals. Fraenkel's goal was to show that by far the bulk of the plays, and what made them funny and charming, was comic style and language *in Latin*. Elements that had been seen, from the time of Gellius, as coarse accretions to the fine bones of the Greek plays, were in fact something new and worthy of appreciation in themselves.[12] We have no contemporary witnesses but the self-conscious remnants of the *palliata* itself; the silence is again suggestive. An emerging scholarly consensus has moved away from a linear, stemmatic model for the *palliata* whereby a single Latin playwright translates a play by Menander or Diphilus – somehow, like Terence in Suetonius's biography, getting his hands on a script, which he copies. Our understanding of the circulation of performance genres is no longer so often based on text, as consciousness of the multiple components of performance has grown.[13] An important tenet of the Freiburg school has been its emphasis on the status of Italian forms as improvisatory, unscripted performance (*Stegreifspiel*), which would explain the paucity of contemporary traces. Positions now vary according to the degree to which a scholar believes the plays translated Greek originals, or represented improvisation through a scripted play, or allowed actual improvisation onstage, as part of the play (see Petrides 2014 for an overview).[14]

---

[12] Gellius 2.23, on Menander's *Plokion* and Caecilius Statius' *Plocium*. Quintilian (10.1.99–100), rejecting Aelius Stilo's admiration for Plautine Latin, held that Latin itself was incapable of reproducing Attic charm. On translation as transformation, see Bettini 2012: 32–60; Feeney 2016: 45–91; McElduff 2013: 61–82.

[13] Forcefully and lucidly laid out by Martin Revermann (2006: 8–17); his focus is almost entirely on Old Comedy, but his arguments can well be applied to the *palliata*. My summary here jumps over an old question on the construction of the individual plays of the *palliata*: did each play derive from a single Greek "original"? W. Beare, in a classic discussion, opined that "there is no evidence at all that Plautus, Naevius or Ennius drew on more than one original at a time" (1964: 312). It is a premise of this book that comedy circulated orally, through actors, who combined jokes and scenes from their repertoire; so Leigh 2004: 37 n. 55, "the comic gag or routine is an important unit of composition for Plautus." See McElduff 2013: 85–94 on the question of translation and multiple sources, taking it back to Leo.

[14] For theory on the circulation of oral performance forms, see Davis 2011 on burlesque, with examples illustrating how oral material was taught and learned.

I do not engage here with scholars who treat Plautus as a read text; probably that is how Gellius knew Plautus, and this approach might well be fruitful for understanding the reception of the *palliata* in antiquity, but, as Niall Slater observed in his influential study of metatheater, a purely text-based approach is inadequate, for "the performance is as important as the poetry"; "a play is not a text but rather a total artistic event which exists only in a theatre during a performance," the actors and the audience being essential components (1985: 4–5). Obviously my book depends on scholars whose chief interest was in words, Fraenkel above all, but very importantly John Wright on the stylistic unity of the *palliata*, and Gonzalez Lodge, whose brilliant *Lexicon*, compiled eighty years before computers, makes it possible for scholars to understand the networks of meaning in the Plautine corpus.[15]

C. W. Marshall, who argues that the texts we have are not scripts but performance transcripts, begins his book with a spiderweb chart showing all the performance genres that influenced the *palliata*, organized century by century. Along with Greek comedy from Old to New, he lists mime, Atellan farce, and Latin tragedy (Marshall 2006: 2). The Freiburg school adds various kinds of verbal dueling and insult: *flagitatio*, Fescennine verses, the songs soldiers sang at triumphs. To this we can usefully add the *thaumata* that show up in Xenophon's *Symposium* (late 360s) and in Theophrastus's *Characters* (probably datable soon after 319 BCE): variety shows at street fairs.[16] If Herodas, as scholars believe, picked up the unscripted mime for his literary mimes in Alexandria in the 270s – so that, in his work, we can see what it might have looked like – the mime added a large portion of sex and violence to the mix. At the other end of the social scale, actors and comedians like the *gelôtopoios* in Xenophon performed at the dinners of rich men and the courts of Hellenistic kings, especially at banquets (Panayotakis 2014: 379–81; Richlin 2016). In the pages below, we will encounter the musician Stratonicus, famous for his barbed jokes, who was killed in the late 300s for insulting a king (which king, what year, different reports), and the poet Sotades, inventor of cinaedic verse, who was killed some time in the 270s for insulting Ptolemy II Philadelphus. Or so

---

[15] On Lodge, see Mavrogenes 1994. He taught at Teachers College of Columbia University, 1900–30, and is best known for the *Gildersleeve-Lodge Latin Grammar*, written with his teacher, the famous Basil Lanneau Gildersleeve, champion of the German style in advanced education. Mavrogenes describes Lodge: "progressive in the best sense: He wanted to relate schoolwork to life, place language in its context of history and ethnology." On Gildersleeve, who fought for the South in the Civil War, see duBois 2003: 13–18.

[16] On Theophrastus, see Rusten and Cunningham 2002: 68–9, 130–1. For details on Xenophon and Theophrastus, see Richlin 2017b: 173–4.

the story goes. These characters resemble comedians, and itinerant Cynics, and the *parasiti* of the *palliata*, themselves stand-ins for the comic poet; Sotades also evokes the Ionic dancers whose campy bump-and-grind pops into Plautus here and there. Each of these performance venues and types implies performers, each with his own skill set, all of them vulnerable to enslavement, for at the low end they would not have been protected by the privileges awarded to the "Dionysiac *tekhnitai*," the great professional associations. Fraenkel took the circulation of human cargo for granted, as part of his model of how Plautus made his plays: "Finally one must not forget that the numerous Greek slaves and freedmen in Rome had brought with them the wondrous tales of their people and undoubtedly found eager listeners" (Fraenkel 2007: 67).

It is important to bear in mind that there were many Greek playwrights, some of whose fragments – particularly those of Antiphanes, from the mid-300s – sound much more like Plautus than Menander's do, and that most of these performance types were ongoing, in revivals now well attested, rather than historically sequential.[17] Thus we often see in the *palliata* a kind of echo-chamber effect: Greek comedy from Old to New parodied Attic tragedy, in the form known as "paratragedy"; Roman tragedy transposed Attic tragedy; so, when Plautus does paratragedy, he is not resuscitating something long dead, and his lines set off multiple reverberations. Indeed, some nuances of these echoes are completely beyond us; *The Rabbit of Seville* sends up the high art of opera, but *The Barber of Seville* is itself a comedy. The Menandrian framework of the *palliata* may well be, not translation, but paracomedy.[18] In most cases, the parodied text is not extant, so we can only guess; judging by the way similar jokes show up in very different performance contexts, we should not in any case be thinking in terms of a single original. In comedy, as Terence complained, there is nothing original (*Eun.* 41). Livius Andronicus, Naevius, and Ennius are credited with tragedies as well as comedies, and in Latin the two forms have large lexical overlaps. As the timeline in Appendix 1 shows, the presence onstage of the *Nea* coincides with a period of intense warfare and incidents of mass enslavement that continues into the reported lifespans of Livius, Naevius,

---

[17] Revivals: Le Guen 2014: 361–2, 365, and esp. 369 for instances from the mid-200s, including at least one from Middle Comedy; Scafuro 2014: 200–1 (from 340/39 onward), 205, 207 (Philemon's [*Misa?*]*nthropes* revived, 237/6). Le Guen notes that evidence for revivals of Old Comedy is lacking (369), but her concern is mainly with the eastern Mediterranean; for comedy in Sicily and southern Italy, see Bosher 2013: 206–7, and Revermann 2006: 68–85. Certainly some varieties of Sicilian comedy resemble some aspects of Old Comedy, nor was the influence unidirectional.

[18] For the concept, see Hunter 1995, discussing mime and the *palliata* in relation to higher dramatic forms.

Plautus, and Ennius; Livius just overlaps with the long-lived Philemon (and new *Nea* continues on into the 100s and beyond; see Millis 2014). By the time Livius Andronicus emerges into the historical record with two plays at the *ludi* in 240, the *palliata* had had several generations to take shape. This is particularly important for historians to realize, since the plays are often identified with Plautus, who is then commonly located between 200 and 180 : after the Second Punic War. This is much too late; the material developed in the *palliata* grew up over a long time, during the 200s. Naevius, who fought in the First Punic War (or says he did), could have begun his career in the *palliata* as early as 252 if, as it seems likely all the playwrights did, he began as a youthful actor. The skills required by the *palliata* preclude late blooming. In any case, Naevius' first recorded production at the *ludi* took place in 235, and Gellius places Plautus' *floruit* during the Second Punic War.[19]

A basic premise of this book is that theater is a social practice, an ongoing production shaped by actors and audience in ever-shifting historical circumstances, and that popular culture circulated with people. The texts we have, in the original circumstances of production, were not read quietly by scholars sitting in a room, with the help of a dictionary. They were performed, on some kind of stage, in costume, and to understand them we must ask: Who were the actors? Who was in the audience? How did these lines work interactively? For the audience, I will take the prologue to Plautus' *Poenulus* as a touchstone; as will be seen in chapter 2, the prologue speaker addresses a list of people that includes several kinds of slaves, alongside married women, while those women's husbands are mentioned only obliquely. It has been suggested that these and other lines generally held to be addressing slaves are only jokes, but I think they are better explained as "shout-outs" – teasing recognition.[20] The presence of Latin-speaking slaves in central Italy is attested outside of the plays by the makers' names inscribed on Cales ware (mid-200s); slaves worked alongside freed slaves and freeborn men in the pottery workshops, and Cales, a Latin colony in Campania (founded 334), is just the place for a hybrid troupe

---

[19] More accurately, Gellius says that Naevius "produced plays for the *populus*" (*fabulas apud populum dedit*) in 235, and that Varro says that Naevius fought in the First Punic War and that Naevius says so in his poem on that war (17.21.45); Plautus' *floruit*, 17.21.46–7.

[20] For different interpretations of the *Poenulus* prologue, see Brown 2013, who gives a full refutation of the arguments for the presence of slaves, adducing Cic. *Har. Resp.* 26; Fitzgerald 2000: 42–3; Slater 1992. Columella, over two hundred years after Plautus, complains that urban slaves waste time at the theater (*Rust.* 1.8.2); see chapter 4 on "free spaces."

to put on a hybrid show, aimed at the grits-eating *opifex barbarus* (*Mos.* 828; see chapter 7).[21] The loquacious signatures borne by made objects in this period attest to what might be called "banausic identity" across the same terrain covered by the acting troupes; if, as G. E. M. de Ste. Croix notes, it has been remarked that there is no talk of the "dignity of labour" in ancient society, still signed work surely expresses pride. Even a building might be signed by slave workers in a hidden corner, as Amica and Detfri, slaves of Herennius Sattius, stamped the roof tile they made.[22] The plays themselves might be seen as objects inscribed with *tituli loquentes*, as actors put the stamp of their author's name onto the prologues. Jokes in several plays imply that a slave character has been to the theater: Mercurius in *Amphitruo*, Chrysalus in *Bacchides*, Gripus in *Rudens*, possibly Tyndarus in *Captivi*. The actors themselves are more elusive; that at least some were slaves is suggested by jokes in the plays, as noted above. Although the only actor's name firmly associated with the plays has the format of a free man's name – T. Publilius Pellio, in the *didascaliae* to *Stichus* – Pellio ("Tanner") might well be a freedman's name, and certainly smells low; banausic. Most elusive of all are the musicians, and here the one name attested for the early *palliata* is resoundingly servile: Marcipor Oppii, again in the *didascaliae* to *Stichus*. As in the case of Retus Gabinius, slave of Gaius, one of the Cales potters (*CIL* I².2.412), Marcipor's skill marks his product; although, as Timothy Moore notes, some later *tibicines* became stars in Italy as they were in Greece, Marcipor's name suggests that his craft was, in 200 BCE,

---

[21] For a brief overview of Cales black-glazed ware and the significance of the inscriptions, see Morel 1989: 484–7; a good example may be seen in the collection of the British Museum (1928, 0117.71). The inscriptions are listed at *CIL* I².2.405–17, 2487–93; see Wachter 1987: 400. The distribution of standardized black-glazed ware has been taken as an index of Roman cultural hegemony, now in dispute; see Jean-Paul Morel's response (2009) to Roman Roth's book (2007a), and Roth's rejoinder (2013), which, however, barely mentions the inscriptions. On Cales artisans and local cultural dynamics, see Ciaghi 1993: 272–3. Lore Benz makes Roman expansion within Italy from 338 BCE onwards part of her account of how Italian improvised theater formed the *palliata* (1995: 145–9), with particular attention to colonies south of Rome. For Roman colonies and their identities separate from Rome, see Bispham 2000.

[22] For a comparison between the Cales ware *tituli loquentes* and some earlier examples in Oscan from a workshop in Teanum, see Vine 1993: 134–41. There is a nice implementation of such implements at *Rud.* 478, as the slave Sceparnio worries he will get into trouble if found with the water-jug from Venus' temple: *nam haec litteratast, eapse cantat quoia sit* ("for she's lettered – she herself sings out whose she is"; see chapter 6 on possessive adjectives and objects as subjects). Just possibly, *litterata* is also a joke on the tattooing of runaway slaves, if Jones 1987: 153 is right about two other possible instances (chapter 7). See below on tattooing. On such objects as pilgrimage souvenirs, see Padilla Peralta in progress; on the Pietrabbondante roof tile, Richlin 2014a: 1. On "dignity of labour" see Ste. Croix 1981: 201.

still banausic.[23] A tight mix of slave and free(d), then, characterized the workshop, the acting troupe, and the audience.

Elusive again is the question of actors' gender, about which the jokes are not so explicit; the idea that they were all male is based on what we know from elsewhere and from later periods about norms in comic acting (see Marshall 2006: 94). All the names of actors we have from the mid-Republic are male, but then we have very few names. This is an important issue, and it is vexing to have to base an argument on what can only be a hypothetical claim; if it is true that all the actors were male, then the portrayal of female characters in these comedies can be analyzed as a form of drag. In any case there was nothing naturalistic about this performance, all the less so if, as seems likely, the actors were masked. Again, on this basic point we have little direct evidence. Scholars today generally accept that the actors were male and wore masks, and I will follow suit, but readers must realize that all such arguments are provisional. At least it is clear that actors wore the Greek *pallium* or *palla*, a short poncho, over a tunic or dress, along with *socci*, flimsy lace-up shoes; these items of clothing feature in many jokes in the plays.

That we have so few names is again significant, an index of a theatrical scene with rules of its own – most of it lost. From the time of Alexander onward, acting grew in prestige in the Greek east, and theatrical festivals and elaborate stone theaters popped up from southern Italy and Sicily to Ecbatana. The history of these actors, whose doings are recorded in honorific inscriptions, has been traced by Brigitte Le Guen. But the linguistic frontier that began in Campania seems also to have marked off central and northern Italy as a theatrical backwater; there were no stone theaters, and scholars like Sander Goldberg and Christopher Johanson have been working to hypothesize how plays might have been staged in Latin in the 200s: in the city of Rome, probably on a temporary wooden stage in the space in front of a temple, with the audience sitting on the steps; probably also in the Forum Romanum, with the audience sitting on some kind of temporary bleachers, or just on benches; possibly, in a similar arrangement, in other public spaces. (Actors refer to the audience space as the *cavea*, the "chicken coop"; see chapter 8.) The widely held idea that plays were produced only at the official festivals of the city of Rome – the *ludi* – and then only once, cannot stand; neither can the often-repeated idea that instaurations of *ludi*

---

[23] On *tibicines*, see Moore 2012: 27–35. Of course another *tibicen* is attested in the *didascaliae* of all the plays of Terence – still, even in the boom times after Pydna, a slave: Flaccus Claudi. For names in *-por*, see Cheesman 2009, and further in chapter 2.

(repetitions for religious reasons) were really held because officials who had commissioned comedies wanted "to ingratiate themselves with the people," the idea being that otherwise people would have only one chance to see the play. An instauration usually meant the extension of the entire festival. Our idea of the importance of comedic performances at the *ludi* is much skewed by the fact that they are all we have left; the *ludi* featured all sorts of other performances, leading up to the giant spectacle at the Circus on the last day; as Moore pointed out, the joke about Pellio in *Epidicus* means that this play may well have been performed not only more than once but by a troupe other than Plautus'.[24] If so, then all the rest as well; certainly revivals were normal in the Greek-speaking theater in this period. Both Naevius and Plautus are credited with a *Colax*. Meanwhile, we do not have enough plays attested to cover the most limited performance model; there must once have been many more plays than Plautus' extant twenty, for, although we have bits of thirty-three additional named plays ascribed to Plautus, as well as bits of the plays of Livius Andronicus, Naevius, Ennius, and Caecilius Statius, at least ten plays per year would have been needed just for the regular *ludi*, if at least two troupes competed (see above on the *palma*): a minimum of 320 plays from 216 to 184.[25] The persistence of the idea of limited occasions for performance is an example of "dogmatic drag," the unquestioned repetition of common opinion, as is the idea that the *palliata* belonged exclusively to Rome.[26]

For, based on jokes in the plays and fragments, it seems certain that plays were produced in the other towns of central Italy. The Praenestine cooks *cista*, showing a comic-strip sequence of slaves in the kitchen, just possibly attests to the impact there of the *palliata*.[27] Another *cista*, found

[24] On multiple performances at the *ludi*, see Goldberg 1998: 15–16, 2012; for shows at the temple of Magna Mater, see Goldberg 1998, and in the Forum, Goldberg 2012, Johanson forthcoming: ch. 5, also Wiseman 2015: 50–7; on possibilities for performance at other times and elsewhere, see Richlin 2014b: 214–16, 220, grounded in Taylor 1937 and Rawson 1985; on instaurations, I quote here de Melo 2013: 3; on productions of *Epidicus*, Moore 2001: 313 (cf. Marshall 2006: 89–90). The focus on Greek drama as enacted at the Attic festivals has been similarly expanded in recent work, notably by Martin Revermann (2006: 70–2, esp. on Sicily); by David Roselli on shows in the Attic demes (2011); by Kathryn Bosher and others on shows in Sicily and southern Italy (2012, 2013); and by Brigitte Le Guen (2001, 2014) and Benjamin Millis (2014) on actors, playwrights, and shows all over the Greek-speaking world.

[25] For the Plautine canon, see Gellius 3.3; he says that "about a hundred and thirty" plays are circulating under Plautus' name (3.3.11). See Appendix 2 for a list of the names of comedies with extant fragments attributed to Livius Andronicus, Naevius, Plautus, Ennius, and Caecilius Statius.

[26] On the concept of "dogmatic drag," see West 2011: 15–16.

[27] Brussels Mus. Roy. A 1159. For this *cista*, see Foerst 1978: 16–17, 116–17, and plates 11b–c; Foerst stresses its uniqueness. The figures, identified as slaves by their short hair and loincloths, are unmasked, but the scene is clearly meant to be funny, as are the lines that come out of the figures'

at Toscanella in northern Latium, has a handle made of two comic slaves.[28] Opportunities for performance would have included not only formal *ludi*, but *nundinae* – weekly market days – as well as periodic mercantile fairs. The nexus of trade, trafficking, travel, and performance structures the *palliata*, and is treated here briefly in chapter 7, but awaits the attention of an economic historian; for example, the sendup in a speech by the prostitute Adelphasium in *Poenulus*: "At the temple of Venus today is the Prostitute Fair: / the traders are gathering there" (*apud aedem Veneris hodie est mercatus meretricius: / eo conveniunt mercatores*, 339–40).[29] The *palliata* incorporates jokes also found in Alexandrian mime in the 270s and in Sicilian comedy back to Epicharmus and Sophron in the mid-400s.[30] In the 200s, a time when ongoing wars created numerous paths to hybrid identity, a bilingual native speaker of Latin and Greek – perhaps from Campania, like Naevius – might have learned the *Nea* in Sicily and brought the scenarios back north with him. Or a native speaker of Greek who learned Latin as a slave – perhaps taken from Tarentum, like Livius Andronicus – might have been bought by an actor and trained. The wars and the hazards of travel could have brought slaves from anywhere in the Mediterranean, with performers of all kinds in the mix, bringing with them in turn their gibes and gambols. Comic and tragic actors would have been sold on the same block. Those who were free were low, although not yet officially so. In later periods, actors, along with pimps and dishonorably discharged soldiers, were stigmatized by the praetor's edict as *infames*, thus lacking in certain civil rights. But actors in the plays do not joke about themselves as *infames*; the words *infamia* and *infamis* appear in the Plautine corpus only

mouths. This odd object is best known for these inscriptions (*CIL* I².560), on which see Vine 1993: 206–8 (dating probably after 200, despite the earlier date usually given), 336–7; Wachter 1987: 166–9. Note the lexical overlap between the *cista* and the comic vocabulary of cooking at *As.* 178–80, *Aul.* 398–405, *Per.* 87–98; the pun on *assum* on the *cista* and at *Poen.* 279–80 and probably *Frivolaria* fr. 80 (with 79 and 81, a probable cooks scene); and the *cista* spit vs. the visual pun on Gripus' spit (*verum*) at *Rud.* 1299–1304 (chapter 8), also the spit sought as a weapon by belligerent slaves at *Bac.* 867, *Truc.* 628. See also Franchi De Bellis 2005: 121–9, who ties the cooks *cista* with comedy but, because she accepts a fourth-century date, thinks mainly of Greek writers, despite a gesture towards the *Poenulus* pun (cf. 27–31 on a possibly comic amatory scene on a Praenestine mirror). On Praenestine *cistae*, see Holliday 2002: 167–8 and 251 n. 57 on "a specifically Latin artistic world, between Rome, Tibur, and Praeneste."

[28] British Museum 1839, 1116.3. Bieber dates this *cista* "probably late third century B.C." (1961: 162, fig. 585); accepted in Rawson 1985: 109.

[29] See the authoritative discussion of trade in the *palliata* by Matthew Leigh (2004: 132–57); also Richlin forthcoming b. On *nundinae* (occurring every ninth day), see Michels 1967: 24–5, 84–9, 105, with discussion at Richlin 2014b: 215. On trade fairs, see Andreau 2002: 119–22; Callataÿ 2015 (with maps) takes the plays of Plautus to reflect Athenian culture and the Athenian economy.

[30] See Richlin 2016: 83–92 on the circulation of comedians; Richlin 2017b on the circulation of jokes both geographically and across performance genres.

to denote bad reputation among the *populus*, who pass judgment on bad behavior.[31] Law and magistrates do not come into it. In this period, when most actors were not Roman citizens in the first place, they were outside this law, or beneath it.

The ironic self-labeling of Italy as *barbaria* in the plays (chapter 7) is part of a defiant claim to hybrid identity, an instance of what the Jamaican writer Michelle Cliff called "claiming an identity they taught me to despise." So, for the early Principate, Sandra Joshel cites Erving Goffman's observations in *Stigma* to show how a freedman might "make virtues of the characteristics that stigmatize him."[32] In the plays, bilingualism is in itself treated as suspicious, a sign of duplicity, in scenes where the one so accused has a claim on the audience's sympathy; like *barbaria*, this is an ironic joke, for the plays are inherently bilingual, hybrid.[33] Page duBois comments, "The Greeks associated tattooing with barbarians, and then with those barbarians among them, their chattel slaves" (2003: 107–8). If *barbaria*, for a Greek, was where slaves came from, what did it mean to a native speaker of Greek to become a slave in *barbaria*? The formation of these concepts belongs to the geographic range of the *palliata*: to the actors who (were) moved across it and to the audiences tumbled about in it.

That the *palliata* belonged to the lowly is not, nowadays, a widely voiced opinion. As E. P. Thompson said, "I have been conscious, at times, of writing against the weight of prevailing orthodoxies" (1966: 12). Most influential in the Anglophone world have been Kathleen McCarthy's *Slaves, Masters, and the Art of Authority in Plautine Comedy* (2000) and Michael Fontaine's *Funny Words in Plautine Comedy* (2010). McCarthy argues that Plautine comedy helped the audience, whom she takes to be Roman citizens and slave-owners, to overcome the anxieties caused by what she calls

---

[31] See Brown 2002, Richlin 2014b: 210–12 on the status of actors before the 180s, and Garton 1972: 231–65 for a list of Republican actors. Cf. Boyle 2006: 16–18, who sums their status up as "banausic," and believes that *infamia* would have applied at this point in the Republic. This is a commonly shared belief (e.g. Fitzgerald 2000: 43), but not supported by the Plautine corpus, where the words *infamia* and *infamis* appear only in *Persa* (the Virgo worries about her father's reputation if he sells her to the pimp, 347, 355), *Trinummus* (much concern about reputation among the *populus*, 121, 689, 739), and *Bacchides*, where the slave Lydus worries about his own reputation along with that of the rest of the family (381). Poverty or bankruptcy are at stake in all three situations. See Feeney 2016: 65–6 for Livius Andronicus as an "entrepreneur," and 92–151 for a survey of the cultural worlds through which he moved. Citizen actors' eligibility for military service is discussed in a famous passage in Livy on the history of Roman theater (7.2.3–13, at 12) that can at best attest to his own time. On actors' separation of themselves from the *populus*, see further in chapter 3.

[32] See Cliff 1985b; Joshel 1992: 65, 198 n. 7.

[33] On bilingualism, duplicity, and ethnicity in scenes involving Syrians and Carthaginians, see Starks 2010: 59–60.

the "burden of mastery." She invokes James C. Scott (on whom see below), but simplifies his ideas on the public transcript so that they support her contention that "Because these plays were performed at publicly funded religious festivals, it is difficult to categorize them as the self-expression of those who were normally without a voice in Roman public life. ... By definition, this public transcript expresses the dominant's view of their own domination" (2000: 17–18). McCarthy adduces American blackface minstrelsy, as analyzed by Eric Lott (1993), as an analogue for the *palliata*. But the actors Lott studied were Irishmen putting on the identities of Southern black slaves for audiences made up of Northern immigrants – playing the other, for reasons of their own. The actors in the *palliata* were not usually, as far as we know, borrowing the identity of an abjected outgroup, and you have to work very hard to delete the slaves from the Plautine audience. McCarthy's views have found favor with many, including William Fitzgerald (2000), who was writing about Latin literature, and Sara Forsdyke (2012: 59), who was not; Fitzgerald was interested in slavery as a metaphor, Forsdyke wanted to explain the double audience for utopian visions in Greek popular culture. DuBois, in a short book on ancient slavery, quotes with approval McCarthy's dictum on Plautus and the minstrel show: "Both kinds of entertainments provided the soothing spectacle of slaves who were content in their servitude."[34] A close acquaintance with Plautus should forestall such arguments: "I'm just as much a person as you," as the slave Leonida says to his free interlocutor (*tam ego homo sum quam tu, As.* 490). Claude Pansiéri was right to fasten on *homo*, here and elsewhere, as a word "qui abolit toute hiérarchie" (1997: 522). McCarthy's views have been attractive because they explain what an upperclass Roman might have gotten out of the plays; for readers who believe the plays were literature and that all Latin literature belonged to the upper class, this is what needs explaining.

Fontaine's arguments depend on bilingual puns he perceives in the text of the plays, which he treats as attesting to a high degree of literacy in the audience. I say "text" advisedly, because it seems to me that most of these puns would only be perceptible to someone who had the OCT in front of him and a lot of time to think about it. I do not think most of them would play onstage (see chapter 7 for an example). His understanding of

---

[34] McCarthy 2000: 212, quoted in duBois 2009: 99. The discussion of Roman slavery there is very brief (2009: 94–108). For more on McCarthy, see Richlin 2014b: 179–81. For dismissal of the possibility that the plays could offer anything to slaves or the "small citizen," see Sharrock 2016. For an aesthetic argument fully attentive to the plays' address from below, see Dressler 2016.

the demographics of central Italy in the late 200s CE does not incorporate mass enslavement or other population shifts, so that Greek words in the plays need another explanation. In the historical justification for his reading (Fontaine 2010: 183–7), he argues that (a) Plautus' audience was small, and therefore "predominately elite"; (b) "Plautus and Ennius, like Naevius and Livius Andronicus before them, were all catering to essentially the same sophisticated, interested, and educated Roman elites"; and (c) this audience knew Greek through education, "a bourgeois cultural concern." This model does not account for the development of formulaic shtick in Latin before Livius. Yet as for Fontaine's claims about cultural circulation – for example, the idea that Phronesium in *Truculentus* is really named Phrynesium, and is meant to remind the audience of the high-priced Greek prostitute Phryne and her story; or that the slave-woman Milphidippa's description of her lovelorn owner (*Mil.* 1270–73) is meant to remind the audience of Sappho 31: as seen above, I certainly agree that all kinds of performance forms (along with people, and popular culture) reached central Italy not only from Athens and Sicily but from Alexandria, so there is no reason why other sorts of poetry should not have arrived there, as well; their dissemination is as much of an unknown to us as the dissemination of the Atellana. The elegies the old man fears will be written in hot coals on his door in *Mercator* (409) perhaps allude to such circulated verse.[35] All cultural forms are grist to the comedian's mill. Still, you do not need to have seen *The Barber of Seville* to find *The Rabbit of Seville* funny; highly allusive comic forms, like *Shrek*, are funny on different levels to different viewers. Parody, moreover, tends to deflate the original, and circulation itself changes meaning, even for Sappho. Where I part company with Fontaine: "An audience whose own enthusiasm for comedy drew them to performances of the *palliata* would, then, perhaps naturally be drawn to study texts of Greek comedy in their acquisition of the language" (2010: 191). This model cannot account for the plays' mixed audience.[36]

---

[35] On Phryne, Fontaine 2010: 24–7, 187–90; on Milphidippa and Sappho, 2010: 194. Fontaine helps his argument by calling Phryne "the Marilyn Monroe of fourth-century-BC Athens" (24); Phryne is said to have lived into the late 300s, which would put her into the stream of popular culture no earlier than Stratonicus (who shows up in *Rudens*), and her reputation lived on in Greek comedy. Her persistence into the *palliata* would be no more of a stretch than the appearance of Mata Hari (1876–1917) in Warren Zevon's song "Genius" (2002). For the elegies on the door, see chapter 3.

[36] Fontaine, however, gave it as his opinion at the 2011 APA seminar on the Plautine audience that slaves in this period did not understand Latin. See above on Cales ware, and Richlin 2014b: 217 n. 52 on Fontaine's historical understanding of Plautus' audience (with reference to Livy 34.44.4–5 and 34.54.3–8).

Fontaine's well-read audience populates Denis Feeney's large-scale study of the cultural upheavals of the 200s BCE (2016), which, throughout, takes the forms that grew into Latin literature as a project of the "bilingual governing élite." The content of the *palliata* poses no problems for his argument because he does not consider it; after accepting the traditional geographical origins of Livius Andronicus, Naevius, Plautus, Caecilius Statius, Ennius, Pacuvius, and Terence (65–6), he nods briefly to Fontaine (88), and says little else about comedy.[37] A rich and otherwise well-informed model of the possible movement of actors through the Italian peninsula from 364 to 241 (Feeney 2016: 105–10) makes no reference to the many metatheatrical self-descriptions in the extant corpus of the *palliata*, perhaps because Feeney takes them to refer only to performance after 240. It seems unlikely to me, however, that the status of actors before 240 was *higher* than it was thereafter.

To be clear about the relation between the status of these actors and the content of the plays: these were low-status performers, highly skilled but socially marginal. Their art made freedom thinkable, but they were not freedom fighters themselves, nor would they necessarily have been nice to know, or noble, or inspiring; if comedians today are slightly crazy, factor in slavery and starvation. Nor were they scholars. The subversive jokes they made were cooked up in the comic soup of shtick in the Mediterranean, going back to Sophron and Old Comedy, and repurposed by the troupe to fit conditions in central Italy in the 200s. They had to be good at their craft to get picked up by the state officials who hired for the *ludi* – great timing, great singing and dancing, the best lines, the funniest body movement – all aimed at one thing: making each member of the audience laugh. They brought "themselves" as actors into many metatheatrical jokes, but who each one was, his history, his desires, are doubly unknowable: we cannot go back for an interview, and, if we could, beneath the mask we would confront the comic's impenetrable facade. "Tell them how your slave made a spectacle out of you," says Tranio to his owner in *Mostellaria*, defining the essence of the comic plot: *dicito is quo pacto tuo' te servos ludificaverit* (1150). The life experience of actors in the *palliata* made them well able to put that across.

---

[37] Brief mentions of Plautus: the names of the gods in *Amphitruo* (Feeney 2016: 60–1); geographical jokes in the plays on their putative Greek location, and linguistic jokes on *barbare* (141–2; cf. chapter 7 below); the relation of Greek myth in Plautus to "the developing education system" (184).

History of Slavery

Orlando Patterson, in *Slavery and Social Death*, began his classic study with three basic elements: the forms of violence that coerced slaves into submission; the "natal alienation" that detached slaves from their kin lines; and dishonor (1982: 1–14).[38] Patterson himself had Roman slavery in mind, and turns to Plautus for a few slave voices – Sosia in *Amphitruo*, Phaniscus in *Mostellaria*, Palaestra in *Rudens* – which he juxtaposes with American ex-slave narratives (12). In a discussion of the freed Roman mime-writer Publilius Syrus, Patterson even suggests "that it was for the slaves who looked on from the fringes that he coined his finest maxim: 'What is left when honor is lost?'" (78). Patterson's focus on the subject position of the slave, and his insistence on the original subject position of enslaved persons, typify an approach to slavery that looks at the experience from the slave's point of view, a challenge for Roman historians since upper-class slave-owners have left the majority of the textual sources available to us. Certainly few have followed Patterson's lead in treating Sosia as an actual slave or looking for slaves in the audience. Moses Finley, one of the most authoritative historians of ancient slavery, perhaps foreclosed this possibility when he wrote (1998[1980]: 185), "I have sedulously avoided any reference to overt statements in ancient literature about the psychology of slaves, for the simple reason that they represent the views and hopes of the slaveowning class, not of the slaves themselves, and have no unequivocal standing as evidence, except about the ideology of the free."[39] This has become a widely shared perception, all the more pressing in a socially conscious academy. Thus the work of Keith Bradley and Sandra Joshel constitutes a determined effort to extrapolate, to fill in the silence, focusing on modes of resistance (Bradley) and on the identity slaves and freed slaves built for themselves in their epitaphs (Joshel). In general, however, Finley's dictum has kept the *palliata* in historians' danger zone, as "literature."[40]

---

[38] To a Latinist it is hard to believe that Patterson's theory is meant to *replace*, for cultures outside the reach of Roman law, the definition of a slave as human property, and has been widely accepted as such for Greece; see Lewis 2017 for a thorough refutation, and Bodel 2017 for an overview.

[39] Already in 1967: 5: "Ancient writers, virtually without exception, reflect the views and sentiments and prejudices of the educated classes, which means the upper classes." Both axioms overstate the homogeneity of the groups "slave-owning class" and "educated classes." See Vlassopoulos 2016 for a critique of Finley's top-down approach.

[40] Historians of slavery and Plautus: Bradley (1984: 28–9, 38–9, 146–7, and esp. 136; 1989: 27–30, thoroughly documented) makes a cautious effort to see what the Plautine corpus does tell about slave life, particularly about the presence of slave-women in contemporary Rome; Joshel's work has focused largely on the Principate. Patterson evidently only read a few plays, and in translation (he cites only Watling's 1964 Penguin, which included *Amphitruo, Mostellaria, Rudens*, and

One of Finley's most profound arguments was his conclusion that "a genuine 'synthesis' of the history of ancient slavery can only be a history of Graeco-Roman society" (1998[1980]: 134). That is, slavery was a structural element that affected every aspect of life. This is a truth obvious to historians of slavery as it has not always been even to other social historians, much less to political and literary historians. Page duBois begins from this point of Finley's at the outset of *Slaves and Other Objects*, where she argues that "slavery informed every aspect of life in ancient Greek society, and ... idealization of the Greeks has led modern scholars often to overlook both slavery and slaves" (2003: 6). She stands here with social historians who have "sought to restore to public view the invisible of the past, those social actors in the quotidian realm who have not had a voice – women, the poor, slaves" (45). Here one might instance Virginia Hunter's examination of the Attic lawsuits, despite their elite bias, along with Aristophanes and Menander, in order to access "the lowest levels of society," in which she includes children, working women, and household slaves (1994: 5–6). In extensively documented chapters on household slaves and the corporal punishment of slaves, she sets pertinent elements of comedy in the social context provided by the lawsuits, which bridge the temporal jump from Old Comedy to New (1994: 70–95, 154–84). She makes no claim to have found a slave voice, however, and duBois, who cites as a "gesture of solidarity" Keith Bradley's endeavor to try to find out "what they thought, or felt," doubts that this is possible (2003: 22, cf. 102). This judgment perhaps looks mainly to evidence in Greek.

In the present study, adherence to the slave's perspective has inflected some basic terminology. First of all, I have avoided the English term "master," preferring "owner" for its clear statement of the power position linking slaves with the person who owned them. Finley emphasizes that "as a commodity, the slave is property," and so, "reciprocally, the old Latin word *erus* also implies the peculiarity of a slave-property" (1998[1980]: 141; cf. Shaw 1998: 12). "Master" in English has some heavy baggage: it connotes innate superiority (dogs have masters); it is used to mean both the owner of a slave and the employer of a servant ("servant" itself being a common

---

Trinummus). Finley's reading of Plautus was selective (1998[1980]: 142 on rights, 143 on kinlessness, vs. 187–8, onstage slaves no index of offstage experience); see below on Finley's training, which was not literary. Spranger 1961 focuses directly on Plautus, but his account shows the influence of his teacher Joseph Vogt, the great advocate for the idea that ancient slavery was comparatively humane. Political historians tend to rely on Erich Gruen's two classic essays (1996a, 1996b); he trained many historians of the Republic working today, and Morstein-Marx and Rosenstein dedicated their 2006 *Companion* to him.

mistranslation for *servus*); and, in the US, it evokes plantation slavery. All these ideas are to be avoided for a clear understanding of the *palliata*, so I have translated referential uses of *erus* and *era*, by far the most commonly appearing terms, as "owner." *Erus* and *era* have no close linguistic relatives in Latin, apart from their own derivatives, and denote only this relationship. The terms *dominus/a*, much rarer in the corpus, I have rendered, according to context, as "householder" (ruler of the *domus*) or "legal owner" (ownership, in Roman law, is *dominium ex iure Quiritium*), with useful results.[41] The actors who speak of the troupe as a *grex* with *dominis*, then, are, once again, claiming a despised identity.[42] Translations like "master" – worse, projecting "master" as a title, as in "master Demaenetus," a usage that does not exist in Latin – falsify the slave's onstage subject position, which consistently treats slavery as an imposed, unnatural, and escapable condition.[43] The owner is the person from whom a slave could purchase his or her freedom, hardly a person viewed with awe, and often shown by the action of the play to be a fool, sometimes something worse. As the slave Paegnium says in a resonant line, *scio fide hercle erili ut soleat inpudicitia opprobrari*: "God, I know how owners' trustworthiness is always accused of sluttishness" (*Per.* 193).[44]

This attitude is manifest even when *erus* and *era* are used in the vocative. Of thirty-five instances of *ere* and eight of *era* (voc.) in the plays, only one prefixes a name, and that one addresses an owner not present: *o ere Charmides* (*Trin.* 617). The line is spoken by the slave Stasimus, who has just mentioned his younger *erus* (616); this use, then, differentiates them. When Charmides does return, Stasimus subjects him to a volley of abuse, before a final recognition and formal greeting – cut off by Charmides (1072–3): the formula is old hat. Five other instances also come from scenes of greeting – related to the slave's duty to go out to meet the owner (*advorsum ire*), often spoofed onstage – and connect with other

---

[41] So also Finley on the commonness of *erus* in the Plautine corpus "in preference to *dominus*" (141). Largely Republican; see Dickey 2002: 78–9. Indeed *erus* takes up nine columns in the *Lexicon Plautinum* vs. less than two for *dominus* (Lodge 1926: 1.514–19 vs. 422–3). *Dominus* in this book: chapter 2, *Am.* 170, *Poen.* 535; chapter 4, *Ps.* 472; chapter 6, *Men.* 443, *Mil.* 744; chapter 7, *Rud.* 745, 969. *Domina*, chapter 3, Hor. *S.* 1.5.55, 67. Nussbaum 2014: 244–5 argues that the etymological meaning of *erus* is "owner," matching the original sense of its Hitt. correspondent.

[42] See Marshall 2006: 84 on *dominis* at *As.* 3: perhaps the "(free) principal actors," perhaps the owners of slave actors, perhaps the troupe's backers, with reference to Peter Brown's work on actor-managers (2002).

[43] "Master Demaenetus": Stewart 2012: 111 and similarly *passim*.

[44] The adjective *erilis* is used by far most commonly in the phrase *erilis filius/a* (21 of 45 instances); next is *erilis amica* vel sim., all in *Mil.* (10 instances): largely relational. On Paegnium's line and *fides* as a theme in the plays, see chapter 3.

formulaic vocabulary: *exspectatus, gaudeo quom salvo' sis, salve,* and *o* (*As.* 619, *Epid.* 202, *Mos.* 448, *Poen.* 1127, *Rud.* 1052).[45] But *ere/a* are certainly not mandatory address forms from slave to owner. Nor do they often show respect. An index of the nature of owner/slave relations in the *palliata,* many instances are spoken by slaves arguing (*Am.* 570, 578), voicing hypocritical respect (*Epid.* 202, *Mos.* 448, cf. 442–3), or reproaching an owner (*Bac.* 668, about to address his owner as *stulte; Cur.* 146; *Trin.* 512). Several come in clusters in joking scenes where the slave dominates (*As.* 619, 641, 714; *Poen.* 280, 296, 384). These instances and others (*Cas.* 311, 313, 632, 646–7; *Cist.* 776; *Ps.* 4) occur in markedly disrespectful contexts, and very markedly in the lexical repertoire of Lampadio in *Cistellaria,* who is consistently disrespectful of his owner but ma'ams her more than any other slave (544, 695, 712, 727): smarmy. Of the few respectful instances, some come from scenes of bargaining (*Aul.* 820, 821, 826; *St.* 419), one again addresses an owner not present (*St.* 655), one is spoken by a prostitute's *ancilla* playing the part of a lady's maid (*Mil.* 1216), and a whole cluster comes from the respectful Messenio in *Menaechmi* – an extended joke (1001–24), because he is addressing the wrong twin. He ends by requesting the manumission he has earned (*ere, te servavi,* 1024): reversal. The closest English translation of this ambivalent vocative, then, would be "boss" or "sir"/"ma'am," which, however, obfuscate the condition of servitude.

Eleanor Dickey deals with *dominus* and *erus* in a chapter on titles, comments on the absence of *domine* as an address from slave to owner, and hypothesizes that slave (characters) "preferred *erus* ... because it referred less harshly to their own status": "something of a euphemism." Since *dominus* means "owner," *erus* then has to mean something "less harsh": "master" (Dickey 2002: 78–9). The principle here is right, but, in my opinion, "master" is worse than "owner," and perhaps it would be useful to defamiliarize *ere* with a non-idiomatic translation. Dickey also notes that slaves onstage commonly address their owners by name, and sees "little difference in the tone between names and *ere,* though one would expect the latter to be more deferential" (234–5). It isn't. If slaves offstage in the 200s called their owners *ere,* they doubtless showed more respect than what is shown onstage, where slaves speak freely (chapter 6); if that is so, then the onstage usage packs extra punch. A choice of the *grex.*

Servus is here translated "slave," since the term in Latin is both unmarked and generic for a male slave; the generic term for "female slave" in the plays

---

[45] On the slave's duty to greet, see chapter 6 on "good slave" speeches; on greeting formulae (but not these), see Poccetti 2010, and chapter 8 below on *iubeo te salvere.*

is *ancilla*, which I have translated "slave-woman," to keep the one-word term. The less common *serva* I have translated "female slave."[46] None of these appear as a normal term of address in the singular.[47] The vocatives of *puer* ("boy") attest mainly to the presence onstage of nine or ten nonspeaking characters, perhaps eye candy; they knock on doors, serve as waiters, fetch and carry, and, in *Pseudolus*, serve as a prop (170–252). The exception is a scene in *Mostellaria* which starts with the old man addressing Phaniscus and Pinacium with *heus vos pueri*, to which the rude Pinacium replies, *heus senex*, "Hey, old man"; here the continued use of *puere* is met with repeated insults and a disrespectful *pater* (939–91). Dickey comments that the common use of παῖ ("boy") to address adult male slaves in Greek comedy has no equivalent in Roman comedy (235), and the uses of *puere* provide no certain contradiction. This is especially interesting because in Greek comedy the fact that the vocative of παῖς and the imperative of παίειν ("beat") are homonyms grounds several extant jokes: no Latin equivalent.[48]

As for the many female characters in the sex trade in the plays, I have translated *meretrix* as "prostitute" and *scortum* – an insulting term in Latin – as "whore," and I have not used the term "courtesan" at all, since it has no place in the world of the *palliata*. We are not talking about the king's mistress here; Phronesium is not Ninon de l'Enclos; whether "courtesan" is even a good translation for *hetaira* is debatable, and that was in another country.[49] I have also avoided the phrase *servus callidus*/"clever slave," in common parlance among historians of Roman drama; although "clever" is superficially a complimentary term, the phrase can be read as patronizing – as such, an oxymoron – and feeds a tendency to view the plays from the perspective of an upper-class slave-owner. As will be seen

[46] Relative frequency: about a column and a half for *ancilla*; only eight instances for *serva*, which Lodge lists with *servus* (six and a half columns). The fact that "slave-man" does not work as a translation for *servus* is due to the gender troubles of the English language.

[47] For *mea ancilla* at *Cas.* 646, see discussion of *mi*/*mea* in Dutsch 2008: 54. This is an echoic joke, responding to Pardalisca's double *ere mi* (632, 646–7), not, I think, a normal term of address. Similarly, although *servi* as a group are sometimes given orders (*Capt.* 456, 919; *Cist.* 649; *Poen.* 1319), *serve* appears only in two joke greetings to bad slaves (*bone serve*, *Bac.* 775; *serve Athenis pessume*, *Ps.* 270).

[48] See Golden 1985: 102–4 on Aristophanes, *Knights* 451, 453 and *Wasps* 456, 1297–8, 1307, also the odd joking addresses at Menander, *Dys.* 459–64, 911–12; Hunter 1994: 166. The only named characters addressed as *puere* are Phaniscus in *Mostellaria* (947, 949, 965, 990) and Paegnium in *Persa* (771, 792), whose youth is well established.

[49] For other discussions of this terminology, see Brown 1990; Marshall 2013: 174–8; Rosivach 1998: 10–11; and esp. Witzke 2015, with a thorough review of scholarship. She rejects both "courtesan" and "prostitute" as inadequate terms, and provides a chart detailing characters and the circumstances of their sex work. See Leigh 2004: 17 nn. 79–80 for discussion of Republican applications of the term *nobilis* to prostitutes.

below (chapter 7), "clever" is too simple a translation for *callidus*, which connotes learning through hard experience.

Slaves' claims to full humanity in the plays tie in with the first of several arguments that have occupied the attention of historians of slavery and occupy mine as well. It is a major contention of this book that not only did slave characters in the *palliata* tell how they thought and felt, but the *palliata* itself constituted a reservoir of anger, helping audience members to keep alive the memory and hope of freedom, of wholeness. As Brent Shaw sums up, liberal and Marxist approaches "have placed a great deal of emphasis on struggle and resistance"; he argues that historians should be looking not only at uprisings but at "the potential denial of the system ... a covert rejection of it," and measuring resistance by the size of the constraints needed to keep it in check: "systemic compulsion" (Shaw 1998: 48–9). A search for the slave's perspective motivates Roberta Stewart's study of Plautus and slavery (2012: 2), but, since she does not seriously consider the circumstances of production, she reads the plays as a reinforcement, rather than a critique, of systemic compulsion.[50] Certainly the plays offer a wealth of information about the constraints Roman owners placed upon resistance; the owners and their constraints, however, are the butt of the joke, as Tranio says, and in fact the rejection of slavery is not that covert in the plays (see chapter 6). Above all, in interacting with the audience, slave characters expect empathy with the slave's point of view.

A second argument concerns the geography of slavery in the ancient world. As will be seen in chapters 7 and 8, the plays involve a great deal of travel, some of it fantastical, and it is a good question what that onstage geography means; I argue here that it relates to human trafficking. Historians since Finley have been concerned to show that "the Greeks of the Hellenistic age exported slavery only *within* the context of their settler cities, and not to the vast rural lands outside of them" (Shaw 1998: 20). Certainly, however, these Greeks exported slaves to Italy, as suggested by Saskia Roselaar's study of Italian traders "all over the Eastern Mediterranean" from the early 200s onward (2012), and the vast rural

---

[50] So, for example, Stewart 2012: 116: "The portrayals of violence against slaves in publicly performed drama show the slave subordinated to the entire community of free citizens. This public representation of such claims naturalizes the logic of slavery. ... The staging of the slaves' thinking about violence – typically in monologue to the audience – allowed Roman audiences to imagine hearing the secret world of the slave's sincere sentiments." Stewart nods to the presence of slaves in the audience (16, 19), but takes the plays to be serving "the interests of the elite" (17). Similarly Erik Gunderson (2015), who remarks, "so is the slave a symptom – the master's symptom" (241); even on *Captivi*, where "the servile object is a subject," still "the fact of subjection to a paternalistic order nevertheless abides" (116–17). His account is not directly concerned with the circumstances of production.

lands were a prime hunting ground for slaves. If Finley's argument were right, knowledge of a terrain outside the reach of chattel slavery might have circulated with slaves taken in the hinterlands, alongside the stories of maroon colonies. On the other hand, as David Lewis notes, specialists in Near Eastern studies are unconvinced by Finley's argument (2011: 105–8), and slavery flourished not only throughout the Near East but in Carthage (Lewis in progress), so there was no real-life conceptual "outside" to slavery in the ancient world – just islands, mountains, and the frontier, or maybe just the big city (see chapter 8).

Among the "constraints" analyzed by historians is sexual exploitation, an issue here fully explored. It is surprising that Shaw in 1998 remarked that the study of the sexual exploitation of slaves had "seen only modest improvements … since Finley's call for more investigation" (1998: 47). He cites only a few exceptions. In 1980, Finley was right that the subject had not been dealt with, but the 1980s saw great changes; perhaps Shaw had in mind Foucauldian readings of ancient sexuality, for it is certainly true that Foucault was not interested in slavery. In any case, by 1998 the co-implication of the sex/gender system with slavery was well understood by many in the field, represented, for example, by Hunter's 1994 study, as well as by important discussions by Sandra Joshel (1986, 1992: 25–34) and Keith Bradley (1984: 116–18), none mentioned by Shaw. Several landmarks in the field do postdate Shaw's 1998 essay, among them the discussion in *Slaves and Other Objects* (duBois 2003), with reference to Old Comedy and oratory, and, on the Roman side, Sandra Joshel and Sheila Murnaghan's collection, *Women and Slaves in Greco-Roman Culture* (1998); Thomas A. J. McGinn's two books on prostitution (1998, 2004); and more recently Kyle Harper's *Slavery in the Late Roman World, AD 275–425* (2011) and the first installments of Kathy Gaca's remarkable work on the rape of war captives (2010, 2010–11, 2011, 2014, 2015). Gaca covers the Greek world from Homer through Byzantium, amassing the details and attitudes from many obscure chronicles as well as from literary sources, and leaves no doubt about the effects of shock and awe on civilian populations, especially women. This is important for understanding the mindset of audiences in the 200s BCE, when so many cities in Italy were taken and the survivors of those cities and others all over the Mediterranean were dispersed into the slave trade. Harper, who devotes almost 200 pages to sexual exploitation in the empire before and after Christianity, speaks of "systemic sexual exploitation" (2011: 290) in a system where the free woman's honor was constituted by the slave-woman's dishonor, and goes so far as to call the Roman slave system "a sex racket established by and for men of the higher classes" (442). Oddly, in 2011, he repeats not only Finley's complaint but Shaw's – "substantially true to this day"; he claims that the study of ancient sexuality has failed to see the exploitation of slaves as an historical and systemic problem because it grew out of the study of canonical texts (283). Cryptic: very few of the texts considered by historians of ancient sexuality were considered canonical when they began to be studied, and most still are not. It is true that books on ancient sexuality continue to appear that do not integrate slavery, just as many *Companion* volumes on ancient history have separate chapters on slavery and "women," or "gender," topics which are not necessarily integrated into other chapters. But in fact work on the history of Roman sexuality treated the exploitation of slaves as systemic from the early 1980s onward.[51]

In this book, the discussion of "what was given" (chapter 2) deals with sexual exploitation alongside the beating of slaves and adds a third constraint: deprivation of food. Although hunger is a constant theme in the plays, and one that crosses the line between slaves and the free poor, I do not know of a full discussion of this issue by historians of slavery, even though it has the ideal pedigree in Cato's *De agricultura*.[52] What appears in chapter 2, then, constitutes a first step.

What Harper wants is research on "the social forces which were at work in the history of sex," rather than on sex as a "cultural problem," and this again points to the fundamental issue in history-writing of what to do with literature. When Erich Gruen says at the end of an often-cited essay

---

[51] Of my own work on sexuality, I can cite, before 1998, Richlin 1992b[1983]: xviii, xx, 34, 37, 44, 46, 51, 54, 55, 65, 82 (a graffito), 89, 93, 194, 217, 223, 224, 226, citing only the historical discussions; social hierarchy was a central concern of the book, as spelled out at xxii, "Most of all, this book considers the implications of the ideological construction of Roman male sexuality for nondominant Romans: women, slaves, foreigners, boys." Still before 1998: 1993b *passim*, esp. 534, 536–7, 545–6; 2014a: 197–240 (on class and the body in women's religion; originally publ. 1997). Since 1998, Richlin 2013b, 2015a, the article "Sexuality" in the 2012 *OCD*, and the article "Sex, Roman" in the 2010 *Oxford Encyclopedia of Ancient Greece and Rome*, from which I cite the second sentence: "First, Rome was a slave culture, and Roman sexual categories are thoroughly enmeshed in status categories." See also Parker 2007; Walters 1997. Among work Harper cites as acceptable: Bradley 1984: 116–18, duBois 2003, McGinn's work, and Williams 2010: 15–40. Somewhat unfairly, he omits from this list Joshel and Murnaghan 1998, from whom he borrows a major axiom, duly cited (291 n. 69). For an overview of the non-integration of ancient women into ancient history, see Richlin 2014a: 23–34.

[52] Cato's handbook on farm management has fascinated historians of slavery, and must attract the reader of the *palliata*, since Plautus and Cato were coevals, although the book is not datable and may have been written well after Plautus' death (see Astin 1978: 190–1; cf. Leigh 2004: 148–52 for detailed discussion). Further background on Cato's interactions with his slaves is often drawn from Plutarch's *Life of Cato*, also tempting, but Plutarch lived in Greece three hundred years after Plautus. The best evidence for the conditions of life in the 200s BCE must be the texts then written. On slave rations in Menander, see Cox 2013: 165; differential feeding is listed among techniques in the management of slaves by Bradley (2015: 156).

that Plautus "illuminates and elucidates the central cultural experience of his age: the tension created by interaction between the Greek world and Roman sensibilities" (Gruen 1996a: 157), perhaps he names Hellenism instead of slavery because slavery, to him, is not a *cultural* experience; it has nothing to do with literature, and Plautus is literature. Moreover, as seen above, there is a widespread tendency among historians of culture to use the word "literature" as coextensive with all canonical texts as property of the upper classes, who are taken to be coextensive with "Romans," as if there were no nonelite culture. We are back with Finley's dictum on avoiding literary statements about slaves; this is why it is crucial to deal with the remains of the *palliata* as the remains of performances, a nexus of social forces and historical persons. In any case, surely slavery *is* cultural, just as culture is historical. Page duBois remarks on the tendency of scholars in the field to repeat familiar opinions and to read within well-worn grooves (2003: 23–5), as in dogmatic drag; mutually exclusive disciplinary boundaries have certainly tended to keep the *palliata* out of history. Few classical literary critics have much training in history, and at least within Classics the two areas often keep an uneasy distance from each other, so that it is not at all surprising that a book on Plautus might manifest at most a consciousness of the Second Punic War, or that an historian might not have read more than one or two plays.

The work of writers like duBois and Hunter, when joined with that of theater historians, makes it plain how what went on in Italy in the 200s BCE is part of a large-scale historical picture in which theater and human trafficking are co-implicated. Virginia Hunter was ahead of her time, in 1994, in treating Attic comedy alongside the Attic orators as a way to get at the lived experiences of slaves. She provides a catalogue of corporal punishments, including deprivation of food, chains, beatings both onstage and in threats, and tattooing (166–8), and analyzes what she calls "slave laments" (167).[53] This category is of great interest to the *palliata*, especially the opening of Aristophanes, *Wealth* (1–7), spoken by the slave Kariôn:

> ὡς ἀργαλέον πρᾶγμ' ἐστίν, ὦ Ζεῦ καὶ θεοί,
> δοῦλον γενέσθαι παραφρονοῦντος δεσπότου·
> ἢν γὰρ τὰ βέλτισθ' ὁ θεράπων λέξας τύχῃ,
> δόξῃ δὲ μὴ δρᾶν ταῦτα τῷ κεκτημένῳ,

---

[53] From Hunter's catalogue: slaves talk about being beaten, *Frogs* 542–8, 741–8, 812–13, and Menander, *Heros* 1–5; list of tortures, *Frogs* 618–21; beatings, *Samia* 306–7, 321, 440–1, 663, 679–80; puns on παῖς/παίειν (above). On slave laments, also *Knights* 4–5, 64–70, and *Wasps* 1292–5. Compare Fraenkel, on *Poen.* 823–44: "a motif so beloved since Old Comedy" (2007: 101). For Hunter's long discussion of the mill as a "house of correction," see chapter 8.

μετέχειν ἀνάγκη τὸν θεράποντα τῶν κακῶν: 5
τοῦ σώματος γὰρ οὐκ ἐᾷ τὸν κύριον
κρατεῖν ὁ δαίμων, ἀλλὰ τὸν ἐωνημένον.

Oh, Zeus and gods, what a tough job it is
to be the slave of a master who's out of his mind!
For, even if the servant offers the best advice,
and his owner still decides not to follow it,
the servant has to have a share in the bad results. 5
Fate doesn't let him rule as master
of his own body – that belongs to the one who bought him.[54]

This speech, which opens the play, is closely comparable in format and content with Sosia's entrance song in *Amphitruo* (chapter 2), and with the speech of the boy prostitute in *Pseudolus*, which is, like Kariôn's speech, in iambic senarii; comparable, in fact, with a whole group of complaints by slaves about their owners' faults (chapter 4). This is, then, a type of shtick that first becomes visible to us late in Old Comedy, and stays in the mix through the *palliata*; it is significant that the example in *Wealth* is much more like what is in the *palliata* than are other examples in Aristophanes, for in *Frogs* and *Wealth*, as has often been remarked, a slave takes center stage for the first time (that we know of). The opening scene of *Frogs* revolves around the metatheatrical point that jokes where slaves complain about carrying a heavy burden are old and corny (1–37); Jeffrey Henderson translates ἐστ' ἤδη χολή (*Frogs* 4) as "It's a groaner."[55] Old Comedy was performed in southern Italy and was part of theatrical revival culture through the 300s, although not thereafter (Revermann 2006: 68–85), so that the presence of the same shtick, in Latin, and long after *Wealth* was first performed, attests to traditional circulation by actors, but adapting to local conditions. David Konstan, writing on the "banality of violence" in New Comedy, opens with methodological cautions on taking comic lines to be a reflection of contemporary reality, but concludes (with regard to the opening of Menander's *Aspis*, where the slave Daos leads in a group of war captives): "The violence implicit in the institution of slavery shows through as part of the backdrop, taken for granted, of the social world of Menandrean comedy" (Konstan 2013: 158).[56]

---

[54] Trans. Henderson, with slight modifications. On Kariôn and his significance, see Revermann 2006: 268–9, 272.
[55] For an overview of jokes about old jokes in Old Comedy, with bibliography, see Ferriss-Hill 2015: 74–5.
[56] For a treatment of *Aspis* that takes the play as critique rather than acquiescence, see James 2014. On the methodological point, see Parker 1989: 234.

That the beating of slaves was shtick in Old Comedy is attested in the often-cited lines from the parabasis of *Peace* (742–7) in which the chorus boasts that Aristophanes will not play the beating of slaves for a laugh, as all his rivals do. This is the same kind of joke as the one in the *Frogs* opening scene, and is itself a form of shtick, a laugh line. What is important is that the list of beating jokes in Old Comedy and New Comedy combined, although vivid, is short, about twenty instances all told, a point Hunter brings up herself (169; cf. Parker 1989: 233). There are also places where Greek and Roman jokes do not overlap, as in the list of punishments in *Frogs*, which resembles the one at *Asinaria* 548–50, but does not match it; in brief, few traces of tattooing in Rome, and, as Holt Parker observed, no crucifixion in Athens (1989: 239–40). On the other hand, although the instances of violence in Greek are rarer, they are markedly more violent than the ones in Roman comedy, and that is especially true of the violence in Herodas: not only *Mim.* 5, with its onstage torture of a slave, but the even more violent *Mim.* 3, with its onstage flogging of a schoolboy, at his mother's behest, as she looks on with approval.[57] Similarly, the heavy-burden jokes show up in the *palliata*, as when Leonida says it is the slave's job to carry the burden (*As.* 660), or when Syncerastus complains about the paraphernalia he has to carry (*Poen.* 852–63, incorporating a beating joke and an adultery-punishment joke), or when Syra in *Mercator* makes the same complaint as she trudges in with the luggage (672–5, figurative). But there are few of these jokes, and they are totally devoid of the Aristophanic punchline, which is, as Dionysus puts it, "when you shift your baggage and say you need to shit" (*Frogs* 8, trans. Henderson). Fart jokes, yes; a few jokes about urination; no poop jokes. The biggest change is in the perspective: slaves in Old Comedy, by and large, are jokes; slaves in the *palliata* are the jokers. What has changed from Old Comedy to the *palliata* is underscored by the resurfacing of a line from *Frogs* at the climax of *Asinaria*: κατάβα, πανοῦργε, says Dionysus to the slave Xanthias, telling him to get down off the donkey – "Get down, smartass" (35); but "Stand still so I can get down now on the slope, although you're worthless," says Libanus to his owner, as he jumps down off his back (*asta ut descendam nunciam in proclivi, quamquam nequam es, As.* 710; see chapter 4). The burden of the joke has shifted, so to speak.

Hunter also points out that the scarred and tattooed bodies of punished slaves are object lessons for their fellow slaves, as are the acts of

---

[57] On Herodas *Mim.* 3, see duBois 2010: 94–7; on *Mim.* 5, see Fountoulakis 2007, and duBois 2007: 435–9, contextualizing this violence in the Macedonian regime in Alexandria.

punishment themselves; in Herodas, as in the *palliata*, slaves grab the one about to be punished and help with the punishment. Moreover, she argues (1994: 176–81), state punishments constitute a "systematic humiliation," in display tortures like the stocks and pillory, and in the actions of the *agoranomoi* (178), who have the condemned dragged across the agora. The *agoranomoi*, then, become in this context the equivalent of the Roman *tresviri* (chapter 2), which casts a new light on their presence in Curculio's list of officials who must make way for him (*Cur.* 285). The *palliata* also stages punishment by forced disappearance – Hegio sends Tyndarus off to the quarries to "teach the other prisoners a lesson" (*captivis aliis documentum dabo, Capt.* 752) – yet *Persa* opens with Sagaristio's return from the mill. Likewise, although less explicit stress is placed on public humiliation in the *palliata*, still it must underlie the boasting by bad slaves like Leonida and Libanus in *Asinaria* and Sagaristio in *Persa* (chapter 6), proud to claim a despised identity. If, as many have argued, torture is a way to divide slave from free, and, as Hunter puts it, a way to make slaves known to themselves as slaves, then the onstage declaration that the process has failed is a radical move, for it is Leonida who says, *tam ego homo sum quam tu* (above).[58] Konstan, in a subtle reading of similar boasting in *Aspis* (2013: 157), ponders its meaning to the citizen audience and the question of what "manliness" could have meant for a slave at that time; again, in the *palliata*, the burden of the joke has shifted.

DuBois (2003: 101–25) also surveys the beating and mistreatment of slaves in comedy and Greek oratory, taking a close look at some of the scenes listed by Hunter. In particular, she adds to a category Hunter deals with in her chapter on slaves in the household: sexual vulnerability. Apart from the many jokes about prostitutes in Old Comedy, she shows how the assumption of household slaves' availability is taken for granted in Aristophanes, even in small details (duBois 2003: 103, 104–5) – still onstage in the *palliata*, where slaves make it an issue (chapters 2, 4, 5 below). Her book's title, *Slaves and Other Objects*, points to the pervasive structural effect of the objectification of human beings in classical Greece: slaves become invisible because they are not agents. In what I think of as the "toile effect," they are like the pattern in upholstery fabric: you are sitting on agricultural workers, but notice them only as decor. Yet they are there

---

[58] Slaves as object lessons: Hunter 1994: 173, 182. Torture the dividing mark between slave and free: duBois 2003: 106 ("marks that set apart the bodies of the unfree"); Finley 1998[1980]: 161–3; Hunter 1994: 176, 181; Saller 1994: 133–53; and Cox 2013: 161 (on slaves in Menander), following Hunter. On the meaning of Libanus' boasting, contrast Fitzgerald 2000: 40 (discussed in the introduction to Part II, below).

to be seen, should we choose to, outside the window. Expanding Hunter's observations, duBois sees the marks on beaten and tattooed slaves as "part of the visual landscape of the ancient city and its households" (2003: 108), and she wants Hellenists to stop airbrushing that landscape: "The slave pops up to defy the idealization of antiquity which has defined modernity's relationship to ancient Greece" (30). In central Italy, too, some bodies bore the marks of slavery, and even if tattooing was not a standing joke in what remains of Plautus, the title of Naevius' *Stigmatias* suggests that tattooed slaves at least circulated into Latium in the 200s: *caveat emptor*. Punitive tattooing wrote the name of the slave's crime across the face; the actor's mask, then, might mask a permanent mask.[59] Most of all, duBois wants scholars not only to *see* the slaves in the texts we study, but to realize the ways in which those texts *un-see* slaves; she wants both to rematerialize slaves and deobjectify them, to understand what it meant to think in a world before abolition.

Adele Scafuro, in an overview of the transition from the late 300s to the 200s in Greek drama, set up a thought-experiment: "an Athenian septuagenarian theater-goer in 305 BCE looks at comedy" (2014: 202–7). What it meant to have a particular lifespan must be a concern for any historically grounded study of theater audiences. Susan Lape (2004) sets New Comedy in the context of the rule of Athens by the successive regimes of Demetrius of Phalerum and Demetrius Poliorcetes (see Appendix 1); her book opens with the words, "Athenian history between the battle of Chaeronea in 338 B.C. and the end of the Chremonidean War in 260 is punctuated by one military disaster after another" (2004: 1). She argues that comedy reacted to the Macedonian occupation by reinforcing, or "reproducing," the norms of the democratic polis, helping to preserve these norms until the final collapse of the democracy in 260. This process, however, was a failure, for comedy's push towards greater inclusivity of marginal groups (women, slaves, foreigners) was outweighed by its repeated return to the "foundational principles of nativity and legitimacy," and the same was true for the city as a whole. Thus, despite moves to enfranchise slaves who had fought for the city in 403/2, and Hyperides' proposed expansion of citizenship after Chaeronea (338), concern for pure bloodlines prevented radical change.[60] This is a major point of difference between Athens and Rome,

---

[59] For facial tattooing, see Jones 1987: 148, and chapter 7 below.
[60] Lape on the bottom line of New Comedy: 2004: 252–3. On Athens and Macedon in this period, 2004: 1–10, 40–67; on Menander and ideology, with further bibliography, 10–12, and esp. 13–39 on the contemporary politics behind his apparently apolitical plays.

where the plot is driven by slaves' desire for manumission as well as by the hope of return for lost citizens. In the *palliata*, both actors and audience inhabited a world not centered on Athens, a world affected from Ionia to Alexandria to Sicily to Italy by the wars of Philip II, Alexander, and the *diadochoi*, while the wars of Italy were gaining the momentum to surge eastward in an opposing shock wave. But not yet.

History of the 200s BCE: War, Poverty, Class Conflict

Knowing where to stop is as important as knowing where to start. Emma Dench highlighted (2003: 295) "the obvious dangers in writing an overly teleological account of ancient Italy, one that constantly projects the future greatness of Rome." The *palliata* developed during a century in which Roman hegemony was not a foregone conclusion; for some of that time, many must have thought Rome's days were numbered. Again, Gellius placed Plautus' *floruit* during the Second Punic War, and the prologue speaker in *Cistellaria*, at least, cheers the audience on to victory against the *Poeni* (202). The modern reader needs to bear in mind how long these wars lasted: the First Punic War, twenty-four years, by Polybius' reckoning; Hannibal's invasion of Italy, fifteen years, or more than three times the length of the German occupation of France in World War II – the repercussions of which are still felt, and still expressed onstage. A look at the timeline in Appendix I shows the constant barrage of wars and incidents of mass enslavement in Italy and around the Mediterranean in the 200s: the aftermath of Alexander, and indeed Alexander casts a long shadow across this book. If the *palliata* belongs to central Italy and not to Rome alone, it also displays a perspective not only Italian but what might be called "trans-Mediterranean," for its jokes, its geography, and its dance steps come from all over. Even its New Comedy framework may well be more second-hand than new, arriving in central Italy travel-stained, not pristine.

Stephen Oakley says in his commentary on Livy book 10 that, after agriculture, "warfare ... is the single most important factor in Roman history in this period" (2005: 4). The timeline depends on the *fasti triumphales*, which have some gaps, but, as Oakley notes, "The Romans went to war with extraordinary frequency, virtually every year between 343 and 242" (20); "our sources for the 280s and 270s are full of references to fighting in southern Italy" (25). This idea has been central to the work of historians like Nathan Rosenstein (2004, 2006, 2012) and to Arthur Eckstein's view of Rome in the Hellenistic context of "an exceptionally competitive and cruel interstate system, a militarized, multipolar anarchy" (2006a: 315, cf.

2006b). Eckstein argues that the bellicose Romans were surrounded by equally bellicose states; certainly the warlords of the eastern Mediterranean make their presence felt in the *palliata*. Roman historians citing monuments of public honor in this period look to the *elogia* of the Scipios and the funeral eulogy of L. Metellus, and Plautus' plays often spoof these virtue and conquest lists, but equally often the plays spoof the grandiose statues set up by Seleucid kings and the conquest lists of their chroniclers (chapter 8). As with paratragedy, the audience picks up a double reverberation here, for the successor kings set the tone for aspiring Roman *nobiles*, in their different ways. Stefan Weinstock charted the development of the cult of Victoria from the 290s through the 180s, and traced its iconography back to Alexander; at the outset of the century, he argues, "The earthquake in the east … opened up a new era, and … the Romans themselves did not yet really know where those gods would lead them" (1957: 247). It is in this uncertain time that the *palliata* began to form. As we will see in chapter 3, the gods of victory, as Mercurius reminds the audience of *Amphitruo*, appeared on the Roman stage; his metatheatrical fancy footwork in this prologue typifies the plays' view of the state from below, as slaves play gods.

The 200s began, in Rome, with the Third Samnite War (298–290), which provided L. Cornelius Scipio Barbatus, cos. 298, with a few lines for his *elogium*; but war was accompanied by continued mass agitation within the city. Activism in the late 300s resulted in the abolition of *nexum* (debt-bondage) in 326 or 313, but this cannot have solved the underlying problem, as witness the Third Secession of the Plebs in 287 and Livy's notice that debtors in chains were freed for military service in 216. Hence the recurring theme of debt and bankruptcy in the *palliata* (noted by Gruen, but located, as usual, "in the early 2nd century," because he is talking about Plautus; rarely noticed by historians of the 200s, doubtless for the same reason).[61] The adjudgement of debtors to their creditors is not only a stock plot point but common parlance in the plays. The *palliata* had to have been in existence during the First Punic War (264–241), a war fed by slave and proletarian rowers; the indemnity exacted by Rome from Carthage doubtless helped fund the *ludi* at which Livius Andronicus staged two plays, but

---

[61] Livy on debtors: 23.14.3, *quique pecuniae iudicati in vinculis essent*; pointed out by Ste. Croix (1981: 572 n. 65), among others. Gruen on usury: 1996a: 146–8, repeated in capsule form in Gruen 2014: 611, where the problem is associated with "the aftermath of the Hannibalic war." Certainly so for the performance of *Pseudolus* in 191 (cf. Feeney 2010), but, as Gruen himself argued, the jokes in the *palliata* cannot safely be pinned down to single dates. See discussion in chapter 3, including a loan joke from Naevius.

it was nothing compared to the indemnities that poured in from the 180s onward. Meanwhile in Carthage, a runaway Roman slave named Spendios became one of the leaders of the Mercenary War that almost brought the city down; possibly a deserter.[62] And meanwhile in Athens, while the *Nea* rolled on, the people of the city endured great hardships as Greece fell apart, and the remains of Menander already attest to the commonness of poverty and hunger. The freed shepherd Tibeios in *Heros* is casually said to have "withered away" (ἀπέσκλη) because he borrowed money to feed his foster children in a time of hunger (λιμός), ran out of money, and could not get a further loan (28–30).[63] All warfare involved crop disruption and food shortage; siege warfare, very common in the 200s, depended for its effectiveness on starvation of the besieged. So the Italian wars likewise left people hungry – if not always in Rome itself, in other towns the actors knew. When the *parasitus* Gelasimus says he was born *per annonam caram*, "at a time when bread cost dearly," he is pointing to a fact well known to the audience: in times of food shortage, the cost goes up, and rich and poor are affected differently.[64] Endemic hunger is embodied onstage by the hungry Dossennus in the Atellan farce that came up to central Italy from the south, and by the hungry *parasitus* in the *palliata*; Horace, at least, took Plautus to be conflating the two (see chapter 3). The role of Manducus, with his hungry jaws, is invoked in *Rudens* as a gig for the *ludi*.[65] The *ludi* – and not only the public *ludi*, but votive and funeral *ludi* – gave the people not only plays but free food, and the implication of these gifts in popular politics and corruption (*ambitus*) is attested already in 328 BCE: the rumor that a *visceratio* (a communal feast on sacrificial meat) was given to pay off

[62] Plb. 1.63.4 (the length of the First Punic War), and 1.62.9–63.3 on the indemnity; on its relative size, see Kay 2014: 37–8. On Spendios, see Hoyos 2007, Walbank 1957: 135, and Welwei 1988: 59; Polybius identifies him as Καμπανὸς ηὐτομοληκὼς παρὰ τῶν Ῥωμαίων δοῦλος (1.69.4). He is a major character in Flaubert's *Salammbô*. On slaves in the military, see chapter 2.

[63] On hunger in Athens in the early 200s BCE, see Momigliano 2012[1959]: 41–3; in Olbia on the Black Sea around 200, Austin 1981: 170–4, with Garnsey 1988: 14–15, 83–5 on Olbia, Samos, and elsewhere; and cf. Raaflaub 2014, esp. 37–8, on conditions in Athens from the end of the Peloponnesian War to Chaeronea. War's hunger is onstage already in the starving Megarian who sells his daughters in *Acharnians* on account of λιμοῦ (743).

[64] On the vocabulary of hunger, see Garnsey 1988: 18–19; for the relation between popular unrest and grain prices, see Thompson 1966: 18–19 on the eighteenth century. On differential experience according to class and status, Garnsey 1988: 24, 32–4. For the connection between war, hunger, and politics in early to mid-Republican Rome, Garnsey 1988: 167–97, esp. on Sp. Maelius (177) and on Plb. 9.11a (192); in Italy in the late 200s, Erdkamp 1998: 280–9. For hunger onstage, see chapter 2 below.

[65] On Manducus and Dossennus – often taken to be the same stock character, on the basis of an emended passage in Varro (*L.* 7.95) – see Beare 1964: 139–42, Manuwald 2011: 172–3. Paul the Deacon's digest of Festus (115L) shows Manducus as a funny/scary, gape-mouthed, noisy *effigies* carried in the *pompa*, with reference to *Rud.* 535 (cf. chapter 2).

an acquittal on a charge of rape, the donor later being elected tribune of the plebs.[66] Regular distributions of free grain long postdate the *palliata*. Peter Garnsey argues that the feeding of the plebs in times of shortage was regarded by the Republican senate as its own prerogative, a process not stabilized until the conquest of provinces that paid a substantial grain tax (so, not before 210), and even then opposed by some "on principle" (Garnsey 1988: 197).

The figure of the *summus vir* comes up repeatedly in the *palliata*, not in a good way; sympathetic characters view the *summi viri* with scorn and suspicion, while the figure of the "people's man at the top," *vir summus populi*, is scorned by nasty characters like the pimp Dordalus (below, especially chapters 2 and 3).[67] The census property classes placed citizens into military classes – the less property, the less well armed – and the plays reflect the effect on morale. P. A. Brunt comments, "A secession was essentially a military strike" (1971a: 640). At the same time, public art linked military service, manumission, and a square meal: a painting in the Temple of Libertas on the Aventine portrayed the public banquet held at Beneventum for the conscripted slaves who had won their freedom in 214.[68] Livy records that, in 293, people first watched the *ludi Romani* wearing laurel wreaths (10.47.3, *coronati ... spectarunt*, see Oakley 2005: 461–2): what did the wreaths mean to civilians? According to a joke made by Cato a century later, when the practice was still ongoing, they meant the difference to the *populus* between safety and sale by a victorious enemy: a fate to be feared by slaves as well as free.[69] The character addressed contemptuously as *vir summe populi* is the slave Toxilus, who wants to buy his girlfriend out of slavery. Onstage, at least, the *populus* includes slaves, and indeed from the

---

[66] For the story (Livy 8.22.2–4) and an account of distributions of food from 291 to 174 BCE, see Kajava 1998: 112–15; and in connection with theatrical shows, the list in Taylor 1937: 292–3 n. 21. Another *convivium publicum* is recorded in December 217 at Livy 22.1.20: a chronological headache, connected by Livy with the simultaneous founding (!) of the Saturnalia, and placed in his narrative between the panic caused by Hannibal's victories at the Trebia (December 218) and Lake Trasimene (June 217), in a year of particular friction between senate and *populus*. See chapter 4 on public banquets, public space, and the *palliata*.

[67] Contrast Sharrock 2016: 101, "Plautus appears to have little interest in citizen poverty"; 116, "the one place where Plautus does show an interest in the relative positions of different citizens is *Aulularia*."

[68] On these slaves, known as *volones*, see Leigh 2004: 26–8, who comments that spectators who saw slaves partying onstage in the *palliata* could have seen this painting as well; also Stewart 2012: 125–9, Welwei 1988: 5–18, and, on the painting, Koortbojian 2002.

[69] On Polybius, the census, and military classes, see chapter 2; on the laureled *populus*, see chapter 3, with Richlin 2017a for more detail on both, and work by Kathy Gaca (above) on what they had to fear.

stage the word *populus* sums up the audience (*As.* 4, *Poen.* 11, *Rud.* 1251), which, as we know, included slaves.

Voicing a widely held view, Oakley writes of Rome in the 290s, "Festivals and the games were the only forms of leisure organized by the state (or indeed by anyone) for the masses; the latter, for which a large proportion of the state was gathered together, provided notable occasions for celebration and display" (2005: 4). This description locates the *ludi* squarely in what James C. Scott called "the public transcript" (below), but I would stress the word "organized," note the top-down view in "display," and question the parenthesized "anyone." "Anyone we know about" would be more accurate; and there is a difference between "art *for* the masses" and "art *of* the masses," who in any case think of themselves not as "the masses" but as "us" (Trinh 1989: 11–15).[70] Nor is "the state," even in the sense "the government," so monolithic in this period, and scholarship follows its fracture lines.

The political history of the 200s in Rome is hotly contested ground, roughly divided between those who focus on poverty, class conflict, and the urban plebs, and those who focus on the upper reaches of Roman society, often identified by these scholars with "the state," as, after all, was done by Althusser: the holders of power are "the state." The first group includes Lily Ross Taylor, with her interest in the urban tribes (2013[1960]); T. J. Cornell, whose history (1995) perhaps most faithfully outlines what Polybius saw as a mixed constitution; Peter Wiseman, whose work often turns to cultural forms like theater; and, most controversially, Fergus Millar (especially 1989). Millar's emphasis on democracy in Rome triggered an emphatic rebuttal from Karl-Joachim Hölkeskamp (2010); along with Nathan Rosenstein, Hölkeskamp has maintained that what held the Republic together was the "acquiescence" of the *populus* to management by the *nobiles*. Discussions of "Roman political culture" revolve around this central point, in which the monuments of public honor, admired by all, serve as cultural glue – *the* glue – that stuck everyone together. So Oakley: "the steady stream of Roman victories and growth of Roman power proved to the populace at large that the government of the state was in good hands" (2005: 12, with an approving footnote to Hölkeskamp). As will be seen below, low characters onstage – slaves and *parasiti* – deliver speeches critical of current political practice (chapter 6). "Slavery" is not in the index of Hölkeskamp 2010, and as far as I can tell he mentions slaves only once in the book (2010: 34); an account of the *populus* in the 200s that

---

[70] On problems with the idea of "art for the masses," see also Parker 2011.

omits slavery cannot be a full account.[71] A polity includes everyone; all are agents; no one could maintain that all agents in the 200s were acquiescent.

The appearance of Matthew Leigh's *Comedy and the Rise of Rome* in 2004 marked a new departure in the historical study of the *palliata*. Grounding his argument in a reading of the whole corpus, Leigh stated his aim as setting history and comedy "in dialogue with each other" (1); like Susan Lape, he begins from war. The difference between the Macedonian occupation of Athens and the net rise in Roman fortunes from the First Punic War to the time of Terence suggests the difference in dynamic between Lape's story and Leigh's. Not that his perspective is triumphalist; he emphasizes that he has "found the comic texts most eloquent … in the expression given to perspectives which assimilate uneasily to those propounded by the senate and the Roman ruling class." Although he does not consider the presence of slaves in the audience, he does not treat the audience as unitary, either; rather, it includes people affected in various ways by the big wars. He traces the point at issue in the plot of *Captivi* – the return of captured soldiers – through historical events of the 200s from Pyrrhus to Cannae, and beyond to the triumph of Flamininus in 194. Fundamental to this book is his observation that the senate's decision not to ransom the soldiers taken captive at Cannae, and Flamininus's recovery of 1,200 of them who had been enslaved in Greece, meant that "large numbers of Romans of the age of Plautus had experienced slavery from both sides" (88). When Pseudolus, as Leigh notes (52), speaks to his owner the famous words of Brennus the Gaul – *vae victis* – what would that mean to an audience member who had come to Rome as part of the spoils?

The plays make it clear that the signs of the state looked different from below. Livy's annalistic notice of the laurel wreaths (293 BCE) is immediately followed by a notice that the same curule aediles who had put on the *ludi Romani* that year also fined some *pecuarii* and, with the money realized, paid to have the road paved from the temple of Mars to Bovillae (10.47.4): that is, they fined some ranchers and hired, or bought, workmen to pave part of the via Appia (Oakley 2005: 266, 463). This concisely ties together the aediles, the *ludi*, the roads, the wars, the issue of land transport, and agribusiness. Invisible behind the *pecuarii* are the slave herdsmen who, 160 years later, would be at the center of the slave revolts. Likewise, as will be seen below (chapters 7 and 8), Roman histories almost never tell who built the roads, except when it comes to forced labor under the

---

[71] For a debate on what sources count in political culture, see Hölkeskamp 2014, Wiseman 2014. See Crawford 2011 for a critique of Hölkeskamp 2010.

Tarquins; the roads facilitated not only trade but, more importantly in this
period, the movement of troops. The roads that, like other public works,
bear the names of Roman politicians and cost so much to build, meant
something different to those who walked down them. In the *palliata*, they
said so.

Free Speech

How could a troupe of low-class actors voice a critique of the state? Or of
the treatment of slaves by owners? Many have felt such a critique to be out
of the question, and certainly not what was going on in the *palliata*.[72] The
state paid for the performances at the *ludi*, it is argued, and so the content
of the *palliata* must be pro-state; the *ludi* served the purposes of the "elite";
the audience was restricted to slave-owning Roman citizens (an instance
of dogmatic drag). A short answer is provided by an important fragment
of the comedy *Faeneratrix*, attributed to Plautus by the first-century-BCE
scholar Sinnius Capito (Festus 512L = Plautus fr. 71–3):

> "Vapula Papiria" in proverbio fuit antiquis, de quo Sinnius Capito sic
> refert: tum dici solitum est, cum vellent minantibus significare se eos neg-
> ligere et non curare, fretos iure libertatis. Plautus in *Feneratrice*: "Heus
> tu! in barbaria quod fecisse dicitur libertus suae patronae, ideo dico
> <tibi>: 'Libertas salve, vapula Papiria.'" in barbaria est in Italia.

> "Get beat up, Papiria" was a saying they had in the old days, on which
> Sinnius Capito reports as follows: "They used to say this, when they wanted
> to convey to people threatening them that they held them of no account
> and did not care, relying on the rights of liberty. So Plautus in *She Charged
> Interest*: 'Hey you! Like they say the freedman in barbarian-land did to the
> lady who used to own him, so I say to you: "Hello liberty; get beat up,
> Papiria."' 'In barbarian-land' is in Italy."

Apart from what Sinnius Capito thought this meant: Plautus here expresses
the idea of snapping your fingers in the face of power, but at a triple
remove. A masked character says the line; he compares himself (or herself)
to a freedman speaking to his *patrona*; the freedman is in *barbaria*. The
character speaks the freedman's line to "you": first "Hello, liberty," then the
enigmatic *vapula Papiria*. Whoever or whatever Papiria was, she/it is vehemently disrespected in this catchphrase. The expression *libertas salve* is a
meta-expression of the greeting to the newly freed slave (chapter 8); *vapula*

---

[72] Most widely cited is McCarthy 2000 (see above).

Papiria, satisfyingly onomatopoeic, adapts a verb that, in the first person, means "I get beat up" (so Sosia in *Amphitruo*), but which, as an imperative, means something like "Fuck you!" For a freedman to say it to a *patrona* is a marked reversal of roles; we do not know what character was addressed as "you," but it seems safe to assume the speaker is expressing defiance. The shift in person is a protective device, just like the shift in place that turns Italy into *barbaria*: here, but not here.

The best explanation for how the *palliata* might have worked is provided by James C. Scott in *Domination and the Arts of Resistance* (1990). Scott argues here against Victor Turner's widely accepted view that rituals of reversal are conservative, a view I myself enthusiastically embraced in analyzing Roman satire as analogous to Roman institutions like the soldiers' songs at triumphs, or the Floralia (Richlin 1992b[1983]: 10–11, 75–76, 228–30). My main concern there, however, was with how the sex/gender system was perpetuated, and in that respect, I think, the *palliata* was as conservative as Turner might wish. The *palliata* in fact provides a prime example of how slavery constructed sexuality in central Italy in the 200s BCE, since the sexuality on show is not only the marriage plot that sometimes runs the story-line, or the still hegemonic plot involving control of a prostitute, but the desires created by the enslavement of boys and men (see chapter 5). Where Scott's model surpasses Turner's is in its flexibility, for, in the spectrum of transcripts he lays out at the outset (Scott 1990: 26), he suggests how speech could shade between "hidden" and "public" meanings. On the one hand, as he says, "power relations are ubiquitous," so that even among themselves slaves have constraints and hierarchies; on the other, "a partly sanitized, ambiguous, and coded version of the hidden transcript is always present in the public discourse of subordinate groups" (19). This feeds into Scott's definition of "infrapolitics" (198): forms of "disguised, low-profile, undisclosed resistance," among which he instances "masked appropriations" by "disguised resisters," "carnival symbolism," and "myths of social banditry and class heroes."

It is generally felt that the performances at the *ludi* were high-profile (so, for example, Holt Parker, below), but the performers were certainly low, and, by definition, disguised, probably masked; it seems fair to describe the slave Epidicus as a class hero, especially since the slave Chrysalus likes *Epidicus* so much (*Bac.* 214), and the *grex* baldly instructs the audience to applaud for Epidicus at the end: "the person who found freedom through his own bad behavior" (*Epid.* 732; see chapter 4, and chapter 6 on "editorials"). What is really important in Scott's graphic showing "resistance below the line" (198) is that he locates there, as a form of "public declared resistance," "public assertion of worth by gesture, dress, speech." As will be seen throughout this book, assertions of worth by slaves are common onstage, a direct counter to the definition of slaves as without honor (see Part II introduction). As Scott says, the hidden transcript is formed by the "systematic *frustration of reciprocal action*," leading to "an acting out in fantasy ... of the anger and reciprocal aggression denied by the presence of domination" (1990: 37–8). Onstage, vengeance is possible.

Turner's argument hinged on the idea that rituals of reversal (for instance, carnival) are temporary, and reinforce order by being extra-ordinary: all goes back to normal the next day. Similar ideas have had a major influence on readings of Plautus since the publication of Erich Segal's *Roman Laughter* (1968); his argument there that "clever" slaves onstage do not even want to be manumitted has been widely repeated even though it is easily falsifiable (see chapter 8). Following Segal on this point, many have said that, in the plays, the normal order is maintained when civic norms are validated at the end of each play. But the bulk of most of the plays is taken up with gross breaches of norms, so that, for individual audience members, scenes can trump the narrative arc, in keeping with Michel de Certeau's ideas about "tactics" (1984; see Richlin 2014b: 178). Nor are the endings so normal, since the ending regarded by many as standard (in fact, occurring in only five of the extant plays) involves a prostitute or slave-woman marrying a young citizen: Cinderella, or *Pretty Woman*. This fantasy belongs to those whose civil status has been erased.

The problems of speech for dominated groups have been widely discussed, nowhere more so than in the history of slavery in North America. This is both an historical problem, with local features, and a transhistorical problem, articulated by anthropologists and sociolinguists: at all times and places, lack of power means lack of free speech. This issue has engaged Hellenists interested in *parrhêsia* in Old Comedy and in the lack of it in New Comedy; Romanists have fastened on Naevius in our period. From the time of Julius Caesar onward, the issue of coded expression by performers runs into the problem of "how to talk to a king," a preoccupation in antiquity for upper-level bureaucrats. But the problem as it appears in the *palliata* is emphatically one of slave speech; there is some indication that, in contemporary tragedy, the problem was one of free speech for plebeians. In particular, the discussion in chapter 6 of *mussito* and related words – all denoting subvocal utterance – identifies a vocabulary specific to the issue of slave speech, one that had antecedents in Aristophanes and Herodas but arrives at a full-blown expression in the *palliata*; this lexical association was anticipated in passing by Elaine Fantham (2005: 223), in a discussion of *libertas* in the mid-Republic. A rare extension of the verb *mussito* to a non-slave in the plays applies it to soldiers in the army rank-and-file (*manipulares, Truc.* 491), suggesting that this critique might extend to the predicament of the relatively powerless confronting those above them; certainly Polybius' description of the Roman army of his day makes it clear that the common soldier went in fear of his officers (6.37–8).[73]

In a parable titled "The Rock that Changed Things," the science fiction writer Ursula Le Guin imagines a slave society in which the job of the slaves is to make beautiful paved terraces for the owners, who look down from above at the patterns in the stone. The owners read the patterns as variations in the shape and size of stones; finally, one slave recognizes that there are patterns in color and begins to make new ones, which the owners do not perceive, even when a slave points out the color patterns to them. The owners' lack of perception, an aspect of their cruelty, finally results in a slave revolt, which the owners do not see coming. The possibilities for subversive viewing are often pointed out by members of muted groups, as for example by bell hooks in "The Oppositional Gaze" (1992: 116):

> Even in the worst circumstances of domination, the ability to manipulate one's gaze in the face of structures of domination that would contain it, opens up the possibility of agency. ... Subordinates in relations of power learn experientially that there is a critical gaze, one that 'looks' to document, one that is oppositional.

Slaves and freed slaves in the *palliata* critique the arrogant owner by "playing the owner," and the same could be said of the *palliata* as a whole. They show what the *summi viri* look like from below. They "look" to document, to bear witness. As Tranio says, making a spectacle of the owner is the essence of comedy.

Humor Theory

Freud, in *Jokes and Their Relation to the Unconscious*, described "the mechanism of the pleasurable effect" in jokes as stemming from the lifting of an inhibition, from "a purpose being satisfied whose satisfaction would otherwise not have taken place" (1960: 143–5). It is true that he gave more weight to jokes that help to overcome an internal obstacle (e.g. politeness learned in childhood) than to jokes that overcome an external obstacle (e.g. fear of powerful people). As Plautus' plays attest, however, external obstacles

---

[73] See chapter 2, and Richlin 2017a:233–4 on this passage and in general on army jokes in the *palliata*.

were a big issue for the audience of the *palliata*, as might be summed up in the stunned reaction of the Mercator in *Asinaria*: "You, a slave, insult a free person?" (*tun libero homini / male servos loquere?*, 477–8). In this scene, and in many others like it, slave characters lay claim to equal rights, as the slave Leonida does here: "You insult another, and you're not to be replied to? / I'm just as much a person as you" (*tu contumeliam alteri facias, tibi non dicatur? / tam ego homo sum quam tu*, 489–90; see chapter 4). The basic joke that underlies *mussito* and its lexical kin, as well as the rest of the jokes in chapter 6, is that slaves are not supposed to speak their grievances aloud. As with "playing the owner," the *palliata* itself does just that. For audiences in the 200s, the biggest inhibition – and so the biggest laugh – belonged to those ordinarily forbidden to say this kind of thing, and then to those who had experienced that prohibition at one time. Of course, since neither audiences nor social groupings are monolithic, any members of the highest census class who were sitting in that audience might well have had a laugh themselves, just by separating themselves from arrogant behavior: they know they are not like that. The historical presence of Roman politicians who wished to champion the *populus* – to be the *vir summus populi* – is amply attested, well into the 200s. That anyone in this period would have understood the exchange between the Mercator and Leonida as metaphorical, as actually being about a senator insulted by his political rival, seems unlikely to me, but all texts are open to interpretation (see further on this in chapter 6).[74]

It does make a difference who you think was in the audience. Holt Parker argued in 1989, "For the Roman, the free slave was the most terrifying of oxymorons. … The Roman of Plautus' age had good reason to fear his slaves" (236), and "the vast number of references to punishment constantly remind the audience of the absolute power of life and death it holds over these slaves" (238). That is, "the Roman" is a slave-owner, and the idea, following Freud, is that people laugh at what they fear (236). William Fitzgerald explicitly expanded Parker's model to suggest that onstage

---

[74] For discussion of Freud's theories, see Beard 2014: 38–40, 214; Henderson 1975: 10–11, 36–55, on Freud and Old Comedy; Parker 1989: 235–6, on Freud and Plautus; Richlin 1992b[1983]: 59–63. On the "Richard Pryor in Long Beach" model, based on a concert video in which a white audience rolls with laughter while Pryor mocks white people onstage, see Richlin 2014b: 178–9. The metaphorical interpretation of Plautus is most closely associated with McCarthy 2000, but circulates in the meme, "Slaves are good to think with." This was indeed a cultural practice in antiquity, as discussed for classical Athens by duBois (2003: 117–30 and *passim*), and was a favorite figure in Latin love elegy and in Roman Stoic philosophy, particularly in the work of the younger Seneca (see Fitzgerald 2000: 11, on "slavery as a model or metaphor for other institutions"; also on Plautus' slaves as "fantasy projections of the free"). But sometimes a slave is just a slave.

violence "reminded the free of the vulnerability of their own bodies," helping them to cope with their fear of pain (2000: 39). I have suggested,
in response to Parker, that "Perhaps, more straightforwardly, slaves in the
audience laughed to quell their fear of beatings" (2014b: 181). In his 1927
essay "Humour," Freud focused on this kind of gallows humor, arguing
that such joking rejects the pain that would otherwise be felt; this constitutes "the triumph of narcissism, the victorious assertion of the ego's
invulnerability ... Humour is not resigned; it is rebellious" (2001[1927]:
162–3). Or, as the slave Sagaristio belts out, "It'll be bam! pow! on my
back, but I don't care" (*Tuxtax tergo erit meo, non curo, Per.* 264). The
point was made more starkly in a classic study by the refugee sociologist
Antonin Obrdlik, arguing on the basis of his recent experiences in Nazi-
occupied Czechoslovakia: the humor of the oppressed expresses "hope and
wishful thinking," "bravado and defiance"; it belongs to those who "have
to persuade themselves that their present suffering is only temporary";
it indicates "the spirit of resistance" (1942: 710, 712). And, he observes,
"if [the oppressors] can afford to ignore it, they are strong" (716). Parker
today might well concede that "the Roman" is as reductive a figure as the
monolithic audience ("it"), and says as much in his essay on popular culture, advising social critics: "resist the temptation to treat 'the people' as
a lump," "resist creating a monolithic Them as well as an indivisible Us"
(Parker 2011: 167–8). And indeed in the plays the free man with no money,
the *parasitus*, experiences hunger and takes a beating alongside slaves.

It is comedians who make comedy, and Freud, although he loved
a joke, was no comic. Yet what comedians say about their art bears out
Freud's ideas about the hostility that underlies many forms of humor, and
makes explicit the often-noted dark side of comedy. In an interview, Jerry
Seinfeld said, "Well, all comedy starts with anger" (Steinberg 2008: 34).
Eric Idle, of the Monty Python group, set epigraphs to each chapter in
his novel *The Road to Mars* (2000), most of them from famous comedians: Anna Russell ("The reason that there are so few women comics is that
so few women can bear being laughed at," 34); Edmund Kean ("Dying is
easy. Comedy is difficult," his supposed last words, 101); Warren Mitchell
("Comedy comes from conflict, from hatred," 119; he played Alf Garnett);
Billy Wilder ("When I am very sad, I make a comedy, and when I am
very happy I make a serious drama," 128); Pamela Connolly ("Famous
people are very often traumatized individuals with a deep-seated sense
of unworthiness. ... They believe that fame will mean an end to pain,
and access to love," 131; a onetime comedian married to the comedian
Billy Connolly, she is now a psychologist); Joan Rivers ("There is not one

female comic who was beautiful as a little girl," 207); Lenny Bruce ("All my humor is based upon destruction and despair," 230); Samuel Beckett ("Nothing is funner than unhappiness, I grant you that. ... Yes, yes, it's the most comical thing in the world," 233); Lenny Bruce again ("Satire is tragedy plus time," 238, a formula attributed to many); Charlie Chaplin ("Life is a tragedy when seen in close-up, but a comedy in long-shot," 242, also attributed to Buster Keaton); the fifth Marx brother ("History repeats itself, first as tragedy, second as farce," 250); Dudley Moore ("People who indulge in comedy tend to be more and more isolated as the years go by," 271; a line I read on August 13, 2014, the day after Robin Williams hanged himself); Woody Allen ("I think being funny is not anyone's first choice," 275); Buddy Hackett ("I don't want to hear advice from anybody who hasn't walked the fifteen yards," 295, on comedy executives); and, from the fictional *De Rerum Comoedia* that is the McGuffin in Idle's novel, "The strange alchemy of comedy that takes anger and turns it into humor" (173). I parade these modern standup comedians to evoke the ones who built the Latin shtick that made the *palliata*; as W. G. Arnott himself argued, many of the techniques used in the *palliata* "belong to the gag repertoire of pairs of stand-up comics at all periods" (1996b: 67), what is known as the "double act" (see chapter 3). Although it has forerunners in Greek comedy, in central Italy in the 200s it came into full bloom.

　　The apocryphal nature of many of the lines Idle used is a reminder of the way jokes circulate.[75] Even without the grim boost given to Roman oral culture by the slave trade, jokes move on their own, over astonishing distances in space and time. Mary Beard points to one that appears in Freud's *Jokes*, featuring a "Royal Personage," that was also told about Augustus, or so we hear from Macrobius four hundred years later (2014: 214; cf. Freud 1960: 79–80). The uncomfortable relationship between the folklorist and the lore, the grammarian and the *palliata*, does not undercut the reality of oral tradition, which, like a muon, becomes visible only in the cloud chamber of the observer's record. Sara Forsdyke shows how the story of the maroon leader Drimakos meant one thing in its context in Athenaeus's collection in the early 200s CE, and another when it was told to the historian

---

[75] The famous line from Karl Marx picked up by Idle comes from *The Eighteenth Brumaire of Louis Napoleon* (1852), his essay about the coup that followed the 1848 revolution in France. For an entertaining demonstration of Marx's line as a meme before 1852, see the leading source of apocryphal circulation, Wikipedia, juxtaposing the line with a letter of Engels from December 1851 and a passage in Marx's unfinished novel of 1837, *Scorpion and Felix*, in which "Caesar the hero leaves behind him the play-acting Octavianus." http://en.wikipedia.org/wiki/The_Eighteenth_Brumaire_of_Louis_Napoleon, accessed Dec. 2014. For Finley on the *Eighteenth Brumaire*, see Tompkins 2014: 205.

Nymphodorus of Syracuse when he visited Chios in the late 300s BCE, and another, she hypothesizes, to slaves on Chios (Forsdyke 2012: 73–7, 85–9; see chapter 8 below). Like the south Italian vases that show scenes of theater, the *palliata* has a long history of being treated as a knock-off, a poor imitation of a much more sophisticated commodity from the metropole. This view is now undergoing revision: "Foreign objects and concepts tend to be brought into existing value systems and are reinterpreted and used for the benefit of the adopters, usually to send messages to others within their own societies."[76] All the more so in the case of comic performance, where not only does the language have to be translated, and with it the jokes, which famously do not translate well, but all the other elements as well: dance, music, masks, costumes, staging, body language. As Fraenkel demonstrated, it is precisely the jokes, the comic language, and the routines that were added into the framework of the *Nea* in the *palliata*. As many vaudeville memoirs recount, all stage acts are worked out by constant testing in front of an audience, in a process of reciprocal feedback.

Performance Theory

In his introduction to *The Theater of Plautus*, Timothy Moore lays out the ways in which theatrical performances communicate with audiences, which he sees as a relay: "all communication between playwright and audience is accomplished through the actors"; he intends to show "how Plautus molded his actors' relationship with their audience" (1998: 2). On the hypothesis, however, that Plautus, like Livius, acted in his own plays, we might draw less of a distinction between author and actor, and think about what the audience sees, and what the actor sees. The audience sees the actors; the actors see the audience's reactions. "I killed," says the successful standup: she made everyone laugh. The joke-writer, if she has one, gets no credit onstage, and in fact his existence is deliberately suppressed. In the extant plays of Plautus, the prologue speakers quite often give Plautus the credit, but to some extent this is itself a joke; he has a joke name; like Naevius, he is a *poeta barbarus*. The Latin of the *palliata* is wildly exuberant, and the songs are far too intricate to have been improvised, so that a person, "Plautus," is a felt presence behind the words that are all we have

---

[76] Robinson 2004: 207; see Richlin 2017b: 173. With Robinson's model compare Nicola Terrenato's ideas on "cultural *bricolage*" (1998), arguing for regional idiosyncrasies against both the old nationalist portrait of Roman triumph going back to Niebuhr, and Marxist economic models (the discussion in Roth 2007a: 21–4 overstates Terrenato's particular interest in elites): useful for an understanding of variations in local audiences. See above on Cales.

left; at the same time, Marshall's point about the *grex* as a team has important implications for the ways in which meaning was produced onstage, especially since, as he notes, "actors' roles need not correspond to their status offstage" (2006: 87–8). Like the setting, he argues, the acting embodies hybridity, indeterminacy (91); specific, I would add, to its time and place.

When Joel Grey sang "If You Could See Her through My Eyes" in the film *Cabaret*, he was part of a double act: a song and dance with a partner in a gorilla suit, dressed up in a frilly pink outfit. The gorilla, mute, kept perfect time in the dance. If all we had were the words of the song, we would be missing not only the sight gag that plays into the anti-Semitic joke in the last line ("She wouldn't look Jewish at all") but the tune (a perfect sentimental ballad), the dance, and the grotesquerie of a gorilla in pink dancing slippers doing a *pas de deux*. Again, we do not know about masks in the *palliata*, but if they were there, and if the costumed actors looked like the ones we see on earlier Italian vases and terracottas, then most characters looked grotesque; the actors' bodies were grotesquely padded; perhaps they even wore a dangling phallus, and, for the female characters, big false breasts. Gaze theory usually dwells on the specularized performer as the object of desire, a thing of beauty, but there is also a specularization of the grotesque, and this is what draws the objectifying gaze of comedy: Charlie Chaplin, Groucho Marx, Harpo Marx, Phyllis Diller. The actor, already low, animates a low costume that is also a disguise, a form of protection: grotesque Tranio makes a fool of his grotesque owner.[77] Paradoxically, then, the disguise that re-objectifies a person already an object is also the means by which he is able to say whatever he wants to. It is also what allows the audience to laugh; if Leonida made his speech to the Mercator with both of them in a naturalistic getup, Freud's conditions would not be met: no laugh.

The objectifying gaze also works within the diegesis of the play in the specularization of female characters. This is a large element in what, I argue in chapter 5, is a form of drag act. Like Joel Grey with the gorilla, male characters onstage often introduce their female love interest with

---

[77] See Wrenhaven 2013: 136–43 on class and the grotesque on south Italian vases and in Attic and south Italian figurines; Revermann 2006: 145–59, esp. at 152, on the "egalitarian element of uglification": "the grotesque body of fifth-century comedy is a shared body. It is only when young and respectable men and women lose the hallmarks of comic ugliness during the second half of the fourth century that ugliness starts to function as a social differentiator, with grotesque corporality beginning to be the preserve of the socially inferior." It is not clear how, or if, this differentiation was retained in the *palliata*; see chapter 5 on drag. See Dutsch 2015 on Astaphium's makeup; note that the jewelry Astaphium wears is ridiculed as an imitation of rich women's jewelry (discussed in chapters 3, 5, and 8 below).

what I will refer to as a "deictic reception": "Isn't she lovely!" The encasement of the actor in the costume and full head-mask, like the gorilla suit, ensures that all onstage gender is acted – for female characters, the desired beauty as well as the grotesque old woman. Here I differ somewhat from scholars like Dorota Dutsch and Sharon James, who have used the onstage speech and embodiment of women to get at the offstage speech of real, embodied women (Dutsch 2008), and who have worked from the experiences of women in New Comedy to social realities in antiquity, with attention both to slaves (James 2010, 2012, 2014) and to general family relations (James 2015a, forthcoming). There were no women onstage – just comedians. Drag is an eminently historical phenomenon; it works differently in different cultures; in the *grex* of the 200s, drag is grounded in the conditions of slavery and sex trafficking. Accordingly, in the *palliata*, this objectifying gaze is also applied to *pueri*, not only to Paegnium in *Persa*, who, as Marshall points out, is sized up by his flirting partner as weighing only eighty pounds (2006: 94), but perhaps also to Libanus, whose sparring partner jokes that he weighs one hundred pounds naked, chains and all (*As.* 299–305). Certainly the gaze objectifies other *pueri* onstage, and perhaps also other male characters when they dance like a *cinaedus*. For a slave actor, the experience of being up on the stage platform must have been a reminder of the experience of being up on the auction block, and so for audience members as well, from their different perspectives.

But *their* faces were not masked – they were visible to each other, and plainly visible to the actors, from the stage. This amounts to a double gaze, another kind of reverberation, something akin to the *Verfremdungseffekt* that was Brecht's goal, for, in the bright daylight, the audience can see those masked faces looking at them, and indeed often addressing them: disorienting.[78] Moore shows how the actor positions himself as both above and below the audience, in terms of power, and what the *grex* has to say is sometimes fairly insulting. Yet you can see the delight of the front-row audience member insulted from the stage in any concert tape of standup. This is a clown's trick – Cirque du Soleil does it – and it works well with the old device of a plant in the audience; it was old in the 200s, a favorite gambit of the Old Comedy actor singling out the *euruprôktoi* in the audience. This is part of the deal in comedy, and Fitzgerald is not wrong

---

[78] See Kruschwitz 2013, on theater in the late Republic, arguing for a mixed audience and an actively reciprocal exchange between audience and stage, and for the theater as a place where the *populus* found "both a voice and a soundbox." For the audience as "co-producers of the theatrical event," see Revermann 2006: 159–64, and 33–6 on "theatrical reciprocity."

to argue that the audience takes pleasure in self-abjection. It all whizzes by, after all. There it is, however; the actors are objects for the spectators' delight, and the audience are objects for the actors' judgment.

Early in his career, Brecht had a brief fling with slapstick, a short silent film called *Mysterien eines Friseursalons* – "Mysteries of a Barbershop" (1923). Brecht was a great admirer of Chaplin, and the film starred the famous comedian Karl Valentin: a chance echo of ancient comedy, where the barbershop was often mentioned among the "free spaces" where a slave could relax (chapter 4; and see above on *The Rabbit of Seville* – odd how this keeps coming up). What Brecht had that the members of the *grex* did not was a revolutionary political theory, although a couple of references to Cynic philosophers perhaps indicate where the *grex* might have found one (Richlin 2014b: 207). The kind of "people's theater" suggested here for the *palliata* is commonly associated today with practical theorists like Augusto Boal, whose agenda for theater is firmly grounded in Marxist thought (1985: 53):

> [The knowledge transmitted by art] is revealed according to the perspective of the artist or of the social sector in which he is rooted, or which sponsors him, pays him, or consumes his work – especially that sector of society which holds the economic power, controlling with it all the other powers and establishing the directives of all creativity ... This sector is evidently interested in the transmission of that knowledge which helps it to maintain its power ... This does not, however, prevent other sectors or classes from fostering also their own art, which translates the knowledge necessary to them, and in doing so [they] are guided by their own perspective. But the dominant art will always be that of the dominant class, since it is the only class that possesses the means to disseminate it.

This hardly stood in his way, and he spent his career fostering, as in his book's title, the theatre of the oppressed. The history of popular culture is at the root of my project, and the question of whether or not the *palliata* was "dominant art" is the chief point at issue in current debate.

Plautus and Theories of Popular Culture

All study is motivated; all history is contemporary history. Finley, in *Ancient Slavery and Modern Ideology*, takes on Joseph Vogt and the Mainz school (too eager to find "humanity" in ancient slavery) as well as the Marxist historians of the eastern bloc (doomed); as for his own motives, he vouchsafes, "To locate slavery within ancient society, in order to understand that society, is a much more difficult and more rewarding enterprise." Born in 1912, Finley was an economic historian, influenced by the work of Karl Polanyi; he took his MA in public law from Columbia in 1929 at the age of seventeen, entering the workforce in the teeth of the Depression. He studied ancient history with W. L. Westermann, and, while teaching at CUNY from 1934 to 1942, did editorial work for the Institute for Social Research, under Horkheimer; in any case, in New York in the 1930s, it would have been impossible not to be involved in the intellectual atmosphere of the Frankfurt School. Finally completing his PhD on the ancient Greek economy in 1950, he found work at Rutgers–Newark (the urban branch campus, incorporated 1946, of the New Jersey state university), and was fired two years later for taking the Fifth when questioned by the McCarran Committee. He emigrated to England and took a job at Cambridge. The eminence of the second half of his life, culminating in a knighthood in 1979, should not obscure the marginality of the first half. Finley was born Moses Finkelstein; not only he and Polanyi, but many economic historians in this period, had reason to be strongly conscious not only of the living politics of Marxism but of the Jews in the Nazi death camps, and the implications of the words "Arbeit Macht Frei" over the gate of Auschwitz: could a stronger resistance have broken down the gate? Finley had nothing but scorn for the supposedly motiveless endeavor of antiquarianism, which, quoting Darwin, he compared to counting pebbles in a quarry, but even antiquarianism is motivated, even if its motives are mystified. As Darwin continues, on Finley's page: "How odd it is that anyone should not see that all observation must be for or against some view if it is to be of any service!"[79]

---

[79] Finley on his own motives, and quoting Darwin: 1998[1980]: 133; he recurs to the image of counting pebbles at 265–6. The outline of Finley's life here comes from the *ODNB* article by F. W. Walbank (cf. Reinhold 1994a); for much further detail see essays in Harris 2013, esp. Schrecker on Finley's testimony before the Senate, and the special issue of *AJPh* on Finley (135.2: 2014), esp. essays by Naiden, J. Perry, and Tompkins. The papyrologist William Linn Westermann taught at Columbia in 1923–48, where he built up the now famous collection; for a scathing review of his book on slavery by Brunt, see *JRS* 48 (1958): 164–70 (a review essay, of which pp. 164–9 are taken up with a fact-filled drubbing of Westermann). Finley himself did not hesitate to criticize his old teacher (1998[1980]: 120–1). Westermann, despite the name, was a midwesterner who took his BA from Nebraska in 1894 and briefly taught high school Latin in Decatur, IL; he was president of the American Historical Association in 1944, for the implications of which see Novick 1988. His Nebraska degree, followed by a stint studying with Diels in Berlin (1899–1902), follows a pattern discussed further below; according to Finley, in Germany he came under the influence of Finley's bugbear, Eduard Meyer. For Westermann, see Reinhold 1994b, who blandly observes of him, "His most important students were Sir M. I. Finley, Naphtali Lewis, and Meyer Reinhold." On the motivations of anthropologists, historians, and classicists, see Richlin 1993a (updated as Richlin 2014a: 289–317). On the motivations of historians of ancient slavery, the position of McKeown in his overview (2007) is indicated by the question mark at the end of his title, confirmed by his Magritte-like announcement, "I am not necessarily a postmodernist" (2007: 9). His motive appears

The desire to find a subject position for slaves in any period is a desire to give voice to the silenced, comparable with similar projects in women's history, subaltern studies, and working-class history.[80] Andromache Karanika begins her book on Greek women's work songs: "To give silence a voice is the main task I undertake in this book" (2014: 1). The study of "popular culture," as it has been practiced in western Europe and North America, has a similar motive, also related to the *Annales* school, the study of history from below, and the New Historicism: a desire to study what has not previously been deemed worthy of study, as for example also sex and the body (see Richlin 1997b, 2013b). The theoretical basis for the study of popular culture is the work of Marx and Engels on ideology, Antonio Gramsci on hegemony, and the Frankfurt School on the culture industry, a set of readings foundational first in the UK, where they influenced the Birmingham school and helped to form the field known as "British cultural studies," and then in the US. As the New Left grew up out of the Old Left and the labor movement via the civil rights movement, and, after 1968, former radical activists joined academic departments of sociology and history, a Marxist theory inflected by the consciousness of American slavery pushed for changes to the canon and the curriculum, and turned the focus of study towards the struggle against oppression. Already, the dawn of the civil rights movement after World War II had politicized the study of American slavery, raising huge questions for the study of all slavery (Finley 1998[1980]: 285–308, a stirring essay; Shaw 1998: 7). In the UK, class was for a long time the main issue, until a postcolonial consciousness arose and complicated things. Starting around 1990, postmodern debates over representing the Holocaust and other atrocities spurred the writing of the history of "communal memory" in reaction to trauma, as scholars looked for forms of resistant memory (Friedlander 1992; Olick et al. 2011).

For all these endeavors, the goal was to uncover, not only voices, but resistant voices – voices pushing against the hegemonic discourse described above by Boal. Hard as it may be to believe now, all these scholars hoped, and some explicitly claimed, that doing academic research on the history of the silenced would somehow constitute activism in the present, and help to bring about revolution, still seen as a possibility in the 1980s. This is difficult to believe for any historian, and became a particular problem

---

to be to teach his students to distrust all scholarship because it is motivated ("This book was partly born of frustrations in trying to convince students of some of the current orthodoxies about ancient slavery," 2007: 159).

[80] For a similar account of the history of the field, see Forsdyke 2012: 8–15. On cultural studies and British Marxism, see Turner 1996: 22–6, 38–77.

for classicists, at least speaking from my own experience as a feminist. Yet, viewed through the lens of memory studies, it is also hard to believe it has not made a difference, for, before the 1970s, women were almost totally absent from handbooks and textbooks, as was the topic of sexuality. This is where antiquarianism can be seen to be political after all, since, as in Le Guin's story, it does matter which pebbles you catalogue. "Making visible" has been a simple but powerful motive for many, from E. P. Thompson's stated purpose in *The Making of the English Working Class* (1966: 12–13), to the authors of the early feminist textbook *Becoming Visible* (Bridenthal and Koonz 1977), to Page duBois in 2003, to Sandra Joshel and Lauren Petersen in 2014; they borrow China Miéville's idea of "un-seeing" from *The City and the City* to describe the process whereby Roman slaves have been erased from the historical record. This is my own motive, as well, and this is why I want to shift the focus onto the actors and the audience and away from the shadowy figure of Plautus, the author.

Those who entered the academy in the generation before 1968 had another, related set of influences, in the anti-war movement that went hand-in-hand with the entry of folk music into mass culture in the 1950s and early 1960s, in what is known to musicologists as the American folk revival. The civil rights movement bridged the two eras, which is why Joan Baez was at Woodstock, why she had "Joe Hill" and "We Shall Overcome" on her playlist there, and why Bob Dylan started out with Leadbelly as well as with Woody Guthrie. My own childhood was saturated in folk music, as will be obvious from the footnotes in this book. The roots of the study of folklore in nineteenth-century Romanticism were faintly visible in the section of Child ballads in the *Joan Baez Songbook*, as the national-istic political motives of the study of *das Volk* were not; the romanticism, however, had never gone away.[81] As they had been for William Morris and the Arts and Crafts movement in the 1880s, and to some founding mem-bers of the Fabian Society (named for the Fabius Cunctator who fought Hannibal), folklore and the study of popular culture were emphatically part of the dream of a lost golden age; it is obvious in Bakhtin, and, as Holt Parker points out, Marx himself saw the Middle Ages as "a time of

---

[81] See Williamson 2004: 72–120 on folklore and German national spirit in the *Vormärz* (with thanks to Sebastian Matzner for the recommendation); Marchand 1996: 152–87 on related uses of Roman archaeology. On Francis James Child, son of a sailmaker, who became Professor of English at Harvard, see M. Brown 2011; Child ballads appear in *The Joan Baez Songbook* (New York: Ryerson Music Publishers, 1964) at 47–70. For national characteristics and the politics of folktales, see Darnton 1984; the title of this essay ("Peasants Tell Tales") bespeaks its influence on Forsdyke 2012 (*Slaves Tell Tales*).

not yet alienated craftsmen" (2011: 150; cf. 148 n. 5, 159). Cynical historians, fed up with this misty-eyed view, have been quick to object that not all that is pre-industrial was lovely; E. P. Thompson himself revised his earlier view of the liberating qualities of rough music, which can be hard to differentiate from a lynch mob (1992: 18); as Parker puts it, "When the rock of hegemony is overturned not all that crawls out is life-affirming. Fascism was a genuinely popular movement" (2011: 154 n. 43). The reader will have noticed that I took pains to say that my imaginary *grex* were not figures of romance. This book will end with a look forward from the *palliata* to the bloodstained slave revolts that began to take place in the 130s BCE, the first ones that made a real mark in the historical record, but what they needed was abolition, and, even now, that's been a long time coming. Meanwhile, it is our job to remember.

Parker's major 2011 essay, "Toward a Definition of Popular Culture," establishes a basis for discussion; after a comprehensive survey and analysis of definitions to date, from Marx through Gramsci to Dick Hebdige and the Birmingham school, he describes his contribution as "a few piñatas big enough for everyone to take a swing at" (158), and I want to take him up on it. His first goal was to emphasize that there *was* popular culture in antiquity, since historians of modern periods have tended to treat popular culture as a new development, whatever their starting point. This probably matters more to classicists than to modernists, but his intervention is timely. The post-millennial surge in work on ancient popular culture backs him up, here most pertinently Sara Forsdyke's 2012 *Slaves Tell Tales* and the 2013 conference at Glasgow on popular comedy, organized by Costas Panayotakis and Ian Ruffell. There is, of course, a long tradition of work on ancient folk culture, going back to Friedländer, Usener, and the movement towards *Sittengeschichte*, and in the twentieth century primarily anthropological in its grounding (I think here of Carlin Barton, Maurizio Bettini, Anthony Corbeill, Donald Lateiner, and many historians of religion); things seem to be getting more political, spurred on the Greek side by discomfort with the idealization of Athens, now seen in work by Kostas Vlassopoulos (2007, 2010, 2011) as well as in duBois.

Parker proposes a new definition of popular culture as "products that require little cultural capital and [are] unauthorized" (2011: 169–70). He postulates three levels of discourse: "unauthorized utterance, the voice … of those without access to cultural capital," instancing Pompeiian graffiti; "the authorized utterance in search of as large an audience as possible," instancing Aristophanes and Plautus; and "the elite speaking to the elite," instancing Tacitus. The middle level, in which we find Plautus, Parker identifies with mass culture – "commercial, commodity, consumer culture." Only the first level counts as truly popular; Parker cites Bakhtin's emphasis on "unofficial" culture (165), and says, "Popular culture ceases to be popular when it is authorized. Recognition is death" (166, on "selling out"). Is there hope for Plautine popularity? Earlier, Parker lists Plautus as fitting Dick Hebdige's definition of popular culture as "generally available artifacts" (153). It all depends how you think the *palliata* worked in the 200s: the sort of market-day performance that I postulate here, and for which I have only the evidence gathered in this book, would be only minimally authorized; if you believe that Plautus' *grex* performed only at the *ludi*, then they were authorized by definition. The difference is between what we can see – Herodas, Plautus, the fragments – and what we cannot – the unscripted mime (Panayotakis 2014), the *thaumata*, and the hypothetical unscripted Italian forms, the *Stegreifspiel* of the Freiburg school. Surely the unscripted forms would make it into Parker's first category.

There is, however, no evidence that any playwright before Terence pulled in the fees Parker documented for Terence, a point Parker had made himself (1996: 591–2); it is thought-provoking that, several times, characters say they have rented their costumes, called *ornamenta*, from the aediles, which perhaps implies that at other times they had less authorized costumes of their own. Did working the *ludi* count as "selling out"? I have thought so (2005: 24). Still, the shows were free, the stage, however authorized, was temporary (not requiring the outlay aediles might apply to something important like a road); even the (cheap) food concessions seem to have been off-site, perhaps along with the sellers of (cheap) souvenir terracotta figurines. The little figure on the cover of this book would fit in your hand. It might be argued that the actors were commodified, in the sense that they were objects of the gaze, and so thereby (as attested in later times) were felt to have sold their bodies, like gladiators or prostitutes.[82] But this is too abstract. Parker quotes from *The World of Goods*: "Goods are primarily needed … for making visible and stable the categories of culture" (Parker 2011: 159: n. 65); when an actor bought a boy to train, when an actor was shipped from Alexandria to Capua and sold in the forum, the people themselves are commodities, so, in the flesh, the culture is the people, who make visible the categories of culture, but do not necessarily make them

---

[82] On terracottas as theatrical souvenirs, see Bosher 2013: 207, citing J. R. Green ("The figurines were made for fans and at the same time encouraged people to become fans"); Wrenhaven 2013: 138–40 (esp. on old nurses, including discussion of a figurine from Tarentum c. 300 BCE); cf. duBois 2003: 68–9. See Richlin 2016: 85–6 on the commodification of comedians in anecdotes and of jokes in jokebooks.

stable. Except when it comes to sex: as seen in the case of the Syracusan impresario in Xenophon's *Symposium*, when you bought a boy to train, you could use him for sex (4.54).

Even for unscripted forms, it is a problem that Parker takes "cultural capital" to entail skill and training. If popular culture is without cultural capital, then what to do with what might be called the street end of the performing arts, the skills of the *thaumata*: dance, acrobatics, juggling, puppetry, and the manifold skills of the comedian and the clown – even the pig imitator who drew the attention of both Mary Beard and Peter Kruschwitz. These skills are authorized within their own calling, by endless practice, training, competition, but the authorities of the street are not recognized by the authorities of the state. The *palliata* was intrinsically stateless, while slave performers lacked not only state-authorized cultural capital but state-authorized *caput* (see chapter 8).

Moreover, cost plays a part here. At the *ludi*, nothing could compete with the show at the Circus, so nothing else was scheduled for the last day; and, if it is possible to believe the description in Dionysius of Halicarnassus, the spectacle of the parade before the races, the *pompa*, was wildly extravagant, and must have been wildly expensive.[83] This is not implausible, since outright displays of money itself were characteristic of the period. Gruen lists some mind-boggling examples starting with Scipio Africanus at the end of the Second Punic War (1996a: 133–4), but such display was well established in the 200s: after his naval victory in 260, C. Duilius listed on his column not only his bold deeds in battle but what we might call the dollar amounts he seized in specie, the lines of figures prominently displayed; at Marcellus's *ovatio* after the sack of Syracuse in 211, according to Livy, the *praeda* in the parade included a scale model of occupied Syracuse, siege weapons, and the *ornamenta* "of royal wealth": piles of worked silver and bronze, furnishings, costly fabrics, many famous statues, eight elephants, and the two Greeks who had betrayed the city, wearing gold crowns (26.21.7–10). This kind of thing is the target of ridicule onstage in the *palliata*, as Gruen himself noted (137, 139–40; cf. chapter 8 below). Of Polybius' account of Marcellus's parade, all that remains are his moral

---

[83] On the pig imitator, Beard 2014: 126, Kruschwitz 2013, also Henderson 2001: 119–28, 223–6; on the *pompa*, Dionysius of Halicarnassus 7.69–73, with fantastic details about an omen involving the cruel public punishment of a slave, and the presence at both the *pompa* and at aristocratic funerals of satyr-dancers doing the comic Greek dance called the *sikinnis*. Dionysius claims the details of the *pompa* go back to the annalist Q. Fabius. For discussion, see Bernstein 2007: 228–9, who takes Dionysius at his word as to the "Greekness" of the *pompa*; on *pompae* in Plautus' plays, Fraenkel 2007: 280–1, Prescott 1936: 103–4.

observations; none of the specifics are left, only a mention of gold and silver, paintings and reliefs, and objects that cause the hearts of those who have been robbed of them to fill with envy and anger as they look on (9.10). It is a strange thing that the maxim with which Polybius begins this passage, οὐκ ἐκ τῶν ἔξω κοσμεῖται πόλις, ἀλλ' ἐκ τῆς τῶν οἰκούντων ἀρετῆς, was spoken before him by the nameless Virgo in Plautus' *Persa* as she was led onstage, dressed as an Arabian captive, to be sold to a pimp: *si incolae bene sunt morati, id pulchre moenitum arbitror*, "If the inhabitants have good ways, I think the town is well guarded" (*Per.* 554). A saying in oral circulation: common knowledge.[84] Or a slave-woman citing philosophy for her own purposes. The *palliata* was different in kind, as it was in cost, from the mass entertainment of the *pompa* and the *ovatio*.

Parker also reviews the importance of recycling and circulation in popular culture, and the way in which cultural forms change levels from high to low as they are re-used (2011: 151, 155): surely philosophy in the mouth of an actor in double drag would count. These issues surface in the *palliata* not only through pastiche, as in paratragedy, but in all the descriptions of food. Does "popular" mean "lower-class"? The slave attendants (*pedisequi*) are told by the *Poenulus* prologue speaker to run to the *popina* while the *scribilitae* are hot, and this all sounds very low, but then Cato has a recipe for *scribilitae* in *De agricultura*, while the slave Syncerastus in *Poenulus* says the pimp's house is full of men of every class, from *equites* to runaway slaves – just like in a *popina* (chapter 2). Prostitution was evidently popular; recall Parker's remarks on what is under the rock of hegemony. If folk culture can be associated with the lore of isolated villages, hence not in general circulation (Parker 2011: 153), then what about exemplarity, and oral circulation, and the way jokes travel, as well as stories and songs? Acting troupes must have been a prime vector. Here again, circulation is complicated by the slave trade, as American popular music was, under different circumstances.[85]

Finally, Parker surveys theorists' insistent claim that the culture of the oppressed must be the locus of resistance to the dominant culture,

---

[84] See Woytek 1982: 345, who takes this thought, like her whole opening speech, to come from the Greek original. The parallels he collects include one that partly overlaps with Polybius' line, a fragment of Zeno (c. 300 BCE), though he misses Polybius; he concludes, "sie gehörte also wohl in den Bereich der Popularphilosophie."

[85] On the circulation of high-art texts with their commodified authors, see Jefferson 2012: 316–18, Yarrow 2006: 37–44; on Attic *skolia* in comparison with the European "little tradition," G. Jones 2014; on the circulation of folktales, Darnton 1984; on exemplarity and jokes as "portable," Langlands forthcoming; on American popular music and the slave songs, L. Jones 1999; on the traffic in comedians, Richlin 2016, 2017b.

a claim perhaps overly romantic (2011: 153–4), and the reaction against that position. It is interesting that the description of dominant cultures in the *German Ideology*, as developed by Gramsci and by Althusser (1971), assumes a passive mass culture, literally prone to manipulation (Parker 2011: 156–7), for this is essentially the view of the Roman state put forward by Hölkeskamp and some others who work on Roman political culture, whose models do not derive from Marx. This position in turn has been critiqued as too monolithic, and certainly lacks the explanatory power of James Scott's model.[86] As seen above, Augusto Boal explicitly resisted this view by his life in the theater. The appropriation of the *palliata* form by Latin-speaking comedians to serve a popular audience is an instance of the reading "up from the bottom" that Rebecca Langlands sees as an inherent potential in exempla, where complicity and insubordination exist in tension, and "even the most coercive exempla always also offer means of resistance." Cultural memory, she holds, is a framework, belonging to and defining a specific culture, within which written texts are generated and to which they also contribute.[87] *A fortiori*, then, performance, especially when it incorporates songs and jokes. It is the argument of this book that the *palliata* constitutes a locus of resistance, and says so itself explicitly, many times over. This is, historically, in itself a marginal view.

The Politics of Reading Plautus

The historian is, as E. H. Carr said, "a social phenomenon, both the product and the conscious or unconscious spokesman of the society to which he belongs" (1961: 42). All writing is of its time. Just as this book argues that the *palliata* must be understood in its historical period and in terms of lifespans, so must classical scholarship, which is no more free of motives than is history-writing. Attention to biography is central to the understanding of the politics of reading Plautus. Erich Gruen, as seen above, believes that the plays do have political meaning, and do critique cultural phenomena like usury and ostentatious generals; he argues, however, that "Plautus … maintains a safe and sardonic distance" (1996a: 157). That is what comedians do; yet at the same time they necessarily locate themselves (see chapter 3 below on actors as outsiders). Few have tried to read Plautus as speaking for a lower-class audience or as offering any kind of critique of the conditions of slavery, and the two major spokesmen for this point of

---

[86] See Forsdyke 2012: 11–12, and her arguments based on Scott at 14–15, 40–1, 47–9, 162.
[87] See Langlands forthcoming.

view, Paul Shaner Dunkin and Claude Pansiéri, are usually mentioned, if at all, with derision: hard acts to follow.[88] Like Plautus, like all of us, they need to be understood in their historical context, which, as it turns out, tells a good deal about the politics of reading Latin literature in the twentieth century.

Paul Shaner Dunkin (1905–1975) was an exact contemporary of his chief critic, George Eckel Duckworth (1903–1972), and a close contemporary of Moses Finley (1912–1986). The lives of the three men illustrate the part played in the twentieth-century US by the politics of regionalism. Dunkin, born in Flora, Indiana, took his BA from DePauw University in 1929 and went on to do graduate work in Classics at the University of Illinois, where his teacher was the famous William Oldfather. While there, Dunkin decided to become a librarian; when he left Illinois in 1937 with a PhD in Classics, it was to take up a post at the Folger Shakespeare Library in Washington, DC. He became an award-winning cataloguer and expert on rare books, and was hired as Professor of Library Science at Rutgers University (New Brunswick, not Newark) in 1959. Duckworth, meanwhile, born in Little York, New Jersey, took his BA from Princeton in 1924, followed by an MA and PhD (1931), and was hired there as an assistant professor while still ABD, spending almost his entire career there (he retired in 1971, my sophomore year; I still remember his office). He was President of the APA in 1955–6 and a Guggenheim Fellow in 1957–8.[89]

Dunkin's *Post-Aristophanic Comedy: Studies in the Social Outlook of Middle and New Comedy at Both Athens and Rome* (1946), was published as volume 31 of *Illinois Studies in Language and Literature*, for which Oldfather was the head of the editorial board. The book is based on Dunkin's doctoral dissertation, written in the mid-1930s, that is, during the Depression. In his brief acknowledgments, Dunkin thanks Oldfather, who had died the previous year, "for a social outlook in certain respects not altogether uninspired by him." This debt is indicated in the text by a series of extraordinary footnotes that quote from Oldfather's notes on Dunkin's work.[90] If Dunkin is odd, Oldfather now appears much more so, despite the fact that Oldfather himself was a towering figure in Classics, not only in the US but in Germany, through his involvement with the *RE*: Sather Professor, 1933–4; APA President, 1937–8. After a Munich PhD (1908), he spent almost his

---

[88] For instances, see Gruen 1996a: 128 n. 16; Segal 1968: 214 n. 35; and discussion in Spranger 1961: 11–15.

[89] On Dunkin, see Hickey 1975, 1993, Griffiths 1978–9: 152; on Duckworth, see Luce 1994.

[90] These start with a bang at Dunkin 1946: 18–20 n. 3, on Glycera and Menander and the general history of older women and younger men, with remarks on Errol Flynn and Charlie Chaplin.

entire career at the University of Illinois, serving as department chair from 1926 to 1945. He directed forty-six doctoral students. His biographer says, "He saw classics primarily as the study of historical and cultural, rather than linguistic and literary, phenomena." He was also, astonishingly, a socialist. Oldfather's politics derive from his time in Munich and the idealistic socialism in Germany before World War I, with its ties to the Fabians, and in 1917 he and other faculty at Illinois underwent Federal investigation for "Socialist and pro-German sentiments"; unlike Finley, Oldfather kept his job. His first major publication, in 1909–10, had been a series of articles in a Chicago periodical adorned with amateur Art Nouveau decorations and voicing a radical socialism not again espoused by American assistant professors until the 1960s. An excerpt from an editorial: "If the *Progressive Journal of Education* could be placed in the hands of a majority of the teachers of the country it would shortly cause a revolution in education that could not help but hasten the final economic revolution that will free mankind." This was the time of the Lawrence Mill Strike (1911), of the Pankhursts in England, of the IWW (founded 1905). From these first articles through the 1930s, Oldfather evinced an interest in slavery, social and economic problems, and what he called in his 1938 APA presidential address the "gross maldistribution of wealth." By all accounts he had a strong influence on his students; he is the immediate context for Dunkin's work.[91]

Dunkin's style is marked by its use of capital letters: "[Plautus'] Characters are generally rogues. The Rich Men are an Ancient Gallant and a Spineless Young Man, smug moralizers if they are good, sometimes grasping, often stupid, always less important than in Menander, always more ridiculous. ... The Slave is the important Poor Man" (1946: 102). He concludes his chapter on Plautus with a socioeconomic reading (103–4):

---

[91] Excerpt: Peyton Boswell, "Editorial," *Progressive Journal of Education* 1.2 (Dec. 1908): 20. On Oldfather, see Armstrong 1994; on his international standing, Calder 1994: xxviii; on his politics, Armstrong 1993, which provides a full discussion of a complex personal history. For a fictional account of the Arts and Crafts movement in Munich before World War I, its politics, and its ties with the English Fabians, see A. S. Byatt's novel *The Children's Book* (2009). Brecht was a student in Munich in 1917, and met Karl Valentin there a few years later. It was a socialist uprising in Munich (1918–19) that led, via a general fascist backlash, to Hitler's power in Bavaria; see Bronner 2012: 119–34, Byatt 2009: 674. On the German Spartacists involved with this uprising and their adoption of Spartacus as a model, see Shaw 2001: 14–19. Adam Weishaupt, who founded the Munich Illuminati in 1776, took as his lodge name "Brother Spartacus" (*ADB*; his friend von Zwack was "Cato"; see Shaw 2001: 19–22 on Spartacus in the Enlightenment). Another case of a region with its own political traditions.

The plays of Plautus are adaptations from Middle and New Comedy along the lines dictated by the bias of a poor man who wrote in order to earn a living. ... His characters are one great rogues' gallery of common folks forced into meanness by their economic position. This is not to say that Plautus was a 'radical'; he was not even a 'liberal.' He has no panacea, no thought-out scheme of reforming the world; he makes no consistent propaganda. ... Plautus was always in need of money. So much of Horace's otherwise captious criticism may be granted; it is obvious enough anyway on internal evidence. But he was a poor man, and in his work may be seen the instinctive reaction of a vigorous poor man to an oppressive capitalistic system.

Dunkin himself has no explicit political agenda; Marx indeed shows up early in the book (15), probably as a significant instance, alongside Adam Smith, in an argument that modern theories may be used to analyze ancient texts ("whatever is true in either economist's theories is just as applicable to the fifth century before Christ as it is to the twentieth century after"). This view was still being debated in the 1980s (see Parker 1989: 234 n. 10), although Brent Shaw observes that the day when economic history governed the study of ancient slavery may be over (1998: 52). But maybe not.

What Dunkin's prose immediately evokes is not Marx but George Ade's 1899 *Fables in Slang*, from which I select the moral of "The Fable of the New York Person Who Gave the Stage Fright to Fostoria, Ohio": "*A New York Man never begins to Cut Ice until he is west of Rahway*" (21). This joke is funnier if you know where Rahway is (see chapter 7 on geographical jokes), but the principle is clear: the Midwest and the East Coast have issues regarding the East's claims to cultural superiority. Ade's politics could best be described as "populist," but he was a searing social critic, and his column in the *Chicago Record* was immensely successful and influential.[92] Dunkin's prose also has echoes of Carl Sandburg's *The People, Yes* (1936); Sandburg may be taken as representative of Midwestern Socialism, and his *American Songbag* reappears here (chapter 8) as one of the authoritative texts of the American folk revivals. The division between East Coast and heartland, still active in the US, goes back at least to William Jennings Bryan's "Cross of Gold" speech, delivered in 1896 but kept alive by Bryan

---

[92] Ade continued to be read through the 1940s and beyond, as perpetuated by the influential East Coast intellectual Louis Untermeyer (1946: 5–13); he quotes Carl Van Doren's praise of Ade (5). Nothing is simple: Untermeyer was a socialist; Van Doren, who taught at Columbia, took his BA from Illinois in 1911. Untermeyer's collection was the source of my own knowledge of Ade in the 1960s; my copy of *Fables in Slang* came from a used bookstore in New Brunswick, NJ, where I was in my first academic appointment, at Rutgers. Gordon Williams's remark when I got the job – "Good; wasn't that where Finley worked?" – turned out to be oddly prophetic, although at the time I thought it just showed how little he knew about New Jersey.

on the Chautauqua circuit into the 1920s. Bryan, a former Congressman from Nebraska when he gave the speech, was the champion of the "hardy pioneers" against "the Atlantic coast," of the farmers and miners against "the encroachments of aggregated wealth," in "a struggle between the idle holders of idle capital and the struggling masses who produce the wealth and pay the taxes." His speech belongs to the time of the Populist Party, of the depression of 1893–6 that triggered in 1894 the protest march on Washington known as "Coxey's Army." Nebraska was the heart of the heartland; Oldfather's power was enhanced by his coalition with his brother, the ancient historian Charles Oldfather, who was chair of History at the University of Nebraska from 1929 to 1946; the hero of Willa Cather's 1918 novel *My Ántonia* studies Classics there, until his Latin professor convinces him to join him in moving to Harvard. This history might explain the fact that George Duckworth spent two years as an instructor at Nebraska (1926–8).[93]

In all other respects Duckworth stands in opposition to Dunkin. Holt Parker approved of his strictures on Dunkin, whom Parker quotes to illustrate the wrong way to write historically grounded criticism (1989: 234). Indeed Duckworth interwove criticisms of Dunkin throughout his authoritative book, *The Nature of Roman Comedy: A Study in Popular Entertainment*, as is helpfully shown in his detailed index. A sample (Duckworth 1952: 278):

> The nature of the Plautine delineation derives from the playwright's conception of comedy, not from a desire to ridicule wealth or the rich man as such. There are in Plautus passages of a serious nature, as well as an abundance of fun, but that a Roman audience would find in his comedies "the Poor Man's complaint against ruthless exploitation" [reference to Dunkin 1946: 107, 137] is incredible. Such a view is an unwarranted ascription of modern socialistic beliefs to an ancient dramatist whose treatment of his characters for comic purposes lends no support to the theory.
>
> On the contrary, the spectators of Roman comedy, being practical, business-minded persons, would follow with interest the financial transactions of the comedies …

Here speaks the voice of the East Coast establishment, firmly ensconced at Princeton in the 1950s – specifically, in 1952, the year in which Finley

---

[93] My copy of Duckworth's book comes from the North Platte (Nebraska) Senior High School Library, from which it was deaccessioned. This library now no longer contains either a copy of *The Nature of Roman Comedy* or any book about or by Plautus, and only four books even tangentially about Rome: testimony to the cultural gutting of what are now hinterlands.

was fired. The meaning of "popular" has clearly undergone a shift, between the New Deal populism of the 1930s and the anti-communist conservatism of the 1950s.[94] When Dunkin moved to Rutgers seven years later (the main campus, founded 1766), his position up the road in working-class New Brunswick relative to Duckworth's in Princeton expressed in spatial terms what separated them in terms of scholarly credibility. Even in the revolutionary year 1968, even the modish Erich Segal, in *Roman Laughter*, singled out Dunkin's politics for ridicule, though conceding that "Dunkin is not the only critic to overlook the fact that no slave is ever ill-treated during a comedy" (1968: 152).[95] Dunkin was an easy target. His ideas about Plautus sound quaint today, but, as will be shown at length below, in fact the plays are full of poor men's complaints against ruthless exploitation, especially if, like Dunkin, you include slaves among "poor men" (proof, if needed, that Dunkin was no textbook Marxist); and, really, who poorer? This was long before the day of the emperor Claudius's freedman Narcissus. Nor is it incredible that persons sitting on the *subsellia* would have found in the *palliata* echoes of the beliefs that led, for example, to the Third Secession of the Plebs, or to the election of C. Terentius Varro – a butcher's son, says Livy – as consul in 216.[96]

Claude Pansiéri published his monumental book, *Plaute et Rome, ou, les ambiguïtés d'un marginal* (1997), as the culmination of a long journey. He was born at Tunis in 1932 into the Italian-Jewish community that, in Tunisia, went back to the late 1600s and flourished under the French protectorate that began in the 1880s. As is vividly described in Albert Memmi's autobiographical novel *The Pillar of Salt* (1992[1955]), and analyzed in *The Colonizer and the Colonized* (1991[1957]), Jews in Tunis formed a set of subcultures among the multicultural colonized. Through secular education, they moved into the professions and a measure of security, interrupted by the Vichy government that began in 1940 and was succeeded by

---

[94] Duckworth's cultural constraints are also indicated by his identification of characters like Ballio as "slavedealers," viz. the index heading "slavedealer (*leno*)": evidently the word "pimp" was not suitable for the Princeton University Press in 1952, nor even the then-current polite term "procurer," which Dunkin did not hesitate to use.

[95] Not actually a fact; see discussion in chapter 2. Segal was teaching at Yale when he wrote *Roman Laughter,* and moved from there to Princeton. Helpfully, he cites studies from behind what was then the Iron Curtain that also treated Plautus as "a champion of the oppressed lower class" (214 n. 35).

[96] For more on these beliefs, and on the tribunes' *subsellia*, see Millar 1989. Livy depicts Terentius Varro (held responsible for the defeat at Cannae) as brought up *loco non humili solum sed etiam sordido*, engaged in *servilia … ministeria*, and appealing to *sordidis hominibus* (22.25.18–26.4); see chapter 2 on labor onstage.

the German occupation that lasted from November 1942 to May 7, 1943, when the city was liberated by the Allies – that is, just before Pansiéri's eleventh birthday. Due to protection by the Italian government representative and the French resident general, the treatment of Jews in Tunisia was at first less drastic than what was going on in France at the time, until the Germans, in their brief stay, set up forced labor camps and began arrests and executions. Memmi says of that time, "Immediately, with the arrival of the Germans, came disaster" (1992[1955]: 273). Perhaps the vividness of Pansiéri's discussion of what happened to Sarsina when the Romans invaded Umbria owes something to this childhood trauma, although his son generally credits his father's approach in the book to the "esprit méticuleux" which led him to visit Sarsina on the track of Plautus.[97]

In Tunis Pansiéri attended the lycée Carnot, of which the long-lived Memmi is also a graduate, and went on to study for a *licence* in Classics while teaching at the lycée Emile Loubet. He went to Paris to complete his *licence*; this was Paris in the early 1950s, a heady time; like Finley in New York in the 1930s, like students in Munich in 1908 and Paris in 1968, like his classmates, Pansiéri was drawn to the political left. He signed the Stockholm Appeal, but separated from the Party over the atrocities under Stalin. He returned to Tunisia in 1954, where he made a reputation as a professor of French; in 1961 he earned a *diplôme d'Etudes Supérieures* for a thesis on Camus, a choice both Parisian and African. Under the Bourguiba presidency in the 1960s conditions for the French and Jewish communities in Tunisia deteriorated, and in 1963 Pansiéri and his family left in a hurry for Marseille, where they were naturalized. His son writes, "il faut imaginer le déracinement et la nouvelle vie qu'il faut reconstruire." Perhaps this chain of experiences led Pansiéri to see in the *Poenulus* a critique of Roman racism (1997: 515–16), a "provocation à l'égard de la xénophobie antipunique de la foule romaine": an argument far ahead of its time. After all, Tunis stands where once stood Carthage. Pansiéri and his wife both found jobs as teachers, and in 1971 Pansiéri began work towards an advanced certification in Latin so as to be able to teach in higher education; his *thèse* was on Plautus' *Casina*, juried in 1976. All this time he was teaching Latin to students in the *faculté des lettres* at Avignon. He then began work at the University of Provence, under the direction of Jean-Pierre Cèbe, on the

---

[97] For a brief history of the Jews of Tunisia in the twentieth century, see Saadoun 2003; as well as the more famous Memmi, the novelists Nine Moati (b. 1938) and Claude Kayat (b. 1939) evoke Pansiéri's Tunis in their work. I am indebted to Dr. Olivier Pansiéri for an account of his father's life.

thèse d'état that would become *Plaute et Rome*, defended in 1991 under the title "Plaute et son temps." It was Cèbe who suggested that he should publish the thesis as a book, and Pansiéri cut the thesis down to its published length of 807 pages.

He died in 2000, thus sparing himself the sight of the reviews. Among those he thanks in his acknowledgments is Mario Torelli, who discussed the project with him in 1982 in Perugia before taking him to visit Sarsina, where the Mayor showed them Plautus' home town. The historical Plautus and his actual relation to Sarsina are themselves part of a regional politics: Sarsina has a yearly Plautus festival and academic conference, which has its own series of collected essays titled *Lecturae Plautinae Sarsinates* (as of 2014, reaching volume 17, on *Rudens*). Pansiéri's critical perspective, indeed his whole project, marks his distance from Paris, where, in the 1980s and 1990s, the focus was emphatically on Greece and philosophy, and Foucault in the *Histoire de la sexualité* skipped the Roman Republic altogether. This may explain why Pansiéri cites as an authority Rattray Taylor's 1954 *Sex in History* (1997: 608), evidently without advice from Paul Veyne, who served on his *jury de soutenance*. His perspective on Plautus is based on the Varronian biography, and so he reads the plays as social commentary by a man who came from the hinterlands and had experienced life at the bottom. This leads him, on the one hand, into close engagement with the long list of scholars who have tried to locate specific passages as references to specific historic events, and on the other into the detailed history of what Rome did to Sarsina in the mid-200s BCE. That I find the first unproductive and the second useful is a product of my own perspective.[98]

A firm follower of Erich Segal's ideas about the safety-valve effect of the Saturnalian world-upside-down, Pansiéri maintains that there could be nothing subversive in Plautine comedy; he cites Dunkin, alongside Philippe-Ernest Legrand's 1910 *Daos*, as part of a pre-Segal era in which readers did not understand that the temporary sanction accorded to free speech defused it (599). Plautus, like his fellow writers, was controlled by the senate, whom it suited to have the *masses populaires* let off steam and have a good time at the *ludi*, not get stirred up (753). Fantasy screened harsh reality for audience, characters, and writer (756):

---

[98] Reviews: see esp. Timothy Moore, *CR* 52 (2002): 175: "at 807 pages, most painful to read." Pansiéri (1997) on the Varronian biography, 43–57, 95–146; on life at the bottom, 223–50, 409–76, 627–732; on specific historic events in the plays, 346–90; on Rome and Sarsina, 58–94.

Les disgraciés du temps historique, sans prise sur leur destin, peuvent, dans
ce temps mythique du théâtre, mener une entreprise toujours réussie de
délivrance et d'assouvissement vindicatif, et y ont prise sur le hasard même.
Entre lui-même et l'histoire de son temps, Plaute interpose ce temps intem-
porel et malléable à souhait de la fiction, comme un écran compensateur de
ses propres hantises et des misères d'autrui.[99]

All comedy starts with anger. Whatever its ends, Pansiéri did not doubt
that Plautus was in sympathy with those at the bottom (248–9):

L'ancien travailleur au moulin connaît bien cette lie de Rome, dont beau-
coup de membres sont des paysans ruinés ... Dans cette cour des miracles
du Forum où se côtoient riches et pauvres ... vivent aussi, par delà l'*infima
plebs*, ceux à qui n'est pas reconnue la qualité d'hommes: esclaves, prostitués
mâles ou femelles ... À ces inquiétantes figures de la déchéance humaine,
à elles surtout peut-être, son théâtre offrira subrepticement, le temps d'un
ludus, une dérisoire et utopique revanche.[100]

As in Pansiéri's vision, the chapters below will travel from the *infima plebs*
in the Forum, through scenes of revenge, happiness, free speech, and
homecoming, to the fantastical reaches of a slave's utopia, where those in
chains could fly away like birds.

Ancient Slavery and Current Ideology

Moses Finley, writing on utopian thinking, ended his essay with a call
to move on to the next stage: "Utopia must therefore take the next tran-
scending step"; and he quotes Oscar Wilde, from *The Soul of Man under
Socialism*: "a map of the world that does not include Utopia is not worth
even glancing at. ... Progress is the realization of Utopia." His essay was
published in 1967; I don't suppose Finley saw Monique Wittig coming up
behind him in the fast lane, but *Les Guérillères* lay only two years ahead,

---

[99] "Those on the losing side of history, with no grip on their fate, could, in the mythic time of the
theatre, put into play a project of deliverance and vindicatory satisfaction, always successful, and
there they got a grip on luck itself. Between himself and the events of his time, Plautus interposed
this timeless and endlessly malleable time of fiction, like a compensatory screen for his own ghosts
and the miseries of other people."

[100] "The one-time worker in the mill well knew these dregs of Rome, many of whom were peasants
who had lost everything ... In this beggars' quarter of the Forum where rich and poor rubbed
shoulders ... there also dwell, beyond the lowest class of the *plebs*, those for whom even the status of
human being goes unrecognized: slaves, prostitutes male or female ... To these troubling embodi-
ments of human downfall – to them above all, perhaps – his theater offered by stealth, just for the
time of the festival, a derisive and utopian revenge."

across the barricades of 1968. Ursula Le Guin's parable about slave art and owners' blindness to it ends with revolution (1994: 67): "He heard the singing, but only as a noise without significance. It was not until the first rock flew through his window that he looked up and cried out in agitation, 'What is the meaning of this?'" Rome never had an effective slave revolution, or a war to end slavery, but the thoughts and feelings of slaves and the free poor were voiced in the *palliata*, as this book aims to show.

PART I

What was Given

In *Work, Identity, and Legal Status at Rome*, a study of inscriptions mostly dating to the Principate, Sandra Joshel used Paul Willis's category of "what was given" to talk about the ways in which enslaved people took the social situation in which they found themselves and made of it an identity of their own – an identity from their own point of view. Although, like the working-class boys Willis studied, Joshel's Roman freedmen claimed an identity defined in terms of labor, still they were historical agents, and they represented their labor as their own action. Their construction of a self from the experience of slavery, manumission, and work was quite different from the interpretation of that experience by the elite slave-owners whose remarks on their human property have come down to us, an accident of survival that has conveyed the misleading impression that all slave-owners were members of the elite. In fact this was far from the case, as thousands of inscriptions show, with some *colliberti* commemorating the former owners with whom they had worked, and some owners marrying their freedwomen – who were sometimes their former fellow slaves.

Joshel traced slaves' and freed slaves' sense of themselves in their work through what was written on their graves; an epitaph like *Zena cocus*, in which a slave cook's work-label plus his name sum up his life, stands as a sort of autobiography. Like all autobiographies, this one is hardly the whole story, but it reminds us that slaves did have a point of view – they were not in life "things" as they were in law, and their subjective experience, their motivations, were not the same as those imputed to them by people who thought of them as objects. Nor were they without kin, or husbands and wives, even when still enslaved, no matter what the law said; nor were their lives always so separate from their owners' lives. Slavery, as seen in chapter 1, was not a static condition; nor were "slaves" a social class, but persons who, though all grievously affected by their civil status, would have had a wide range of experiences, pasts, and hopes within that civil status, low as it was. As this book will show, the owners that slaves onstage complain about are often the rich men, the *summi viri* or "top men"; slaves onstage lay claim not only to family but to personhood, as they tell what abuse feels like and say what it is they want.

Joshel's first chapter takes an epigraph from Willis: "The point at which people live, not borrow, their class destiny is when what is given is re-formed, strengthened and applied to new purposes."[1] Willis was talking about work and workers and I will be talking about plays and players, but his formulation exactly describes what happened as comedians in the 200s BCE made the *palliata* out of the rubble of war, in collusion with their audiences: "articulating the innermost self with external reality," as Willis says. The *palliata* constitutes the prehistory of the later epitaphs Joshel studied, and tells a different kind of story – more complex, perhaps more slippery. Yet the players and the plays, as best can be told from the extant transcripts, in their interactions with the audience do chart a range of points of view approximating the low end of those present in Rome around 200. Part I looks at what the *palliata* does with what was given – how the actors, their lines, and the staging engage the audience in inside jokes about life at the bottom of the heap. Certainly most of these jokes would have been intelligible, even funny, to those higher up in the heap, even the "top men" so disparaged in the plays, for whom slaves onstage were indelibly marked as low. Such audience members, however, would have had to take it all from the position of outsiders, at best seeing an analogy with their own lives; there are no jokes in these plays about the boredom of senate meetings or the problems of a would-be consul. Menaechmus I's complaint about his problems with *clientes* is a rarity, and does not make him look good. Rather, the plays joke about the hardships experienced by slaves and the free poor (chapter 2); they use metatheatrics to separate the actors, as low-status professionals, from the local citizens in the audience, and also use forms of indigenous folk invective – related to debt, prostitution, and crowd justice – to align themselves with popular discourse and show what a professional can do with it (chapter 3). The players were playing to a mixed audience, but their jokes are grounded in experiences they shared with slaves, freed slaves, and the poor.

---

[1] Joshel 1992: 3, quoting Willis 1981: 2.

CHAPTER 2

The Body at the Bottom

At the most basic level, slavery affected enslaved persons' physical experience. Enslavement itself implies captivity and bondage, and slaves were subject to bondage, torture, and physical punishments specific to their condition. Slaves were commonly trafficked for sex and were available for their owners' sexual use; how much they were fed also depended on their owners. Enslavement due to capture in war, kidnapping, or sale or exposure by parents broke familial bonds and erased natal identity, while those born into slavery had family ties and natal identity unlike those of freeborn people. As seen in chapter 1, the mixed audience of the *palliata* in the 200s BCE in central Italy is likely to have included a sizeable proportion of freed slaves, alongside people whose family members, neighbors, or fellow townspeople had been enslaved. As in Freud's argument that we laugh at what we fear, slaves in the audience could laugh when characters joked about beatings, while, sitting next to them, free(d) people in the audience could laugh at threats of physical violence from which they were themselves (now) safe. Jokes about sexual abuse targeted the collage of stains it left behind, certainly on slaves and freed slaves, and evidently on the poor as well, considering what happens to poor girls in *Aulularia, Cistellaria, Epidicus,* and *Persa.* Rape as a plot device is a holdover from the *Nea,* yet still fresh in Latin. Similarly, during the war years, when armies seized the crops and food shortages haunted the cities, the free poor shared the hunger of slaves. A lot of Plautine humor depends on the audience's recognition of these issues, even on their firsthand experience of them, in varying ways and degrees. Empathy begins under the skin.

This empathy is further complicated by the probability that both actors and playwrights, during this period, came from the lower classes and had some experience of slavery. The actor's mask is an emblem of changed identity; the *Poenulus* prologue speaker ends with "I'm going; I want to turn into someone else now" (*ibo, alius nunc fieri volo,* 126); so slavery

71

changed people's identities and changed their names. The most common joke in the plays, and perhaps the most taken for granted, is the characters' names; since you can't tell the players without a program, let us start there.

Names

The most threatened identity in Plautus is that of the slave Sosia in *Amphitruo*, who spends the very long opening scene having his identity stolen by Mercurius: the god, costumed as Sosia's double, also beats him up. Asked to identify himself by Mercurius with the words "Whose are you?" (*quoius sis*, 346), Sosia repeatedly claims an identity as his owner's slave (*eri sum servos*, 347; *Amphitruonis ego sum servos Sosia*, 394; *alienabis numquam quin noster siem*, 399; *non sum ego servos Amphitruonis Sosia?*, 403). He exists as a possession. But also as a body; he sees Mercurius' appearance, in detail, as what he has often seen in the mirror (442); matching their scarred backs will prove the likeness (446).[1] He doubts the evidence of his senses at length, adducing his recent beating as a proof of his own existence (407); he says he will have to find a new name (423); at the end of the scene, he asks the audience to tell him what has become of him (455–9):

> ... di immortales, obsecro vostram fidem,
> ubi ego perii? ubi immutatus sum? ubi ego formam perdidi?
> an egomet me illic reliqui, si forte oblitus fui?
> nam hicquidem omnem imaginem meam, quae antehac fuerat, possidet.
> vivo fit quod numquam quisquam mortuo faciet mihi.

> ... Immortal gods, I'm begging you, honest fellow citizens,[2]
> when/where did I die? When/where was I transformed? When/where did
>   I lose my shape?
> Or did I myself leave me there, if maybe I forgot?
> This guy here has hold of my whole image, what it was before.
> While I'm still alive it's happening, what no one ever will do for me when
>   I'm dead.

---

[1] On Sosia's body and the actor's body inside the costume, see Dutsch 2015: 18–19; Slater 2014: 119–20. On Sosia's identity as a form of property, see Dressler 2016: 43; on his loss in the context of the lament for the fallen city, see Jeppesen 2016: 139–40.

[2] On the formula *obsecro vostram fidem* and the practice of *quiritatio*, see chapter 3. Sosia here appeals ironically to the gods – he has one standing next to him, beating him – and, conflating gods and audience, to the audience, shading into the formula whereby one citizen appeals to others for help in a public place. But Sosia is not a citizen; as will be seen, he is not the only slave onstage to make such an appeal.

His erasure is a death, a transformation, and a loss of body; he fears that he has somehow left himself behind in the land of the enemy, even that he has forgotten himself. Since his double has his *imago* – his likeness, but also his mask – the slave now has what he will never have in death: a look-alike, to march at his descendants' funerals wearing his *imago*, his life-mask. Sosia, as in other slaves' jokes, can be no one's ancestor; he here also takes a passing swipe at the *imago* of the *summus vir*, which must have seemed funny to comedians.[3] This speech concludes with Sosia's wish that this adventure may end in his manumission (460–2), but no such luck; instead, he spends the rest of the play in a morass of pronouns (597 *mihimet Sosiae*, 598 *Sosia illic egomet fecit sibi uti crederem*, 607 *egomet memet*, 625 *Sosia ... ego ille*). His identity, like the actor's mask, is detachable.

The name change for slaves is a mark of natal alienation, and was literally understood as such in Roman custom, whereby even adoption into another family, with the resulting name change and rupture of agnatic bonds, constituted a type of *capitis deminutio* – literally, "diminishment of person," *caput* here standing for the whole person, as it does elsewhere both in law and in the *palliata*.[4] Enslavement constituted *capitis deminutio maxima*. As best we can tell from later periods of Roman history, slave dealers renamed slaves to make them appealing to buyers, often using Greek names no matter what the origin of the slave; whereas Roman citizens in the mid-Republic had at least a first name and a family name,

---

[3] The commonly held belief that the *imagines* at an aristocratic funeral in this period were worn by actors appears to be a chimaera; Polybius in his famous account says no such thing, only that the masks were placed on men who most closely resembled the ancestors (not the dead man) in size and general appearance (6.53.6; surely either relatives or hired mourners). The dead man was there in person, as a corpse (6.53.1; see Johanson forthcoming). The two other passages generally cited in support of this idea are dubious, and both much later: Diodorus Siculus (a habitual fantasist, here represented by Photius's summary) says that famous men had body doubles (*mimêtas*) who followed them around all their lives to learn the role (31.25.2); Suetonius in the *Life of Vespasian* (19) says the *archimimus* Favor played Vespasian at his funeral, but this comes in a paragraph about Vespasian's fondness for performers, and it is the imitation that is customary, not the actor. Pliny, *HN* 35.6.2, also sometimes cited, says nothing about who wore the *imagines*. Toynbee has this right (1971: 47–8); Walbank (1957) *ad* 6.52.7–8 expresses surprise that Polybius left out the actors, but has only Diodorus and Suetonius to adduce. Actors are assumed by Christenson 2000 *ad loc.*, and in current standard accounts like Bodel 1999 and Flower 1996. And by myself (2014b: 186). For Sosia's joke, cf. *Mos.* 427–8, *ludos ... vivo ... seni/ faciam, quod credo mortuo numquam fore* ("I'll hold games for the old man while he's alive, which I think will never happen when he's dead"): Tranio disrespecting his owner.

[4] On the concept, see Lee 1956: 76, 85–6. For discussion, see Leigh 2004: 37 (*capitis deminutio* and prisoners of war); Richlin 1999: 193–5. The *Institutes* of Justinian state baldly, "A slave has no *caput* to be lost or changed" (1.16.4). Buckland (1908: 3–6), enlarging on Paulus's famous line, *Servile caput nullum ius habet* ("A slave's *caput* has no rights," *D.* 5.3.1), emphasizes that the slave's lack of *caput* did not in fact mean rightlessness, and that, although slaves were classified by law as things, they were also classified as persons.

slaves had just this one name. Most of the enslaved persons and all the freed slaves in the audience would have lost their birth names, while slaves born in the household – *vernae* – would have been named by their owners, officially having no parents. A common type of renaming was the use of "ethnonyms" – names based on the slave's putative country of origin – and, onstage, in keeping with the ethnic stereotyping of Syrians as servile, a typical slave name was "Syrus"; picked, in a metatheatrical joke, as a stock name by the slave Chrysalus in *Bacchides* (649), just as Sosia says his father was "Davus" (*Am.* 365, 614).[5] The slaves we know of in this period have names like the old-fashioned "Marcipor" (literally, "Marcus Boy") and Flaccus ("Floppy"), and perhaps "Statius" and "Pellio" ("Tanner").[6] This system of nomenclature would have affected the meaning to the audience of the funny names of the characters in the *palliata*, which are often funny in a significant way: soldiers have long, bombastic names, *parasiti* and cooks have names connected with food, bankers and pimps have nasty names like "Wolf."[7] The names of prostitutes, their *ancillae*, and *lenae* are sex- or liquor-related and usually in a diminutive form, as are some names of other *ancillae* and of *pueri* (see table 2.1) – a comically overdetermined marking of their market purpose. Torturers, themselves slaves, have names connected with force, while other adult male slaves, the old men and their wives and sons, tend to have less obvious names; the sheer variety of the male slaves' names is evident when they are lined up with the cooks and torturers (table 2.2), or with those in table 2.1, and these names seem to be designed, not for the market, but for dramatic effect and memorability, like "Nicely-Nicely" and "Groucho" and "Curly."

---

[5] On slave names, see Joshel 1992: 35–7, with bibliography; note esp. Varro, *L.* 8.21, on how owners might change the names of a newly bought slave. Compare the "inconsiderate man," in the character sketches of Ariston of Keos (Plautus' contemporary): "when he buys a slave, he doesn't even ask for his name, or give him one himself, but merely calls him 'slave'" (for the translation and attribution, see Jeffrey Rusten in Rusten and Cunningham 2002: 185). On slave onomastics see Tordoff 2013: 23–7, following the in-depth study of the range of meanings found in Athenian slave names, real and fictional, in Vlassopoulos 2010; for real-life Roman slave onomastics see the critique of the concept of "onomastic *apartheid*" in Cheesman 2009: 523–8. See further below, chapter 7, on ethnonyms and the geography of the slave trade.

[6] Marcipor Oppii, the *tibicen* for Plautus' *Stichus*, and Flaccus Claudi, Terence's *tibicen*, both known from the *didascaliae* (see Moore 2012: 27); Caecilius Statius, Gellius 4.20.12–13, Robson 1938, Cheesman 2009: 516, and further in chapter 7 below; T. Publilius Pellio, Garton 1972: 260. On the names of theater personnel in this period, see Richlin 2014b: 210–11. On the meaning of "Marcipor," see Cheesman 2009 (*Marci-* is not a genitive). On the name "Flaccus," see Parker 2000, who argues that its literal sense is not usually felt.

[7] See Brown 2004: 6 for brief but telling remarks on the disparities between military names and military characters, despite Donatus's theory that names must match characters.

Table 2.1 *Names of prostitutes,* ancillae, *and* pueri *in the* palliata

For those names not in the dramatis personae for the indicated play, or otherwise there identifi ed, line numbers are given. All plays are attributed to Plautus unless otherwise noted.

Name	Meaning	Status	Play
Acropolistis	Woman of the Acropolis	pimp's *fidicina*	*Epidicus*
Acroteleutium	End Bit	freed *meretrix*	*Miles Gloriosus*
Adelphasium	Little Sister	pimp's *meretrix*	*Poenulus*
Aeschrodora	Dirty Gifts	pimp's *meretrix*	*Pseudolus* 196
Ampelisca	Little Grapevine	pimp's *meretrix*	*Rudens*
Anterastilis	Rival Lover Woman	pimp's *meretrix*	*Poenulus*
Archilis	[generic slave-woman][a]	*ancilla* of a *meretrix*	*Truculentus* 479
Astaphium	Little Raisin	*ancilla* of a *meretrix*	*Truculentus*
Bacchis	Bacchic Woman	free *meretrix*	*Bacchides*
Bromia	Bacchic Woman	household *ancilla*	*Amphitruo*
Canthara	Wine-Glass	household *ancilla*	*Epidicus* 567
Casina	Cinnamon	household *ancilla*	*Casina*
Cleareta	Famous Virtue	free *lena*	*Asinaria*
Crocotium	Little Saffron	household *ancilla*	*Stichus*
Delphium	Little Dolphin	free *meretrix*	*Mostellaria*
Eleusium	Little Eleusinian	*tibicina*	*Aulularia* 333
Erotium	Little Love	free *meretrix*	*Menaechmi*
Giddenis	[Punic name]	*nutrix*	*Poenulus*
Gymnasium	[Place to get a workout]	free *meretrix*	*Cistellaria*
Halisca	Little Salty	old household *ancilla*	*Cistellaria*
Hedylium	Little Sweetie	pimp's *meretrix*	*Pseudolus* 188
Leaena	Lioness	pimp's doorkeeper	*Curculio*
Lemniselenis	Moon Goddess of Lemnos	pimp's *meretrix*	*Persa*
Lucrio [This character's name might be "Lurcio"; he appears in only one scene (813–66), where he is not clearly marked as a *puer*]	Foxy[b]	*puer?*	*Miles Gloriosus*
Lucris [Hybrid formation from Greek *Lukaina*, "Little She-Wolf," and Latin *lucrum*, "profit," "wealth"]	Casha	war captive/trade goods	*Persa* 624
Melainis	Dusky	freed *lena*	*Cistellaria*

(continued)

Table 2.1 (*cont.*)

Name	Meaning	Status	Play
Milphidippa	Eyelid-disease-mare	*ancilla* of a *meretrix*	*Miles Gloriosus*
Paegnium	Little Toy (or, Skit[c])	*puer*	*Captivi* 984
Paegnium	Little Toy (or, Skit)	*puer*	*Persa*
Palaestra	Wrestling Match	pimp's *meretrix*	*Rudens*
Pardalisca	Little She-Leopard	household *ancilla*	*Casina*
Pasicompsa	Lovely to All	sex slave	*Mercator*
Phaniscus	Little Torch	*puer*	*Mostellaria* 947
Phidullium	Little Thrifty	*ancilla*	*Cornicula* fr. 66
Philaenium	Little Loves-to-Chat	free *meretrix*	*Asinaria*
Philematium	Little Kiss	freed *tibicina*	*Mostellaria* 971
Philocomasium	Little Loves-to-Party	free *meretrix*	*Miles Gloriosus*
Phoenicium	Little Red	pimp's *meretrix*	*Pseudolus*
Phronesium	Little Brainy	free *meretrix*	*Truculentus*
Phrugia	Phrygian Woman	*tibicina*	*Aulularia* 333
Pinacium	Little Picture	*puer*	*Mostellaria* 949
Pinacium	Little Picture	*puer*	*Stichus*
Pithecium	Little Monkey	*ancilla* of a *meretrix*	*Truculentus* 477
Planesium	Little Traveler	pimp's *meretrix*	*Curculio*
Scapha	Rowboat	old *ancilla* (?)[d]	*Mostellaria*
Selenium	Little Moon Goddess	free *meretrix*	*Cistellaria*
Sophoclidisca	Little Bitty Smart Girl	*ancilla* of a *meretrix*	*Persa*
Stalagmus	Dangle	*puer* (now grown)	*Captivi*
Staphyla	Bunch of Grapes	old household *ancilla*	*Aulularia*
Stephanium	Little Party Garland	slave *meretrix*	*Stichus*
Syra	Syrian Woman	old household *ancilla*	*Mercator*
Syra	Syrian Woman	*tonstrix*	*Truculentus*
Syra	Syrian Woman	*vilica* ?	Caecilius Statius *Titthe* 222 R₃
Telestis	Perfect Woman	war captive	*Epidicus*
Thessala	Thessalian Woman	household *ancilla*	*Amphitruo* 770
Xytilis	Scratchy[c]	pimp's *meretrix*	*Pseudolus* 210

[a] See Schmidt 1902a: 178.

[b] See Schmidt 1902a: 193–4. Schmidt takes the name to be the ethnonym *Lokrión*, "Man from Locris," but concedes that the sense of *lucrio* as "out for profit," "wily" clings to the word; see Paulus 49L, **Cercopa** *Graeci appellant lucrari undique cupientem, quasi* κέρδωνα, *quem nos quoque lucrionem vocamus.* κέρδων is also an epithet for the fox; see Forsdyke 2012: 63 for the famous image of Aesop chatting with a fox, in the context of fox fables.

[c] As the male slave name "Stichus" has a theatrical sense, so "Paegnium," as well, may have a double sense: "sex toy" and "[low erotic dramatic form]"; see Davidson 2000 on *paignia*, esp. 56 on Hellenistic symposium culture.

[d] For discussion of Scapha's status, see chapter 8.

[e] See Schmidt 1902b: 386, who reads *Xystilis* and defines accordingly (although not by any reference to shaving); he rejects a sense involving scratching, on the grounds that "ξύω in obscönem Sinne ist mir nicht bekannt." But with κνίζω scratching is strongly associated with foreplay.

Table 2.2 *Names of adult male slaves in the* palliata

For those names not in the *dramatis personae* for the indicated play, or otherwise there identified, line numbers are given. All plays are attributed to Plautus unless otherwise noted. Slaves who play a central role are marked with an asterisk.

Name	Meaning	Status	Play
Acanthio	Thorny (? Hedgehog)	personal slave	*Mercator*
Anthrax	Coal	slave cook	*Aulularia* 310
Artamo	Butcher	*lorarius*	*Bacchides*
<A>s<pa>s<i>us	Welcome	? house slave	*Vidularia*
Cacistus	Worst	fisherman	*Vidularia*
[Status unspecified in the extant fragments]			
Cario	Carian Man	(probable) slave	*Miles*
		cook	*Gloriosus*
*Chalinus	Horse-bit	armor-bearer	*Casina* 55
*Chrysalus	Golden	house slave	*Bacchides*
Colaphus	Punch	*lorarius*	*Captivi* 657
Collybiscus	Cookie	*vilicus*	*Poenulus*
Congrio	Eely	slave cook	*Aulularia* 310
Corax	Hook[a]	*lorarius*	*Captivi* 657
Cordalio	Heart Attack	*lorarius*	*Captivi* 657
Cyamus	Bean	house slave	*Truculentus*
[Addressed as *Geta*, "Getic Man," *Truc.* 577]			
Cylindrus	Rolling Pin	slave cook	*Menaechmi* 300
*Epidicus	Under Litigation	house slave	*Epidicus*
*Gripus	Fishnet	fisherman	*Rudens*
Grumio	Clod[b]	farm slave	*Mostellaria*
Harpax	Grabber	*cacula* or *calator*	*Pseudolus* *Pseudolus* 1009
Lampadio	Torchman	house slave	*Cistellaria*
*Leonida	[Spartan hero-king]	house slave	*Asinaria*
*Libanus	Frankincense	house slave	*Asinaria*
Lydus	Lydian Man	*paedagogus*	*Bacchides*
Lydus	Lydian Man	?	*Cornicula* fr. 68

(*continued*)

Table 2.2 (*cont.*)

Name	Meaning	Status	Play
*Messenio	Messenian Man	personal slave	*Menaechmi*
*Milphio	Eyelid-disease Man	house slave	*Poenulus*
*Olympio	Olympian Man	*vilicus*	*Casina*
*Palaestrio	Wrestler	house slave	*Miles Gloriosus*
Palinurus	[helmsman of Aeneas]	house slave	*Curculio*
Pistus	Fido	*vilicus*	*Mercator* 278
*Pseudolus	False	house slave	*Pseudolus*
*Sagaristio [Sounds like Latin *sagus*, "prophetic," and *sagum*, "soldier's cloak"]	? Man from Sangaros[c]	house slave	*Persa*
Sangario	Man from Sangaros	house slave	*Trinummus* 1105
Sangarinus	Man from Sangaros	house slave	*Stichus*
Saurea	Lizard	*atriensis* (fake)	*Asinaria*
Sceledrus [Sounds like Latin *scelus*, "crime"]	Dung[d]	house slave	*Miles Gloriosus*
Sceparnio	Axe-man	manual laborer	*Rudens*
Simia	Ape	house slave	*Pseudolus* 727
*Sosia [Common comic slave name]	Safe	house slave	*Amphitruo*
Sparax	Tear 'Em	*lorarius*	*Rudens* 807
*Stalagmus[e]	Dangle; see table 2.1	house slave?	Naevius *Stalagmus*
Stasimus	Steady	house slave	*Trinummus*
Stichus	Line	house slave	*Stichus*
Stichus	Line	*vicarius* (imaginary)	*Asinaria* 433, 437
Strobilus	Spinning Top	house slave	*Aulularia*
Syncerastus	Pork Stew[f]	pimp's slave	*Poenulus*
Syrus	Syrian Man	pimp's slave (fake)	*Pseudolus* 636
Thesprio	Thesprotian Man	armor-bearer	*Epidicus* 29

(*continued*)

Table 2.2 (*cont.*)

Name	Meaning	Status	Play
Thyniscus [This name is a conjecture, but the *Th-* and the *-scus* ending are present in the text.]	Little Bithynian	house slave	*Cistellaria* 283
*Toxilus	Man from Scythia[g]	house slave	*Persa*
Trachalio	Deltoids	*calator*	*Rudens* 335
*Tranio	Rower's Bench[h]	house slave	*Mostellaria*
Truculentus	Truculent	farm slave	*Truculentus*
Turbalio	Mess	*lorarius*	*Rudens* 798
*Tyndarus	? Man from Tyndaris[i]	house slave	*Captivi*

In addition, the unassigned fragments possibly attributable to Plautus include a reference to a house slave with the classic name *Davus* (Gell. 18.12.3, compare Sosia's self-identification as "son of Davus," *Am.* 365, and chapter 7), and a list of house slaves called to come out of the house with clubs (fr. inc. 173–4, cf. *Poen.* 1319–20): *Cilix, Lycisce, Sosia, Stiche, Parmeno* ("Cilician Man, Little Lycian Man, Safe, Line, Faithful").

[a] *Corax* literally means "crow," and in that sense connotes "carrion eater," which might be in play here (common in Aristophanes), although the main function of the name here is its resonance with "Colaphus" and "Cordalio." The word is transferred to a range of hook-shaped things; the sense "torture hook," attested only later (Lucian, *Menippus* or *Nekyomantia* 11), makes *korax* one of a class of animal names that are used to denote instruments of torture (see chapter 3 on the dog, chapter 6 on the mouse). However, *korax* had topical resonance in the 200s as the word for the advance in naval weapons that helped Rome win the First Punic War, a kind of grappling hook (Plb. 1.22.3).

[b] Or maybe "Pocket"; see Schmidt 1902b: 369–70.

[c] See Schmidt 1902a: 204–5 on this and the next two names as ethnonyms located in northern Asia Minor, including the city of Sangaros in Bithynia, although "Sagaristio" poses problems.

[d] See Schmidt 1902b: 381–2, who rejects a formation from *skel-* "thigh" and traces this name to vernacular words for human and animal excrement.

[e] Wright (1974: 51) speculates that Stalagmus was the title character of this play, based on parallels between 70 R₃ and lines spoken by Pseudolus and Palaestrio.

[f] See the probably Plautine *Phago* (fr. 100), with Varro *L.* 7.61.

[g] Or maybe "from India"; see Schmidt 1902a: 211, who argues that this must be an ethnonym, since "Sagaristio" is an ethnonym (see above). A connection with names in *tox-* suggesting "Bowman" is surely also felt here.

[h] See Schmidt 1902b: 386. A conjecture of Bergk's, who thought *thraniōn* would be a plausible (presumably comic) name for a slave oarsman in the Athenian navy; Schmidt also suggests "Tanner's Bench."

[i] See chapter 7.

Not everyone onstage has a name; this includes some major characters, like the *lena* in *Cistellaria* and the Virgo in *Persa*, but often namelessness is an index of objectification, the lot of supernumeraries, non-speakers: *pueri*, cooks, *servi*.[8] But even the named characters in the plays have just one single name, almost always Greek. Therefore, the crucial change whereby a slave named "Pellio," once manumitted, would take his former owner's *praenomen* and *nomen* and become "T. Publilius Pellio" is invisible onstage; Acroteleutium, who is a freedwoman, does not have a freedwoman's name, because her owner does not have a Roman name himself. The single Greek names align the characters with Greeks, certainly, but they also align them with slaves. This was a meaning overwhelmingly present to any audience members sitting in Rome in the 200s, whether they were native speakers of Greek, Latin, or another language; the onstage action may pretend to be set in Greece, but the Greek names are set in a Latin text and take the form of Latin names. We are in *barbaria* now, where a Greek name means something different from what it meant back in Athens, or Sicily.[9]

Like all slave names, the many prostitutes' names in the plays mark a social placement – even more so. As the *nutrix* Giddenis in *Poenulus* says of the threat hanging over her former charges, now owned by a pimp: "Indeed, today their names would be changed / and they would be making their living with their bodies, a living unworthy of their birth" (*namque hodie earum mutarentur nomina / facerentque indignum genere quaestum corpore, Poen.* 1139–40). Fraenkel gives this as an instance of a common kind of riddling joke – the "name change" is from *virgo* to *meretrix* – but, both onstage and off, this joke has a clanging resonance.[10] The names on the list in table 2.1 show how consistently sex workers onstage are labeled to attract customers; yet most female household slaves onstage have similarly sexy names, as do *pueri*, underscoring the sexual vulnerability of both groups and the intentions of sellers and buyers, familiar offstage as well. Many end in the diminutives *-ium* and *-isca* or *-iscus* (all based on Greek endings); this makes a joke out of the name of the prologue speaker in *Cistellaria*, the god Auxilium

---

[8] For statistics, see Prescott 1936, Duckworth 1938. Duckworth, however, excludes the mute characters (even those with names), on whom see Klein 2015. Many of these are slaves, and their presence onstage constitutes a significant element in the plays' meaning; see also Prescott 1937 for analysis of major characters who are onstage for long periods without lines.

[9] A much-discussed question; see Adams 2003: 351–4 on Plautine Greek in general; Chalmers 1965: 31–3, Feeney 2016, Fontaine 2010.

[10] The interpretation goes back to Ussing; see Fraenkel 2007: 22–3. His comments – "If one loses the qualities one has had till now or acquires completely new ones, then one must also change one's name. … an expression for the deterioration of the current situation" – recall in this case Patterson's concept of social death.

("Help"), who appears in a play with two prostitutes named Gymnasium and Selenium.[11] The literal translations given in table 2.1 do not deal with the bilingual aspect of the names, itself bearing overtones of the luxury trade and the *langue d'amour*, or with the tone of the diminutives and the resemblance of these names to those of historically attested prostitutes; "Leaina," for example, was the name of a famous *hetaira* in the late 300s BCE.[12] Milphidippa's ungainly name, however, does not mean she is unattractive (see below), while the three *ancillae* named "Syra" (*Mercator, Truculentus,* Caecilius Statius *Titthe*) are thus marked as members of a sterotypically ugly, servile ethnic group (see Starks 2010). Presumably this was not their birth name; the soldier in *Truculentus* presents his beloved Phronesium with two unnamed Syrian *ancillae,* "both queens back home," whose *patria* he has destroyed (*adduxi ancillas tibi eccas ex Suria duas, / ... sed istae reginae domi/ suae fuere ambae, verum <earum> patriam ego excidi manu, Truc.* 530–2).

The renaming process is partly spelled out in *Captivi,* when it comes out that the recaptured runaway slave Stalagmus – himself formerly used for sex by his owner – had kidnapped his owner's son Tyndarus as a child. He addresses Tyndarus' former owner: "Your father gave him to you / when you were a boy, as part of your *peculium,* and he was a little tiny four-year-old. / ... / He was called 'Paegnium,' but afterwards you all called him 'Tyndarus'" (*nam tibi quadrimulum / tuo' pater peculiarem parvolum puero dedit. / ... / Paegnium vocitatust, post vos indidistis Tyndaro, Capt.* 981–4). It seems impossible that Tyndarus' birth name could have been *Paegnium* ("Little Toy"), the name of a flirtatious *puer* in *Persa,* and at least possible that it was Stalagmus (whose name means "Dangle") who renamed him for sale after kidnapping him: payback.[13] Meanwhile, all the boys

---

[11] *Cist.* 154; self-identified as *deus* in the previous line. See Clark 2007: 86 on Auxilium and the contemporary trend towards deified abstractions, and on the gender tensions in the name, although they are, if anything, male/female, not male/neuter.

[12] On the names of *hetairai* both historical and comic, see Henry 1992: 265, McClure 2003: 59–78; Kurke 2002: 33–40 on Leaina and other *hetairai* hired by Demetrius Poliorcetes and featured in the *Chreiai* of Machon in the mid-200s BCE, on which see Richlin 2016: 86, 91. On Greek, the *sermo amatorius,* and the luxury trade, see Hough 1934, with discussion by Leigh 2004: 5. This used to be a standard explanation of what is going on here – "Greek" means "expensive party," as signified by the term *pergraecari* and its gloss by Paul the Deacon (235L); the idea was popularized by Segal 1968: 31–41. Note esp. his judgment, "[Plautus'] audience knew perfectly well what a Greek was like: he was their exact opposite" (37): a paradigmatic treatment of the audience as monolithic, with the elder Cato as its representative. Surely the situation was much more complicated than that, considering the varieties of hybridity both onstage and in the audience (and in Cato). See Richlin 2016, forthcoming a. On the sexual vulnerability of *ancillae,* see Marshall 2015.

[13] On the renaming of Tyndarus in *Captivi* and on Stalagmus in the play, see the detailed discussion at Leigh 2004: 90–1. For "Paegnium," Lindsay's translation "Pet" (1921: 114, *ad* 984) and Watling's translation "Laddie" (1965: 93) are optimistic; defended by Philippides 2011.

have grown up, and the free boys are named Philocrates ("Loves to Rule") and Philopolemus ("Loves War"), but the adult Stalagmus still bears the label of a *puer*. The same might be implied of the *vilicus* Collybiscus in *Poenulus* and the house slave Libanus in *Asinaria*: "Cookie," both edible and diminutive; "Frankincense," a desirable luxury, like Casina.

The unnamed Virgo in *Persa*, playing an Arabian slave, makes up her own natal name on the spot ("My name in my fatherland was 'Lucris'," *Lucridi nomen in patria fuit*, *Per.* 624); evoking Greek prostitute names like *Lukainion* ("Little She-Wolf") in a *para prosdokian* ("Luc ... ris"), and making a Greek name out of the Latin *lucrum*, the name means "Casha," and becomes a selling point (625). When the pimp's slave Planesium in *Curculio* is reunited with her brother at last, he gives his father's name as "Periplanes" (636), a comic patrilineage for a girl far from home, who, despite her supposedly virginal status, already has a prostitute's name. So the kidnapped Adelphasium ("Little Sister") and Anterastilis ("Rival Lover Woman") in *Poenulus*, despite what Giddenis says, already have names like those of other prostitutes, again presumably given to them by their kidnapper before he sold them to the pimp (*Poen.* 86–90). So does the kidnapped Palaestra ("Wrestling Match") in *Rudens*. Contrast the names of the unmarried girls in *Aulularia* and *Vidularia*, Phaedria ("Shining") and Soteris ("Savior Girl"), or of the *matronae* Cleostrata ("Famous Army," *Casina*), Dorippa ("War Horse," *Mercator*), Eunomia ("Good Order," *Aulularia*), and Phanostrata ("Shining Army," *Cistellaria*), along with that of Planesium's long-lost mother, Cleobula ("Famous Counsel," *Cur.* 643). Her *nutrix* Archestrata ("Army Leader," 643) might then be conceived of as free, while the free *lena* Cleareta ("Famous Virtue," *Asinaria*) has a name that belies her nature. But most of these names connect with the characters they denote only insofar as their lack of denotative force and, in some cases, their military/cavalry/government elements label the characters as free, possibly as well-born.[14] The names of the young wives in

---

[14] On the spelling of "Cleostrata," see MacCary and Willcock 1976: 95. On the name of the *matrona* Artemona in *Asinaria*, see Schmidt 1902a: 178–9, who holds that it is just the female form of the fairly common man's name "Artemôn," the literal sense of which was long weakened: "Der schon verblasste Name war Plautus aus dem Leben bekannt." The name's resonances include the alarming *artamos*, "butcher," as well as the goddess Artemis: no clear label. Interestingly, Schmidt notes that "Artamo" and "Artemon" are names associated with slaves and freedmen (Artamo is the *lorarius* in *Bacchides*). The *locus classicus* on comic names denoting class in association with an upper-class wife is Aristophanes, *Clouds* 46–70, where the Alcmaeonid wife wants to name her son something ending in "horse" (63). Artemona has the dowry but not the name. The resonance of the wives' names is something like that of Margaret Dumont's roles in the Marx Brothers' movies, like "Mrs. Gloria Teasdale" in *Duck Soup*, "Mrs. Suzanna Dukesbury" in *At the Circus*. Like other elements of shtick in the *palliata*, this is a holdover from a meaning system elsewhere, much as "Lady Bracknell"

Stichus – Panegyris ("Festival") and Pamphila ("All-love") – are then sus-
piciously juicy, while the war captive Telestis in *Epidicus*, bought from the
spoils, evidently still has her birth name ("Perfect Girl"). Perhaps capable
of a lecherous misprision, as the boys give her the once-over: "Take a look
at her, look her over, Epidicus: / from her toetips to her topmost curl, she's
the most built for fun" (*aspecta et contempla, Epidice: / usque ab unguiculo
ad capillum summumst festivissuma, Epid.* 622–3).[15] Pretty as a picture, her
new owner concludes, to which the slave Epidicus replies that she will
cause his skin to be painted by "Apelles and Zeuxis with paint made of
clubs" (*pigmentis ulmeis*, 626).

In a repeated joke, a slave expresses fear of punishment as fear of a name
change – from Sosia to "Quintus" (a common *praenomen*, but, in context,
"fifth man [to be beaten]," *Am.* 305), from Chrysalus to "Cross-alus" (*Bac.*
362), from Syncerastus to "Broken Leg" (*Crurifragium, Poen.* 886). Hegio says
Tyndarus' name will be changed to *Sescentoplagus*, "Six Hundred Lashes,"
when he is in the quarries (*Capt.* 726). The starving *parasitus* Gelasimus says
he is going to change his name to Miccotrogus, "Eating Little" (*St.* 242).
Renaming, as Fraenkel demonstrated, is a basic comic technique in the *palliata* (2007: 17–44); the plays' play with personal names makes a joke out of
something that was, in real life, painful to bear. "I'll now make this same play,
if you like, from a tragedy / into a comedy, with all the same verses," says
Mercurius in the *Amphitruo* prologue (*eandem hanc, si voltis, faciam <iam> ex
tragoedia / comoedia ut sit omnibus isdem vorsibus*, 54–5).

Names mark the poor as well as slaves in the *palliata*. Luxuria in the
Trinummus prologue explains (18–20) that Philemon called the play
Thensaurus ("Treasure"), but, when "Plautus turned it the barbarian way"
(*Plautus vortit barbare*), he made the name *Trinummus* – "Thirty Bucks" –
thus choosing to name the play after a poor man's wages and the first funny
scene in the play (the long overdue Act 4, scene 2). Here we meet the hard-
up, unnamed Sycophanta, who, as Timothy Moore points out, is repeatedly identified as an actor (1998: 11–12). The *parasitus* in the *palliata*, like
his Greek forebears, is a professional funny man, telling jokes in return
for a meal, but the *palliata* emphasizes his hungry poverty rather than his

changes meaning from England to North America. See discussion of Robinson 2004 in Richlin
2017b: 173.

[15] The connection is drawn by Schmidt 1902a: 210, who remarks of the name, "hier im guten Sinne."
The once-over is complicated by the presence of the male actor inside the costume, as the lines take
the form of the typical deictic reception (see chapter 5).

status as a party sidekick.[16] Like prostitutes, *parasiti* have professional names that identify them with their social placement in meaningful ways. The names given to *parasiti* in the plays relate to eating (Curculio, Artotrogus in *Miles*, Saturio in *Persa*), comedy (Gelasimus in *Stichus*), or sex (Peniculus in *Menaechmi*, Ergasilus in *Captivi*). Gelasimus says that his father gave him his name (*St.* 174), underscoring his freeborn status, but slaves also lay joking claim to parents, and it should be emphasized that *parasitus* names are demeaning, clownish: "Weevil" (compare the joke at *Cur.* 586–7 about weevils in the flour, product of the mill), "Bread-eater," "Fatso," "Funny," "Little Penis" or "Little Brush," "Working Boy." Ergasilus, as will be seen below, admits to the nickname "Whore" (*Scortum, Capt.* 69); his supposed real name already likened him to a prostitute (cf. Greek *ergasimos*; Schmidt 1902b: 367–8). Through their very appellations, the characters in the *palliata* make light of conditions embodied in both actors and audience.

Addressing the Body of the Audience

The plays' direct appeal to fellow-feeling in the audience is evident in numerous monologues, some famous, some less so. Starting with one of the best known: in the prologue to *Amphitruo*, the god Mercurius addresses the audience in a speech of over 150 lines. He opens (1–7) by addressing the audience as traders – buyers and sellers – who desire his help in business, as befits his contemporary cult on the Aventine, in a neighborhood of tradesmen (Andreussi 1993). He goes on to introduce himself by name (19), saying he has been sent at his father's bidding. Then he inserts a parenthesis (26–31):

> etenim ille quoius huc iussu venio, Iuppiter
> non minu' quam vostrum quivis formidat malum:
> humana matre natus, humano patre
> mirari non est aequom sibi si praetimet;
> atque ego quoque etiam, qui Iovis sum filius,   30
> contagione mei patris metuo malum.

> Indeed that Jupiter by whose command I come here
> fears a beating no less than any of you does:

---

[16] *Parasitos* speeches retailed in Athenaeus's *Deipnosophistae* show a character with his own shtick, already well developed in the time of Epicharmus (480s BCE; *Hope* or *Wealth* fr. 32, Ath. 6.235f–236b). These monologues list behaviors prominent among which is assistance in komastic brawling (not found in the extant *palliata* before Terence); Greek *parasitos* names both real and comic tend to denote things to eat or physical violence, unlike anything in the *palliata*. See esp. the monologues at Ath. 6.238b–c, 238c–d, 238d–f, and cf. Richlin 2016; Tylawsky 2002: 59–77, 122.

born of a human mother, a human father –
it's no fair being surprised if he's anxious on his own behalf;
and I too, even, who am the son of Jupiter,   30
fear a beating from infectious contact with my father.

These lines are commonly taken as a metatheatrical joke about the status of "Jupiter" and "Mercurius" as actors, who might be slaves, behind their masks; the line "born of a human mother, a human father" is then doubly transgressive, not only in allotting human parents to the king of the gods but in allotting any parents to a slave.[17] The insistence on the fictionality of natal alienation is, as will be seen, a recurring theme in the plays. An even bigger recurring theme is slaves' fear of a beating, "the bad thing," *malum*; what is important here is that "Jupiter" fears a beating "no less than any of you does." Mercurius is talking to people in the audience who have reason to fear a beating – slaves, first and foremost.

As a character in the play, Mercurius is subject to a double come-down, forced to take on a new identity not only human but servile. As seen above, he becomes an exact physical replica of Amphitruo's slave Sosia, and in their opening scene together both of them comment on the experience of slavery. Immediately after the prologue, Sosia enters, without noticing Mercurius, and begins to address the audience. He cracks a few jokes about the dangers of walking around at night, and how he fears he will be thrown into the *carcer* by the *tresviri*, where he expects "eight strong men would beat on me like an anvil" (160); then he blames his situation on his owner (163–75):

> haec eri immodestia
> coegit me,
> qui hoc noctis a portu
> ingratiis excitavit.
> nonne idem huc luci me mittere potuit?   165
> opulento homini hoc servitus dura est,
> hoc magi' miser est diviti' servos:
> noctesque diesque adsiduo satis superque est
> quod facto aut dicto adest opus, quietu' ne sis.
> ipse dominu' dives operis, [et] laboris expers,   170
> quodquomque homini accidit lubere, posse retur:
> aequom esse putat, non reputat labori' quid sit,
> nec aequom anne iniquom imperet cogitabit.

[17] On these lines as metatheatrical, see Christenson 2000: 141–2; Lefèvre 1999: 21; Moore 1998: 111, commenting "'Mercury' is a slave, pretending to be a god, pretending to be a slave"; Slater 1990: 120. On Mercurius' opening speech, see esp. Slater 2014: 113–20.

ergo in servitute expetunt multa iniqua:
habendum et ferundum hoc onust cum labore.   175

My owner's lack of self-control
forced me to do this,
he who woke me up when I didn't want to
and made me leave the harbor, at this time of night.
He couldn't send me here in daylight?   165
Slavery to a wealthy man is hard in this way,
yes, in this way the slave of a rich man is more miserable:
night and day, nonstop, there's enough and to spare
of what he needs said or done right now, so you shouldn't get a rest.
The rich householder himself, unfamiliar with chores or work,   170
thinks that whatever a person happens to feel like, can be done;
he thinks it's fair, he doesn't think about how much work it is,
or reflect upon whether what he commands is fair or unfair.
And so in slavery many unfair things happen:
and this burden has to be lived with and borne along with the work.   175

The song appeals to the audience's judgment about what is fair, with
forms of *aequom* repeated four times in three lines (172–4; compare
Mercurius in the prologue, above). Sosia's rhetorical question – "He
couldn't send me here in daylight?" – calls on the audience's fellow-feeling,
the *nonne* that leads his question looking forward to a sympathetic "Yes, he
could!" The villains here are, not owners in general, but rich owners, who
do not know what it is to work.[18]

Mercurius, also addressing the audience, interrupts Sosia's song,
although continuing in the same meter (176–9):

satiust me queri illo modo servitutem:
hodie qui fuerim liber, eum nunc
potivit pater servitutis;
hic qui verna natust queritur.

It's more proper for me to complain about slavery in this way:
I who was free today, me, now
my father has put me into slavery's possession;
while this guy who was born a *verna* is complaining.

This interjection appeals to the audience to confirm that a person
born free and then enslaved has more to complain about than one born
into the household, a *verna*; the presence of both points of view side by

---

[18] On the resemblance between this song and the "slave laments" analyzed by Virginia Hunter, esp.
Kariôn's opening speech in *Wealth*, see chapter 1; on points also found in a *parasitus* speech from
Epicharmus's *Hope or Wealth* (Ath. 6.235e–236b), see Richlin 2016: 87.

side onstage implicitly appeals to a division of opinion in an audience among whose members this difference is an issue. Sosia, although he has not officially heard what Mercurius is saying, duly picks up Mercurius' line and proclaims himself *vero verna verbero*, "a real flogworthy *verna*" (180); the word *verna* appears only rarely in Plautus, and is used mostly of Sosia (*Am.* 179, 180, 1033; elsewhere, *Mil.* 698). Meanwhile, Mercurius has reframed the setup of the play as surrender of a son into slavery; the experience of being sold by a parent is acted out at length in *Persa*, where the Virgo's double-edged speeches blame her father for her sale to the pimp (615–55; see chapter 5). The element of sexual use is not lacking from the scene in *Amphitruo*, either: Sosia sings of his hard use by a rich owner in ionics, a notoriously sexy beat.[19] If the audience was conscious of *vernae* as always possibly the offspring of an *ancilla* and her owner, then Sosia as well as Mercurius act as slaves to their fathers (see chapter 3 on the *Captivi* prologue). The voices of the slaves Mercurius and Sosia go on to occupy the first 498 lines of this 1146-line play, so that the audience is primed to see the rest of the action through their eyes as well. As will be seen in chapter 3, numerous other prologue speakers are slaves, actors, or servile in some way – the Lar Familiaris in *Aulularia*, Auxilium in *Cistellaria*, Palaestrio in *Miles Gloriosus*, the star Arcturus in *Rudens*, the actors in *Captivi* (52), *Casina* (13), *Poenulus* (126) – while other plays open with expository conversations or verbal duels between slaves (*Epidicus*, *Mostellaria*, *Persa*).

Indeed, the paired opening songs in *Persa* introduce a play in which all the characters are slaves except for a pimp, the *parasitus* Saturio, and Saturio's unnamed daughter, the Virgo who dubs herself "Lucris" as she is sold onstage. The first song is sung to the audience by the lead character, the slave Toxilus, whose love affair with a slave prostitute, transgressively, will propel the play; the second, also sung to the audience, comes from Toxilus' best friend Sagaristio, who will play the *Man from Persia* of the title. Toxilus' song is about love; Sagaristio's is about how much he hates being a slave, full of sarcasm and jibes at his owner. This setup precedes the pair's mutual recognition. Thus it is no surprise when Sagaristio, returning to the stage with the money Toxilus needs, launches into a song of thanksgiving that turns into a vehement attack on his owner (whose money he is lifting). *Tuxtax tergo erit meo, non curo*, he sings – "It'll be bam! pow! on my back, but I don't care" (264), and then (266–71),

---

[19] Bettini 1995; Moore 2012: 113, and further below, chapters 4 and 5.

nam id demum lepidumst, triparcos homines, vetulos, avidos, ardos
bene admordere, qui salinum servo opsignant cum sale.
     virtus est, ubi occasio
     admonet, despicere.[20] quid faciet mihi?   268a
verberibus caedi iusserit, compedis impingi. vapulet,
ne sibi me credat supplicem fore: vae illi! nihil iam mihi novi   270
     offerre potest quin sim peritus.

See, that's what's really charming, to get these super-stingy, little old,
    greedy, dried-up guys,
and bite 'em well – the kind of guys who lock the silverware away from a
    slave and the salt with it.
     Virtus is, when the chance gives the word,
     to despise them. What'll he do to me?
He'll have me flogged, he'll have me put in leg irons; let *him* take a beating,
he shouldn't think I'll beg him for mercy: *he's* doomed! Nothing new now
     he can do to me that I'm not already an expert in.

This speech justifies Sagaristio's theft by portraying his owner as a member of a particular set of owners: old, harsh, and stingy with food. In contrast, Sagaristio boasts of his ability to take a beating, a point of pride he shares with other strong slave characters in the plays, just as the plays repeatedly denigrate owners who begrudge food to slaves, as will be seen. He uses violent language against his owner: *vapulet* (269), *vae illi* (270). Compare the fragment of *Faeneratrix* seen in chapter 1, where a freedman character uses the expression *vapula Papiria* in defying his former owner; or Pseudolus' *vae victis* to his owner's face (*Ps.* 1317). In closing out his triumph-song to the audience with these lines, Sagaristio offers the spectators a set of moral definitions: *nam id demum lepidumst* (266), and, very plainly, *virtus est* (268); compare Leonida's *em istaec virtus est*, of the ability to lie, cheat, and steal, as long as you can take a beating (*As.* 323), and the extended praises of such virtues offered in turn by Libanus and Leonida (*As.* 545–77). Sagaristio's definition takes the *virtus* that, as will be seen in chapter 3, belongs to a conquering soldier, and redefines it for a slave who is not himself classed as a *vir*. These are outlaw virtues, resistant virtues, virtues from low down. Sagaristio's song leads immediately into a funny and perhaps sexy scene between him and Toxilus' slave-boy Paegnium (below), sealing Sagaristio's moral code into a bubble as the play rolls on;

---

[20] Reading *despicere* for the text's *dispicere*; see Woytek 1982: 260 for justification of *dispicere*, along with a useful list of parallel passages for the moral definition. With *occasio* here, compare *Poen.* 42 *dum occasio est*; see chapter 7 for *moneo* used in commands. For *despicio* used absolutely, see Marcus to Fronto, *M. Caes.* 4.13.1 (*cum video, despicit*, 67,20 van den Hout), in a lively letter that ends with a promise to read *istum histrionum poetam*; Marcus and Fronto were great readers of early comedy.

his point is made, however, and nothing that follows unmakes it. He has something to say to slaves with a grievance – you know who you are.

The *Poenulus* prologue most directly addresses the audience according to their social roles, and has been widely taken to confirm the presence of slaves in the audience.[21] The prologue speaker declares himself *imperator histricus* (4), "actor-general," and proceeds to give a series of commands to the audience on how to behave. His addressees include theater staff (11, 19–20), along with the lictors who appear elsewhere among those who punish slaves with a beating (18); prostitutes, probably male (17); slaves (23–7); wet-nurses with babies (28–31); married women, with, by implication, their husbands (32–5); and *pedisequi* – slave attendants (41–3).[22] Of these, all are slaves except some of the babies, the married women, and their husbands, who are not described as elite in any way, and perhaps the lictors, lower-level civil servants, who are directed in language usually addressed to slaves (*neu … muttiant*, cf. chapter 6); contrast the speaker's oblique appeal to the *ludorum curatores* at 36–7 ("as for those in charge of the games, / let the prize not be awarded to any *artifex* unjustly").[23] Although it has been doubted, I think it is safe to say that the speaker is addressing persons actually present, and recognizably so, in the theater space, who are expected to laugh and be tickled when recognized from the stage. Unsurprisingly, the generic "slaves" (*servi*, 23) are threatened with a beating, either in the

---

[21] For doubts, see Brown 2013, who discounts each set of lines here taken to be addressed to slaves. Taking this prologue to include slaves among those present: Beare 1964: 173 ("a tumultuous crowd of every age and condition"), Manuwald 2011: 98 (cautiously); Marshall 2006: 75–6, firmly ("The audience of Plautine comedy was composed of individuals from every social station in Rome. Metatheatrical reference by stage characters to the audience provides a reliable gauge," with reference to the *Poenulus* prologue); Moore 1994/5: 114–17 (there but standing); cf. Moore 1998: 195–6 on the *Captivi* prologue.

[22] The *scorta exoleta* at 17 are usually taken to be male prostitutes past their prime (*exoleta*), that is, well past adolescence, on the basis of the well-established use of *exoletus* in later periods with this sense (see Williams 2010: 91, with brief mention of this passage). However, the possibility that these are female prostitutes in late adolescence cannot be ruled out, since a speaker in the probably Plautine *Parasitus Medicus* states plainly, *domi reliqui exoletam virginem* ("I left a grown-up girl at home," fr. 105). Female prostitutes in Plautus certainly have a prime capable of being passed; see below on the *meretrix adulescentula* in *Miles Gloriosus*, and, for example, Scapha's speech to Philematium in *Mostellaria*. On *scorta exoleta* in the Forum Romanum (the only other use of this phrase in Plautus), see below.

[23] Purcell's classic study of the *apparitores* (1983), focused as it is on epigraphic evidence, does not go back before the late Republic; he demonstrated that, from then on, the magistrates' servants, who included *praecones* as well as lictors, were predominantly freed slaves: an upper civil service rank, a position for strivers. But in Plautus the lictors, sometimes specified as eight in number and linked with the *tresviri* and the *carcer*, are associated exclusively with beating slaves; the two who are said to accompany the praetor at *Epid.* 27b–28 are conflated with these other lictors as a joke. No magistrate is mentioned in the *Poenulus* prologue except the *imperator histricus* himself; is this part of his joke? See below, and chapter 8 on *lorarii*.

theater or at home (26); they are told to move over and make room for
free people, or to pay for their freedom (*capite*, 24), and, like others, they
are told to obey the command or go home, but the *imperator histricus* is a
joke figure, and these are joke commands. What is perhaps less obvious,
the theme of hunger and starvation comes up repeatedly in this allocutory
section of his speech (6–10, 14, 30–1, 41–3), and the speaker goes on to
dub Plautus *Pultiphagonides* (54), "Son of an Eater of Grits" – that is, poor
people's food (for more on hunger, see below).

Beyond these introductory shout-outs to people sitting in the audience
who recognize the experience the actors are talking about lies the huge
mass of lines and scenes that address the same experience. Let us begin
with the beatings, which have drawn the most attention. As will be seen,
the fear of a beating belongs not only to slaves but to the poor, as represented onstage by the hungry figure of the *parasitus*.

Beating

It is commonly said that slaves are not beaten onstage in Roman comedy,
but sometimes they are; the stage directions are implied in the lines, indeed
are formulaic, with the beater's *em tibi* followed by a statement by the
beaten of what is happening (*verberas, caedis, tactio est*).[24] Usually this is a
mock beating, the equivalent of being hit with the slapstick of *commedia* or
the rubber chicken of vaudeville; but in the black comedy *Captivi*, always
the exception, the two bound men explicitly act out pain (200, *oh! oh! oh!*).
Even these "ow"s are the equivalent of the "boo hoos" of the characters
led off for purchase, but both are playing for laughs an experience shown

---

[24] Slaves not beaten: influentially, Erich Segal (1968: 152–5, 162–3), esp. 152, "the fact that no slave is
ever ill-treated during a comedy"; 163, "only the agelasts are whipped" (he cites three free characters – Labrax in *Rudens*, Dordalus in *Persa*, and the soldier in *Miles*). Segal was arguing against what
he saw as the then prevailing view "that Plautine slaves are generally beaten in retribution for their
misdeeds"; he cites only a 1955 article by Bernard Knox. In so doing, he does a lot of special pleading on the obvious exceptions to his generalizations; his point is that *clever* slaves are not beaten
for being clever (see chapter 8 for his arguments on manumission). Following Segal is the equally
influential Holt Parker (1989), who says flatly, "There are no instances of the actual torture of slaves,
on or off stage" (233), with a promise to deal with "the cases of blows on and off stage" (233 n. 6).
The subsequent discussion (241), however, uncharacteristically for Parker, gives only a partial list,
allowing him to argue that the ones beaten are "the figures ... whom Erich Segal terms 'agelasts'."
Many of the onstage beatings are indeed slapstick, but not all, and certainly not all are meted out
to blocking characters; see below on the groaning captives in *Captivi* and the *ancillae* in *Truculentus*
who say plainly that the straps hurt their arms. No onstage crucifixions, but plenty of everyday
violence; nor is slapstick meaningless.

as painful. As the Virgo in *Persa* says to her father when he explains she is going to be sold to the pimp and then reclaimed as free (360–4):

> ... cogita hoc verbum, pater:
> eru' si minatus est malum servo suo,
> tam etsi id futurum non est, ubi captumst flagrum,
> dum tunicas ponit, quanta adficitur miseria!
> ego nunc quod non futurumst formido tamen.

> ... A word, father – think about it:
> if an owner has threatened a beating to his slave,
> even if it's not going to happen, when the whip is picked up,
> while he strips off his shirt, what misery he feels!
> I – now, what's not going to happen, I fear it still.

The Virgo empathizes with the imagined slave, the audience empathizes with the Virgo. As Freud says about humor, it is "a means of obtaining pleasure in spite of the distressing affects that interfere with it; it acts as a substitution for the generation of these affects, it puts itself in their place. ... [It] arises from *an economy in the expenditure of affect*" (1960: 284; italics original). The more immediate the prior experience of pain, the bigger the economy. The Virgo's lines, on the page, are serious, poignant; spoken onstage by a male actor in drag, pleading with the grotesque *parasitus*, they are distanced from their literal meaning, and bent by the audience's possible consciousness of the possibly slave actor behind the mask, but the Virgo appeals to her father to imagine the scene of a beating – possibly even a "saying" (*verbum*) about beating – as something familiar to him, and the scene onstage appeals to the same familiarity among the audience members. Few present will not have known what she meant – some as beaten, some as beaters, some as both, all as witnesses. Nor would their recognition be only mental. Like Sagaristio, Libanus in *Asinaria* boasts of his capacity for bearing pain: *qui mest vir fortior ad sufferundas plagas?* "Who is a braver man than me at taking blows?" (557). This follows a black-comedy list of tortures (548–50): "cattle-prods, red-hot metal plates, crosses and fetters, / irons, chains, prisons, yokes, shackles, collars." "Familiar with our backs," he says to his friend, "they have often put scars (*cicatrices*) on our shoulder-blades" (551–2). The serious beatings and tortures so luridly described here are everywhere present in the lines of the plays; they take place offstage, but, like Libanus, the slave characters bring them along in the form of scars. Sosia, checking out Mercurius' body part by part to compare with his own, ends with a "scarred back" (*tergum cicatricosum, Am.* 446) as conclusive identifying mark; the slave Milphio

complains that he is carrying around a back that is "ridged with sores like
an oyster" because of his owner's romance (*quasi ostreatum tergum ulceribus
gestito, Poen.* 398).²⁵ The scarred back would have been physically present
in the theater as well as in these lines: in the physical carriage of an actor
playing a slave like Sagaristio, in the bodies of slaves and freed slaves on the
stage and sitting in the audience.

Onstage, owners do beat slaves and workers, and the lines emphasize
the action: the miser Euclio beats the old slave-woman Staphyla (*qur me
miseram verberas?*, "Why are you beating poor me?" *Aul.* 42); he chases
and beats the cook Congrio (406–14 offstage, then *tuom nunc caput sentit,*
"Your head is feeling it now," 426); he beats the Slave of Lyconides (*qua
me caussa verberas?* "What reason do you have for beating me?" 632).
Phaedromus in *Curculio* beats Palinurus (*em tibi male dictis pro istis,* "Take
that for those ill words of yours," 195; *pugnis caedis,* "You're hitting me with
your fists," 199). Charinus shakes or hits Acanthio (*placide ... priu' quam
vapulem,* "Take it easy, before I take a beating," *Mer.* 167). Agorastocles
beats Milphio for sweet-talking his beloved (*em voluptatem tibi!/em mel,
em cor, em labellum, em salutem, em savium,* " 'Pleasure!' – take that! And
that for 'honey,' and that for 'heart,' and that for 'lips,' and that for 'life,'
and that for 'kiss'!" *Poen.* 382–3, and four more in 384–5; *verberas,* says
Milphio – "You're beating [me]," 384). A blow perhaps punctuates the
final dismissal of Tranio by the *senex* in *Mostellaria* at his son's friend's
intercession: *age abi, abi inpune. em huic habeto gratiam* ("Go on, get out
of here, get out, no penalty. Pow, thank that guy," 1181). Ballio beats his
slaves, then beats one of them again for expressing pain (*doletne? em sic
datur, si quis erum servos spernit,* "Oh, that hurts? Pow, that's what you get,
if any slave looks down his nose at the owner," *Ps.* 155). The onstage bonds
of Chrysalus in *Bacchides,* of Tyndarus and Philocrates in *Captivi,* and of
Epidicus in *Epidicus* – all of whom triumph in the end – are often noted,
but the two slave-women in *Truculentus* are brought on in chains as well
(*vinclis,* 784) and released only after an inquisition (838), and Tyndarus'
chains, as *Captivi* closes, will be removed only to be placed on Stalagmus.
As Hegio's commands make clear, the process requires a blacksmith (*Capt.*
1027). One of the slave-women in *Truculentus* exclaims at the pain of leather restraints (*lora laedunt bracchia,* "the straps hurt our arms," *Truc.* 783);

²⁵ Cf. references to bruising, like the "painted" back at *Epid.* 626 (above), or Ballio's threat to make his
slaves' backs polychrome like tapestries (*Ps.* 145–7), and other jokes on the word *varius* ("spotted"/
"bruised," esp. *Epid.* 17–18). For display of scars, cf. the probably Plautine *Fugitivi* fr. 89: A *age age,
specta, vide vibices quantas!* B *iam inspexi. quid est?* ("Come on, come on, look at this, see how many
welts!" # "Now I've had a look: and?").

her owner brings the two women onstage after stringing them up for a flogging inside the house (777). Libanus calls the house doors his *conservas* because they are threatened with a beating (*As.* 386); Pseudolus grandly steps forward as the doors' *patronus* (*Ps.* 606).

Slaves and workers also beat each other up: so Leonida, masquerading as the *atriensis*, beats Libanus (*As.* 431, *em ergo hoc tibi*, cf. 416–17, and below); Olympio and Chalinus fight as proxies for their owners (*Cas.* 404–12); the *lena*, if her line cues a stage action, gives her daughter a clout on the ear (*Cist.* 118–19); Messenio and Menaechmus I beat up the slaves of the *senex* (*Men.* 1011–18 – note 1018, *em tibi etiam*); Tranio beats Grumio ([TR.] *em, hoccine volebas?* GR. *perii! qur me verberas?*, *Mos.* 9–10); and, at spectacular length, Mercurius (not really a slave) beats up Sosia (*Am.* 295–454 – many cues, most simply *vapula*, 395; attested to by Sosia afterwards, 606, 624). Sometimes slaves hit free people, and this is legitimate when they are ordered by their owners, as when the house slaves are called out to beat the soldier in *Poenulus* (1319–20, cf. fr. inc. 173–4), or when the soldier is tortured at the end of *Miles*. Otherwise, this constitutes an outrageous reversal: the pimp Dordalus is beaten and sexually humiliated by the slaves Toxilus, Sagaristio, and Paegnium (*Per.* 810, 846–8); the pimp Labrax is beaten offstage by *lorarii* as the slave Trachalio cheers them on and gleefully comments on the sound effects (*Rud.* 658–62); Leonida, masquerading as the *atriensis* (himself a slave), hits the Merchant (*As.* 477). These transgressions go along with a long list of defiant words and actions taken by slave characters against owners onstage (chapter 4); always, however, onstage commentary defines the slave as the one who is supposed to be the one beaten, and epithets like *verbero* and *mastigia* depend on that axiom.

The physical punishment of slaves imports real-life bogeymen into the plays – men who carry out the punishments as part of their job definition. Some are state officials, like the *tresviri*, who have people to do the beating for them (*Am.* 155–62, *Aul.* 416, *Per.* 72); or the lictors, who have their own rods (*As.* 574–5, *Epid.* 27b–28, *Poen.* 18, 26).[26] A joke about the *tribunus vapularis* (*Per.* 22) hints at the experience of the army rank-and-file, including slaves, at the hands of the *tribunus militaris*.[27] Other bogeymen belong to the private sector, like the horrific *carnufex*, the "meat-maker," and the *tintinnaculos ... viros* (*Truc.* 782), Ballio's *lanios ... cum tintinnabulis*, "the

---

[26] There is no trace in the plays of the lictor as the one who frees the slave before the praetor by touching him with another sort of rod, the *festuca* or *vindicta*, although the *festuca* itself is mentioned (*Mil.* 961); cf. Persius 5.175 with the scholiast *ad loc.*, and see Nisbet 1918 for further sources.

[27] On the *tribunus militaris* as the agent of punishment, see Plb. 6.37.1–4, 7–8; see Richlin 2017a: 217–20 on class difference and slaves in the Roman army in the 200s, and below.

butchers with the bells" (*Ps.* 332). The common use of *carnufex* as an insult bespeaks the presence of the professional torturer in the everyday lives of actors and audience, and on their streets – the *carcer*, domain of the *tresviri*, right in the Forum Romanum, while the torturers were segregated "outside the gate" (*extra portam, Ps.* 331, cf. *Mil.* 359–60), which in Rome meant the Esquiline Gate in the Servian Wall.[28] But some bogeymen live right in the same house with the rest of the *familia*: the tyrannical *atriensis* of *Asinaria* (cf. *Ps.* 609), and the "strap-men," the *lorarii*.[29] Similarly, the *vilicus*, who enters the onstage world as a visitor from the *villa*, is never a sympathetic character: Olympio (identified as *vilicus, Cas.* 52, 98) threatens Chalinus with hard labor and deprivation at the *villa* (120–40), knows that his special relationship with the owner makes him disliked, and fears what will happen to him when his "Jupiter" dies (328–37); Collybiscus in *Poenulus*, whose name perhaps indicates early training in submissive behavior, is happy to be used as a stooge in the schemes of Milphio and his owner, cheerfully agreeing that he is Agorastocles' slave (797). Grumio in *Mostellaria* might perhaps be identified as a *vilicus*, judging by his threat to punish Tranio in the country (4) and the strings of (ironic) imperatives he unleashes (20–4, 63–5). His triple-barreled string of rhetorical questions (25–7) follows the format used by Leonida playing the *atriensis* (*As.* 424–6; chapters 4, 6). Oddly, the *lorarii* are not blamed for their actions; as will be seen in chapter 8, they perform onstage a display of muscle that supports the owner's power, but speak no cruel words, indeed hardly a word at all.

Thus the speeches – and song – of the *lorarius* in *Captivi* are highly unusual, adding extra emphasis as his words poignantly remind the audience that these men are slaves themselves. His opening conversation with Hegio lays out the difference between the owner's and the slave's subject position (116–24):

[28] Like other death-related activities, torture and execution were located outside the city walls, although later sources attest to their presence in the Subura, in the center of the city. The phrase *extra portam* is probably not site-specific, since the Puteoli inscription also places torturers outside the gates, incidentally mentioning that they were required to wear bells when dragging off corpses (II.11–14, *cum tintinnabulo*); Ballio's bells are often taken to be chains, but they might, then, simply be bells. For general discussion, see Bodel 1994: 72–80 (tentatively redating the inscription to the first half of the first century BCE), 2000: 145–6 (incl. the bells); Hinard and Dumont 2003; Castagnetti 2012. For placement of Roman executions outside the Esquiline Gate in particular, see Suetonius, *Claudius* 25.3 (*in campo Esquilino securi percussit*), Tacitus, *Ann.* 2.32.5 (*extra portam Esquilinam ... more prisco*); Coarelli 1996a.

[29] The word *lorarius* does not appear in the plays themselves, but in the superscripts to scenes involving these characters; see Prescott 1936: 100–3, and further in chapter 8. Still these slaves appear to be differentiated from other house slaves by the task they are assigned to do.

[HE.] liber captivos avi' ferae consimilis est:
semel fugiendi si data est occasio,
satis est, numquam postilla possis prendere.
LO. omnes profecto liberi lubentius
sumu' quam servimus. HE. non videre ita tu quidem.   120
LO. si non est quod dem, mene vis dem ipse – in pedes?
HE. si dederis, erit extemplo mihi quod dem tibi.
LO. avi' me ferae consimilem faciam, ut praedicas.
HE. ita ut dicis: nam si faxis, te in caveam dabo.

[HE.] A free captive is just like a wild bird:
if he gets one chance of running away,
that's enough, you could never catch him after that.
LO. We all surely feel like being free
more than slaving. HE. You don't seem like it, I must say.   120
LO. If I don't have anything to give, you want me to give myself – to
    my feet?
HE. If you do, I'll have something to give you, on the spot.
LO. I'll make myself just like a wild bird, like you foretell it.
HE. Just like you tell it: because if you do, *I'll* give *you* – to a cage.

This interchange plays with several terms that are repeated in various regis-
ters within the Plautine lexicon. Unchained captives are like "wild birds" –
the paradigmatic *res nullius*, which can be owned once caught, but which
break the bonds of ownership once they are set free.[30] The *lorarius* is ready
to fly away with them, or run. The *cavea* doubles as cage and space for the
(captive) audience; as will be seen below, the trapping of birds also recurs
in the plays as a figure for the trapping of men by slave traders, prostitutes,
and tricksters, and the caging of slaves for sale. The axiom delivered by
the *lorarius* – all people want to be free – is used by Hegio as an occasion
for making him a counterexample ("you don't seem to"); the jingle *liberi
lubentius* is significant, as will be seen in chapter 4. The *lorarius* takes this as
taunting him with his inability to buy his way out of slavery, and he picks
up Hegio's wild bird simile like a parried insult in verbal dueling; compare
the duelists in Horace's *Satires* 1.5, "like a wild horse, that's what I say you

---

[30] Definition of the *res nullius*: Justinian, *Institutes* 2.1.12–13, cf. Lee 1956: 110. Stewart 2012: 59 n. 41
adduces the section of the *Digest* that includes wild birds (41.1.1–5), but classifies Hegio's thought
here as part of the play's reinforcement of the idea of natural slavery, in the person of the "seasoned
slave," the *lorarius*, whom Hegio does not credit with the desire to be free. *D.* 41.1 in fact includes
the spoils of war among things capable of being owned instantly (41.1.5.7), and free men who escape
the enemy as capable of regaining their freedom (41.1.7.pr.). See Leigh 2004: 57–97 on *Captivi*
and *postliminium* (the process whereby captured free men regained their freedom, and its history
in the 200s BCE), and chapter 8 below on Gripus in *Rudens*. On the *lorarii* in *Captivi*, see Moore
1998: 192–3.

are," "I take that" (*equi te / esse feri similem dico, accipio, S.*1.5.56–8; see
chapter 3).[31] His *quod dem* at 121 is usually taken to refer to his *peculium*,
although, as seen in a threat Toxilus makes to his slave Paegnium (*Per.* 192),
sex is currency between owner and slave. And, in return, for Hegio, *quod
dem* is a beating. He doubts the reality of the *lorarius'* desire for freedom,
but *quod det* recurs as a description of its price in *Trinummus*, when the
old man Philto explains what the slave Stasimus has been muttering to
him about (563–4): *quid censes? homost: / volt fieri liber, verum quod det non
habet* ("What do you think? He's a person: / he wants to be made free, but
he doesn't have what he needs to give," *Trin.* 564–5, and cf. below on *Poen.*
833, 843). A *homo* here is a "person" in the legal sense – a body acknowledged as a legal subject; as will be seen in chapter 4, this word is often used
in association with the rights of *libertas*. Philto here in fact is lying about
what Stasimus has been saying to him, but that does not undercut the logic
of his lines – and indeed Stasimus has already instanced manumission as
something he desires in vain (440).

The *lorarius* later sings to the chained men some words of comfort
(195–200):

> Si di inmortales id voluerunt, vos hanc aerumnam exsequi,   195
> decet id pati animo aequo: si id facietis, levior labos erit.
>   domi fuistis, credo, liberi:
> nunc servitus si evenit, ei vos morigerari mos bonust
> et erili imperio eamque ingeniis vostris lenem reddere.
> indigna digna habenda sunt, erus quae facit.   200

> If the immortal gods wanted this, that this tribulation
>   should pursue you,   195
> make it look good, bear it with a fair spirit: if you do this,
>   the work will be lighter.
>   At home you were free, I believe it:
> now if slavery has befallen you, the right way for you is
>   to do your duty to it
> and to your owner's command, and use your wits to make
>   slavery easy on you.
> Treat the unjust things the owner does as just.   200

After the prior scene with Hegio, the audience knows the *lorarius* speaks
from his own experience. When he urges the two young men to do their
duty to slavery, he uses a verb – *morigerari* – that appears repeatedly in

---

[31] As explicitly depicted by Horace (*S.* 1.5.58), and as in Syncerastus' joke at *Poen.* 871 (chapter 8), this
poignant line is probably accompanied by body movement.

Plautus to mean both "obey" and "be sexually compliant."[32] He explicitly says that the owner's actions are unjust, but slaves must pretend they are just; compare Sosia's critique of what is fair (*aequom*) and unfair. Their spirit should be fair, the *lorarius* advises (*aequo animo*), even though the owner's is not. The captives and the *lorarius* are bound together – as are the actors, of whom the prologue speaker says, *haec res agetur nobis, vobis fabula* ("this action will be real for us, a play for you," 52 – see chapter 3).

Like the body of the slave, the body of the *parasitus* is open to punishment – indeed, rough treatment is repeatedly stated to be part of the job. Ergasilus in *Captivi* calls his kin *plagipatidas* ("blow-sufferers," 472); this is the same word Tranio uses when appealing to the audience for someone who will agree to be tortured in his place for pay (*Mos.* 354–60, esp. 356 *plagipatidae, ferritribaces viri*, "blow-sufferers, shackle-chafing men").[33] So Ballio addresses his slaves, *plagigera genera hominum*, "you blow-bearing type of person" (*Ps.* 153). Tranio sees such volunteers as like those who take a fee of three *nummi* for letting themselves be transfixed by spears (357–8): in the army? In a show of some kind? The Sycophanta in *Trinummus* hires himself out for *tribu' nummis* (844); the similarity between slaves, the free poor, and actors is fairly explicit in both cases (see Moore 1998: 11).[34] In particular, *parasiti* can expect to have a jar broken over their heads (*Capt.* 89), perhaps the equivalent of the clown's cream pie in the face, only harder, for the banker in *Curculio* speculates nastily that a jar filled with ashes might have dug out Curculio's eye, and Curculio tells the audience that such jars have often hit him (396–8). The same projectile, again ash-filled, is (verbally) brandished in a fragmentary scene in *Amphitruo*, either by Amphitruo against Mercurius/Sosia or, in keeping with the outrageousness of what remains of the scene, by Mercurius against Amphitruo (fr. iv). Sosia fears what the *iuventus* may do to him if he goes out at night (*Am.* 153–4); the *parasitus* Ergasilus depends on the *iuventus* and fears they may

---

[32] On *morigerari*, see Williams 1958: 19–22; with this, see Clark 2015 on the *morigerus* slave who paradoxically wins a measure of self-respect by agreeing to his own sexual use. Clark demonstrates that the adjective *morigerus* is more often used of male slaves and in relation to sex than it is of dutiful wives.

[33] Brown (2013) points out that *Mos.* 356 has been taken as a direct address to slaves in the audience – wrongly, as he argues: like similar jokes elsewhere in the plays, not aimed at actual audience members. Certainly Tranio's words appeal to audience members of all statuses, the reaction of each deriving from experience.

[34] On the fee, see Callataÿ 2015: 26–7, 41, arguing that this was "a very high wage" (clearly it means a lot to the Sycophanta, at least). The value of a *nummus* is controversial, as Callataÿ's bibliography shows; probably silver, see the more accessible Mattingly and Robinson 1935.

cease to feed him (*Capt.* 69–92, 104–6, 461–95; cf. Corbett 1986: 15–16, 33).
He sums up the alternatives for a man like him (*Capt.* 88–90):

> et hic quidem hercle, nisi qui colaphos perpeti
> potes parasitus frangique aulas in caput,
> vel ire extra Portam Trigeminam ad saccum licet.   90

> And here, by God, indeed, unless you can put up with punches
> as a *parasitus*, and having pots broken on your head,
> you might as well go out the Triple Gate to hold the bag.   90

This was the gate that led, perhaps, from the Forum Boarium out to the
docks and the pons Sublicius: a joke based on the audience's recognition
of the neighborhood.[35] The alternative to the comedian's life is the life of a
laborer, or a beggar.

What was in the bag? The phrase *ire ... ad saccum* (90) used to be translated "to hold the beggar's bag," and is now taken to mean "to carry a
porter's sack"; impossible to say, since the work *saccus* appears only here
in Plautus. So Bonnell Thornton translates (1769: 1.258): "We must sub-
mit to sit among the beggars / Without the city gate"; so W. M. Lindsay
glosses (1921: 76), thinking of the docks: "Then hey! for Three Arches
and the dock-porter's sack" – that is, the dock-worker as stevedore. It
all depends on what you imagine lay outside the gate; Plautus' audience
knew. Contempt is displayed for porters in the plays in the words *baiiolus,*
baiiolare, most conspicuously by the soldier in *Poenulus* when insulting
Hanno: "Who is this person with the long tunic like a tavern boy? / ... /
Isn't the girl ashamed to put her arms around a *baiiolus* in the middle of
the road?" (*quis hic homo est cum tunicis longis quasi puer cauponius? / ... /
non pudet puellam amplexari baiiolum in media via?*, 1298, 1301). The basic
meaning of *baiiolus* seems to be "man who carries sacks," "stevedore," but
in the plays, perhaps by extension or joking, the *baiiolus* is just a man who
carries a customer's baggage for him, even just his wallet; a servile occupation, as is implied by Leonida's teasing insistence that an *erus* should not
carry a wallet (*As.* 657–61, cf. *Men.* 265, *Ps.* 170); hard labor, as is implied

---

[35] For the location of the Porta Trigemina, see Coarelli 1996b (conjectural; near the Forum Boarium,
at the foot of the Aventine). On the hotly contested relation between the Porta Trigemina and the
pons Sublicius, see Tucci 2011/12 (a reference I owe to Matthew Roller). Otto (1965[1890]: 304),
who says *ad saccum* is not proverbial, takes *saccum* to mean "beggar's bag." It is hard not to think of
the famous line of Anatole France about "the law, in its majestic equality" forbidding rich as well
as poor to sleep under bridges, as cited by Justice Frankfurter and in turn by Justice Brennan. For
the association between the pons Sublicius and beggars, see Seneca, *De vit. beat.* 25.1; for bridges in
general, Mayor *ad* Juvenal 4.116, who comments, "Still at Rome beggars haunt the hills and bridges"
(1872: 236). The only bridge in Plautus, however, is the one that falls down at *Cas.* 66.

by Pasicompsa's protest in *Mercator* (508); shameful labor, perhaps also associated with low inns, as in *Poenulus*.[36]

Ergasilus lives on the edge. In the view of later Romans of the upper class, to sell your body, to live in a sold body, a body for sale, was little different from being a slave; Cicero famously remarks, "Unbefitting a free man and dirty are the ways of making a living of all wage-earners whose labor rather than skill is bought; for among those people the wage in itself is a pledge of slavery. ... And all craftsmen (*opifices*) are employed in a dirty skill; nor can a workshop, indeed, contain anything befitting a freeborn person" (*inliberales autem et sordidi quaestus mercennariorum omnium, quorum operae, non quorum artes emuntur; est enim in illis ipsa merces auctoramentum servitutis. ... Opificesque omnes in sordida arte versantur; nec enim quicquam ingenuum habere potest officina*, Cic. *Off.* 1.150). So much for the *opifex barbarus* (see chapter 1); nor are Cicero's ideas inconsistent with upper-class attitudes in the 200s BCE, at least in the Greek world, as "the list of acceptable and unacceptable professions stands in a long aristocratic tradition" (Dyck 1996: 331).[37] Sosia, we recall, complains that the "rich householder" (*dominus dives*) does not know the meaning of labor. Rather than taking the contempt for the *baiiolus* in the *palliata* to prove

[36] For *baiiolus* (also *baiulus*) as porter, see Ernout-Meillet s.v. *baiulus*. Cf. also *Poen.* 1354 for the overtones of paying through the body; *Mer.* 508 is discussed in chapter 5. At Gell. 5.3.2, *baiulus* is a translated label for Protagoras when he was a hired laborer carrying a load of firewood on his back: another rags-to-riches biography (see chapter 1). Paul. 32L has *Baiulos dicebant antiqui, quos nunc dicimus operarios*; *operae* means "work for hire," although onstage (Plautus, *Vid.* 21, 24, in a back-and-forth about rural labor), and very commonly in Cato's *De agricultura*, the word *operarius* is associated with agricultural labor, without the generic contempt it acquired later. What Lindsay meant by "porter": "Coal was still carried on men's backs up the long ladders from ships' holds: in Birmingham men could still, in the 1830s, be hired at 1*s.* a day to wheel sand in barrows nine miles by road, and nine miles empty back" (Thompson 1966: 313). For slave baggage-carriers, see *Men.* 435–6, 445, 986; *Mer.* 672 (also in chapter 5); *Poen.* 978–81 (the butt of shtick); more examples in Prescott 1936: 114–17, who adduces Aristophanes *Frogs* (1–11, a metajoke about slave porters; see chapter 1). See Ketterer 1986b: 105 for the provocative suggestion that stage baggage was exaggeratedly complicated and burdensome – a sight gag which would turn these usually mute characters into Buster Keaton. On unskilled labor in Rome, see Brunt 1980 in relation to the building trade, updated in Padilla Peralta 2014; and esp. Brunt 1966: 14–16 on dockworkers, porters, and artisans' organizations.

[37] See in particular the story about Gnathainion and the bronze-smith in Machon's *Chreiai* (fr. XVII, ll. 349–75 Gow), discussed in Kurke 2002: 48–51, where she adduces Aristotle, *Pol.* 1337b8–15, a dismissal of *technas ... banausous* and wage labor as abject. Dyck reviews Cicero's ideas in the context of Panaetius, the main basis of *De officiis*, as well as of Aristotle; note esp. his remarks on Cicero's equation of wage labor with slave labor, and his observation that in Roman custom *mercennarii* and *opifices* were excluded from the Senate, with comments on alienated labor (Dyck 1996: 331–6). See further Dressler 2016: 34 n. 3 on art and materiality; Joshel 1992: 63–9, with bibliography; Rose 2012: 8; Ste. Croix 1981: 122, 197–8 on Cicero, and 197–203 on wage labor in general, with 579 n. 39 on *operae*. Feuvrier-Prévotat 2005 offers a brief overview of words for "work" onstage, and very brief overviews of workers, with bibliography.

its upper-class orientation, then, we should see here an internalization that complicates both the pride of the *artifex* in his work and the fears of slaves. G. E. M. de Ste. Croix argues that the ideology of the ruling class trickles down: "there is every reason to think that even humble folk (who of course were far from despising all work, like the propertied class) really did regard hired labour as a less dignified and worthy form of activity than one in which one could remain one's own master, a truly free man" (1981: 199). Those "hired from the forum," like cooks and the Sycophanta, are commodified even when free, and some cooks identify themselves as slaves (*Aul.* 309–10, *Men.* 300); as Ste. Croix pointed out, the area of Roman law known as *locatio conductio* (contracting and hiring) maps relative respect and power, and the range of *locare* and *conducere* in the Plautine corpus bears this out. Slave cooks are hired from an (unmentioned) owner for a fee, just as slave prostitutes' fees go to their pimp; indeed, the cooks in *Aulularia* are hired along with two music girls and arrive along with the groceries, like other outside cooks. The stock characters include no smiths, no butchers, no millers, although *faber, lanius, pistor* populate the plays' language; comedians are the sole spokesmen for free labor, and they do not work for wages.[38] Even the chorus of starving fishermen in *Rudens* express pity for men who have no skill (290–305, below) – complicated, because their fellow fisherman Gripus is a slave. The worth of the Tiber fishermen's skill was recognized every June at the *piscatorii ludi*; they must have loved this scene, indeed the whole play.[39]

Beggars, who have neither skill nor work, occupy an even more abject place than the *baiiolus* in the onstage world. In a run of jokes focused on the audience's status and census class, the *Captivi* prologue speaker complains about being forced to beg (13, *histrionem cogis mendicarier*): the joke is in the clown's pride. As will be seen in chapter 8, *pauper, mendicus, rex, parasitus* appear side by side in a list of stock characters in the *Menaechmi* prologue (76) – alas, no beggars onstage in the extant *palliata*. The beggar is the polar opposite of the rich man, the king; the word itself resonates with its cognates: *menda*, "stain"; *mendax*, "liar," which, along with *mendacium*, is a favorite word in the Plautine lexicon, even spawning *mendaciloquos* (in

---

[38] On the civil status of cooks in Greek comedy, see Wilkins 2000: 408–9 (slave cooks a Macedonian development, according to Athenaeus); "an agent for hire" (370). Greek cooks boast of their labor and skill and so does the cook in *Pseudolus* (790–891), but the *palliata* is more interested in cooks as thieves – a trait closely associated with slaves in general.

[39] These games are attested at Festus 232L and 274L, with tantalizing details; part of the rich discussion in Brunt 1966 (at 15). Bispham 2000: 163–4 discusses these games as possibly attracting fishermen from Ostia.

connection with "those whom tax-paying city citizens call *scurrae*," *urbani adsidui cives quos scurras vocant, Trin.* 200, 202–3; and with the poverty-stricken Sycophanta, available for hire in the Forum, *Trin.* 765, 769, 815). Like the *baiiolus*, the beggar stands for what no one wants to be. For a young man whose father has money, "begging" means losing it (*Bac.* 508, 514); for a father with a lost son, a fate worse than death: "I'd rather my kin should die than go out begging; / good people pity the dead, bad people laugh at a beggar" (*malim moriri meos quam mendicarier / boni miserantur illum, hunc irrident mali, Vid.* fr. vii (xvi)). A selfish young man in love would (hyperbolically) rather let his father be sold than allow his beloved "to be in need or beg" (*venibit, Mos.* 229; *egere aut mendicare*, 230). A (fictional) stingy man would rather his son were a slave with a full belly (abroad, at someone else's expense) than a beggar, at home, to shame the family (*ubi minime honestum est, Capt.* 321–3). Wealth-conscious characters contrast the *mendicus* with *rex, opulentissumus, divites* (*St.* 132, 133; *Trin.* 493, 829–31), equate him with "plunderers" (*latrones, St.* 135), and suggest that giving money to beggars does them no favors (*Trin.* 339–40).[40]

The word "beggar" can be a punchline all by itself, as in a spelling joke in a run of shtick between Gripus and the shipwrecked pimp Labrax (*Rud.* 1304–6):

> GR. medicus, quaeso, es?
> LA. immo edepol una littera plus sum quam medicus. GR. tum tu
> mendicus es? LA. tetigisti acu. GR. videtur digna forma.

> GR. What, you're a doctor?
> LA. No, by god, I'm one letter more than a doctor. GR. Then you're
> a beggar? LA. You put your needle on it. GR. You look like one.

An insult; perhaps an emaciation joke, a sight gag. The slave cook Congrio calls Euclio *mendice homo* during their fight (*Aul.* 423), asking him the classic question "How dare you lay a finger on me?" (*quid tibi nos tactiost*). Euclio is not his owner, not even his renter; you should not hit what you do not own, and the property knows the difference.[41]

As in Freud's theory of humor, where fear is a source of laughter, the frisson is in the narrow escape, the hair's breadth that separates the character from begging in the street. The *parasitus* Saturio makes a sardonic joke about his daughter's dowry of jokebooks fitting her to marry a *mendicus*

---

[40] On Plautus' critique of the morality of selfishness, see Pansiéri 1997: 286, 517–21.
[41] Cf. similar questions at *Aul.* 744; *Cas.* 406, 408; *Cur.* 626; *Men.* 1016; *Poen.* 1308: all protest a breach of status or property boundaries.

(*Per.* 396), and he also likens himself to the needy Cynic philosopher, with his *marsuppium*, in a list of props (123–6) evidently shared with the *parasitus*, himself obviously like a beggar. The *marsuppium* is for "a little assistance / to comfort his home life" (*paullum praesidi / qui familiarem suam vitam oblectet*). The *parasitus* Gelasimus, auctioning off his worldly goods, includes in his inventory "a rusty strigil, a wrinkly reddish pouch, / an empty *parasitus* in which you can store the leftovers" (*robiginosam strigilim, ampullam rubidam, / parasitum inanem quo recondas reliquias*, *St.* 230–1). What was in the bag? The props belong to the Greek *parasitos*, with his strigil and oil flask, but Plautus' *parasiti* carry a doggy bag. Ergasilus, too, both sees the likeness (*ad saccum*) and rejects it. In any case, neither portering nor begging is *liberalis*, in Cicero's terms, and the *parasiti*, like the *Captivi* prologue speaker, are jealous of their class standing. They have a skill.

So, likewise, although they see the resemblance between their lives and a slave's, *parasiti* do not welcome it, and Curculio is insulted when the soldier, taking him for a slave, denies his ability to serve as a witness (623); *em ut scias me liberum esse!* retorts Curculio, initiating a brief slugfest ("Take that, so you'll know I'm free!" 624–7). Like the freed Advocati in *Poenulus*, he is touchy about the recognition of his status. The *parasiti* bear one general resemblance to the audience members watching them in that, instead of reclining on *lecti* at what dinners they can get, they are men of the *subsellia* – "men of the one-man bench" (*unisubselli viros*, *Capt.* 471; *unisubselli virum*, *St.* 489); compare the *Poenulus* prologue speaker's injunction to the audience that they "keep calm and sit on the benches" (*bono ... ut animo sedeant in subselliis*, 5; cf. *Am.* 65). In this, they resemble also the slaves at the end of *Stichus*; as Stichus comments, "Like Cynics, we are received on the bench rather than on *lecti*" (*potius in subsellio / cynice accipimur quam †in lecticis†*, 703–4). Here, like Saturio, Stichus compares his way of life with the bare-bones existence of a Cynic philosopher.[42]

There was, then, a community marked by scars; unwilling, but recognized from the stage. It included even soldiers. The banker insults Curculio as one-eyed (392) because the *parasitus* has disguised himself as a war veteran, evidently wearing an eyepatch.[43] He represents a surprisingly common stock character onstage – the soldier's slave (here, a freedman) – and it

---

[42] For the stock props of the *parasitus*, see Csapo and Slater 1994: 71–2, with plate 10A. On *parasiti* and Cynics, see Richlin 2014b: 207, Tylawsky 2002: 54–7. Tylawsky traces *parasiti* back to Iros the beggar in the *Odyssey*.

[43] Eyepatch: so Marshall 2006: 153; rather than a change of mask.

is similarly surprising to find Polybius making casual mention of slaves in the army on a routine basis (6.33.1), presumably as servants or teamsters or laborers (as opposed to the much-discussed emergencies when slaves were drafted into the army or fleet). In addition, Polybius makes it clear that a soldier's place in the census classes determined how much body armor he would have: the poorer (and younger) the soldier, the less armor. The lowest census class, in the army, served as *velites* – light-armed troops – while those below this class, the *proletarii*, served in the navy as rowers. Of navy discipline Polybius makes no mention. But he goes into detail on army discipline, which was directed ordinarily at failure to keep watch, theft, self-prostitution ("if any one of those in the bloom of youth were found misusing his body"), and cowardice, all punishable by the *fustuarium* – beating with clubs and stones. All veterans in the audience would have been familiar with this calculus. The army was one place where the dividing lines of honor broke down, for there the free could be beaten as well as slaves, and not all their scars came from battle. The joke seen above on the *tribunus vapularis* plays with this familiarity, and the army language in the *palliata* appeals to the experience of the lower ranks.[44]

The fear of a beating and the fear of sexual abuse are closely connected in Roman comedy, both being painful breaches of the body's boundaries. That actors might be beaten is most clearly stated – in a joke, of course – at the end of *Cistellaria*, where the whole troupe tells the audience not to wait around for the characters/actors to come off the stage: *ubi id erit factum, ornamenta ponent; postidea loci / qui deliquit vapulabit, qui non deliquit bibet* ("When their business is done [backstage], they'll take off their costumes; after that / the one who's messed up will get a beating, the one who hasn't messed up will have a drink," 784–5). Compare the joke at the start of *Amphitruo* discussed above, and Mercurius' further recommendation to the audience, in the prologue, that an actor who plants his own fans in the audience "should have his costume (*ornamenta*) cut to pieces – and his

---

[44] Polybius says it is the tribunes who administer "to all in the camp, slave and free alike," the oath not to steal (6.33.1); the details on the *fustuarium* are given at 6.37.8–10; beyond this lay the terror of decimation (6.38). Some evidently survived a beating (6.37.4). On the oath, see Welwei 1988: 57, and 56–80 on noncombatant slaves in the Republican army. On the sexual behavior treated as criminal, I accept here Walbank's interpretation (1957: 720). On servile punishments for soldiers, see Walters 1997. On the emergency drafting of slaves into the Roman army, see Leigh 2004: 216–28, Stewart 2012: 125–9, and Welwei 1988: 5–18; postwar manumission was sometimes offered as an incentive, and a similar offer after Arginusae (on which see Welwei 1974: 65–104) touched off a joke in Old Comedy (*Frogs* 33–4), but there are no such jokes in the *palliata*. See chapter 1 on Spendios. For the adoption of light-armed soldiers into the comic army, and a joke at the expense of the well-armed, see the probably Plautine *Frivolaria*, fr. 79, 80, 81 (*legiones Lavernae; rorarii … accensi; triarii*), and others listed in Richlin 2017a: 231–2, with discussion of resistance to militarism onstage and off.

hide as well" (*Am.* 85; see chapter 3). More metatheatrically, the audience at the end of *Asinaria* is urged to clap loudly *si voltis deprecari huic seni ne vapulet* ("if you want to beg this old man off from a beating," 946). The prologue speaker in *Casina* similarly conflates character and actor (82–6) when he says that the title character – who never in fact appears in the play, but is impersonated onstage by an actor playing a male slave in drag –

> ... neque quicquam stupri
> faciet profecto in hac quidem comoedia.
> mox hercle vero, post transactam fabulam,
> argentum si quis dederit, ut ego suspicor,
> ultro ibit nuptum, non manebit auspices.   85

> ... will not perform any illicit sex act,
> I'm sure, in this comedy, at least.
> But, God, soon, in fact, after the show is over,
> If anybody gives her cash, as I suspect,
> she'll volunteer to get married, and won't wait for a ceremony.   85

A hint that the actor's body is available to the public for sex, at a price, as well as vulnerable to a beating.[45] Onstage, threats to beat could easily be played as threats to rape, as in the dance/fight between the pimp and the *puer* Paegnium at the end of *Persa*, where Paegnium taunts the pimp, "Take this thick rope and hang yourself," and the pimp replies, "Don't you touch me, or I'll give you a big beating with this stick" (PA: *restim tu tibi cape crassam ac suspende te.* / DO: *cave sis me attigas, ne tibi hoc scipione / malum magnum dem*, 815–17). Such threats would be facilitated if, as some think, actors in the *palliata* wore a phallus.[46] The cook Congrio, beaten by Euclio, says, *fustibus sum mollior magi' quam ullu' cinaedus*, "Due to your cudgels, I'm much limper than any fag" (*Aul.* 422; same joke at *Mil.* 1424). The relation between slavery and sexual use in Rome in this period can be judged mainly from the *palliata*, but the plays assume the audience knows that the bottom position in the social hierarchy entails the bottom position in the sexual system. When the Virgo is sold onstage, when Chalinus emerges in his rumpled bridal gown, the audience sees a takeoff on the everyday slave market. The actor's charisma on the Plautine stage lies partly in his blatant sexual ambivalence.

---

[45] For discussion of this passage, with bibliography, see Richlin 2015b: 50, 63 n. 12; the argument goes back at least to Forehand 1973.
[46] So Marshall 2006: 62–4, with other examples.

Sex

Cicero, as seen above, held that bodies for sale were thereby servile; he singles out for special opprobrium all skills "that are the servants of the pleasures" (*quae ministrae sunt voluptatum*). In the *palliata*, the adjective *venalis*, "for sale," is used as a substantive to mean "slave," and is also associated with the flesh trade. Both slaves and prostitutes say what that feels like, expecting the audience to get it, and indeed many of the prostitutes in the plays *are* slaves or freed slaves; the *lena* in *Cistellaria* draws a direct connection for young Selenium: "Because we are freedwomen, both I and your mother, we both / were prostitutes" (*quia nos libertinae sumus, et ego et tua mater, ambae / meretrices fuimus, Cist.* 38–9). Prostitution is rarely glamorized in the *palliata*, so that the term "courtesan," commonly in use among scholars, seems inappropriate for these women, as well as anachronistic (see chapter 1). The women and boys who appear, or are mentioned, as prostitutes and sex slaves belong to a system in which a character like Telestis in *Epidicus* could be captured by the army and bought from the spoils (*praeda*) by a young soldier for his sexual use (*Epid.* 43–4, 91, 108); or in which characters like Planesium in *Curculio*, the Virgo as "Lucris" in *Persa*, Adelphasium and Anterastilis in *Poenulus*, and Palaestra in *Rudens* could be captured or kidnapped and sold to a pimp. Others, like Philaenium in *Asinaria*, Gymnasium in *Cistellaria*, and Pasicompsa in *Mercator*, along with the shipload of unnamed female musicians in *Stichus*, are passed from man to man.[47] Moreover, household slaves both male and female, in the plays, could be as open to sexual use as prostitutes; the old man in Caecilius Statius' *Plocium* complains that his wife has sold a pretty slave-woman out of jealousy (Gellius 2.23.10), and the premise of *Casina* is that a male slave-owner could have free access to the "wife" of a male slave he owned.[48] In the extant plays, however, it is the male slave characters who talk about their sexual use by owners, and in *Casina* they are the ones used. An actor playing a slave-boy or a prostitute, then, was doubly degraded, first by playing roles for pay (if he was free), then by playing *these* roles. His

---

[47] On trafficking Pasicompsa, see James 2010; more generally on sex trafficking in New Comedy, Marshall 2013, 2015, and chapter 7 below. On Roman soldiers' ownership of slave-women under the empire, see Phang 2001. A similar system underlies Greek comedies like Menander's *Sikyonios*, in which a four-year-old Athenian girl is captured by pirates and taken to Karia, where she is sold in the marketplace to a mercenary soldier from Sikyon.

[48] See Marshall 2015 for discussion of the blurred line between *ancillae* and prostitutes in a slave system in which all slaves were sexually open.

civil status was ambiguous behind the mask, his sexual status was thereby doubly dubious.

That male slaves had to provide sexual services to their owners is the basis of numerous jokes in Plautus, especially but not exclusively for slaves addressed or spoken of as *pueri*. Anticipating sex with Casina, Lysidamus uses his *vilicus* Olympio for a warmup onstage (*Cas.* 451–66), as the slave Chalinus calls the play-by-play for the audience: "By God, I believe he wants to dig out the *vilicus*'s lady-parts"[49] (*credo hercle ecfodere hic volt vesicam vilico*, 455); "By God, I think they're going to tangle their feet together today; / sure, this old man likes to chase after guys with beards" (*hodie hercle, opinor, hi conturbabunt pedes: / solet hic barbatos sane sectari senex*, 465–6). He remarks on the reward system whereby sexual compliance with the owner means promotion, based on his own experience (460–2):

> illuc est, illuc, quod hic hunc fecit vilicum!   460
> et idem me pridem, quom ei advorsum veneram,
> facere atriensem voluerat sub ianua.

> That's the reason, that's the reason, why he made this guy a *vilicus*!   460
> A while ago, when I went to welcome him home, he wanted
> to make me the overseer (*atriensem*) under the doorway.

That these lines include a double entendre is suggested by the line that precedes them: "Back off, lover; get yourself off my behind" (*ultro te, amator, apage te a dorso meo*, 459), says Olympio, as the owner goes too far. *Atriensis* literally means "entryway-man." After Chalinus' aside, Olympio picks up, cravenly, "How I did my duty to you today, what a pleasure I was to you" (*ut tibi morigerus hodie, ut voluptati fui*, 463). The *senex* Simo, in a fragmentary exchange, seems to be horsing around similarly with the less cooperative Tranio (*Mos.* 719–27, esp. 724–5, *morem geras. / vita quam sit brevis simul cogita*, "you should do your duty, / and think about how short life is, while you're doing it"; cf. also *quod solet fieri hic / intu'. ... scis iam quid loquar*, "what usually happens inside here / ... you know what I'm talking about," 722–3, with formulae below). It is not surprising that slave-owners onstage cast this vulnerability up to slaves: so the slave Toxilus to his slave Paegnium, "I'm going to give you a little advance on your allowance," *aliqui te peculiabo, Per.* 192; the pimp Ballio to his *puer*, "Watch

---

[49] Or "dig this *vilicus* some lady-parts." For the use of *vesica*, "bladder," to mean "vagina" in Latin, see Adams 1982: 91–2, and 116 on the insulting use of *cunnus = culus*. Perhaps here, as at Juvenal 2.10, a word that means by metonymy "female receptacle" is substituted for the anus in an invective context.

out nobody takes a poke at your purse," *ne quisquam pertundat cruminam cautiost, Ps.* 170.

But it is fascinating to see slaves taunting each other with their use for sex. So, most tellingly, Sagaristio and Paegnium (*Per.* 284–6):

> SAG. video ego te: iam incubitatus es. PA. ita sum. quid id attinet ad te?
> at non sum, ita ut tu, gratiis. SAG. confidens. PA. sum hercle vero.   285
> nam ego confido liberum fore, tu te numquam speras.

> SAG: I see you: you just got laid – on. PA. So I did. What's it to you?
> At least I don't do it for free, like you. SAG: You're sure of yourself. PA.
>   By God, I am,   285
> because I'm sure I'll be free, but you've got no hope.

Here Paegnium, who has just come out of the pimp's house, parries Sagaristio's insult by owning it, saying he prostitutes himself as a way to earn the money with which to buy his freedom; earlier, Sophoclidisca, slave of a slave prostitute, trying to seduce him in a long flirtation scene, says "you need to wake up this little teen body, so you don't always slave away the nasty way" (*hanc vigilare oportet formulam atque aetatulam,* / *ne … foede semper servias,* 229–30). The scene between Sagaristio and Paegnium immediately follows Sagaristio's boasting song in defiance of his owner, discussed above; the two modes of getting by are strongly contrasted, so that Paegnium's oblique suggestion that Sagaristio is used by his owner (285) is extra-insulting. Meanwhile, when the already-specularized Paegnium teases Sagaristio, there is an element of sexual teasing: "If you want someone to obey you, you have to pay for him" (*emere oportet, quem tibi oboedire velis,* 273). As will be seen below and in chapter 3, money is very much at issue here, as are the *fides* on which the ability to get money is based and the confidence that exceeds a slave's expectations, making *confidenter* a reproach: "Some nerve!" (see chapter 6).

- The accusation of having sex with the owner is also made against Chalinus by Olympio – some nerve (*Cas.* 362):

  > CH. comprime istunc. OL. immo istunc qui didicit dare.
  > CH. Stuff that guy! OL. No, that guy, who's learned to give it up.

- Again, jokingly, against Epidicus by the slave Thesprio: "He loves her more than he ever loved you" (*plusque amat quam te umquam amavit, Epid.* 66), to which Epidicus reacts indignantly, as if to an insult.
- Again, with a nasty double meaning, against Tranio by Grumio: "not everybody can lie next to his betters" (*non omnes possunt … / … superiores*

accumbere, *Mos.* 42–3; for the usage and the implication, compare *Bac.*
1188, *scortum accumbas*, with 1192–92a; *St.* 750–3).

- Again, clearly, against the boy Phaniscus by the boy Pinacium (*Mos.*
885–98), especially 894–5:

  PHA. novit erus me. PI. suam quidem culcitulam oportet.
  PHA. The owner knows me. PI. Sure, he ought to know his own mattress.

- Again, against the soldier's slave Harpax by the pimp Ballio and the *senex*
Simo (*Ps.* 1180–1):

  [BA.] noctu in vigiliam quando ibat miles, quom tu ibas simul,
  conveniebatne in vaginam tuam machaera militis?

  [BA.] At night when the soldier went on watch, when you went along,
  did the soldier's sword fit into your sheath?

- They think he is an impostor, however, and also accuse him more generally of using his body to get what he wants, 1187–8:

  ... [HA.] mea quidem haec habeo omnia
  meo peculio empta. BA. nemp' quod femina summa sustinent.[50]

  ... [HA.] All these things I have are definitely mine,
  bought with my own *peculium*. BA. Yeah, the one the top of your thighs
  holds up.

  As in Toxilus' jibe to Paegnium (above), the slave's savings account is
  here equated with his body as sexual capital.
- Again, against Trachalio by Gripus (*Rud.* 1073–75):

  ... TR. comprime hunc sis, si tuost.
  GR. quid? tu idem mihi vis fieri quod erus consuevit tibi?
  si ille te comprimere solitust, hic noster nos non solet.

  ... TR. Please stuff this guy, if he's yours.
  GR. What? You want the same thing to be done to me that your owner's
  used to doing to you?
  Even if *he's* used to stuffing *you*, this owner of *ours* doesn't do it to *us*.

---

[50] For an overview of literary texts that bring up the sexual use of male slaves by soldiers, and a consideration of possible documentary evidence, see Phang 2001: 266–77. On this point, she deals
with materials going back to Plautus, including this passage in *Pseudolus*. The comic slave who
accompanies his soldier owner goes back at least to Daos in Menander's *Aspis* (see James 2014); on
soldiers' slaves in Plautus, see Richlin 2017a: 229–30. Evidence that individual soldiers in the settled,
professional army of the Principate owned slaves, both male and female, is extremely common, as
Phang shows; on slaves in the Republican army, see above.

This back-and-forth closely resembles the one between Olympio and Chalinus above. Puns on *comprimo* ("repress"/"rape," here translated "stuff"), and formulae using *soleo* and *consuesco* to mean "you're used to it," and *dare* to mean "put out," "allow oneself to be used sexually" – all also appear in insults to owners (chapter 4). They are uniquely applied to two women by the slave Truculentus, turning what he takes to be Astaphium's insulting suggestion that he should rape her *era* into an accusation that Astaphium regularly does just that (*eam ... tu, quae solita's, comprime, Truc.* 262). The accusation of being used for sex in this instance flips: the female owner here uses the female slave as a dildo rather than as a receptacle.[51]

Slaves' openness to sexual use structures the world within the plays in a way that meshes with the *cavea* and the city. One of the cooks rented from the forum by Strobilus' owner in *Aulularia* takes Strobilus' plan to "divide" the groceries as a threat to his sexual integrity, as seen in the pickup lines of his fellow cook (285–6):

> bellum et pudicum vero prostibulum popli.
> post si quis vellet, te hau non velles dividi.
>
> What a pretty and moral public whore, I'm sure.
> If anybody wanted to later, you wouldn't mind getting "divided."

Compare the wording in the *Casina* prologue (84–6): *mox hercle vero, post transactam fabulam, / argentum si quis dederit, ... / ultro ibit nuptum* (above). Strobilus tells the first cook he did not mean "that" (*istuc*, 288), a common lead out of a double entendre, squeezing it for a second laugh, and drawing the audience into complicity by verifying the obscene meaning. Similarly, in *Cistellaria*, as the slave Lampadio enters and discovers the *cistella* lying onstage, he ends his brief monologue with a gratuitous laugh line about the sexual use of boy slaves: "I have to do what boys have to do: I'll bend over for the box" (*faciundumst puerile officium: conquiniscam ad cistulam, Cist.* 657).[52] Everybody knows what boys have to do. This is one thing that separates the slave Tyndarus ("brought up well and

---

[51] On this passage, see Dutsch 2015, Richlin 2015, and chapter 5 below on how this scene plays out in drag. On slaves as dildos, see duBois 2003: 82–100.

[52] On the "bend over" joke in *Cistellaria*, see discussion in Richlin 2015: 57, 64 n. 21. Pomponius *Prostibulum* fr. vi, *ut nullum civem pedicavi per dolum / nisi ipsus orans ultro qui occuinisceret* ("just as I buggered no citizen under false pretenses / unless the kind who himself was begging for it of his own free will as he bent over," Frassinetti 154–5) is surely related in both content and vocabulary, and suggests that *Ps.* 864, *si conquiniscet istic, conquiniscito*, was a laugh line. Fraenkel, following F. Skutsch, took the *Cistellaria* line to be a reference to children's games (2007: 298 n. 38, cf. Fraenkel 1964[1920]), but this seems strained, in light of the commonness of abuse jokes in Plautus. See chapter 4 on a similar joke in *Asinaria*.

chastely," *Capt.* 992) from the slave Stalagmus; the contempt for Stalagmus enacted onstage at the end of the *Captivi* is associated with his status as Hegio's former sex slave (954, 956, and esp. 966, *bene morigerus fuit puer, nunc non decet,* "He was very dutiful as a boy, now it's not fitting"). As seen above, it seems unlikely that "Paegnium" was Tyndarus' birth name. Thus it is a bitter joke when *parasiti* own up to nicknames that liken them to those used for sex: Ergasilus' opening monologue begins (*Capt.* 69), *Iuventus nomen indidit "Scorto" mihi,* "The young guys call me 'Whore'." He follows this with a lame explanation, then a startling description of those who feed *parasiti* as "those whom [*parasiti*] lick" (*quos ligurriant,* 84). Peniculus' opening monologue begins with the same joke formula (*Men.* 77), *Iuventus nomen fecit "Peniculo" mihi* – with the explanation that, when he eats, he cleans the table (his name could mean "Little Brush"). It more obviously means "Little Tail"; looking at the explanation for the name "Scortum" in *Captivi*, it seems clear that the obscene sense of "Peniculus" is felt.[53]

Sitting in the audience were many people who knew what the actors were talking about. Just as the familiarity of beatings implies the presence onstage and in the audience of scars, so the familiarity of sexual abuse implies the presence onstage and in the audience of the traces of sexual abuse. Addressing a mixed audience of slaves, freed slaves, and slave-owners – all overlapping categories – the plays joke, as with beatings, about a familiar fear, with a strong undercurrent of condemnation of slave-owners who so use their slaves: in *Casina*, the owner Lysidamus is ridiculed, as is his stooge Olympio, while Chalinus serves as their chief vilifier and the direct agent of their eventual humiliation – although he must dress up as their bride to do so. The news of the former use of Stalagmus adds a sour taste to the final scene of *Captivi*; after all, Hegio is no saint in this play, and is criticized from the outset for slave-trading (98–101, *quaestum … inhonestum*). Stalagmus' revenge might have rung a bell, here and there, in the audience; certainly his parting shot, as Hegio calls for a smith "so I can give this guy those fetters" (*istas compedis / … huic dem*), recalls the speeches of the *lorarius* early in the play: "A guy with no *peculium*, you're doing right

---

[53] On the name, see Gratwick 1993 *ad* 77–8 (it means "Tail" or "Appendage," following Festus 260L); Damon 1997: 57 (it means "sponge," evidently following, among other sources, Paulus 231L; but this specifies that the sponges are long, and so called because they look like tails). The main point of all the kinds of *peniculi* in Festus is that they are long, tail-shaped things, as Festus says, "possibly so called *a pendendo.*" De Melo, following Gratwick, analyzes the explanation as a *para prosdokian* exploiting the anticipated obscene sense of the name (2011b: 435 n. 4). See above on *parasitos* names in Greek comedy.

by" (*quoi peculi nihil est, recte feceris,* 1027–8). Indeed Stalagmus' days of increasing his *peculium* by selling his body are long gone, as Hegio makes clear. Gripus' jibe at Trachalio turns the standard insult into a contrast between a good owner and a bad owner – as well as a disclaimer for himself, for, in general, onstage, imputations of having been used are indignantly denied. The self-hatred and defensiveness suggested in the exchange between Sagaristio and Paegnium address audience members who can see both points of view; those who have put this threat behind them still feel the effects, and know how vulnerable they still are, as they watch the Virgo and her father, Ergasilus and Peniculus. Yet not all audience members were equally addressed; women in the audience knew they were watching men play women, and rarely saw these men play household slave-women subject to their owner's use. Instead, when the plays dealt with the issue of use by owners, the focus stayed mainly on men dressed as female prostitutes and on men dressed as male house slaves.

Plutarch in the *Life of Cato* says Cato made his male slaves pay to have sex with his female slaves (21.2). Even if this story does not date back to Cato's lifetime, access to sex with women might have been limited for the male slaves present at the *palliata* – actors, audience, theater staff – and freed slaves would have known about that. Certainly the situation in the *palliata* attests to a chronic hunger for women among male slaves – a running joke. Indeed, most of the male characters onstage lust after the female characters played as beautiful, but it is notable that few household slave-women are played as beautiful, and almost no male slaves gain access to beautiful women, Toxilus in *Persa* being the outstanding exception (he pays his beloved's pimp to set her free). Trachalio in *Rudens*, once freed, will get to marry the sexy second female lead, once she is freed: another ex-prostitute. As Amphitruo and Sosia arrive home and Amphitruo anticipates a warm welcome from his wife, Sosia echoes him: "Don't you think my arrival is awaited by my girlfriend?" (*me non rere expectatum amicae venturum meae? Am.* 659). But Sosia has no visible girlfriend. Stichus and Sangarinus in *Stichus* will have to pay for sex with their fellow household slave Stephanium, who (like Paegnium) makes money by selling her body. Again, the premise of *Casina* depends on the ability of owners to control sexual access to female slaves, and the anxiety-ridden desire of male slaves forms the basis of the play's humor: Olympio threatens to torment Chalinus by making him listen as he and Casina have sex (*Cas.* 132–40), and Chalinus himself comments ironically on his sexual frustration as the play ends: "I married two men, but neither one did what's usually done to a new bride" (*duobus nupsi, neuter fecit quod novae nuptae solet,* 1011). This frustration drives the fantasies about slave sex and marriage in the *Casina* prologue (68–78) and in *Stichus* (446–8), and the situations in which slaves claim to party with their young owners (below, chapter 4); it also must play a part in the constant expressions of desire for prostitutes and resentment of their high prices, and of the hatred expressed for pimps. The pimp Ballio is Pseudolus' longstanding enemy (*Ps.* 233–4).

We must ask what it would have meant to the audience as a whole to watch comedies in which the female parts were played by masked men. And what did it mean to these male actors to dress up as desirable women and flirt with male characters onstage and with men in the audience? What did it mean to that audience to be flirted with? To see two masked faces pressed together in a stage kiss? The meaning of the *palliata* as a form of drag will be explored in chapter 5. Meanwhile, we can say that the sex in Plautus, at least superficially, is androcentric and heterocentric, directed at males for whom sex with women is a chief goal. The plays, although loaded with double entendres, are not often sexually explicit, but when they are they talk about sex with women from a male point of view: the *paedagogus* Lydus gives the young man's father a graphic account of his charge fondling Bacchis (*Bac.* 478–83); Calidorus quotes from Phoenicium's letter to him (*Ps.* 64–8); Pseudolus talks about what goes on at parties (*Ps.* 1259–61). In all these speeches, and in scattered lines throughout the plays, the focus is on kissing, tongue-kissing, breasts, and sexual clinches – as Pseudolus puts it, "If they feel like it, they go body to body" (*si lubet corpora conduplicant*, 1261). Women, as usual, do not talk about what it is that they desire in men, even the besotted Selenium in *Cistellaria*, even the clinging Alcumena (Jupiter: *qur me tenes?*, *Am.* 532), eager as she is to keep Jupiter in her bed (502, 512–14, 530, 531–2, 544). Prostitute characters do not talk in person about their own desire, although Phoenicium's letter provides a case of double ventriloquism.

Nor does anyone speak at length about the desire for *pueri*, much less the desires of *pueri* themselves. The monologue of the *puer* in *Pseudolus* – a very rare voicing of the experience of pederastic sex from the point of view of the *puer* – says that it hurts (*Ps.* 786–7; see chapter 4). Famously, the one playwright to put boys at the center of his plays as love objects, Afranius, was censured for it by Quintilian (10.1.100), and there are no examples among the extant plays of the *palliata*. Libanus, in a joking reply to his owner, rejects his sidekick Leonida as a possible sex partner: "I've got no use for his embrace, and he shuns mine" (*ego complexum huius nil moror, meum autem hic aspernatur*, *As.* 643). Yet boys are all over Plautus' plays, often flirting, and male actors played both the boys and the beautiful women; arguably, both are equally specularized, and there are no women onstage (chapter 5).

The question of whose desire motivates the *palliata* casts in a new light the often-quoted lines from *Curculio* in which the slave Palinurus lectures his owner Phaedromus on how not to get castrated for having illicit sex (29–32). Palinurus approves of buying from the pimp and gives Phaedromus a list of illicit sex objects expressed in terms of real estate (33–8):

> ... nemo hinc prohibet nec votat
> quin quod palam est venale, si argentum est, emas.
> nemo ire quemquam publica prohibet via;   35
> dum ne per fundum saeptum facias semitam,
> dum ted apstineas nupta, vidua, virgine,
> iuventute et pueris liberis, ama quidlubet.

> ... PA. Nobody prohibits you or forbids
> that you should buy from here what's openly for sale, if you have the cash.
> Nobody prohibits anybody from going down the public road;   35
> as long as you don't make a pathway through posted land,
> as long as you keep yourself off a married woman, an unmarried woman,
>   a maiden,
> the youth and free boys, love whatever you feel like.

This speech is bracketed by Phaedromus' interjected reminder that his beloved lives in a pimp's house (33, 39). Palinurus' list is a joke – most desirable bodies are off limits – but even what is licit is only so with a qualification: you can have what's "openly for sale" (*palam ... venale*) if you have the money to buy it: *si argentum est, emas*, a conditional that recurs in other contexts, as will be seen below. The list is certainly a valid reminder of what was off limits to citizen males – *a fortiori*, to male slaves – but also serves as a tacit reminder of the openness of low-class bodies, again using the charged word *venalis*, and of the preciousness of money for those who were themselves merchandise, for whom money was the ticket to manumission, carefully hoarded savings. So the slaves Stichus and Sangarinus make clear, responding to the entrance of their fellow-slave Stephanium: "My *peculium*'s taking a beating, it's a deal," says Stichus; "Freedom's running away from this *caput*," says Sangarinus (STI. *vapulat peculium, actum est.* SA. *fugit hoc libertas caput*, St. 751; see below on the pimp's house in *Poenulus*). The fact that it is a male slave who lays down the rules in *Curculio* should come to mind when we deal with double speech in Plautus (chapter 6). That the romance of the young owner means something different to his male slaves is demonstrated by Milphio in *Poenulus*, who gives a table of equivalences (392–4): "his honey, my gall" (*mel huiius, fel meum*, 394). "I'm wildly in love," says Milphio's owner; "My shoulderblades feel it," replies Milphio (*amo immodeste. #meae istuc scapulae sentiunt*, 153).

What, then, did it mean to the audience to see so many prostitutes at the center of these plays? What needs were served by the Cinderella stories of the girls reclaimed as citizens, the triumph of a few powerful women like Phronesium in *Truculentus*? In the *Poenulus* prologue, the *imperator histricus* starts off his list of injunctions with "Let no overripe whore sit on the stage" (*scortum exoletum ne quis in proscaenio / sedeat*, 17–18).[54] This line emphasizes the nature of the stage as a display space: the audience looks at the actors as buyers look at slaves for sale and as customers look at cheap prostitutes (cf. the vocabulary used in *Poen.* 265–70, below, associating cheap prostitutes with standing out in public). Cheap *male* prostitutes. As Chrysalus, turning the tables, says to the old man Nicobulus, "You don't know you're now for sale, / and you're standing on the very stone where the auctioneer does his sales pitch" (*nescis nunc venire te, / atque in eopse astas lapide, ut praeco praedicat, Bac.* 814–15).[55] The Choragus in *Curculio* locates *scorta exoleta* and other prostitutes at particular spots in the Forum Romanum (473, 482, 484), while the young man in *Truculentus* locates pimps and *scorta* among the bankers' stalls (62a–73), which, onstage, belong to the Forum as well (see chapter 3, chapter 7). As seen in chapter 1, the stage itself may well have been in, or in sight of, the Forum; the theater space overlays the public space, the public space shows through the theater space. So, onstage as just offstage, prostitution plays a central role in Roman comedy, a change from Greek New Comedy, where the shows were staged in purpose-built stone theaters (over one hundred of them, throughout the Greek world).[56] Unsurprisingly, that role is deeply enmeshed in problems related to slavery. All three cultural forms – the *palliata*, prostitution, and slavery – exploded alongside each other in the course of the 200s BCE, as wars brought home their human spoils and shoved people around the Mediterranean.

Prostitutes and sex slaves motivate the action of *Asinaria, Bacchides, Cistellaria, Curculio, Epidicus, Menaechmi, Mercator, Miles Gloriosus, Mostellaria, Persa, Poenulus, Pseudolus, Rudens,* and *Truculentus*, and possibly *Vidularia* – fourteen of the twenty extant plays. Other options

---

[54] On *scorta exoleta* here, see Moore 1998: 141, 220 n. 26; cf. above, n. 22.

[55] For the degradation experienced by slaves on the auction block, see Bodel 2005, with illustrations; Bradley 1984: 115–16; Bradley 2011a: 242, on the stele of M. Publilius Satur at Capua, with references at 262; Joshel 2010: 95–110; and further in chapters 5 and 7 below. The Capua stele is discussed in Binsfeld 2009, with bibliography; for the image, also Joshel 2010: 98.

[56] See Csapo 2014: 52–6, for the estimate and an overview.

were available in the plotlines of New Comedy; this is what Plautus thought would please the crowd, if what we have is a representative sample. Naevius seems to have gone in this direction at least in his *Corollaria* (fr. 36–8, 41–2), *Paelex*, *Tarentilla* (fr. 75–9, 90–1), and *Triphallus* (fr. 96–8). Prostitution and sex slavery seem also to have featured in, at the least, the probably Plautine *Cornicula* (fr. 66), *Gemini Lenones* (fr. 90), *Nervolaria* (fr. 96, 100), *Schematicus* (if that is its title: fr. 112, *numquam ... limavit caput*, cf. *Bac.* fr. xvi *nec ... limares caput*, *Poen.* 291 *numquam limavi caput*, Livius Andronicus, *Tereus*, *Trag.* 28–9 R.$_{2–3}$ *numquam limavit / caput*, a good example of a joke circulating through comedy and tragedy), *Sitellitergus* (fr. 115), and whatever play featured a request to Davus to spruce up the house in anticipation of a visit from "our Venus" (fr. inc. 164–5), or talked about a "pimp law" (fr. inc. 140). Almost all the prostitutes in the extant plays are female, with male prostitutes appearing only in small parts and passing mentions (see below on the *Gemini Lenones* fragment). The prostitute characters range from ingenue to femme fatale, from non-speaking (Phoenicium and the others in Ballio's house in *Pseudolus*) and unnamed (the second *fidicina* in *Epidicus*) to star (Phronesium). A certain degree of validation is accorded to them simply as the focus of so much attention. Although attacks on their reputed bad qualities (greed, deceit) are common, they are repeatedly credited with a particular sort of agency: they have power over men's desire.

This agency is several times described in a set of related and significant metaphors: bird-catching, sheep-shearing, and fishing (*As.* 178–85, 215–26; *Bac.* 102, 1121a–1148; *Mer.* 517–27; *Truc.* 35–9, 42, 964). As seen above, bird-catching relates to the capture of slaves as wild things, *res nullius*, and to the double sense of *cavea* as [bird]cage/audience space (see further in chapter 8); sheep-shearing relates to the common sense of *tondeo* in Plautus as "fleece" and *mutilo* as "clip" – the action performed upon the free dupe by the trickster (esp. *Capt.* 267–9; see chapter 4 on barbershops). Fishing, as seen especially in the central scene in *Rudens*, is a powerful metaphor for the slave trade (see chapter 7). All these cases involve turning the tables: the exploited person becomes the exploiter. In *Mercator*, the *senex* actually volunteers himself as a sheep, pushing the sense of *tondeo* towards the sexual overtones in *tonstrix*, "female barber." Within their historical context, these plotlines and scenes mean something more specific than jolly Saturnalian fun, laughable for all, and something less cruel than the dead-end stories of Greek symposia that filled the pages of Hellenistic anecdote collectors and the jokes of Middle Comedy. Sex slaves in the *palliata* are simultaneously low and sought-after, specularized and feared, so that their agency cuts both ways for slave and freed actors and audience.[57]

The categories "prostitute" and "slave" overlap in the plays; some of the prostitutes are slaves, some are free or freed, a few are slaves or foundlings who turn out to be capable of legitimation: Selenium in *Cistellaria*, Planesium in *Curculio*, the captive Telestis (but not the *fidicina* Acropolistis, though she plays the part) in *Epidicus*, the sisters Adelphasium and Anterastilis in *Poenulus*, Palaestra (but not Ampelisca) in *Rudens* (see chapter 7). The con game in *Persa* with the unnamed Virgo as "Lucris" replays this plot-line, as does the unplayed story of the household slave Casina (*Cas.* 81–2, 1013–14), although we notice that the Virgo expects that, for her, just being involved in the fake sale will wreck her marriageability, never mind growing up in a pimp's house like Planesium, Palaestra, or the *Poenulus* sisters. In most of the plays involving prostitution, the central prostitutes stay prostitutes, the happy ending consisting in being allowed to stay with a preferred customer for a year or so, with or without manumission, or just in completing a successful cash transaction: Philaenium in *Asinaria* (free), the Bacchis sisters (free), Acropolistis in *Epidicus* (freed), Erotium in *Menaechmi* (free), Pasicompsa in *Mercator* (slave), Philocomasium in *Miles* (free), Philematium in *Mostellaria* (freed), Lemniselenis in *Persa* (freed), Phoenicium in *Pseudolus* (freed), Phronesium in *Truculentus* (free).[58] To varying degrees, the *ancillae* of prostitutes do business themselves on the side: Erotium's *ancilla*, flirting with Menaechmus II while demanding jewelry, specifically *stalagmia*, "danglers" (*Men.* 541–3); Sophoclidisca, suiting her conduct to life in a pimp's household (*Per.* 213); Astaphium, giving a warm welcome to one of her owner's clients, perhaps also her own (*Truc.* 94, 126) and teasing the slave Truculentus (*Truc.* 256–314, 672–98), who taunts her for being paid in cheap jewelry (*accepisti armillas aeneas*, 272). Acroteleutium's *ancilla* Milphidippa is said to be "outstandingly clever" (*prime cata*, *Mil.* 794), and attracts the soldier in her own right (988–9, 999–1000, 1006). Philematium's attendant Scapha is old now, but recalls her glory days, and remarks that she was pretty once herself (*Mos.* 199–202; see chapter 8 on her status). Some of the slave prostitutes are shown as belonging to a pimp – Cappadox in *Curculio*, the unnamed owner of Acropolistis in *Epidicus* (47, 352), Dordalus in *Persa*, Lycus in *Poenulus*,

---

[57] On prostitutes in Athenaeus's comic fragments and symposiastic anecdotes, see Henry 1992, 2000; McClure 2003.
[58] For discussion of the status of Acropolistis, see chapter 5.

Ballio in *Pseudolus*, Labrax in *Rudens* – and the houses of Lycus and Ballio are portrayed as brothels.

The conditions of prostitutes' lives are not shown as pleasant, despite the romance and parties (both depicted as goods onstage, though criticized), despite the clothing, jewelry, and makeup. Several of them weep as they are led off to a purchaser (Planesium, *Cur.* 520; Pasicompsa, *Mer.* 500–1, anticipating housework; "Lucris," *Per.* 622, 656; Phoenicium, *Ps.* 1038–9). Their tears are attested by scorn or cruel jokes: "Why are you crying, dummy?" (*quid stulta ploras, Cur.* 520); "Don't cry, please; you'll be free soon, if you fall over frequently" (*ne sis plora; libera eris actutum, si crebro cades, Per.* 656); "Don't cry, you don't know how things are, Phoenicium; / but I'll see to it you find out when you're lying down" (*Ne plora, nescis ut res sit, Phoenicium, / verum ... faxo scibis accubans, Ps.* 1038–9 – just teasing). There is, perhaps, a trace of the sale of a weeping boy onstage in a fragment of the probably Plautine *Gemini Lenones*: "This boy is sad that he is being led off to be sold" (*dolet huic puello sese venum ducier*, fr. 90). The Virgo's own father in *Persa* tells her to shut up as she begs him not to sell her: "Shut up, dummy" (*tace, stulta*, 385). Even a preferred customer or purchaser will harp on the cost of purchase and on the prostitute's status as merchandise, notably Philolaches in *Mostellaria* (297–305), Toxilus in *Persa* (834–42); they are like Ballio in *Pseudolus*, who says, "Your girlfriend's been turned into silver" (*amicam tuam esse factam argenteam*, 347).

At the end of the Virgo's sale as "Lucris," she has to stand there while the pimp makes a joke about her clothes coming off (*Per.* 670); when (now back in her identity as the Virgo) she asks for notice and reward from her co-conspirators, they ignore her (674–5). When she tells her father at the outset that his use of her will deprive her of any hope of marriage (383–4), he makes it clear that he regards her as his property (*quae sis mea*, 340; see chapter 6 on the force of possessive adjectives). Free women are occasionally treated as things elsewhere: one long scene in *Aulularia* depends for its humor on a confusion between Euclio's daughter and his pot of gold (731–802). But prostitutes are repeatedly treated as objects: the slave Strobilus equates the *tibicina* Phrugia with the ingredients for lunch (*Aul.* 332); Agorastocles refers to the sisters in *Poenulus* as merchandise (341–2); the brothers' cargo in *Stichus* includes female musicians (*fidicinas, tibicinas/ sambucas*, 380–1) along with silver and gold, textiles, perfumes – and *parasiti* (388): comedians are commodities, too.

Prostitutes who are free may still be under the control of their mothers, who have brought them up to the trade and are sometimes said specifically to take a fee (*As.* 751–2): Cleareta and Philaenium in *Asinaria* (504–44), the unnamed *lena* and Gymnasium in *Cistellaria* (2 and *passim*), the unnamed *lena* and Philocomasium in *Miles* (106–12). Phronesium's mother is involved in her schemes (*Truc.* 401, 802). This setup appears elsewhere in literature notably in Lucian's *Dialogues of the Courtesans* (3, 6, 7), and enters the historical record in the story of a court case from late ancient Egypt.[59] As noted above, the *lena* in *Cistellaria* associates the occupation of *meretrix* with her freedwoman status. Other freedwoman sex workers in the plays include the unnamed *fidicina* in *Epidicus* (proud of her non-slave status, 497–8) and, in *Miles*, Acroteleutium, brought into the plot by the *senex* and described by him as his *clienta*, a "teenage prostitute" (*meretricem adulescentulam*, 789, cf. 915, where she calls him *patrone*). This makes it interesting that the *senex* Daemones sees Palaestra and Ampelisca as his potential *clientae* – young, cute ones, too (*ambas forma scitula atque aetatula*), who make him worry about his wife's jealousy (*Rud.* 893–6): edgy, when Palaestra turns out to be his daughter. The old man in *Epidicus* turns out not to be the father of the *fidicina* Acropolistis, but he is her *patronus*, leaving her future in some doubt, as is the future of Lemniselenis in *Persa*, whose *patronus* is her former pimp – another shadow over that play's dark ending. And indeed Epidicus tells his young owner that he need not fret when Telestis turns out to be his half-sister, for "You surely have something to love right at home, the *fidicina*" (*tibi quidem quod ames domi praesto est, fidicina, Epid.* 653). Handy! So much for the defiant speech Acropolistis makes to the old man (see chapter 5).

Despite the romance plot, prostitutes in Plautus are often shown as having sex with more than one customer, not always by choice, or are treated as fungible. The mean old man in *Stichus* begs his sons-in-law to give him four *scorta* from their supply of imported goods (542–73); at the opposite extreme, the Parasitus and his patron in *Asinaria* draw up a detailed "law" for Philaenium that would keep her severely confined (751–808). Menaechmus I, in contrast, is unperturbed to find that his brother has had a party with his own particular *meretrix* Erotium (1140–5). The young owner's father in *Asinaria* demands a share in Philaenium (736–9, 830–3, 847–50, 882–911), and almost gets it; the Parasitus intends to arrange a

---

[59] P. Berol. 1024.6–8, translated in Lefkowitz and Fant 2016: 152: the mother has given her daughter to a pimp, the girl has been murdered by a customer, her mother seeks restitution because she depended on her daughter's earnings for her support. On this case and its possible relation to reality, see esp. Harper 2011: 308, who classes it with the general sale of children by their parents into prostitution, and comments, "the life of shame, like the life of slavery, entailed social death"; also Strong 2012. On the mother-daughter pairs in comedy, see James 2015a, Marshall 2013: 177, Rosivach 1998: 51–75, and esp. Dutsch forthcoming on *lenae* and their daughters.

timeshare in her for his patron and the young owner (*As.* 915–18, *alternas
… noctes*); the father in *Mercator* tries to buy Pasicompsa, and succeeds
in groping her (203–4). As Sharon James points out (2010), she is passed
along multiple times in the play. Ballio famously exhorts his stable of prostitutes to get out there and drum up business with a usual clientele that
is made up of entire business organizations – the grain-dealers (*Ps.* 188),
the butchers (197), the olive-oil sellers (210–11) – or just "men at the top"
as a group (*summatum virum*, 227); similarly, Toxilus promises the pimp
Dordalus that crowds of the "best men" will besiege his house to have fun
with Lucris (*optumis viris, Per.* 567). Stephanium in *Stichus* plans to let
two slaves take turns with her, and says she loves both of them (742–4,
750–1); when Sangarinus asks if both he and Stichus are welcome to her,
she replies, "I'll do my duty, my darlings" (*morigerabor, meae deliciae,* 742).
Phronesium exits with two customers, and says she will "do her duty" (*mos
geratur, Truc.* 961) not only with them but with anyone in the audience
who wants to join in (965–6) – an offer reminiscent, again, of the *Casina*
prologue, and the cooks in *Aulularia*. The whole point of Scapha's advice
to Philematium in *Mostellaria* is that it is unwise for a prostitute to devote
all her attention to a single customer, because she had tried that herself –
"I did my duty to just one man" (*uni modo gessi morem,* 200a) – and he
left her when her hair turned grey. The Bacchis sisters seem resigned to letting their two young customers' fathers join in, although the second sister
remarks that it is repellent to put your arms around death (1152). The level
of grossness implied here is spelled out by a *senex,* the neighbor Lysimachus
in *Mercator* (574–6):

> iaiunitatis plenus, anima foetida,
> senex hircosus tu osculere mulierem?   575
> utine adveniens vomitum excutias mulieri?

> Full of an empty stomach, with stinky breath,
> you goaty old man, should you be kissing a woman?   575
> So you'll go up to her and make the woman puke?

These lines would be particularly funny to audience members who had
been forced to kiss an owner, achieving a tidy economy in the expenditure
of affect.

Prostitutes generally refer to themselves as *meretrices,* "earning girls,"
while others refer to them casually or disparagingly as *scorta,* or, very
rarely, as *lupae* (*Epid.* 403; *Truc.* 657). Both words are crude, equivalent
to "whore" in tone: a *scortum* literally is an animal's hide, a *lupa* is a she-
wolf. "I can make love or hire a whore now," says Truculentus eagerly to

Astaphium; "Heavens, you put it charmingly," she replies: he is rude, as usual ([TR.] *vel amare possum vel iam scortum ducere. / AS. lepide mecastor nuntias, Truc.* 678–9). She is similarly sarcastic to his equally crude owner (*lepide facis*, 668). Although Stephanium in *Stichus* is a household slave (431–3), she generalizes about what should and should not be done by a *mulier meretrix* (746), an unusual variant on the common practice of male slaves who generalize about what a *servus homo* can and cannot do (see chapter 6). The term *meretrix* must resonate with the constant use of *mereo* and its cognates in Plautus to refer to just deserts (see especially *Capt.* 1020, *Cas.* 1015, *Epid.* 711–12), and in turn with the idea of earning pay for work (*Vid.* 49). That there are levels among prostitutes is set out most vividly in *Poenulus*, where Adelphasium protests that she does not wish to rub shoulders with the whores who have sex with slaves (265–70):

> an te ibi vis inter istas vorsarier   265
> prosedas, pistorum amicas, reginas alicarias,
> miseras schoeno delibutas servilicolas sordidas,
> quae tibi olant stabulum statumque, sellam et sessibulum merum,
> quas adeo hau quisquam umquam liber tetigit neque duxit domum,
> servolorum sordidulorum scorta diobolaria?   270

> Or do you want to be pushed around   265
> with those streetwalkers? Mill-slaves' girlfriends! Queens of the land of grits!
> Poor little dirty groupies of slaves, smeared and stinking with eau de
>   camel –
> girls who reek of cheap hotel rooms, and streetcorners, and public toilets!
> Girls no free man ever touched at all, never mind took home with him,
> dirty little no-good slave boys' two-dollar cash-on-the-barrel whores![60] 270

Along with the low price and public availability, note the implication that there were prostitutes forced to exploit even the men in the mill (paradigmatic place of slave punishment); the association with dirt and smells; and the ironic use of *regina*. Adelphasium's remarks cause the slave Milphio,

---

[60] For the translation, see Richlin 2005: 208, with notes; here reading *reginas* in 266 with Lindsay, although the MSS alternate, *reliquias* ("leftovers"), is just as good. Paulus, preserving what is probably a gloss of this line, says that, in Campania, the *meretrices* who used to stand outside the grain mills to do business with *alicarii* were called *alicariae* (7L), and *alicarius* shows up as an abusive term in Lucilius, 496M (see Marx *ad loc.*); cf. Adams 1983: 335–7 for an alternate interpretation. "Eau de camel" translates *schoeno delibutas*, literally "smeared with the aromatic eastern grass called 'camel's hay'"; cf. a similar invective list at *Cist.* 405–8 that includes *diobolares schoeniculae*, "two-dollar eau-de-camel girls," 407; also the disturbing fragment *ulcerosam, compeditam, subverbustam, sordidam* (fr. inc. 155, possibly Plautine: "a woman full of sores, wearing fetters, covered with beatings, dirty"), akin to the probably Plautine *Nervolaria* fr. 100, *scrattae, scrupipedae, strittabillae, sordidae* ("retching, flint-footed, screeching, dirty women"; see de Melo 2013: 455 for sources for this line's alternate attributions to *Aulularia* and *Cistellaria*).

eavesdropping, to protest vehemently against her nerve in scorning slaves (271; see chapter 8). But she has a point: slaves onstage do not wind up with prostitutes like Adelphasium. The slave Truculentus is seduced, not by Phronesium, but by her *ancilla*, Astaphium (*Truc.* 669–98), whom he has previously taunted for dressing above her station (270–5), a stand-in for her owner: "So you can buy the big-ticket items, that's why you're always wearing those bronze rings?" *mancupion qui accipias, gestas tecum ahenos anulos?*, 274).[61] Similarly, Ampelisca, not Palaestra, will be freed to be given as a wife to the freed slave Trachalio (*Rud.* 1220, 1405–9), and Palaestrio admires and wishes to marry Milphidippa, the *ancilla* of the freed prostitute Acroteleutium (*Mil.* 1007–8, 1139–40). There are levels among male slaves, too; when the slave Sceparnio, whom we see doing manual labor, tries to kiss Ampelisca, she protests (*Rud.* 424), *non sum pollucta pago*, "I'm not offered up to the district." Ballio, in his great song, warns his four female sex workers that, unless they earn him a big birthday present from their regular customers, the rich men and merchants, he will prostitute them "to the public" (*poplo*, 178, cf. *Aul.* 285, above, *prostibulum popli*); thus Calidorus wants to free Phoenicium not only for himself but "so that he won't turn out my girlfriend" (*ne amicam hic meam prostituat*, 231). Note the use of *pop(u)lus* to mean "poor men," "all and sundry." Stichus says reproachfully to his fellow slave Sangarinus (765–6) that kissing Stephanium while standing makes her a *prostibilis*; for similar motives, Gymnasium goes inside because "for a *meretrix* to stand alone in the street is the sign of a *prostibulum*" (*Cist.* 331); so Toxilus, threatening Lemniselenis at the end of *Persa* and claiming to be her *patronus* because he has arranged for the pimp to free her, lectures her: "By God, without me / and my rescue, this guy would have made you a street hooker any day

---

[61] The issue is not, as is sometimes claimed, that Astaphium as a slave was not entitled to participate in an act of *mancipatio*; slaves who did so simply acquired for their owners (Buckland 1908: 712–13). What was bought by *mancipatio* was *res mancipi* – houses, draft animals, slaves, and Italic land – and that is what is bought with the phrases *mancupio dare* and *mancupio accipere* elsewhere in the corpus (*Cur.* 494–7, 617, *Mer.* 449, *Per.* 524–5, 532, 589, female slaves; *Mos.* 1091, *Trin.* 421, houses; *Mil.* 23, the speaker – facetious). Still, both the text (these lines are vexed in P) and the interpretation that the rings are to be used as the bronze bar in an act of sale by *mancipatio* seem strained, especially since the phrase elsewhere needs an object, if only implied (see de Melo 2013: 297). The interpretation goes back at least to Ussing in 1886; see overview in Enk 1953: 2.74–75. The point is that her jewelry is fake – bronze for gold; 274 picks up the often-bracketed 272, *an eo bella es, quia accepisti armillas aeneas?* On the further meaning of Astaphium's Victoria earrings or brooches, see chapter 3. Like Milphio, Truculentus rejects what he cannot have (compare *Poen.* 274, *Truc.* 277–9). For jokes based on slaves' legal incapacities, see *Bac.* 880–4, *Ps.* 116–18 (*stipulatio*). A description of the process of sale "by bronze and balance" appears, oddly enough, in Varro's discussion of *nexum* (*L.* 7.105), on which see chapters 3 and 4.

now" (*hercle apsque me / foret et meo praesidio, hic faceret te prostibilem pro-pediem*, 836–7).[62] At the other end of the spectrum, the terms change: the soldier in *Epidicus* wants to free Acropolistis and make her his *concubina* (465–6), as the soldier in *Poenulus* wants to do with Anterastilis (102–3). The soldier in *Miles Gloriosus* keeps Philocomasium as his *concubina* (*passim*); Phronesium remarks that she was held by her soldier "like a wife" for a year (*quasi uxorem, Truc.* 392–3).

The difference between respectable women and prostitutes is spelled out repeatedly by characters of different status: by the *matrona* Cleostrata in *Casina* (585–6); by the *lena* in *Cistellaria*, in a long opening song (23–37); by the soldier and Palaestrio in *Miles* (free and freed, 961–3); by the attendant Scapha in *Mostellaria* (188–90); by the *senex* Periphanes in *Epidicus* (400–3), harshly referring to the hired *fidicina* as a *lupa* and ordering her to be kept apart from Acropolistis, the girl he thinks is his daughter Telestis. It is ironic, then, that Telestis' mother reacts with disgust when she meets Acropolistis: "puppies smell one way, pigs smell another" (*aliter catuli longe olent, aliter sues, Epid.* 579), or possibly "piglets smell one way, sows smell another" (see chapter 5). The Virgo in *Persa*, as seen above, fears she will never be able to marry once she has been sold, even if falsely (383–4). This is why the guardians of foundlings and the owners – even pimps – of women reclaimed from slavery insist that they have kept them *bene ac pudice*, "well and chastely" (*Cas.* 44–6, 81–2; *Cist.* 172–3; *Cur.* 518; compare the joke Sosia makes about his tongue, *Am.* 349). This is why lovers similarly insist that they have never had sex with their beloveds (*Cur.* 51–60 – doubted by the slave Palinurus, 57; *Epid.* 110; *Poen.* 281, 292–4, 1096, and vouched for by the prologue speaker, 98–101).

The plays, however, like to blur this line; the innocence of Adelphasium and Anterastilis in *Poenulus* is drastically undercut by their eagerness to display themselves for sale to the *mercatores* at the *mercatus meretricius* at the temple of Venus (339–40), backed by their elaborate bathing scene (a musical number, 210–54) and a long opening sequence of getting ready to go, with nasty remarks about their competition (320–3), all reprised in their song as they return in Act 5 (1174–95). "What big girls!" says their long-lost father on first seeing them (1167), a probable drag joke; this element, too, was always available to undercut any sentimentality (see chapter 5), and the

---

[62] The same idea appears in contemporary tragedy; cf. Naevius *Danae* (*Trag.* 7 R.₂₋₃ = 12 W. = 8 *TrRF*), *desubito famam tollunt, si quam solam videre in via* ("immediately they start a rumor, whenever they've seen a woman alone in the street"). On the lexicon of prostitution as public, see Adams 1983: 329–32, 343–4.

unladylike demeanor of Planesium in *Curculio* as well makes it unlikely that the virginal Palaestra and Ampelisca in *Rudens* were played as seriously virginal (certainly not Ampelisca, considering the scene at the well where Sceparnio admires her breasts, paws her about, and jokes about his erection, 414–39). The shipwrecked Palaestra, in her opening song, gestures to her costume (*med hoc ornatu ornatam*, 187), presumably wet rags and not many of them, as Ampelisca complains ("with our clothes all wet," *uvida veste*, 251), and the priestess of Venus emphasizes (*cum uvida veste*, 265; *tam maestiter vestitas*, 265a), disapprovingly (*ad istunc modum*, 271). Their genitals appear to be visible, to judge from the laugh line that leads out of the scene where they take refuge at the altar of Venus: "[Venus,]" prays Trachalio, "they say you were born from a *concha*; so don't you turn away from these girls' *conchae*" (*te ex concha natam esse autumant, cave tu harum conchas spernas*, 704). Rather, some kind of naked-woman feature formed part of the actor's costume.[63] The concept of "nice girl temporarily owned by pimp" is a titillating one, a classic of stories in oral circulation; such stories, as produced on the comic stage, incorporate a sort of wink that valorizes the unchaste, and, as will be seen in chapter 5, lead to the only eagerly anticipated weddings in Plautus.

What appear to be the same rules apply to enslaved or kidnapped boys, of whom there are several in Plautus: Tyndarus in *Captivi* (sold, but "well and chastely brought up," *bene pudiceque educatust*, 991–2); Menaechmus I (adopted by his kidnapper, 32–3, 57–62); Agorastocles in *Poenulus* (kidnapped, sold to a rich old man, then freed and adopted by him, 72–7). For they were also at risk; if bought for household use, they might have expected to be used like the other *pueri*; in the plays, adopted girls, like Selenium, are not brought up as chaste citizens, and we might wonder about the intended fate of the baby boy passed off as her own by Phronesium. Along with the *scorta exoleta* of the *Poenulus* prologue and the *Curculio* Forum tour, there are other male prostitutes in Plautus: the banker Lyco in *Curculio* casually professes to be in the market for a *puer* he can rent out for profit (382–3); the *puer* in *Pseudolus* (767–89) gives gritty details of working for a pimp; Diniarchus in *Truculentus* casually admits to having tried male prostitutes as well as female, and he and Astaphium discuss the differences (149–57). As seen above, a boy seems to have been sold onstage in a play titled *Twin Pimps*. Nobody, however, undercuts the

---

[63] On the naked-woman costume in Old Comedy, see Callier 2014, Zweig 1992; in the *palliata*, Dutsch 2004, Marshall 2006: 64–5. On this *concha* joke, see Richlin 2017b: 174.

claims of the kidnapped boys to have spent their youth chastely: an index of what could be undone and what could not.

"What ain't we got? / We ain't got dames!" sang the chorus of sailors in *South Pacific* in 1949, to an audience of World War II veterans and their wives. Not all the members of that chorus, and not all the male members of that audience, of course, were interested in dames, but the situation was recognizable, indeed a fond postwar heteronormative ideal. In the same way, the substantial presence of prostitutes onstage in the *palliata* and the desires and frustrations associated with them addressed an audience familiar with the desires and issues specific to wartime Italy in the 200s BCE. This was not Luther Billis in a grass skirt and a pair of coconuts. The fact that these sex symbols were played by men speaks to a situation in which male prostitution was common, cinaedic dance was another Alexandrian import, and young men in the army who engaged in illicit sex were liable to the *fustuarium*. Whereas violence and, as will be seen, hunger affected different kinds of people in similar ways, prostitution affected different kinds of people in ways keyed to their past, current, and hoped-for social roles. For the *matronae* addressed in the *Poenulus* prologue, *meretrices* were the natural enemy, and indeed the *palliata* itself posed problems for wives: in the plays, wives are conventionally physically repulsive, domineering, old, sometimes greedy, and in metatheatrical moments the actors suggest that the audience is full of men who like to hire *scorta* (*Am.* 287–8, *Mer.* 1015–26, *Ps.* 203–4, *Truc.* 98–105), and that husbands want to hire *scorta* behind their wives' backs (*As.* 942–5; *Cas.* 1016, mischievously identifying those who applaud with such husbands; *Men.* 128–9, such a husband onstage asking for approval from *amatores mariti* in the audience).[64] From all women not in the sex trade, including slave-women, prostitutes onstage might have elicited a degree of Schadenfreude. From all men, they were supposed to elicit lust; again, for slaves and freed slaves, this lust would be complicated by Schadenfreude coupled with the anger and ache inspired by an unaffordable treat.

The whole troupe speaks the closing lines of *Bacchides*, in which they say "We wouldn't have made all this up, if we hadn't seen it happen before now, / that fathers rival their sons in the houses of pimps" (*neque adeo haec faceremus, ni antehac vidissemus fieri / ut apud lenones rivales filiis fierent patres*, *Bac.* 1209–10). The pimp's slave Syncerastus in *Poenulus*, who hates

---

[64] On invective against women in Latin, and especially against old women, see Richlin 2014a: 62–80. On these audience appeals, see Moore 1998: 8–49. On hostility between classes of women onstage, see further in chapter 5.

his owner, presents a lurid description of what goes on in his house (830–8), claiming you might see there "a cavalry officer, a footsoldier, a freedman, a thief or a fugitive slave ... / beaten, bound, or debtor slaves; any guy who's got the price, / all kinds are accepted here" (*equitem, peditem, libertinum, furem an fugitivom ... , / verberatum, vinctum, addictum: qui habet quod det, utut homo est, / omnia genera recipiuntur,* 832–4). "When I see these things happen, it's torture," he sums up; "slaves bought for the highest prices are losing their *peculia* for their owners at our house" (*haec quom hic video fieri, crucior: pretiis emptos maxumis / apud nos expeculiatos servos fieri suis eris,* 842–3). That is, like the *lorarius* in *Captivi,* or like Stichus and his friend, they will lack what they need to pay for their manumission – *quod det* here pays the pimp for sex. Both Syncerastus and the *Bacchides* troupe emphasize what they have seen themselves, exploiting the double gaze of the theater, whereby the masked actors inspect the audience: "We've seen you at it" (chapter 1). From Syncerastus' perspective, the pimp's house is hell (831). For different reasons, prostitution was also a nightmare scenario for parents of children lost to human trafficking. Yet again, these were not real women or boys onstage, but masked caricatures, and their sexiness was played for laughs. Specularized and grotesque, they were open to anybody's desire, of whatever gender or status, whether for the mask or the actor under it.

Prostitutes were also important recurring characters, with a lot to say for themselves; there is no reason why actual prostitutes should not have been in the audience to enjoy all that attention, as they are among the crowd that welcomes the legion home in *Epidicus* (206–54) – a passage that includes a lengthy comic catalogue of women's fashions (223–35). Philaenium in *Asinaria* often gets, as Sugar says in *Some Like It Hot,* the fuzzy end of the lollipop, but in her final scene she leads the old man on to insult his wife with the wife onstage (894–5), evidently consciously (901 – if this is her line), and then taunts him (930, 939–40). The Bacchis sisters in *Bacchides* never lose control, and, in the end, lace into their two elderly customers (*Bac.* 1120–54); Phronesium dominates *Truculentus.* Her *ancilla* Astaphium sings a whole song justifying prostitutes' greed (*Truc.* 209–45), here resuming an argument she makes in her opening song (95–111): it is the customers who swindle the prostitutes, not vice versa. "Gee, that's how it is, and, gee, some of you sitting in the audience know I'm not lying about it," she sings (*fit pol hoc, et pars spectatorum scitis pol haec vos me hau mentiri,* 105). A laugh line, but presumably some of them do – from various perspectives. This is a Forum audience, not a Broadway audience; they had lived through, or were still living through, the First Illyrian War, the Second

Punic War, the First and Second Macedonian Wars, and the Aetolian War, survivors of battles, invasion, devastation, mass enslavements and displacement of populations, and hunger.

Hunger

The *Poenulus* prologue speaker, as seen above, knits hunger into the fabric of his speech, and ties it firmly to comedy itself. His first command after he introduces himself divides the audience between hungry and full (5–10):

bonoque ut animo sedeant in subselliis 5
et qui essurientes et qui saturi venerint:
qui edistis, multo fecistis sapientius,
qui non edistis, saturi fite fabulis;
nam quoi paratumst quod edit, nostra gratia
nimia est stultitia sessum impransum incedere. 10

They should keep calm and sit on the benches, 5
both those who have come hungry and those who have come full:
you who have eaten, you acted much more wisely,
you who haven't eaten, make yourselves full on *fabulae/fabuli*;
indeed, somebody who has on hand food to eat, it's just too much stupidity
for him to go take a seat without breakfast, for our sake. 10

As seen above, *subsellia* are where *parasiti* sit to get whatever dinner they can; for the contrast between *essurientes* and *saturi*, compare the scene where Saturio says to Toxilus, who he hopes will feed him, that Toxilus is wrong to call him "Saturio," because he has arrived as "Essurio" (*Per.* 103). The naming of the group *quoi paratumst quod edit* (9) suggests that not everybody does have food on hand to eat, an idea that is confirmed throughout the corpus of the *palliata*; the *parasitus* in a fragment of the probably Plautine *Boeotia* says that, when he was a boy, people ate when their belly (*venter*) told them to, "except when there was nothing to eat" (*nisi quom nihil erat*, at Gellius 3.3.3 = fr. 27). The prologue speaker makes a significant pun in telling those who are hungry that they must fill up on *fabulis*: *fabuli*, "little beans," were the popcorn of Roman theater (Gowers 1993: 59–60), and form part of the slave feast at the end of *Stichus* (690); *fabulae*, of course, are the plays themselves. Food for the hungry, food for the poor; beans were subsistence food.[65] So the prologue speaker says to

---

[65] See discussion of legumes and the common diet in Garnsey 1998: 226–52, esp. at 241–2; 1999: 12–21, esp. at 15 on legumes as "the poor man's meat," and 43–61 on malnutrition in relation to class, status, and gender.

the *praeco*, "Unless you shout, starvation will catch you while you're silent" (*nisi clamabis, tacitum te obrepet fames*, 14); so he tells the wet-nurses that their babies are in danger of starving, or might get hungry (*ne ... pueri pereant fame, essurientes*, 30, 31); so he injects a drooling moment by telling slave attendants to hurry over to the *popina* "while the cheese pastries are hot" (*dum scribilitae aestuant*, 43). *Scribilitae*, for which Cato provides a mouth-watering recipe in *De agricultura* (76–8), were puff-pastry cakes made with cheese; as for the *popina*, Syncerastus says of the pimp's house, "It's dark and dim, they eat and drink there just like in a *popina*, no different" (*tenebrae, latebrae, bibitur, estur quasi in popina, hau secus*, *Poen.* 835).

As seen above, when it comes to violence and sex, slaves in Plautus have points in common with *parasiti*, prostitutes, comedians, and occasionally with the free poor, groups which in any case overlap. They also share the simple hunger for a full belly; food is the main motivator for all *parasiti*, who earn food by telling jokes, just like comic actors and writers. Even the *parasitus* Artotrogus, who appears so briefly and never approaches a meal, says it is his belly that drives him (*venter, Mil.* 33). Hunger makes Saturio sell out his daughter (*ventris caussa, Per.* 338). Hunger and poverty are likewise repeatedly said to be the motivating factors for prostitution: so the *lena* Cleareta tells her daughter Philaenium ("we'd die of hunger," *ne nos moriamur fame, As.* 531), and her angry customer confirms it ("you used to live happily on dirty bread, in rags, in want," *sordido vitam oblectabas pane, in pannis, inopia*, 142), wishing he could put the women back where he found them, "at the far limit of poverty" (139); so the unnamed *lena* explains why she pimps out her daughter Gymnasium ("so I wouldn't go hungry," *ut ne essurirem*; "She gets married every day ... / if she didn't keep marrying, the household would die of sad starvation," *cottidie viro nubit ... / nam si haec non nubat, lugubri fame familia pereat, Cist.* 41, 43, 45); so Scapha warns Philematium that she needs a permanent meal ticket (*victum sempiternum*, 224); so Astaphium tells the audience in her solo ("We remember when he was rich and he remembers when we were poor," *nos divitem istum meminimus atque iste pauperes nos, Truc.* 220). Philippa in *Epidicus* was a poor girl when Periphanes raped her, as he recalls ("the poor girl I remember I stuffed in Epidauros," *in Epidauro pauperculam memini comprimere, Epid.* 540a–b, cf. 554–7, and chapter 7).

Hunger is used to control slaves: the *vilicus* Olympio threatens to starve Chalinus (*Cas.* 126–9):

> post autem ruri nisi tu acervom <ervi> ederis
> aut quasi lumbricus terram, quod te postules

gustare quicquam, numquam edepol ieiunium
ieiunumst aeque atque ego te ruri reddibo.

> But later, in the country, unless you eat a heap of hay,
> or dirt, like an earthworm, when you ask
> to have a bite to eat, by God, hunger itself is never
> so hungry as I'll make you in the country.

This threat goes along with others to bend Chalinus in two from carry-ing water "so they could make a crupper out of you" (125), and to make him listen while Olympio and Casina have sex, trapped in the wall like a mouse; the starvation is part of a general program to transform Chalinus into an animal or an object. Not a happy object, either; a crupper is a band that holds a saddle on a horse by looping under its tail. Olympio will be hungry himself before his wedding (801–3). Philolaches, eaves-dropping, threatens Scapha with "hunger and cold" (*fameque atque algu*, *Mos.* 193) and specifies that he will stop her food and drink for ten days (237–8). Milphio envies Syncerastus for his access to both plentiful food and free sex in the pimp's house (*Poen.* 867–8, esp. *domi sit quod edis, quod ames adfatim*, "At home you've got something to eat and love til you're full"). Sceledrus resents Palaestrio because his sycophancy has endeared him to the owner's live-in *amica*: "He is called first for food, the meat bits are given to him first" (*primus ad cibum vocatur, primo pulmentum datur, Mil.* 349).[66] Meat here is the bonus, the good part that they might run out of. Hunger makes slaves as unscrupulous as a comedian, a poor man; Pinacium calls the *puer* Phaniscus a *parasitus* because he can be made to do anything for food (*Mos.* 888). Or less scrupulous: as Stasimus' impov-erished owner politely argues about what food he would accept from a rich man's *clientes* at a public dinner, a *cena popularis*, Stasimus bursts out ravenously (*Trin.* 474–7):

> ST. at pol ego etsi votet
> edim atque ambabus malis expletis vorem,   475
> et quod illi placeat praeripiam potissumum

---

[66] *Pulmentum*, according to Varro, was so called because it was what you ate with *puls*, and *pulmen-tarium* was derived from this (*L.* 5.108); *puls*, he says, was "the most ancient of foods" (*de victu antiquissima*, 5.105). It was a kind of porridge; Varro repeats an etymology that attributes the word to the sound it made when immersed in boiling water, as if it were called "plop" or "blurp." The sense of *pulmentum* as "meat" is deduced mainly from the specific instances of *pulmentarium*, all strongly flavored, hence usually translated "relish." *Pulmentum* itself, however, was evidently only a supplement to the main food item. This suggests the force of the meat meals craved by *parasiti* in the plays: extraordinary fare. See Briscoe 2010: 156–7, on *pulmentum/pulmentarium* in Cato's *Origines*; on *puls*, Gowers 1993: 53–6, and esp. Purcell 2003: 332–6 on foodways and cultural identity, with brief discussion of Plautus at 335. Compare Gripus' restricted diet (*Rud.* 937–37a), chapter 8 below.

neque illi concedam quicquam de vita mea.

> ST. But, by god, even if he said no,
> I'd eat and gobble it down with both cheeks stuffed,   475
> and what he liked, I'd grab that first of all
> and I wouldn't give him a bit of what meant life to me.

Stasimus' owner is arguing about what favors he might take from a rich man (*opulentus*) with a rich man who wants to do him a favor; Stasimus, like an unrepressed id, cannot be so polite. Times are hard, he explains (*hac annona,* "with the price of groceries this high," 484).[67] His attitude, in a play centered on class tensions, bespeaks a general anxiety, not unrealistic.

Verifying Sagaristio's complaint about men like his owner, "who lock the silverware away from a slave and the salt with it," owners comment grudgingly on the cost of feeding slaves. That this has some grounding in social circumstances is suggested by the budget Cato sets up in *De agricultura* for the allocation of food, drink, and clothing to farm slaves, including those in chains (56–9), and by the provisions made for chaining and feeding debtors in the XII Tables (*Tab.* III, Gellius 20.1.45): fifteen pounds of chain minimum, one pound of grits (*far*) per day.[68] Neither Cato nor the XII Tables makes any mention of *pulmentum* – Cato's diet is basically bread and *pulmentarium,* "relish" (figs, olives, fish sauce, vinegar, oil, salt). In any case, the urban households in the *palliata* are portrayed as subject to food control. The *senex* Antipho in *Stichus* exits his house, threatening beatings to a household he calls "pigs" (64), and taunting them with their eagerness to accept their monthly allowance of food – a slave cannot remember his duty, but "You all remember on the first of the month to look for your food rations" (*vos meministis quotcalendis petere demensum cibum,* 60).[69] The pimp Dordalus in *Persa* (who has a similar entrance speech, 731–2) rejoices to get Lemniselenis off his hands so he will no longer have to

---

[67] For the expression *hac annona* and the vocabulary of hunger, and on public banquets and distributions of food, see chapter 1, and further in chapter 4 below.

[68] See further Gowers 2012: 203–4 on Hor. *S.* 1.5.68–9, discussed in chapter 3 below. On the feeding of slaves in Cato, see Dalby 1998 *ad loc.* The use of hunger as a form of social control onstage has not been much addressed by historians of ancient slavery, who do usually discuss the agricultural handbooks on this point; so on management techniques in general, Bradley 2015: 155–9. See Hunter 1994: 162 on Xenophon, *Mem.* 2.1.15–17, where Socrates says owners use starvation to curb slaves' lust; Cox 2013: 165 on food deprivation as a slave punishment in the *Nea*.

[69] This joke is the cousin of a joke at Herodas, *Mim.* 6.4–7, where the slave is waiting for her rations, described as *alphita*; Purcell 2003: 333 n. 9 says that when Pliny (*HN* 18.84) opposes Greek *polenta* to Latin *puls,* he means *alphita,* which he is calling by its Latin name. *Krithê,* "barleycorns," which are ground into *alphita,* were the punishment rations assigned to the survivors of a decimation in the Roman army, a source of shame (Plb. 6.38.3). See chapter 7 below and Richlin 2017b: 181–2 on the joke: as the joke circulates, the food changes.

feed her: "Today I've saved myself two loaves of bread a day / ... today, now, she'll be dining off somebody else, she won't taste anything of mine" (*ego hodie compendi feci binos panis in dies / ... iam hodie alienum cenabit, nihil gustabit de meo*, 471–3). Ballio taunts his slaves and prostitutes with eating too much in the midst of his long tirade (*Ps.* 139–42, 183–4), while Phronesium in *Truculentus* complains repeatedly about the cost of supporting her staff, both permanent (the two new Syrian *ancillae* "to eat up my food," *quae mihi comedint cibum, Truc.* 534) and temporary (903–4). Even a *parasitus* can begrudge food like an owner; so an unnamed *parasitus* to an unnamed *puer*: "You can eat up a loaf of bread three feet wide, / but you don't know how to knock on a door" (*comesse panem tris pedes latum potes, / fores pultare nescis, Bac.* 580–1). Daemones defines himself to his slave Sceparnio as "the one who gave money for you" (*qui pro te argentum dedit, Rud.* 98), and tells him he has to keep his mind on Daemones since Daemones is the one who feeds him (183). The slave fisherman Gripus sings of his own hunger (*Rud.* 937–37a), and of how he works to relieve "my owner's poverty and my own slavery" (this same Daemones, 918), the two of them, then, not being so far apart in terms of bodily comforts.

Thus in the same play the chorus of fishermen sing a song about their hunger (290–305), with the opening lines, "In every way, poor people live miserably, / especially those who have no livelihood, who have learned no trade" (*omnibu' modis qui pauperes sunt homines miseri vivont, / praesertim quibu' nec quaestus est neque didicere artem ullam*, 290–1). Unless they make a good catch, "we go to bed without dinner" (*dormimus incenati*, 302). Evidently they share Gripus' occupation and hunger, even though they are not slaves; the lack of *quaestus* or *ars* addresses a city full of the displaced poor, who, as seen above, inhabited a world in which *quaestus* and *ars* earned varying degrees of respect. The slave Trachalio – a rich young man's body servant, better off than they are – greets them as "you starving breed of persons" (*famelica hominum natio*) and asks them "How are you doing? How are you dying?" (*quid agitis? ut peritis?*, 311); they reply, "As is fair for a fisherman: of hunger and thirst and false hope" (*ut piscatorem aequomst, fame sitique speque falsa*, 312). The hunger of the free poor likewise appears in the fragments of *Vidularia*, as the evidently shipwrecked (fr. i), city-soft (35) Nicodemus begs Dinia for work as a farm laborer. Dinia tells Nicodemus that anyone he hires will work a lot, earn little, and eat little (49); Nicodemus assures him that he will need minimum food and provide maximum labor (*cibique minimi maxumaque industria*, 42), and that Dinia will have to feed him only breakfast plus his wages – no lunch, no dinner (50–3).

In contrast, the freed slave Advocati of *Poenulus* take great pride in their ability to feed themselves and tell Agorastocles he is foolish for complaining that they would work harder if he were feeding them (533–9):

> ADV. an vero non iusta caussa est qur curratur celeriter
> ubi bibas, edas de alieno quantum velis usque ad fatim,
> quod tu invitus numquam reddas domino de quoio ederis?   535
> sed tamen cum eo cum quiqui, quamquam sumu' pauperculi,
> est domi quod edimus, ne nos tam contemptim conteras.
> quidquid est pauxillulum illuc, omne nostrum id intus est,
> neque nos quemquam flagitamus neque nos quisquam flagitat.

> Well, really, isn't it fully justified for someone to run fast
> where you can eat and drink off somebody else as much as you want,
>   til you're full,
> what you'll never have to repay, if you don't want to, to the
>   householder off whom you're eating?   535
> But howsomever and wherefore, although we're poor guys,
> we have something to eat at home, no need for you to grind us down
>   so snootily.
> Whatever that little bit is, it's all ours, at our house.[70]
> We don't dun anybody and nobody duns us.

Like the envied Syncerastus (*quoi domi sit quod edis*), they "have something to eat at home" (*est domi quod edimus*), like the man *quoi paratumst quod edit* in the *Poenulus* prologue; like Milphio, their desire is to eat until they feel full (*ad fatim* expresses a subjective feeling). They have internalized the grudging owner's idea that slaves eat "off" the owner (534 *edas de alieno*, 535 *domino de quoio edis*, compare Dordalus *alienum cenabit*, *Per.* 473, and Daemones' *de illarum*, *Rud.* 181), while implying that the owner expects something in return which, as slaves, they did not want to give (535, *invitus numquam reddas*). Their indignant assertion that they are self-supporting likewise recalls Harpax's insistence that he has bought all his gear out of his own *peculium* (above); as will be seen in chapter 3, a good credit rating and fiscal respect are hard for a slave to come by, while the public shaming of *flagitatio* (539) could ruin a reputation: not theirs. At the end of their scene with him, the Advocati say of Agorastocles to the audience, "This one demands a markedly insulting injustice: / he thinks we should be his slave and buy our own lunch" (*iniuriam illic insignite postulat: / nostro servire nos sibi censet cibo*, 809–10). Poor as they are, they accuse the rich man of *iniuria*, an affront to honor. *Iniuria* in law was a delict,

---

[70] Retaining MSS *intus est*; see further below on *domi* (chapter 3).

an actionable offense; offstage, not a claim available to the low against the high, thus a radical claim when invoked by the low onstage.[71]

Doubling down, the Advocati step out of character during their scene and let on to the *spectatores* that they, along with Agorastocles and the *vilicus*, are all actors who have rehearsed together (550–4). As Moore comments (1998: 12), like the Sycophanta in *Trinummus*, they not only say they are actors but identify themselves as poor: *sumu' pauperculi* (536). Indeed, from the outset, after Agorastocles ends a long list of insults for their slowness by asking them if they learned to walk that way from wearing fetters, they vigorously present their own class perspective (515–21):

> ADV. heus tu, quamquam nos videmur tibi plebeii et pauperes,   515
> si nec recte dicis nobis dives de summo loco,
> divitem audacter solemus mactare infortunio.
> nec tibi nos obnoxii istuc quid tu ames aut oderis:
> quom argentum pro capite dedimus, nostrum dedimus, non tuom;
> liberos nos esse oportet. nos te nihili pendimus,   520
> ne tuo nos amori servos esse addictos censeas.

> ADV. Hey, you, although we look to you like plebeians and poor men,   515
> if you don't talk right to us, you rich man, from your topmost position,
> we know how to stick a rich man with bad luck, no fear.
> We're not liable to you for what you love – or what you hate,
> when we gave cash for our *caput*, we gave our money, not yours;
> it behooves us to be free men. You carry no weight with us,   520
> so don't think we're slaves bonded out to your love problems.

Like Sosia in *Amphitruo*, they blame the *dives* for his restricted point of view; unlike him, they say they know how to make rich men suffer, and can tell Agorastocles to his face that he carries no weight with them (517, 520).[72] Their label of Agorastocles as *dives de summo loco* invokes a common pejorative label in the plays (chapter 3). They reject both the position of being *obnoxii*, which, as will be seen, is part of slavery (chapter 6), and the status of debt-slave (*addictos*, 521); and they identify

---

[71] The delict of *iniuria* was grounded in the XII Tables (Paul. *Sent.* 5.4.6); see Frier 1989: 177–200. One main use was to repress *clamor* and *convicium*, especially in verse; perhaps in play in Metelli v. Naevius. The popular courtroom of the *palliata* staged both the *clamor* and the charge. Onstage, *iniuria* is invoked by slaves against owners (*Epid.* 715; *Rud.* 669–70, 1138; *Truc.* 836); by actors against officials (*Poen.* 37); associated with *quiritatio* (*Men.* 1008; *Rud.* 626, 643) and with rape (*Aul.* 794; *Cist.* 180). Note esp. *As.* 497, Leonida to the Mercator, claiming respect *quamquam ego sum sordidatus* (see chapter 3, and, on dark, dirty clothing as a mark of the working class, Richlin 2014a: 283–4).

[72] Fantham 2005: 222 chose this speech to illustrate her argument that "What we do find in both Plautus and Ennius is not criticism of any named grandee but the language of popular protest."

themselves as freedmen who saved up to buy themselves out of slavery, claiming their *peculium* as "our money" (519; compare the *quod dem* of the *lorarius*, discussed above). Their pride resonates with Paegnium's jeer that he is working towards freedom, even if by prostituting himself, and with the *Poenulus* prologue's suggestion to slaves that "they should give coin for their *caput*" (*aes pro capite dent*, 24). Everybody wants to have *quod det*.

Parasiti liken themselves, or are likened, to slaves, most elaborately Peniculus on the similarity between economic dependency and slavery (*Men.* 77–97):

> PE. Iuventus nomen fecit Peniculo mihi,
> ideo quia mensam quando edo detergeo.
> homines captivos qui catenis vinciunt
> et qui fugitivis servis indunt compedis,   80
> nimi' stulte faciunt mea quidem sententia.
> nam homini misero si ad malum accedit malum,
> maior lubido est fugere et facere nequiter.
> nam se ex catenis eximunt aliquo modo.
> tum compediti ei anum lima praeterunt   85
> aut lapide excutiunt clavom. nugae sunt eae.
> quem tu adservare recte ne aufugiat voles
> esca atque potione vinciri decet.
> apud mensam plenam homini rostrum deliges;
> dum tu illi quod edit et quod potet praebeas,   90
> suo arbitratu ad fatim cottidie,
> numquam edepol fugiet, tam etsi capital fecerit,
> facile adservabis, dum eo vinclo vincies.
> ita istaec nimi' lenta vincla sunt escaria:
> quam magis extendas tanto astringunt artius.   95
> nam ego ad Menaechmum hunc <nunc> eo, quo iam diu
> sum iudicatus; ultro eo ut me vinciat.

> The young men have given me the name "Peniculus,"
> because ... when I eat I wipe the table right off.
> Those who bind captive persons with chains
> and who put fetters on fugitive slaves,   80
> act really stupidly, at least in my opinion.
> For if a miserable person gets beating after beating,
> his desire is greater to run away and act badly.
> For they get themselves out of the chains somehow –
> even if they're fettered, they grind off a link with a file,   85
> or break off the pin with a stone. That's all foolishness.
> If you want to keep a guy in check right, so he won't run,
> he should be bound with edibles and drinkables.

> At a full table you'll tie up the guy's snout;
> while you offer him something to eat and something to drink,   90
> until he feels full, in his judgment, every day,
> by God he'll never run, even if he's committed a capital crime,
> you'll easily keep him in check, while you bind him with this bond.
> So those edible chains are only too clingy:
> the more you stretch them out, the tighter they grip him.   95
> See, I'm going to this Menaechmus now, whose debt-slave
> I've long been – I go voluntarily, for him to bind me.

The sexual body of the *parasitus* here leads to his stomach via bondage: he is clear that he has sold himself for food, just as Stasimus professes his willingness to take a handout, and the Advocati say they would like to eat at another's expense. Like the Advocati and Milphio, Peniculus sees it as desirable to eat until you feel full (*ad fatim*, 91), using the vocabulary of satiety like the *Poenulus* prologue speaker. Figuratively speaking, Peniculus has been "adjudged" to Menaechmus (*sum iudicatus*, 97) – that is, he is his debt-slave; Plautus is said to have written a play called *Addictus* while working in the mill (see chapter 1), there are *addicti* in Syncerastus' owner's brothel, the Advocati say indignantly "Don't think we're slaves *addicti* to your love problems" (*ne tuo nos amori servos esse addictos censeas, Poen.* 521). Peniculus himself compares himself to an animal with his snout tied to a feed-trough (89).

So other *parasiti* describes themselves as saleable, as objects, even animals, as the *vilicus* Olympio animalizes the slave Chalinus in *Casina*. Gelasimus, who claims that *Fames* is the mother he has carried in his belly for more than ten years, like an elephant (*St.* 160, 163–70), says he is ready to sell himself – "I'm for sale, with my whole outfit" (*venalis ego sum cum ornamentis omnibus*, 172) – as prostitutes are sold with their accessories (part of their costume).[73] He proceeds to line up all his goods – his jokes and his pitiful trappings – for an auction (218–33); his misery suggests what made the auctioneer (*praeco*) such a despised figure, and underlines the irony of the dutiful Messenio's transformation into a *praeco* at the end of *Menaechmi* (1155–62). Compare the auction that punishes the pimp at the end of *Poenulus* (1364), and the slave auction described by Chrysalus (*Bac.*

---

[73] So Planesium costs thirty minae plus ten for her gold and clothing, *Cur.* 344; Lucris costs sixty, again plus ten for her clothing (*Per.* 665–9); Phoenicium has been sold for twenty minae, "without her outfit, just with everything inside her skin" (*sine ornamentis, cum intestinis omnibus, Ps.* 343). The *senex* Periphanes at first volunteers to throw in the lyre (*fides*) with the *fidicina* (*Epid.* 473–4); then, when it turns out she is the wrong *fidicina*, and already free, to boot, he refuses to return it to her (514) – he must have been clutching it the whole time, a sight gag, for this musical instrument marks the player as sexually available. For the prices, see Callataÿ 2015: 25, 40.

815, above), or the slave auction in the probably Plautine *Hortulus*: "Let the *praeco* be there; let him/her be sold with a wreath for whatever price s/he will fetch" (*praeco ibi assit; cum corona quiqui liceat veneat*, fr. 91). Festus quotes this alongside Cato's joke about the wreathed *populus* at risk of sale (400L; chapter 1). Ergasilus in *Captivi* compares *parasiti* to dogs (85–7), and to mice (77), as does Saturio in *Persa* (58 – same line), and says he will bind himself over to Hegio, auctioning himself "as if I were a farm" (*quasi fundum vendam, … me addicam*, 181); Saturio in *Persa* is ready to sell not only his daughter but himself for a meal (145–6). The other play Plautus is supposed to have written in the mill was called *Saturio*, and Paul the Deacon has a shred of it: "That the Romans 'liked to eat' dog flesh, that is they ate it up, Plautus reports in *Saturio*" (*catulinam carnem esitavisse, hoc est comedisse, Romanos, Plautus in Saturione refert*, Paulus 39L = fr. 110): a joke, perhaps, like other complaints of *parasiti* about how they are abused – the biter bit, as it were.

When the shipwrecked pimp in *Rudens*, teeth chattering with cold, jokes, "Why don't I hire myself out somewhere as a Manducus at the games" (*quid si aliquo ad ludos me pro manduco locem*, 535), he brings onstage the toothy mask of the starving man, played for pay by a hungry actor (chapter 1). The unnamed Sycophanta in *Trinummus*, who is hired (for three *nummi*) from the forum like a cook or a *fidicina*, says he is driven to his work by poverty (*egestas*, 847); likewise, Gelasimus says he was born in hard times (*per annonam caram*, *St.* 179), and that he got his name from poverty, which made him be funny (175, 177). When he begs for a place at a long-awaited dinner, saying he would take up only the room a caged dog might lie down in, his patrons insult him like a slave (619–27); they tell him to go to the *carcer*, and, when he says that he will go there, but after dinner, they say he would crucify himself for a dinner or lunch. "That's my nature," he says; "I'll fight it out with anyone much more easily than with Starvation" (*ita ingenium meumst. | quicumvis depugno multo facilius quam cum Fame*, 626–7). They go off without him, and he interrogates himself (and the audience): "You see how heavy the cost of groceries is?" (*vides ut annonast gravis*, 633–5). The cost of food, the *annona*, marks the poor man's distance from the rich man.[74] Gelasimus goes off to hang himself, saying he will fill up his gullet with a "hemp drink" (*potione iuncea onerabo gulam*, 639), so no one will say he died of hunger. Pain makes comedy: the

---

[74] See chapter 1. Phrases with *annona* are associated with hunger also by the *parasitus* Ergasilus (*Capt.* 495) and the slave Stasimus (*Trin.* 484). On poverty, hunger, and the *parasitus*, see Pansiéri 1997: 409–33.

ancilla Crocotium, admiring his desperate rant early in the play, remarks, "There's nobody as funny as he is when he's hungry" (*ridiculus aeque nullus est, quando essurit*, 217).

The Comedian's Body

The name "T. Maccius Plautus" seems, like a slave name, not to be a name given at birth; all three names belong to the world of low theater, of the phallus, the flatfoot mime, and the Atellan fool. If the comedian chose it for himself – a stage name – he was putting a sendup of the *tria nomina* on the marquee: so much for the *summi viri*. The prologue speaker of *Casina* calls him "Plautus with the barking name" (*Plautus cum latranti nomine, Cas.* 34), perhaps aligning him with the itinerant Cynic philosophers with whom the *parasitus* Saturio claims kinship (*Per.* 123–6). Conversely, the famous riddling invocation of the "barbarian poet" (*poetae … barbaro*), who was taken in antiquity to be Naevius, is part of the description of the slave Palaestrio thinking (*Mil.* 209–12). Palaestrio here is the spirit of comedy; he poses *euscheme … et dulice et comoedice* (213), "becomingly, like a slave, like a comedian." Palaestrio's pose, chin on fist, was mass-produced in souvenir terracottas of slaves on altars.[75] The *parasiti* repeatedly define their work as telling jokes in return for food, and treat their words concretely as their stock in trade: a trunk full of "books" with "six hundred stories, / all Attic, not one Sicilian one" in lieu of a dowry (*librorum … plenum soracum,/ … sescenti logei/ atque Attici omnes; nullum Siculum, Per.* 392–95); an auction of "funny stories" (*logos ridiculos, St.* 221–33); "books" (*libros*) with "funny stories" (*ridiculis logis, St.* 454, 455; cf. *Capt.* 482–3). When he thinks he will be fed, Gelasimus cries, "I'm not selling my stories" (*non vendo logos, St.* 383); when he hears his patrons have imported *parasitos ridiculissumos* in their Asian cargo, he laments, "Now my stories are for sale, that I said I wouldn't sell" (*venales logi sunt illi quos negabam*

---

[75] On Plautus' biography and the story of Naevius, see chapter 1; on Plautus' name, see Gratwick 1973, esp. 82 on the class implications of the *tria nomina* in this period. Gratwick is agnostic on the meaning of the "barking name" (78 n. 6, on Paulus 259L), but surely it recalls the self-comparisons by *parasiti* to dogs and to Cynic philosophers, the Dog-men (see above). For the pertinent sources on Naevius and the *Miles* passage, see Beare 1964: 40–1; the link to Naevius comes from Paulus (32L): *Plautus Naevium poetam Latinum 'barbarum' dixit*, "Plautus called Naevius, the Latin poet, 'barbarian.'" For the identification of slave and writer here, see Fitzgerald 1995: 56–8. The slave sits chin in hand (209, *aedificat: columnam mento suffigit suo*); the poet does something else (210–12, *non placet profecto mihi … / nam os columnatum poetae esse indaudivi barbaro/ quo bini custodes semper totis horis occubant*), a typical Plautine analogical joke. Allen was surely right to see here a reference to some kind of pillory (1896: 37–40, 54–64; *contra*, Corbeill 2004: 78–9). For figurines in this pose, see Csapo and Slater 1994: plate 9, and the image on this book's cover.

vendere, 393).[76] Comedians themselves were part of the traffic in shtick. The arch-slave Pseudolus also compares himself to a *poeta* who writes from his imagination onto the page (*Ps.* 401–4), and tells his dupe Simo that Simo can write any due punishment on his body (544a–45):

> quasi in libro quom scribuntur calamo litterae,
> stilis me totum usque ulmeis conscribito.
>
> Like when letters are written in a book with a pen,
> you can write me all over with elmwood styluses.[77]

The *Poenulus* prologue speaker calls Plautus *Pultiphagonides*, "Son of an Eater of Grits" (*Poen.* 54). These are good doorposts, says Tranio; "no *puls*-eating barbarian workman did this work" (*non enim haec pultiphagus opifex opera fecit barbarus, Mos.* 828).[78] The old men he is fooling think he means a carpenter, but Tranio is making them into doorposts, as the audience can see, and he is the *puls*-eating *opifex barbarus*. The polenta eaten by the *Graeci palliati* so despised by Curculio is poor men's food, and the *palliati* are standing on the stage – Curculio is one of them (*Cur.* 288–95). The drooling speeches, the cast of characters, the facts of life, bespeak writers, players, and audience that have known hunger and physical pain.

---

[76] On the commodification of comedians and jokebooks, see Beard 2014: 202–9; Richlin 2016, 2017b. See chapter 1 on the *opifex* and the Cales potters.

[77] On Pseudolus and other central slaves as figures for the comic poet, see Sharrock 2009: 116–40; Slater 1985: 118–46.

[78] On *pultiphagonides* and *pultiphagus* as emblems of the Italian comedian, see Gowers 1993: 53–7.

CHAPTER 3

Singing for Your Supper

The satirist Horace did not like Plautus, and based his critique on money (*Epistles* 2.1.168–76):[1]

> Creditur, ex medio quia res arcessit, habere
> sudoris minimum, sed habet comoedia tanto   170
> plus oneris, quanto veniae minus. Adspice Plautus
> quo pacto partes tutetur amantis ephebi,
> ut patris attenti, lenonis ut insidiosi,
> quantus sit Dossennus edacibus in parasitis,
> quam non adstricto percurrat pulpita socco.   175
> Gestit enim nummum in loculos demittere, post hoc
> securus cadat an recto stet fabula talo.

> Comedy, because it summons its subject matter from what's at hand,
> is believed to take minimal sweat, but, [compared with tragedy],   170
> it's as much more work as it is less easily liked. Look at Plautus,
> how he tends to the characters of the young man in love,
> of the frugal father, of the tricky pimp,
> what a Dossennus he is among his voracious *parasiti*,
> how he runs across the stage with his *soccus* untied.   175
> See, he's astretch to put coin in his cash-box, after that
> he doesn't care if his play falls down or stands up straight.

As Juvenal remarked a century later, Horace had a full belly, thanks to his full moneybox (7.62); the satirist can afford to look down on Plautus, and sets him onstage, in the guise of a stock character from Atellan farce, among the *parasiti*, running like a slave, wearing the shoes of a comic actor,

---

[1] "The satirist Horace": I make no claim about the historical Horace. This passage, with *Ars Poetica* 270–4, has been very widely discussed; for overviews, see Ferriss-Hill 2015: 197–8; Manuwald 2011: 172; and esp. Lowe 1989, Stärk 1995. The comparison between comedy and tragedy and the comedian's claim that comedy is harder go back at least to Antiphanes' comedy *Poiêsis* (fr. 189, Ath. 6.222c–223a): Horace here knocks comic shtick by appropriating comic shtick. For adumbrations in Aristophanes, see Ferriss-Hill 2015: 72–8; on the Antiphanes fragment, Slater 2014: 108–9.

all for money.[2] In fact the plays themselves make it a point of pride: actors are professionals, onstage to make their living; highly skilled, but low in the social scale. They wear *socci* as a badge of honor. As seen in chapter 2, actors, like *parasiti*, sing for their supper, to an audience that knows what labor costs. As seen in chapter 1, they did so in a wartime economy. This chapter ties the song to the supper: poverty, debt, and hunger, and the fears of a *populus* in times of war, found expression in oral forms that actors in the *palliata* took to the bank.

Despite commonalities, then, between actors and some audience members, a constant theme in the plays, especially in prologues, works to separate the players from the audience: actors are "us," the audience is "you." As seen in chapter 1, this distance is a structural element of all theater and endows the actor with authority and glamor. In Roman theater generally, already by the time vernacular tragedy and the *palliata* become visible to us, this distance allowed those on the stage to speak of political issues in coded terms that audiences could pick up on, despite the danger; in later periods, we know they did.[3] In the *palliata*, this distance, augmented by the use of masks, allowed the players to speak of themselves and the circumstances entailed by their social position, and to set themselves apart from the official endeavors of the Roman state, or any state. As Timothy Moore has demonstrated (1998), the actors, by both pleading with and commanding the audience, fluctuate between a marked lower position and a marked usurpation of power. This is the quintessence of the comedian's art.

Moreover, the plays are permeated by familiar popular forms that put the audience into the familiar position of onlookers at a shouting match. What is at stake, often: honor, credit, money, civil status. Just as the presence of prostitutes on the city stage overlaps with the everyday presence of prostitutes in the city streets and market spaces, so the insult matches and scenes of dunning in the plays superimpose the audience, essentially sitting in the street, over the same space where they might see the same kind

---

[2] Comedy shoes: wearing *socci* – soft-soled shoes – is a running joke in the *palliata*. They leave tracks onstage (*Cist.* 697–8); Epidicus' owner swears to supply him, as he frees him, with clothing (including the comedian's *pallium*) and *socci* (*Epid.* 725); a rich man is said to have had soles fastened onto his *socci* with gold (*Bac.* 332); Stasimus, about to run away with his young owner to join the army, says he must have "stiffeners" (i.e. ankle supports) fastened into his *socci* (*Trin.* 720; see chapter 8); Saturio says that a *parasitus* has to be like a Cynic philosopher, whose accessories include *socci* and a *pallium* (*Per.* 124). Clown shoes, metatheatrical shoes: omnipresent *socci*, freedmen's *socci*, rich men's *socci*, soldiers' *socci*, Cynic *socci*. A joke similar to Atellana titles like *Maccus Miles* (attested in the later literary Atellana), or the title of the probably Plautine *Parasitus Medicus*.

[3] See, for later periods, Bartsch 1994; on political interpretations of drama by audiences in the Republic, Kruschwitz 2013.

of scenes enacted by amateurs on any given day. As best we can tell from
later sources, these scenes occupied a well-demarcated space in the social
hierarchy: low.[4] Cheers, dunning (*flagitatio*), and cries for help (*quiritatio*)
are uniformly associated with crowds in the street, while *occentatio* (a sort
of charivari) is performed by a crowd unruly if not always low-class. Yet
these practices followed a set format, with rules of its own, and the actors
are amazingly good at it – professionals – courting the audience's admiration. These verse forms as preserved in the record of the *palliata* are, in the
terms used by Giulio Colesanti (2014) and Riccardo Palmisciano (2014),
"emerged texts," as opposed to the "submerged texts" that enjoyed scarce
transmission. The actors and their comedy, then, mark themselves as low
by means of formal elements as well as by explicit metatheatrical speeches
to the audience, but also claim to be worth watching. Both as actors and as
professional jokers, they repeatedly insist that this is how they feed themselves. Prostitute to *parasitus*: "You're talking trash!" *Parasitus*: "I always
do – trash is what I live on" (*nugas garris. #soleo, nam propter eas vivo
facilius, Cur.* 604).

The prologue speaker of *Captivi*, an actor, in explaining the plight of
Tyndarus, pauses for some editorial comment (50–2):

> ita nunc ignorans suo sibi servit patri;   50
> homunculi quanti sunt, quom recogito!
> haec res agetur nobis, vobis fabula.

> So, now, in ignorance, he is a slave belonging to his own father;   50
> how much are little guys worth, when I come to think about it!
> This action will be real for us, a play for you.

Lindsay translates line 52, "fact on the boards, fiction for the benches"
(1921: 74). *Res* here surely has a double meaning: "the matter of our play,"
"the internal reality of the play," and "reality for us actors," with the consciousness of the presence of slaves and freedmen behind (some) masks.
Moore puts it strongly, spelling out the prologue speaker's meaning: "'To
you free spectators,' he says, 'this is only a fiction, but we (the slave actors
and the previously-mentioned slave spectators) know the reality of slavery'" (1998: 196). Lines 50–1 are the more emphatic in that they repeat an
idea expressed earlier in the prologue, as the speaker points to one of the
two men standing in chains on the stage: "He now, back home here, is a
slave belonging his father, nor does his father know; / it's a fact that the
gods use us human beings like balls" (*hic nunc domi servit suo patri, nec scit*

---

[4] For the low register, see Fantham 2005: 223, allocating *flagitatio* to "the humble."

pater; / enim vero di nos quasi pilas homines habent, 21–2; the reference is to a game of catch).[5] Indeed, the speaker, as he begins to speak, points first to the two men (line 1), then to those in the audience who are standing (line 2), and then to the house that forms the backdrop (4), and poses the question of "how this guy comes to be a slave belonging to his own father" (*is quo pacto serviat suo sibi patri*, 5) as the subject of the prologue (*apud vos proloquar*, 6).[6] The ambiguity of *homunculi quanti sunt* (51) is hard to convey in English: *homunculi* are persons for whom the speaker feels compassion, seeing them as small, weak, or obscure; *quanti sunt* means "are worth how much," "what is the price of," and here cues an exclamation. If line 51 continues the thought in line 50, it opens up an issue rarely discussed openly in Latin: not the play's far-fetched situation whereby a father unknowingly purchases his own lost son, but the everyday situation in which owners impregnated their own slave-women, the resulting *vernae* then not being acknowledged as sons and daughters. Plautus' audience would have been conscious of this as we are not, and from many angles. Likewise, the movements of the speaker's masked face, his gestures, would enable him to include some audience members in *homunculi quanti sunt* and *nobis*, others in *vobis*. Explicitly, however, this play is about war captives who are sold as slaves, a description that applies roughly to at least some of the comic writers we hear about: Livius Andronicus, Caecilius Statius, Terence. This is the players' story; this is what war means to them. And, as they took their show on the road, they moved through a war-torn landscape, belonging nowhere now themselves – an experience also shared by some in their various audiences.[7]

The plays are set in the street. Accordingly, they are full of street noise. Italian oral forms belong to the time and place the actors moved through; the content of the form derives meaning from its historical location. The choice by actors and playwright to adopt these forms into the *palliata*

[5] Cf. *Truc.* 706, Naevius *Tarentilla* 75–79R with discussion in Wright 1974: 35–6, and *Cur.* 296–7, in a double entendre. Notably, all these passages are metaphorical.

[6] The question of what is meant by *illi quia astant*, "because those men are standing here" (2), has been the topic of much discussion; see Moore (1994/5: 114, 118–19; 1998: 11, 195) for the argument that it means audience members without seats, accepted by de Melo (2011a: 511). Moore identifies these persons with "slaves and other poor spectators," in connection with income distinctions in the subsequent lines, and that must be the case in the *Captivi* prologue. There is no real reason, however, to think that general seating was usually differentiated by civil status rather than first-come-first-serve; see Marshall 2006: 78 on the dynamics of seating in the *cavea*, and further below, in the section on debt.

[7] All three came from war zones; if not taken directly in a siege (Terence was certainly born between the wars), they were part of the collateral damage. On *Captivi* and audience members with kin amongst the Roman soldiers taken at Cannae, see Leigh 2004: 86–96.

marks the plays as not-Greek; also, like the popular stories studied by Rebecca Langlands, the forms are a kind of "shared language." In turning now to verbal dueling, *flagitatio, occentatio, quiritatio*, and what I here call "cheerleading," I hope to show how the relationship between form and history takes shape, and what the forms have to do with the lives of actors and audience.

Cheerleading

Among the fourteen extant prologues, six incorporate a sort of cheerleading, in which the prologue speaker praises the prowess of the audience and the state in war, and/or wishes them success in their current military endeavor. In all these wishes, the speaker uses the second person plural: this is *your* war. Of course all the prologues, which address the crowd directly, naturally use the second plural throughout, but there is still something about the way these wishes are framed that separates them from the actors, and makes the whole endeavor of war – or the audience's wars – something from which the cast is separated.

There is some reason to think that that would in fact have been the case for Rome itself. (As will be seen, the cheerleading speeches are quite generic, and could have been played as well in Praeneste or any other town the troupe visited; both Praeneste and Tibur had their own cults to Victoria.[8]) As noted in chapter 1, most of the actors in the *palliata* were not Roman citizens at all, so that the civil disabilities that later attended actors, keeping them out of the military, would have been irrelevant for them: too low, too outside, to be eligible for the Roman army in the first place. So were the poorest citizens, the *proletarii*, who held only an unenvied eligibility to row in the fleet. This is not to say that slaves, freedmen, and outsiders had no experience in the Roman armed forces, for all these categories had such experience, at times, throughout the 200s and to Polybius' day, in various capacities; moreover, the army itself was divided into ranks according to census classes determined by property, so that property differentiated the military experience of male citizens and their families – especially so in the city (see chapter 2).[9] Onstage jokes using military language addressed this wide range of experience. But onstage victory cheers addressed the whole

---

[8] Weinstock 1957: at Praeneste, 215 n. 19; at Tibur, a cult for Hercules Victor, 217. On Victoria at Rome, see also Clark 2007: 56–8. On touring, see chapter 7.

[9] Welwei concludes his discussion of *calones* (free and slave workers on the infantry supply train) with the observation that at least some of them had combat experience (1988: 77).

audience, many of whom could only be civilians, for whom defeat meant the sack of the city, ruin, and a strong chance of death or enslavement. As seen in chapter 1, audiences at the *ludi Romani* wore the laurel crowns of victors from 293 BCE onwards, and Cato made a chilling joke about this practice: "That the *populus* might rather go hold a thanksgiving ceremony wearing wreaths, for a battle well fought by their own effort, than be sold wearing the wreath if the battle were badly fought" (*ut populus sua opera potius ob rem bene gestam coronatus supplicatum eat, quam re male gesta coronatus veneat*). The mass appeal of the goddess Victoria is suggested by an onstage joke in which the slave Truculentus jeers at Astaphium, a prostitute's slave-woman, betting her that her "Victorias" are made of wood (*Truc.* 275) – cheap ornaments made to look like gold, indicating that rich women wore Victoria, too. Rich women had more to lose; slave-women had already lost. It cannot be too often emphasized that Gellius put Plautus' *floruit* during the Second Punic War, when Hannibal was at the gates.[10]

The actors are removed from the war effort, yet they, with the audience, are engaged in something that has to do with it: the *ludi* themselves. The lengthy *Amphitruo* prologue brings in the audience's success, at home and "abroad" (*peregri*), in several places (1–14, 39–49, 73–80); as seen in chapter 2, the god Mercurius, the prologue speaker, takes credit for their success in trade, and gives credit to Jupiter for their success both generally and, specifically, in war. He then makes an elaborate series of metatheatrical arguments that locate Mercurius and Jupiter as actors inside the god costumes and suggest how familiar a sight were the gods of war on the wartime stage in the 200s BCE.[11] We will look at this prologue in detail before turning to the more formulaic cheerleading speeches in other prologues.

---

[10] Laurel wreaths for the audience: Livy 10.47.3; see Oakley 2005: 461–2 (probably only in years when there was a victory, but, in the 200s, that was most years) and Weinstock 1957: 216–17. Cato's joke is at Festus 400L, Gell. 6.4.5; cf. 6.4.3, explaining the expression *sub corona venire*, which refers to the sale of war captives (see Welwei 2000: 12–14 on this passage). The surprising attribution of this joke to Cato's lost *De re militari* (fr. 2) derives from explicit attributions in Festus and Gellius. See Astin 1978: 184–5, 204–5 on *De re militari*, and Richlin 2017a for further discussion. Victorias: usually taken to be earrings; Enk quips, "Truculentus contendit Victorias ex auribus Astaphii pendentes non aureas esse" (1953: 2.75), but there are no *aures* here. Perhaps *fibulae*? The next line is *ne attigas me* (276), so he has moved his hands towards them; brooches would cue a classic grope. Dutsch 2015: 21–2 comments on 276 but takes the Victorias to be bracelets. On "direct military appeals" in the prologues, see Gunderson 2015: 108–17; on the plays in the context of the lament for the fallen city, see Jeppesen 2016.

[11] For a detailed discussion of the *Amphitruo* prologue, see Moore 1998: 110–15; he shows how Mercurius builds rapport with the audience and notes that "Mercury speaks more lines of monologue than any other Plautine character" (115). See Beard 2003: 41–3 for the notion that *Amphitruo* is basically a "parody of triumphal mimesis," in that, at the *ludi Romani*, the presiding magistrate dressed as a

After Mercurius' remarks on how Jupiter fears a beating "no less than any of you" (27), he says he comes in peace, bringing peace (32), makes some general remarks on justice, and then, as prologue speakers do, asks the audience to pay attention – still in character as an actor in a god costume (38–45):

> nunc iam huc animum omnes quae loquar advortite.
> debetis velle quae velimus: meruimus
> et ego et pater de vobis et re publica;   40
> nam quid ego memorem (ut alios in tragoediis
> vidi, Neptunum, Virtutem, Victoriam,
> Martem, Bellonam commemorare quae bona
> vobis fecissent) quis benefactis meu' pater,
> deorum regnator, architectust omnibus?   45

> Right now, all of you turn your attention here, to what I'm saying.
> You ought to want what we want: we've earned it,
> both I and my father, from you and from the state;   40
> for why should I remind you (the way I've seen others,
> in tragedies, remind you – Neptune, Manliness, Victory,
> Mars, Bellona – of what good things
> they'd done for you) – [why should I remind you] of what good deeds
> my father, ruler of the gods, is the architect for all?   45

On the surface, the joke is that the god Mercurius is standing there on the stage asking the audience to be grateful to him and Jupiter, and doing so (appropriately for this god) in the language of the market: *meruimus*, "we've earned it." But, as seen in chapter 2, earned rewards are often laid claim to in the plays by those who hope to improve their lot, and what Mercurius asks for here is for the audience to pay attention to the play; the benefit is to the actors, not to the gods, unless spectatorship is worship. In a way, that is just what the *ludi* were, but Mercurius is also reminding the audience of the good that actors (as well as gods) do for "you and the state" – a move familiar from Aristophanes, except that this petition is on behalf of an outsider social group rather than a competitive playwright (contrast what Terence does in his prologues). The list of gods on the tragic stage who remind the audience how they have served "you" is a list of gods of war, a topic appropriate to tragedy rather than comedy, as the *Captivi* prologue speaker notes (58–62); war is present in the *palliata* everywhere, but obliquely, expressed in the form of jokes and the cast of characters. Yet

---

triumphator – who was dressed as Jupiter; a costume not attested, however, before the empire, and only ambiguously there, cf. Beard 2007: 281–4.

Neptune and the rest are also actors in god costumes.[12] When Mercurius claims to have seen these gods onstage himself (*vidi*, 42), the joke involves triple speech: as the god Mercurius, as the actor who plays him, and, in both guises, as a slave (he comments self-consciously on his costume's "servile appearance," 116–17). So he joins the group of theater-going slave speakers: Chrysalus (*Bac.* 213–15), Gripus (*Rud.* 1249–53).

Mercurius moves smoothly from this point to a string of jokes – famous, see chapter 6 – about tragedy and comedy. From there he goes on to convey Jupiter's requests to the audience on the subject of angling for theatrical prizes, which he treats as if it were *ambitio*, "crooked campaigning," using grand legal diction: the presence of claques among the audience is to be policed by *conquistores*, here "investigators," who are to go around the *cavea*, to all the spectators on the *subsellia*, and take the toga away from any claque members (*favitores*) they find, to be held as security (64–71).[13] This unique mention of the toga in Plautus constitutes a strong identification of noisily applauding members of the audience, or hecklers, with voters (male Roman citizens), erasing, for the moment, the others present; the toga, of course, made its wearer conspicuous. The joke works the same way as those that tease the audience by identifying those who clap with those who would like to have a *scortum* (above, chapter 2); in a similar move, without using the word "toga," Euclio in *Aulularia* says to the audience, "Why are you laughing? I know you all, I know there are a lot of thieves here, / who hide themselves in their chalky outfits and sit there as if they were prudent" (*quid est? quid ridetis? novi omnis, scio fures esse hic compluris, / qui vestitu et creta occultant sese atque sedent quasi sint frugi, Aul.* 718–19; cf. Moore 1998: 19, 45–7). The investigators are likewise to make sure that the aediles do not "give [the prize] to anyone" *perfidiose* (72); as will be seen, *fides* in the plays is a central preoccupation: "good faith," "trustworthiness," "fiscal integrity." Here the aediles' trustworthiness is also under scrutiny.

Then Mercurius returns to his double address, in the role of god/actor, to the audience as victorious in war (73–80):

> sirempse legem iussit esse Iuppiter,
> quasi magistratum sibi alterive ambiverit.

[12] See Holliday 2002: 186–8 for a late-fourth-century *cista* possibly showing a theatrical staging of a triumph, featuring a *triumphator*, multiple *paterae*, and "the triumphal chariot of Jupiter," with remarks on its relation to theater history.

[13] *Conquistores* at a later period are military recruitment officers, enforcing the draft; for the call-up process in the city and on-the-spot penalties in a story from 275 BCE, see Brunt 1971a: 628–9 n. 5, with sources. In that context, the verb *respondere* has the technical sense "answer when called"; see below on its theatrical sense.

virtute dixit vos victores vivere,　　　　　　　　　　　　　　75
non ambitione neque perfidia: qui minus
eadem histrioni sit lex quae summo viro?
virtute ambire oportet, non favitoribus.
sat habet favitorum semper qui recte facit,
si illis fides est quibus est ea res in manu.　　　　　　　　80

Jupiter has ordered the same law to hold [for the aediles],
　　as if one of them engaged in crooked campaigning for office, for
　　　　himself or another.
He said, you are victorious because of your manliness,　　　75
　　not by crooked campaigning nor by breaking faith: how less
should there be the same law for an actor as for a man at the top?
It's right to campaign by manliness, not by claques/partisans.
A man who does right always has enough fans/partisans,
　　if those who are in charge of all this have *fides*.

Mercurius goes on (81–5) to stipulate that actors, too, should be
inspected to make sure they do not have supporters planted in the audience – if they do, they are to be beaten in costume, stripped, and beaten
again (*eius ornamenta et corium uti conciderent*, 85), a marked differentiation from the audience member who is to lose his toga (and whose war
it is – who is part of the *vos victores*). The whole thing, with its legalistic
language, must be a send-up of ever-current efforts to control electoral corruption; *virtute ambire* (78) is an oxymoron picking up *virtute
… victores vivere* (75).[14] Here what is at stake is some kind of prize for
actors and playwrights (*palmam*, 69), satirically compared with elected
office. Again, the contrast between players and what the Advocati in
Poenulus called "a rich man from the topmost position" (*dives de summo
loco*, 516) is explicitly marked by Mercurius' double-edged rhetorical
question: *qui minus / eadem histrioni sit lex quae summo viro?* (76–7).
Histrio and *summus vir* are polar opposites here, just as the *virtus* of
Sagaristio and Leonida sends up this kind of *virtus*. The argument is
clownish, the sentiment serious, insisting on *fides* just as Sosia's song, as
seen in chapter 2, insists on what is *aequom*. The structure of the section
strongly suggests that the troupe had at least one plant in the audience who was wearing a toga and had it ripped off his struggling body
by other troupe members acting as *conquistores*, here clown policemen.

---

[14] See Gruen 1996a: 148 n. 126, part of a general treatment of political issues in the *palliata* as recyclable
rather than specific; and chapter 1 for a case of *ambitus* in 328 BCE.

Funny, like the jokes about the *tresviri* and the lictors and the *carcer*, a building also located in the Forum.

This section of the prologue concludes, before moving into the by now long-awaited outline of the plot, with a last reminder of the actors inside the god costumes (86–95):

> mirari nolim vos quapropter Iuppiter
> nunc histriones curet; ne miremini:
> ipse hanc acturust Iuppiter comoediam.
> quid? admiratin estis? quasi vero novom
> nunc proferatur Iovem facere histrioniam;   90
> etiam, histriones anno quom in proscaenio hic
> Iovem invocarunt, venit, auxilio is fuit.
> praeterea certo prodit in tragoedia.
> hanc fabulam, inquam, hic Iuppiter hodie ipse aget
> et ego una cum illo. nunc <vos> animum advortite   95

> I wouldn't want you to wonder why Jupiter
> now cares about actors; don't you be surprised:
> Jupiter himself is going to act in this comedy.
> What? You're surprised? As if indeed it was a new thing
> to put Jupiter onstage to play an actor's part;   90
> why, when the actors on this stage last year here
> invoked Jupiter, he came, and helped them out.
> Anyway he certainly appears in tragedy.
> This play, I say, Jupiter himself will act in here, today,
> and I along with him. Now you all, pay attention   95

The fact that Jupiter and Mercurius will be acting in the play is stated twice in this section (88, 94–5), and will be repeated again in the prologue's last lines (151–2). Mercurius again here jokes on a triple level: it should not be a surprise to see Jupiter onstage, because Jupiter often appears in tragic scenes when the characters invoke his aid; likewise (this?) actor playing Jupiter helped out the other actors in a performance the audience is called on to remember, when he was needed onstage; literally, the god Jupiter manifested himself onstage when the actors needed him. There is a hint, in *auxilio*, of the *quiritatio* formula that invoked help from the *populus* or from the gods (see below). Furthermore, a sense cued by Mercurius' earlier lines about war gods onstage, the tragedies themselves display the world of victorious soldiers, aided by Jupiter. This joke relates to the *Poenulus* prologue, where the *imperator histricus* announces in his opening lines that he is here to rehearse the *Achilles* of Aristarchus, a play Ennius transposed to the Roman stage, evidently not long before *Poenulus* was staged. It was tragedy's job to play kings and gods, comedy's job to play the slave, as Mercurius says himself (60–3; see chapter 6).[15]

The *Amphitruo* prologue, then, embeds victory wishes in a complex argument; other prologues are more direct. The *Captivi* prologue speaker, as seen above, also says war has no place on the comic stage – ironic, in a play that deals entirely with the aftermath of war – and takes himself offstage by differentiating himself from the warrior audience: "goodbye, most just judges / at home, and best of warriors in warfare" (*valete, iudices iustissumi / domi, duellique duellatores optumi*, 67–8).[16] Again here, as in the *ambitio* jokes in *Amphitruo*, the prize-voting audience owns the war. The actual audience is not entirely composed of *duellatores* any more than is the all-male cast of *Captivi*, which includes a *parasitus* who is starving in wartime; the prologue speaker indulges in flattery (we are used to this in the barker's ubiquitous "Ladies and gentlemen," once also flattery, and the great bebop comedian Lord Buckley did the same with "M'Lords, M'Ladies" – not so bellicose, equally fictive).[17] Likewise, the *Casina* prologue speaker, fresh from his jokes about what "Casina" might do after the show, incongruously wraps up with two lines of flattering cheerleading: "Goodbye, do well, and conquer by true manliness, as you've done so far" (*valete, bene rem gerite, [et] vincite / virtute vera, quod fecistis antidhac*, 87–8).

The delayed *Cistellaria* prologue is spoken by the self-proclaimed god Auxilium, "Help," whose serious name, as seen in chapter 2, is undercut not only by late arrival (line 149) but also by its resemblance to prostitute and *puer* names. Auxilium rattles off a story of rape and travel between Lemnos and Sicyon, with the occasional "take my wife" joke thrown in, and ends with an elaborate set of wishes for the audience to beat Carthage (197–202):

> … bene valete et vincite
> virtute vera, quod fecistis antidhac;
> servate vostros socios, veteres et novos,
> augete auxilia vostris iustis legibus,   200

---

[15] Compare, in respect to stage effects, the probable reference to an *Alcumena Euripidi* on the Roman stage at the opening of *Rudens* (Fraenkel 2007: 50–1), where the rude slave Sceparnio, in his entrance speech, says his household's roof has been blown off, not by the wind, but by this play (*Rud.* 86), setting up a reference to the thunderous ending of *Amphitruo* as well as to a visit to the tragic theater. If so, he thereby becomes yet another slave with experience as an audience member.

[16] On the formulaic speeches that follow, see Leigh 2004: 38–9, with discussion of the definition of *virtus vera* in Ennius' *Phoenix* (*TrRF* 109). In that passage, the verbal similarity of this Ennian tragedy to Plautine cheers is close (*virum vera virtute vivere*); note also the speaker's alignment of *virtus* and courage with *libertas* as opposed to servitude.

[17] On Lord Buckley, see Trager 2002.

perdite perduellis, parite laudem et lauream,
ut vobis victi Poeni poenas sufferant.

> ... Goodbye and be well, and conquer
> with true manliness, as you have done so far;
> preserve your allies, both old and new,
> augment your auxiliaries by your just laws,   200
> destroy your enemies, give rise to fame and glory,
> so that the *Poeni*, conquered, should pay the price to you.

Along with the wish for victory, Auxilium self-referentially begs consideration for *auxilia*, and looks to the law. Does he mean the *auxilia* offered by
the tribunes of the plebs? Could *legibus* be dative – do the laws themselves
need help? Elsewhere the *populus* is strongly associated with the rule of
law.[18] Probably, in this martial context, he means the non-Romans (*socii*),
who provided the non-citizen troops (*auxilia*, 200) that fought alongside
the Roman army. Both senses were available to the audience. The *Rudens*
prologue ends with a one-line cheer: "Goodbye [= be strong], so that your
enemies lose faith in themselves" (*valete, ut hostes vostri diffidant sibi*, 82).
Considering that Arcturus's whole complaint in the first part of this prologue has to do with his job of supervising the *fides* of mortals, this is
an appropriately framed wish, resembling Auxilium's appeal on behalf of
auxilia. The *Asinaria* prologue speaker, after a short string of jokes about
Plautus and the play, similarly exits on a two-line simple *quid pro quo*: "pay
attention to me, benevolently, / so that Mars will help you equally now
as he has done at other times" (*date benigne operam mihi / ut vos, ut alias,
pariter nunc Mars adiuvet*, 14–15).

These appeals to the audience have several points in common, beyond
the obvious echoes in the wording. Continued success is offered in return
for paying attention to the play, and is said to depend on a set of virtues.
These virtues involve fairness and justice, a constant concern throughout
Plautus' plays, always a concern of the less powerful, and often a concern
of actors speaking as actors in the prologues. And war is always spoken
of as your (pl.) concern, not ours: "the *Poeni*, conquered, should pay the
price to *you*" (*vobis victi Poeni poenas sufferant, Cist.* 202), but "*We* will
give you an old-time comedy of his" (*nos ... anticuam eiius edimus comoediam, Cas.* 11–13): this revival prologue attests to the temporal as well as
locational re-usability of cheerleading. The "you" addressed here are the

---

[18] See *As.* 600, *Bac.* 438, *Cur.* 509, *Poen.* 725, *Ps.* 126, *St.* 353, 490, 492, *Trin.* 482, 1146, and esp. *Trin.*
1028–58. For legislation onstage as ineffectual, see Gruen 1996a: 141–2.

populus, including the slaves and free women who, though not agents in the war, needed victory.

The obvious echoes in the wording, however, perhaps constitute more than the regular tendency of the *palliata* to quote itself and re-use jokes. Mercurius tells the audience that Jupiter says *virtute ... vos victores vivere* ("you are victorious because of your manliness," *Am.* 75); the *Casina* prologue speaker exits on *vincite / virtute vera, quod fecistis antidhac* (*Cas.* 87–8); Auxilium in *Cistellaria* winds up for the lead-out with the exhortation, *vincite / virtute vera, quod fecistis antidhac* (*Cist.* 197–8). Could this be a slogan? A crowd chant to the departing legions? If so, *parite laudem et lauream* (*Cist.* 201) sounds like part of another. Taken as a whole, with the stress on the last syllable of *vincite* at the end of the iambic line, *vincite ... antidhac* imitates the trochaic septenarius, the beat common in known Roman street chants, here embedded in two lines of senarii.[19] Virtus and Victoria themselves appeared onstage (*Am.* 42): did they elicit cheers for the soldiers?[20] Did the audience pick the cheer up as the prologue speakers addressed them? This would make sense for audiences who were wearing the laurel crown of victors on their heads. Meanwhile, the repeated references to past success, and the purpose clauses, sound like prayers: *ut vos, ut alias, pariter nunc Mars adiuvet* (*Asinaria*); *ut vobis victi Poeni poenas sufferant* (*Cistellaria*, a terrible pun, with obvious currency until 201 BCE); *ut hostes vostri diffidant sibi* (*Rudens*). The widespread use of orchestrated or spontaneous chants in the street, sometimes in the theater after permanent theaters were built, has been well established for later periods.[21]

If he was echoing a popular chant, Mercurius would (ironically) have been taking on the role of a *fautor* himself. "Cheerleading" both does and does not translate what he is doing. Like cheerleaders, the prologue actors

---

[19] Cf. below for Gilbert Highet's theory on the repeated taunt *libertino patre natus* in Horace's *Satires*: in Horace, part of a line of hexameter; but also readable as part of a trochaic septenarius. Gerick, in his book on *versus quadratus* (a special form of this meter), does not consider *Cas.* 87–8 or *Cist.* 197–8, and notes in his section on soldiers' songs that the earliest ones attested in this meter come from Julius Caesar's Gallic triumph (1996: 35); as will be seen below, however, he treats *versus quadratus* as a characteristically folk/popular meter. Moore 1998: 15–16 treats *Captivi* 67–8 to illustrate the actors' strategy of combining flattery with manipulation of the audience; compare Leigh 2004: 79–80, setting this address in the context of war.

[20] On the increasing importance of the cult of Victoria in the 200s BCE, see Weinstock 1957; the chronology he traces keeps step with the development of the *palliata*. See also the brief discussion in Dench 1995: 73–4, and Richlin 2017a. Weinstock cites the god-list in *Amphitruo* (217 n. 30) in a discussion of conjoined groups of war gods.

[21] Aldrete 1999: 101–64, focusing on the relation between the urban plebs and the emperor, but acknowledging the long history of the custom; note esp. "the existence of a body of well-known acclamation formulas and the rhythmic nature of many of the acclamation chants themselves" (103).

lead a crowd of spectators to yell for a contest which the actors themselves are ineligible to join. Like rabble-rousers, they are of the crowd and incite the crowd. This was a position integral to several better-attested Roman street practices. If public or mass speech formulae are indeed present in the cheerleading speeches, they tally with a far larger group of popular speech formulae present throughout the plays, in the more entertaining form of insults; here, too, the actors would be performing as experts in drawing a crowd.

Verbal Dueling

In 36 or 35 BCE, Horace published, in his first book of *Satires*, a poem about a road trip that may have taken place in 38 or 37, in which he and Vergil traveled from Rome to Brundisium in the entourage of Maecenas. Although festooned with vivid historical and geographical details, the poem, according to the commentator Porphyrio in the 200s CE, was based on an earlier satirical poem, the *Iter Siculum* by Lucilius (c. 180–102 BCE), thus at the earliest about a generation after the death of Plautus. Lucilius in turn may have looked to the *palliata* for a scene in his poem, where Horace, despite his professed dislike of Plautus, may have followed him. Lucilius, a Campanian, came from an equestrian family; Horace, an Apulian, made both his home town and his class placement a central part of his poetic persona, repeatedly calling himself *libertino patre natus*. In this respect, his satirical oeuvre constitutes a gigantic expansion of the speeches of the touchy freed Advocati in *Poenulus* – with typically second-generation assimilation, for the *dives de summo loco* is now the speaker's admired friend and patron, although the speaker manifests a painful self-consciousness about his origins, and shows off a concomitant envious consciousness of Lucilius' higher status.[22] The class position of both Lucilius and Horace, then, should be kept in mind when considering a central vignette in Horace's poem.

At this point in the road trip still in Campania, entering Samnite country, Horace and his friends stop for the night at a villa belonging to one of the travelers, L. Cocceius Nerva, ancestor of the future emperor, and

---

[22] On the date of *Satires* I, see Gowers 2012: 3–4; on the historicity of the trip to Brundisium, Gowers 2012: 182–3; on Horace's status as a freedman's son, Williams 1995, Gowers 2012: 4 ("the poverty and ex-slave status of his father are now regarded sceptically"); on *Satires* 1.5, Gowers 1994, Cucchiarelli 2002, Wallochny 1992: 91–5. Lejay 1911: 136 and Cucchiarelli 2001: 35 n. 69 argue that there were contests like the singing match at *S*. 1.5.15–17 in Lucilius' *Iter Siculum*. Fraenkel pointed out the similarity between the animal insult at 1.5.56 and a line of insult in the *Iter Siculum* (2007: 42).

are entertained at dinner by a pair of comedians whose language evokes
Plautus in certain ways (*S.* 1.5.50–70):

> hinc nos Coccei recipit plenissima villa,   50
> quae super est Caudi cauponas. nunc mihi paucis
> Sarmenti scurrae pugnam Messique Cicirri,
> Musa, velim memores et quo patre natus uterque
> contulerit lites. Messi clarum genus Osci;
> Sarmenti domina exstat: ab his maioribus orti   55
> ad pugnam venere. prior Sarmentus "equi te
> esse feri similem dico." ridemus, et ipse
> Messius "accipio" caput et movet. "o tua cornu
> ni foret exsecto frons" inquit "quid faceres, cum
> sic mutilus minitaris?" at illi foeda cicatrix   60
> saetosam laevi frontem turpaverat oris.
> Campanum in morbum, in faciem permulta iocatus,
> pastorem saltaret uti Cyclopa rogabat:
> nil illi larva aut tragicis opus esse cothurnis.
> multa Cicirrus ad haec: donasset iamne catenam   65
> ex voto Laribus, quaerebat; scriba quod esset,
> nilo deterius dominae ius esse; rogabat
> denique cur umquam fugisset, cui satis una
> farris libra foret, gracili sic tamque pusillo.
> prorsus iucunde cenam producimus illam.   70

> From here, the lavish villa of Cocceius received us,   50
> which stands above the cheap inns of Caudium. Now, o Muse,
> I wish you'd sing me the brawl of the *scurra* Sarmentus
> and Messius Cicirrus, and of what father born
> each joined the dispute. Glorious the stock of Messius, an Oscan,
> while Sarmentus' lady legal owner lives: sprung from these ancestors   55
> they came to the brawl. First Sarmentus: "Like a wild horse,
> that's what I say you are." We laugh, and himself,
> Messius: "I take that" – and moves his head. "Oh, your forehead –
> if the horn hadn't been cut off," he says, "what would you do, when
> you threaten us so, even mutilated?" But the other had a disgusting scar 60
> disfiguring the bristly forehead on the left side of his face.
> Having made a lot of jokes about the "Campanian disease" and his face,
> he kept asking him to dance the Cyclops shepherd:
> he'd have no need of a mask or tragic boots.
> Cicirrus said a lot back to this: had he already given his chain   65
> to the Lares, as he had vowed; if he was a *scriba*,
> his legal owner still had the right to him, nonetheless; finally
> he kept asking why he had ever run away, when one pound
> of *far* was enough for him, so skinny and weak as he was.
> Right merrily we enjoy that dinner to the last.   70

The main difference between verse satire and the *palliata* as literary forms is well illustrated here: the satirist writes for readers or declaims for listeners, a one-man show; the satire speaker stands outside the action, describing it from the point of view of a particular spectator; most of the lines of insult are in indirect discourse, preserving no formal elements from the fictive original. When Horace did a reading for friends, he was performing a scene of performance. At the same time, his text specifies the scene's setting (dinner, Cocceius's villa), along with audience reactions (*ridemus*, 57, *prorsus iucunde … producimus*, 70), and indicates action as well as words (*caput et movet*, 58). The performance transcripts of the *palliata*, in contrast, while they give the performers' lines, offer us only clues about a setting that was immediate to the audience and also a public space – open; just as the performance left each audience member free to laugh as he or she saw something funny.

Verse satire is not so open; the speaker in Horace's satire differentiates himself from the performers he reperforms by a series of sneering comic moves that amplify the performers' insults of each other. He locates himself in a "lavish" (*plenissima*) villa, belonging to the aristocratic Cocceius, that is set "above the cheap inns" (*super … cauponas*, 51); then he belittles the performance and the performers by casting the event in mock-epic language (53). It is a *pugna* (fistfight, 52, 56) or *lites* (lawsuit, 54), no epic battle; Sarmentus is a *scurra*, Messius Cicirrus has a funny name, like a rooster crowing (52); their parentage is low (Oscan ethnicity is a joke, an outsider ethnicity, so *clarum genus* is a sneer, 54; Sarmentus has a female owner in place of a parent, 55); neither of them has *maiores* in the Roman sense, so that the attribution of *maiores* to them (55) is a dig. As is his wont, the speaker has it both ways, with the question *quo patre natus* (53) recalling the numerous times this question is asked about Horace himself in the *Satires* and *Epistles*.[23] Contrast Mercurius' question to Sosia (*Am.* 346), *quoius sis* – "Whose are you?" – and Sosia's dignified assertion that he is *Davo prognatum patre*, "born of my father Davus," a classic comedic slave name (365; see chapter 4). In the *palliata*, a player gets to answer the question; Horace, caught between Lucilius and Maecenas, gives a top-down view. Sarmentus was a real person, an actual freed slave associated with

---

[23] *Quo patre natus*, Hor. *S.* 1.6.29, cf. 1.6.7, 58–60, 64, *Ep.* 1.20.19–28; cf. Gowers 2012: 222. See above on cheerleading; note esp. Gilbert Highet's idea, pointed out by Gowers, that *libertino patre natus* (*S.* 1.6.6, 45, 46; *Ep.* 1.20.20) might have been the start of a street taunt in trochaic septenarii (a passing thought, Highet 1973: 268 n. 1: "an accentual form of the *versus quadratus* used in popular taunts").

Maecenas, well attested; if, as Emily Gowers argues, he is a surrogate for the satirist Horace, he is an abject one.[24]

Certainly the speaker's own body in *S.* 1.5 is grotesque itself, so that the grotesqueries of the insult match do not entirely set the performers apart from him. But grotesque the insults are, based on animal comparison, facial disfiguration, disease, the monstrous onstage, and slavery – chains, the Lares, being a runaway, being owned, thinness associated with controlled feeding (*una / farris libra*, 68–9). "Short commons," as Gowers notes, citing the ration for chained debtors in the XII Tables (2012: 203; cf. chapter 2). Adding a layer of invective, the speaker verifies some of these insults, labeling Messius as Oscan, giving Sarmentus a *domina*, describing Messius' scar as disgusting (*foeda*), his forehead as *saetosam*, "bristly," like a boar. Compare *saetosi caput hoc apri*, "this head of a bristly boar," in Vergil's seventh *Eclogue* (29) – a poetry-book closely akin to Horace *Satires* 1, and a poem that produces its own (Theocritean) song contest in alternating verses (*alternis … versibus*, 18), just as Sarmentus and Cicirrus here take turns (56–64, 65–9).

These literary duels, layered with intertexts like puff pastry, aim at a reading audience that can pause to savor the aftertastes. Yet Horace's poems also bear simple witness to insult matches as a part of the culture he lived in and to the staging of insult matches as a popular form of entertainment, sometimes associated with eating dinner, often associated with laborers, nor is he the only witness. On the passenger barge on the way to Brundisium, the *pueri* and the sailors insult each other (*S.* 1.5.11–13), chiastically: *tum pueri nautis, pueris convicia nautae / ingerere* ("then the boys upon the sailors, upon the boys insults the sailors / heap," 11–12). A sailor and a traveler (*viator*) take turns praising their girlfriends, *certatim* (17). In *S.* 1.7, duels within a duel: a proscribed man named Rex and a "half-breed" (*hybrida*) named Persius, arguing their case before Brutus in Asia in 43 BCE, are sneeringly contrasted with pairs of epic warriors (10–18) or gladiators (19–20); again, everybody laughs at them (*ridetur ab omni / conventu*, 22–3), and animals are invoked, if only figuratively, as Persius compares Rex to "that Dog, the star hated by farmers" (25–6). Rex, identified as from Praeneste (28), retorts with "Italian vinegar" (*Italo … aceto*, 32), like "a hard / grape-harvester undefeated, to whom often the traveler / would have yielded, as he reviled him as a 'cuckoo' in a loud voice" (*durus /*

---

[24] Gowers 2012: 200; cf. Richlin 2015a: 361 for further contemporary abuse of him. Like Plautus' *parasiti*, and like the Greek comedians attested at Hellenistic courts (Richlin 2016), Sarmentus was a clown for the powerful. See further below.

vindemiator et invictus, cui saepe viator / cessisset, magna compellans voce cuculum, 1.7.29–31).[25]

Almost two hundred years later, the young Marcus Aurelius, after a long day at the vintage, dined with his mother and his adoptive father the emperor in the wine-press room, and "We all enjoyed listening to the yokels insulting each other" (*rusticos cavillantes audivimus libenter, M. Caes.* 4.6.2). Or so he writes to his beloved teacher Fronto, in a letter full of the consciousness that he is acting like a person in (what is to him) a book: he gargles like someone in an Atellan farce by Novius, and he picks grapes with a quotation that is taken to be from Novius, perhaps from his play *Vindemiatores*, "Grape-harvesters" (4.6.1). He probably was well aware, then, that *cavillationes* are among Gelasimus' goods for sale (*St.* 228), and were associated onstage with shtick (*Aul.* 638) and jesting (*Mil.* 642, *Truc.* 684–5). Two hundred years later still, Ausonius, in a highly self-conscious portrait of the river Moselle, shows the vineyard-workers "competing with crude yells" (*certantes stolidis clamoribus*), while the traveler on the riverbank and the bargeman on the river "sing insults to the belated farm-workers" (*probra canunt seris cultoribus*), raising the echoes (*Mosella* 165–7). The agricultural writer Columella, a contemporary of the younger Seneca, opines in his section on the best slaves for vineyard work that they must have a "quick mind" (*velocior animus*) and a "strong intelligence" (*acuminis strenui*), but that it is just the dishonest ones (*improborum*) who are likely to be so endowed – "which is why vineyards are usually cultivated by men in chains" (*ideoque vineta plurimum per alligatos excoluntur, Rust.* 1.9.4). To what extent this idea is present to Horace, Marcus, or Ausonius cannot be known, but the status of the *vindemiator* for them must be low, probably servile, and the same goes for the bargemen and the farm-workers, while the *viator* is no grandee.

The *palliata* is full of insult matches like these and the one reported in *S.* 1.5, but much more elaborate, carefully structured – and produced onstage before a mixed audience, not at dinner to entertain the *summi viri*. Rather than think of literary parallels, then, the spectators could be caught up in the swing of it, as they might be on the street, only without danger. In doing so, they were participating in a folk form that exists in cultures around the world, known to anthropologists and folklorists as "verbal dueling." The slave Libanus, a champion practitioner, calls it

---

[25] I must agree with commentators who find the explanation offered by the elder Pliny forced (*HN* 18.249; cf. Morris 1909: 115 *ad loc.*); *cuculus* is a common term of abuse in Plautus, cf. *As.* 923, 934 (associated with a trochaic refrain), *Per.* 282, *Ps.* 96, *Trin.* 245–6.

"word-skirmishing" (*verbivelitatio, As.* 307), an image from light-armed troop combat, with its stinging jabs; Pompeius Festus sums up the main structural element as "the throwing back and forth of insults" (*ultro citroque prob<r>orum obiectatio*, 507L). (Libanus' term might also have evoked for his audience the class placement of the *velites* in the lowest census bracket.) Two specialized Roman forms, *flagitatio* and *occentatio*, were analyzed long ago by Usener (1901) and will be discussed further below. The elements of the form common to many cultures are as follows: men, usually in pairs, take turns insulting each other; there is a conventional verbal format, and the opponents score points by good use of the format; conversely, it is possible to lose by being unable to reply in kind; this takes place before an audience in a public place, with locally recognized temporary boundaries; and in conventional circumstances (at dinner, after dinner, while drinking, at a bar or other party venue). The most widespread form today is the rap battle. The content is often obscene and, as in most forms of humor, often involves play with recognized social norms.[26] Thus Horace stages his written duel as after-dinner entertainment featuring local semi-pro talent, like the one mentioned by Marcus at which actual "yokels" performed, while the poetic vignettes of grape-harvesters are set in a particular outdoor workplace; the duels in Plautus, like almost all the action in the *palliata*, take place in the street outside the house doors. That this location was associated with verbal dueling in real life is suggested by passing remarks within the plays.

It should be emphasized, in light of some commonly made arguments about the *palliata* as *Kunstsprache* rather than "colloquial" speech, that verbal dueling, like many other folk forms, is often metrical and subject to elaborate formal conventions, while still being considered by native speakers to be low in register – even contemptible, as in "truly frivolous talk" among the Chamula (see Gossen 1976). Low forms are not *ipso facto* artless. As scholars have noted, the shtick that recurs in Roman comedy is highly formulaic, in characteristic ways quite different from what appears

---

[26] For verbal dueling around the world, see Pagliai 2009, and Pagliai 2010 on traditional verbal dueling in central Italy, with comprehensive bibliography; for rap battles, see formal and historical analyses in A. Bradley 2009, Neff 2009, and Wald 2012; for formal and historical analyses of protest music, see A. Moore 2013 and Peretti 2013; on ancient invective and rap, Rosen and Marks 1999; on Roman verbal dueling, Richlin 1992b[1983]: 74–5. Among classic studies, Gossen 1976, on verbal dueling in Mexico, makes a good comparative example for Rome on both formal and social grounds. Among numerous analyses of verbal dueling in Plautus by the Freiburg school, see Lefèvre 2001 on the opening duel in *Epidicus*; Wallochny 1992: 142–80, 189–93 focuses on *verbivelitatio* as a type of argument scene and analyzes its "tactics." For Greek versions, see below on *skolia*; accounts of comedians at Greek symposia do not include this kind of team act (see Richlin 2016).

in related jokes in Greek comedy. Since Parry and Lord, any Homerist would be startled to hear that orality is inconsistent with sophisticated formal structure.[27]

A duel in *Persa* between the slave Toxilus and the pimp Dordalus incorporates two telling cues that underscore the level of skill needed to perform these duels onstage (405–27). Dordalus greets Toxilus as he emerges from his house, and at once Toxilus launches his attack:

... DO. oh,	405
Toxile, quid agitur? TO. oh, lutum lenonium,	
commixtum caeno sterculinum publicum,	
inpure, inhoneste, iniure, inlex, labes popli,	
pecuniai accipiter avide atque invide,	
procax, rapax, trahax – trecentis versibus	410
tuas inpuritias traloqui nemo potest –	
accipin argentum? accipe sis argentum, inpudens,	
tene sis argentum, etiam tu argentum tenes?	
possum te facere ut argentum accipias, lutum?	
non mihi censebas copiam argenti fore,	415
qui nisi iurato mihi nil ausu's credere?	
DO. sine respirare me, ut tibi respondeam.	
vir summe populi, stabulum servitricium,	
scortorum liberator, suduculum flagri,	
compedium tritor, pistrinorum civitas,	420
perenniserve, lurcho, edax, furax, fugax,	
cedo sis mi argentum, da mihi argentum, inpudens,	
possum [a] te exigere argentum? argentum, inquam, cedo,	
quin tu mi argentum reddis? nihilne te pudet?	
leno te argentum poscit, solida servitus,	425
pro liberanda amica, ut omnes audiant.	
TO. tace, opsecro hercle. ne tua vox valide valet!	

[DO.] ... Oh,	405
Toxilus, what's up? TO. Oh, you pimping dirtbag,	
you public shithouse, with extra dung on top,	
you unclean, immoral, illegal, unjust, people's grease stain,	
you greedy, beady-eyed, evil-eyed money vulture,	
you mouthy, grabby, pushy – nobody could	410
run through your unclean garbage in three hundred lines –	

---

[27] On formulae in shtick, see Richlin 2017b: 179–92, Vogt-Spira 2001; on "truly frivolous talk," Gossen 1976. For an (uncharacteristic) example of a misleading opposition between "orality" and "stylised forms of language" affected by meter and song, see Halla-aho and Kruschwitz 2010: 128. They are dealing with early Roman tragedy, and it is fascinating to speculate on overlaps in personnel, training, and method between tragedy and comedy in this period.

Will you take your cash? Please take your cash, shameless!
Please have your cash, your cash, are you even going to have it?
Can I make you take your cash, dirtbag?
You didn't think I could get my hands on that much cash,   415
so you wouldn't risk giving me credit unless I swore to it?
DO. Hey, let me breathe, so I can do the response to you.
The people's man at the top! You slave-girls' motel,
you savior of whores, you're making the whips sweat,
you're wearing out the shackles, you flour-mill city,   420
you permanent slave, you slurper, you food-grubbing, thieving runaway!
Hand me my cash, please, give me my cash, shameless!
Can I squeeze the cash out of you? The cash, hand it to me, I'm saying,
won't you give me back my cash? Have you no shame?
The pimp is asking you for cash, you solid slavery,   425
to set your girlfriend free – everybody listen up!
TO. Shut up, please – my God, your voice is mighty mighty!

The echoing "oh"s that initiate the duel suggest the drawing of breath, and
that is just what Dordalus says he needs to do in order to launch into his
reply to Toxilus, in a metatheatrical pause (417) that courts the audience's
anticipatory laughter. When he is done, Toxilus remarks on the strength of
the pimp's voice (427), and we might guess that the actor playing Dordalus
performed his speech on a single breath (I cannot myself get beyond line
424).[28] In response to Toxilus' admiring exclamation, the pimp says, "Salt
costs me as much as it costs you"; his tongue must defend him or never taste
salt (428–30). Like the slaves in chapter 2, the tongue has to earn its keep;
or, as an actor, the man under the pimp mask has to display this skill to eat.

The two actors not only put on a bravura display of breath control; not
only do they employ a full set of the insults commonly aimed at slaves
and pimps; first and foremost, they take turns showing off, as the first
speaker sets up an intricate pattern, and the second speaker matches and
outdoes it (*tibi respondeam*) – a style familiar in modern tap-dancing and
in improvised vocal and musical forms. (Indeed, the final scenes of both
Persa and *Stichus* feature brief competitive dance-offs.[29]) So Olympio says
to Chalinus at the end of their verbal duel, topping off a barrage of threats,

---

[28] For a possible parallel in Greek, dated to the mid-300s – "nearly sixty lines of anapaestic dim-
eters without break and so possibly spoken in one breath by a virtuoso slave/cook" – see Scafuro
2014: 201.

[29] Habinek 2005: 117 thinks the slaves of *scurrae* who *ludunt datatim* at *Cur.* 296 are doing a "competitive dance" and Curculio is outdoing them as he runs past; followed by Moore 2012: 124. The use
of *datatim* there, with parallel uses of *dato* to mean "oblige sexually," seems to me to rule out that
option, but it certainly comes up elsewhere. See chapter 4 on *Stichus*; for an overview of competitive
dance in the *palliata*, Moore 2012: 126–7, and 195–6 on "reciprocal choreography" and "banter."

"Now, so you don't ask that you should respond to me, / I'm going inside; I'm bored with your conversation" (*nunc ne tu te mihi respondere postules, / abeo intro. taedet tui sermonis, Cas.* 141–2) – a laugh line, because Chalinus has said nothing but "What will you do to me?" and "What will you do?" for the last twenty-odd lines (*quid tu mihi facies?* 117, *quid facies?* 132): straight lines. But Toxilus and Dordalus give a full performance. The verb *respondeo*, then, has a technical sense in a verbal duel like this; it also works as a cue in runs of shtick, as straight man and funny man feed each other lines, and *responde mihi* appears already in one of the few fragments of Livius Andronicus' comedies. As in "double acts" in modern Anglophone popular theater, two comedians work together, developing a fast-paced rhythm grounded in recycled material.[30]

In the *Persa* duel, each of the duelers does four lines of insults, followed by five lines of patterned, thrusting questions; as will be seen below, these follow a format peculiar to the dunning performance called *flagitatio* and widely attested elsewhere. Toxilus' four lines start with a half-line (406), then three full lines, then another half-line (410), followed by a metatheatrical comment that takes up a half-line plus a line (410–11), saying how many lines he would need to cover all the pimp's *impuritias*, his uncleanness; dirt has been a main component in Toxilus' insults against the pimp. Dordalus begins with his metatheatrical breath-taking line (417), which he follows with four continuous lines of insults. Both speakers make much use of alliteration – a feature of contemporary poetic diction here put to forceful use. Each also has a group of three adjectives ending in *-ax* (410, 421), Toxilus at the start of his line, Dordalus at line end, each time capping the run of insults before the speaker moves on, Toxilus to metatheater, Dordalus to his *flagitatio*. Each insults the other in relation to the people: Toxilus' disgusted *sterculinum publicum* (407) and *labes popli* (408) are opposed to the pimp's sneering *vir summe populi* (418). The figure of the "man at the top" – as we have seen, a problem figure in the *palliata* – here, as elsewhere, has the respect of pimps, which gives this insult a boomerang quality like the "exploding cigars" in chapter 6, for Toxilus makes no claim to be a *vir summus*. Toxilus' insults recall the cook-to-cook insult *prostibulum popli* in *Aulularia* (chapter 2), and, in keeping with his theme, associate Dordalus with dirt. Dordalus here and in all his insults

---

[30] On verbal dueling as an enjoyable game, where the players seem more like partners than opponents, see Wallochny 1992: 182. Just so; see Arnott's review (1996b: 67), quoted in chapter 1 above. Wallochny uses the proverbial *par pari respondere* (cf. *Per.* 223, Paegnium to Sophoclidisca) to stand for a category of duel; see esp. 1992: 65–72, 166–71. On *responde* as a cue and its appearance in Livius, see Richlin 2017b: 185–6.

attacks Toxilus for his civil status, focusing, as in slaves' verbal duels, on Toxilus's history of punishment (*suduculum flagri*, 419; *compedium tritor*, *pistrinorum civitas*, 420), the unlikelihood of his manumission (*perenniserve*, 421; *solida servitus*, 425), his hunger (*lurcho, edax*, 421), and the likelihood that he will try to escape (*fugax*, 421). Toxilus pulls off almost a whole line of insults beginning with the negating *in-*, emphasizing all the righteous things Dordalus is not (408), along with an animal metaphor incorporating a play on *avide/invide* (409). On the other hand, he falls back on a repeat of *lutum* (406, 414) and forms of *impur-* (408, 411). Dordalus repeats an idea in *perenniserve* (421) and *solida servitus* (425), and again in *inpudens* (422, borrowed from Toxilus, and in the same position – line end, first line of *flagitatio*, cf. 412) and *pudet* (424); but his four lines of insults dance and weave, the first line picking up Toxilus' *sterculinum publicum* with *stabulum servitricium* (418), the next two lines alternating pairs of nouns in the vocative and genitive in an elaborate chiasmus: ABBA, ABAB. He ends with five vocatives in one line. The chiasmus of his insults meshes with the chiastic patterns in both characters' *flagitatio*, and, if this contest were being judged, Dordalus would win on points.

Insult matches like these fill the plays in order to fill the seats: made to order. The *grex* at the end of *Bacchides* claims to have made the plot from firsthand knowledge (*neque … haec faceremus, ni … vidissemus*, 1209), and the actors commonly describe the play as something they are doing or making (the basic meaning of *ago*). As seen in chapter 1, the plays show signs of improvisation by the players. Improvise what? Beatrix Wallochny sums up: Plautine characters have *Streitlust* – they love to argue (1992: 189). Evidently this was fun to watch. And fun to hear: Dordalus' mighty lungs, the content of these duels, and the marked term *clamor* (below) suggest delivery at full volume, useful to overcome what must have been considerable ambient noise in an open-air theater. Form follows function; location and demand shape form. (Think of the instructions to Nicholas Nickleby on the elements to include in his translation of a French play, all determined by the props, skills, and egos of Mr. Crummles's troupe.[31]) A major structural element in the plays is evidently there to facilitate the players' display of verbal dueling skills like the ones on show for the characters Toxilus and Dordalus.

Moreover, the plays are full of scenes that involve two slaves, or a slave and an adversary. As seen in chapter 2, many of the prologue speakers

---

[31] Charles Dickens, *Nicholas Nickleby*, chapters 22–4; see McElduff 2013: 61–2 for an entertaining application of this episode to the rise of Roman comedy.

are slaves, actors, or workers. What is the effect, what is the motive for this procession of humble figures? The prologues are all in senarii, spoken; perhaps, then, more intimate with the audience than sung lines accompanied by music (see Moore 1998: 31). Though some prologues are funny, a prologue constitutes a sort of talking program (for productions unlikely to have had written ones), performs a service for the audience and the play, and serves as a transition between pre-play and play, like a verbal curtain (for productions that never mention curtains). The prologue sets the tone; the tone is low.

In a smooth transition, then, once the prologue is over, and in cases when there is no prologue, the opening scenes of the plays very commonly involve slave or other low characters engaged in low joking. Of the nineteen plays that have extant opening scenes, only *Trinummus* and *Truculentus* open with free male characters, and even the boring old men in *Trinummus* do a run of old-wife jokes (51–66). Five plays feature opening dialogues between two slaves: *Amphitruo* 153–462 – with Mercurius' prologue, over a third of the play; *Casina* 89–143; *Epidicus* 1–103; *Mostellaria* 1–83; *Persa* 1–52. *Rudens* opens with a brief monologue by the slave laborer Sceparnio (83–8). Six more opening scenes feature dialogues between owner and slave, all lively and more or less antagonistic (*Asinaria* 16–126, *Aulularia* 40–119, *Curculio* 1–95, *Mercator* 111–224, *Poenulus* 129–209, *Pseudolus* 1–132), as well as (probably) the lost opening scene of *Bacchides*, while Sceparnio's monologue in *Rudens* continues into a scene in which Sceparnio insults not only his owner but an arriving visitor (89–147).[32] Two plays open with monologues by *parasiti* (*Captivi* 69–109, *Menaechmi* 77–109), one with a dialogue between a *parasitus* and his soldier patron (*Miles* 1–78). The two that open with female characters together (three prostitutes, *Cistellaria* 1–119, followed by a monologue by the *lena*, 120–48; two young wives, *Stichus* 1–57) are, then, anomalous, possibly a novelty, unexpected. It seems safe to guess that low joking was what the audience preferred to see, because the opening scene needs to grab the audience's attention.

Accordingly, several spectacular and memorable examples of duels occur in opening scenes: Mercurius and Sosia in *Amphitruo*, Olympio and Chalinus in *Casina*, and Tranio and Grumio (who disappears thereafter) in *Mostellaria* (cf. also the scene between Palaestrio and Sceledrus at *Mil.* 272–344, which at times follows dueling format, e.g. 315–18). Verbal duels take place almost exclusively between slave characters, not all of them male,

---

[32] On the *Bacchides* opening see de Melo 2011a: 364–9.

although the maleness of the actors complicates gender in scenes involving female characters.[33] There is a lot of this in the plays – more than 229 of 947 lines in *Asinaria* include dueling between the slaves Leonida and Libanus (267–380, 407–90, 545–78, and *passim*); *Persa* includes duels between Sophoclidisca and Paegnium (200–50) and, as seen in chapter 2, Sagaristio and Paegnium (272–301), as well as the one between Toxilus and the pimp (405–26); and there are minor duels between Phaniscus and Pinacium in *Mostellaria* (885–98) and Astaphium and Truculentus in *Truculentus* (256–314, 669–98). There are some brief duels involving free characters, like the flurry of insults between the neighbor *senes* Alcesimus and Lysidamus (*Cas.* 591–612) and the tirade of the soldier towards the end of *Poenulus*, with replies from Agorastocles and the visiting Carthaginian, Hanno (1296–1320). All instances of formal *flagitatio* onstage involve mixed slave/free groups, while sections of the duel between Toxilus and Dordalus follow this specialized format, as will be seen further below. Agonistic elements like the tug of war in *Rudens* or the lot-casting scene in *Casina*, which itself incorporates some verbal dueling and a proxy fistfight between the slaves of husband and wife, should remind us that paired combat is the most famous Roman spectator sport, the combatants in both tending to be servile or free poor. As is the case today, specularized physical combat for pay was not an upper-class occupation; as seen in chapter 2, Tranio gives a shout-out to men who get hurt for three *nummi*, perhaps performers (*Mos.* 357–8), and Gelasimus, taxed with a willingness to go *summam in crucem* for a meal, says, "I'll fight it out with anyone much more easily than with Starvation" (*St.* 627) – a probable reference to paid combat.[34]

A word about meter. Although the duel between Toxilus and Dordalus is set in senarii, and duels can be found in a range of meters including polymetric songs, a great many of the examples in this chapter are in trochaic septenarii (tr7), traces of which are seen above in cheers and which are attested later for the soldiers' songs at triumphs, familiar from Suetonius.

---

[33] On slaves and parasites as the main participants in duels, see Wallochny 1992: 62, with bibliography; 83.

[34] De Melo translates *quicumvis* as "with anything," but the sense of *depugno* leans heavily towards single combat. For the gender of *quicum*, cf. Cic. *Off.* 3.77, *dignum esse … quicum in tenebris micas*, which he calls "a proverb worn with antiquity" among "rustics." The gladiatorial pair as model for duelists appears explicitly at Horace *S.* 1.5.56 *pugnam*, 1.7.19 *par pugnat*, and has an obvious parallel in Aristophanic images of fighting cocks. The points of similarity between *Clouds*, *Knights*, and Plautine verbal dueling have long been noticed; see Fraenkel 1927: 366–7, 1961: 50 n. 16, with further bibliography. He took the relationship to be cousinly rather than ancestral, as does Wallochny, who believes Plautus had no knowledge of Old Comedy. But what did the *actors* know? Where had they been? See Richlin 2016, 2017b.

Those songs taunted the triumphant general the soldiers had followed; as a marching beat, they invite comparison with jodies, the call-and-response "cadence calls" used in the US military. Jodies, in turn, go back to African-American work songs, and the best known of them, "Sound Off," is also called the Duckworth Chant, after an African-American soldier, Pvt. Willie Duckworth, in the Second World War.[35] The tune of "Sound Off," however, resembles the tune of familiar children's taunts, also in trochaic septenarii, like "John and Mary sitting in a tree, K-I-S-S-I-N-G," or (from my own childhood in the mean streets of New Jersey in the 1950s), "Car, car, C-A-R, stick your head in a jelly jar," "You can't catch a nanny goat" (from playing tag), or just the basic "Nah, nah, na-nah, nah" – or, for that matter, "Ring Around the Rosie," or sports taunts like "We want a pitcher, not a glass of water." The oral circulation of such taunts is a major area of study in the subfield of children's folklore, most famously by Iona and Peter Opie; whether there is something cross-culturally and transhistorically irritating about trochaic septenarii is a matter for sociolinguists.

Timothy Moore argues that trochaic septenarii are so common in Roman comedy that they should be viewed as "unmarked" – "the default meter of Roman comedy" – the very stuff, then, of which the *palliata* is made. They are among the stichic meters that were, like polymetric songs, accompanied by the *tibia*; Moore suggests that these lines may have been delivered between speech and song, with rhythm as the most important element. (Although accompanied stichic meters are often compared with operatic recitative, perhaps an analogy with rap would be closer, as in "My Shot" in *Hamilton* – agonistic, polyvocal, full of resolution, more rhythmic than melodic, popular, and, like much rap, set in trochaic septenarii.) Certainly taunts onstage in the *palliata* are often set in this meter, and it seems at least possible that the cadence would trigger a deep recognition in the audience, also that the "tune" often associated with taunting by Roman commentators (below) was recognizably present onstage. As will be seen, the jingling segmentation characteristic of the *versus quadratus* – a variety of trochaic septenarius associated with nonliterary forms – also structures both taunts and *flagitatio*. Nonliterary examples range from children's rhymes to soldiers' songs to crowd chants at the theater, several of which, like this one, single out the Sarmentus we met in Horace, *Satires* 1.5:

---

[35] For historical background and bibliography, see Burke 1989: 424–5. Burke focused on the extremely violent content of cadence calls she collected at the US Naval Academy and other service academies; scholarship on the history of the form remains scarce. Interestingly, Burke documented many Vietnam-based calls and songs, circulated among trainees in the late 1980s by contact with "prior-enlisted" men: an example of the persistence past currency that characterizes popular forms.

digna dignis | sic Sarmentus | habeat crassas | compedes
people get what they deserve | so Sarmentus | should have thick | fetters

As these are reported, they were directed at Sarmentus "by the people," *a populo*, attesting to the possibilities for spontaneous composition and rapid circulation in public spaces: not just actors in the audience but comedians.[36] Again, this capacity for jingling among members of the audience, if it was present in the 200s as it was in the 30s, suggests opportunities for interaction between insult-slinging actors and echoing audience. Several of the forms to be considered here – *flagitatio, occentatio,* and *quiritatio* – depend on group participation; as with the cheerleading discussed above, the audience might well have gotten into the act.

Lost to us are conventional taunting gestures, of which Roman sources name very few other than the extended middle finger that has enjoyed such a long history. They are robustly attested in Italian culture from the 1700s onward, so perhaps they were also present onstage in the *palliata*. For their effectiveness, I need only turn to the taunting scene in *Monty Python and the Holy Grail*, where John Cleese as the French soldier, having exhausted a fund of parodic yet irresistibly funny insults, beats a sort of tattoo on his own head: a climactic point.[37]

Formal characteristics of verbal dueling in Plautus include:

• line-for-line exchanges, as at *As.* 274–7 (tr7). Here, of the two combatants, Leonida has entered without seeing Libanus, who has already struck up a relationship with the audience in a monologue (249–66), so that Leonida's lines are straight, Libanus' are jokes:

> LE. aetatem velim servire, Libanum ut conveniam modo.
> LI. mea quidem hercle liber opera numquam fies ocius.　　　　　275
> LE. etiam de tergo ducentas plagas praegnatis dabo.
> LI. largitur peculium, omnem in tergo thensaurum gerit.

---

[36] On children's playground chants and street culture, see Opie and Opie 1969. Fraenkel 1927 argues that trochaic septenarii came into Latin from Greek, although long before the 200s BCE, through popular circulation; for independent indigenous evolution, see Gerick 1996: 12–26, esp. the closing remarks on popular stress-accented verse. On the chants in Suetonius, with many examples of Roman taunts, chants, and games, see Gerick 1996: 27–58; the taunts of Sarmentus are discussed in Courtney 1993: 473–4, along with numerous examples of *versus populares* and *triumphales* (470–85). On the unmarked nature of trochaic septenarii onstage, see Moore 2012: 172–4, and 93–103 for the relation between rhythm and song. For association between this meter and insults onstage, see the full survey of *versus quadratus* in Plautus, Gerick 1996: 84–185. For "actors in the audience," see Bartsch 1994.

[37] On taunting gestures in Rome, see Conington 1872: 18–19, *ad* Persius 1.58–60; Corbeill 2004: 6, 38; Richlin 1992b[1983]: 90, 132. On such gestures in Italy in the eighteenth to nineteenth centuries, in connection with the Society of Dilettanti, see Carabelli 1996: 66, 95–106; understanding of the portrait of the Dilettanti is now considerably advanced by Coltman 2009: 159–90, esp. at 175–6.

LE. I'd be willing to slave all my life, if I could just meet up with Libanus.
LI. With my help, surely by God you'll never be free sooner.   275
LE. I'll even give two hundred fat whip-strikes off my back.
LI. He's giving away his *peculium*, he carries his whole fortune on his back.

Here the audience is pulled one way by Leonida, the other by Libanus, who has the advantage of being able to riff on Leonida's lines while Leonida remains oblivious.[38]

- name-calling, as at *As.* 297–8 (still tr7; here the combatants meet):[39]

LE. gymnasium flagri, salveto. LI. quid agis, custos carceris?
LE. o catenarum colone. LI. o virgarum lascivia.

LE. Workout gym for the whip, greetings. LI. What's up, guardian of
    the jail?
LE. You chain farmer. LI. You rod romp.

In line 297, the second player matches the syntax of the first, again with chiasmus: vocative-genitive-verb, verb-vocative-genitive; then again in 298, *o* genitive-vocative, *o* genitive-vocative. As seen above, much of the duel between Toxilus and the pimp in *Persa* consists of name-calling, sometimes, as here, in vocative-genitive pairs, sometimes just a barrage of two-syllable adjectives (*edax, furax, fugax*), although, again, symmetrically placed. This is seen also in the *flagitatio* of the pimp Ballio below; compare a fragment of Naevius, unfortunately without context: *pessimorum pessime, audax, ganeo lustro aleo* ("Worst of the worst, bold, glutton, barfly, gambler," *Com. inc.* 118).

- capping insults within lines, as at *Per.* 287–90 (continuing on from the exchange discussed in chapter 2):

SAG. potin ut molestus ne sies? PA. quod dicis facere non quis.
SAG. abi in malam rem. PA. at tu domum: nam ibi tibi parata praestost.
SAG. vadatur hic me. PA. utinam vades desint, in carcere ut sis.
SAG. quid hoc? PA. quid est? ...   290

SA: Could you possibly not be annoying. PA. You're talking about what
    you can't do.
SA: You go to hell. PA. No, you go home – hell's there already and waiting
    for you.

---

[38] On this line-for-line structure see Wallochny 1992: 69–71, 166–71 on Plautus, and 13–21 on amoibaic competition in Old Comedy.
[39] On this passage, see Wallochny 1992: 61–2, on the commonness of insult exchange in scenes of greeting.

SA. This baby'll bail me out. PA. I wish there was no bail, so you'd be
in jail.
SA. What's this? PA. Yeah, what? ...   290

The speed of the exchange here is augmented by elisions at the change
of speaker (288, 289), forcing the audience to shift along, willy-nilly. The
pace also tests the players' (or the characters') ingenuity; when at a loss,
they fall back on echoic insults, as Paegnium essentially says "No, *you* are"
to Sagaristio (287); Sagaristio himself then falls back on a formula (288).
Paegnium scores a point by picking up *vadatur* with *vades* and making
the "go" in "go to hell" literal, then turning it into a cut at what awaits
Sagaristio at home; Sagaristio responds with a figurative threat to punch
Paegnium (289). Paegnium again scores by developing Sagaristio's metaphor (and fist) into a threat of the *carcer*; then both of them take a rest
with place-holding lines (290).[40] Compare Sophoclidisca and Paegnium,
briefly at a loss: PA. *heia*! SO. *heia*! (*Per.* 212).

• interruptions, where one character starts a line and the other cuts in and
gives his words an insulting twist, as at *Cas.* 389–90 (tr7):

   OL. taceo. deos quaeso – CH. ut quidem tu hodie canem et furcam feras.
   OL. mihi ut sortito eveniat – CH. ut quidem hercle pedibus pendeas.

   OL. I am silent. I pray to the gods – CH. That indeed you might bear the
   dog and yoke today.[41]
      OL. That it may fall to my lot – CH. That indeed, by God, you might be
   strung up by your feet.

The same technique shows up as Sagaristio and Paegnium continue
their duel (*Per.* 292–3). Sagaristio begins an oath: "May all the gods and

[40] On this scene, see Wallochny 1992: 71–2. The meter is iambic septenarii (ia7), on which see Moore
2012: 184–9; this exchange forms part of a run of ia7, incorporating most of the duel between
Sagaristio and Paegnium (280–99) plus a teasing scene involving Toxilus, Sophoclidisca, and
Sagaristio, that lies partly outside Moore's grouping of ia7 runs involving the romance plot.
Arguably, the association between Sagaristio and this meter in *Persa* (also) relates to his role as
sarcastic sidekick; cf. Moore's remarks on the Roman association between this meter and comedy
(2012: 184).

[41] *Canis* here is evidently yet another sort of slave punishment; compare *Cur.* 691–2, *cum catello ut
accubes, / ferreo ego dico* ("that you should lie next to a puppy – the iron puppy, I mean") – a play on
catella, "small chain." Other uses of "dog" in Plautus suggest that the instrument itself is the object
of contempt, suggesting further that all the instruments of torture and punishment are demeaned
by association with those punished, rather than elevated by association with those who decree the
punishment, just as those who physically inflict the punishment are themselves demeaned, as seen
in chapter 2. See esp. Allen 1896: 45–6 on *canis, catulus, catellus* and Greek *skylax*; also Headlam
2001[1922]: 156 on animal names for instruments of torture in Greek, and Hunter 1994: 177–81 on
instruments of torture in Greek and the relation of the instruments to degradation (on which in
general, see duBois 1991, 2003: 103–13).

goddesses destroy me – " (*di deaeque me omnes perdant*); Paegnium cuts him off before he gets to "if": "I'm your friend, I want all your prayers to come true" (*amicus sum, eveniant volo tibi quae optas*). The oath in shtick, then, is a setup for this kind of joke. As performed in verbal dueling, this is a variation on the "technique of the pregnant pause" (*bedeutungsvolle Pause*, Lefèvre 2001: 116), also often used in oaths, as in Paegnium's "God bless … me" (*Per.* 205): suitable for a single speaker or a double act.

- back-and-forth insults, four to a line (*Am.* 344, tr7):

> ME. ain vero? SO. aio enim vero. ME. verbero. SO. mentire nunc.
> ME. So you say? SO. So I do say. ME. Flogbait. SO. Now you're lying.

The pace here is even faster, again with elision at the change of speakers, this time in combination with a pun – another quick-shifting move that demands quick response from the audience to get the joke. Picking up Sosia's *vero*, Mercurius morphs it into the insulting term *verbero*, and Sosia re-interprets it as the verb *verbero*, "I'm flogging you," which is not true at the moment, although Mercurius does beat Sosia at some points during this duel, hence Sosia's stress on "now." See next.

- fistfights, or threats of blows, as at *Amphitruo* 395 (tr7); throughout the long exchange between Mercurius and Sosia, there are repeated verbal cues for Mercurius to hit Sosia, like this:

> SO. pacem feci, foedus feci. vera dico. ME. vapula.
> SO. I made peace, I swore a truce. I'm telling the truth. ME. You take a
> beating!

This single line manifests repetition, parallel structure, alliteration, and a clean segmentation into four units, the fourth being emphasized by a blow.

The duel between Grumio and Tranio in *Mostellaria*, in its opening lines, combines many of these elements and sets up a more elaborate framework of call-and-response, including marked use of imperatives and questions (1–10):

> GR. Exi e culina sis foras, mastigia,
> qui mi inter patinas exhibes argutias.
> egredere, erilis permities, ex aedibus.
> ego pol te ruri, si vivam, ulciscar probe.
> <exi,> exi, inquam, nidoricupi, nam quid lates?   5
> TR. quid tibi, malum, hic ante aedis clamitatiost?
> an ruri censes te esse? apscede ab aedibus.

abi rus, abi dierecte, apscede ab ianua.
em, hoccine volebas? GR. perii! qur me verberas?   9–10

GR. Get out of the kitchen and outdoors, please, you whipping post,
since you're showing me how smart you are among the lasagne pans.
Step outside, the ruin of your owner, out of the house.
Gee, when I get you in the country, if I live long enough, I'll fix you right.
Get out, get out, I'm saying, you oven-smell-lover, and what are you
      hiding for?
TR. What's all this yelling from you, damn it, here outside the house?   6
Do you think you're in the country? Get away from the house.
Get back to the country, get strung up, get away from the doorway.
Pow! Is that what you wanted? GR. I'm dead! Why are you
      hitting me?   9–10

Here the elements of verbal dueling are refashioned to fit the spoken lines
of senarii (ia6), as in the duel between Toxilus and Dordalus. Notice particularly the repetition of *exi* (1, 5), along with forms of *ex* and *e-*, and
the balanced ABC, ACB structures of lines 1 and 3: imperative – adverbial phrase – name-calling; imperative – name-calling – adverbial phrase.[42]
Compare the repetition of *abi* and *apscede* in 7–10 and the triple imperative in 8; and compare the opening duel between Olympio and Chalinus,
another rural/urban pair, in *Casina*: "Get back to the country, get back to
your military zone to be hanged" (*abi rus, abi dierectus tuam in provinciam*,
103). The setting before the house door is significant; as will be seen, the
house door is the main location for *occentatio*, and one location for *flagitatio*. The same goes for the word *clamitatio* (6): *clamor* is yelling with a
purpose, yelling intended to shame the addressee (compare Dordalus, *ut
omnes audiant*, *Per.* 426; Chrysalus paying off the soldier, *ne clamorem hic
facias neu convicium*, *Bac.* 874). Grumio wants to get Tranio out of the
house; it works, with *quid lates* cuing a magnificent eruption out the door.
Grumio will lose the duel. "Why are you hitting me?" asks Grumio (9–
10); *quia vivis*, "Because you're alive," retorts Tranio, and Grumio answers
patiar, "I'll let that go" (11), like Messius Cicirrus saying *accipio* in Horace's
satire: a missed point. The use of *patior* here, with its use in double entendres elsewhere (*Capt.* 867, see chapter 4), reveals the implicit sexual stakes
in these duels: the winner is top, the loser is bottom, which would become
a marked characteristic of later Roman humor.

---

[42] Lindsay has *nidoricupi nam* at 5 for MSS *nidor culine*; de Melo takes Pylades' *nidor e culina*, punc-
tuating *exi, inquam, nidor, e culina*, which would produce another variant on lines 1 and 3: imperative – parenthesis – name-calling – adverbial phrase.

The content in verbal duels, as already illustrated, takes a familiar shape: slaves accuse other slaves of having been frequently punished, or threaten that punishment lies ahead; slaves argue about who is more likely to gain manumission; slaves accuse each other of having been used for sex; a "good slave" like Grumio accuses another of harming the owner. Slaves are not supposed to insult free people, although onstage they frequently do (chapters 4, 6). The Mercator in *Asinaria* is stunned when Leonida and Libanus insult him: "You, a slave, insult a free person?" (*tun libero homini / male servos loquere?*, *As.* 477–8). Menaechmus I, trying to placate his wife, guesses that she is angry because their slaves have broken this rule, and promises to punish them: "The slave-women or the male slaves haven't talked back to you, / have they? Tell me. They won't get away with it" (*num ancillae aut servei tibi / responsant? eloquere. inpune non erit*, *Men.* 620–1). The power to insult, on the other hand, is freely available between slaves: "You crime, are you still insulting me?" says Sagaristio to Paegnium; "Since you're a slave, it should at least be okay for a slave to insult you," Paegnium replies (SAG. *etiam, scelus, male loquere?* PA. *tandem uti liceat, / quom servos sis, servom tibi male dicere*, *Per.* 290–1).

Insult matches between free characters are less common. The back-and-forth between the neighbors Alcesimus and Lysidamus plays mostly on a series of questions, especially a barrage introduced by *quin* (*Cas.* 604–9, ia6), which elsewhere commonly introduces insulting or sarcastic questions (see chapter 8). The teasing exchange between Agorastocles and the Advocati in *Poenulus* (721–40, ia6) perhaps mocks forensic cross-examination; the tense introductory scene between Agorastocles and this anomalous chorus ends in a brief exchange of body-part curses (570–1, tr7):

> [AG.] quin etiam deciderint femina vobis in talos velim.
> ADV. at edepol nos tibi in lumbos linguam atque oculos in solum.

> AG. In fact, I wish your thighs would fall right on your ankles.
> ADV. But, gee, us to you: your tongue on your crotch, and your eyes on the ground.

The soldier Antamoenides in *Poenulus*, astounded to see the Carthaginian Hanno with his arm around the prostitute the soldier plans to buy, launches into a series of single insults that use Hanno's foreign dress to liken him to a working man in a long tunic – an inn's boy or a porter (*puer cauponius*, 1298; *baiiolum*, 1301, tr7) – or an effeminate man: "womanish," "African hussy," "woman" (*mulierosum, amatricem Africam, mulier*, 1303–5,

switching into senarii at 1304).[43] Then, in a brief barrage, the soldier compares Hanno to a list of squashy, smelly, foreign things (1309–14):

> ANTA. ligula, in' malam crucem?
> tune hic amator audes esse, hallex viri,   1310
> aut contrectare quod mares homines amant?
> deglupta maena, sarrapis sementium,
> manstruca, halagora, sampsa, tum autem plenior
> ali ulpicique quam Romani remiges.

> ANTA. You shoelace, will you get crucified?
> You dare to set up as a lover here, you fish-sauce man,   1310
> or put your filthy paws on what male persons love?
> You skinned sardine, you seedy Levantine,
> you smelly sheepskin, you fishmarket, you smashed olive,
> you're more stuffed with garlic and Punic garlic than Roman rowers.[44]

The items on his list are exotic, in a cheap way, but also produce a magnificent outpouring of brick-like syllables: the glop of *deglupta*, the hiss
of *sarrapis sementium*, the eruptive *manstruca, halagora, sampsa*. The triple epithet recalls the cadence of the duel between Toxilus and Dordalus.[45]
The list evokes, like the *puer cauponius* and the *baiiolus*, the detritus of the
marketplace, what Virginia Woolf called "bargaining and cheapening";
the *malam crucem* and the *remiges* evoke the direst precincts of slavery and
poverty. The soldier is not a sympathetic character, while Hanno has been

---

[43] On *baiiolus* (or *baiulus*) and unskilled labor, see chapter 2. The soldier goes on to say that Hanno
smells like a rower in the fleet; similarly, one of the speakers in Cicero's *De oratore* cites a scrap of
Caecilius Statius that seems to pair *remigem … aut baiulum* (*De orat.* 2.40; but see Caecilius 274
R₃, where Ribbeck takes only the oarsman to belong to Caecilius). For *mulierosus* "womanish,"
not "womanizing," compare, among many common formations in *-osus* in the Plautine corpus,
hircosus ("goaty," *Mer.* 575), *radiossus* ("radiant," *St.* 365) – both, like *mulierosus*, hapax – and the
repeated forms *latebrosus* "shadowy," *rabiosus* "crazy," *ventriosus* "paunchy." The soldier goes on
to call Agorastocles a *cinaedus* who should have a *tympanum* (1317–18) like the eunuch priests of
Cybele, continuing to impugn his opponents' masculinity in opposition to his own (cf. *Bac.* 845).
The idea of womanizers as effeminate, however, does appear in another insult by a soldier, calling
his rival a *moechum malacum, cincinnatum, / … tympanotribam* ("soft adulterer, with curled hair, …
a drum-banger," *Truc.* 609–11).

[44] For translation and brief notes on the text, see Richlin 2005: 270; Starks 2000: 177–81, who emphasizes the low-class associations of the items on the list, and argues that all have an insulting sexual
sense. *Hallex* at 1310 is a guess for the MSS semi-legible *fallax*. On the vegetables in line 1314, see
de Melo 2012: 159, who translates *ulpici* as "Phoenician garlic," citing Columella, *Rust.* 11.3.20 (who
in fact says that some people call *ulpicum* "Punic garlic"); perhaps more pertinently, Cato (*De agr.*
71) recommends it for use in cattle medicine. On the "Roman rower," see above on slaves and poor
men in the Roman fleet; after the sack of New Carthage in 210, there were plenty of Punic slaves
rowing; on the ethnic implications of their double diet, see chapter 7.

[45] The triple epithet is peculiar to the early *palliata* (cf. above on Naevius, *Com. inc.* 118) and is found
neither in early tragedy nor in Ennius *Satires*.

established as good; the soldier's top-down insults backfire. After this tirade, following up on his feminization of Hanno, the soldier accuses the young owner Agorastocles of being a *cinaedus* rather than a *vir* (1317–18), which leads to physical threats from Agorastocles (1319–20). Both the soldier and Agorastocles threaten punishments usually reserved for slaves (*excruciandum ... carnufici dabo*, 1302; *fustis*, 1320), a move characteristic of many exchanges of insults, even between free characters. As with the instruments of torture and punishment, invective itself, as a tool, belongs at the bottom.

Flagitatio, Occentatio, Quiritatio

The Roman folk form *flagitatio* appears throughout the plays, not only acted out but also referred to as a feared form of communal policing through shame.[46] That it was a kind of street theater is evident, and implied by Diniarchus' bitter threat against the prostitute Phronesium outside her house, which begins, "I'll put on a show by shouting in the street" (*ludos faciam clamore in via*, *Truc.* 759–63); compare Tranio's *ante aedis clamitatio* (above). The street-scene setting of most Roman comedy places the spectators exactly where they would normally be for optimum real-life rubbernecking – a fact brought out at the end of *Mercator*, after a scene of *flagitatio*, as one of the shouters says, "Let's go inside, this place isn't serviceable for your deeds / (while we're discussing them), that passersby should be their arbiters" (*eamus intro, non utibilest hic locus, factis tuis, / dum memoramus, arbitri ut sint qui praetereant per vias*, 1005–6). [All look at audience.] The pimp Ballio in *Pseudolus* connects the dots between real-life *flagitatio* and stage comedy (1081–3, ia6), referring to an extended *flagitatio* scene earlier in the play as

> nugas theatri, verba quae in comoediis
> solent lenoni dici, quae pueri sciunt:
> malum et scelestum et peiiurum aibat esse me.
>
> theater nonsense, the words that by custom
> are said to the pimp in comedies, even children know them:
> he said I was "bad" and "criminal" and "an oath-breaker."

---

[46] On *flagitatio*, shaming punishments, and Roman honor, see Barton 2001: 18–21, who refers to the censor as "a sort of chief shamer." For *flagitatio* in the context of self-help punishment in early law, see Kelly 1966: 22–3. Wallochny 1992 deals with *flagitatio* only briefly (95 n. 162) and credits the roots of verbal dueling in the *palliata* to Fescennine verses, mime, and Atellane farce (88–97, 189–93). Since almost nothing remains of any of these forms from the mid-Republic, and the word *Fescenninus* does not appear in the extant *palliata*, I will not make use of them here.

His lines not only make a metatheatrical joke but suggest, again, the presence of children among the *palliata* audience, or at least the childhood socialization of people living in the cities where the *palliata* played – socialization into both the language of the *palliata* and the language forms the *palliata* re-enacted.[47] As with the late Republican audience's taunts of Sarmentus (above), the exchange of insults potentially incorporated the audience, not just as bystanders but as participants. The process itself, moreover, had specific associations.

Flagitatio was a way of dunning a debtor or a dispossessor; a century and a half after Plautus, the equestrian poet Catullus uses this form, whereby an owner demands his property back, to make one of the invectives among his lyric poems (c. 42). First he summons friends to help him – here, metapoetically, the friends are the verses themselves (1–2):

> Adeste, hendecasyllabi, quot estis
> omnes undique, quotquot estis omnes.

> Come here, hendecasyllables, as many as you are
> all of you, everywhere, as many as you are, all of you.

Then he says what he has lost (his notebook), and calls the woman who has taken it a "foul adulteress" (*moecha turpis*, 3). Then he asks his friends to act with him in dunning her: *reflagitemus* (6). Then, after some more nasty descriptions of the woman, comparing her with a dog, he gives his friends the direct command, and they all chant together (10–12):

> circumsistite eam, et reflagitate,   10
> "moecha putida, redde codicillos,
> redde, putida moecha, codicillos!"

> Stand on each side of her, and shout for them back: 10
> "Adulteress putrid, give me back my notebook;
> give back, putrid adulteress, my notebook!"

More name-calling: now she is "dirt, whorehouse" (*lutum, lupanar*, 13); then, "in a louder voice" (*altiore voce*, 18), the chant is repeated (19–20).

The hendecasyllabic meter was sometimes used for Greek *skolia*, convivial verses that featured back-and-forth verse-capping, and was a favorite of Catullus in his polymetric collection; moreover, theft is a general theme in Catullus' poetry book (cf. esp. c. 12 on the napkin thief, where the alternatives are return of the object (*remitte*, 12.11), or "three hundred

---

[47] That these lines attest to the presence of children at the plays is viewed with skepticism by Peter Brown (2013); Ballio's words can be taken to mean simply that the insults were childish.

hendecasyllables" (10; cf. *Per.* 410–11)).[48] But in this one poem, Catullus uses elements already familiar from verbal duels in Plautus, both in content (the comparison to a dog; the words *putidus* and *lutum*) and in form: the chanted refrain here takes the chiastic form seen above in verbal duels, which is characteristic of *flagitatio*: "a stylistic device of popular eloquence," as Fraenkel says (1961: 48). In Plautine *flagitatio*, verbs like *redde*, "return," often appear, and the performance is said to take place either in the forum (*Epid.* 118–19, *Ps.* 1145) or in the street outside the debtor's front door: "like a *flagitator* he's always standing in front of my house," *quasi flagitator astat usque ad ostium* (a lame joke about the sun, *Mos.* 768); cook to Euclio, "If you don't order my pots to be returned right this second, / I'm going to tear you apart by squawking here in front of your house" (*te <iam> iam, nisi reddi / mihi vasa iubes, pipulo hic differam ante aedis*, *Aul.* 445–6).[49] When *flagitatio* takes place onstage, it is, then, in the right place: outside the front door. If the creditor has supporters, they surround the debtor (like Catullus and his hendecasyllables), with the verb *circumsisto* or forms of the adverb *altrinsecus*, and occasionally *clamor* or *flagitium*, *appello* or *compello*, used as a cue. In Plautus' plays, slave characters sometimes serve as the little hendecasyllables do in Catullus' poem.

So Libanus and Leonida surround their young owner, in a clinch with his beloved: "Let's stand on either side of them, and, one of us from this side, from the other side, the other, let's call them out" (*circumsistamus, alter hinc, hinc alter appellemus*, *As.* 618, ia7), a double chiasmus – here you can see how the sentence structure echoes the physical act of surrounding. The neighbor *senex* and the young man's friend in *Mercator* surround the young man's lecherous father, who has bought the young man's *amica*: "I'll stand next to him from here, on the other side. / Let's both keep loading

---

[48] On hendecasyllabic meter in *skolia*, see Ellis 1889: xli; on *skolia* and verse-capping, Griffith 1990: 192–3. The association between *skolia* and the aristocratic symposium has been challenged by Gregory Jones, who associates them with "the voice of the demos" (2014: 257). Certainly *skolia* are picked up in Old Comedy in non-elite contexts. On verbal dueling in Catullus 42, see Fraenkel 1961, following Usener 1901: 20–1 and arguing that Catullus used the form in the spirit of Plautus and popular custom rather than that of Callimachus and antiquarian preciosity. Chiastic structure appears in invective in Catullus 16.2; 58.1, 2; 61.124–8 (Fescennines), as well as in *Catalepton* 12.1–3 (Fescennines; note *putidum caput*, 12.1). Triple epithets like those in Naevius, *Com. inc.* 118 and *Persa* appear at Catull. 29.2, 10 (*impudicus et vorax et aleo*); this poem has a second refrain (29.5, 9, *cinaede Romule, haec videbis et feres?*).

[49] On *pipulo* here and in other testimonia as the racket made by *flagitatio*, see Usener 1901: 23. Usener compares *obvagulatum ito* in the XII Tables (2.3; Festus 262L), where the place of a subpoena is served by shouting outside the house door; *vagulatio* is defined as *quaestio cum convicio*, Festus 514L. Warmington, fond of a quaint translation, renders *obvagulatum* as "waul" (1938: 437). Compare *Poen.* 31, where the hungry babies *obvagiant* "like kids." Usener notes the theme of animal noise comparison, and compares the term "Katzenmusik" as applied to the charivari (1901: 27).

him with the words he deserves" (*ego adsistam hinc alterinsecus. / quibus est dictis dignus usque oneremus ambo, Mer.* 977–8, tr7). Then the two of them take turns with the refrain "Are you still talking, you ghost?" (*etiam loquere, larva? Mer.* 981, 983); like the wife's refrain at the end of *Asinaria* – "get up, lover, and go home" (*surge, amator, i domum,* 921, 923, 924, 925), also in tr7 – this one seems suitable for being picked up by the audience. Finally the friend says, "Give her back to him" (*redde illi*), and the father says, twice, "He can have her for himself" (*sibi habeat; sibi habeat licet,* 989) – relinquishing ownership.[50] When the slave Pseudolus and his young owner Calidorus move to attack Ballio, Calidorus orders Pseudolus, "Stand next to him on the other side and load him with insults" (*Ps.* 357, tr7, *adsiste altrim secus atque onera hunc maledictis*). The probably Plautine *Cornicula* seems to have had a scene in which characters surrounded a soldier to insult him, as Varro quotes from it: *quid cessamus ludos facere? circus noster ecce adest* ("Why hesitate to hold our games? Look, our Circus is here," tr7, fr. 62); the soldier is the *circus,* Varro explains, because, when he enters, "those mocking him surround him" (*circumeunt ludentes, L.* 5.153). Again, here, *flagitatio* is a form of theater. Entertainingly, as the *senex* Periphanes in *Epidicus* realizes that the *fidicina* he has been trying to palm off on the soldier is freed and not saleable, and refuses to hand back to her the *fides* he has been holding, she threatens to dun him for it: "You're not returning my *fides?* / … I'll leave. / But with a louder outcry you *will* return it later" (*fides non reddis? … / … abiero. / flagitio cum maiore post reddes tamen,* ia6, *Epid.* 514–16). Presumably she plans to come back with helpers.

The spectacular attack on Ballio takes the simple form of a rapid fire of epithets in the vocative case, spoken alternately by Calidorus and Pseudolus, each insult being smugly accepted by the pimp. The scene is prompted by the discovery that Ballio has sold something Calidorus wants – his *amica* (*Ps.* 347) – much as Charinus in *Mercator* wants his *amica* back, and Toxilus wants his *amica* to be freed. Money, however, is the basic problem; Ballio cues the barrage by pointing out that he, the wicked pimp, has money, while the self-righteous, well-born Calidorus has none (*ego scelestus nunc argentum promere po<ti>s sum domo; / tu qui pius,*

---

[50] For the insulting response *etiam loquere,* see the insult duel between Sagaristio and Paegnium above (*Per.* 290), and below, chapter 6. This scene in *Mercator* is the only instance of *flagitatio* discussed by Scafuro (1997: 185–6), who is mainly interested in what this scene has to do with the lost Greek original: "The *flagitatio* has replaced the mechanism of reconciliation that probably belonged to the Greek original. … Here we have another instance of the parody of Attic social practice and theatrical convention." Citing Usener, she sees *flagitatio* as related in general to "the public shaming of a wrong-doer," and does not tie it in with the problem of debt (see below), which was not part of the purview of her study.

istoc es genere gnatus, nummum non habes, 355–6). Calidorus and Pseudolus take up their positions and set upon Ballio (359–68, tr7):

> CALI. ingere mala multa. PS. iam ego te differam dictis meis.
> inpudice. BA. itast. CALI. sceleste. BA. dicis vera. PS. verbero.   360
> BA. quippini? CALI. bustirape. BA. certo. PS. furcifer. BA. factum optume.
> CALI. sociofraude. BA. sunt mea istaec. PS. parricida. BA. perge tu.
> CALI. sacrilege. BA. fateor. PS. peiiure. BA. vetera vaticinamini.
> CALI. legerupa. BA. valide. PS. permities adulescentum. BA. acerrume.
> CALI. fur. BA. babae! PS. fugitive. BA. bombax! CALI. fraus populi.
> BA. planissume.   365
> PS. fraudulente. CALI. inpure. PS. leno. CALI. caenum. BA. cantores
> probos!
> CALI. verberavisti patrem atque matrem. BA. atque occidi quoque
> potius quam cibum praehiberem: num peccavi quippiam?

> CALI. Heap a lot of bad things on him. PS. Now I'll tear you apart with
> my words.
> Shameless slut.[51] BA. Yup. CALI. Criminal. BA. You're right. PS. Flogbait.
> BA. Why not? CALI. Tomb-robber. BA. Sure. PS. Yoke-wearer. BA.
> Well done!
> CALI. Embezzler. BA. Done that, too. PS. Killed your parents. BA.
> Keep going.
> CALI. Temple-robber. BA. I confess. PS. Oath-breaker. BA. Old news.
> CALI. Law-breaker. BA. Very much so. PS. Young men's ruin. BA. So glad
> to do it!
> CALI. Thief. BA. Oh yeah. PS. Runaway. BA. Yowza. CALI. Cheater of the
> people. BA. So obviously.   365
> PS. Cheater. CALI. Unclean. PS. Pimp. CALI. Filth. BA. Honest
> eulogy, guys!
> CALI. You flogged your father and mother. BA. And killed them, too,
> rather than give them food: did I do something wrong?

The pounding beat of trochaic septenarii fosters the litany of single-word insults while the long line makes room for changes of speaker; compare the long scene between Mercurius and Sosia at the beginning of *Amphitruo* (263–462, tr7, demarcated by change of meter), or between Libanus and Leonida at *Asinaria* 267–380 (tr7), or between Paegnium and Sophoclidisca at *Persa* 200–50 (tr7). The terms of abuse are familiar from the verbal duels seen above, and add a calendar of the worst crimes in Roman culture: tomb-robbing, temple-robbing, breaking an oath, fraud, killing parents. In addition, Ballio is called by names usually reserved for

---

[51] See Usener 1901: 25 n. 48: "*Impudicus* steht geradezu für *pathicus*" (with some later parallels). This duel inspired Usener's essay, as Fraenkel noted; Usener discusses it in full at 1901: 25–7.

slaves (*verbero, furcifer, fugitive*), and accused of doing what pimps do for
a living – ruin young men (364); indeed, "pimp" itself is used here, self-
reflexively, as an insult (366) – the ultimate insult, for Pseudolus. Ballio's
winning technique takes the novel form of acceding to each insult, usually
the mark of a lost point in a duel, as seen above with *accipiam* and *patiar*.
That Ballio feels no shame is part of his onstage identity as a pimp, as he
says himself (1081–3, above); as Toxilus says to Sagaristio when Dordalus
charges him extra for a moneybag: "He's a pimp, he's not doing anything
surprising" (*quando lenost, nihil mirum facit, Per.* 688).

That being shouted at in public was normally shameful is implied by
jokes. When young Stratippocles in *Epidicus* asks his friend Chaeribulus
for a loan, Chaeribulus first says, "God, if I had it, I'd <promise you>" (*si
hercle haberem <pollicerer>*, 116); pressed further, he replies, "But I myself,
by God, am torn apart by shouting, I am dunned" (*quin edepol egomet
clamore differor, difflagitor*, 118; for *differor*, compare *Aul.* 446, *Ps.* 359,
above). Stratippocles' reply shows how bad this is: "I'd rather my friends
like you were burned up in the oven than flamed in the forum" (*malim
istiusmodi mi amicos forno occensos quam foro*, 119.[52] He has the bakehouse
on his mind; two lines later, he threatens the eavesdropping Epidicus with
the *pistor*). Chaeribulus is like a slave here in that a slave has no money, but
also in that he is shouted at; Epidicus, at the end of the play, complains,
"I'm being shouted at like a slave" (*inclamitor quasi servos*, 711; a joke,
since he is still a slave). For a free person, this is degrading, and not only
metaphorically so, for an audience familiar with debt bondage (below).
The prologue speaker in *Menaechmi* says he can remember Menaechmus'
grandfather's name the more easily "because I saw him dunned by shouting" (*quia illum clamore vidi flagitarier, Men.* 46) – a laugh line. When the
soldier's slave Harpax first sees the *senex* Simo and the pimp Ballio, he asks
Simo if he is the pimp, pointing at him; Simo gets angry, threatens him
with a beating, and clears things up: "*He's* the pimp [points at Ballio], but
this guy [points at self] is an honest man" (*hic leno est, at hic est vir probus,
Ps.* 1144). Ballio picks him up on this: "But you, Mr. Good Man, are often
dunned by shouting in the forum, / when there's never a nickel, except
what this pimp assists you with" (*sed tu, bone vir, flagitare saepe clamore in
foro, / quom libella nusquamst, nisi quid leno hic subvenit tibi, Ps.* 1145–6)
– the same point he scores off Simo's son Calidorus in the *flagitatio* scene.

---

[52] *Occensos* is Usener's emendation for the MSS *mensos* (1901: 12 n. 20), engineering a play on *occensus*
"burned up" (only in Ennius, *Ann.* 14.9 [v. 387 Skutsch], attested by Festus 218L) and *occentatio*, the
process of chanting at someone, on which see below.

Charinus in *Mercator* complains that his own father "sets up a shout all over the city" to announce that no one should trust him if he asked for a loan (51–2; *conclamitare tota urbe*). As seen in chapter 2, the Advocati in *Poenulus* say proudly, "We don't dun anybody and nobody duns us" (*neque nos quemquam flagitamus neque nos quisquam flagitat*, 539).

The basic problem is credit, and a public reputation for trustworthiness. In an extended scene in *Mostellaria*, the moneylender Misargyrides ("Son of Cash-hater") sets out to dun Philolaches for the interest on the money he has loaned him (all in senarii). He makes it clear that he wants the interest first, and then the principal (592, 598–600), and Tranio, to his face, calls this free man "beast" (*belua*, 569, 607–8, 619); both in Misargyrides' presence and after he exits, Tranio expresses loathing for moneylenders as a class: "a man who's a *danista*, the class that's most dishonest" (*danista qui sit, genu' quod inprobissumum est*, 626); "By God, no class of persons is more disgusting today / nor less legitimate than the moneylending class" (*nullum edepol hodie genus est hominum taetrius / nec minu' bono cum iure quam danisticum*, 657–8). Misargyrides is identified throughout the scene as a *danista*, and this Greek occupation-type enters the forum along with the cash-flow problems endemic in the Hellenistic world, as seen in chapter 1.

Onstage, Misargyrides is standing in front of Philolaches' house, and he begins to shout for his money: "I know you have a good voice, don't shout so much," says Tranio (*scio te bona esse voce, ne clama nimis*, 576); "By God, but I'm really going to shout," replies the moneylender (*ego hercle vero clamo*, 577); "Whoa, vigorous! / You're enjoying good fortune now that you're shouting," says Tranio, cutting him off in mid-yell (*eugae strenue! / beatus vero es nunc quom clamas*, 587–8); the moneylender threatens to shout for Philolaches by name (*iam hercle ego illunc nominabo*, 587), and to stay in front of the house until midday (582). Tranio brings up and dismisses the idea that Philolaches might go into exile on account of the debt (596–7); that the dunning is a cause of shame is explicitly stated by Tranio's owner: "Why is this man calling out (*compellat*) my son Philolaches so / and why is he making an insulting outcry (*convicium*) in your presence?" (616–17). Misargyrides, although without any helpers, is warming up for a full-fledged *flagitatio*, and tells Tranio that, if he will only pay up, this will put an end to all his *responsiones* (591) – a reminder of *respondeo* in the insult match between Toxilus and Dordalus. Sure enough, when no money is forthcoming, the moneylender begins to chant (*Mos.* 603–5):

cedo faenus, redde faenus, faenus reddite.
daturin estis faenus actutum mihi?
datur faenus mi? ...

Give me the interest, return the interest, the interest – you guys, return it.
Aren't you going to give me the interest right now?
Will the interest be given to me? …

"Interest there, interest here!" says Tranio, reduced to mimicry (*faenus illic, faenus hic!*, 605).

The moneylender's chant picks up on the earlier exchange between him ("Will the interest then be returned to me," *reddetur igitur faenus?*) and Tranio ("It will return: now go away," *reddet: nunc abi, Mos.* 580), which is continued by Tranio's line, "No, go home, by God, I'm telling the truth, just go away" (*immo abi domum, verum hercle dico, abi modo*, 583). The injunction to go away repeats the duel between Tranio and Grumio and the duel between Olympio and Chalinus; as for the format, it can now be seen that, in the duel between Toxilus and Dordalus, each of their speeches ends with a classically chiastic *flagitatio* refrain. Each uses the *flagitatio* format to cap his stream of insults; returning to the duel in *Persa*, we can now see how Toxilus ironically reverses the usual demand by dunning the pimp to *take* the money to free his *amica* (*Per.* 412–14):

accipin argentum? accipe sis argentum, inpudens,
tene sis argentum, etiam tu argentum tenes?
possum te facere ut argentum accipias, lutum?

Will you take your cash? Please take your cash, shameless!
Please have your cash, your cash, are you even going to have it?
Can I make you take your cash, dirtbag?

Dordalus returns to convention (422–4, *cedo sis mi argentum, da mihi argentum, impudens*), and underscores the point by saying he is shouting for his cash "so all may hear" (426).

Money is the basic problem, but female slaves are also a commodity. The practice of *occentatio* in Plautus consists of a mob first clamoring for a woman outside the doors of a house and then setting fire to the doors; the woman's owners are shamed by the process. The scene somewhat resembles the charivari as attested in modern Europe, in that it enforces community values, although *occentatio* more blatantly expresses the crowd's straightforward desire for the woman.[53] The *senex* in *Mercator* paints a picture of what is likely to happen if his son presents his mother with Pasicompsa as an attendant (405–11, tr7):

---

[53] On the charivari, see Davis 1971 (on sixteenth-century France), esp. 52–3; Barker 2013 (on seventeenth-century Italy); Thompson 1992 on the English equivalent, "rough music," esp. on the

... illa forma matrem familias 405
flagitium sit sei sequatur; quando incedat per vias,
contemplent, conspiciant omnes, nutent, nictent, sibilent,
vellicent, vocent, molesti sint; occentent ostium:
impleantur elegeorum meae fores carbonibus.
atque, ut nunc sunt maledicentes homines, uxori meae 410
mihique obiectent lenocinium facere. ...

        ... A shape like that, if she were accompanying 405
a married lady, it'd be a public scandal; when she'd be walking down the
   street,
they'd all stare, they'd look at her, they'd nod, they'd wink, they'd whistle,
they'd pinch her, call her, they'd annoy her; they'd set up a chant outside
   the door:
my front door would be filled up with coals of poesy.
Also, the way people are given to insult these days, they'd be accusing 410
my wife and me of setting up in the pimp business.

The *flagitium* he fears here is related to the *flagitium* the *fidicina* threatens to use to get her *fides* back: something simultaneously disgraceful and loud. According to Cicero, the XII Tables included strictures against anyone "who had performed *occentatio* or made up a song whereby he caused disrepute or *flagitium* to another" (*si quis occentavisset sive carmen condidisset, quo infamiam faceret flagitiumve alteri, De rep.* 4.2 = XII Tables 8.1), and Festus says, retailing the opinion of Verrius Flaccus in the late Republic (190L),

> *Occentassint* antiqui dicebant quod nunc convicium fecerint dicimus, quod id clare et cum quodam canore fit, ut procul exaudiri possit. Quod turpe habetur, quia non sine causa fieri putatur. Inde cantilenam dici †querellam, non cantus† iucunditatem, puto.[54]

> The ancients used to say *occentassint* ["they sang against"] to describe what we now would call *convicium fecerint* ["they made an insulting outcry"], because this is done loudly and with a certain melodic quality, so that it can be heard from far off. It is considered shameful, because it is thought to be

---

use of rhyming, memorization of format and elements, the relation of folk to "dignified" forms, and the "total publicity of disgrace" (8); also Davis 1975: 139, on "truth-telling." Usener ended his study of "folk justice" with a note on the persistence of these forms into medieval Italy, as attested by the city ordinances of Bergamo. See below on the parallel with some Greek customs, and Forsdyke 2012: 144–70, for comparison between Greek and early modern customs.

[54] I print Lindsay's text with the dubious parts obelized; the noteworthy word in the last sentence is *cantilenam*, with its suggestion of singsong and repetition. *Querellam* is a conjecture for MSS *quia illam*, already in Paulus; as *cantus* is for *candus*.

done not without cause. Hence I think the [grievance?] is so called [because it takes the form of?] a refrain, [not for the] pleasingness [of the song?].

The elements of loudness and the refrain format, in these definitions, link together *occentatio* and *flagitatio* with the abstract terms *flagitium* and *convicium*, seen above in *Bacchides* and *Mostellaria*.[55] Again here in *Mercator*, capping the mostly non-verbal street harassment, there is some kind of chant in front of the house door, and the house is treated as a brothel, the family as brothel-keepers like Ballio. A married lady should have an ugly maid, the old man argues, one because of whom "no *flagitium* would come to our front door" (*neque ... quicquam eveniet nostris foribus flagiti*, 417).

The *carbones* at the climax of the attack on the house are sticks of charcoal to write with, scrawling the *elegea* (a unique use of this term in Plautus) onto the door like a slave tattoo, a visual version of the chanting in *occentent* (cf. Catull. 37.10). Yet their fiery origin is strongly suggested by the description of *occentatio* that Toxilus uses while persuading Dordalus to buy the Virgo (all in tr7). He paints a picture of how rich she will make him, and how many of the "best men" (*optumis viris*) will come to him for a party (*Per.* 564–8); Dordalus, slow on the uptake, says he will keep them outside; Toxilus then cannot resist a swerve aside into threatening the pimp: "But then they'll chant in front of your door at night, they'll burn down your front door" (*at enim illi noctu occentabunt ostium, exurent fores*, 569): an elite mob. The extreme act of arson is connected in Greek performance texts with the climax of komastic revelry (implicitly upper-class), and *parasitoi* in Middle Comedy boast of their ability to help their patrons attack a house: climbing ladders, fighting, prying doors open, rushing in. The pimp in Herodas *Mim.* 2 complains about such behavior, again with a class inflection (33–9, cf. 52). In the *palliata*, parties are not so violent.[56] But fire and the charivari underlie Usener's suggested emendation of *occensos* seen above, in a context that combines an oven

[55] For discussion, see Lintott 1999: 8–9; Usener 1901: 3–5, with reference to this passage in *Mercator* and to the passage below in *Persa*. On the fear of public disgrace over failed *fides* expressed in *flagitium volgo dispalescere* at *Bac.* 1046, see Owens 1994: 397.

[56] In Middle Comedy: Aristophon, *Iatros* fr. 5 = Ath. 6.238b–c; Antiphanes *Progonoi* fr. 193, = Ath. 6.238c–d. For a wide array of sources, see Headlam 2001[1922]: 82–4, on Herodas *Mim.* 2.36–7: "one of the most picturesque features of Greek and Roman life, the practice of young men in the evening after their wine ... sallying forth alone or in bands" (82). In the *palliata*, violence at the house door only at *Bac.* 1118–20 (no fire, just a threat of axes, instantly quashed) and Terence, *Eun.* 771–91 (a comic military assault, with a very faint suggestion of fire in the invocation of King Pyrrhus, 783 – "Burns").

with *flagitatio*. A connection with burning, although not based in etymology, hangs around both terms: *flagito* with *flagro*, *occento* with *incendo*. The infatuated young man at the pimp's door in *Curculio* is at the right address when he cues himself, "Suppose I go up to the front door and set up a chant?" (*quid si adeam ad fores atque occentem*, 145); the polite and silly serenade that follows, then, is something of a surprise.

The practices of *flagitatio* and *occentatio* have points in common with *quiritatio*, the public cry for help whereby a person in trouble could appeal to all others in earshot to defend him against hostile force. By the time of Varro, it had this name, with its basis in citizenship: *quiritare dicitur is qui Quiritium fidem clamans implorat* ("That man is said to 'quiritate' who shouts to invoke the *fides* of the *Quirites* [Roman citizens]," *L.* 6.68). This is certainly the sense it bears in sources from the later Republic; in the *palliata*, however, the practice is not so restrictive, although the conjoined terms *fidem*, *clamo*, and *imploro* have a well-established technical sense onstage. Possible interactive staging is suggested by several direct appeals to the audience for help (*auxilium*) in cases of theft, all of which invite the audience to point and shout out directions: the slave-woman Halisca calls on "my dear people, my dear spectators" (*mei homines, mei spectatores*, *Cist.* 678); the soldier in *Curculio* offers a reward (590); the miser Euclio beseeches the audience, "I beg you, ... / I plead, I call you to witness" (*opsecro ego vos ... / oro, optestor*, *Aul.* 715–16). Fear of violence, however, rates full *quiritatio*, perhaps inviting a barrage of *fabuli* from the audience. The *parasitus* Curculio, who has been treated as a slave by the soldier, first starts a fistfight and then calls on the citizens for help: *o cives, cives!* (*Cur.* 626). Menaechmus I, attacked by the slaves of the *senex*, appeals to the citizens of Epidamnus for help: "I beg your loyal help, / Epidamnians, rescue me, citizens!" (*opsecro vostram fidem, / Epidamnienses, subvenite, cives!* *Men.* 999–1000). In a way, he performs a counter-*flagitatio*, as he asks of the crowd attacking him, "Why are you surrounding me?" (*quid me circumsistitis?* 998). In the event, it is the loyal slave Messenio who comes to the rescue. As seen in chapter 2, Sosia slips in a bit of *quiritatio* when he calls out to the audience (or to the gods), *obsecro vostram fidem* (*Am.* 455); the formal cry was *pro fidem, Quirites!* Indeed Sosia has made use of the formula earlier, as Mercurius beats him: *pro fidem, Thebani cives!* (376), at which Mercurius jeers, "Are you still shouting, you executioner?" (*etiam clamas, carnufex?*) – an ironic insult to choose, in the circumstances. Sosia, of course, is no citizen, but he is certainly being forcibly abused, and needs rescuing; he is not the only slave in the *palliata* to make such an appeal, either. The slave Trachalio in *Rudens* appeals to the citizens of Cyrene to come to the aid of the two slave prostitutes who have taken refuge in the shrine of Venus, in an elaborate *quiritatio* (615–26, erupting into tr7 in an entrance cued by *quid hic … clamoris oritur*, 613–14):

> TR. Pro Cyrenenses populares! vostram ego imploro fidem,   615
> agricolae, accolae propinqui qui estis his regionibus,
> ferte opem inopiae atque exemplum pessumum pessum date.
> vindicate, ne inpiorum potior sit pollentia
> quam innocentum, qui se scelere fieri nolunt nobilis.
> statuite exemplum inpudenti, date pudori praemium,   620
> facite hic lege potius liceat quam vi victo vivere.
> currite huc in Veneris fanum, vostram iterum imploro fidem,
> qui prope hic adestis quique auditis clamorem meum,
> ferte suppetias qui Veneri Veneriaeque antistitae
> more antiquo in custodelam suom commiserunt caput;   625
> praetorquete iniuriae priu' collum quam ad vos pervenat.

> TR. Help! Fellow-countrymen of Cyrene! I invoke your *fides*,   615
> farmers, neighbors, who are nearby in these parts,
> bring help to the helpless and do your worst to the worst kind.
> Deliver them, lest the power of the impious be more powerful
> than of the innocent, who do not want themselves to be made notorious
>   by crime.
> Make an example for the shameless, give a prize to chastity,   620
> make this a place where it's permitted to the vanquished to live by law
>   rather than by force.
> Run to the shrine of Venus here, I invoke your *fides* again,
> you who are nearby here, and you who hear my outcry,
> Bring help to those who have entrusted their *caput* to Venus
> and to the guardianship of Venus' priestess, in the age-old custom;   625
> wring the neck of *iniuria* before it comes to *you*.

Indeed he makes quite a ruckus (*clamorem* 623 picking up 614), and Daemones, as he interrupts and Trachalio flings himself at his knees, expresses annoyance, ordering him, "Explain to me why you are starting a riot" (*quid sit mi expedi / quod tumultues*, 628–9). This cues a loop of shtick, punctuated by the repeated cue *ut mi istuc dicas negoti quid sit quod tumultues* (638); *tumultus* was civil unrest necessitating an emergency call to arms: the owner's view, just as Daemones' *clamoris* differs from Trachalio's *clamorem*.[57] All Trachalio's language, however, resonates with themes seen

---

[57] Wallochny 1992: 68–9 comments on the loop of shtick but not on the *quiritatio*. On *tumultus* and the call to arms it justified, see Lintott 1999: 91, 153–4; Brunt 1971a: 629–30 on tumultuary levies, for example the one held on the occasion of the slave uprising in 198 BCE. In the plays, *tumultus/*

above: he appeals to his *populares*, fellow members of the *populus*; he asks for help for the helpless (lit. "those without resources"), expressed in terms of *opes* and *inopia* (contrast the *opulento homini* of Sosia's song), while the wicked are to be punished as a correct *exemplum*; power should not threaten the innocent; the two girls are credited with *caput*, as if they were free (see chapter 2); notoriety for victimhood is feared; merit should be rewarded; and *vi victo vivere* is here rejected for the rule of law and custom – the reverse of the cheerleading *virtute victores vivere*. Law and *mos* belong to the *populus* (cf. *Cur.* 509–11, below; *Trin.* 1028–58, which also reclaims *mos*); *iniuria*, damage to honor, threatens all, low as well as high (see chapter 2). In a typically Plautine personification, Trachalio calls on the people to "wring the neck" of *iniuria*, implying a powerful gesture; he employs the powerful verb *vindicare*, which, as will be seen in chapter 8, is the word for what a person does who reclaims a person wrongfully enslaved; and indeed Trachalio is calling for help for two slave-women clinging to an altar and beset by a pimp (cf. 643–5). Here *clamor* serves as a defense, and *fides* stands guard; in *quiritatio*, *fides* is more than faith, trust, or a good credit rating, and appeals to a network of persons, of legal subjects.[58] It is important that slave characters onstage can appeal to the *populus*; these speeches blur the line between slaves and the free poor.

Yet *fides* poses a major problem for a slave. A slave's promise, or oath, has nothing to back it, for a slave officially has no honor to lose, a slave has no *fides*. In return, a slave cannot expect *fides* from an owner; as seen in chapter 1, Paegnium makes a significant complaint about this. His owner Toxilus, exasperated, says to him, *peculiabo* – "I'll peculiate you" (*Per.* 192). This is a probable sexual threat framed as a promise of money, and Paegnium's joking response takes off from the promise and returns the threat, with a wink to the audience (see chapter 6 on face-out lines): "God, I know how owners' *fides* is always accused of sluttishness / but they can't ever be forced to bend – to judgment on that *fides*" (*scio fide hercle erili ut soleat inpudicitia opprobrari / nec subigi queantur umquam ut pro ea fide habeant iudicem*, *Per.* 193–4, tr7; see chapter 1 on *erilis*). The wording

---

tumultuo are associated with loud noise at the house door (*Bac.* 1120, *Mil.* 172, *Poen.* 207, *Trin.* 1176) and the beating of hated characters (*Mil.* 1393, *Rud.* 661); the political sense is explicit in a joke at *Poen.* 524–5 (*non decet tumultuari*; see chapter 7). In all cases, these words describe disorderly conduct.

58 See Fantham 2005 on the relation between *quiritatio* and popular freedom in Livy; Lintott 1999: 11–14 on *quiritatio*, esp. Trachalio's speech, 7 on stoning as "a form of angry demonstration." Fraenkel cites the Plautine instances of *quiritatio* in arguing that *fides* was invoked by the weak seeking help from the strong, the appeal to the gods in expressions like *obsecro vostram fidem* being modeled on human relations (1916: 193, 195).

inpudicitia opprobrari is startling, and suggests a common (*soleat*) off-stage resentment. An owner's meaningless promises form a running gag in *Mostellaria* (174–5, 184–5, 252–3) and in *Poenulus* (133–7, 428–44). The chief promise arousing anxiety in slaves onstage is the promise to manumit (chapter 8), which is why Chrysalus (an expert on the legal process of promising) predicts that his owner will endow him with freedom, "to the extent that I'll never get it" (*ego adeo numquam accipiam, Bac.* 828–9).[59] This anxiety, in turn, is directly related to the poor man's anxiety over debt.

Debt and Shame, *Fides* and Credit

The prologue speaker of *Casina* defines the *ludi* as a time and place where the audience can forget their worries and their debts, and the bankers have been eluded (23–8):

> eicite ex animo curam atque alienum aes*,
> ne quis formidet flagitatorem suom:
> ludi sunt, ludus datus est argentariis;   25
> tranquillum est, Alcedonia sunt circum forum:
> ratione utuntur, ludis poscunt neminem,
> secundum ludos reddunt autem nemini.

> Throw your worries out of your mind, along with your debt,
> and don't let anyone be afraid of the man who duns him:
> it's time for the games, and we've played a game on the bankers;
> it's peaceful – in the forum it's like the Alcedonia.   25
> They're calculating; during the games they don't hound anyone,
> but after the games they won't pay a thing back to anyone.

These lines address the audience in general, and assume that bankers are the common enemy, dishonest dealers who deserve to be tricked, and that debt is a common problem. Certainly it was a problem for some people. The prologue speaker in *Captivi* jokes that he must pay the audience the "balance" of his story because he does not want to be in debt (*accipite reliquom: alieno uti nil moror*, 16). As seen above, he has focused from the start of his speech on vertical differences in the audience, saying that the two chained men are standing (onstage) "because those guys are standing

---

[59] For Chrysalus' legal expertise in the context of *fides*, see Owens 1994: 392. Chrysalus' line is commonly taken to mean that he would refuse to be manumitted; surely *accipio* here has its technical sense in the context of money and legal promises (like its counterpart *reddo*), and means "receive" and not "accept" (despite de Melo 2011a: 453 and many school texts and translations available online). See chapter 1 for the idea that there are "slaves content in their servitude" in comedy. For *accipio* as a technical term, see examples below.

there" (*illi quia astant*, 2), as he points to audience members without seats. Then he singles one out at the back (*illic ultumus*) who says he didn't "get it" and calls him to the front (*accedito*): "if you don't have a place to sit, there's a place you can take a walk, / since you're forcing an actor to be a beggar" (*si non ubi sedeas locus est, est ubi ambules, / quando histrionem cogis mendicarier*, 12–13) – surely a plant, as in the *Amphitruo* prologue discussed above. The speaker specifically addresses the "balance" of his explanation to "you who can be assessed for your wealth" (*vos qui potestis ope vostra censerier*, 15), as if the seated audience were his potential creditors, or as if the rest of the audience could not hear: another joke, and not a friendly joke. An entire segment of the city population, the *proletarii*, were defined – as opposed to *assidui* – precisely by their lack of wealth to assess.[60] A related joke is made by Auxilium in *Cistellaria*, speaking his (late) prologue: "Now I want to pay off the balance remaining, / so that my name will be taken off the ledgers, and I won't be in debt" (*nunc quod relicuom restat volo persolvere / ut expungatur nomen, ne quid debeam*, 188–9). Toxilus in *Persa* caps his reverse *flagitatio* with financial language: "You didn't think I could get my hands on that much cash, / so you wouldn't risk giving me credit unless I swore to it?" (*non mihi censebas copiam argenti fore / qui nisi iurato mihi nil ausus credere?* 415–16). These lines are full of significant terminology: *censebas*, "assess" (like a censor); *copiam argenti*, "plenty of ready cash"; *iurato*, "sworn on oath" (with legal implications – not something a slave could usually do); *credere*, "give credit." His words here, and a major theme in *Persa* as a whole, address a situation that plagued most ancient cities and became particularly pressing during the wars of the 200s BCE: poor people were mired in debt.[61]

---

[60] For discussion of this passage, see Moore 1994/5: 118–19; Moore 1998: 195; above, n. 6; and Dressler 2016: 37–41, on the economic relations in play. An unspoken joke on *assidui*, "those with enough wealth to be assessed by the census"/ "those sitting down," may be in play; although *assiduus* in its class sense does not certainly appear in the corpus (? *Trin.* 202), it appears in the XII Tables (1.4 = Gell. 16.10.5). Gellius' antiquarian interlocutor opines that "property and family money were held to be like a hostage and security to the state, and there was in it a certain *fides*, a guarantee of patriotism" (*amorisque in patriam fides quaedam*, 16.10.11).

[61] On debt in the 300s–200s BCE, see Andreau 1999: 64–70 (on slaves and their *peculium*); Andreau 2002: 115, 123–5; Millett 1991: 74–9, on poverty and debt in Athens; Richlin 2014b: 207–10; Walbank 1981: 167–75; and below on *nexum*. On credit problems for the "new poor" in classical Athens as denizens of the *emporium* (including prostitutes), see Vélissaropoulos-Karakostas 2002: 132–3, with Vlassopoulos 2007, and compare Leigh 2004: 118–23 on the significance of the port in the *palliata*. On the procedure for bankruptcy, during which the bankrupt was sold *sub hasta*, see Mayor *ad* Juvenal 3.33 (*et praebere caput domina venale sub hasta*), with many legal references. Procedure for bankruptcy in Plautus involves the *parasitus* Gelasimus who auctions his belongings (see below), as well as the pimps in *Curculio* and *Poenulus* who are threatened with bonds and litigation (*Cur.* 718–23, *Poen.* 1338–66, 1408–9). Livy, at least, connected debt problems in the Republic with mandatory

Legally, moreover, slaves could not own property at all; everything they acquired was for their owner (this is Gripus' problem with the suitcase, as later with his finder's fee, in *Rudens*). This is what makes it such a radical claim when the Advocati in *Poenulus* say they paid their own money for their *caput*. Slaves onstage, as also later attested in law, were allowed to accumulate money in a *peculium*, which they were expected to apply towards purchasing their freedom from their owner; hence that particularly Roman virtue, *frugi*, means, for a slave, simultaneously "thrifty" and "good" (cf. *Capt.* 956–7).[62] So Syncerastus describes slave customers in his owner's brothel as losing their *peculium* "for their owners" (*Poen.* 843); the owner is expecting to get this money in the end, to make up for the money he spent on the slave's purchase price, if any, and on his keep over the years. (He would get it one way or another, for the money was his if the slave died before manumission; three hundred years later, the younger Pliny indulgently let his slaves make wills, as long as they kept the money in the household: no loss to him [*Ep.* 8.16].) Lack of a *peculium*, in the plays, is thus counted as a moral failing on a slave's part: so Lysidamus says that Chalinus has none, as opposed to the *frugi* Olympio (*Cas.* 254–8), and Stalagmus bitterly accepts chains as the correct pay for a slave without one (*Capt.* 1028). The cost of desired goods had to come out of the *peculium*; Stichus' owner means it when he says Stichus' *amica* must be paid for "out of your pocket" (*de tuo, St.* 426), and, as seen in chapter 2, Stichus and Sangarinus, when Stephanium tells them she will lie with both of them, know what that means to their savings towards freedom (751). The owner here incentivizes abstinence. Evidently Stephanium's "love" for the rivals will be adding to her own *peculium*; Sangarinus is her *conservos* (433), but she is making money on the side (cf. Paegnium, *Per.* 192, 285). While *in patria potestate*, sons also had *peculia*, of which slaves might form a part, as Tyndarus was given to Philocrates (*Capt.* 988); slaves (called *vicarii*) might also be part of a slave's *peculium*, as Sophoclidisca belongs to Lemniselenis (*Per.* 201, 248) and Paegnium belongs to Toxilus (247) – just as slaves might form part of a woman's dowry, like the unseen *atriensis* in *Asinaria* (85). Indeed, Leonida, pretending to be that *atriensis*, is credited with a *vicarius* by his henchman, as part of the effort to make him appear fiscally sound (*As.* 433–4).

---

army service; see Brunt 1971a: 642; Fantham 2005; *contra*, Rosenstein 2004: 54–5. For an extended analogy between the *palliata* and Depression-era film comedy, see Gunderson 2015: 243–50.

[62] On the custom of the *peculium* in the mid-Republic, see Watson 1971: 45, citing *As.* 539–41 as "very significant" (the prostitute Philaenium to her mother: "even the shepherd who tends another man's ewes, Mother,/ has one for his own [*peculiarem*], to comfort his hope with").

Therefore, for a slave, cash was the best good thing of all, convertible into food, love, and freedom, the key to getting goods for oneself; this is perhaps the most extraordinary thing about the ending of *Pseudolus* – that Simo feels forced to give the slave twenty minas, rather than torture him "as in other comedies," and he hands over the money onstage (1238–45, 1313–17). Big money very rarely comes into slaves' possession in the plays; a plot point, as the golden Chrysalus himself observes (*Bac.* 676). Gripus' hopes of hanging on to the money in the suitcase, or even to his finder's fee, are repeatedly denied by his owner, in the end with cold finality: "By God, there's nothing here for you, don't get your hopes up" (*nihil hercle hic tibi est, ne tu speres, Rud.* 1414). From the start, Gripus knows he will have to make a deal with his owner for his freedom before he lets on about his find (928–9). Likewise, the Slave of Lyconides hopes vainly to convince his owner to let him use the pot of gold to buy his freedom (*Aul.* 816–17, cf. 823). In the normal course of events, rarely do slaves even obtain temporary control of large sums (shaving a bit off small sums is a joke, as at *Truc.* 562). Sagaristio's owner entrusts the cattle money to him (*Per.* 260–1), but Leonida and Libanus, despite elaborate efforts (*As.* 407–503), cannot get the Mercator to entrust the donkey money to Leonida, who is pretending to be the *atriensis* Saurea. Leonida makes a show of asking about money owed to the household (432–45); they both claim the owner trusts Leonida (456–62); Leonida calls the money "My twenty minas" (*viginti minas meas,* 468); they boast of Leonida's reputation for fiscal probity at Athens and in high-value trade (492–3, 499–501). Standing on his dignity, Leonida/Saurea finally accuses the Mercator of *iniuria,* a public assault on his honor, and says, "Although I wear a working man's clothes, / I am prudent (*frugi*) nonetheless, and my *peculium* is immeasurable" (*quamquam ego sum sordidatus, / frugi tamen sum, nec potest peculium enumerari,* 497–8; see chapter 2). None of it works; to get the money, they need their owner to vouch for Leonida (579–84). When they finally have the *crumina* full of money in their possession, they dangle it before their young owner to make him crawl for it (see chapter 4).

Even Pseudolus, pretending to be Ballio's slave Syrus, cannot get the soldier's slave Harpax to give him the money owed the pimp. He claims to be, not the *atriensis,* but the one who gives orders to the *atriensis* (609); he says he handles the pimp's accounts, receiving and paying out money (*accepto, dato,* 626–7); he claims that six hundred times as much is habitually entrusted to him (*soleant credier,* 632). "You had to come stick a fork in my credit!" he laments (*inventu's … meam qui furcilles fidem,* 631). "I'll never trust you," says Harpax (*numquam credam,* 629); "I wouldn't trust you" (*ut ne credam tibi*, 633); "I'll never trust a dollar to anyone but Ballio himself" (*nummum credam nemini*, 644). (He, at least, has been trusted with money, and is last seen on the way to pick up much more; he thinks, however, that he can trust the pimp, a self-professed perjurer, and has trusted Pseudolus with something more valuable than money, providing an object lesson in the superiority of brains to obedience.) Chrysalus, the embodiment of cash flow (*copiam, Bac.* 639a), only handles money directly once, among all his schemes (1066). The *vilicus* Collybiscus in *Poenulus* is given the "three hundred golden Philips" only in order to trick the pimp, and happily lets the Advocati inspect his bankroll (*Poen.* 597); they let the audience know it is only stage money, "comic" money (598–9). All he gets from the deal is an unexpected meal (802–4). Money is scarce.

The problem of debt and the need for credit pervade the *palliata*. Previous discussions of *fides* have treated it as, by definition, a virtue of the powerful (the *summi viri*, the Roman state) in relation to the weak (dependents, conquered states): asymmetrical.[63] But within the world of the *palliata*, *fides* is commonly treated as something everybody needs: a reciprocal value, inherently even (*aequom*) rather than uneven. For people at the bottom, survival is at stake, before politics. Their world is hazardous. The Choragus in *Curculio*, before he begins his tour of the Forum, worries about having trusted the rented costumes to Phaedromus (464, 466 *credidi*); the Forum as he sees it is full of untrustworthy characters – perjurers (470), liars (471), false accusers (478–9), moneylenders (*qui dant quique accipiunt faenore*, 480), and just "those you should not trust" (*quibu' credas male*, 481). Soon after this scene, Curculio, disguised as the freedman "Thunder God," exclaims that associating with pimps causes people to lose their credit rating (502–4, ia7):

> nec vobiscum quisquam in foro frugi consistere audet;
> qui constitit, culpant eum, conspicitur, vituperatur,
> eum rem fidemque perdere, tam etsi nil fecit, aiunt.

> Nor does anyone prudent dare to stand with you in the forum;
> anyone who's done so, they blame him, he's stared at, he's insulted,
> they say he's lost his assets and his credit, even if he's done nothing.

---

[63] On the pervasiveness of the issue: "credit is everywhere in the plays of Plautus and Terence" (Callataÿ 2015: 36), though he takes this to reflect Menander's Athens; the lucid account in Kay 2014: 1–7, 107–25 is grounded in the Roman historical context. The issue is central in only six extant plays (*Asinaria, Curculio, Epidicus, Mostellaria, Persa, Trinummus*, presumably also in the lost *Addictus* and *Faeneratrix*), but numerous casual remarks on banking show up elsewhere. On *fides*, see Owens 1994: 387 for a review going back to Fraenkel 1916 and Heinze 1929; on the religious roots of *fides*, Burton 2011: 40–1, with further bibliography.

The honest man here is *frugi* – a virtue elsewhere consistently associated with good slaves who save up their *peculium* to pay for their manumission – and two things are at stake: *res* and *fides*. The Virgo in *Persa*, pleading with her father not to sell her to the pimp, even falsely, points out to him that poor people need a good reputation: "for, if *infamiae* move in with poverty, / poverty gets heavier, and your *fides* gets weaker" (*nam ad paupertatem si admigrant infamiae, / gravior paupertas fit, fides sublestior, Per.* 347–8). The vulnerability of monetary, personal *fides* is a constant sore point in the plays; its loss is effected, Curculio says, through public shaming, just as the too-pretty slave-woman is harassed in the street.

Likewise, in a face-to-face society, bankruptcy was performed in public, so that a man who had lost everything was subjected to the scrutiny of rubberneckers. Gelasimus, setting out his goods to the audience for auction, complains of his disgrace (*St.* 198–204, 207–8):

> sed curiosi sunt hic complures mali,
> alienas res qui curant studio maxumo,
> quibus ipsis nullast res quam procurent sua:　　　　　　200
> i quando quem auctionem facturum sciunt,
> adeunt, perquirunt quid siet caussae ilico:
> alienum aes cogat an pararit praedium,
> uxorin sit reddenda dos divortio.
> …
> dicam auctionis caussam, ut damno gaudeant;
> nam curiosus nemo est quin sit malivolus.

> But there are a lot of bad busybodies here,
> who look after other people's assets with the greatest zeal,
> though they have no assets of their own to look after.　　　　200
> These guys, when they know someone is going to hold an auction,
> they come, they ask what might be the reason, right there:
> whether debt forces him, or he's bought a farm,
> or if the dowry has to be given back to his wife in a divorce.
> …
> I'll tell the cause of my auction, so they can take pleasure in my loss;
> for there's no busybody who isn't also an ill-wisher.

The *curiosus* was a figure of particular dislike in later Roman culture, often tied, as here, with the evil eye; the social critique in Gelasimus' speech has Greek ancestors as well, in the traditional dislike of *polypragmosunê*. It is clear that the experience of having your goods auctioned had a punitive aspect in itself, of public shaming.[64] What Gelasimus is doing onstage once

---

[64] On the *curiosus* and the evil eye, see Barton 1993: 85–98, 189, on *polypragmosunê, curiosi,* and magic;

again overlays the performance of a common street scene onto the common street, with editorial comment. That debt was *aes alienum* – literally, "somebody else's bronze" – shows how grounded this problem was in the location of money. The auction turns the house inside out; Gelasimus says, "I have to sell out of the house whatever I have" (*foras necessumst quidquid habeo vendere*, 219). Despite the presence of *curiosi* "here," he starts to hawk his possessions to the audience: "I'm selling funny stories. Go on, set the price. ... [to one audience member] Hey, did you nod?" (*logos ridiculos vendo. age licemini. / ... ehem, adnuistin?* 221, 224).

Where would a slave keep his *peculium*? In a cash-box, as Horace says of Plautus' money? Bankers in the *palliata* hold money on deposit, but not for slaves. Another idiom associated with money, then, perhaps has a more literal significance than might at first appear: *domi* means "in my pocket," but *domi* is where the cash is. Sagaristio, asked for money, says, "If I had it at home (*domi*), I'd promise it now" (*Per.* 45). In the same play, the *parasitus* Saturio says that a *parasitus* who has any money at home (*si quid domist*, 122) just wants to spend it on a meal. In a variant on the common joke in which a character says he can pay for something "out of his back" (that is, by being flogged), Chrysalus boasts that he has plenty of "back at home" (*mihi tergum domi est, Bac.* 365) – here also a joke on his owner's threat of "rods in the country" (*virgae ruri*). Milphio envies Syncerastus because he has food and women at home (*domi, Poen.* 867). The Advocati are proud that they have food to eat at home (*domi, Poen.* 537). Leonida/Saurea boasts that he made a debtor bring a banker to the house (*domum*) to pay up – although, in keeping with Leonida's grandiose airs, the banker will make a written transfer (*scribit nummos, As.* 440). Tellingly, Ballio is also proud that he has plenty of money in the house (*domo, Ps.* 355). The house then is not only identified with the self ("at *my* house"), even with the body, but with availability; this is ready money, money a person actually has, and does not have to go to the forum to get – to borrow; or to withdraw from a credit account, as wealthy persons are able to do onstage.[65] The Slave of Lyconides takes the pot of gold home to secure it (*condam domum, Aul.* 712), and later confesses that the gold is "in a moneybox at my house" (*in arca apud me*, 823). The house is "my house" even for slave characters.

Leigh 2013: 79–84, and 30–2, 45–52, 60–7 on the *polypragmôn* in comedy and related genres. On auctions as a form of public shaming, see Ste. Croix 1981: 166; Callataÿ 2015: 42–3.

[65] On where money was kept, and the relatively large amounts kept at home, see Callataÿ 2015: 32–6; on the scene in *Asinaria* and ledger transactions, see Kay 2014: 121.

Bankers, in contrast, belong in the forum. Indeed, in the extant *palliata*, they never live behind the door in the scenery, but enter from the forum; less domestic, even, than pimps, although, as seen above, Diniarchus puts the tables of money-men (*argentariae*) right next to the pimps (*Truc.* 66–7), and draws an analogy between prostitutes and the ledgers recording "interest-bearing money" – "deposits, not loans" (70–2, *aera … usuraria; accepta dico, expensa ne qui censeat*).[66] The moneylender in *Mostellaria* enters with a comic speech about how poor business is these days (a laugh line – the audience is not expected to sympathize), and pictures himself toiling away, "from morning til night, I spend all day in the forum" (*a mani ad noctem usque in foro dego diem*, 534), trying to lend money at interest. Leonida, playing the *atriensis*, makes a similar complaint (*As.* 428–9). The banker in *Curculio*, with his wolfish name, makes no bones about his crookedness (371–83):

> LY. Beatus videor: subduxi ratiunculam,
> quantum aeris mihi sit quantumque alieni siet:
> dives sum, si non reddo eis quibu' debeo;
> si reddo illis quibu' debeo, plus †alieni† est.
> verum hercle vero quom belle recogito,   375
> si magi' me instabunt, ad praetorem sufferam.
> habent hunc morem plerique argentarii
> ut alius alium poscant, reddant nemini,
> pugnis rem solvant, si quis poscat clarius.
> qui homo mature quaesivit pecuniam,   380
> nisi eam mature parsit, mature essurit.
> cupio aliquem <mi> emere puerum qui usurarius
> nunc mihi quaeratur. usus est pecunia.

> LY. I appear to enjoy good fortune; I've cooked up a little calculation,
> re: how much of my money is mine and how much is other people's.
> I'm a rich man, if I don't pay the people back I owe money to.
> If I do pay them back what I owe them, there's more I can borrow.
> But, by God, how nice it feels to bear in mind   375
> that if they start to press me, I can just go to court.
> You'll find that plenty of money-men have this custom –
> they hound this one and that one for money, but pay nobody back,

---

[66] On *argentarii* as small-scale operators, see Andreau 1999: 30–49. See Kay 2014: 116–24 for Plautine banking in its economic context, with attention to several passages discussed here, including an elucidation of *Truc.* 66–73; on the Forum location, see Moore 1998: 130–6. Kay (113 n. 30) accepts the arrival in Rome of *argentarii* as bankers by the late 300s despite the ambiguity of Livy 9.40.16, on which, see Richlin 2017a: 220–2.

and they settle accounts with their fists, should anyone hound them too
    loudly.
Any person who's made his money quick,   380
unless he gets stingy quick, gets hungry quick.
I want to buy myself some boy who could be marketed
for rental from me. There's money in rentals.

Evidently Lyco is on his way to the pimp's house to do some shopping;
the surprise ending to his speech confirms Diniarchus' observation on the
kinship between bankers and pimps, with their cozy forum location. Lyco
is identified in *Curculio* as a *trapezita*, a "table-man" – a Greek occupa-
tional title that evokes the way moneylenders set up in the forum. He says
outright that he plans to return none of the money he holds, matching
the observation made by Pseudolus that bankers "look to get their own
back, but pay back a deposit to no one born" (*suom repetunt, alienum
reddunt nato nemini, Ps.* 297; the same wording found at *Cas.* 27, above).
Lyco's self-professed fiscal policy is acted out, offstage, by the pimp Lycus
in *Poenulus*, although he loses confidence that going to court will solve his
problems. (Note the shared name.) Lyco confirms the relationship between
lack of money and hunger (*essurit, Cur.* 381), and suggests how a rich man
could overcome *flagitatio*: by meeting loud outcries (*poscat clarius,* 379)
with force. Curculio completes his rant against pimps with a rant against
men like Lyco (*Cur.* 506–11, ia7):

CU. eodem hercle vos pono et paro: parissumi estis hibus:
hi saltem in occultis locis prostant, vos in foro ipso;
vos faenori, hi male suadendo et lustris lacerant homines.
rogitationes plurumas propter vos populus scivit,
quas vos rogatas rumpitis: aliquam reperitis rimam;   510
quasi aquam ferventem frigidam esse, ita vos putatis leges.

By God, I lump you right in with them, you're just the same as they are;
at least they set up shop in shady places – you're right in the forum;
they mangle people by luring them into their lairs – you do it with interest.
The *populus* has passed plenty of bills on account of you,
which you dodge as soon as they're passed; you always find
    some loophole;   510
as if boiling water were freezing, that's what you think the laws are.

If Curculio, unlike Diniarchus, locates bankers and pimps in different
parts of the city, Lyco is standing next to him in front of the pimp's house
as he says these lines, and indeed touches off the attack on bankers by
appreciating the attack on pimps. This speech is one of those places in the
plays that refer (semi-)explicitly to contemporary issues and conditions,

siding with the *populus*; that lending money at interest was also viewed negatively offstage in this period is most obviously attested at the outset of Cato's *De agricultura*, where Cato compares *faeneratores* unfavorably with thieves, claiming that "our ancestors" set a double penalty for thieves but a quadruple penalty for moneylenders (*De agr.* pr.1–4).[67] The title of *Faeneratrix*, with its resonant fragment (chapter 1), suggests the impact of *faenus* as a buzzword. Dinia in *Vidularia*, making a private loan to a poor man, says flatly, "It's not fitting to wear out a needy person with interest payments" (*defaenerare hominem egentem hau decet*, 89) – probably with a wink to the audience (see chapter 6). Money-men are the enemy; even Cappadox the pimp calls them untrustworthy (*Cur.* 679–85, tr7):

> CA. Argentariis male credi qui aiunt, nugas praedicant:
> nam et bene et male credi dico; id adeo ego hodie expertu' sum.   680
> non male creditur qui numquam reddunt, sed prosum perit.
> velut decem minas dum solvit, omnis mensas transiit.
> postquam nil fit, clamore hominem posco: ille in ius me vocat;
> pessume metui ne mihi hodie apud praetorem solveret.
> verum amici compulerunt: reddit argentum domo.   685

> CA. People who tell you you can't trust bankers – they're just talking trash.
> I say it's both good and bad to trust them; that's how it went today
> for me.   680
> Money's not badly trusted to people who never pay it back – it just
> disappears.
> Like when this guy is paying my ten *minas*, he went to every banker's table.
> After nothing happens, I hound the guy with shouting: he summons me
> to court;
> I was scared in the worst way that he'd settle with me today in front of
> the judge.
> But my friends made him do it: he's paying back the cash from his home
> savings.   685

Even the pimp can hound his debtor in public; even when the money-man tries his favorite move of dragging things into court, the pimp's *amici* can force the issue, and the money-man has to pay with real money, *domo*.

For a slave, the problem was much worse, acting, as slaves must, without real *fides*. This is the joke when the old man in *Epidicus* refuses to give back the *fides* (lyre) to the freedwoman *fidicina*, and she threatens to dun him for it – to make him give her back her *fides* – for she is entitled to it, in

---

[67] On the date of *De agricultura*, see chapter 1. In any case, Cato's attitude here is representative of his lifetime; see Astin's detailed discussion of moneylending in the early 100s, 1978: 319–23. On Cato's own involvement in shipping loans in this context, see Leigh 2004: 148–52.

both senses. Hence, as seen in chapter 2, *confidenter* is used as a reproach to
slaves who act free (see further in chapter 6). Toxilus and Sagaristio have little prospect of getting a loan (*Per.* 5–6, 43–5); Sagaristio, when Toxilus asks
him for money, replies just as Chaeribulus (possibly) does in *Epidicus*: "if
I had it at home, I'd promise it to you right now" (*si id domi esset mihi, iam
pollicerer, Per.* 45); but, unlike Chaeribulus, who is free, he does not say he
is being dunned.[68] Instead, he says it is a ridiculous amount of money to
ask him for, more than he would get if he sold himself (40) – not that he
owns himself; pressed to look for a loan somewhere, he replies, "I'll look
for one myself – if anyone would give me credit" (*si quis credat*, 44). Slaves
thus can dun, but are not dunned themselves, because you have to have
credit to get into debt. The pimp Dordalus has made Toxilus swear an oath
that he will pay in cash for Lemniselenis (400–3), and, at the end of the
play, concludes that Toxilus has swindled him because he would not give
Toxilus credit, would not trust a slave (*quia ei fidem non habui argenti, eo
mihi eas machinas molitust*, 785): revenge. Indeed, Toxilus makes a point of
this mistrust in their duel (416), and again afterwards, as he and Dordalus
exchange ideas on credit and banking (431–6). He leads by expressing his
anger (*tibi suscensui*, 431) as a low credit rating (*tibi sus-censui*):

> TO. iam omitte iratus esse. id tibi suscensui
> qui te negabas credere argentum mihi.
> DO. mirum quin tibi ego crederem, ut idem mihi
> faceres quod partim faciunt argentarii:
> ubi quid credideris, citius extemplo a foro   435
> fugiunt quam ex porta ludis quom emissust lepus.

> TO. Now stop being angry. I low-rated you
> because you said you wouldn't trust me for the money.
> DO. Strange if I wouldn't trust you – so you'd do the same
> to me that the money-men mostly do:
> when you trust them with any, they run away from the forum faster
> than a rabbit out of the starting gates at the games.

He sounds like Cappadox; another pimp insulting bankers. Toxilus then
hands Dordalus the money; although Toxilus says it is "honest, counted
out" (*probi, numerati*, 438), the pimp wonders aloud how he can get it
checked to be sure it is not counterfeit (440). Toxilus wants Lemniselenis
(441): "Maybe you're afraid to trust her into my hand?" (*fortasse metuis*

---

[68] *Pollicerer* is Mueller's addition to the text at *Epidicus* 116, on the analogy of *Per.* 45 (also *Bac.* 635,
   Pistoclerus to Mnesilochus); the two situations are certainly parallel, except that the two speakers in
   Epidicus are free and the two in *Persa* are slaves. See chapter 4 on slave friendships.

in manum concredere?). The pimp remains focused on the tendency of bankers to disappear (442–3). But when he returns from the forum, in a good mood, he exults about how many people he has trusted today (*ut ego multis credidi*, 476), and he repeats forms of the verb *credo* nine more times in the next thirteen lines (477, 478, 482 twice, 484 twice, 485–6, 487, 490). Toxilus, pretending to be grateful, calls down blessings upon him and promises never to wish harm to the pimp from now on (a big lie); the pimp replies, magnanimously, "Go on, don't swear an oath, I trust you enough" (*abi, ne iura, sati' credo*, 490). He will soon find out his mistake. Chrysalus in *Bacchides* leverages his own untrustworthiness to make his owner hand over the money: *nolo ego mi credi*, he protests (*Bac.* 1062, cf. 1064–5). It is part of the grandiosity of Leonida's claims as *atriensis* that he complains that a merchant was slow to pay back "what I gave him on credit, before" (*priu' quae credidi, As.* 439). Like Toxilus, he wants to be thought credit-worthy.

Again, the audience would have been fully conscious that, for a free person, the enforcement of a debt could end in a form of slavery or house arrest, after a trip to the praetor's court, as seen in the threats against the pimp Cappadox at the end of *Curculio* (689–93, 718, 721–3) and against the pimp Lycus at the end of *Poenulus* (1341–2, 1361–5, 1409).[69] Debt led to the last secession of the plebs, in 287. When the pimp says he will become Agorastocles' *addictus* (*Poen.* 1361) and hold an auction tomorrow (1364), Agorastocles threatens him explicitly with imprisonment in his house: "so you'll be with me meanwhile in wooden custody" (*ut sis apud me lignea in custodia*, 1365).[70] Any free person can turn into a slave. At the same time,

---

[69] Although the contract for *nexum* was abolished by the Lex Poetelia in 326 or 313 BCE, private imprisonment for debt and debt servitude persisted afterwards; see Brunt 1971b: 56–7; Ste. Croix 1981: 165–9; Watson 1971: 163, 1975: 111–24, esp. at 115. See Livy 23.14.3, where those who were "in chains, having been adjudged for a cash amount" were set free to fight in the army in 216, with Ste. Croix 1981: 572 n. 65. Oakley 1998: 688, on Livy 8.28, emphasizes the vastness of the legal scholarship spawned by this problem. Varro, in discussing the term at length, defines the nature of the servitude involved: "a free man who bonded his work into slavery in place of the money he owed, until it was paid off, is called a *nexus*" (*liber qui suas operas in servitutem pro pecunia quam debebat <nectebat>, dum solveret, nexus vocatur*, L. 7.105). This chapter of *De lingua latina*, in which Varro mentions the ending of *nexum* in the dictatorship of C. Poetelius (313 – Livy 8.28 gives the earlier date), begins as a gloss on the word *nexum* in a play titled *Colax*; as remarked by Terence (*Eun.* 25), Plautus and Naevius each wrote one, though the fragment is conventionally attributed to Plautus (Varro does not explicitly identify the author). Plautus also wrote an *Addictus*, and the *addictus* shows up in Plautus at *Bac.* 1205, *Capt.* 181, *Poen.* 521, 720, 833; with a court judgment, at *Poen.* 186, 564, 1341, *Rud.* 891. Watson 1975 differentiates *nexi* from *addicti*. See chapter 4 on the story of Publilius. On "the prominence of debt as a cause of political change under the Roman Republic," see Kay 2014: 114–15.

[70] On the form of confinement, see Allen 1896: 48–51.

this fantasy of torturing the pimp in your own back yard belongs less to any senators in the audience – what Philip Kay calls "Rome's aristocratic plutocracy" – than to those who actually might have been in trouble for debt at this level.[71]

Actors and Audience in the Wartime Economy

In an early scene in *Asinaria*, the *lena* Cleareta gives a young man a lesson in what John Henderson calls "marketplace economics in the sexwork industry"[72] (*As.* 198–201, tr7):

> diem, aquam, solem, lunam, noctem, haec argento non emo:
> cetera quae volumus uti Graeca mercamur fide.
> quom a pistore panem petimus, vinum ex oenopolio,　　　　　　200
> si aes habent, dant mercem: eadem nos discipulina utimur.

> Daylight, water, sun, moon, night – these things I don't buy for cash:
> the other things we want to use, we trade by the rules of Greek *fides*.
> When we want to get bread from the baker, or wine from the
> 　　　wineseller's shop,　　　　　　200
> if they get the coin, they give the goods: well, we here go by the same
> 　　　rulebook.

The *lena* sees this as fair exchange: "equal recompense given for equal, work in exchange for money" (*par pari datum hostimentumst, opera pro pecunia, As.* 172). Her economics describe, as well, the format of verbal dueling, where contestants return like for like (*par pari respondent*); her economics also describe, on a larger scale, the bargain between actors and audience, where performance earns applause, and applause earns military success, in the quid-pro-quo terms of cheerleading. That "cash on the barrel" evidently went by the oxymoronic *Graeca fides* makes perfect sense for the *Graeci palliati* onstage and in the street. They all had to eat; they all had credit problems.

The actors cheering on the audience and putting on magnificent displays of invective were singing for their supper. Usener and Fraenkel looked

---

[71] Kay 2014: 17; see full discussion at 15–18 of evidence for high levels of wealth in Rome's upper classes during the Second Punic War.

[72] Henderson 2006: 107, and see his discussion at 139–41. On this scene, see esp. Dutsch forthcoming; she argues that the speeches of the *lena* "suggest that an imaginary cultural structure is determining her position," achieving a "quasi-Brechtian effect of distancing from a dominant ideology," and that her arguments to her daughter invert the Roman moral system "under conditions of penury," being "class-specific rather than universal." See further Dressler 2016: 27 on representation as simultaneously economic and rhetorical in Plautine thought.

at their chanted forms as interesting survivals of *Volk* rituals, part of the "self-help" nature of Roman law; Andrew Lintott looked back on these scenes from the perspective of the late Republic, where there are eyewitness accounts of orchestrated shouting, with well-attested political goals (see Richlin 1992b[1983]: 86–7). We do not have contemporary witnesses to tell us how a performance of *Persa* at a given date and venue was interpreted by the audience. But we have some idea of the offstage world. In the 200s BCE and the early 100s, the *palliata* addressed an audience for whom debt was not quaint, shame was a real threat, and slavery was directly tied with the fortunes of war as well as with debt; indeed, the *palliata* itself took form in a Mediterranean world racked by war and debt. The circulation of jokes and actors to central Italy came about, at least in part, through war and debt. The importance of the idea of credit in *Pseudolus* (datable to 191) has been tied with an effort to regulate banking in 193–192, and that certainly would have been an association present to spectators of the 191 performance, but the onstage search for credit would have had a political edge throughout the 200s. A joke about loans appears in the *Triphallus* of Naevius, who was born in the 260s and probably died before the end of the Second Punic War. Plautus' plays in general are full of moneylenders, while Terence's, all produced after Pydna, have none. The plays' concern, seen in chapter 2, with beating, sexual abuse, and hunger is related to the question of money and credit in a century when the first mass enslavements hit the market, the *populus* had some voice, and central Italy was in flux. The *populus*, says Curculio, has passed laws to control the flow of credit, and this is in keeping with the development of legislative power by the tribal assembly after 287, in a crisis itself triggered by debt; even if the wealthy Cato also disapproves of moneylenders, the attacks on them in the plays most directly address people with money problems.[73] If Plautus was "astretch to put coin in his cash-box," as Horace chided, so were a lot of people onstage and in the audience.

The actors operated in a fiscal climate in which pimps and money-lenders were a threat to people with limited cash, people already traumatized by war. Comic actors are there to cheer people up, hence the

---

[73] On *Pseudolus* and the crisis of 193–192, see Feeney 2010: 295, who traces the idea back to Kiessling in 1868; also Feeney 2010: 296 on Jean Andreau's observation on Plautus and Terence; and cf. Kay 2014: 114–15, 119, who notes the similar arguments made to date *Curculio* to this crisis. On the year 287 and the tribal assembly, see Brunt 1971b: 57–8. Naevius' loan joke: *Com.* 96–8 R₃; see Wright 1974: 48. As Kay's overview shows, the widespread attitude towards banking across the extant plays suggests an ongoing issue; see esp. his remarks (2014: 114) on the number of known bills aimed at regulating interest during this period (twenty-seven).

cheerleading: *your* city will not be sacked. The prologue speaker of *Casina* opens with a formal greeting: "Hail, best of spectators, / you who hold *Fides* in the highest esteem, as *Fides* holds you" (*Salvere iubeo spectatores optumos,* / *Fidem qui facitis maxumi, et vos Fides,* 1–2); soon he will bring up their debt problems. The whole last third of *Aulularia* centers on the Temple of Fides, and it is here that the Slave of Lyconides finds the pot of gold he hopes he can use to buy his freedom.[74] The star Arcturus begins the *Rudens* prologue by explaining how he and other stars walk the earth by day, spying out who acts with *pietas* and *fides,* who gets a boost from *opulentia,* and who reneges on loans and acts falsely in court: Jupiter will punish wrongdoers, he promises (1–30).[75] Slaves, for whom access to cash meant so much, had no credit; *fides* and *credo* are highly charged terms for them in the plays. Meanwhile, sex trafficking, as these plays and their Greek cousins show, was a major part of the slave trade; hence pimps do business with bankers, and hence the central role of pimps onstage. The pimp says to the weeping Planesium, as he sells her to the man she thinks is the soldier's agent, "Just be a good prudent girl" (*fac sis bonae frugi sies, Cur.* 521). Save up your tips. The process of *occentatio* and the street scene described by the old man in *Mercator* show what the public life of a young prostitute or *ancilla* was like. At the same time, the process of *quiritatio* onstage allows the powerless to try to get redress; the audience participates, as slave and free together are appealed to as the *populus.*

Behind *flagitatio* lies a threat of enslavement between free people; verbal dueling between slaves onstage uses some of the forms of *flagitatio* in a performance by people who had already lost everything but their skill, for an audience at risk. In onstage duels, as in their occasional appeals to "fellow citizens," slave characters act free, they push towards freedom, often at the expense of a rival; they compete to be upwardly mobile, to be treated with respect. This is the driving force behind the desires to which we will now turn.

---

[74] On the deified *Fides* and the temple of Fides onstage, see Clark 2007: 58–62, 73–5, 82–5, 101–5.

[75] On this odd passage, see Fraenkel 1942, following an extensive treatment by Friedrich Marx (1959[1928]: 52–62); Marx credits the whole concept of stars as spies to Diphilus, while of course the idea of celestial record-keeping goes back to Hesiod, lending this passage a strong flavor of the folktale. Neither Fraenkel nor Marx comments on the Roman topicality of the language here, particularly of *pietas, fides,* and *opulentia* (which I here take as nominative, with de Melo. Although the range of *opulentia* and *opulentus* in connection with prayers for money makes Marx's translation "daß er jeden mit Reichtum segne" attractive, these words are more often used of rich people as opposed to the poor).

PART II

What Was Desired

Paegnium in *Persa*, a *puer* and slave's slave, holds a low position in the onstage world. Yet, as seen in chapter 3, he addresses to his owner a jeering reproach that lays claim to an expectation of better treatment: "God, I know how owners' *fides* is always accused of sluttishness / but they can't ever be forced to bend – to judgment on that *fides*" (*scio fide hercle erili ut soleat inpudicitia opprobrari / nec subigi queantur umquam ut pro ea fide habeant iudicem, Per.* 193–4). These lines drew the attention of Moses Finley, who perhaps oversimplifies their meaning: "no master can be brought to court over a promise to a slave" (1998[1980]: 142). Orlando Patterson held dishonor to be among the chief losses inflicted by enslavement, and it is sometimes argued by historians, based on statements by survivors, that slaves do not expect honor, that they internalize a belief in their own worthlessness. But Paegnium makes a generalization – *soleat inpudicitia opprobrari* – and the implied critical voices behind it are those of slaves, who, throughout the plays, clamor for honor. Legal process is not their only concern; they unman the owner, as the owner has unmanned them. The *palliata* is full of similar voices, issuing from the mouth-holes of slave masks: "How unworthy does this really seem?" says Leonida to his owner; "How unworthy do I really seem?" says Libanus (*As.* 669, *indignum*; 697, *indignus*). Antonin Obrdlik's "spirit of resistance" (1942; chapter 1) surely breathes in lines like these. They are suited for delivery with a wink to the audience – the "face-out" lines discussed below in chapter 6; they look for affirmation. The chapters that follow will survey many forms of "resistance" in the sense used by historians of slavery: a contestation of owners' rights, as opposed to "accommodation" (Bradley 2011b). Slaves onstage express a desire for trustworthiness (*fides*), both that they themselves should be trusted and that they should be able to trust their owners; they desire to be deemed worthy (*dignus*) of good things. They often speak of *virtus* as something they have, and, if the *virtus* they claim is sometimes a parody or reversal of the *virtus* claimed by a Roman general, that does not make the claim less serious. Insofar as *virtus* was felt to retain its root sense of "manliness," it constituted one of the chief things taken from a male slave. Verbal dueling, just as much as oratory, was a form of counting coup, and the risk for a slave who insulted his owner to his face offstage was greater than that for an orator who insulted another orator.

It gives me pause, then, that a reader of Plautus might say of Libanus' boasting about how much punishment he can bear, "This appropriation of the language of honor by the one who is outside the society of those who claim honor neither reflects, nor is it meant to represent, a slave culture; it is entirely a fantasy of the free" (Fitzgerald 2000: 40). Richard Saller, in a classic discussion of corporal punishment as marking the difference between slave and free, speaks of "the essential opposition between *dignitas* and *servitus*." No Roman author, he comments, "argued that slaves possessed a sense of honor that made corporal punishment wholly inappropriate" (1994: 145). He has been speaking of the elder Cato, and it well may be that few upper-class Romans put in writing any misgivings about the aptness of violence against the enslaved. However, that slaves possessed a sense of honor is claimed repeatedly onstage in the *palliata*, while an array of slave and freed characters charge their superiors with *iniuria*: actionable damage to honor. Epidicus and the unnamed Ancilla in *Truculentus* do so precisely in response to corporal punishment. Sosia delivers a straightforward reproach to his owner: "Amphitruo, this is the most miserable misery for a good slave, / when he tells the truth to his owner, if that truth is conquered by force" (*Am.* 590–1). The audience knows that Sosia is, in fact, telling the truth, while his owner is wrong.

Carlin Barton picks Saller up on this point in her book on Roman honor: "emotionally the slave was every bit as sensitive to insult as his or her master" (2001: 11). The low, she argues, have reason to guard an integrity that is constantly at risk. The chapters that follow will show how slaves onstage made up for what had been taken from them. They acted it out, whether in jeers like Paegnium's or in outrages like the riding scene in *Asinaria*; they said what they wanted, and commented on it in metatheatrical moments, as in the riff on slave marriage in the *Casina* prologue (chapter 4). The actors even acted out what slave-women wanted, although this message is undercut by the maleness of the *grex* (chapter 5). They found ways to say what they wanted, and commented on those ways; although slaves onstage are constantly being told to be quiet, they go right on talking, just as the *palliata* itself is the place where slaves talk back (chapter 6). In their creation of an onstage geography, and in their use of memory, they try to undo natal alienation (chapter 7). And they dream of freedom, or of the wealth that will buy that freedom, or of escape off the map altogether (chapter 8). Off the grid, rather; beyond the reach of *dominium*. Michelle Cliff, in "Claiming an Identity They Taught Me to Despise," speaks of the history that was taught her as a girl in Jamaica, and the facts that were taught her about race and mixed race, and the meaning of the word *creole* (1985b). The *palliata*, with its shimmering Latin, was made by a hybrid *grex* trying to get by in *barbaria*. What they made grew out of who they were. What follows will show how what slaves, freed slaves, and the free poor wanted was acted out onstage in the *palliata*. We have seen what was given; now we will see what was desired.

CHAPTER 4

Getting Even

One of the largest fantasy elements in Plautine comedy, the Saturnalian element so often commented upon, is the way in which slave characters get the better of owners. As seen in chapter 1, Tranio in *Mostellaria* defines this as the essence of comedy; giving a flip answer to his owner when the owner asks him what to do now, he replies (1149–51):

> si amicus Diphilo aut Philemoni es,
> dicito is quo pacto tuo' te servos ludificaverit: 1150
> optumas frustrationes dederis in comoediis.

> If you're friends with Diphilus or Philemon,
> tell them how your slave made a spectacle out of you –   1150
> you'll give them the best thwartations for their comedies.

In fine metatheatrical form, not only does the arch-trickster Tranio here tell the audience what comedy is, with reference to the Greek godfathers of the *palliata*; not only does he as a character give a tip to writers; he also does so while instantiating what he recommends: he evades the old man's question with an answer that emphasizes his own agency, marked as a joke by the immediate pickup line, *tace* ("shut up"). *Frustrationes* are deceptions, tricks, frustrations – blocking moves, the banana peels of slapstick; the verb *ludifico*, very commonly used to describe what is done to the dupes onstage, picks up the ludic element in the *ludi* that featured comic plays.[1] Tranio's answer is the kind of thing someone sitting in the audience might wish he or she could say to the person giving orders. Some of the most common types of slave misbehavior in Plautus directly address the experience of enslaved people and, in Freudian terms, would have caused

---

[1] The word *frustratio* is itself a comic formation, used elsewhere in Plautus only once – when Jupiter first appears in *Amphitruo*, in a metatheatrical monologue in which he says, "Today I'll throw the biggest thwartation onto their household" (*in horum familiam / hodie frustrationem iniciam maxumam*, *Am.* 874–5): Jupiter as slave/comedian. Many of the reversals in this chapter are discussed in Segal 1968, who interprets them as funny insofar as they are temporary.

the maximum release of inhibition in people who were themselves forbidden to do what was being acted out onstage; of course, freed slaves also owed their *patronus* a dutiful obedience, nor did the memory of slavery end with manumission.

Putting the Owner Down

The disrespect shown by slaves for owners in Plautus is so pervasive as to be invisible, and is shown in a wide variety of ways. That most of the owners shown in the plays do not deserve respect in the first place, as a plot element, confirms the validity of the single lines and shtick that give verbal form to a general contempt. As James C. Scott says (1990: 37–8), the hidden transcript acts out fantasies of vengeance; in the plays, this vengeance appears onstage.

Slaves very often speak disrespectfully of their owners or other free people, as in Sosia's opening song (chapter 2). Strobilus and the cooks in *Aulularia* run a whole series of jokes about how stingy Euclio is (294–320), and in scenes like this the audience is in on what goes on below stairs, as it were – in *Persa*, such scenes make up most of the play. Palaestrio in *Miles* views the soldier who now owns him with complete scorn: "My owner is bound with elephant hide, not his own, / and he doesn't have any more sense than a stone" (*eru' meus elephanti corio circumtentust, non suo, / neque habet plus sapientiai quam lapis*, 235–6); "My owner is such a big thief of other men's women as I believe / nobody ever was or will be" (*eru' meus ita magnus moechus mulierum est ut neminem / fuisse aeque neque futurum credo*, 775–6); and (to the audience, with the soldier onstage) "No rock is stupider than this guy" (*nullumst hoc stolidiu' saxum*, 1024). In a similar vein, Sophoclidisca compares her owner's wits unfavorably with those of a sheep (*Per.* 173–4). The *puer* Phaniscus in *Mostellaria*, failing to recognize the *senex* at whose door he has been knocking, tells him to mind his own business (940) and says to the audience, "This old man is crazy for sure" (*senex hic elleborosust certe*, 952). Pseudolus refers to his older owner as an "old tomb" (*sepulcro vetere*, 412). The slaves of young men who have fought as soldiers depict them as cowards (*Epid.* 29–38; *Trin.* 722–4), much as they describe themselves as cowards in battle (*Am.* 199–200, 427–32; *Trin.* 725–6). And, repeatedly, slaves say they will sell (their) owners, or buy them as slaves: so Stasimus of Philto, "I wish this guy'd be made / my slave, along with his *peculium*" (*ego istum velim / meum fieri servom cum suo peculio, Trin.* 433–4); so Chrysalus of Nicobulus, "I'll sell this *comptionalis* old man, / whom I have for sale, the minute I sack this town" (*comptionalem*

*senem / vendam ego, venalem quem habeo, extemplo ubi oppidum oppugnav-
ero, Bac.* 976–7). Extra disrespect is vented in *comptionalem*: "worn-out
goods, for sale cheap." Note the stress on sale in connection with the sacking of a town (see Jeppesen 2016: 150–1).

These claims have a counterpart in the many lines in which a free person
announces himself to be enslaved to a slave or prostitute: so Pistoclerus to
Bacchis, "I make myself over to your ownership: / I am yours, I give over
my services to you" (*tibi me emancupo: / tuo' sum, tibi dedo operam, Bac.*
92–3); so Nicobulus to both Bacchis sisters, "Lead us off wherever you like,
just like we're your debt-slaves" (*ducite nos quo lubet tamquam quidem
addictos, Bac.* 1205). Both use legalistic language (*emancupo, dedo operam,
addictus*), and, as will be seen, statements like *tuo' sum*, as well as the verb
lubet, figure prominently in the language of slavery and freedom. Words
like *addictus*, along with *mercennarius* (soldier to pimp, *Poen.* 503), were
spoken to an audience painfully aware that debt could lead to slavery;
ready to laugh at jokes about degrading work or beggary; conscious that
elite Roman attitudes towards labor could be contemptuous (see chapter
2 on Cicero's *De officiis* 1.150–1, where Cicero calls the wages for manual
labor a "pledge of slavery"). When a free person identifies himself (and it
is always a male) as enslaved, this is meant patronizingly rather than literally, although often the free person is about to get a nasty surprise that
will take him down a peg: this relabeling is more predictive than he knows
(Lysidamus to Olympio, *Cas.* 738). Similarly, when a free person calls a
slave *patronus, erus,* or even *pater,* he usually really owes the slave something big, though he cannot be relied upon to show his gratitude in any
material way (so Philocrates to to the suspicious Tyndarus, *Capt.* 238–9;
Lysidamus to Olympio, *Cas.* 739).[2] And that is the point: slaves who help
free people onstage rarely receive a reward in proportion to their efforts, a
sour note that jangles along with the many other vices of owners onstage.

Moving the hostility up a notch, Plautine slaves very commonly speak
disrespectfully *to* free people, especially their owners. These lines can be surprisingly harsh. Sexual insults by slaves against free characters are uncommon, but they do exist – only between males, and rarely to owners – and
focus on accusations of passive sexual use in boyhood; these taunts reverse
owners' taunts against male slaves (see chapter 2). The unnamed Slave of

---

[2] These reversals are discussed in Segal 1968: 111–16. Note that in the *servitium amoris* of elegy and
Catullan love lyric, it is the poet who professes his own abjection; onstage, doting lovers are fools or
worse (Diniarchus in *Truculentus*), with the interesting exception of Chalinus in *Casina* and Toxilus
in *Persa*.

Lyconides insults the miser Euclio by deliberately misconstruing his *pone*, "put it down," as "behind," and replying, "Gee, I think that's what you're used to giving out, old man" (*id quidem pol te datare credo consuetum, senex, Aul.* 637). The *puer* Paegnium, in the midst of a brawl, similarly insults the pimp Dordalus, who is crying out that his buttocks are being pinched: "I'm allowed; they've been well perforated for some time now" (*licet: iam diu saepe sunt expunctae, Per.* 848). The slave Libanus insults his owner, whom he is about to ride like a horse (see below). The *vilicus* Collybiscus, aside to the audience, insults the (freed slave) Advocati: "They do what *scurrae* are used to doing: they put guys behind them" (*faciunt scurrae quod consuerunt: pone sese homines locant, Poen.* 612). (Note here the imputation of sexual passivity to *scurrae*, cousins of *parasiti* as comedians; this probably accounts for Curculio's insult against the slaves of *scurrae* "who play give-and-take with each other in the street, / both the ones who take it and the ones who do it" (*qui ludunt datatim ... in via, / et datores et factores, Cur.* 296–7).)[3] Free speakers formulate insults that follow similar patterns, again from less powerful to more powerful speaker, like the retort of the *parasitus* Ergasilus to Hegio (*Capt.* 867): HE. "I can easily bear that" (*facile patior*). ER. "I think you used to do that when you were a boy" (*credo, consuetu's puer*), a line omitted by Lindsay from his 1921 school text. The pimp Cappadox in *Curculio*, in a scene that establishes his relative physical weakness, even effeminacy, says to the soldier, "Oh, you lost your ring?" And then to the audience, "This soldier was rightly enlisted in the perforated corps" (*perdidistin tu anulum? / miles pulchre centuriatus est expuncto in manipulo*, 584–5), playing on *anus* "ring/anus." The audience here is itself being enlisted, welcomed into an attack on the soldier. The formulaic nature of these insults suggests that the lexical items *consuesco*, *dato, patior, pone, soleo* all might have carried with them the potential for double entendre. This leads in turn to the reflection that double entendre, especially with such common and innocuous words, is a useful medium for a type of speech always aiming at plausible deniability (see chapter 6 on double speech and slave speech). Not all that deniable, as Lindsay's expurgation attests.

Most direct insults are not so risky – although it is essential to note that onstage insults carry little risk; that is the whole point, that is the magic

---

[3] Cf. Naevius *Tarentilla* 75–79R, discussed in chapter 3 above; Corbett 1986: 34–5, 57 (on *Cur.* 296–7: they are playing ball games); Damon 1997: 110 (on the joke in *Poenulus*: a "hint of passive homosexual relations"); Habinek 2005: 117 (on *Cur.* 296–7: competitive dance moves), followed by Moore 2012: 124. Moore 1991: 356–8 rejects a sexual sense for what I take to be a similar joke at *Cur.* 484.

of the stage. The dynamic is that of the "straight man" and the "funny man" in comic double acts (chapter 3): the funny man says outrageous things, the straight man sets up the jokes and reacts. In this display, the audience is always conscious that *both* characters are comedians, so that the norms expressed with outrage by the straight man are as ludicrous as the excesses of the funny man – rather, the comedians make the audience laugh through their relation to each other. In the *palliata*, this disjuncture from actual figures of authority would have been augmented by the grotesque masks and the foreign getup. Free characters often comment in outraged amazement on what has happened; so the old man in *Epidicus*, after he is sassed by the *fidicina*, cries out, "Ouch! To be tricked like this, to my face, out in the open!" (*ei! seic data esse verba praesenti palam!*, 521); they sometimes make threats of a beating, but rarely reply with an effective comeback, and sometimes do not even take notice (and, of course, insults aside are inaudible – the actor in cahoots with the audience). Furthermore, a reply like *ne molestu's*, "Don't be annoying," not only ends a run of jokes or stops an insult but can serve as an acknowledgment of defeat, like a safe word. The joke about Euclio's sexuality is set up by Euclio himself, when he responds to the question "What do you want?" (*quid vis tibi?*) with the ambiguous *pone* (*Aul.* 636–7). When the Slave of Lyconides interprets this to mean that Euclio likes to take it from behind (*pone*), Euclio's next line picks up *pone* with *pone hoc* ("put *this* down!"), in a triple-barreled version of the cue to end a run of shtick: "Put *this* down, please, enough with the cracks, I'm not interested in trash right now" (*pone hoc sis, aufer cavillam, non ego nunc nugas ago, Aul.* 638).[4] Often the owner is the straight man, while the slave or *parasitus* is the funny man, sticking it to the boss, and indeed the Slave here makes another joke on *pone* (639). There are no repercussions.

So all kinds of insults are plentiful. Chrysalus, tied up for an imminent beating, tells Nicobulus to his face, "You don't know you're for sale now" (*nescis nunc venire te, Bac.* 814, cf. 816), and, to the audience, says he is senile, overdue for death, "a blot on the landscape," "worth as much as a rotten mushroom" (*terrai ... odium, fungus putidus, Bac.* 820–1). Sosia turns the sight gag of Alcumena's pregnancy into jokes made to Amphitruo, the straight man, about her gluttony (*Am.* 664–7) and having to haul the water when she goes into labor (668–73); he repeatedly speaks disrespectfully of her to Amphitruo in her presence (Act 2, Scene 2), and finally to her face

---

[4] On the verbal cues involved in runs of shtick, see chapter 3 on *respondere*, and in general Richlin 2017b: 179–92.

(739–41). She now calls him on it ("He's speaking to me impolitely again," *iterum hic in me inclementer dicit*), and tells Amphitruo that he needs to discipline Sosia (742). The egregious Leonida, pretending to be the *atriensis*, orders Libanus to abuse the hapless Mercator, and the two slaves insult him in terms familiar from verbal dueling, some of them usually used on slaves: "unclean, worthless" (*inpure, nihili, As.* 472); "you disgrace of a person" (*flagitium hominis*, 473); "this slut," "you slut" (*impudicum, inpudice*, 475); "criminal" (*sceleste*, juxtaposed with *mihi scelesto*, 476); "executioner" (*carnufex*, 482); "flogbait," "yoke-bearer" (*verbero, furcifer*, 484–5). The Mercator, puzzled, explains how they are supposed to behave: "A slave person is not supposed to be arrogant" (*non decet superbum esse hominem servom*, 470); "You, a slave, insult a free person?" (*tun libero homini / male servos loquere?*, 477–8). Leonida, losing patience, hits him (*vapula*, 478). As the quarrel winds down, he lays claim to equal rights: "You insult another, and you're not to be replied to? / I'm just as much a person as you" (*tu contumeliam alteri facias, tibi non dicatur? / tam ego homo sum quam tu*, 489–90). He here ups the ante from what Paegnium says to Sagaristio during their verbal duel: "Since you're a slave, it should at least be okay for a slave to insult you" (*tandem uti liceat, / quom servos sis, servom tibi male dicere, Per.* 290–1).

The *puer* Pinacium tells the *parasitus* Gelasimus to mind his own business and teases him about his hunger (*St.* 319–25); Pinacium keeps it up in front of his owner Panegyris, and Gelasimus complains to her about it ("I've been letting this guy speak unjustly," *istum patior dicere iniuste*, 344), but then allows Pinacium to make him help sweep the doorway, with further digs about his hunger and poverty (345–60). Pinacium is equally rude to Panegyris herself, and she sums up, dimly: "By gosh, you're not submissive enough to your owner" (*non ecastor ... satis erae morem geris*, 361). The smarminess of the slave Lampadio in *Cistellaria* (chapter 1) shows as he turns his owner's prayer as she exits into a prayer that she would leave (*uti abeas domum*, 596); he insinuates she is drunk (667); he mimics her instructions not to interrupt (*ne obloquere rusus*, 754). The old slave-woman Staphyla taunts her owner Euclio with their poverty (*Aul.* 83–4). The freed *fidicina* Acropolistis, having been discovered not to be the long-lost daughter of the *senex* Periphanes, puts the blame flatly on him: "That's your fault, not mine" (*tua istaec culpast, non mea, Epid.* 587) – even though, since he is the one who freed her (504–9), he is now her *patronus*.[5] Palinurus calls his owner Phaedromus "crazy" (*insane, Cur.* 19),

---

[5] For discussion of the status of Acropolistis, see chapter 5.

and insults Phaedromus' beloved Planesium to her face in front of him
(190–92); Milphio does the same thing to Adelphasium in front of
Agorastocles (*Poen.* 392–9), replacing his previous endearments on behalf
of his owner – what she means to Agorastocles – with what Adelphasium
really means to him as a slave: "hatred," "enemy," "ill-wisher," "eye disease,"
"bile" (*odium, inimica, malevola, lippitudo, fel*). If she cannot take pity on
Agorastocles, says Milphio, she should hang herself along with the pimp
and his whole household, because "I now see I'll have to be staying alive
by sips" – that is, his jaw will be broken (*mihi iam video ... victitandum
sorbilo*, 397) – and "I'm walking around now with my back ridged like an
oyster-shell with sores" (*iam quasi ostreatum tergum ulceribus gestito*, 398),
"because of you" (*propter te*, 397), "because of the love you two share"
(*propter amorem vostrum*, 399). He relabels her, and tallies up the cost to
his own body of what his owner calls "love."

Milphio repeatedly tells Agorastocles off, although he often at the same
time describes how Agorastocles has beaten him (*Poen.* 135–53, 378–9,
397–8, 410–13); the two of them, though, interact like an old vaudeville
team (158–63, 279–80, 290–6, 311–13). Pseudolus calls his young owner
"cuckoo," like Horace's vineyard worker (*cucule, Ps.* 96); tells him not to
be annoying (*molestus ... ne sis*, 118 – a common exit cue from a run of
jokes, here a shock from slave to owner); and implies he is asleep at the
wheel (*qui vigilans dormiat*, 386). Acanthio tells his young owner to drink
hot pitch (*Mer.* 140): just a joke! Milphio, reproved by Hanno for mocking an arriving foreigner, reacts with echoic and direct insults: he answers
Hanno's contrast between *servom ... et nequam et malum, / hominem peregrinum atque advenam* ("a slave both worthless and bad, / a person foreign and newly-arrived," *Poen.* 1030–1) with *hominem et sycophantam et
subdolum* ("a person both a con-man and a sneak," 1032); he then calls
Hanno "you double-speaker, / with forked tongue like a crawling beast"
(*migdilix, / bisulci lingua quasi proserpens bestia*, 1033–4).[6] He is chastised
by his owner ("I don't want you to speak unjustly," *nolo te iniuste loqui*,
1037 – the same adverb used by Alcumena of Sosia). Similarly, Sceparnio,
on meeting Plesidippus, calls his gender into question (*utrum tu masne
an femina es*, "are you male or female?", *Rud.* 104), says the gods will send
Plesidippus a beating (108), and accuses him of being a thief (110–11);
Plesidippus responds with pompous remarks on what would entitle a slave
to speak at all, much less speak rudely to a free man, especially when his

---

[6] Accepting de Melo's interpretation of *migdilix* as derived from Greek *migda* "in a mixed way" plus
Latin -*lix*, "tongue" (2012: 129 n. 58).

owner is present (*peculiosum esse addecet servom et probum*, "a slave would have to have a big *peculium* and be honest," 112; cf. *ubi erus assit*, 119, and *deludificavit me ille homo indignis modis*, "that person has made a spectacle of me in unworthy ways," 147). Like Milphio, Sceparnio responds in turn with echoic insults, impugning Plesidippus' sexual morality (*et impudicum et impudentem hominem addecet*, "a person would have to be both slutty and shameless," 115). As Plesidippus tries to talk to Sceparnio's owner Daemones, Sceparnio keeps interjecting insults – suggesting Plesidippus help him re-roof the house (122–3), taunting him as a man who hangs around temples to get a meal (140–1), suggesting he belongs in the mill (144–6). Sceparnio offers an equally rude welcome to the pimp and his Sicilian friend, trying to steal the Sicilian's clothes and ill-wishing him (580–3); to the Sicilian's request for dry clothes and shelter, a favor to be returned at some vague future point, Sceparnio says he would never give him credit without a deposit (581) – an insult, as seen in chapter 3 – and rejects him as a "barbarian guest" (*barbarum hospitem*, 583).

Pomposity like Plesidippus' is itself the target of abuse in scenes where slaves caricature the behavior and speech of owners or their slave deputies. Sagaristio, arriving with the money Toxilus needs, signals his intention to act grand (*Per.* 307, *amicibor gloriose*, 308 *magnufice conscreabor*, "I'm going to dress in style," "I'm going to hawk and spit like a bigshot"), struts up to Toxilus (who says he looks as if he has handles, 308), and responds to Toxilus' greeting with a string of commands: "Get over here. It'll be seen to. I want it done. Come. Move it" (*adito. / videbitur. factum volo. venito. promoveto*, 310–11).[7] For the string of imperatives, compare the very typical commands of Daemones to his slave Gripus: "Get inside, don't be annoying, hold your tongue" (*abi intro, ne molestu's, linguae tempera, Rud.* 1254). The luckless Olympio, playing the owner to his own owner in a whole scene in *Casina* (720–58a), insults the cook, assumes with pomp a stately demeanor ("I am slow to dress in style and in the manner of a gentleman," *cesso magnufice patricieque amicirier*, 723), and insults his owner: "Pee-yew! When you speak, it stinks"; "Can you get away from me, / unless you want me / to throw up today"; (*fui fui! foetet*

---

[7] *Promoneto*, "remind me," is the reading of APL, accepted by Leo, Lindsay, and de Melo; Leo adduces *promonebo* at Cicero, *Att.* 4.12. *Promoveto* is the reading of FZψ, and must be right (cf. Shackleton Bailey 1965: 188, who emends the Cicero text to *praemonebo* and adds that *promoveto* should be accepted at *Per.* 311, with Ritschl, "against Leo and Lindsay"). In commands, owners are the ones who do the reminding (see chapter 7). *Promoveo* occurs in Terence with the right sense (*And.* 639, *Eun.* 913, *Hec.* 703). On the association between the imperative mood and speech by owners to slaves in late ancient school exercises, see Bloomer 1997: 71–4.

tuo' mihi sermo, 727; *potin a me abeas, / nisi me vis / vomere hodie?* 731–32a); "What do I need with a slave so worthless?" (*quid mi opust servo tam nequam?*, 741). The two lapse into a bilingual duet, peppered with Olympio's imperatives: "Remember, remember," "Stop it," "Let (her)," "You just go," "Just go," and, to the cooks as well, "Hurry up and go inside and hurry up and hurry," "Please go," "Make (dinner)" (*memento, memento* 737, *omitte* 737, *sine* 753, *tu i modo* 755, *i modo* 758; *cito intro ite et cito deproperate* 744–5, *i sis* 749–50, *facite* 746–7). They squabble over who is the slave and who is the owner (734–8), as Olympio claims free status (*servus ego?*), and Lysidamus moves from *eru' sum* to *servos sum tuos.* Lysidamus interjects his own imperatives: "Wait," "Wait," "Wait and stay put," "Just you go," "Take a look" (*mane* 727, *mane* 733, *mane atque asta* 737, *i tu modo* 756, *perspicito* 756). But he finally caves in: "If you're ordering me, / watch out, you'll have company" (*si tu iubes/ em ibitur tecum*, 758–58a).[8]

In a similar mimicking of rank, Leonida tells how he imitated the manner of the *atriensis* ("At once I make myself a smooth-talking man, a bigshot," *extemplo facio facetum me atque magnuficum virum, As.* 351); he warns Libanus that, continuing in this role, he (Leonida) will have to strike Libanus with his fist (371–2). Later, acting the part, he says sarcastically to the play-cowering Libanus, "Did I hail you as Libanus the freedman today? Are you manumitted now?" (*hodie salvere iussi / Libanum libertum? iam manu emissu's?* 410–11) – hitting him between questions, to judge by the Mercator's response (417).[9] This is a bitterly mimicked taunt: slave onstage mimics *atriensis* aping owner mocking slave's hope of manumission. Leonida continues his angry rhetorical questions based on commands (424–6):

> iussin, sceleste, ab ianua hoc stercus hinc auferri?
> iussin columnis deici operas araneorum?   425
> iussin in splendorem dari bullas has foribus nostris?

> Didn't I order this shit, you criminal, shoveled away from the doorway?
> Didn't I order the spiders' work to be cleaned right off these columns?   425
> Didn't I order these knobs on our doors to be polished til they glisten?

---

[8] See Moore 2012: 113, who points out that Olympio and Lysidamus here sing in ionics "as the *Senex* states openly and repeatedly that Olympio is now free and the *Senex* is his slave (731–41)" – a use of the association between the ionic meter and transgressive role reversal.

[9] In this sequence of bossy speeches, the *iubeo* in the formal greeting *iubeo salvere* awakens within the idiom. This expression normally greets and recognizes a person by name and/or station, and forms part of the formula for manumission, as here; see further in chapter 8.

The anaphora works like slaps, the *stercus* like a kick, the iambic *bullas has* like bangs, and the speech ends with another blow ("So, pow, this is for you," *em ergo hoc tibi*, 431). In this scene, slaves and freed slaves in the audience could watch a [slave] actor play a slave who caricatures the *atriensis*; along with the plot-driven purpose of the scene (to cheat a merchant out of money in order to aid the slaves' owners), there is pleasure in public exposure of a slave-driver.

The verb *fastidio*, "turn one's nose up," "show disdain," is often used in comments that a character has exceeded his authority or acts with arrogance, some of which use the catchphrase formula *ut* + verb + subject [derogatory term], as in *ut fastidit gloriosus* (*Cur.* 633, *parasitus* to soldier), "How the boaster turns his nose up!" So Lysidamus to the above-himself Olympio ("But wait, although you turn your nose up," *mane vero, quamquam fastidis, Cas.* 727); so the young wife Panegyris to her back-talking *puer* Pinacium: ("Do you turn your nose up at me, you shameful thing?," *mihin fastidis, propudiose?, St.* 334). When Chrysalus tells the story about the rich man who has had soles fastened onto his *socci* with gold, Nicobulus, playing the straight man, says, "Why is he so fussy?" (*qur ita fastidit?, Bac.* 333). Answer: because he is so rich. When a slave acts this way onstage, the other characters re-enact owners' astonished reactions to slaves' self-assertion, with an effect something like that of the word "uppity" in English. Usually, however, the slave maintains the upper hand, and the accuser looks foolish.

Similarly, the adjective *magnuficus* and its adverbial form show up, as seen above, when characters onstage talk about the affect of a person who makes superior claims to power – an affect they are mocking as they imitate it. It is associated with soldiers: by Chrysalus, himself boasting (*Bac.* 966); by Pseudolus as he watches the slave Simia enter, pretending to be a soldier ("How he goes, how he carries himself like a bigshot!," *ut it, ut magnufice infert sese, Ps.* 911); and by the pimp Cappadox, who places his onstage soldier on a social scale we will revisit in chapter 5: "I don't count your bigshot words … / as worth any more than my slave-woman who cleans the toilet" (*tua magnufica verba … / non pluris facio quam ancillam meam quae latrinam lavat, Cur.* 579–80). (Simia is only impersonating a soldier's slave, but he introduces himself grandly as a "famous military man," *stratioticus homo … cluear, Ps.* 918). The pimp Ballio, planning his birthday party, shows his nature when he says he wants "to receive the top men like a bigshot, so they'll think I'm a wealthy man" (*magnufice volo me viros summos accipere, ut mihi rem esse reantur, Ps.* 167); listening to him go on, Calidorus says sarcastically to Pseudolus, "Does he seem like enough of a bigshot to you?" (*satin magnificus tibi videtur*, 194). Pimps dream of impressing the top men (compare Toxilus' sales pitch to Dordalus in *Persa*), while characters like the Advocati distrust them. The word also has generic overtones; Pseudolus, talking to himself about his triumphant return to his young owner, says, "I'll accost the guy like a bigshot" (*magnifice hominem compellabo*, *Ps.* 702), before launching into a proud speech to the "tyrant"; watching him, the young owner's friend says, "How that executioner sends up tragedy!" (*ut paratragoedat carnufex*, 707). Comedy mocks the *summi viri*, tragedy takes them seriously; the politics of tragedy are known to us only through fragments, but a fragment of the probably Plautine *Blind Man*, or *Robbers*, suggest that ostentation by the audience at the games was likewise the target of mockery: "I watched the games like a bigshot, like a wealthy man" (*spectavi ludos magnifice atque opulenter*, *Caecus* or *Praedones* fr. 36). Even if the *ludos* here are figurative, the speaker must be an unprivileged person flaunting his temporary privilege. This line looks for a laugh from the people in the cheap seats – that is, all the seats. As Sosia points out, "Slavery to a wealthy man is hard" (*opulento homini … servitus dura est*, *Am.* 166).

Pervasively, slaves say to free interlocutors, "You're stupid" – *stultu's*. So Lydus to his owner, the *senex* Philoxenus, *stultus es* (*Bac.* 464); Chrysalus to his owner's son Mnesilochus, *stulte* (*Bac.* 673); Chrysalus to his owner, the *senex* Nicobulus, *o stulte, stulte* (*Bac.* 814); Epidicus to his owner's son Stratippocles, "You're stupid, shut up" (*stultu's, tace*, *Epid.* 652); Scapha to Philematium as she tends her, "You really are an exceedingly stupid woman" (*nimi' tuquidem stulta es mulier*, *Mos.* 176), and again "Now you're a stupid woman, acting stupidly" (*te … nunc stultam stulte facere*, 186–87), and again, "You are just plain stupid" (*stulta es plane*, 194). Tranio says to his owner, "Sometimes you're ridiculously stupid" (*interdum inepte stultus es*, *Mos.* 495); Toxilus says to the pimp Dordalus, "You are a childishly stupid person" (*tu … homo stultus es pueriliter*, *Per.* 591) and "Shut up, stupid" (*tace, stulte*, 830); Milphio says to his owner Agorastocles, "You are stupider than a flint stone" (*tu es lapide silice stultior*, *Poen.* 291). In a rare cross-sex instance, the bold slave-woman Astaphium says to her owner's customer, *stultu's*, not once but twice (*Truc.* 730, 743). Epidicus' early reproach to his owner's son shows what is at stake: "Do you think it's right for me to be the guilt-offering for your stupidity, / so that you use my back as the substitute sacrifice for your stupidity?" (*men piacularem oportet fieri ob stultitiam tuam, / ut meum tergum tuae stultitiae subdas succidaneum?*, *Epid.* 139–40). He begins to beguile the two *senes* with the polite conditional "If it'd be fair / for me to be wiser than you two" (*si aequom siet / me plus sapere quam vos*, *Epid.* 257–8); they will indeed turn out to be stupid, as Periphanes concedes of his friend ("I've seen a hammer that was smarter," *malleum / sapientiorem vidi*, 524–5).

The slaves who mastermind their plays often give orders to free characters. Tranio, trying to get his owner to get rid of the moneylender, moves from "I beg you" (*Mos.* 618) to a string of imperatives ending in "I order you" (634–5, *ego iubeo*). Pseudolus, an outstanding example, says starkly to old Simo at the end, quoting the famous words of Brennus the Gaul after the sack of Rome, "Woe to the defeated" (*vae victis*, *Ps.* 1317); also just "Do what I order you" (*fac quod te iubeo*, 1327).[10] Having forced Simo to tears of supplication (*heu heu heu*, 1320), he explains why he is so implacable: "You would have had no mercy for my back" (*neque te mei tergi misereret*, 1324). Not only have they switched roles, but, as Pseudolus says outright, justifiably so, in an earlier exchange with Simo (471–3):

> PS.   age loquere quidvis, tam etsi tibi suscenseo.
> SIMO.   mihin domino servos tu suscenses? PS. tam tibi
> mirum id videtur? ...

> PS.   Go on, say what you want, though I'm still angry with you.
> SIMO.   You, a slave, are angry with me, your legal owner? PS. Does that seem
> so amazing to you?

An important question, and one with many echoes in the *palliata*, as will be seen; just as Sosia's question about Amphitruo expects a sympathetic "yes" from the audience (chapter 2), so this one expects a resounding "no" from (some in) the audience, based in a shared anger. This anger onstage at times manifests itself in physical ways. A repeated feature of the stock "running slave" routine is the emphasis on shoving people out of the way, and the speaker often makes the point that people of rank must make way for him. In fact both slaves and *parasiti* speak these lines, so that the issue is not civil status but relative (net) worth. Mercurius makes a metatheatrical *a fortiori* argument (*Am.* 984–90):

> Concedite atque apscedite omnes, de via decedite,
> nec quisquam tam av<i>dax fuat homo qui obviam opsistat mihi.   985
> nam mihi quidem hercle qui minus liceat deo minitarier
> populo, ni decedat mihi, quam servolo in comoediis?
> ill' navem salvam nuntiat aut irati adventum senis:

---

[10] On *vae victis*, Pseudolus, and Brennus, see Leigh 2004: 52. Pseudolus' line suggests the circulation of the story of Brennus as part of Italian folk tradition, in line with Rebecca Langlands's work in progress on exemplarity; see esp. Festus 510–12L on the status of *vae victis* as *proverbium* and its recycling in the story of Camillus. Compare the catchphrase *vapula Papiria* (chapter 1).

ego sum Iovi dicto audiens, eius iussu nunc huc me adfero.
quam ob rem mihi magi' par est via decedere et concedere.   990

Yield and get out of the way, all of you, get off the road,
nor let there be any person so bold as to block my way.   985
For indeed, by Hercules, how should I, a god, be less permitted to threaten
the people, if they don't yield to me, than the little slave in comedies?
That guy announces the ship's back safe or the arrival of an angry old man;
I myself take orders from Jupiter, by his command I now betake
        myself here.
So it's all the more fair to get off the road and yield to me.   990

The jingle *populo/servolo* (987) emphasizes Mercurius' real position, while
dicto audiens (989) emphasizes the slavery he has been forced to put on.
Compare Pinacium (*St.* 274–5), who, as he runs in, compares himself to
Mercury; or Ergasilus, who proclaims, "Let no one block my way" (*ne mi
opstiterit obviam*, *Capt.* 791), followed by a long string of physical threats
(like "My fist is a ballista, my elbow is a catapult," *meumst ballista pugnum, cubitus catapultast mihi*, 796), leading into specific threats against
millers, fishmongers, and butchers. Curculio asserts, "Nor is there anyone
anywhere so wealthy as to block my way" (*nec <usquam> quisquamst tam
opulentus, qui mi opsistat in via*, 284), followed by physical threats ("that
he won't fall down, that he won't stand on his head," *quin cadat, quin
capite sistat*, 287) against a jumble of officials, as well as "Greeks wearing
the *pallium*" (*Graeci palliati*, 288–95) and the slaves of *scurrae* (296–7).
Acanthio urges himself on against the crowd of those coming towards him:
"Push 'em away, / force 'em down, tumble 'em into the street" (*aspellito,
/ detrude, deturba in viam*, *Mer.* 115–16). The *puer* Pinacium displays the
range of powers assumed by the runner (*St.* 284–7):

> … nunc, Pinacium,
> age ut placet, curre ut lubet, cave quemquam flocci feceris,   285
> cubitis depulsa de via, tranquillam concinna viam;
> si rex opstabit obviam, regem ipsum priu' pervortito.

> … Now, Pinacium,
> do as you please, run as you like, don't give a damn for anyone,   285
> push 'em off the road with your elbows, pacify the street;
> if a king blocks the way, flip the king himself over first.

These speeches, always accompanied by music, are often made while
the speaker is alone onstage or observed by kibitzers, and so are mainly
directed at the audience; it has been suggested that the runners might have
entered *through* the audience, which would have allowed for clowning

like the toga-snatching horseplay in the *Amphitruo* prologue (chapter 3).[11] Often they are in trochaic septenarii, perhaps evoking soldiers' mocking parade songs, although these are attested only later in the Republic (see chapter 3): the running slave or poor man, then, a one-man army.[12] The runners' speeches must have involved a lot of miming; as in Pinacium's speech, the characters often give themselves stage directions, and it is hard to believe these were unaccompanied by gestures or dance movement. Indeed, Timothy Moore argues (2012: 122–4) that the scenes in which characters enter running should be understood as dance scenes, and that Curculio describes actions he might not only mime but parody: the Greeks wandering around with their books and bundles, drunk; the slaves of *scurrae* fooling around with each other in the street. Consistently, however, what was mimed was knocking over important men. Both Pinacium and Ergasilus use their elbows, as does Curculio (*Cur.* 282), perhaps recalling the "bigshot" stance adopted by Sagaristio that makes him look to Toxilus as if he had handles: bigshots take up extra space on the street. Pinacium sees his run as expressive of liberty (see below on *lubet*), and takes on even the paradigmatic "man at the top," the *rex* (see chapter 8).

In some plays, slave characters physically humiliate their owners, as in Pseudolus' subjugation of Simo above. Startling examples come from *Asinaria*, which begins with the *senex* Demaenetus ordering his slave Libanus to steal money from him (91), and includes a scene (646–731) in which Libanus and Leonida force the young owner Argyrippus and his prostitute *amica* to promise them freedom, beg them for money, and go down on their knees; the *amica* is made to call each of them sweet names and is asked to kiss and embrace them. Each time, this final move makes the young owner angry enough to protest – "She should kiss you, flogbait? … She should embrace you, executioner?" (*ten osculetur, verbero?*, 669; *ten complectatur, carnufex?*, 697), and each time the slave addressed responds with a question: LE. *quam vero indignum visum est?*, 669; LI. *quam vero indignus videor?*, 697: "How unworthy does this really seem?" "How unworthy do I really seem?" – compare Pseudolus to Simo, above.

---

[11] Entering through the audience: Wiles 1991: 59–61, focusing on Curculio's entrance. The running-slave scenes are widely discussed as shtick dating back to Greek comedy (see Marshall 2006: 193–4), but, as Wiles and Marshall point out, the shape of the *palliata* stage allowed for vigorous interaction with the audience.

[12] Mercurius' song is in iambic octonarii rather than trochaic septenarii; Moore associates this meter both with slaves bearing messages and with tragic parody, singling out Mercurius' speech (2012: 183) – especially apt, considering Mercurius' self-association in the prologue with *tragicomoedia* (see chapter 6).

And then Libanus commands his owner to carry him on his back (698–710):

[LI.] ne istuc nequiquam dixeris in me tam indignum dictum,
vehes pol hodie me, si quidem hoc argentum ferre speres.
ARG. ten ego veham? LI. tun hoc feras \<hinc\> argentum aliter a me?   700
ARG. perii hercle. si verum quidemst decorum erum vehere servom,
inscende. LI. sic istic solent superbi subdomari.
asta igitur, ut consuetus es puer olim. scin ut dicam?
ARG. inscende actutum. LI. ego fecero. hem quid istuc est? ut tu
     incedis?   705
em sic. abi, laudo, nec te equo magis est equos ullus sapiens.   704
demam hercle iam de hordeo, tolutim ni badizas.
ARG. amabo, Libane, iam sat est. LI. numquam hercle hodie exorabis.
nam iam calcari quadrupedo agitabo advorsum clivom,
postidea ad pistores dabo, ut ibi cruciere currens.
asta ut descendam nunciam in proclivi, quamquam nequam es.   710

[LI.] So you won't get away with saying such an unworthy thing to me –
by God, today you're going to carry *me*, if you hope to bear off this cash.
ARG. *I* should carry *you*? LI. Are you going to get this cash from me any
     other way?   700
ARG. By God, I'm dead. Well, if it's right for an owner to carry a slave,
climb on board. LI. That's the way you show these stuck-up guys
     who's boss.
Stand still, then, like you used to back when you were a boy. Know what
     I mean?
ARG. Climb on, already. LI. I am. Hey, what's this? Can't you get a move
     on?   705
So – pow! Get going, good boy, no horse is smarter than you, horse.   704
By God, I'm going to take away your feed unless you vamoose like a trotter.
ARG. Please, Libanus, lovey, that's enough. LI. By God, you'll never beg
     off today.
In fact, now I'm going to spur you at the gallop up this hill,
then I'll give you to the millers so you can be tortured while you're running.
Stand still so I can get down now on the slope, although you're
     worthless.   710

That it is the slave's job to carry burdens and the owner's to go unbur-
dened has been established already when the owner began to beg for
the wallet full of money that Leonida was carrying (657–60): the scene
intensifies the irony of the name Argyrippus ("Cash Horse"). Here the
degradation of the owner is the direct response to his denial of sex to the
slave, who sees this as a question of worth and justice (*indignum* 669,

indignus 697, *indignum dictum* 698). The owner sees this as a breach of social rules (701); Libanus, probably aside, points the moral to the audience in terms of conquest and subjugation (702), of what to do with the "men at the top," here the *superbi*. Telling the young man to bend over, he implies that Argyrippus was habitually used for sex as a boy – an accusation, as seen above, also made to an owner by the Slave of Lyconides in *Aulularia*, and to Hegio by the *parasitus* Ergasilus, and used elsewhere against slaves (compare Ballio to Harpax, *facere solitun es – scin quid loquar? Ps.* 1178; the use of the verb *asto* here suggests possible overtones akin to those of *morem gerere*, as also in the many "After you!" "No, after *you*!" exits).[13] The insult here turns the riding into a rape; although Libanus is not identified in the text as a *puer*, as seen in chapters 1 and 2 both his name (~ "Chanel") and his small size (one hundred pounds stripped naked, *As.* 299–305) might have suggested his sex-object status to the audience. This would then be revenge as well as rape. Once astride his owner, Libanus makes some kind of physical move, spurring or slapping or using an improvised riding crop: *em sic* (704; surely this line belongs after 705).[14] When his horse will not go fast enough, Libanus threatens to take away his food (706), imitating the stingy owners seen in chapter 2; then he will drive him even faster uphill, and, once he is worn out, send him to the mill to be killed with running (708–9), as owners threaten slaves with the mill. That this ride is another caricature of owners' abuse of slaves is underlined by the final *nequam es* (710) – what owners say to slaves; so Olympio to Lysidamus (*Cas.* 741), playing the owner to his owner. Argyrippus has to beg Libanus to get off, using the conciliatory *amabo* – "please, lovey" (707) – that belongs normally to women's speech.[15] The scene winds up with the two slaves being worshiped as gods, but the slave's riding of the owner avenges on the owner's body all the injustices of owner to slave.

Similar terms arise in other instances in which the slave reverses the balance of power. Acanthio makes Charinus beg to hear his message (*Mer.* 171–2):

---

[13] Interpretations of this line as referring to leapfrog, going back at least to Riley's 1852 Bohn translation, can perhaps be recognized as overly innocent; cf. Henderson 2006: 191–206, 235–8, with discussion of line 703 at 202, and see chapter 2 on "bend over" jokes about *pueri*. For a pertinent analogy between slave-owners and horse-owners, see Finley 1998[1980]: 141, and, for Apuleius's *Metamorphoses* as an allegory of the slave as quadruped, Bradley 2000.

[14] B has lines 703 and 704 reversed, so it does not seem impossible that the order of lines here is off; and surely *inscende* (705) must precede *abi* (704).

[15] On *amabo*, see Dutsch 2008: 50–3 and James 2015a: 108–9.

[CH.] ... mihi supplicandum servolo video meo.
AC. tandem indignus videor? CH. immo dignus.

[CH.] ... I see I must beg my little slavey.
AC. At long last, do I seem unworthy? CH. No, worthy.

Charinus, like Argyrippus, needs something from his slave here. Pinacium in *Stichus* proclaims that his *era* ought to supplicate him in order to receive his message, again using the language of fairness seen in Sosia's opening song in chapter 2, and many times since then (*aequiust ... aequom censeo*, 290–3). *She* should come out to greet *him*, he says (*advorsum veniat*, 299), testifing to the social meaning of this typical slave duty (chapter 6). A less spectacular episode than the *Asinaria* riding scene, but structurally similar, comes from *Cistellaria*. Just as Demaenetus in *Asinaria* orders Libanus to steal from him, so Alcesimarchus in *Cistellaria* orders his slave to insult him (233); as the slave nervously complies, he begins to berate his owner as owners usually berate slaves, with escalating violence, from "By God, you really *are* worthless" (*nihili hercle vero es*, 238), repeating his owner's self-accusation, to "By God, you are worthy of calamity" (*dignus hercle es infortunio*, 239), to "You'll never be prudent" (*frugi numquam eris*, 240), to "You ought to wear shackles and never take them off" (*compedis te capere oportet neque eas umquam ponere*, 244), to "For this, you are worthy to wear the yoke ten times" (*ob istuc ... dignu's deciens qui furcam feras*, 248), to a final command: "You should hang yourself" (*suspendas te*, 250). The similarity of this gimmick to the scene where Leonida orders Libanus to insult the Mercator (*As.* 471, above) suggests that this was shtick: funny to have a slave compelled to insult a free person. Punishment is expressed here, and often, in the language of worth (*nihili, dignus, frugi, dignu's*), and slaves' speeches throw this into question.

Above all, when Periphanes finally confronts his slave Epidicus (*Epid.* 682–731), Epidicus insists that he bind him and Periphanes winds up begging Epidicus to let him free him.[16] The balance begins to shift as Epidicus begins to claim free status (711–12):

EP. etiam inclamitor quasi servos? PE. quom tu es liber gaudeo.
EP. merui ut fierem. PE. tu meruisti? ...

---

[16] Cf. the analysis of this scene in Segal 1968: 109–11, emphasizing Epidicus' wish to humiliate his owner; he goes on, however, to instance this scene as an illustration of the principle that "the clever slave does not even desire manumission" (164). On this point, see chapter 8 below. Ketterer (1986b: 100) argues that the onstage presence of the straps (*lora*) used to bind Epidicus – foreshadowed at 612 and specifically defied at 684 – labels the scene as one of torture; this has wide implications for many other torture-related props in the plays.

EP. Am I still being shouted at like a slave? PE. I rejoice that you are
    a free man.
EP. I've earned that I become one. PE. You've earned it?

Periphanes here uses sarcastically one of the formulas by which an owner
recognizes his new freedman (compare Leonida as the *atriensis* above);
Epidicus takes him up on it (see chapter 8). To a bystander, he spells out
what he has done to deserve better: "By God, it's by the most insulting
injustice / that I stand here tied up, I by whose efforts this daughter of
his was found today" (*maxuma hercle iniuria / vinctus asto, quoius haec
hodie opera inventast filia*, 715–16). He protests here an assault on his honor
(*iniuria*), as if he had any (see chapter 2). Eventually Periphanes responds
to these claims of merit (721–2), and comes to a bargain with Epidicus
(723–31):

EP. ne attigas. PE. ostende vero. EP. nolo. PE. non aequom facis.
EP. numquam hercle hodie, nisi supplicium mihi das, me solvi sinam.
PE. optumum atque aequissumum oras. soccos, tunicam, pallium   725
tibi dabo. EP. quid deinde porro? PE. libertatem. EP. at postea?
novo liberto opus est quod pappet. PE. dabitur, praebebo cibum.
EP. numquam hercle hodie, nisi me orassis, solves. PE. oro te, Epidice,
mihi ut ignoscas siquid inprudens culpa peccavi mea.
at ob eam rem liber esto. EP. invitus do hanc veniam tibi,   730
nisi necessitate cogar. solve sane si lubet.

EP. Don't you touch me. PE. Really, show me your hands. EP. I don't want
    to. PE. You're not being fair.
EP. By God, never today, unless you pay me a penalty, will I let myself be
    unbound.
PE. You beg for what's very good and very fair. I'll give you   725
socci, a tunic, and a *pallium*. EP. And then what? PE. Freedom. EP. But
    after that?
A new freedman needs something for num-nums. PE. It will be given, I'll
    provide food.
EP. By God, never today, unless *you've* begged *me*, will you unbind me. PE.
    I beg you, Epidicus,
to forgive me if I did wrong, by my fault, heedlessly.
But for that reason: be thou free. EP. Against my will, I do this favor for
    you,   730
so I won't be forced to by necessity. All right, unbind me if you feel like it.

The *grex* then immediately closes the play with an endorsement: "This is
the person who found freedom through his own bad behavior. / Applaud
and be well" (*Hic is homo est qui libertatem malitia invenit sua. / plaudite
et valete*, 732–3). This bald ending might be compared with the moral at

the end of a fable, or with exempla as what Langlands (forthcoming) calls "working stories" – stories to which community members return repeatedly, because they "convey moral complexity without needing to resolve or collapse it." Open, not closed; a reminder that theatergoers have a post-audience existence during which they discuss what they have seen, a feature emphasized by the slave characters who talk onstage about what they have seen at the theater – Chrysalus, for one, talking about this very play (below).

In this closing scene of *Epidicus*, the tense of *merui* and *meruisti* (712) emphasizes the process by which the slave works his way towards freedom; the sum of his actions makes a case for manumission, and the slave's favorite adjective *aequom* is now picked up by the owner, first teasingly, then placatingly (723, 725). Counter to later convention, or any evidence for the 200s BCE, Epidicus claims a *patronus* owes his freed slave support, here in the form of a meal, and the owner agrees; ironically, the clothing offered by the owner to pay his "penalty" is what Epidicus is already wearing, the comedian's garb (725–6).[17] Epidicus asks not only for a meal, but for *quod pappet* – lip-smacking baby talk, a reference to the pap that a *nutrix* chewed for her charge – emphasizing the desire to be served by the (feminized) owner. The offer of food picks up on the fear of hunger so often expressed in the plays, and makes an alternate model to the much-deplored behavior of the stingy owner (chapter 2), as well as to the negligence of *patroni*, fleetingly mocked in *Curculio*, where the banker Lyco says to the soldier, in something of a non sequitur, "You act more wisely / than some pimps, who have freedmen and abandon them" (*faci' sapientius / quam pars lenonum, libertos qui habent et eos deserunt*, 547–8; see chapter 6). Support is what Palaestrio disingenuously begs the soldier for (*ne me deseras*, *Mil.* 1363); support is what Scapha wishes for, lamenting her misplaced love (*reliquit deseruitque me*, *Mos.* 202). Dordalus in *Persa* rejoices over freeing Lemniselenis because now he will no longer have to feed her (471–3). Periphanes' promises evoke the fantasies of a life of plenty that flare up sometimes in the *palliata*, alongside the hope of manumission (chapter 8). The main thing here, however, is that Periphanes actually apologizes, admits he has behaved badly, and begs Epidicus to accept his manumission – performed onstage in this play as it is, less generously,

---

[17] Treggiari 1969: 16: "The freedman would usually support himself, taking the burden of finding food and lodging from the shoulders of his patron." Indeed, by law, it was freed slaves who owed their *patroni*, not only an agreed-upon amount of work during their lifetime, but a portion of their estate upon death. On manumission, see further in chapter 8.

at the end of *Menaechmi* (1146–50) and, sketchily, at the end of *Rudens* (1410–23), where an invitation to dinner is also thrown in. Epidicus sets conditions, using punitive language (*supplicium mihi das*, 724); a *supplicium* is not just a penalty but a humiliating penalty, akin to the verb *supplico*. The whole binding scene constitutes a refusal to beg for mercy: "I'm not supplicating. You want to bind me? Here, I'm holding out my hands; / you have the straps, I saw you buy them: what are you waiting for?" (*nec tibi supplico. vincire vis? em, ostendo manus; / tu habes lora, ego te emere vidi: quid nunc cessas?*, 683–4). A bravura reversal of the norms of punishment: self-abasement rejected, the *em* that marks the blow re-used for passive resistance, the reminder that slaves see the mechanics of brutality, the seizure of the initiative. Epidicus' *me orassis* (728) corrects Periphanes' *oras* (725). His lordly attitude towards his new *patronus* must have come to mind, for some in the audience, when Chrysalus in *Bacchides* said how much he loved the play.

A special case of owner abuse is only partially extant towards the end of *Amphitruo*. Here Mercurius, pretending to be Amphitruo's slave Sosia, meets him at the door of his own house with a torrent of abuse. Mercurius has first dressed up as a drunk (1007) and speaks from the roof of the house (1008), emphasizing the reversal of roles as he stymies his owner below. He takes further shots at the already shaky identity of Amphitruo: AM. "It's me!" ME. "What 'it's me'?" (AM. *ego sum*. ME. *quid "ego sum"?* 1021); and again, "What person are you?" (*quis tu es homo?*, 1028), eliciting from Amphitruo a maddened "You still keep asking me who I am?" (*etiam quis ego sim me rogitas*, 1029). He calls Amphitruo "fool" and "dummy" (*fatue*, 1026; *stolide*, 1028). He makes a sarcastic metatheatrical joke about Amphitruo breaking down the house doors by knocking: "Were you thinking they're provided to us at public expense?" (*censebas nobis publicitus praeberier*, 1027): playing the owner. And, seemingly, he dumps something liquid on Amphitruo's head ("I'm sacrificing to you," *sacrufico ego tibi*, 1034), cued by "I'll make him soused while he's sober" (*faciam ut sit madidus sobrius*, 1001), and Amphitruo's "You keep pouring words" (*verba funditas*, 1033); possibly he calls Amphitruo "chamberpot" (*matula[m]*, fr. v).[18] In any case, it must be Mercurius, on the roof, who threatens to pour water on Amphitruo's head (fr. v), and, as seen in chapter 2, one of

---

[18] I here agree with Christenson's ideas on the text of fr. v and on Mercurius' actions, and with his suggestion that Nonius' *matulam* in fr. v should be the vocative *matula*, although I think that, both here and at *Per.* 533 (Toxilus to Dordalus), it should retain its sense "chamberpot" (cf. *Mos.* 386) rather than "jug." See chapter 3 on Toxilus' association of Dordalus with filth. On this scene, see Slater 2014: 123–4 on the physical reversal here: slave high/king low.

them threatens the other with a pot full of ashes (fr. iv). Mercurius is not Amphitruo's slave, indeed he is a god; but Amphitruo believes he is Sosia, and threatens to beat him.

The pimp Dordalus is thoroughly beaten and humiliated in the final act of *Persa* – taunted, danced at, and showered with insults – and his lines underscore the stage action: "Ow! He's punching me!" (*ei! colapho me icit*, 846); "Ow! He's pinching my buttocks!" (*ei! natis pervellit*, 847). But Toxilus closes the play with a laconic summary that, as Moore notes (1998: 14), anticipates the audience's approval: "The pimp is done for" (*leno periit*, 858). An unsympathetic character also features in the most violent punishment of a free man, at the end of *Miles Gloriosus*: the soldier. Here the *senex* Periplectomenus and the cook Cario, with the help of a *lorarius*, beat and threaten to castrate the soldier in revenge for his supposed attempted adultery. The cook threatens to use his knife to cut off the soldier's testicles and hang them around his neck like a baby's amulet (1398–9); the old man has him beaten with clubs (*fustibus*, 1401; cf. 1403, 1405, 1406, 1412, 1415, 1418, 1424) and spread-eagled for castration (1407). The soldier has to beg for his own body, and pay a fine to secure its safety (1420). It seems possible that the hostile treatment of most *gloriosi* in the plays – with this the most extreme – voices resentment towards army officers; that stage soldiers' boasts evoked contemporary generals is widely surmised.[19] But perhaps the officer more immediately evoked here was the *tribunus militaris*, who authorized the *fustuarium* (chapter 2). That castration in the 200s BCE was more of a threat to slaves than to free men is suggested by the casual response of the *lena* Cleareta in response to a client's request to have her daughter be his (figurative) slave (*mihi … serviat*, *As.* 235) exclusively for a year: "Why, if you want it, I'll castrate the men among my household slaves" (*quin, si tu voles, domi servi qui sunt castrabo viros*, 237).

Overall, the Plautine stage provided its audience with the occasional spectacle of the degradation of owners, sometimes to an outrageous degree. Such actions by slaves go unpunished onstage, gratifying what was presumably a widely shared fantasy. The wording in such scenes often takes pains to put the owner in a slave's place – begging for fair treatment, being struck, being reduced to tears, being told he is worthless, threatened with a beating or the mill or even castration, taxed with sexual use in childhood;

[19] See Gruen 1996a: 129–40, on this theme as a critique of military matters in contemporary Rome; cf. Richlin 2017a: 231.

even, in *Asinaria*, being subjected to a virtual rape onstage. The slave changes places with the owner. Sometimes he even rises above the owner.

Raising Up the Slave

The triumphs of the trickster slave have been catalogued at least since Fraenkel, who made this particular expansion of the slave's role the centerpiece of his array of things Plautus inserted into the plots or scripts he adapted from Greek New Comedy. The slave who describes himself as *architectus, imperator,* or *rex* often boasts of his brilliance, and in particular speaks of his exploits as those of a great (Greek) military leader, historical (Greek) king, or even a hero of (usually Greek) mythology: not the contemporary Fabius, nor the mythical Romulus. Fraenkel's argument that these Greek names were derived, not from book learning or Greek originals, but from material in longstanding oral circulation and folk tradition (2007: 45–71), is surely right, as is his association of one strand of this tradition with the importation of human cargo to central Italy (67). These were names the audience could be expected to recognize, some of them clearly proverbial.[20]

As will be seen in chapter 8, the figure of the *rex* circulates insistently through the plays and is related to onstage slaves' most fantastical yearnings. For now, I still want to focus on the particular verbal forms in which ordinary slave desires were expressed in a positive way in the plays. The figure of the mock-heroic slave works to enable certain lines to be said and understood: if the exceptional slave can make a spectacle of himself, the average onstage slave can make a wish, and the audience will be ready to hear it. That the figure of the heroic slave served to inspire slaves in the audience – and that this was common knowledge – is, I think, proven by the famous lines of Chrysalus in *Bacchides* (213–15):

> non res, sed actor mihi cor odio sauciat.
> etiam Epidicum, quam ego fabulam aeque ac me ipsum amo,
> nullam aeque invitus specto, si agit Pellio.   215

> Not the action, but the actor hurts my heart with hatred.
> Even *Epidicus*, a play I love like I love my own self –
> I don't watch any play less willingly, if Pellio's acting.   215

---

[20] On the expansion of the slave's role and the slave as military hero, see Fraenkel 2007: 159–67, and further in chapter 8 on folk tradition; among many discussions, see Segal 1968: 129–35.

This self-referential joke, probably half-aside, is dragged into a back-and-forth about Chrysalus' willingness to listen to an account of his young owner's success. Chrysalus, in character as a slave, says he loves a play which features a slave who wins his manumission at the end. He loves it *aeque ac me ipsum* not only because he is a parallel literary creation but because, from his onstage perspective as a slave, Epidicus is his hero, his role model; he likes to go to the theater (*specto*), and repeatedly (he has seen more than one play, and this play more than once, with different casts, whom he recognizes), and watch Epidicus win his freedom by trampling all over his owner. Moreover, the eruption of the (real-life) *Epidicus* and Pellio into the spoken line serves as an abrupt shove into the metatheatrical; the line reminds the audience again of the actor inside the slave costume, whether Pellio or a well-known rival was playing Chrysalus. So not only the characters but the actors who played them could have been an inspiration to slaves in the audience, and Chrysalus' lines look for recognition among the spectators. Perhaps this explains the profusion of cheap terracotta figurines of actors in slave costumes: not just souvenirs, but mascots. Chrysalus as he speaks these lines is simultaneously a slave talking to his owner's friend, a slave character in a play, and an actor, status masked.[21]

Heroes like Chrysalus, Epidicus, Pseudolus, and Tranio are exceptionally uninhibited in their expression of self-esteem and dominance over their world (see Segal 1968: 102–36 for a classic discussion). They pave the way, as it were, for lesser figures to deliver tirades about the injustice of owners and the pains of slave labor and to proclaim their own point of view and moral superiority.[22] These speeches are surprisingly forthcoming, and, like Chrysalus' speech about Pellio, often look towards the audience for recognition, although of a more general nature; many of them are monologues or solos, like the songs by Sosia and Sagaristio seen in chapter 2, in which Sosia asks why his owner had to send him off so early, and Sagaristio redefines *virtus* for those he sings to. Sagaristio's opening song also expresses a bitter disgust with the conditions of his life. It starts

---

[21] Attention to this passage has focused mostly on the historicity of Pellio and on metatheatricality. See Marshall 2006: 89–90, 120, and chapter 1 above on reperformance. Brown 2013 believes that this passage, along with others in which slave characters say they have been to the theater, is purely metatheatrical. See chapter 3 on Mercurius in *Amphitruo* and Sceparnio in *Rudens*, chapter 6 on Gripus in *Rudens*, and probably also the line from *Caecus* or *Praedones* (fr. 36) discussed above: "I watched the games like a bigshot."

[22] Here I argue, then, directly against Finley 1998[1980]: 188, following Spranger: "never did the slave, for all his superiority as an intriguer, exceed his master in morality."

out like the "good slave" speeches we will see in chapter 6, but twists into
a bad slave speech (*Per.* 7–12):

> qui ero suo servire volt bene servos servitutem,
> ne illum edepol multa in pectore suo conlocare oportet
> quae ero placere censeat praesenti atque apsenti suo.
> ego neque lubenter servio neque sati' sum ero ex sententia,   10
> sed quasi lippo oculo me eru' meus manum apstinere hau quit tamen
> quin mi imperet, quin me suis negotiis praefulciat.

> A slave who wants to slave for his owner like a good slave
> slaving away,
> by God, he needs to store up a lot of things in his heart
> that he thinks will please his owner, whether he's there to see it or not.
> But I don't slave because I feel like it, and I'm not just what my owner
> expects,   10
> but just like a case of pinkeye, my owner can't keep his hand off me,
> without giving me orders, without stuffing me in his business.

The repetition *servire ... servos servitutem* (7) must be sarcastic; the jingle
servitutem servire is something of a formula onstage, here in inverted commas; as always, *lubenter* (10) relates to the free will of a free person, as will
be seen below. The analogy between the slave and an eye infection (11),
also used by the *senex* Nicobulus in reaction to Chrysalus (*Bac.* 913–15),
is here used by Sagaristio to boast of the beatings he provokes. Sagaristio
soon afterwards tells Toxilus that he is just back from a year in the mill
(20–3); later, in his speech of triumph, he voices his disdain for corporal
punishment and for his owner, as seen in chapter 2. He there vows never to
beg for mercy (270), recalling the Virgo's description of the fear normally
felt by a slave anticipating a beating (chapter 2), and the times when the
plays make owners beg for mercy from slaves, and Epidicus' refusal to
beg. Sagaristio is unquestionably a positive character in *Persa* – the leading male's best friend, and, when the play is staged, the co-star – but his
attitude towards punishment (*nihil ... novi / ... quin sim peritus*, 270–71)
is paralleled by that of the very bad slave Stalagmus in *Captivi*: "Whoa, I
believe you're threatening a beating to me, like I never had one" (*heia, credo
ego inperito plagas minitaris mihi*, 963). He is also kin to the shady slave
Libanus, at the end of his great catalogue of slave punishments: "Who is
a braver man than I am at bearing beatings?" (*qui mest vir fortior ad sufferundas plagas?, As.* 557). They are all bad boys, which, in comedy, makes
them good (see chapters 6 and 8).

The complaints of Sophoclidisca in *Persa* (168–81), of Syncerastus
in *Poenulus* (823–44, 870), and of the *puer* in *Pseudolus* (767–87) are

complicated by their involvement in sex work – no one is expected to like
working for a pimp, and prostitutes in the plays are not that sympathetic.
These slaves still, like Sosia, have a point to make about the injustice they
feel is done to them by their owners' treatment of them; they occupy the
moral high ground – even Sophoclidisca, who otherwise occupies a particularly abject position as part of the *peculium* (*Per.* 201) of a slave prostitute who in turn belongs to a pimp. Her entrance song, nonetheless, marks
her as vigorously able to speak for herself, and her ensuing scene with
Paegnium is one of the highlights of the play. She launches into a sarcastic
protest against her owner's lack of confidence in her, in light of her own
intelligence (168–76):

> SO. Sati' fuit indoctae, inmemori, insipienti dicere totiens,
> nimi' tandem me quidem pro barda et pro rustica reor habitam esse aps te.
> quamquam ego vinum bibo, at mandata non consuevi simul bibere una.   170
> me quidem iam sati' tibi spectatam censebam esse et meos mores.
> nam equidem te iam sector quintum hunc annum, quom interea, credo,
> ovi' si in ludum iret, potuisset iam fieri ut probe litteras sciret,
> quom interim tu meum ingenium fans atque infans nondum etiam
>   edidicisti.
>   potin ut taceas? potin ne moneas?   175
>   memini et scio et calleo et commemini.

> SO. It was enough to explain it to a "brainless, mindless, witless girl" so
>   many times,
> but I think you even take me for a dumb country girl on top of it.
> Maybe I drink wine, but I don't drink away what you tell me with it.   170
> I thought at least you'd had a good enough look at me and my character.
> In fact I'm chasing after you five years now, and that's enough time, I think,
> if a sheep went to school, it'd be able to learn to read and write,
> but in all this time you still couldn't figure out my brainpower, you
>   dumb baby.
>   Can you shut up? Could you stop nagging?   175
>   I remember and I know and I've learned the hard way and I'm
>   keeping it in mind.

The song continues into a sarcastic declaration of the woes of lovers,
wrapped up by a statement of Sophoclidisca's errand: "It befits me to go,
so I'll be all obedient to my owner, so she'll be free faster due to that" (*ire
decet me, ut erae opsequens fiam, libera ea opera ocius ut sit,* 181). As will be
seen in chapter 6, *decet* is a loaded word in relation to "good slave" behavior; the whole tone of her previous lines makes it clear to the audience that
Sophoclidisca feels much the same as Sagaristio does about obedience, and

that she does not actually feel an altruistic wish for her owner to become free. This sense is firmly borne out by the scene that follows.

Her entrance song is an expansion of a frequent impatient reaction onstage to owners' orders, the equivalent of an eyeroll, here emphatically stated at 176; Sophoclidisca's claim to comprehension includes the slangy *calleo*, literally "I'm toughened," which she repeats later in a burst of exuberant language when taking orders from Toxilus (305): *magi' calleo quam aprugnum callum callet*, "I'm tougher than a boar's tough hide is tough."[23] This locution suggests the active sense for *calleo*, "It's been beaten into me" – compare Ballio's sneering comparison of his slaves to donkeys, *ita plagis costae callent*, "so tough are their ribs from beatings," *Ps.* 136.[24] At the start of the scene that follows, Toxilus and the slave who forms part of his own *peculium*, Paegnium, go through an extended back-and-forth about unnecessarily repeated orders (183–96), in which, as seen above and in chapter 3, Paegnium gives voice to a marked statement of the differential access to justice experienced by slave and owner. Sophoclidisca's point here is that she is smarter than her owner, who nonetheless treats her as stupid. Her opening line quotes her owner's words, which use one of the common formats seen in verbal dueling (chapter 3): with *indoctae, inmemori, insipienti*, compare *Persa* 408, *inpure, inhoneste, iniure, inlex*. The effect of this echo is to throw the insult back at her owner. Sophoclidisca lays claim to *mores* and *ingenium* (171, 174); she metatheatrically denies that the consumption of wine associated onstage with slave-women interferes with her abilities. She contemptuously describes her period of servitude with her owner as *te ... sector* (172), using a verb that elsewhere in Plautus involves chasing around after forbidden sex objects, or a fugitive, or an animal, and indeed she compares her owner with a sheep (173) and calls her *fans atque infans*, perhaps meaning a person who speaks but makes no sense.[25] Thus she not only echoes but mocks her owner's nasty words to her. This kind of mimicry, as seen above, constitutes in the plays a running critique of owners' behavior.

Syncerastus, as seen in chapter 2, paints a lurid picture of the interior of the pimp's house and what is wrong with it; throughout, his attitude is that of one who deplores what he sees. He would rather spend his life in chains

---

[23] Slangy: "mot populaire," Ernout-Meillet s.v. *callum*.

[24] I owe this reading to Mary-Kay Gamel in performance notes for *Persa*, June 2004; confirmed by Naevius, *Com. inc.* 115 R₃, *utrum scapulae plus an collus calli habeat nescio* ("I don't know whether my shoulderblades or my neck have more scar tissue"). See chapter 7 on the metatheatrical use of *calleo* in scenes of command.

[25] On the meaning of this phrase, see Woytek 1982: 222–3.

in the quarries or the mill than be a slave to the pimp (*Poen.* 827–9); the sights he sees in the brothel torture him (*crucior*, 842); he expresses a wish that the whole household would die (*ut ego hanc familiam interire cupio*, 870). The slave Milphio, at first eavesdropping as Syncerastus tells it to the audience, undercuts him by telling the audience that Syncerastus is himself no good – *quasi ipse sit frugi bonae*, 845; *ignavus*, 846. He names the usual owner-oriented faults here, but Syncerastus goes on to provide the crucial information that will move the plot forward, and, while he is onstage, he addresses the feelings of those whose subordination feels wrong to them because of the low quality of those who own them.

In a short monologue in *Pseudolus*, a most abject member of such a *familia* also gets to tell the audience what it is like to be a pimp's slave, only here the speaker is an unnamed boy prostitute and not a house slave. This scene brings the audience back to the extended scene early in the play in which Ballio parades his household onstage, berates them, threatens them, and tells them what they must do to earn money for his upcoming birthday party, as they all stand there in silence (133–229); that scene in turn leads directly into the taunting of Ballio (230–380; see chapter 3).[26] When the boy enters, Ballio has been offstage for almost 400 lines; the pimp is about to return, but first the boy re-introduces him to the audience. The preceding scene has ended with Pseudolus' trochaic septenarii; the music stops; and the boy begins to speak in senarii. Perhaps, then, as the boy takes the stage and speaks alone, directly to the audience, the silence emphasizes his aloneness.[27] So he begins with an appeal to the audience's sympathy, in an unusual version of the slave's lament (767–78):

> PU. Quoi servitutem di danunt lenoniam
> puero, atque eidem si addunt turpitudinem,
> ne illi, quantum ego nunc corde conspicio meo,
> malam rem magnam multasque aerumnas danunt.   770
> velut haec mi evenit servitus, ubi ego omnibus
> parvis magnisque miseriis praefulcior:
> neque ego amatorem mi invenire ullum queo
> qui amet me, ut curer tandem nitidiuscule.
> nunc huic lenoni hodiest natalis dies: 775
> interminatust a minimo ad maxumum,

---

[26] For brief but trenchant comments on the parade scene, see Marshall 2013: 177; see also Rosivach 1998: 93–5, who stresses the prostitutes' youth (*aetatulam*, 173), on which see chapter 8; Hallett 2011: 185–90, on the language used in the scene.

[27] See Moore 2012: 174–6 on the range of overtones of iambic senarii; 1998: 31 on intimacy as a possible effect.

si quis non hodie munus misisset sibi,
eum cras cruciatu maxumo perbitere.

A boy to whom the gods give slavery to a pimp,
and if they give him ugliness as well,
I swear, as far as I can figure it out in my heart,
they give him a big bad thing, and many troubles.   770
Like, this slavery happened to me, where I'm stuffed in
all kinds of small and big miseries:
nor can I find myself any lover
to love me, so I can at least be taken care of a little more shinily.[28]
Now today is this pimp's birthday: 775
he's threatened everyone from the smallest to the biggest,
whoever hasn't sent him a present today,
will perish tomorrow with the biggest torture.

The full speech has been called "perhaps the weirdest scene in Plautus"
(Feeney 2010: 284), but it is, as I hope to have shown here, not at all
unusual in its denunciation of an owner's injustice and harshness. Like
other slaves onstage, the boy describes slavery as something the gods have
given him (767, 770) or something that has happened to him (771). Like
Sagaristio, he uses the verb *praefulcio* to describe the way he is stuck (*me
suis negotiis praefulciat, Per.* 12; *miseriis praefulcior, Ps.* 772) – the only two
appearances of this verb in the Plautine corpus. The boy's speech goes on
to describe in luridly suggestive language what sex acts he will have to
perform (779–87), and appeals to the audience's sympathy with the line
"Alas, how tiny I still am now for that thing" (*eheu, quam illae rei ego etiam
nunc sum parvolus,* 783). This was an audience, as seen in chapter 2, well
acquainted with the slave trade and with the public sale of slaves, including children – an audience among whom were people who had become
separated from their children in the wars, or who had abandoned a child,
or knew of an abandoned child, or, indeed, had been sold as children
themselves. *Parvolus* elsewhere refers to kidnapped children under the age
of six. When this scene was played in Rome, it might have resonated with
the (possibly) traditional story of the beautiful young boy C. Publilius,
taken into debt bondage by the wicked *faenerator* L. Papirius who wanted
him for sex (Livy 8.28), an act which caused a public outcry and the passage of an (ineffectual) law against debt bondage in 326 BCE. In Livy's
story, the boy resists sexual use, is stripped and flogged, and runs out *in*

---

[28] The unusual adverb used by the boy here, *nitidiuscule*, picks up *nitidiusculum* at *Ps.* 220, used by
Ballio to describe what the heads of Xytilis' fellow slaves would look like if she had extorted more
oil from her clientele, the oil-dealers.

publicum telling his injuries; he draws a "huge force of people" (*ingens vis hominum*), who gather in the forum and then, *agmine facto*, march on the senate-house, forcing the consuls to convene the senate, with dramatic demonstrations of the boy's injury as the people plead with the senators.

Livy's tale is at least consistent with the kinds of public protest seen in chapter 3, and with the continuing presence of debt as a theme in the plays. If this story is in play here, then the appearance of a boy prostitute onstage – a class of persons rarely even mentioned in the plays – and one played by an actor wearing an ugly mask (indicated by the boy's self-identification as ugly), an actor who speaks in gross terms, and perhaps in a squeaky voice, about what a boy prostitute might have to do: is this a joke?[29] The *puer* is no Publilius. Might Publilius have been the hero of a *fabula praetexta*, that rarity of the Roman stage? Possibly even that mythical beast, the *praetexta* in oral tradition? Livy's account is certainly melodramatic; would that make this scene parapraetextate?[30] Indeed the whole spectacle of a character like Palaestra wailing about the besmirching of her pure young maidenhood, like Verginia, would have seemed like a joke to all the *vernae* in the audience. The *puer* is the ugly truth, a standing indictment of Ballio, speaking for all the prostitutes in the earlier scene in *Pseudolus*.

A particular critique of slaves' subordination is delivered by the *paedagogus* Lydus in *Bacchides*, who is in the position of having to discipline the owner's son. The problems this poses are set up in an early scene between Lydus and his grown-up charge, Pistoclerus (109–69): "Am I your slave or are you mine?" (*tibi ego an tu mihi servos es?*, 162), says Pistoclerus, and,

---

[29] See chapter 5 on the boy's appearance as a sight gag, and the sense of *turpitudinem* here as "ugliness."
[30] On the rarity of the *fabula praetexta*, see Beare 1964: 39–43; Manuwald 2011: 140–4, with bibliography, pro and con, on Wiseman's theory of the unscripted *praetexta* (141): "a way of transmitting and spreading Roman history." See Wiseman 1998: 1–16, and *passim*. On the resemblance of the Publilius episode to other stories of rape and political change in Livy, see Oakley 1998: 691; on the dramatic quality of such episodes in Livy, see Feldherr 1998: 169–77 (with remarks on the *praetexta* at 172), 203–11 on the story of Verginia; and esp. Fantham 2005: 213–18 for an overview of Livy's stories on the abolition of *nexum* and the use of *quiritatio* both at 2.23.8 and in the story of Verginia. On the ancestry of the *praetexta*, it seems significant that Naevius is credited with two; if the *palliata* developed for some decades before surfacing at the *ludi*, accreting oral performance forms as it went, there is no reason why the *praetexta* should not be imagined as developing similarly. On Publilius as a possible hero of a *praetexta*: Lucretia featured in a *Brutus* (Varro, *L.* 6.7, 7.72 = Accius 41 K; in senarii; see Erasmo 2001: 110 for assignment of the play from which Varro quotes to Cassius of Parma, one of Caesar's assassins, rather than to Accius, with Boyle 2006: 158–9, 257 n. 44, La Penna 1979, and esp. Manuwald 2015: 180–1). On an oral tradition for the Publilius story: the fact that the story appears with different character names and no mention of the abolition of *nexum* in Valerius Maximus (6.1.9) aligns it with stories in oral transmission, on which see Langlands forthcoming (on "sites of exemplarity" and "popular knowledge"); the *Pseudolus* scene might be, in her terms, a "remediation." On the persistence of *nexum*, see chapter 3.

to end the scene, cuts off his old teacher's reproaches: "You've been given freedom to make your plea so far, Lydus. / That's enough" (*istactenu' tibi, Lyde, libertas datast / orationis. satis est*, 168–9). Later, Lydus has the chance to complain to Pistoclerus' father (419–34, 437–48). First he claims that the father, in his youth, would never have so defied his *paedagogus*, who would have controlled his movements (423) and kept him busy with a regimen of exercise and study (424–33). The climax of this argument is a claim that the boy would have been beaten by his teacher for the slightest error: "Your hide would get as full of spots as a wet-nurse's *pallium*" (*fieret corium tam maculosum quam est nutricis pallium*, 434) – a non-heroic simile that gives a shout-out to another set of caregivers in the audience, and also a reminder of free children's debt to the slaves who raised them. It is also a reversal of the kind of language used to describe a slave's bruised skin.

After a mild rejoinder from the father ("Lydus, customs are otherwise today," *alii, Lyde, nunc sunt mores*, 437), Lydus goes on to describe how things are now: a boy of six, if the teacher so much as touches him, will break the teacher's head with his *tabula* (440–1); if the teacher appeals to the father, he will commend the boy, and rebuke the teacher ("Hey, you low-value old man," *eho senex minimi pretii*, 444). Lydus concludes: "Here, with a system like this, can / the teacher exert authority, if he himself takes a beating first?" (*hocine hic pacto potest / inhibere imperium magister, si ipsus primus vapulet?*, 447–8). Unsympathetic a character as Lydus may be, he expects audience support here. The schoolroom, in a long Roman tradition expressed, after the 200s, both in literature and in treatises on child-rearing, was the one place where a slave or a lower-class free person could hit a higher-class free person, and Lydus voices the teacher's predicament – a rarity.[31] If Lydus reflects the presence in Rome of Greeks purchased to teach the children of senators, he speaks for the learned in *barbaria*: justified, but something of a stuffed shirt. He is doomed to failure in the

---

[31] On slave nurses and their charges, see Joshel 1986; on physical chastisement of children and slaves, Saller 1994: 144 n. 42 (referring obliquely to this scene), 147, 148–9; 1998: 90. Saller argues that Roman sentiment (but who counts as "Roman"?) was against the beating of citizen children, on the grounds that beating was inherently servile, a chief dividing mark between slave and free; he cites Plutarch's *Life* of the elder Cato among other sources, but many parents must have delegated this power to teachers and child-minders, thereby creating a major social tension. Indeed, Quintilian (*Inst.* 1.3.17) hints that teachers might use the threat of punishment to coerce students into sex. See Herodas, *Mim.* 3 for a scene where a schoolboy is violently beaten by his schoolmaster at the behest of his (lower-class) mother: it was in the comic repertoire, but not in the *palliata*. The association between schoolmasters and beating resurfaces in Roman satire (Hor. *Ep.* 2.1.70, Juvenal 1.15); see Kaster 1995: 134 on Suetonius's account of Horace's teacher Orbilius at *Gramm.* 9.4. Juvenal 7.203–41 presents a similarly heartfelt complaint on behalf of schoolmasters, here conceived as free but poverty-stricken.

play; as he speaks, the eavesdropping friend of Pistoclerus gets a laugh by saying that he is only surprised that Pistoclerus has not hit Lydus with his fists (450), and the deluded Lydus goes on to praise this eavesdropper; but Lydus makes his point.

The most defiant speech of all comes from Astaphium in *Truculentus*, another prostitute's slave-woman. Her song (209–55) speaks up for prostitutes' right to squeeze their customers dry and rebuts what "men say among themselves" (*praedicant viri … secum*, 237). Her words are marked as addressed to the audience not only because this is a solo, but by the axiomatic or gnomic quality of what she says (not uncommon in solos); they are marked as privileged speech for a slave by her lead-in (209–12):

> Hahahae! requievi,
> quia intro abit odium meum.
> tandem sola sum. nunc quidem meo arbitratu
> loquar libere quae volam et quae lubebit.

> Ha, ha, ha! I'm relieved,
> because the one I hate's gone inside.
> Finally I'm alone. Now, really, as I see fit
> I'll speak out freely what I want and what I feel like saying.

What she "feels like saying" is that the progressive impoverishment of the customers and the enrichment of her owner only demonstrate the natural circulation of wealth: "a human deed's been done" (*humanum facinus factumst*, 218). Once Diniarchus was rich while they were poor, now things are reversed (220–1). Criticism is stupid: "He would be a stupid man who'd be surprised at this" (*stultus sit qui id miretur*, 221). The audience is drawn by her line *sola sum* directly into the hidden transcript, into collusion with the stage as a place for free speech. Naevius' much-discussed line, *libera lingua loquemur ludis Liberalibus* ("We will speak with a free tongue at the games of the Liberalia," 113R), suggests the essential relation between ludic speech and freedom.[32] Apart from the bold cynicism of her message, Astaphium's song stands out for her emphasis on free speech and free will (*meo arbitratu, libere, quae volam*), anchored by the verb *lubebit*.

In the language in which slave characters lay claim to power, forms of the verb *lubere* play a central role.[33] When, in the denouement of a scheme,

---

[32] For detailed discussion, see Wiseman 1998: 35–51.

[33] Gunderson (2015: 185–8) connects *lubet* with *lubido* and relates it to desire; the category "What Was Desired" in chapters 4–8 here is more concrete but no less grounded in the emotions. As Gunderson says (2015: 188), Sosia voices at *Am.* 395 "the (made) truth that power grants possession. … The powerful do as they wish. The powerless are reduced to clutching at the scraps of their selfhood." See chapter 6 on *decet* and *oportet*.

the dupe finally expresses outrage and asks, "How could *you* do this to *me*?" – that is, how could you have power over me, when the reverse should be true – the victor responds smugly, *lubuit*. The tone is impudent, as in "I felt like it," but the connection between *lubere* and *libertas* is strongly felt, as seen in the songs of Sosia and Sagaristio: the rich owner thinks that "whatever a person happens to feel like, can be done" (*quodquomque homini accidit lubere, posse retur, Am.* 171); Sagaristio, ironically, sings "I don't slave because I feel like it" (*ego neque lubenter servio, Per.* 10). *Lubere* expresses free will, the unfettered volition that belongs to a free person, as would be explicitly stated in the *Institutes* of Justinian, seven hundred years later: "Liberty indeed is that by which free men are so called, the natural power to do what a person wants to do, except what is prohibited by force or law" (*libertas quidem est, ex qua etiam liberi vocantur, naturalis facultas eius quod cuique facere libet, nisi si quid aut vi aut iure prohibetur, Inst.* 1.3.2). So, when his owner asks, "On what assurance did you dare … ?" (*qua fiducia ausu's,* 697), Epidicus replies, "I felt like it: on that assurance" (*lubuit: ea fiducia,* 698); the play on the legalistic *fiducia* and the term *confidens*, often applied to an "uppity" slave, as by Sagaristio to Paegnium (*Per.* 285, chapter 2), are appropriate in a system where, as seen in chapter 3, a slave has no *fides*. When Epidicus' owner asks, "Why did you dare to give [the money]?" (*qur dare ausu's?,* 710), he replies, "Because I felt like it" (*quia mi lubitum est*). So Pseudolus, belching into his owner's face (*Ps.* 1299): *lubet*. So, more discursively, Pinacium, running in with the good news, eggs himself on: "Run as you like, don't give a damn for anyone" (*curre ut lubet, cave quemquam flocci feceris, St.* 285); compare his earlier lines, "I bear a heart laden with gladness and goodwill, / and I don't feel like saying anything except in grand style" (*onustum pectus porto laetitia lubentiaque / neque lubet nisi gloriosse quicquam proloqui,* 276–7). So the slave Cyamus and the prostitute Phronesium in *Truculentus* reply to the soldier's lines, "Why did you dare to speak to me unkindly?" (*qur ausu's mi inclementer dicere,* 604–5) and "Why did you dare [love another man]?"(*qur ausa es …* , 607): "I felt like it" (*lubitumst, Truc.* 604–5); "I don't give a damn for you" (*non ego te flocci facio,* 606); "I felt like it" (*lubitumst,* 607).

The reply is not always made to an owner, as in this early exchange between Chalinus and Olympio: CH. "Why are you crawling in the city, *vilicus* of no great value?" / OL. "I feel like it" (CH. *quid in urbe reptas, vilice hau magni preti?* / OL. *lubet, Cas.* 98–9). Nor is the reply always made by a slave to an owner: so the slave Simia, playing the soldier, when Pseudolus asks him where he has been, replies, "Where I felt like being" (*ubi mi lubitum est*, 913a), and Pseudolus plays the straight man; so Ballio, when Calidorus says, "Why did you dare to do this?" replies, "I felt like it, she was mine" (*qur id ausus facere?: lubuit, mea fuit*, 348). This line, here coupled with the stock assertion of ownership (possessive adjective plus *esse*, chapter 6), shows the range of powers inherent in *lubere*; so Paegnium tells the inquiring Sagaristio that his owner, the slave Toxilus, is "where he feels like being, and / he doesn't need your advice" (*ubi illi lubet, nec / te consulit*, *Per.* 277a–b). The same terms are used by a slave of himself in the response of the boy Phaniscus to the boy Pinacium in their verbal duel: "I belong to myself, I like to eat" (*mihi sum, lubet esse*, *Mos.* 889).[34] Leonida, about to let his co-slave Libanus and their young owner in on his big money-making scam, says he is here "to make them more *lubens* than *Lubentia*" (*ut ego illos lubentiores faciam quam Lubentiast*, *As.* 268) – that is, he will make them eager. He will also empower them, for the one who is *lubens* has rights. When Mercurius asks the newly arrived Sosia whether he is slave or free, Sosia replies, "Whatever my spirit feels like" (*utquomque animo conlibitum est meo*, *Am.* 343). Similarly, Libanus replies to his owner's "Where will you be?" (*ubi eris?*) with "Wherever my spirit feels like" (*ubiquomque lubitum erit animo meo*, *As.* 110). This exchange comes towards the end of a scene in which Libanus and his owner treat each other as familiar friends, in league against the owner's wife; the owner has just ordered Libanus to cheat him (91). The scene closes with Libanus proclaiming he fears no one, not even the owner; the owner then endorses his abilities in a brief monologue. This highly unlikely scenario matches the expression of free will in *lubitum erit*. Contrast the literally meretricious identification of her own will with that of her *patronus* by the freed prostitute Philematium: "What you feel like doing, that's what I feel like doing, / my pleasure" (*quod tibi lubet idem mihi lubet, / mea voluptas*, *Mos.* 296–7). The use of *voluptas* here is ironic; the usual promise of a prostitute is "I will be a pleasure to you" (*voluptati ero tibi*). Whose pleasure? Whose will?

The power implicit in the verb *lubere* is made explicit in a type of assertion that takes the form of paired correlatives, seen above in the response of the slave Leonida to the Mercator, claiming equality: "I'm just as much a person as you" (*tam ego homo sum quam tu*, *As.* 490). So Olympio to Lysidamus in their duet: "My life is as dear to me / as yours is to you"

---

[34] Or, with a probable play on *esse*, "I like to be [what you say]." Pinacium's jokes lead up to an accusation that Phaniscus is used for sex by their owner (894–5); Phaniscus here, then, like Paegnium in *Persa*, lays claim to his own abuse (cf. chapter 2, and, for discussion of the full passage, Gunderson 2015: 71–2 and Richlin 2017b: 189–90).

(*tam mihi mea vita | tua quam tibi carast, Cas.* 757–57a). The balance of
tam mihi quam tibi is compressed into the one word *omnes* with the first-
person plural – "we all," "all of us" – as used by the *lorarius* to Hegio: "We
all surely feel like being free / more than slaving" (*omnes profecto liberi
lubentius | sumu' quam servimus, Capt.* 119–20). The arbitrary nature of
enslavement, of course, is the main theme of *Captivi,* which is full of para-
doxical speeches in which this *tam/quam* balance is expressed, as in this
speech of Tyndarus (who, impersonating his owner Philocrates, does not
know that Hegio is his father, or that he was born free) to Hegio (who does
not know that Tyndarus is his son; *Capt.* 310–12, 316):

> ... tam ego fui ante liber quam gnatus tuos,
> tam mihi quam illi libertatem hostilis eripuit manus,
> tam illic apud nos servit quam ego nunc hic apud te servio.
>
> ...
>
> quam tu filium tuom tam pater me meu' desiderat.
>
> ... I was just as free before as your son was,
> the enemy's hand took freedom from me as it did from him,
> he is just as much a slave among us now as I am a slave here with you.
>
> ...
>
> My father longs for me just as much as you long for your son.

So he later says to another war captive: "You, too, indeed, / are a slave now,
and were once free, and I'm sure I will be" (*et tu quidem | servos es, liber
fuisti, et ego me confido fore,* 574–5) – an echo of Paegnium (*ego me confido
liberum fore, Per.* 286). Moreover, although most readers of Plautus would
associate the enactment of equality primarily with *Captivi,* in fact *Captivi*
is not the only play in which free and slave appear interchangeable: the
god Mercurius in *Amphitruo* looks just like the slave Sosia; the Virgo in
Persa plays a slave; Sagaristio in *Persa* plays himself and the man from
Persia who is his (free) twin brother and who says he wants to buy him
out of slavery (695–6); the *vilicus* in *Poenulus* plays a mercenary soldier,
while the slave music girl Acropolistis in *Epidicus* passes, for a time, as
Periphanes' daughter (and so is freed), her freed friend passes as a slave, and
the freed slave prostitute Acroteleutium in *Miles Gloriosus* plays a *matrona*
(790–3).[35] Yet again, these onstage enactments by slave characters only re-
enact what is happening all the time onstage as actors with masked civil

---

[35] See Marshall 2006: 131–4 on slave masks, and esp. 149–52 on the problems masks posed for the
exchange of identities by owner and slave in *Captivi* and for the transformation of prostitute into
long-lost daughter in several plays; also 87–8, on the paradox that "actors' roles need not correspond
to their status offstage," with discussion in chapter 1.

status play both slaves and owners. Here, too, an issue that concerns slave and free also concerns rich and poor, as the wealthy Philto in *Trinummus* tries to convince the bankrupt Lesbonicus that he means him well: "I'm a person, you're a person" (*homo ego sum, homo tu es*, 447).

Claiming Good Things

In the quest for equal status, the main good thing slaves want in the *palliata* is manumission, or, even better, recognition as a freeborn person and reunion with family. This ultimate dream comes true for both male and female characters in the plays, and will be discussed in chapters 7 and 8. Short of this actual freedom, the plays sometimes assert equality by allowing male slaves to lay claim to the good things of which they are normally deprived, particularly sex with women, sometimes also food or money. *Parasiti* likewise do occasionally get a meal, although Saturio and his daughter are excluded from the final party scene in *Persa*. Slave-women onstage act out no such scenes of gratification, and indeed *scorta* figure as desired objects for male slaves, very much as fungibles; at best, a slave-woman like Leaena in *Curculio* gets to take a drink onstage (120–40): "Do you like it?" says the slave Palinurus to her (*ecquid lubet?*), and she replies, "I like it" (*lubet*), to which Palinurus replies that he would like to stick her with a cattle-prod (*mihi … stimulo fodere lubet te*, 131). Unlike the desire of male slaves for wine, the desire of *lenae* and *ancillae* for wine onstage is a fault (so of Leaena, *Cur.* 76–81 and throughout her scene; the *lena* in *Cistellaria*, 149–50; Sophoclidisca, seen above). Prostitutes both slave and free are seen onstage participating in parties (*Asinaria, Mostellaria, Persa, Stichus*), but the motivating force is not their own when men are present – only the all-female breakfast party in *Cistellaria* represents what a female character wants, as the hostess says: "By God, this was done with a willing spirit" (*lubenti edepol animo factum*, 12). But what she wants is to please her guests.

Although some claims for sex by male slaves are rebuffed, others succeed, sometimes to a fantastical degree. Three of the greatest heroes among the slaves – Chrysalus, Tranio, and Pseudolus – claim to attend parties alongside their young owners. Chrysalus' owner is the one "with whom I drink, with whom I eat and love" (*quicum ego bibo, quicum edo et amo*, *Bac.* 646); in their opening scene, Tranio says to Grumio, "I like to have a few drinks, make love, hire whores. / This all comes out of *my* back, not on the assurance of *yours*" (*lubet potare, amare, scorta ducere. / mei tergi facio haec, non tui fiducia*, *Mos.* 36–7), to which Grumio replies, "How confidently he speaks!" (*quam confidenter loquitur*, 38), and snipes, as seen above, "Not everybody can lie next to his betters" (42–3; see chapter 2). Pseudolus actually does attend a party with his owner Calidorus at the end of his play, although offstage: "This is how I and my young owner / spent this day *con mucho gusto*" (*hoc ego modo atque erus minor / hunc diem sumpsimus prothyme, Ps.* 1268–68a). Leonida says he will share the spoils equally with Libanus and their young owner (*praedam pariter cum illis partiam, As.* 271), because he parties with them on an even footing: "Since they have a few drinks with me equally, and often go whoring with me equally" (*quando mecum pariter potant, pariter scortari solent*, 270). What is envisioned here is not a squalid scene like that described by the (hostile) speaker of *Against Neaira*, where a drunken prostitute accommodates slaves after her owner has passed out (ps.-Dem. *Ne.* 33), or like the pimp's house as Syncerastus describes it, but a drinking party where the slaves recline as the owners do, and, as Pseudolus says, "If they feel like it, they go body to body" (*si lubet corpora conduplicant, Ps.* 1261). He says he has a *scortum* of his own at the party (*meum scortum*, 1272).

Male slaves make passes at their owners' *amicae*, or make jokes about having sex with them: so Libanus to Philaenium, though he takes it back when the young owner upbraids him (*As.* 624–5). Soon afterwards, in the riding scene, Leonida directly asks Philaenium to kiss him (668); Libanus asks explicitly for a more fervent embrace (695–6). Milphio gets carried away when flattering Adelphasium on behalf of his owner, although he is beaten for it: "Let me give you a kiss" (*sine dem savium, Poen.* 375). Sceparnio makes a pass at Ampelisca (*Rud.* 415–37), commenting on her body, skin color, breasts, and kissability (421–3) and fondling her (419, 424–25); he later says of her and Palaestra, "I could love either of them, if I were good and drunk" (*ego amare utramvis possum, si probe adpotus siem*, 566). Tranio jokingly wishes to have sex with the two prostitutes attached to his owner and his owner's friend: Delphium says, "We'll both do our duty to you" (*morigerae tibi erimus ambae*), and Tranio comments as she exits, "Jupiter should only make that happen!" (*ita ille faxit Iuppiter, Mos.* 398). Here, as seen above, the adjective *morigerus* bears the double meaning "obey"/"be sexually compliant"; the combination of these meanings should by now be unsurprising – "to have power over" = "to have sexual access to." Pseudolus promises Simia a party (with food and wine) and a woman to kiss him (*Ps.* 947–48).

The triumph of Pseudolus produces the biggest jackpot. After humiliating the *senex* Simo, Pseudolus invites him to drink with him, even (as seen above) orders him to do so (1327); the two of them end the play by inviting the audience along, Pseudolus only on condition that they applaud, and, even then, maybe tomorrow (1331–3) – the classic comic invitation, as at the end of *Rudens*. At this concluding party, Pseudolus not only has his own *scortum* (1272), whom he calls his *amica* (1277a–1278); he also, famously, dances, in the notorious Ionic style (1274a–1275; see below). Similar elements appear in the two all-slave parties that conclude plays. In *Persa*, the slave Toxilus embraces his *amica* Lemniselenis (763–66a), for whose freedom he has paid the pimp: "This wished-for day has been granted me today by the gods, since it is permitted for me to put my arms around you, a free woman" (*optatus hic mi / dies datus hodiest ab dis, quia te licet liberam med amplecti*, 773a–74) – note the ambiguity of agency in the indirect statement, where *med* could as easily be object as subject. Toxilus and Sagaristio dance in the Ionic style as part of the taunting of the pimp Dordalus (824–6).

In *Stichus*, Stichus begs his owner for a holiday (*eleutheria*, 422 – literally, "freedom festival," cf. *Per.* 29; see chapter 8). The owner grants his request ("go away, wherever you like," *abi quo lubet*, 424), and gives him some wine; the *amica*, however, he says Stichus will have to pay for himself (426). Stichus explains that his *amica* is the *ancilla* of his owner's brother, and that in fact he shares her with her *conservus* Sangarinus the Syrian – "we are rivals" (*rivales sumus*, 431–4). At the party, however, which takes up the last 126 lines of this 775-line play, the model is more sharing than rivalry. Sangarinus at first suggests they play morra (like rock-paper-scissors) to see who sits where (*mica*, 696); this shifts into a quasi-military division of the *provinciae* of wine and water, according to "whichever you feel like" (*utram tibi lubet*, 698); and in turn to a generally benevolent egalitarianism: "Here's to you all [including the audience], here's to us, here's to you, here's to me, here's to our Stephanium, too" (*bene vos, bene nos, bene te, bene me, bene nostram etiam Stephanium*, 709).[36] Indeed, rivalry is depicted *as* egalitarianism, as the two slaves go into a song-and-dance challenge (729–33):

---

[36] The game denoted in Latin by *micare* ("flash [fingers]"), is often identified with morra, a counting-out or gambling game still played in Italy, although continuity cannot be proven; a version is played by Italian-Americans from Connecticut to Pennsylvania as "once, twice, three, shoot" ("I'll choose you for it!") and evidently not elsewhere in the US. The game probably also shows up in Plautus in a taunt at *Per.* 186–7 (Paegnium to Toxilus: *da hercle pignus ... / si scis tute quot hodie habeas digitos in manu* – in context, "it is as safe a bet that I remember your orders as that you know how many fingers you have on your own hand," as opposed to the gamer's bet on the other gamer's hand). See chapter 3, n. 34, for a proverb cited by Cicero in which morra in the dark tests trustworthiness. Perdrizet 1898, on Greek vs. Roman images of morra-players, remarks on having seen the game played in Italy.

[STI.] haec facetiast, amare inter se rivales duos,
uno cantharo potare, unum scortum ducere.   730
hoc memorabilest: ego tu sum, tu es ego, unianimi sumus,
unam amicam amamus ambo, mecum ubi est, tecum est tamen;
tecum ubi autem est, mecum ibi autemst: neuter <ne>utri invidet.

[STI.] This is a good joke: that two who are rivals share the love,
drink from a single cup, hire a single whore.   730
This is something to remember: I am you, you are me, we are of one spirit,
we both love a single girlfriend, when she is with me, she's still with you;
but when she's with you, she's there with me, too; neither one begrudges
   the other.

Stichus sets up the situation as a set of definitions or illustrations, as
Sagaristio does when he defines "what's really charming" (*id demum lepidumst, Per.* 266) as taking vengeance on stingy owners. Stichus' language,
however, picks up his egalitarian sense, as in the *tam/quam* lines above, with
repeated use of antimetabole: 730, *uno* – noun – infinitive, *unum* – noun
– infinitive; 731, AB=, B=A, A+B=; 732, the syllable *am* repeated (audibly)
four times, A=, B=; 733, B *ubi autem* =, A *ibi autem* =, CC. Stephanium,
for her part, claims she loves both equally, with the jingle *ambos amo* (750);
in the end, both male slaves dance again, aiming to outdo the "Ionic or
cinaedic" dancers (769, 772), "now both equally" (*nunc pariter ambo*, 772).
And in this play, uniquely, the *tibicen* is invited to drink with the players (715) – although once again the *spectatores* are disinvited (775). In this
markedly triangular setup, in which the two male slaves sing happily about
their bond, dance like *cinaedi*, and have sex with the same woman, it is
hard not to think of Eve Sedgwick's analysis of the way male homosocial
desire can work through a woman as a vector.[37] If Stephanium was played
by a male actor, of course, there were in fact three men on the stage: two
dancing like *cinaedi*, one dancing like a woman. As will be seen in chapter
5, this dynamic permeates the *palliata* as a whole.

Significantly, space for a party is sometimes referred to as a *locus liber*
(*Bac.* 82; *Poen.* 177, 602, 657–8; *St.* 662); the enabling force of this freedom
is seen at the end of *Persa*, where Toxilus eggs on Paegnium to mock the
pimp: "Why don't you make fun of him, the way you always do, since this
is a free place" (*quin elude, ut soles, quando liber locust hic,* 805). Paegnium,

---

[37] Sedgwick 1992: 21–7. For discussion of the meaning of the cinaedic/Ionic dancing here and at the
end of *Persa* and *Pseudolus*, see Benz 2001; Habinek 2005: 117–18, 184–6; and esp. Moore 2012: 106–
14, with some corrections to Habinek's general account; also Williams 2010: 193–4, for a general
overview of *cinaedi* as dancers. Cf. chapter 2 on Sosia's opening song, and Richlin 2017b: 174 for this
dance form in the context of the circulation of comic performance.

assigned to be the pimp's "new *cinaedus*" (804), jumps into a taunting dance.[38] The unreality of such mouth-watering opportunities for slaves is underscored by Sagaristio's incredulity when he hears about Toxilus' problem – "Now slaves fall in love here?" (*iam servi hic amant?*, *Per.* 25) – and by an aside to the audience in Stichus' speech to his owner about his plans for the party (*St.* 446–8):

> atque id ne vos miremini, homines servolos
> potare, amare atque ad cenam condicere:
> licet haec Athenis nobis. ...

> And you all shouldn't be surprised at this, that little slave persons
> have a few drinks, make love, and set up for a dinner:
> these things are permitted to us in Athens. ...

Here "Athens," as "elsewhere" often does in the plays, stands for several things: the notional setting of the Greek original; the stage; the place where slaves in the audience and onstage came from before they were slaves, where they still had rights; a place to which slaves might escape, or at least where they might wish to be.

The sense that desired things are available elsewhere is demonstrated by the lines in the *Casina* prologue (67–78) in which the speaker justifies the plot's dependence on the existence of slave marriage – an even greater leap into unreality, on the Roman stage, than free access to prostitutes for male slaves, and related to other instances of fantasy travel (chapter 8).[39] The speech expresses a strong preference for "elsewhere":

> sunt hic inter se quos nunc credo dicere:
> "quaeso hercle, quid istuc est? serviles nuptiae?
> servin uxorem ducent aut poscent sibi?
> novom attulerunt, quod fit nusquam gentium."   70
> at ego aiio id fieri – in Graecia et Carthagini,

---

[38] The right to hold a drinking party as claimed by slaves in the plays might be tied with the argument that the Attic *skolia* belonged to "middling" Athenians, who held *symposia* of their own (Jones 2014); as at those *symposia*, however, so here there remains a subordinate group who are at the party to pour wine and be used for sex (cf. Jones 2014: 253 on the *pais* in *skolia*). Habinek 2005: 186 points out that the party in *Stichus* includes a Greek drinking song, *cantio Graeca*, cuing a scrap of Greek (707). For the *locus liber*, see further below. On the marked association between these party scenes and the "'slave on top' motif" in Plautus, see Moore 2012: 110, who also adduces *St.* 446–8. Paegnium's taunt to Dordalus at *Per.* 815, *restim tu tibi cape crassam ac suspende te*, is an old joke, seen in Aristophanes, *Wasps* 1343, τῇ χειρὶ τουδὶ λαβομένη τοῦ σχοινίου, also in a party scene; here weaponized.

[39] On the specific metatheatrical point that slaves do occasionally have wives in Greek New Comedy, see Cox 2013: 171–2 (on Menander, *Epit.* and *Her.*; see Arnott 1996a: 5 n. 1 for the legal issues). On the demographic possibility for "familial relationships" in Rome at this period, see Bradley 1984: 146–7: an issue for historians of slavery concerned with sources of slaves and slave breeding.

et hic in nostra terra – in <terra> Apulia;
maioreque opere ibi serviles nuptiae
quam liberales etiam curari solent;
id ni fit, mecum pignus si quis volt dato   75
in urnam mulsi, Poenus dum iudex siet
vel Graecus adeo, vel mea caussa Apulus.
quid nunc? nihil agitis? sentio, nemo sitit.

There are some of you here, I think, who are now saying to each other,
"I ask you – God, what's this? A slave wedding?
Are slaves going to marry a wife, or ask for one for themselves?
They've brought in something strange, that happens nowhere on
   earth."   70
But I say it does happen – in Greece and Carthage,
and here in our land – in the land of Apulia;
why, slave weddings are always seen to there
even more carefully than free people's weddings;
if that's not so, anybody can make a bet with me   75
for a jug of honey-wine, as long as the judge is a Carthaginian
or even a Greek, or for all I care an Apulian.
What now? Nothing doing? I get it, nobody's thirsty.

As often in Plautus, the word *hic* (67) immediately opens up several levels of meaning. It means "here" in the temporary space of the theater,
as well as "here" at this point in the play, in the world of the play; and,
most obviously, it means "here" in Rome, or somewhere in central Italy.
The focus shifts: what is at stake here is a wedding ceremony (travestied
in the play at 798–854); what is at stake in the play is slave marriage and
the sexual use of *ancillae*. The speaker asserts that slaves do get married
somewhere in the world, then moves that east to Greece and south to
Carthage (both war zones productive of slaves – for some in the audience,
"outlandish," even "scary"; for others, "home"), and caps that with *nostra
terra*, specified as Apulia (joke location, identified elsewhere as backward
(*Mil.* 648; cf. Paulus 23L); wrecked by Hannibal; a war zone productive
of slaves). Then he makes a joke that depends on the local identification
of Greeks and Carthaginians as untrustworthy (compare *Graeca ... fide*,
"cash down," *As.* 199; *dissimulat ... / Poenus plane est*, *Poen.* 112–13); finally,
he pretends to bury the whole issue in a joke about drinking. In fact, he
has made an important assertion: "But I say it does happen" (*at ego aiio
id fieri*, 71). For this and the next line to work as jokes, there would have
to be a pause after *fieri* and one after *nostra terra*, allowing for a "What?!"
moment during which the audience was on the hook, then released by the
second half of the line. During that pause, audience members had first to

deal with the proposition that slaves get married, and then define *nostra terra*. The speaker underscores the point by making a bet that finds no takers: everyone knows that what he says is true, and in fact the evidence for slave marriage elsewhere is carved in stone.[40] Some enslaved people in the audience would have been separated violently from their spouses during capture; some women in the audience would not have known if their soldier husbands were dead or enslaved; Apulia after Hannibal was full of slaves. The displacements in this passage nod to the audience's knowledge that whether you can get married depends on what has happened to you and where you are. "Here," then, also means "where we are slaves now," and "slaves" also includes "people who used to be free." "Slaves get married" then points to the realities of "here": slaves did get married, in the sense that they chose permanent partners, as attested in later inscriptions (see chapter 8); and slaves were mated with other slaves by their owners, for example as Cato mentions that farm-owners might provide the slave *vilicus* with a "wife" (*si eam tibi dederit dominus uxorem, De agr.* 143.1). This naturally did not remove the owner's right to have sex with either partner.[41] In fact that is the "marriage" envisioned in *Casina*: each owner tries to get Casina for his own slave's ostensible partner, really so as to have her for himself (52–7). Hence the preference for "elsewhere."

Within *Casina*, both Olympio and Chalinus express strong desire for a wife, although (unlike Stichus and Sangarinus) each conflates this with the desire to beat the other one out – that is how their owners have set it up, after all. Olympio taunts Chalinus with an erotic picture of his wedding night, during which he plans to confine Chalinus in the window frame so he will have to listen (132–40; see chapter 5). Chalinus vows never to give

---

[40] Carved in stone: on a marble stele from Beroia in Macedonia, probably dating to 280 BCE, translated in Burstein 1985, from which I excerpt (p. 73, item 54, lines 4–9): "Payment for their freedom was made by Kosmas, || Marsyas, Ortyx to Attinas, daughter of Alketas, for themselves *v* | and their wives, Arnion, Glauka, *v* Chlidane, | and for their children ..., and for all their possessions, ea|ch fifty gold (staters); *v* and Spazatis for her|self and her possessions paid gold (staters), twenty-five of them." Burstein notes that the inscription is discussed by Westermann (1955: 35), who indeed devotes a page to it as predating the famous manumission documents from Delphi, but says nothing about the wives. Fifty staters = 600 drachmas, or 3,600 obols (Burstein 1985: 74, 150) – about three years' pay at three obols/day, a large sum to be scraped up by unpaid laborers. For further examples of Greek slaves with families, see Zelnick-Abramovitz 2005: 157, 163–70, who emphasizes that the evidence for manumission of families, even parent–child pairs, is rare, supplementing an extended discussion in Bradley 1984: 47–80, who emphasizes the prevailing tendency to break up families.

[41] On the wedding ceremony in *Casina*, see Williams 1958: 17–18, who holds that it is a mashup of Greek and Roman forms. For evidence on slave marriage and on the use by slaves of terms for "legal wife" and "legal husband" on their epitaphs, see Joshel 1992: 46, with further bibliography; cf. 29, 43–5 on "ties that existed regardless of their legitimacy."

up Casina, even when the owner gives him a choice between manumission without her, or marriage to her and remaining a slave – himself and his children – all his life (287–94). His exit line in this scene asserts his right to existence: "You don't want to see me, but I will still be alive" (*invitus me vides, vivam tamen*, 302).

The arrogant Palaestrio warns his current owner, the lecherous soldier, not to love Milphidippa, an *ancilla* belonging to the *meretricula* Acroteleutium: "This one's engaged to me; if the other one marries you today, / I'll make this one my wife immediately" (*mihi haec desponsast: tibi si illa hodie nupserit, / ego hanc continuo uxorem ducam*, Mil. 1007–8). He has no serious intentions; the point is the balance of *nupserit* (for the soldier and the supposed wife of the neighbor) by *uxorem ducam* (for the slave Palaestrio and the wife's *ancilla*). Palaestrio's claim is asserted to mark his ascendancy over the soldier, who replies to him, "I am your slave attendant" (*pedisequos tibi sum*, 1009). The slave Trachalio, although only on pleasantly joking terms with the *ancilla* Ampelisca (*Rud.* 363–4, 372–5), does suddenly develop serious intentions towards her, which then are necessarily conditional: "And that Ampelisca should marry me, when I am free" (*atque ut mi Ampelisca nubat, ubi ego sim liber*, 1220). She is bought from the pimp and freed at the end so that this can take place (1408–9), after his continued insistence (see chapter 8). Within the plays, male slaves do not have wives; but they want them.

The right to legal marriage, the *ius conubii*, was one of the basic rights of Roman citizens, a necessary condition for making more citizens, to whom a legal person could leave legally owned property; slaves could not bequeath anything to their families, which had no legal status. So, very occasionally in the plays, slaves claim family: Sagaristio, although lying, claims to have a free twin (*Per.* 695–6, 830–1); the *nutrix* Giddenis is reunited with her long-lost son (*Poen.* 1141–4). The prostituted sisters in *Poenulus*, kidnapped together, suggest a possible imagined back story for the Bacchis sisters in *Bacchides*. Just as a threadbare *parasitus* claims ancestors, as when Saturio enters extolling "the ancient and time-hallowed profession of my ancestors" (*veterem atque antiquom quaestum maiorum meum*, Per. 53, cf. 54–61, 390; Gelasimus at St. 174, 179), so slaves claim ancestors, too, with the same comic assertion of value: Sosia metatheatrically claims descent from Davus, the classic slave of Greek New Comedy (*Am.* 365, 614); Olympio credits his success to the *pietas* of himself and his *maiores* (*Cas.* 418). Sceledrus claims the cross will be his tomb (*sepulcrum*), as it was his ancestors' (*Mil.* 372–3). That is, he will end up crucified, and just as Sosia's mask will never be bedeck a descendant at a fancy funeral, so Sceledrus has no family tomb, since his ancestors go similarly unmarked. Pseudolus sings that he relies on the *virtus* of his ancestors (*Ps.* 581–2); Pinacium claims his heroic message-bearing will add to the deeds of his *maiores* (*St.* 281–2, 303–4), who, he says pertly to his owner, gave him his name (332): a quick reclaiming of his identity from her, and of his sex-toy name as a family name. Perhaps Epidicus also lays claim to ancestors ("that's how I do it, that's how our people did it," *sic ego ago, sic egerunt nostri, Epid.* 340), as does Pseudolus, speaking for slaves and comedians: "Our kind has always been dry-eyed" (*genu' nostrum semper siccoculum fuit, Ps.* 77). That the profession of *parasitus* is an "honorable and respectable practice" is an old joke, going back at least to the New Comedy playwright Diodorus of Sinope in the 280s (*Epikleros* fr. 2 = Ath. 6.239b–f, trans. Olson); tellingly, Diodorus' speaker instances as forebears twelve citizens selected by the city. The claim of an honored history is, then, peculiarly resonant in a culture in which *maiores* belonged to the powerful. The audacity of such a claim is underlined by the taunt flung at Tyndarus in *Captivi*: "What 'father'? [For] one who's a slave!" (*quem patrem? qui servos est*, 574) – a taunt undermined by the fact that, unknown to anyone onstage but known to the audience, Tyndarus' father is standing next to him. Sosia's joke that there will never be a funeral at which a lookalike wears his *imago* jabs at the slave's distance from the *summi viri* as marked specifically by his inability to be an ancestor (*Am.* 459; see chapter 2).

Conversely, in keeping with his general assumption of free status, Toxilus treats the day of his triumph as his birthday (*Per.* 768–9); compare the less aggressive *parasitus* Ergasilus, who claims today is his birthday in order to get a meal (*Capt.* 174). Enslaved girls are recognized by the birthday gifts they were given as children – Planesium's brother gave her a ring (*Cur.* 656), Palaestra's father gave her a gold *bulla* (*Rud.* 1171); among her other tokens, her father's name is written on one, her mother's on another (1157, 1159): the mark of filiation. Yet Telestis is recognized just by the memory of a birthday gift, a slave's memory and a slave's gift: she was given a *lunula* and a gold ring by her father's slave Epidicus (*Epid.* 639–40; see chapter 7). That gift-giving was a conventional burden on slaves is suggested by the complaints in Terence's *Phormio* (39–50), but Epidicus does not complain. A pimp, repellently in the context of *Pseudolus*, can celebrate his birthday, and extort gifts from his slave prostitutes: "Birthday boy, hey, birthday boy," sings out Pseudolus to his despised enemy (*hodie nate, heus hodie nate, Ps.* 243). Slaves lost their birthdays along with the rest of their natal rights.[42] As they were (legally) nobody's parent, so they were nobody's child.

The issue of friendships between slaves onstage deserves fuller treatment than I can give here: not only Toxilus and Sagaristio, but Leonida and Libanus in *Asinaria*, Epidicus and Thesprio in *Epidicus*, Milphio and Syncerastus in *Poenulus*, Stichus and Sangarinus in *Stichus*, and the always-exceptional pair in *Captivi*, Philocrates and Tyndarus, fellow captives – all male. The female pairs are young prostitutes, Palaestra and Ampelisca in *Rudens* and the sisters Adelphasium and Anterastilis in *Poenulus*, whose onstage relationships revolve around their shared plight – none of their doing; Lucy and Ethel, without the mischief. Slave friendships make perhaps as radical a claim onstage as anything else presented here; where natal alienation has broken family ties, friendships have a special resonance, and later epitaphs testify to what are now known as "families of choice" among slaves and freed slaves. Amica and Detfri, who put their names and footprints on the tile they made, were surely friends.[43] The onstage pairs have a comic function as a double act, with antecedents in Old Comedy (Sosias and Xanthias, who open Aristophanes' *Wasps*; the slaves Demosthenes and Nikias, who open *Knights*; the slaves of Trygaios, who open *Peace*); in Plautus' plays, however, slave friends have complex relationships, often at the center of the action. They fill a gap barely visible in Latin literature, the same kind of gap measured by Virginia Woolf in "Chloe liked Olivia," or by the Bechdel test, only for slaves. There is, however, no female slave pair equivalent to Leonida and Libanus in comedy to play to Amica and Detfri in the audience (see chapter 5 on Plautus' sister). Thinking of onstage bonds between slaves and the free poor, we might include here the friendship between Toxilus and the *parasitus* Saturio, if a relationship based on kitchen handouts counts as a friendship.

Certainly Saturio could use a friend; *parasiti* do not usually have any, hence the poignancy of his daughter's line, "even if our lives are broken, we still have friends" (*etsi res sunt fractae, amici sunt tamen*, *Per.* 655). Indeed, he is the only *parasitus* with a visible family member. *Parasiti* do get some dinners, to consummate all the "drooling speeches": Ergasilus wreaks carnage in the kitchen (*Capt.* 909–21); Curculio exits to enjoy a second feast

---

[42] On slave birthdays, see Joshel 1992: 65. The importance of having a birthday (*dies natalis*) is perhaps reflected in the later legal process whereby the emperor could restore a freed slave's birthrights (*natales*), *D.* 40.11.

[43] For a wealth of later epigraphic evidence on families of choice, see Williams 2012: 259–354; Joshel 2010: 109 discusses an epitaph from one freedman to another, commemorating a friendship dating back to the slave market. On the Pietrabbondante roof tile, see Richlin 2014a: 1–2.

(*Cur.* 365–70); Saturio has been in Toxilus' house, presumably eating, while his daughter has been sold onstage to the pimp (*Per.* 724–6).[44] The desire expressed onstage for a free meal once again superimposes a stage image on top of something present in the streets where the stage was. Beneventum was not the only place where there were public dinners in the streets (see chapter 1); at least one occasion is on record when tables were set up in the Forum Romanum (183 BCE, the funeral games for P. Licinius Crassus), and we also hear of an awning spread over the Comitium in 208, evidently in connection with the *ludi Romani*. Mika Kajava argues that, although public banquets are not attested for all funeral games, "there is no reason to doubt that the Roman people were often fed on such occasions."[45] Banquets, however, were fraught with their own class issues. The *cena popularis* seen in chapter 2, at which the slave Stasimus says he would shove a rich man out of the way to get at the food, is portrayed as taking place in a temple (*aedem*, *Trin.* 468), where it might happen that a rich man (*opulentus*, 469) would be placed next to the bankrupt Lesbonicus and served with lavish amounts of food (*epulae*) by his dependents (*a cluentibus*, 471); Lesbonicus may share in this food only by invitation. For, as well as the general public banquets, there were also religious banquets associated with specific guests, like those held at the Ara Maxima to honor Hercules (only men could attend), or the *epulum Iovis* frequently recorded during the Second Punic War in connection with the *ludi Plebeii*. This dinner, organized by the priestly college of *epulones*, was restricted to upper-class men, who dined alongside an image of the god.[46] Hence the joke in *Persa* when Saturio greets the slave/patron he hopes will feed him: "Oh my Jupiter / on earth, your *coepulonus* hails you" (*o mi Iuppiter / terrestris, coepulonus compellat tuos*, 99–100). The status of each is doubly inverted.

In real life, where slaves woke up in the morning and went about their business, perhaps there were places where they themselves could go that constituted *loci liberi* – not that they were supposed to have free time, for the most part, but where they took time as if free. Columella's vice list for urban slaves suggests, although with a strong owner's bias, what those

---

[44] On parasites and "drooling speeches" – catalogues of rich food, with an even richer vocabulary – see Gowers 1993: 62–4.

[45] The funeral games of 183, Livy 39.46.2; the Comitium covered over, 27.36.8; see Kajava 1998: 114.

[46] On the banquets for Hercules, see Kajava 1998: 119; for the *epulum Iovis* and its guests, Donahue 2003: 429–30 ("senators"), whose sources, however, are largely imperial, in a synoptic account of public feasting; also Habinek 2005: 42 ("leading men"), placing this event as a prime example of upper-class men linking themselves with gods. Instances of this dinner in connection with the *ludi Plebeii*: Livy 25.2.8–10 (also a distribution of oil by the aediles at the *ludi Romani*); 27.36.9; 29.38.8; 30.39.8; 31.4.5–7.

places might have been two and a half centuries after Plautus: "the playing field, the Circus, the theaters, gambling, *popinae*, brothels" (*campo, circo, theatris, aleae, popinae, lupanaribus*, Rust. 1.8.2). Do the plays give us any other ideas?

One, possibly, was the barbershop. Suggestively, Leonida in *Asinaria* comes across the Mercator while sitting in the barbershop (*in tostrina ut sedebam*, 343); as John Henderson points out, "slave stubble sat cheek by jowl with free" (2006: 137). Later, backing up Leonida's story, Libanus tells the Merchant that the *atriensis* has gone to the barber (394); then Leonida, pretending to be the *atriensis*, compains that he had ordered Libanus to come to the barbershop (408, 413). So, too, the slave Geta in Terence's *Phormio* likes to sit in the barbershop while waiting for a young *citharistria* to get out of school, and there he gets into a conversation with a stranger (*Ph.* 88–93). The *tostrina* is repeatedly named as a checkpoint in monologues reporting a search of the city, in the formulaic phrase *in medicinis, in tostrinis* (*Am.* 1011–14, cf. *Epid.* 197–9), and forms one of the Latin elements in these bilingual placename lists, which clearly constitute shtick in themselves: a counterpart to the "running slave" entrance routine. The barbershop as gossip center was a standing joke in Greek going back at least to Aristophanes.[47] In the urban legend of the Athenian barber who (Plutarch says) brought the news of the Sicilian disaster, Virginia Hunter held that the barber must have been thought of as a slave, or he could not have been tortured as he was: "one of a large group who practiced their trades either with or independently of their masters in the industrial districts of Athens and the Piraeus." The *locus*, then, would be not only banausic but servile in itself.[48]

The frequent use of "clipping" to mean "deceiving" in the plays recalls the double sense of "clip joint" in English, as seen particularly in this extended metaphor in *Captivi* (266–9):

nunc senex est in tostrina, nunc iam cultros adtinet.
ne id quidem, involucre inicere, voluit, vestem ut ne inquinet.

[47] So Beard 2014: 188, "that hot spot of ancient popular culture: the place where ordinary men went to get shaved and trimmed and have a chuckle." She is discussing the possibility that the Suda says the jokebook known as *Philogelos* was "the kind of book you would take to the barbershop," herself citing Polybius 3.20.5 (where Polybius scorns the works of inferior historians as κουρεακῆς καὶ πανδήμου λαλιᾶς, "common babbling like what goes on in barbershops") and Plutarch, *Moralia* 508f–509c = *de garr.* 13. Cf. Aristophanes, *Wealth* 337–8, *Eccl.* 303a–b (garland shops, again λαλοῦντες); Menander *Sam.* 510–12, again with λαλεῖν; S. Lewis 1995; further sources in Gowers 2012: 254–5 *ad* Horace *S.* 1.7.3.
[48] Plutarch, *Life of Nicias* 30, *Moralia* 509a–c, in Hunter 1994: 154–5; the story is also discussed in Vlassopoulos 2007: 42–3.

sed utrum strictimne attonsurum dicam esse an per pectinem
nescio; verum, si frugist, usque admutilabit probe.

Now the old man is at the barber's, now at last he's got his hand on
the razor.
He didn't even want to throw a cover over him so as not to stain his clothes.
But whether I should say he's going to shave him close or through the comb
I don't know; but, if he's prudent, he'll clip him good and proper.

Here the captured slave Tyndarus comments to the audience with approval
on the technique of the captured free man Philocrates, who is pretending to
be the captured slave Tyndarus. The verbs *tondeo*, "shear," and *(ad)mutilo*,
"clip," are frequently used elsewhere to mean "deceive," "con"; combing
is used as a metaphor for "beating," as in the phrase *pugnis pectitur*, "he's
being combed with fists" (*Rud.* 661, cf. *Men.* 1017, *Poen.* 358, and *Capt.* 896
fusti pectito, "you can comb me with a club"). Dordalus says to Sagaristio,
"You clipped me all the way down to the skin" (*me usque admutilasti ad
cutem*, *Per.* 829), and the violent overtones of *mutilo* – which also means
"mutilate" – are always present. These processes also evoke the disreputable: one of the female slaves in *Truculentus* who helps get the baby for
Phronesium is identified as *Syra tonstrix* (*Truc.* 405, 771–2, 856), and she
is able to locate an unwanted baby for Phronesium's use because she goes
around from house to house, doing her job (407, *ut opera est*); three hundred years later, *tonstrix* is used by Martial in a riddling description of a
prostitute, whom he places in the Subura, next to the torturer's place and
the cobblers (2.17.1). Closer to Plautus, the Middle Comedy playwrights
Alexis, Amphis, and Antiphanes are all credited with a *Kouris* (*Barber
Girl*), and Polybius sets this figure among other prostitute-equivalents in
a nasty story about the Ptolemaic court c. 200.[49] As seen in chapter 2, the
senex in *Mercator* uses *tondeo* in a double entendre when coming on to the
prostitute Pasicompsa (*Mer.* 526).

The barbershop itself appears later, in the world of Roman satire where
free speech is politically charged, as a site for gossip (Hor. *S.* 1.7.3) and a
place where the satirist goes himself (Juv. 1.25); Persius, in his program-
matic first satire (1.119–20), blurts out the secret that *Mida rex* has ass's
ears and compares himself elliptically to Midas's barber – the mythic para-
digm of the body servant who knows the king's secrets and can tell them

---

[49] Alexis, K-A 112 (107) = Ath. 8.362c; 113 (108) = Ath. 10.443d; 114 (109) = Ath. 10.432e. Amphis,
K-A 23 (23) = Ath. 13.567f; 24 (24) = Ath. 13.591d. Antiphanes, K-A 126 (128) = Ath. 3.120a; 127
(129) = Ath. 7.303f–304a. None of these, unfortunately, concerns barbers. For the story about
Tlepolemus insulting Agathocles at the court of Ptolemy V, see Plb. 15.25.32(24) – very reminiscent
of the kinds of court insults found in tales of comedians in Athenaeus (see Richlin 2016).

(see chapter 6). In traditional barber stories, low is uncomfortably close to high: the barber of the tyrant Dionysius boasts that he often has his razor at the tyrant's throat, and is crucified (Plutarch *Mor.* 508f–509a). So this important image in Persius – it was singled out for revision after his death by his literary executor as being too politically dangerous, since it was an obvious thrust at Nero (Suetonius *Life of Persius* sub fin.) – points to a more politically significant meaning for the barbershop: as Sian Lewis notes, *ergastêria*, "workshops," were thought of in fourth-century Athens as hotbeds of "political disaffection and criminal conspiracies," dangerous because slaves worked there and could mix with free men (1995: 440 n. 19). Kostas Vlassopoulos (2007: 38), borrowing the term "free spaces" from the political theorists Sara Evans and Harry Boyte, argues that, in places in classical Athens where "citizens, metics, slaves and women" mixed, class boundaries became permeable and identities became blurred, and the view from below was vociferously expressed. Commonly mentioned were *ergastêria* and "lounging-places" (*hêmikuklia*), located in the agora. If there is any truth to Varro's story that *tonsores* first came to Italy from Sicily in 300 BCE, then barbers entered the world of the *palliata* alongside comedians, and traveled the same road: even commemorated by an inscription at Ardea, *scriptum in publico*. A narratorial joke, in all likelihood, but, even so, a comic history.[50] The forum in central Italy was an equivalent space to the agora, where you could find shops, bankers, prostitutes, slave markets – and, as was not the case in Greece, plays. The *Poenulus* prologue speaker orders the *pedisequi* off to the *popina* to get a snack (41–3), "while you have the chance" (*dum occasio est*).

The Dream of a Free Place

The *palliata* does a lot for the bodies at the bottom. The hungry are fed; unlike the well-fed Broadway audiences for *Oliver!* who sang along to "Food, Glorious Food," the audience of the wartime *palliata* went hungry. Slaves onstage are principal beneficiaries of the plays' action; the plays lower owners and raise up slaves. Slaves onstage get to say all the things a slave could never say in real life – slaves tell their owners off, face to face.

---

[50] Varro, *R.* 2.11.10, *omnino tonsores in Italiam primum venisse ex Sicilia dicuntur p. R. c. A. CCCCLIII, ut scriptum in publico Ardeae in litteris extat, eosque adduxisse Publium Titinium Menam.* On this odd interjection in a discussion on sheep-shearing, see Nelsestuen 2011: 335; his whole essay usefully complicates Varro's text, usually taken straight. The recurrence of the cognomen *Mena* ("sardine") in Horace's junkman, Volteius Mena, first spied in the empty barbershop (*Epist.* 1.7.50–1), perhaps makes Varro's Mena equally fishy.

They hit free people, and the egregious Libanus even rides his owner, with a conscious suggestion of rape, possibly of payback. Male slaves lay claim to respect, to the rights held by free men; slaves both male and female take center stage and run the show. This was doubtless entertaining to any upper-class people watching, borne along, with the whole audience, on the flow of jokes, songs, and dances. But to slaves and freed slaves it would have been entertaining in a special way, a way close to home. The whole fabric of the plays is made up of things slaves want. Mostly so far, however, of things male slaves want. It is now time to take a look at female slaves in the *palliata* and see to what extent the plays address things women want — if, in performance terms, there were any women onstage at all.

CHAPTER 5

Looking like a Slave-Woman

Virginia Woolf, in *A Room of One's Own* (1929), imagined what would have happened if Shakespeare had had a sister as talented as he was. Left behind at home to do women's work and marry early, finally she cannot bear it any more and runs away:

> The force of her own gift alone drove her to it. She made up a small parcel of her belongings, let herself down by a rope one summer's night and took the road to London. She was not seventeen. The birds that sang in the hedge were not more musical than she was. She had the quickest fancy, a gift like her brother's, for the tune of words. Like him, she had a taste for the theatre. She stood at the stage door; she wanted to act, she said. Men laughed in her face. … She could get no training in her craft.

It was Woolf's choice to end this vision with the writer's suicide: "who shall measure the heat and violence of the poet's heart when caught and tangled in a woman's body?"[1]

About fifty years later, Hattie Gossett wrote a poem called "Is It True What They Say about Colored Pussy?" The theme of the poem is the history of the abuse of the bodies of women of color, and Gossett includes American slavery and American labor:

> they make all kinds of laws and restrictions to apartheid-ize colored pussy
> and then as soon as the sun goes down guess who is seen sneaking out back to the cabins?
> and guess who cant do without colored pussy in their kitchens and fields and factories and offices?[2]

---

[1] Woolf 1929: 82–3. This essay originated as a set of lectures delivered to mostly female audiences at Newnham and Girton on Oct. 20 and 26, 1928; see Rosenbaum's introduction to Woolf 1992 (xiii–xix, and xix–xli for how the lectures came to be published as the article "Women and Fiction"), and Rosenman 1995: 22–5, who notes that the section on Shakespeare's sister, "probably the most famous part of the essay today," was not in the original lectures.

[2] Most readily available in the classic Second-Wave collection *Pleasure and Danger* (Gossett 1984: 411–12); see also n. 8 below.

Gossett's poem tells one of the open secrets also told in Plautus' plays, which, as we have seen, are all about telling open secrets. For women's secrets, however, they do so without any visible input from Plautus' sister. Yet some effort is being made onstage in the *palliata* to tell about slave-women; more than nothing.

The *Poenulus* prologue addresses both *matronae* and *nutrices*, along with (male) prostitutes. Considering the plays' common misogyny, their pervasive objectification of women, and the probable lack of women behind the masks of the *palliata* (see chapter 1), it is a good question what women viewers found to enjoy, although they were certainly there.[3] By far the majority of the plays focus on male characters – *Captivi* has no female characters at all, and *Trinummus* has only the prologue speakers – but a few make a special appeal to the female spectator: *Cistellaria*, which focuses on a group of free and freed prostitutes; *Epidicus*, in which a newly enslaved woman's mother comes to find her; *Stichus*, which opens with two young *matronae* talking; *Truculentus*, in which the central and triumphant figure is female, if not so sympathetic; and the anomalous *Casina*, in which a *matrona*, her friend, and her *ancilla* triumph over the lecherous *senex*. Other plays have large roles for female prostitutes, and *Persa* has several key female characters; still the plays are often male-centered, like the films of Judd Apatow or the Marx Brothers. What slave-women in the audience might have liked perhaps stemmed from what the Combahee River Collective Statement called the "simultaneity of oppressions," now called "intersectionality" – in Plautus' Rome, the double burden of being both a slave and female.[4] As seen in chapter 2, the adjective *morigerus*, "dutiful," is applied to male slaves in reference to a servitude that incorporates sexual compliance; this adjective is also applied to married women in the plays (Alcumena, *Am.* 842; *Cist.* 175, a "dead wife" joke), as well as to the supposed slave bride Casina (897–8), and to female prostitutes (*Men.* 202; *Mos.* 398). On the other hand, "women" was a far from unitary class in Rome as always; the

---

[3] Scholars sometimes remark in passing that theater audiences were predominantly male (Gold 1998: 21, "the predominantly and normatively Roman male audience" of *Casina*; for "the shows" in the time of Juvenal, Gunderson 2005: 235, "an audience of 'the people,' who will have been mostly men"). To my knowledge, there is no reason to think so, for any period, although "normatively" is worth discussion. Cf. Manuwald 2015: 181–2; Marshall 2006: 75–82; Moore 1998. On the plays as testimony to "a significant female presence in the servile population of the second century as a whole," see Bradley 1989: 28–9.

[4] See Combahee River Collective 1983: 280–1: "We are of course particularly committed to working on those struggles in which race, sex and class are simultaneous factors in oppression." This activist group took its name from the region in which Harriet Tubman carried out her operations during the Civil War. On intersectionality, see Hancock 2016; for a collective study of Greek and Roman women and slaves, see Joshel and Murnaghan 1998.

divisions among women produced opportunities for comedy, as spectators saw and heard painful truths stated openly on the stage – a classic trigger for the release of inhibitions.

That gender affects viewing has been the subject of extensive discussion since the 1970s, exploding with the rise of gaze theory around 1985. Chapter 1 deals briefly with the general question of multiple perspectives in any given audience, and of ways in which viewing is affected by status. In particular, starting from John Berger's dictum, "Men look at women. Women watch themselves being looked at. This determines not only most relations between men and women but also the relation of women to themselves" (1972: 47), theorists began to discuss ways in which the gaze itself can be gendered, and to explore the range of options open to women. They argued not only that some women living under such scopic regimes *enjoy* being the object of the gaze – after all, it constructs their sexuality – but that women have a gaze of their own.[5] Taking into account the experience of African-American women living in the aftermath of slavery, bell hooks outlines what she calls the "oppositional gaze," arguing, as seen in chapter 1, that "Subordinates in relations of power learn experientially that there is a critical gaze, one that 'looks' to document, one that is oppositional" (hooks 1992: 116).[6] In particular, with regard to the character of Sapphire in the *Amos 'n' Andy* comedies, she says (1992: 120):

> Grown black women had a different response to Sapphire; they identified with her frustrations and her woes. They resented the way she was mocked. They resented the way these screen images could assault black womanhood, could name us bitches, nags. And in opposition they claimed Sapphire as their own, as the symbol of that angry part of themselves white folks and black men could not even begin to understand.

As this chapter will show, although wives onstage in the *palliata* are often assaulted as bitches and nags, slave-women do occasionally get a chance to speak truth to power. However – and this is a big "however" – if the women onstage in the *palliata* were indeed men in women costumes, that complicates the gaze of every member of the audience, including the women sitting there. At the same time, slave-women in the audience had

---

[5] For the female gaze, see Gamman and Marshment 1988 (influential for current work on popular culture); for the gaze and sexual desire, Caught Looking 1988, and on "sex-positive" feminism, Johnson 2002; for the female gaze and art, Kent and Morreau 1985 (focused on men).

[6] On gaze theory, see Richlin 1992a, with overviews, bibliography, and applications to Greek and Roman material; in particular, see Terri Marsh's essay on different viewing positions among the audience for Greek tragedy. For more recent studies, see Fredrick 2002 and Joshel and Petersen 2014, with reference to slavery and the gaze in the household and in public spaces.

something in common with slave actors, however they were dressed. Our gaze will focus on slave-women in the audience and onstage, in relation also to free women in the audience and onstage, and to the men behind those masks.

As seen in chapter 1, all through the 200s BCE, all over the Mediterranean and in Italy itself, armies Roman and non-Roman contributed to the flow of persons who began their week as (free or slave) inhabitants of one place and ended it as objects for sale, either on the spot or someplace else – many in Rome. Readers today who think in terms of a "master class" and identify the audience with that class should bear in mind, for example, the experience of the upper-class Capuan families sold into slavery in Rome in 210 (Livy 26.34). Kathy Gaca has demonstrated that the sacking of cities in "populace-ravaging warfare" characteristically entailed the rape of captives, particularly women and girls (Gaca 2010–11). In consciousness of this historical context, C. W. Marshall has called for a darker understanding of the relationship between sex trafficking and the plots of New Comedy (2013), and has traced the overlaps between "prostitute" and "household slave-woman" as women bought for sex (2015). Different women in the audience knew firsthand about different experiences produced by the wars of the 200s. Female slaves shared with male slaves the experience of rape and enslavement, of use by owners, and of being prostituted by owners, although onstage we see much more of female than of male prostitutes (chapters 2, 4). Some experiences, however, were gender-specific to women: serving women owners as body servants; producing slave children for the household; nursing the household's children, slave and free; being an *era* (as Lemniselenis has Sophoclidisca in her *peculium*, and Philematium perhaps had Scapha); being a man's long-term love interest, at least while still young (not shown onstage for males, but see chapter 7 on Philippus Poenus in 192 BCE). The loss of children to slavery is shown onstage as affecting both fathers and mothers, but often as involving displacement across the Mediterranean, a violent disruption of place along with family.

Paul the Deacon in the eighth century CE retails the following etymology of the Latin word *ancilla*, "slave-woman": "*Ancillae* are so called from the name of King Ancus Martius, because he captured a great number of women in war" (Paulus 18L). Paul's source for this scholarly fancy reaches back to the first century BCE, where it attests to an ongoing association between slave-women and the processes of enslavement – an association which was present to the inhabitants of the cities of Latium in the flesh, every day. *Ancillae* in Plautus are often, but not always, house slaves, and belong sometimes to women and sometimes to men; of these, some belong to pimps, and, of these, some are prostitutes and main characters in the plays (see Marshall 2013).[7] This chapter will first review a range of female characters, to see how slave-women do have a voice onstage as speaking subjects, and then look at what it means if these characters were acted by men.

Object into Subject

Michelle Cliff, in an essay titled "Object into Subject," wrote of American racism (1982: 34):

> Through objectification – the process by which people are dehumanized, made ghostlike, given the status of Other – an image created by the oppressor replaces the actual being. The actual being is then denied speech; denied self-definition, self-realization; and over-arching all this, denied selfhood – which is after all the point of objectification.[8]

Cliff's project was to analyze the work of African-American women artists as a response to a history of objectification – to show how object turned into subject. The differences between Rome and the Americas as slave societies determine some differences in the process of objectification. On the one hand, slaves under Roman law were literally objects, treated under the Law of Things as well as under the Law of Persons (see Joshel 1992: 28–37).[9] On the other, Roman slaves were categorized not by race but by civil status, and this status was capable of change: a central fantasy in the plays of Plautus. The plays themselves lavishly bestow selfhood on male slaves, and sometimes on female slaves and freedwomen. Nor were these plays created by "the oppressor," in any direct way; they play with slave stereotypes, and often undercut them. Often, as seen here, the actors speak through their masks powerful critiques of the process of enslavement, and tell what it feels like to be a slave. Female characters have some of the best lines. We do not, however, have any Roman equivalent to the art discussed by Cliff;

---

[7] Prostitutes as *ancillae*: Planesium is *ei ancillula, Cur.* 43; Lemniselenis is *ancilla mea, Per.* 472; Palaestra and Ampelisca are *meas ancillas, Rud.* 712.

[8] This scholarly essay, often reprinted, is well worth seeking out in its original venue in the radical feminist journal *Heresies*, where Hattie Gossett's poem "Is It True What They Say about Colored Pussy?" appears in a sidebar on p. 40.

[9] On objectification of *ancillae* onstage, see Marshall 2015: 133–5, adducing the categories of objectification laid out by Martha Nussbaum (1995).

instead, we have the traces of enactments, and these are what we need to understand.[10]

The plays sometimes display the direct association between female slaves and the spoils of war. *Epidicus* concerns one young woman, Telestis, who has been bought from the spoils by a young combatant, and another young woman, Acropolistis, who has been bought and freed by the young man's father Periphanes in the belief that she is his daughter; in reality, she is a *fidicina*, a music girl, palmed off on the father by the slave Epidicus on behalf of the young man, who had wanted her before he saw Telestis. (Compare *Stichus* 380–1, where *fidicinas, tibicinas, / sambucas … forma eximia* form part of the cargo of a trading ship – three kinds of female musicians, all of "outstanding shape.") By the end of the play, Telestis will turn out to be the actual daughter, hence off-limits to the young man. As *Captivi* constantly tests whether slaves are so by nature or by chance, so a sub-theme in *Epidicus* tests whether there is any qualitative difference between Telestis and Acropolistis. The main issue is the title character's quest for freedom, vindicated in the final triumphant scene (chapter 4); still, there are these two MacGuffins.

Telestis shows up as motivating factor near the beginning of the opening scene, as the young man's armor-bearer breaks the bad news to Epidicus (43–4): "He has bought a captive young girl from the spoils, with a charming shape, / worthy of a free woman" (*forma lepida et liberali captivam adulescentulam / de praeda mercatust*). The young man himself, on his first entrance, is being reassured about his purchase by a friend (106–8): "You're stupid, Stratippocles. Are you ashamed because you bought a captive woman from the spoils, born from a good family (*genere prognatam bono*)? Who would blame you for that?" Stratippocles replies that he has not made her have sex with him (110), although we have heard from his armor-bearer that he loves her madly (*deperit*, 65). The adjective *liberalis*, and the bystander's comment that Telestis is "born from a good family," point up the ambiguous status of sex slaves: their attractiveness stems partly from the titillating fact that they *might* be respectable women, that they *look like* respectable women, even that they *recently were* respectable women, before the annihilation of enslavement erased their status.[11] Nevertheless, captives

---

[10] More correctly, we do not know if we have work by women's hands; see Richlin 2014a: 1–2 on the Pietrabbondante roof tile (signed by Amica and Detfri), and Levin-Richardson 2013 on graffiti. The presence of two slave-women in a brickyard opens up the question of who made all those terracotta figurines.

[11] As a Greek cousin of *liberalis*, the adjective ἐλευθερίος appears in Menander (*Her.* 40, ἐλευθερίος καὶ κοσμία), used by the slave Daos to vouch for the virtue of the slave-woman he loves. His point is that she is a suitable mate for him; she indeed turns out to be a citizen, and in the end marries

are loot; when Epidicus reports on the parade of returning soldiers – a triumph-like display, laden with arms and pack-animals (208–9) – each has multiple captives with him, specifically sex-objects: "Then what a bunch of captives they led with them! Boys, virgins, / two apiece, three apiece, one had five" (*tum captivorum quid ducunt secum! pueros, virgines, / binos, ternos, alius quinque*, 210–11). Telestis is part of the loot – even her mother Philippa, when she comes looking for her, defines her as an object: "She's become the property of the enemy" (*hostiumst potita*, 532; *hostium est potita*, 562). If the triumph is in Rome, then the "enemy," to Philippa, is Rome. The Roman location of this slave traffic is also marked in *Captivi*; the father's trading in captives, none too creditable to him (98–101), is made "out of the spoils, from the quaestors" (*de praeda a quaestoribus*, 453).

Telestis herself appears only to be ogled (622–4) and recognized as the long-lost daughter (637), the only point at which she speaks. To Acropolistis is given an excruciating non-recognition scene, when she is presented to Telestis' mother as Telestis (567–606). Conducted out of the house by a non-speaking female slave with the slave name "Canthara" ("Wine-glass"), Acropolistis confronts Philippa, who rejects her with notable disgust: "puppies smell one way, pigs smell quite another" (*aliter catuli longe olent, aliter sues*, 579).[12] Telestis' father Periphanes upbraids Acropolistis (584–90, 93–5):

AC. quid loquar vis? PE. haec negat se tuam esse matrem. AC. ne fuat
si non volt: equidem hac invita tamen ero matris filia;   585
non med istanc cogere aequom est meam esse matrem si nevolt.
PE. qur me igitur patrem vocabas? AC. tua istaec culpast, non mea.
non patrem ego te nominem, ubi tu tuam me appelles filiam?
hanc quoque etiam, si me appellet filiam, matrem vocem.
negat haec filiam me suam esse: non ergo haec mater mea est.   590
...
AC. numquid ego ibi, pater, peccavi? PE. si hercle te umquam audivero

---

a citizen. *Liberalis* (often paired with *lepida*) in Plautus describes not only slave-women who will recover citizen status (*Cur.* 209, *Epid.* 43, *Per.* 521, 546), but respectable free women (*Per.* 130, the Virgo; *Mil.* 967, the purported *matrona* in love with the soldier), as well as the soldier himself, in a fictive ogling speech reported in flattery by the *parasitus* (*Mil.* 64, attributed to female fans): consistently sexy, paradoxically objectifying. For the overtones of *lepida*, see Gunderson 2015: 127–30.

12 The text is uncertain, as is the sense; it seems possible that Philippa says "piglets smell quite different from sows," considering the metaphor at *Truc.* 268 where the slave Truculentus says "I'll trample you with my feet as a sow [tramples on] her young" (*quasi sus catulos pedibus proteram*). *Rus merum*, responds Astaphium, disapprovingly – "country style." If this is what Philippa means, we arrive at an equally insulting differentiation between (dirty) virgins and (dirtier) sexually experienced women, not far from what Periphanes says of the hired *fidicina* at *Epid.* 403. Otto, following a suggested emendation of the text of the codices, which have *suis*, reads <*leonis*> *aliter catuli longe olent, aliter suis* ("the young of the lion smell one way, the young of a sow smell another way," 1965[1890]: 79). On balance, neither puppies nor lions really belong in this line.

me patrem vocare, vitam tuam ego interimam. AC. non voco.
ubi voles pater esse ibi esto; ubi noles ne fueris pater. 595

AC. What do you want me to say? PE. She denies she's your mother. AC.
 Let her not be,
if she doesn't want to be: I, on the other hand, even if she doesn't want
 me to, will still be [my/a] mother's daughter (*ero matris filia*); 585
it's not fair for me to force this woman of yours to be my mother if she
 doesn't want to be.
PE. Then why were you calling me "father"? AC. That's your fault,
 not mine.
Was I not supposed to call you father, when you were calling me your
 daughter?
This woman, too, even, if she'd call me "daughter," I'd call her "mother."
This woman denies I'm her daughter: so she's not my mother. 590
***
AC. Did I do something wrong there, father? PE. By God, if I ever
 hear you
call me father, I'll end your life. AC. I'm not calling you.
When you want to be [my] father, then be; when you don't,
 you won't be. 595

Acropolistis' speeches in this scene repeatedly call to account the falseness
of natal alienation, the fiction whereby enslaved persons have no legal kin
(Patterson 1982: 5–8). Behind Periphanes' bluster lies the truth known to
himself, Philippa, and the audience: that Periphanes had raped and abandoned Philippa, a poor girl (*pauperculam memini comprimere*, 540b), and
only now, belatedly, wants to find their daughter.[13] Acropolistis seemed
plausible enough to him, since he had only seen Telestis once (600).
Acropolistis asserts that she indeed has a mother, she indeed is a daughter
(585) – a point that is later emphatically repeated by Epidicus himself, in a
line cloaked by its status as a joke ("she's *a* mother's daughter," *matris filia
est*, 700); these lines echo the more common claims by male slave characters that they, too, are human beings, that they have parents (cf. esp. *Am.*
28, *humana matre natus, humano patre*, "born of a human mother, a human
father"). She shrugs off the desires of Periphanes and Philippa, which for
her have produced just another set of commands to obey: "That's your
fault, not mine" (587). Her last words in the scene remind everyone present
that Periphanes' status as father has been entirely capricious (595). After a

---

[13] For a close analysis of this scene, arguing that lines 587–8 hint at Acropolistis' suspicious status as a
 fidicina bought and freed by the old man – as if "father" and "daughter" here meant "Daddy" and
 "Baby" – see Slater 2001, followed by Marshall 2015: 132. On Philippa and Periphanes, see James
 2015a: 116–19 (he has "belatedly developed a conscience," 116), and further in chapter 7 below.

series of reproaches by Philippa, Periphanes sends both women offstage, calling Acropolistis "this Circe, daughter of the Sun" (*Circam Solis filiam*, 604): as he calls his son's beloved a witch (*venefica*, 221) before he identifies her with Acropolistis, so now she is a powerful witch with an all-seeing father, although Periphanes still means this as an insult – means she is the daughter of no one.

Periphanes has had an earlier warning about the futility of his actions, although he does not fully understand it. An unnamed *fidicina* has been palmed off on him as Acropolistis, and he tries to sell her to a soldier; presaging the later scene, the soldier rejects the *fidicina* (490; see chapter 3). Checking his facts with the girl, Periphanes gets a snappish answer: "Indeed nobody would have been able to buy me for any money: / I'm free now, for more than five years" (*neque me quidem emere quisquam ulla pecunia / potuit: plus iam sum libera quinquennium*, 497–8). The same is now true, she adds, of Acropolistis, whom she knows "as well as I know myself" (*tam facile quam me*, 504): unity.[14] These two freedwoman characters, like the Advocati in *Poenulus*, insist on the rights their independence gives them. Indeed, the *fidicina* twice tells Periphanes, "You're going to hear it" (*audies*, at line end in 499 and 507) – putting him in the slave's place, as will be seen in chapter 6 – and she exits with a threat to dun him (516), as seen in chapter 3.

It is all the more striking when female slaves, the most objectified characters on the stage, speak truth to power. The most spectacular example is that of the unnamed Virgo in *Persa*, who – twice – tells onstage what it feels like to be sold. Her words are enabled by a quadruple mask: a male actor speaks the lines; he is wearing the mask of a respectable girl; but she is a poor girl, the daughter of a *parasitus*, the only extant example of such a family member for a *parasitus*; and, within the play, the Virgo is made to play an Arabian girl, perhaps enslaved as a war captive, and brought to "Athens" by the equally fictive title character, to be sold to a pimp.[15]

---

[14] Acropolistis' status is debatable; see Marshall 2015: 129–36 for analysis of her as a slave. Neither Epidicus nor Periphanes ever says he has freed her, just that he has bought her (85–90, 154, 563–5), and from a pimp (352, 364–70): later, Periphanes specifies that he understood she was a captive (563–5). But both repeatedly say Periphanes bought her as his daughter (85–90, 171–2, 357, 368, 542a, 568), and he treats her as a *virgo* (400–5); elided, then, onstage is a (fraudulent) father–daughter recognition scene like those in *Poenulus* and *Rudens*, or a ransom as in *Captivi*. That Acropolistis has been freed is stated both as bogus hearsay (243–6, 268) and real hearsay, in the account of the *fidicina* (503–9), which Marshall bluntly rejects: "This woman is lying" (2015: 132). Certainly Acropolistis is not free to go; see chapter 8 on her obligations as a freedwoman.

[15] On class, disguise, and female speech in this scene, see Marshall 1997; for this scene in the context of others in which Plautus elicits sympathy for female characters in distress, Marshall 2006: 189–92; for the geographical dislocations mapped in this scene as a trademark of sex trafficking, Marshall 2013: 180–1; and further below (chapter 8).

If she is a war captive, she is a former resident of the "Arabian City of Gold" (*Chrysopolim ... urbem in Arabia*, 506), part of the *praeda* (508), then (or coincidentally?) "stolen and trafficked from deepest Arabia" (*furtivam, abductam ex Arabia penitissuma*, 522); the pimp asks if her father was captured, too (644). As such, she has been decked out to look "foreign" (*in peregrinum modum*, 158, cf. 464). The remoteness of Arabia is given as a reason why the pimp need fear no rescue effort (541). As the parasite's daughter, she had hoped for a respectable marriage, which she fears even a fictive sale to a pimp will scotch (383–4). As the Arabian girl, she hopes her [Arabian] father will come to rescue her (618, 653–4), as her [Athenian] father will have to do, to undo the sale. (For "Athenian" read "from here.") Her real father has in fact given her to Toxilus "to be used" and to be sold, a process which they both understand to be akin to pimping her (127–46). Her father has, in effect, sold her – in exchange for a single meal – and, in her first scene, she calls him on it: "Would you sell your daughter for the sake of your belly?" (*tuin ventris caussa filiam vendas tuam*, 338).

That first scene hinges entirely on her father's perception of her as "mine" (*quae sis mea*, 340). "Do you take me for your slave-woman or your daughter?" she asks him (*utrum pro ancilla me habes an pro filia*, 341); he claims *imperium* over her (343), and she concedes his *potestas* (344). As seen in chapter 2, she draws a vivid comparison between her fear of being sold and a slave's fear of a beating (360–4). While she is pleading her case, eventually her father says to her, *tace, stulta* ("Shut up, stupid," 385); so Periphanes says to Acropolistis, before she gives him an earful, *quid stas stupida? quid taces?* ("Why are you standing there like a dummy? Why are you silent?" *Epid.* 583).[16]

Like Acropolistis in her unmasking scene, the Virgo gets a chance to speak her mind in the scene in which, disguised as the Arabian slave-girl, she is sold to the pimp Dordalus, as part of the con engineered by the slave Toxilus. As noted in chapter 2, her own lines are full of double meanings; as will be seen in chapter 6, this is an essential quality of slave speech as presented in the plays, and the scene pulls the audience into collusion. Onstage, her double meanings are picked up – sometimes – by Toxilus, who responds with his own double speeches to the pimp and with metatheatrical asides; he appreciates her cleverness, but she shows the audience something else, that he ignores: the pathos of her situation and its repugnance to her. As always, this is there for the taking, and any one

---

[16] These "shut up" lines recur in the plays, often addressed to women; see Dutsch 2008: 46, and compare chapter 4 on the situations in which slaves call their owners *stultus*.

audience member may pick it up or not. Meanwhile, the pimp leaves no
doubt what her fate will be as his possession. Toxilus introduces her to him
as she enters, in words that echo the first we hear of Telestis; the pimp asks,
"Is this that stolen virgin?" and Toxilus replies, "God, she certainly looks
like a free person, whoever she is" (*specie quidem edepol liberalist, quiquis
est*, 546). As with Telestis, *specie ... liberalist* is presented as a selling point;
already, when luring the pimp, Toxilus has described her as "a free-type
(*liberalem*) virgin, with a very choice shape" (521); this is why he wants
her in the first place, as he tells her father – "because she has a charming
and free-type shape" (*quia forma lepida et liberali est*, 130). During the sale
scene, Toxilus urges, "I think she's of high birth (*summo genere*); you'll
make a fortune on her" (651–2); and Toxilus repeats this idea at the end of
the sale: "Does she remember freedom enough, [or what]? She's going to
bring you in a nice haul" (*satin ut meminit libertatis? dabit haec tibi grandis
bolos*, 658). That is, she must be fresh goods if she thinks this way; men will
pay good money to have sex with the former daughter of a *summus vir*; the
pimp will be the beneficiary. Toxilus' assessment is prompted by the final
exchange between the pimp and the girl, as the Virgo repeats that her family will come for her (655–7):

> TO. audin quid ait? VI. nam etsi res sunt fractae, amici sunt tamen.
> DO. ne sis plora; libera eris actutum, si crebro cades.
> vin mea esse? VI. dum quidem ne nimi' diu tua sim, volo.

> TO. Do you hear what she says? VI. Because even if our lives are broken,
> we still have friends.
> DO. Don't cry, please; you'll be free right away – if you fall over frequently.
> Do you want to be mine (*mea*)? VI. As long as I'm not yours too long,
> I want to.

"Even if our lives are broken, we still have friends" ostensibly refers to the
(fictive) war in Arabia, and truthfully refers to the parasite's poverty and
the "friends" (all slaves themselves) who have put her in this position; her
tears are fake (for the play-within-the-play) and real (for what her father
has done to her); appropriately so, as the pimp's consolation ends with the
crude reminder of how a *meretrix* might possibly become a freedwoman.
The pimp, like her father, conceives of her as *mea*; her final words ostensibly express the wishes of the Arabian girl, and in fact express the wishes
of the Virgo that her father should hurry up (cf. 724).
    The doubleness of the Virgo's speeches within the sale scene is repeat-
edly marked by asides, both by herself and by Toxilus, that spotlight her
abilities as a liar (606–8, 610, 622–3, 626, 630, 634–5, 639). Throughout,

Toxilus sees what the pimp cannot, while the audience sees what neither of them can: her resistance. She begins with a statement on slavery and truth-telling (615–16):

> ... TO. heus tu, advigila. VI. satis est dictum: quamquam ego serva sum,
> scio ego officium meum, ut quae rogiter vera, ut accepi, eloquar.

> ... TO. Hey you, wake up. VI. Enough said: although I am a slave-woman,
> I know my duty, that I should tell the truth about what I'm asked, as
>   I received it.

This is essentially what Acropolistis says to Periphanes: I will tell you the truth you tell me to tell you. The Virgo hereby repeats to Toxilus that she will perform as stipulated; she hereby tells the pimp that she is a good slave. As the audience knows, she is also repeating the promise she gave to her father that she will tell the lies in which he had coached her (378–82); yet, exercising her independence as best she can under restraint, she manages to tell the actual truth at the same time – a recurrent characteristic of slave speech in Plautus.

The pimp tells her not to be surprised if they ask her a few questions. She replies, "Why should I be surprised, Mister? / My slavery has forbidden me to be surprised at anything bad that happens to me" (*qur ego hic mirer, mi homo? / servitus mea mi interdixit ne quid mirer meum malum*, 620–1). And she weeps; "Don't cry," says the pimp (*noli flere*, 622). Her *servitus* is both the state she is acting and the state into which her father has thrust her; her tears are, again, both fake and real. Toxilus exclaims his approval; the pimp asks her name. *Lucridi nomen in patria fuit*, she replies (624) – "My name in my fatherland was Casha." Painfully true.

The pimp asks where she was born, and she replies with an old joke: "as my mother / told me, in the kitchen" (*ut mihi / mater dixit, in culina*, 630–1). A similar joke appears in the *Life of Aesop* as a smart answer given by a slave during sale, so, like the girl, it has an appropriate pedigree for a slave (*Vit. Aes.* 25); but she knows that the kitchen is, in truth, where her father's plan originated, and the audience knows she reproved him for it. Toxilus gets only the joke; the pimp gets nothing, and carefully explains that he wanted to know her *patria* (635; same structure in *Vit. Aes.* 25). She replies cagily, "What one should I have, unless this one where I am now?" (636): just what a good slave should say, whose national bonds are broken with her natal bonds – not that the Arabian girl is happy about this; nor is the Virgo, whose *pater* has sold her. The pimp persists: "But I'm asking about the *patria* that was (*fuit*)" (636); she replies (637–8), "I count for nothing everything that was (*fuit*), since it is past (*fuit*);/ just like a person, when he's breathed his last, why would you ask him who he was (*fuit*)?" A concise illustration of what Patterson calls "social death." Toxilus pretends to bully the name of her *patria* out of her, and she answers like a good slave: "Since I'm a slave here, this is my *patria*" (*quando hic servio, haec patriast mea*, 641). Or, she can tell she is in her father's country, because she is enslaved here.

The pimp keeps up the interrogation: "Was your father captured?" "Not captured," she replies, "but what he had, he lost" (*non captus, sed quod habuit perdidit*, 644). Toxilus, still playing salesman, comments to the pimp that this shows she is *bono genere nata*, "born from a good family" (like Telestis), for "she knows nothing but to speak the truth" (*nihil scit nisi verum loqui*, 645) – acknowledging, perhaps, the Virgo's comment on what her father has done to her, and once again pointing to the salability of lost high status. "High status" here means "truthful," with reference to slaves' reputation for lying (hence the shock value of Paegnium's remarks on owners' *fides*); the Virgo, of course, *is* lying, and both Toxilus and the audience can understand her – they speak her language. The pimp insists on having her father's name; she replies that her father should be called *Miser* and that she should be called *Misera* (646–7), speaking for the Arab and his daughter, her father and herself: "Pitiable (male)," "Pitiable (female)."[17] Finally, the pimp asks about her father's standing; the Virgo replies, "Nobody was a more welcome guest: / both slaves and free people used to love him" (*nemo quisquam acceptior: / servi liberique amabant*, 648–9). That is, he was a *parasitus*; "love" in the past tense here is sad, and pushes the pun on *liberi*, "free people," and *liberi*, "his children" – but the Virgo herself used to be free, both as the Arabian girl and as herself. Toxilus' double-edged comment to the pimp echoes *quod habuit, perdidit* in the Virgo's earlier speech: the father is in truth a miserable man, since "he's been thoroughly lost himself, and has lost those who bore him goodwill" (*ipsus probe perditust et benevolentis perdidit*, 650).

Here an audience familiar with natal alienation and social death saw it acted out onstage, in a rare major role for a respectable girl – a technically respectable girl, a poor girl (no dowry but her father's jokes, 389–96), and as such much too close to enslavement. She and the actor whose voice spoke her words told the audience what it feels like to be threatened with a beating, and what it feels like to be sold, far from home one way or the other. Ennius' tragedy *Andromacha* probably told its audience the same

---

[17] On female characters' use of this adjective to describe themselves in Plautus, see Dutsch 2008: 108–10.

thing; what makes this scene funny is the Virgo scoring off the pimp, who, as we know (this is comedy), will lose.[18]

Much more minor slave-woman characters tell the truth in the corners of Plautus' plays, and sometimes not in double language at all. Roles like this in Greek comedy, with its restrictions on speaking parts, were usually mute. We might not expect much of these bit-part players; as the pimp in *Curculio* says to the soldier, "I don't count [you] as worth any more than my slave-woman who cleans the toilet" (*non pluris facio quam ancillam meam quae latrinam lavat*, 580). Like Dordalus (and all pimps), the pimp in *Curculio* is an unsympathetic character, and this line invites a reaction from *ancillae* in the audience in the midst of the general amusement of watching the pimp and the soldier insult each other in this scene. The plays do open up space for the viewpoint of *ancillae*, and even show where the category *ancillae* itself had fracture lines: the sex-slave Pasicompsa says, "I wasn't trained to be a porter / or herd sheep in the country or nurse babies" (*non didici baiiolare* / *nec pecua ruri pascere nec pueros nutricare*, *Mer.* 508–9), while less glamorous *ancillae* do hard labor (see below). As seen in chapter 2, nobody wants to be a *baiiolus*; so it is a shout-out to drudges that the outstanding example of empowered speech by a slave-woman in Plautus comes from the wholly obscure Syra in *Mercator*, first seen carrying luggage: a minor character who appears in four scenes, attendant on the neighbor's wife (670), *nutrix* of her son (809); an old woman of eighty-four (673); by her generic name, a Syrian, considered both the most servile of slaves (*Trin.* 542) and the ugliest of slave-women, fit only for menial work (*Mer.* 415–16; probably *Truc.* 541) – dark-skinned, like Syrian male slaves (Starks 2010: 68; cf. Marshall 2006: 148–9). Out of the blue, she launches into a monologue decrying the double standard for married men and married women. As will be seen below, slave-women in Plautus do not usually express sympathy for *matronae*, but the reverse.[19] This speech is as extraordinary in its way as Medea's famous lines on the lot of women in Euripides' *Medea*, although, fittingly, it is much less well known (*Mer.* 817–29):

---

[18] In fact at least one of Andromacha's speeches from this play became so famous that people still knew it by heart in Cicero's time; see Manuwald 2015: 177, and discussion in Jeppesen 2016: 143–5.

[19] See Dutsch 2008: 118–19, on slave-women who see themselves as extensions of their female owners. On Syra's speech, see James 2012, Dunsch 2014, and esp. Starks, who sets it in the context of Syrian-ness in Plautus generally, arguing that "the comedian employs Syra's name as a first indicator and continuous signifier that she and her ethnicity should symbolize longsuffering slavery for the Roman audience" (2010: 63). Dunsch 2014 focuses on the issue of how much the speech owes to its putative Greek original. The speech has never been included in Lefkowitz and Fant's standard reader on women in antiquity (4th ed. 2016), and its content has only recently aroused much discussion.

Ecastor lege dura vivont mulieres
multoque iniquiore miserae quam viri.
nam si vir scortum duxit clam uxorem suam,
id si rescivit uxor, inpunest viro;   820
uxor virum si clam domo egressa est foras,
viro fit caussa, exigitur matrumonio.
utinam lex esset eadem quae uxori est viro;
nam uxor contenta est quae bona est uno viro:
qui minu' vir una uxore contentus siet?   825
ecastor faxim, si itidem plectantur viri,
si quis clam uxorem duxerit scortum suam,
ut illae exiguntur quae in se culpam commerent,
plures viri sint vidui quam nunc mulieres.

My God, women live by a hard law,
and, poor things, a much less fair way than men.
For if a husband hires a whore and hides it from his wife,
if the wife finds out, the husband goes unpunished;   820
but if a wife goes out of the house and hides it from her husband,
the husband has grounds; she is forced out of the marriage.
I wish the law was the same for a husband as for a wife;
for a wife is satisfied, if she's good, with just one husband:
why shouldn't a husband be satisfied with one wife?   825
My God, I'd fix it, if husbands were hit the same way –
whoever hired a whore and hid it from his wife –
the same way women are forced out who deserve blame,
there'd be more husbands on their own than there are wives now.

Syra never appears again in the play; what did this speech mean when
it was delivered? It is notably out of sync with what happens in the play
itself. The straying husband here (like the husbands in *Asinaria* and *Casina*
and, to some extent, *Menaechmi*) does not step out of line "unpunished";
as seen in chapter 3, the play ends with a *flagitatio* of which he is the target. His neighbor's wife Dorippa (like the wives in *Asinaria* and *Casina*
and *Menaechmi*) has no thought that she is stepping out of line by stepping outside, but uses a complete freedom of movement for strictly matri-
monial ends – as she says of her return from the country to check up
on her own elusive husband, "I've used my brains, / I've come back, to
chase down the guy who's running away from me" (*feci ingenium meum,
/ reveni, ut illum persequar qui me fugit*, 668–9). Syra comes with her, and
indeed is the one who tells her that a *mulier meretrix* is (misleadingly, as
it will turn out) ensconced in her house (685). As for being "forced out of
the marriage": divorce in the plays, when mooted, is most emphatically
brought up by female characters who have been wronged (Alcumena, *Am.*

882–90, 925–30, speaking the words of the divorce formula, cf. her husband at 813, 852; the unnamed wife in *Menaechmi*, 719–807, cf. her husband at 113). Although Cleostrata's neighbor warns her to watch out lest
she hear the words *i foras, mulier* (*Cas.* 210–12), Cleostrata is not worried;
in *Mercator*, Dorippa has just sent Syra to fetch her father, with divorce in
mind (*Mer.* 784–8). Like Dorippa, who speaks of her husband as a runaway slave (*fugit*), the wife in *Menaechmi* addresses (the man she thinks is)
her husband in terms used of slaves (710–11, cf. chapter 6) and repeatedly
describes his behavior as *flagitia* (709, 719, 721, 735, 738), as Dorippa does
of her own husband (784). On the other hand, the plays themselves subject
these wives to cascades of abuse, and Menaechmus I's wife is reproached
by her father onstage precisely for treating her husband as a slave (*Men.*
766–7), in particular for treating him as an *ancilla* (795–97).[20] Yet within
the calculus of the plays, as seen in chapter 2, this means a reversal of an
expected subordination; to an *ancilla* sitting in the audience, the idea that
a *matrona* might make her husband sit with the *ancillae* and card wool, as
the father sarcastically suggests here, might have a certain appeal. Onstage,
then, things work more the way Syra thinks they should.

Thus Syra, in her monologue, joins the group of unlikely characters in
the plays who editorialize on moral issues, showing where injustice lies
(see chapter 6). Plenty of these speeches, as seen in previous chapters, are
made by slaves and *parasiti*: Mercurius on electoral abuse, Sosia on abusive
owners, Curculio on bankers, and, in a way, the *puer* in *Pseudolus* on the
plight of a child prostitute. Syra here uses the language of fairness and punishment first seen in chapter 2 in Sosia's opening song; she appeals to the
rule of law, and adds her voice to those of other slaves who complain about
the use of prostitutes by free men, like Syncerastus in *Poenulus*, or the *grex*
at the end of *Bacchides*. Her monologue follows a scene between her and
her former nursling Eutychus, who identifies himself as her "owner and
nursling" (*erus atque alumnus tuo' sum*), to which she replies, "Hello, little
nursling" (*salve, alumnule*, 809): putting him in his place. Eutychus exits
this scene with the command "Follow me" (*sequere me*, 816), but Syra stays
put, and makes her speech. When she herself first enters, toting Dorippa's
luggage, Dorippa complains because she walks so slowly (670–1), and
Syra answers, as if setting up for a very old joke, that she is bearing a
heavy load (672). "What load?" replies Dorippa, the straight line, and Syra

[20] On the idea of the husband of a wealthy wife as a "dowry slave," often remarked on by scholars as
a stock theme, see Duckworth 1952: 255–6, 282–5; Rei 1998; Stärk 1990; and comments in James
forthcoming.

answers, "Eighty years and four: / and, added to that, slavery, sweat, thirst"
(*annos octoginta et quattuor: / et eodem accedit servitus, sudor, sitis*, 673–4).[21]
A joke – she needs a drink; but she bears witness.

Syra is not unique; other secondary slave-women, here and there, take
center stage. At the end of *Amphitruo*, Bromia has a major song describing
the thunder-accompanied childbirth of Alcumena, and plays the key role
of recognizing Amphitruo and raising him up from the ground, where he
is lying as if dead (1076). She is the one who makes him recognize that he
is wrong to think Alcumena has been unchaste: "I'll make you say otherwise" (*faciam tu idem ut aliter praedices*, 1085). The old woman Staphyla
in *Aulularia* defies the miser Euclio and champions his daughter (74–5).
Pardalisca in *Casina*, in addition to a substantial soliloquy and several big
sung scenes, has a major song reporting on dramatic events, during which
she makes her owner's husband catch her as she pretends to faint (634)
and makes him believe she is making a pass at him (635–42). Halisca in
Cistellaria has a long scene (Act 4, Scene 2) which begins with a song
(671–703) as she searches for the tracks of those who might have taken the
missing *cistella* (who are in plain view onstage) and asks the spectators to
point out which way they went (678–9). At the end of her scene she denies
any authority – "I am just a female slave" (*ego serva sum*, 765) – but (as with
the *lena* in *Curculio*) her one appearance onstage includes a meaty musical number. Stephanium in *Stichus*, although she does not have a song,
does have a metatheatrical monologue addressing the audience (673–82),
in the iambic septenarii that Moore notes are often associated with the
entrance of prostitutes (2012: 185); with her entrance at 673 begins the
major party scene.

The prostitutes' *ancillae* – unnamed in *Menaechmi*, Milphidippa in
Miles, Sophoclidisca in *Persa*, and above all Astaphium in *Truculentus* – are
different from most other *ancillae* in that they make conscious use of sexual
power. Scapha in *Mostellaria*, whatever her status, coaches Philematium on
the use of her body to control her lover. The plays paint no rosy view of
this power; indeed, as will be seen below, women's sexual power is both
exploited and resented onstage (cf. Dutsch 2008: 60–81). Nor do female
slaves, as you might expect, complain about the sexual use made of them
by their owners, although male slaves commonly complain of their own
exploitation, as seen in chapter 2; the substitution of a male slave for the
title character in *Casina* epitomizes the situation. A brief run of lines from
Bromia's interactions with her owner at the end of *Amphitruo* perhaps

---

[21] On slave complaints about their heavy load as an old joke already in *Frogs*, see chapter 1.

constitutes an exception. After her song about Alcumena's childbirth, she recognizes Amphitruo (1075–7):

> [BR.] ibo et cognoscam, quisquis est. Amphitruo hic quidem <est>
> erus meus.
> Amphitruo. AM. perii. BR. surge. AM. interii. BR. cedo manum. AM. quis
> me tenet?
> BR. tua Bromia ancilla. …

> [BR.] I'll go up and see, whoever he is. Indeed this is Amphitruo my owner.
> Amphitruo. AM. I'm dead. BR. Get up. AM. I'm a goner. BR. Give me
> your hand. AM. Who is holding me?
> BR. Your Bromia slave-woman. …

Amphitruo has suffered throughout the play, and particularly towards the end, from confused identity and lack of recognition, especially from the god impersonating his slave Sosia; here Bromia gives her owner what he wants: proper name and status recognition, wound up with her own self-naming. At the same time, she is in control, and perhaps she recognizes more than just his face (1082–4):

> [AM.] scin me tuom esse erum Amphitruonem? BR. scio. AM. vide etiam
> nunc. BR. scio.
> AM. haec sola sanam mentem gestat meorum familiarium.
> BR. immo omnes sani sunt profecto. …

> [AM.] Do you know I am your owner Amphitruo? BR. I know. AM. Look
> again now. BR. I know.
> AM. This woman has the only sane mind among everyone in my
> household.
> BR. No, they're all sane, for sure. …

In performance, the double recognition in line 1082 would have to be justified by a gesture, arguably the lifting of Amphitruo's *pallium* to reveal a stage phallus; Bromia would then be commenting on Amphitruo as the familiar user of his whole household, a surefire laugh line for an audience with comparable experience.[22] More on this below. The parallel with Eurykleia's recognition of Odysseus (*Od.* 19.392–3, 467–8) by the scar "above the knee" (450) suggests the second look is not at Amphitruo's face. Odysseus' scar certainly fuels a joke in *Poenulus* (see chapter 7 on Agorastocles' monkey-bite scar).

---

[22] On the possible use of some form of phallus in Roman comedy, see Marshall 2006: 62–4, 66, and above, chapter 2.

A more explicit, and, to a modern audience, an admirable instance of speaking truth to power is provided by two slave-women in *Truculentus* who barely have names; they are identified only as "Ancilla," and, once again, "Syra" (see Starks 2010: 59–60, on ethnic slurs in this scene). Callicles, husband of the Ancilla's owner, brings them onstage, bound, announcing that he has just interrogated them in the house while they were hung up and flogged (775–9); he wants them to confirm their testimony, or he will kill them (*necem*, 781) or turn them over to the professional torturers, the "men with the bells" (*tintinnaculos … viros*, 782; cf. *Ps.* 332). The Ancilla responds ambiguously to this threat: without Lindsay's punctuation, *vis subigit verum fateri ita lora laedunt bracchia* ("force presses [us] to speak the truth the straps are hurting our arms so," 783). On the surface, this means, "We are forced to speak the truth, because the straps are hurting us." More simply, it means, "We are forced to speak the truth, which is, that the straps hurt us." The Ancilla's testimony reinforces this sense as an important truth later in the interrogation; the two women remain bound throughout the scene (784, 836–8). Meanwhile, as Callicles begins the onstage interrogation, he separates the women and shoves himself between them (*divorsae state – em sic, istuc volo*, 787), telling them not to make signs to each other and blocking their view of each other – "I'll be the wall" (*neve inter vos significetis, ego ero paries*, 788). This blocking sets the three of them up in a sort of reverse *flagitatio*, as Callicles cues each of them to speak (*loquere tu*, 788, 796, 799) or be silent (*tace*, 791 twice; *satis es fassa*, 792; *cave tu nisi quod te rogo*, 801): "Shut up," "You've admitted enough," "Watch out, you, except when I'm asking you something." As in a *flagitatio*, they have nothing pleasant to say to him, although he is the one trying to regain possession of a lost object.

Callicles wants to know what has happened to the baby his daughter gave birth to as a result of her rape, and the two slave-women tell him plainly. He exclaims, "Look, there it is: women's wrongdoing" (*vide sis facinus muliebre*, 809). This leads to an exchange between him and the Ancilla (810–15):

> AN. magi' pol haec malitia pertinet ad viros quam ad mulieres: 810
> vir illam, non mulier praegnatem fecit. CA. idem ego istuc scio.
> tu bona ei custos fuisti. AN. plus potest qui plus valet.
> vir erat, plus valebat: vicit, quod petebat apstulit.
> CA. et tibi quidem hercle idem attulit magnum malum.
> AN. de istoc ipsa, etsi tu taceas, reapse experta intellego.   815

AN. God, this kind of badness has more to do with men than with
    women;   810
a man, not a woman, made her pregnant. CA. I know that myself.
You were a good guardian to her. AN. The one who is stronger has
    more power.
He was a man, he was stronger; he won, he took what he wanted.
CA. And to you, by God, he brought a big beating.
AN. About that, I know myself, even if you'd shut up, because I felt it
    for real.   815

The cowardly Diniarchus has been hiding in plain sight onstage through-out the scene, so that the audience is reminded that Callicles is blaming the wrong people; like the audience, the Ancilla knows he is there (817). The rapist is literally exposed here, and repeatedly confesses his fear of exposure (773–4, 785–86, 794–5, 818–20, 823–4). It is the Ancilla who finally points him out and names him: "I see you" (*video ego te*, 822); "Diniarchus" (825). Callicles cannot see him until he steps forward and speaks (826). After the two men have it out, the Ancilla tells Callicles that he is doing wrong by keeping the two slave-women bound (836–7): "See to it, please, that you don't commit a great and insulting injustice" (*vide quaeso magnam ne facias iniuriam*, 836). He at once unbinds them and sends them offstage. This in a culture where all slave testimony was elicited under torture; like other low characters onstage, the Ancilla lays claim to honor (see chapter 2 on the delict of *iniuria*).

This scene allows the (actor playing the) slave-woman not only to blame men for rape and its consequences – consequences affecting both her own-er's daughter and herself – but to defend herself against a charge of neg-ligence through a critique of power and to testify to her own experience of pain: *de istoc ipsa, etsi tu taceas, reapse experta intellego* (815). She insists on it: *ipsa, reapse, experta*. Her words *plus potest qui plus valet* (812) speak, however briefly, for those in the audience who have been overpowered. At the same time, the owner admits to his own knowledge about how impreg-nation works (*idem ego istuc scio*, 811). What the two slave-women here have done is to conceal the birth of a baby boy to a raped free woman and to give that baby to a *meretrix* – an act similar to those whereby Selenium became the foster child of a *meretrix* in *Cistellaria* and Casina became an *ancilla*. Maybe this suggests why the play gives these two slave-women the job of speaking for all women in this slave society: they know the inside secrets of servile birth. The existence of the word *verna* ("slave born in the household") testifies in part to male owners' sexual use of their house-hold's slave-women, in part to the coupling of male and female slaves, both producing the desirable byproduct of more slaves. As seen in chapter 2, the word is used only rarely in the plays: of Sosia in *Amphitruo;* in a self-loathing abstraction by a *puer* in *Bacchides* (*sine vernilitate,* fr. ix); and by the nasty Periplectomenus in *Miles Gloriosus,* in a long rant explaining why he would never marry. Imitating the speech of an extortionate wife, he includes among the expenses she demands, "Aren't you going to send anything to the *nutrix* who feeds the *vernae?*" (*nutrici non missurus quicquam quae vernas alit,* 698). Phronesium, lying to her soldier, lists wine for the *nutrix* among her expenses (a joke, *Truc.* 903), but evidently does assign slave-women to "give that boy the tit" (*puero isti date mammam,* 448). They could do it because they had given birth themselves. These open secrets about the circulation and nurture of babies in a slave society are, like the rapist Diniarchus, exposed onstage in the *palliata.* As another rapist says of the old slave-woman Staphyla, whom he describes as *pedisequa nutrice anu,* "slave attendant, wet-nurse, old woman": "she knows what happened" (*ea rem novit, Aul.* 807).

Only once in the plays is a slave-woman reunited with her child, and it is the Carthaginian *nutrix* Giddenis, who finds her own son as she assists her old owner in the finding of his lost daughters (*Poen.* 1122–46). Giddenis herself attests to the paradoxes within a *familia* that includes two sets of children, free and slave, both cared for by a *nutrix* alongside an *uxor.*[23] The *Menaechmi* prologue speaker (19–21) credits the twins with two mothers, "their mother who gave the tit" (*mater sua … quae mammam dabat*) and "the very mother who bore them" (*mater ipsa quae illos pepererat*). The *Poenulus* prologue addresses *nutrices* in the audience, complete with babies (28–31), immediately before it addresses *matronae.* The extended meaning of the word *familia* incorporates what all women in that *familia* have in common: they are all expected to be *morigerae.*

Although the plots of the plays sometimes depend, as here in *Truculentus,* on women's networks (see Feltovich 2011; cf. Bradley 1989: 28–9), wives in the plays stand in opposition to their husbands' access to sex objects – slave-women (Casina in *Casina,* Pasicompsa in *Mercator*) or paid prostitutes (Philaenium in *Asinaria,* Erotium in *Menaechmi*). The freedwoman *lena* in *Cistellaria* goes into detail; dispensing sage advice to her friend, the youthful *meretrix* and would-be wife Selenium, she suggests that "our kind"

---

[23] For a survey of the evidence on the *nutrix* as object and subject during the principate, see Joshel 1986. Sharon James reminds me that Terence picks up on the politics inherent in this relationship at the end of *Adelphoe,* where the newly freed Syrus asks that his wife Phrygia be freed as well, because "she was the first to give the tit / to your grandson, this guy's son" (*tuo nepoti huius filio / hodie prima mammam dedit haec, Ad.* 974–5).

(*hunc ordinem*, 23) should cultivate *amicitia* like the "high-born daughters, high-class *matronae*" (*summo genere gnatas, summatis matronas*, 25) – a phrase that recalls not only the "high birth" attributed to the enslaved Telestis and Virgo as a selling point, but also the arrogant *summi viri* seen in chapters 2 and 3. And, indeed, her own words remind her of the lack of *amicitia* between *matronae* and *meretrices*, and she sings (27–37):

> si idem istuc nos faciamus, si imitemur, ita tamen vix vivimus
> cum invidia summa. suarum opum nos volunt esse indigentis.
> > nostra copia nil volunt nos potesse   29, 30
> > suique omnium rerum nos indigere,
> > > ut sibi simus supplices.
> eas si adeas, abitum quam aditum malis, ita nostro ordini
> > palam blandiuntur, clam, si occasio usquam est,
> > > aquam frigidam subdole suffundunt.   35
> > viris cum suis praedicant nos solere,
> > suas paelices esse aiunt, eunt depressum.

> If we'd do the same thing, if we'd imitate them, even so we hardly get along,
> and with the highest degree of ill-will from them. They want us in need of
> their wealth.
> > They want us to be able to make use of our own resources
> > not at all   29, 30
> > and want us to need everything of theirs,
> > > so that we'll have to beg from them.
> If you'd go up to them, you'd prefer the exit to the entrance, the way they
> > openly sweet-talk our kind, then in secret, if they get the chance,
> > > they sneakily pour cold water [on us].   35
> > They say we're always doing it with their husbands,
> > They say we're their rivals, they want to put us down.

This zero-sum game, with one group demanding that the other be subordinated (*supplices*, 32), recalls the power games in scenes acting out male slaves' desires, as when Sagaristio says his owner "shouldn't think I'll beg him for mercy" (*ne sibi me credat supplicem fore*, *Per.* 271), or Epidicus refuses to humiliate himself (chapter 4). The speech of this freed *lena* also strongly recalls, in its terms, the speeches of the freed Advocati in *Poenulus*, proud of their self-sufficiency (chapter 3). That the *lena* twice speaks of "our kind" (*ordinem*, 23; *ordini*, 33), as opposed to *matronae* as a group, perhaps constitutes a sort of class consciousness – certainly solidarity; even in relation to the means of production, since sex work is labor.[24] Onstage,

---

[24] For the evidence of an *ordo matronarum*, see most recently Valentini 2012, with the reviews by James (2015b) and Schultz (2013): some group actions are attested by much later sources. The song of the *lena* is interesting in its treatment of *matronae* as necessarily upper class and freedwomen as forced

matronae do express disdain for prostitutes (see chapter 2). Cleostrata in *Casina*, unprovoked by any *meretrix*, says casually to her grumbling husband, "It's not the job of *matronae*, but of prostitutes, / husband dear, to make sweet talk to other people's husbands" (*non matronarum officiumst, sed meretricium, / viris alienis, mi vir, subblandirier*, 585–6). In *Epidicus*, Periphanes orders a hired *fidicina* to be housed apart from the woman he thinks is his daughter, because "the manners of a maiden are far different from those of a whore" (*divortunt mores virgini longe ac lupae*, 403) – a rare use of *lupa* in Plautus. As it turns out, the "daughter" is the ex-*fidicina* Acropolistis, and the hired *fidicina* is her friend; both have been slaves; they are not different at all, but Periphanes sees what he believes. The audience knows better, though, and the joke is that there is no visible difference between virgin and whore. Has sexual use made Acropolistis different in kind from Telestis? When Philippa – no *matrona* herself – harshly differentiates Acropolistis from the daughter she is seeking, she speaks as a poor woman, raped as a girl, well acquainted with the thin margin that separates poor girls from prostitution. This is what worries the Virgo in *Persa* (383–9): a bad reputation means no marriage, especially when a girl has no dowry.

The divisions among women voiced by the *lena* in *Cistellaria* are well attested, for later periods, in one major area of women's real life. Roman women's religion acted out slave/free divisions among women; throughout the year, festivals encouraged women to make a public display of the relative degrees of licit access to their bodies – for example, the Matralia on June 11, where *matronae* drove a slave-woman out of an enclosure by slapping her, or the Nonae Caprotinae on July 7, when slave-women held a feast and mock battle outside the city, commemorating a time when Roman slave-women saved the *matronae* from being raped by an invading enemy force by standing in for them. Class divisions in worship, even among free women, are attested for the cults of Pudicitia (from 296 BCE) and Fortuna Virilis.[25] While some goddesses' worship included special rituals for slave-women, the cult of Venus – by the first century CE, a prominent women's cult all over

---

into prostitution (38–9), since freedwomen could legally marry, even onstage (Ampelisca in *Rudens*); see Fantham 2011, 2015: 92–3, and, on the legal status of *libertae*, M. Perry 2014. The analysis of sex work here goes back to Engels, *Origin of the Family, Private Property, and the State*, and has a large current bibliography.

[25] On class division in Roman women's religion, see Dolansky 2011; Richlin 2014a: 197–240; Schultz 2007; and the excellent discussion in Clark 2007: 39–69 on Pudicitia Plebeia in the context of the wars and politics of the 200s BCE.

Italy – manifests, like other cults, a marked lack of epigraphic evidence of slave-women's participation, so perhaps the welcoming of the ship-wrecked prostitutes Palaestra and Ampelisca by the priestess of Venus came as something of a surprise in the plotline of *Rudens*. In that case, Ampelisca's monologue describing their welcome has a certain edge to it (408–11):

> ut lepide, ut liberaliter, ut honeste atque hau gravate
> timidas, egentis, uvidas, eiectas, exanimatas
> accepit ad sese, hau secus quam si ex se simus natae! 410
> ut eapse <sic> succincta aquam calefactat, ut lavemus!

> How charmingly, how freely, how respectably and not grudgingly
> she welcomed to herself [us] frightened women, needy, wet, castaway, half-dead,
> not otherwise than if we were born of her! 410
> How she's hiked up her skirt and heats up the water herself, so we can have a bath!

The model is mother–daughter, and at first sight the two prostitutes optimistically hail her as mother (263, cf. chapter 8), but the priestess here ministers to the prostitutes as if she were their *ancilla*; *succincta* marks an action associated in Latin with laborers, and bathing a prostitute is elsewhere the job of her *ancillae* (*Poen.* 222–4). Indeed, the *Poenulus* sisters are getting ready for the "Aphrodisia" festival, viewing it less as a holy day than as as an opportunity for competitive display, like the triumphal return of the legions in *Epidicus*: goodness, as Mae West said, had nothing to do with it.[26] As for the priestess as mother, the recognition of lost girls by their mothers appears within the plays as a rarity, a good thing greatly desired (below); Telestis maintains she is *some* woman's daughter; later in *Rudens*, Palaestra will be greeted by her real mother with open arms, but Ampelisca will go on without parents of any kind.

Scapha in *Mostellaria*, in attendance after the bath, has a different take on what the status of *matrona* means, neatly balancing Cleostrata's dictum on what a prostitute's job is. Reproving the ex-*tibicina* Philematium for her monogamous relationship with her *patronus* Philolaches (188–9), she comments: "It's the lot of a *matrona*, not of a prostitute, to be a slave to

---

[26] See *Poen.* 191, 256, 264–70, 318–22, 336–40, with Henderson's remarks (1999: 8–9) on the relationship between these scenes and the temple of Venus Erycina, a Sicilian import dedicated on the Capitoline in 215 as a counterbalance to the defeat at Lake Trasimene in 217 (Livy 22.9.10, 22.10.10; 23.30.13, 23.31.9). *Ludi* were vowed at the same time. On the fashion show at *Epid.* 222–35, see James forthcoming.

one lover" (*matronae, non meretricium, est unum inservire amantem*, 190). She means this literally; now that Philolaches has freed her, Philematium need no longer care if he loves her or not (209–11). Scapha warns that Philematium will regret it in old age "if you are a slave to him alone" (*si illum inservibis solum*, 216). Philematium does not listen; she feels indebted to Philolaches because he freed her (167, 204–5). He agrees. The practical *lena* in *Cistellaria* likewise tells Selenium that monogamy is for *matronae* (78–81), and observes that, if her daughter Gymnasium does not "get married" on a daily basis, she and the *lena* will starve (42–45). Gymnasium jokes that Alcesimarchus' upcoming marriage should be no barrier to the continuation of his love for Selenium (103); Phronesium in *Truculentus* coolly tells Diniarchus that he can always return to her when he begins to fear his wife (879–80).

The point at issue between *matronae* and *meretrices* is not hard to see, and it is explicitly stated by the *lena* in her opening song (*Cist.* 37): wives fear sexual rivals for their husbands. The sorely tried Artemona complains that her husband (a senator, 871) will not have sex with her, and knows that he is with a *scortum* and "plowing another's field" (*As.* 867, 872–4). The word *paelex* is used not only by the *lena*, but by the old slave-woman Syra in *Mercator*, who urges her owner to go and see the *meretrix* she thinks has been installed in their house, calling her "your *paelex* Alcumena, my Juno" (*tuam Alcumenam paelicem, Iuno mea*, 690). This casual remark throws light on the status of Alcumena as the lead female character in *Amphitruo*: wife of an absent soldier, available for use by a (married) male of higher status. The address *Iuno mea* evokes those who label the top position "Jupiter" (Lysidamus and his *vilicus* Olympio, *Cas.* 331–7, 406–7; Saturio, desiring food, to Toxilus, *Per.* 99–100), sometimes reversing the expected roles (Ergasilus of himself, to his *patronus* Hegio, *Capt.* 863): gods as *summi viri*, a relational term. The *paelex* as a category in relation to the wife is also marked by the old farmer Daemones, explaining to the two shipwrecked slave prostitutes that his wife will kick him out of the house (*extrudat aedibus*) if he gives them shelter: "She'll say I've taken *paelices* before her eyes" (*paelices adduxe dicet ante oculos suos*, *Rud.* 1046–7). Prostitutes are necessarily kept outside the home; that wives had to look for rivals first in their own homes is the central point of *Casina*. Indeed, the substitution of the male slave Chalinus for the slave-woman Casina reminds the audience that females were not the only rivals, an aspect that is underscored in the play by Lysidamus' behavior with his *vilicus* Olympio (452–66, with Chalinus' comment on his own experiences with the owner, chapter 2). But *paelex* is a derogatory term, and restricted in the plays to women.[27]

Jealousy of female house slaves must underlie the running joke in *Mercator* that Pasicompsa is too pretty to be an *ancilla* for the young man's mother (210–11, 395–417). An *ancilla*, argues his father – who fully intends to buy Pasicompsa and have sex with her – should be able to do hard physical labor, cook, and take a beating (396–8); Pasicompsa cannot be his wife's attendant "respectably enough" (404) because, as seen in chapter 3, men will harass her in the street (406–9) and accuse his wife and him of pimping her (410–11). The proper *ancilla* for the young man's mother, says his father, will be (414–16)

> ancillam viraginem aliquam non malam, forma mala,
> ut matrem addecet familias, aut Syram aut Aegyptiam: 415
> ea molet, coquet, conficiet pensum, pinsetur flagro.
>
> some strapping *ancilla* – not a bad woman, but one with an ill shape,
> as befits a *materfamilias*, either a Syrian or an Egyptian: 415
> she'll grind grain, cook, finish her wool quota, get beaten by the whip.

The intersection of slavery/gender/sexuality/ethnicity/color here shows its face for a moment, tying dark skin to drudgery and the lash; one of the two bound women in *Truculentus* (above) is named Syra, like old Syra in *Mercator* itself. Later, the neighbor *senex* teases Pasicompsa as she weeps, fearing she will be expected to carry heavy loads, tend flocks, or act as a wet-nurse (508–9); he then turns a putative discussion of her weaving skills into a speculation on her sexual skills (518–27; cf. James 2010 on Pasicompsa's deployment of flirtation in this scene).

The husband in Caecilius' *Plocium*, in one of the fragments quoted by Aulus Gellius (2.23.10), complains that his wife has nagged him into selling an *ancilla* of whom she was jealous; the wife, he claims, is now boasting that she has done him out of his *paelex*. Gellius quotes this section to show how different Caecilius is from Menander, whom Gellius far prefers, and refers to Caecilius' embroideries as "some kind of other farcical stuff" (*alia nescio quae mimica*, 2.23.12); what Caecilius has added, however, is an elaborate portrayal of the old wife's boasting, ventriloquized by her hostile husband (149–56 R,):

> ea me clam se cum mea ancilla ait consuetum, id me arguit;
> ita plorando, orando, instando atque obiurgando me obtudit

---

[27] At least one antiquarian took it to be gender-neutral; see Paulus 248L (*non solum feminae, sed etiam mares*). See Brown 1990: 263 n. 37 on the rarity of the word παλλακή in Greek New Comedy.

eam uti venderem; nunc credo inter suas
aequalis et cognatas sermonem serit:
"quis vestrarum fuit integra aetatula,
quae hoc idem a viro
impetrarit suo, quod ego anus modo
effeci, paelice ut meum privarem virum?"

She said I was on familiar terms with my *ancilla*, behind her back, and
accused me of it;
so by crying, begging, standing over me, and berating me she beat me
into selling [the *ancilla*]; now I believe among
her own age-mates and female relations she casts such talk:
"Who of you has there been, in the freshness of first youth,
who's brought off the same deed from her husband
that I just did, an old woman:
I deprived my husband of his *paelex*."

The plot point comes from the original, and Gellius, summing up his
readings in both authors, labels the *ancilla* "a girl not unskilled in service
and of an appearance not unsuited to a free person" (*non inscito puellam
ministerio et facie haut inliberali*, 2.23.8); the Menandrian lines he quotes
talk only of the girl's work skills. Caecilius voices the shrew, but parallels
are rare. Cleostrata vents her anger on her husband and not on the absent
Casina; like other *matronae* in the plays, she sees the *ancillae* as her department (261), a kind of top-down solidarity. It is a puzzle that the angry
wives in Plautine comedy do not have more to say about *ancillae*, and that
ancillae are rarely shown complaining of being flogged by a female owner.
Philematium only threatens Scapha (*Mos.* 240), and Artemona admits to
having tortured her *ancillae* – wrongly, she realizes: "the poor things, guilt-
less" (*insontis miseras*, *As.* 888–9). Halisca fears a beating "if my *era* finds
out I'm as witless as I am" (*si era mea sciat tam socordem esse quam sum*, *Cist.*
673–4): a low point of self-abjection in the plays.

Yet just as Gripus in *Rudens* wants to turn into a slave-owner, slave-
women aspiring to liberty must simultaneously aspire to turn into *matronae*, as marriage is the desired or enforced end for all free young women
in the plays (the pregnant daughter of Euclio in *Aulularia*, the Virgo in
Persa, the unnamed young women to whom young men are married off in
Trinummus and *Truculentus*). Scholars today sometimes write of the plays
as if they had a "marriage plot," like romances, but marriage is shown as a
happy ending for young women with speaking roles only when their status
at the start of the play prohibits it.[28] Casina, the only household slave to

---

[28] On the plays as featuring the romance plot, see e.g. Fantham 1975: 52, "almost invariably based on
a sexual relationship frustrated by social obstacles" (writing of New Comedy as a whole); Konstan

achieve this goal (1013–14), remains offstage throughout, expressing nothing, and even the sex slaves are not shown onstage singing "Someday My Prince Will Come" or verbally rejoicing over their upcoming nuptials. They sing about finding customers (*Poen.* 236) and being pretty (*Poen.* 1174–95), or about their fall from respectability and sad plight (*Rud.* 185–219, 664–76); they rejoice to find they are free and have relatives and birthdays (Planesium, *Cur.* 655–8; Telestis, *Epid.* 639–40, 644, 648–9; Adelphasium and Anterastilis, *Poen.* 1257–68; Palaestra, *Rud.* 1144–5, 1175). Only before her birth status is recovered does the free *meretrix* Selenium speak lines that say she desires marriage (*Cist.* 77, 98–9), and she disappears at the end of Act 3. Out of nineteen plays with endings, only four end with Cinderella weddings – five, if you count *Casina*.

It is these women's young lovers who develop an eagerness to marry (Alcesimarchus in *Cistellaria* (485), Phaedromus in *Curculio*, Agorastocles in *Poenulus*, Plesidippus in *Rudens*): hard to explain in the context of comedy. Have they never been to the theater? Do they not know what to expect? Free young women in the plays arouse no such longings. Lyconides in *Aulularia* wants to marry Euclio's daughter because he has raped her and she has just given birth to his baby, while his own father had wanted to marry her because she had no dowry and he could boss her around. Lysiteles in *Trinummus* just wants to marry Lesbonicus' sister to show what a good man he is, while the cynical *senes* who arrange a marriage for the repentant Lesbonicus in the last seven lines of the play speak of marriage only as a bad joke, a punishment for bad behavior. In *Truculentus*, only when publicly shamed (by the two *ancillae*) does Diniarchus ask to marry the girl he has raped. Evidently the sexual fervor aroused by a prostitute can carry over into a betrothal; as Philematium in *Mostellaria* says she "beat" Philolaches into purchasing her freedom by "sweet-talking him" (*id extudi … illi subblandiebar, Mos.* 221), so such behavior is acted out onstage by Planesium in *Curculio* (162–214), who continues on to betrothal – uniquely, she is asked for her agreement, and gives it (*cupio*, 673).

Poenulus, to be sure, ends with hugs (1260–9, 1292–4), but these are non-erotic and include the girls' father Hanno, in contrast with a preliminary

---

1983: 24; Rosivach 1998: 1; Feeney 2010: 282, "The fundamental plot [of *Pseudolus*] resembles virtually every other Plautine plot – boy has met girl but cannot have her, but finally does get her thanks to cunning slave." Even if we do not insist on "thanks to cunning slave," this excludes *Amphitruo, Aulularia, Captivi, Casina, Epidicus Menaechmi, Mostellaria, Stichus, Trinummus*, and *Truculentus*. Peter Brown in 1990 showed in detail the falsehood of this generalization not only for Roman but for Greek New Comedy. On the issue of viewpoint, see Marshall 2015: 124: "any sense of a supposedly 'happy' ending is focalized exclusively in terms of male satisfaction."

teasing sequence in which Agorastocles first pretends to be pimping them
to their unrecognized father and they cooperate (1217–18):

> HA. gaudio ero vobeis – ADE. at edepol nos voluptati tibi.
> HA. leibertatique. ADE. istoc pretio tuas nos facile feceris.

> HA. I will be a source of joy to you – ADE. But, by God, we'll be a
> source of pleasure to you.
> HA. – and of freedom. ADE. At that price, you'll easily make us yours.

The cross-purposes in these interrupted speeches get at a basic paradox in the
enactment of slave-women and sexual desire in the *palliata*: Adelphasium
offers Hanno *voluptas*; he offers her *libertas*; she sees that as a price for
which she and her sister will become *tuas*, as his freedwomen. This is a
closed system; only recognition by a parent can switch a young woman out
of prostitution and into matrimony.

What of slave-women's own sexual desire? Is it voiced or acted out
onstage? In a way, yes: there are several flirting scenes that involve *ancillae*.
The most elaborate one is between Sophoclidisca and Paegnium in *Persa*,
where the teasing, framed as verbal dueling, has a heavy erotic charge; watching this play staged several times demonstrated to me that the words require
a lot of erotic body language and vocalization from actors. An *ancilla* in
the audience might go along with Sophoclidisca's pleasure in specularizing
Paegnium, even as Sophoclidisca is specularized at the same time. Indeed,
she might just want to watch Sophoclidisca, who makes a decidedly bigger
impression than her owner Lemniselenis, despite the use of Lemniselenis
as goal in the play and Lemniselenis' glamorous Act 5 entrance (see further below on love between women onstage and in the audience). Notably,
Sophoclidisca is among the few female characters in Plautus to make physical moves on a male character, as attested by Paegnium's protest, "Don't
you paw me, you gropie" (*ne me attrecta, subigitatrix*, 227). Ampelisca in
Rudens has a similarly sexy scene with Sceparnio (414–39), although he has
most of the erotic lines and makes all the physical moves.

Yet when Ampelisca does call Sceparnio *mea voluptas* ("my pleasure"), a
sort of voicing of desire, it is in a promise to do "what you want" (*quae voles*,
436), and this is a common usage for prostitutes onstage (see chapter 4).
The confusion of will in *mea voluptas = quae voles* epitomizes the problem in slave-women's desire onstage, especially in light of the fact that
it is voiced by male actors. So, mainly, no – slave-women's sexual desires
are not the point in the *palliata*. Astaphium, in the scene where the slave
Truculentus succumbs to her wiles (*Truc.* 669–98), serves chiefly as straight
woman for his solecisms, and when she calls him *mea voluptas* (687) this

is, as so often, untrue. Indeed, in all three scenes these characters are trying to get something, if not money. Ampelisca, who will be freed at the end of *Rudens* just so that she can marry the freed slave Trachalio, has several long scenes with him, but shows no erotic interest in him at all. And the same can be said for the rest of the *ancillae* in the plays: just as the Syrian drudges are imagined by the *senex* in *Mercator*, they are asexual. Whatever sexual desire was felt by *ancillae* in real life, the plays do not try to voice it.

At the same time, the plays know, and the audience knows, that every *ancilla* is some woman's daughter, and several plots foster the fantasy that a lost girl might be returned to her mother someday (*Cistellaria, Epidicus, Poenulus, Rudens*), or at least to her family (*Curculio, Persa*). Some are luckier than others, as emphasized by Ampelisca's last line in *Rudens*. As she and Palaestra exit after Palaestra has been recognized by her father, Ampelisca says: "That the gods love you is a pleasure to me" (*quom te di amant voluptati est mihi*, 1183). She knows her place. One of the most cynical aspects of *Casina* is the way it has Casina's *era* plot (unknowingly) to marry off her best friend's daughter (as she will turn out to be, 1013) to her son's slave, so that her son, rather than her husband, can use the girl for sex (55–9); in this play, the girl's non-appearance leaves the focus on the male slave, who speaks the play's closing speech in drag.[29]

Slave-Woman Drag

One of the problems voiced in Plautus' plays, as seen in chapters 2 and 4, is the sexual frustration of male slaves, for whom women represent a scarce commodity. This overlaps with the related problem that male slaves are themselves the target of sexual use by owners within the plays, and with the meta-problem of the sexual ambiguity of actors outside the plays, although the most direct evidence for this comes from much later sources.[30] Juvenal puts it most plainly (3.96–7): watching an actor play a woman, "you'd say everything was empty and smooth / below his belly (*ventriculum*), and split by a slender crack." The desire voiced by male characters onstage for female characters, then, is somewhat ambiguous, as will be seen, and merges with the unspoken desire of male slave characters for other male characters.

---

[29] For discussion of Casina's parentage, see Arnott 2003: 40–2, a reference I owe to Sharon James. On what the play does with her, see Marshall 2015: 129.

[30] On the actor's *infamia* and suspect sexuality as attested from the late Republic onward, see Duncan 2006: 124–59; Dutsch 2008: 179–84, with remarks on audience/actor as subject/object; Edwards 1997. See chapter 1, however, on the lack of direct evidence for theatrical *infamia* in the mid-Republic.

Pueri, after all, are specularized onstage just like attractive female characters; the soldiers in the *Epidicus* triumph are bringing home *pueri* as well
as *virgines*; the relative merits of *pueri* and female prostitutes feed a joke
onstage (*Truc.* 149–52). Dorota Dutsch argues (2008: 181) that the Plautine
histrio is "in an imaginary space between genders." As seen in chapter 2, the
prologue speaker of *Casina* capitalizes on the blurring of role with actor,
on the blurring of Chalinus with Casina, and on the blurred masculinity
of actors/slaves when he makes his parting joke (79–86): the "exposed girl"
(*puellam expositiciam*) will commit no act of *stuprum* during the play, but
afterwards, "if you hand over the cash, as I suspect, / will become a bride
(*ibit nuptum*) on the spot, and won't stand upon ceremony." *Nuptum* here,
as in the *lena's* speech in *Cistellaria*, is a joke for "have sex." Nor, beneath
the mask, could the audience be certain which of the actors were slaves,
which free: another important ambiguity (see Marshall 2006: 86–9).
Indeed, this would add another layer to what Marshall (2006: 154), following Jacques Lecoq, calls the performance of "mask and counter-mask": the
actor, already playing a role that undercuts the expectations raised by his
mask-type, can also put into play the gender of "the actor," in that time-
honored role, "himself" (think of Steve Coogan). The gendered experience
of members of the audience would have affected how they reacted to what
they saw onstage, and the prominence of male slaves onstage would have
addressed in particular the male slaves in the audience, as was set forth by
Barbara Gold in her discussion of *Casina* (1998: 21). Female slaves in the
audience, along with free women, were left to practice an oppositional
gaze.

Thus, although many of the lines considered above speak specifically
for women, producing slave-women and freedwomen onstage as feeling
subjects, some of them, and many others in the plays, produce a more
ambiguous effect, almost campy, in the sense voiced by one female impersonator quoted by the anthropologist Esther Newton: "Camp has got to be
flip. A camp queen's got to think faster than other queens. ... She's got to
have an answer to anything that's put to her. ... She's sort of made light of
a bad situation" (Newton 1979[1972]: 110–11). Newton's source here means
by "a bad situation" the closeting of homosexuals in the 1950s–1960s; the
"bad situation" in Plautine Rome was the sexuality produced by slavery.
Bromia's joke to Amphitruo speaks for all the *familiares*, and the fact that
the line is delivered by a male playing a female adds to its force. All the
speeches considered so far in this chapter need to be reconsidered as spoken by male actors wearing false breasts, women's clothing, and grotesque

masks: a kind of drag.[31] To unpack the *palliata* – and indeed the Atellana, if Pomponius' title *Maccus Virgo* is any indicator – I would propose a stripped-down definition of "drag" as the playing of a female role by a male onstage such that both actor and audience share the consciousness both of the double gender and of what it might imply. This would lay no claim at all to the highly complex system of gendered meaning described by Esther Newton for the drag queens she interviewed in the 1960s. Without pertinent local written or visual sources from the time of Plautus, and no first-person accounts from his actors – no time machine for Esther Newton – it is not possible to know what drag truly meant to them. By 2010, only forty years after Newton, drag had taken on new inflections (Meyer 2010), so we cannot project, for example, Maecenas' beloved Bathyllus onto the actor who played Bromia two centuries earlier.[32] We also need to think about the full range of female roles and how they might be played.

Based on comparative evidence, it seems probable that actors playing old and/or subordinate slave-women were marked off visually from those playing sex objects; Kelly Wrenhaven argues that, in material representations, old women in particular share grotesque features with slaves.[33] In the Greek New Comedy masking tradition, slaves wore masks that were grotesque when compared with those the central free characters wore – *if* the typology of masks preserved by the sophist Julius Pollux in the late second century CE does go back to an Alexandrian original, as is generally believed. Pollux differentiates characters according to civil status, sexual availability, and age, with a handful of types for male slaves and three for old women, these last being uniformly ugly (wrinkled, two-toothed). Then, *if* those masks were used in central Italy, slave-women like Syra in *Mercator* would have looked grotesque. Another uncertainty: *if* the representational tradition seen in later mosaics, from second-century BCE Pompeii to Syria and Mytilene in the late third century CE, dates back to copybooks based on paintings from Menander's lifetime, then there is strong evidence – since the characters in some of the mosaics are labeled – that sometimes actors in Menander's plays did wear ugly masks to play

[31] See Dutsch 2004, Marshall 2006: 64–5 on big comic breasts; Marshall 2006: 130, 152 on women's masks.

[32] For context and sources on the love of Maecenas for the pantomime dancer Bathyllus, see Mankin 1995: 230–1 (on Horace, *Epodes* 14.9); Duncan 2006: 194–6; Lada-Richards 2007: 59 and *passim*.

[33] See Wrenhaven 2013: 138–40, with remarks on the blurred line between free and slave nurses; chapter 1 above for Wrenhaven and Revermann on the relation between slavery and the grotesque onstage.

old women. Much closer to third-century-BCE Latium are the terracotta theatrical masks and figurines found at Lipari, for which the New Comedy masks have been dated to 300–250 BCE; among these are some unattractive female faces and forms. Unlike some mosaics, however, these objects bear no labels to say what character they represent, if any. The earliest pertinent mosaic is the scene at Pompeii from Menander's *Synaristosai*, which depicts the character Philaenis as a hideous wrinkled crone; she is taken to be the original of the *lena* in Plautus' *Cistellaria*, and shows up five hundred years later in Mytilene looking much the same. In Syrian mosaics showing the same scene, however, Philaenis "lacks the unpleasant grizzled look of the Pompeii and Mytilene procuresses, whose rounder faces are distinctly yellow and wrinkled" (Gutzwiller and Çelik 2012: 600). It is notoriously hard to know how closely any of this corresponds with what went on onstage at various dates in various places, and the documentary value of the mosaics, as far as female slaves go, is limited by the fact that serving-women are often shown half-size and unmasked. The chief point of connection between Pollux and the *palliata* is the red hair of certain male slaves. I here follow C. W. Marshall's dictum that "just as the script has been freely adapted into Latin, so is there a parallel transposition of the Greek masking tradition" (2006: 127); that is, Pollux is not the last word.[34]

Even harder to get at is the possibility that some masks represented particular ethnicities, which would affect multiple characters in *Poenulus* and *Rudens* and all of the slave-women identified as Syrian. Color in theatrical masks is often taken to indicate gender (men are dark because they spend time outdoors, women are pale because they live indoors), as it does on Greek vases. Prostitutes onstage, however, are white-skinned because they have covered themselves in *cerussa*, white lead, as Philematium tries to do in *Mostellaria* (258–64), and pink-cheeked from rouge (*Truc.* 290). Makeup in itself is a kind of mask, a construction of femaleness, so an actor wearing a mask painted to look made-up is constructing two layers of female

---

[34] For discussion of masks, see Wiles 1991, Marshall 2006: 126–58, esp. 133 on the red-haired slaves; on the Pompeii mosaic, see Dunbabin 1999: 38–9 with fig. 44, and Wrenhaven 2013: 138; on theatrical mosaics showing Menander's plays, see Csapo 1999 and Nervegna 2014 (yes, the representations on the mosaics date back to Menander's time) and Gutzwiller and Çelik 2012 (close attention to local variation, and fully illustrated in color; see figs. 22–7, with discussion at 597–606). Marshall (2006: 151–2) works through the ways in which Pollux's list would have had to be modified for female roles in the *palliata*. On the Lipari masks, see Bernabò Brea 1992/3, esp. 28–30; 2001: 285. His alignment of masks with particular characters seems completely fanciful, but much resembles other efforts to match up Pollux, these objects, and the plays, viz. the elaborate charts in Webster 1949, which in turn serve as the basis for further debates. Schwarzmaier 2012: 73–83 revises Bernabò Brea's analysis and moves away from an Athenocentric view of the Lipari objects, but she was unable to view the entire corpus. The standard reference is Webster 1995.

gender over his own face, constructing a construction, a superfemininity. Would ethnic masks have constituted a kind of subfemininity? An alternate femininity? This would have meant a visual contrast between Palaestra and Ampelisca as they first appear, since Ampelisca is later described as dark-skinned (*Rud.* 421–2). What would a Syrian mask have done to the meaning of Syra's speech in *Mercator*? Like old-woman masks, ethnic masks would have complicated the visual effect of a character as "female."[35]

Actors playing women, moreover, shared the stage with actors who played the *cinaedus*, like the boy Paegnium in *Persa* (804–17), or like the actors who drop into an Ionic/cinaedic dance routine at the end of *Persa* and *Pseudolus* and *Stichus*, or like Sosia in *Amphitruo*, who does a little Ionic shimmy as he complains about the hardness of being a slave to a rich man (161–72). As has been remarked, the performance of these dance moves onstage by comic actors, and the citation of famous dancers by name in *Persa*, suggest that the audience was familiar with actual *cinaedi* as performers, along with the music they danced to: another element, then, in the circulation of performers around the Mediterranean. The home base for cinaedic dance was Alexandria, although Toxilus locates the dancer he imitates explicitly in Ionia (*Per.* 826). Either way: like the cargo of musicians in *Stichus*, such dance(r)s would have been exotic, imported, and a local actor doing this dance in Latium would be enacting not only a sexuality but an exotic sexuality – Orientalized, like the belly dance.[36] *Ludii barbari* (*Cur.* 150) do not dance like this.

For, like jokes, performance itself always takes on local meaning. Ethnographic studies of US drag and camp in the 1900s and early 2000s have been at pains to locate these phenomena at a particular historical moment and in a particular relationship to contemporary sexuality. Esther Newton's classic study emphasizes what we cannot do with Roman comedy: she talked to the performers themselves and watched them perform. Similar claims of local specificity characterize accounts of cross-dressed theatrical modes across time and space.[37] Close studies of individual actors

---

[35] On Philematium's makeup, see Dutsch 2015: 27; on makeup as constitutive of gender, see Richlin 2014a: 166–96; on ethnic masks in the *palliata*, see Richlin forthcoming a, Wrenhaven 2013: 135.

[36] See chapter 4 on Ionic and cinaedic dancing in Plautus; Moore 2012: 106–14, with bibliography. Implications about the audience: Habinek 2005: 182; Moore 2012: 111. The original suggestion about Sosia came from Maurizio Bettini in his study of Sotades (1982, 1995); for the Alexandrian location, see Cameron 1995: 18–20, and Richlin 2016, 2017b, on the circulation of jokes, comedians, and performance through the slave trade. On exotic slaves, including the *psaltria*, as luxury imports, see Leigh 2004: 10, part of a discussion of the view from the *togata* involving smaller cities in Italy. On Orientalized sexualities, see Boone 2014.

[37] For detailed comparison between conditions in the *palliata* and findings by Esther Newton, Moe Meyer, and historians of Chinese opera, see Richlin 2015b. On "acting the wench" in the

(e.g. Zhang 2011) point out yet another layer in our ignorance: we can speculate about "the Plautine actor" but have no idea how an individual's desires might have meshed or fought with the role of a slave-woman onstage. What did cross-dressing mean onstage in central Italy in the 200s BCE?

The troupe I imagined in chapter 1 was all male, multiethnic, and malnourished, though strong: thin, small, wiry. Maybe the Gaulish one was taller. The shoes they wore onstage – *socci* – added nothing to their height, and let them move fast. The costumes and masks they wore onstage completely encased them, *if* – another unknown – the costumes used in the *palliata* resembled those seen on south Italian terracottas from the early 200s, or on the actors on the Toscanella *cista* handle (chapter 1). If so, then nothing would be visible of the actor but his ears and hands. His body would be covered by a long-sleeved tunic and leggings, if not by voluminous draperies over padding (big breasts, big hips); his whole head would be covered in a mask with attached hair. This would have helped actors in the *palliata* produce the hidden transcript onstage and give voice to public political critique from below, otherwise highly risky; such disguises, especially women's clothes, are found across western history in connection with popular protest, where anonymity is a precondition for speech, not always liberatory.[38] Camp, too, can be viewed as political critique, as in Brechtian theater, part of the resistance created by power, in Foucauldian terms: a form of "engaged performance" as discussed by Mary-Kay Gamel.[39] The actor's encasement also meant that everyone onstage – as in most ancient drama – was wearing a costume that advertised its own artifice, as Nancy Rabinowitz has argued with respect to male actors playing women in Attic drama (1998). In comedy at least, *all* the roles are in inverted commas: "wife," "rich man," "poor man," "male slave," "slave-woman," "slave-boy," "nanny," "soldier," "pimp," "banker," "torturer," as are the props ("money," "chains," "jewelry").[40] Playing female characters,

nineteenth-century minstrel show, see Lott 1993: 159–68, arguing that working-class men in New York were able to filter their homoerotic desires through the disguise of blackface; on same-sex desire and the Elizabethan stage, see bibliography at Rabinowitz 1998: 20 n. 21; also Robinson 2006: 199–250, continuing into the eighteenth century.

[38] See Davis 1975: 147–50 on the use of popular "women on top" characters and costume by male protest groups in seventeenth- to nineteenth-century England, France, and Ireland, part of an optimistic analysis of the liberatory possibilities inherent in folk forms like the Skimmington ride; cf. Thompson 1992, and chapter 1 above on rough music.

[39] For camp as Brechtian or Foucauldian, see Meyer 2010: 36, 44, 107; on "engaged performance," see chapter 7 below.

[40] For objects onstage as operating within "a set of metaphorical 'quotation marks,'" see Ketterer 1986a: 207, and chapter 7 below on recognition tokens; see Dressler 2016: 23 on drama,

however, involved special skills, and playing some roles involved multiple intersectionality, like the role of Giddenis in *Poenulus*: old/Punic/slave/woman.

Here I will follow Rabinowitz's analysis.[41] Most importantly, she divides the spectators into the "narrative audience," who believe what they see is real, and the "authorial audience," conscious that the play is "a made thing" (1998: 4–5). Not all viewers see the same way; each viewer may view differently at different times; each sort of viewing may fluctuate. Still, with some degree of consciousness, "the cross-dressed actor signals the conventionality of the form and underlines the unnaturalness of the sign"; female costume becomes "emblematic of the artifice of the theater as a whole." Both kinds of audience "would sense the man in the woman" (14). As I have argued elsewhere (2014a: 175), "onstage, each primping whore – and Scapha, too – is a woman with a man inside, played by a man with a woman inside, for behind her mask is the actor's face, and inside his mouth are her words": slave-woman drag. Or slave, woman, drag – double drag, since "Plautus" was as much a performance as "Pardalisca." Dutsch, in a study of the relationship in the *palliata* between the actor's body, the character's staged gender, and the audience's experience, says that the performer is onstage in two ways: as himself, and as his female appearance, so that the actor's *imago* is "a sign for a 'woman'" (2015: 19). Not that this is simple; Plautus, she notes, draws attention to that.

Rabinowitz singles out the actor's voice as a constant onstage reminder of enacted gender (1998: 7–8). References by female characters onstage to voice "constitute cues to the authorial audience" (16); all the more so in the *palliata*, since, as Timothy Moore notes, "the plays of Plautus and Terence consistently associate music with women," who have more accompanied lines than male characters, use displays of metrical agility to dominate the stage, and generally make full use of the *vox muliebris*.[42] Other performative elements likewise distinguish female characters: the attributes Dutsch refers to as *schema*, including posture and gait. Encased in costume and mask, acting the woman, Rabinowitz argues, the Athenian citizen male "experienced what it was to become female" (12). Slave actors

---

representation, and "symbolically symbolic exchanges," and 33 n. 1 for props and the poetics of property.

[41] On the transgressive nature of men playing women in Greek drama, see also Bassi 1995, Zeitlin 1985 on tragedy; Duncan 2006: 32–47, Callier 2014, Taaffe 1993 on drag in Aristophanes. In an essay foundational for feminist theater studies, Sue-Ellen Case (1985) argued that Greek drama erases actual women and that "these roles should be played by men … [they] are properly played as drag roles" (324), the original players having been "male actors in drag" (318). Cf. Gamel 1999.

[42] Moore 2015: 68; cf. Moore 2012: 88–90, 246, 305.

in third-century Italy, however, knew this already, whether or not they had been raped after a siege or on the market; the plays are full of jokes about the sexual use of *pueri* by owners. Amplified like the props, the bit parts and non-speaking roles of slave-women and slave-boys onstage, seen as eye candy by Fraenkel himself, must have been highlighted by sexy costumes and masks; contrast the ugly *puer* who has the surprising solo in *Pseudolus* (767–89), and calls attention to his looks (768, *turpitudinem*): a sight gag.[43] If the production of some members of the encased troupe as eye candy was more notional than real, still *all* the eye candy onstage – male and female – was sexually available, and under the costumes and in the audience were people who knew that from experience.

Dutsch identifies precisely this process – making illusionary candy – as part of the work done onstage by actors performing a "sensory reaction," noting that, in the experience of such performance, no one can tell "when the visible ends and the imaginary begins" (2015: 20). As I will argue, this applies particularly to the possibility of casting body type against role, creating many shades of drag. The extant lines only point the way, or ways. We must work to put ourselves on the benches, watching the *grex* at work: the lead slave with his red hair, the beloved woman with her white, white face, her gaudy dress, her "gold" jewelry. It is fitting that one of the very few clear references to a mask in the early *palliata* is to a woman's mask, the mask of the slave prostitute Planesium in *Curculio*.[44] The slave Palinurus insults her: "You with your owl eyes, you even have the nerve to call me 'disgusting thing'? / You drunken little masky, you rubbish" (*tun etiam cum noctuinis oculis "odium" me vocas? / ebriola persolla, nugae, Cur.* 191–2).

Camp has been seen as closely related to parody, whose "dependence upon an already existing text in order to fulfill itself is reason for its traditional denigration" (Meyer 2010: 41) – a thought-provoking parallel for the *palliata*, with its close relation to the *Nea* and its penchant for paratragedy. Gesine Manuwald points out that the *parasitus* in *Curculio* makes a

---

[43] Fraenkel (2007: 100) says the non-speaking prostitutes in Ballio's parade in *Pseudolus* "would have appealed to the eyes of the Roman audience, as they were young and attractively decked out"; he seems to have been thinking in terms of actual mute women onstage. Cf. Klein 2015 on this scene, and on the ability of extras to affect the meaning of onstage action. For the translation of *turpitudinem* (hapax in Plautus) as "ugliness," cf. the usage of *turpis* in the corpus, occurring only in two scenes concerning female prostitutes' looks, opp. *pulcer* (*Mos.* 288, 291; *Poen.* 306 [= *Mos.* 291], 307, 323, 338).

[44] Naevius' *Personata* perhaps involved a female character wearing a mask, yet another level of metatheatricality – if in fact this is the title of a play. This question has been hopelessly entangled in the controversy over the start date for the use of masks in Italy, so that the title is usually taken to mean "the play where the actors wore masks." See Manuwald 2011: 79–80 for the current state of the question.

misogynistic joke that passes itself off as a line from tragedy, and considers the position of women in the audience watching the exemplary parade in tragedy and the *praetexta*. Paratragedy, indeed, sends up not only the grandiloquence of tragedy but what it does with gender – hence the puzzle posed by Alcumena's big song in *Amphitruo*, or laments like Palaestra's in *Rudens*. Conventions meant to be taken seriously on the tragic stage become comic when burlesqued on the comic stage by a man in false breasts and a dress, *hoc ornatu ornatam*, as Palaestra entertainingly specifies (187) – "dressed in this costume"; her plight, the slave actor's plight. When a Wagnerian soprano sings Brunnhilde, her divine voice is supposed to counteract any incongruities in her physical appearance; when the fat lady sings on the comic stage, the incongruity is the joke, blowing up gender conventions along with genre. Roman comedy has slaves but no kings (*Am.* 60–3), likewise queens but no queens.[45]

That Roman comedy incorporates drag even in the limited sense I propose has rarely been systematically considered. Barbara Gold's study of *Casina* (1998) deals mainly with the cross-dressing within the play. Many have asserted a sort of naturalized fiction of male as female, a common suspension of disbelief. Apart from cues to a disparity between appearance and role (on which more below), the general spoofing of femaleness onstage suggests that audience members, in various ways, derived enjoyment from a consciousness of male impersonation of the female. The plentiful commentary in Latin on the naturalism of gender performance onstage comes from much later periods, and reflects the habituation of Roman audiences to the *pantomimus*. Marshall (2006: 92–3) points to possible "multicultural influences" on the performance styles of two comic actors described by Quintilian in the first century CE, including their skill at various female roles (Quint. 11.3.178–80). The actor's ability to go both ways was still being singled out for praise in the sixth century CE, when the rhetorician Choricius of Gaza described the dancer as "trying to persuade

---

[45] For a similar analysis of paratragedy in Aristophanes, see Callier 2014. Manuwald 2015 provides a brief but authoritative overview of female characters in early tragedy and the *praetexta*; see 2015: 174 on *Curculio*, 181 on women in the audience. Numerous grand speeches by female characters are extant in the fragments of Ennius and might have served as the models for solos like Alcumena's or Palaestra's; see above on *Andromacha*. See Bianco 2007: 155–95, for Palaestra's song in *Rudens*, and 237–61 on Alcumena and Bromia in *Amphitruo* (serious); Dutsch 2008: 128–32 on Palaestra and Ampelisca in *Rudens* ("a series of innuendos regarding the girls' inadequate garb"), noting parallels to Ennius' *Medea*. Scholars are strongly divided as to whether to take Alcumena as tragic or comic: see Bond 1999 (tragic) and Langlands 2006: 211–18 (serious); Bleisch 1997, Christenson 2000: 37–45, Dutsch 2008: 153–6, Moore 1995 (comic); also Gunderson 2015: 198–201, against Christenson and performance criticism in general (tragicomic).

the audience not that he is representing something, but that he really *is* what he allegedly represents" (*Dialexis* 12, p. 248 F.-R., as quoted and translated in Russell 1983: 83). Roman unease with this skill, however, is densely attested in Latin rhetorical handbooks going back to Cicero and the *Rhetorica ad Herennium* (Richlin 1997a; Gunderson 2000: 111–48), and there is no source other than Plautus to tell us whether a Plautine audience watching slave actors viewed the enactment of female characters naturalistically. It is one thing to read the OCT and perceive these female figures as female, and another to sit in the Forum and watch encased actors go into a clinch and press their masks together. What did the audience see in the masked kiss, the costumed clinch?

What follows will necssarily be hypothetical; since we cannot know how the plays were staged, we can only try out different possibilities, as in rehearsal. Nor should we imagine that each performance of each play was identical, since, even as we have them, they incorporate additions (all or part of the *Casina* prologue) and alternate versions (*Poenulus* has two endings). No one steps on the same stage twice. Drag itself comes in different varieties, not only from the viewer's perspective but, as will be seen, from the troupe's: a question of casting. Here I want to show how drag *could* have worked onstage in the *palliata*.

What an actor could do onstage might be suggested by an interchange in *Truculentus* between the prostitute's slave-woman Astaphium and the rustic slave Truculentus.[46] One of the few places in Latin that refers to sex between women at all, never mind between female owners and slave-women, it incorporates a play on the words *era* (female owner) and *ira* (anger) – in itself a suggestive collocation. Astaphium, as seen in chapter 4, is one of the few female characters to make use of the standard Plautine markers for privileged speech. So bold in her ways, she might have been, to a watching *ancilla* in the narrative audience, what Epidicus was to Chrysalus (*Bac.* 214) – particularly so, at this moment in the play, to one who loved women (another hypothetical category). The effect would have been complicated further if Astaphium's mask slipped here.[47] She says to the truculent Truculentus (262–4),

---

[46] Cf. Fraenkel 2007: 25; Dutsch 2015: 20–3 on this scene in full.

[47] "Lesbian existence" is a major issue in the history of sexuality, going back to Rich 1980; see Bennett 2000, Brooten 1996 (despite the title, evenly divided between non-Christian and Christian evidence). Basically, it is a mistake not to postulate the existence of female–female desire in any period, whether it spoke its name or not. Rabinowitz 1998: 20 n. 20 asks whether scholars' emphasis on cross-dressing displaces women, and of course it does; the experience of conjectural male actors receives a great deal more attention in this book than does the experience of conjectural women in the audience. See Richlin 2014a on this problem.

AS. comprime sis eiram. TR. eam quidem hercle tu, quae solita's,
comprime.
inpudens, quae per ridiculum rustico suades stuprum.
AS. "eiram" dixi ...

AS. Please stuff your anger. TR. [Understanding her to have said, "Please
stuff my owner"] No, you stuff her, by God – you're used to it (*quae
solita's*).
You shameless thing, to talk a country boy into a sex crime just to be funny.
AS. I said "anger" (*eiram*) ...

What voice did the actor playing Astaphium use when he said *eiram* the
second time? All he would have to do onstage today is drop his voice an oct-
ave from an in-character falsetto in order to play the man inside the woman,
the actor inside the mask. The actor playing Bromia might have done the
same thing in his second recognition of Amphitruo.[48] A move like this would
only be another kind of metatheatricality, a wink at the authorial audience.

Male slaves' repeatedly voiced desire for women, seen in chapters 2
and 4, sometimes leads them, onstage, into female impersonation, most
memorably in *Casina*. In the verbal duel between Olympio and Chalinus,
discussed above, the main point at issue is that both want to marry the
same slave-woman. Olympio, as befits his status as slave-driver, makes a
series of threats against Chalinus involving forced labor and starvation on
the farm (115–30). But the climactic threat is that Chalinus will be forced
to witness Olympio's nights with Casina. In order to make his threat vivid,
Olympio ventriloquizes his imaginary bride, as Chalinus will do offstage,
at the end of the play; the substitution of male slave for missing woman,
male voice for female, dramatizes a sexual hunger (130–40):

> [OL.] postid, quom lassus fueris et famelicus,   130
> noctu ut condigne te cubes curabitur.
> CH. quid facies? OL. concludere in fenstram firmiter,
> unde auscultare possis quom ego illam ausculer:
> quom mihi illa dicet "mi animule, mi Olympio,
> mea vita, mea mellilla, mea festivitas,   135
> sine tuos ocellos deosculer, voluptas mea,
> sine amabo ted amari, meu' festus dies,
> meu' pullus passer, mea columba, mi lepus,"
> quom mihi haec dicentur dicta, tum tu, furcifer,
> quasi mus, in medio parieti vorsabere.   140

---

[48] See Newton 1979[1972]: 48, 100–1, on such tactics in 1960s US drag, including a drop in vocal register, as part of a characteristic opposition between inside/outside; cf. Rabinowitz 1998 (above) on the
actor's voice. On *solita's* as a common cue in formulaic insults, see chapter 4.

[OL.] After that, when you'll be tired and starving,   130
I'll see to it that at night you get the bedding you deserve.
CH. What'll you do? OL. You'll be shut up close in the window-frame,
where you'll be able to listen when I'm kissing her.
When she'll be saying to me, "My darling, my Olympio,
my life, my little honey, my good time,   135
let me kiss your little eyes, my pleasure,
please, lovey, let yourself be loved, my holiday,
my sparrow chick, my pigeon, my bunny" –
while these words are being said to me, then you, yoke-bearer,
like a mouse, you'll be squirming in the middle of the wall.   140

Olympio voices the elusive Casina here as he imagines the two of them
in bed together, a sort of auto-eroticism; as he speaks her imagined
words, does he break into falsetto? In any case, he here reproduces
what actors did onstage all the time, as they spoke words like those of
Ampelisca and Astaphium: *mea voluptas* (here literally true). The scene
might easily be blocked by having Olympio grab Chalinus and make
him stand in for Casina. At the same time, in Olympio's projected scene
of torture, Chalinus is subordinated here precisely in his role as helpless
eavesdropper, emphasized by his cage-like imprisonment in the case-
ment. Like the attendant slaves at parties – like Paegnium at the end
of *Persa* – Chalinus would have to witness a more powerful male having sex, here with an *ancilla* he desperately wants for himself.[49] He is,
in effect, in the audience, a spectator; so people sitting on the benches
watched male slaves act out scenes where male slaves desire female slaves
acted by male slaves.

Male slaves in the plays sometimes have this voyeur's position onstage,
watching their owners go into a clinch with their beloved prostitutes; they
voice a sort of detached disgust, like Palinurus in *Curculio*: "Do you see
how grimly they're grinding away? They can't embrace each other enough"
(*viden ut misere moliuntur? nequeunt complecti satis, Cur.* 188). Libanus and
Leonida in *Asinaria* go further, extorting their own turn with Philaenium,

---

[49] See also J. Clarke 1998: 88 on "onlooker figures" and the Warren cup, and 97–105 for examples and
discussion of painted scenes of men and women in bed with slaves in attendance. For a response
to Clarke, distinguishing the power politics of "onlooker" scenes in rich men's homes from the
scenes on the walls of brothels, see Green 2015: 145–52, also responding to Severy-Hoven 2012. All
are working with material from the early Principate, when at least one elite writer found the idea
of male slaves' voyeurism titillating (Martial 11.104.13). In *Casina* we see what it looks like from the
onlooker's point of view. The idea that a slave routinely slept in an owner's bedroom seems to be
largely a modern idea, rarely attested in ancient texts, but they are sometimes posted outside the
bedroom door, so that, like Chalinus, they could hear; see Riggsby 1997: 44–6.

and making her beg them in words like those Olympio invents for Casina
(*As.* 662, 664–8, 686, 691–6):

> LE. hanc, quoi daturus hanc, iube petere atque orare mecum. 662
> …
> PH. da, meus ocellus, mea rosa, mi anime, mea voluptas,
> Leonida, argentum mihi, ne nos diiunge amantis. 665
> LE. dic me igitur tuom passerculum, gallinam, coturnicem,
> agnellum, haedillum me tuom dic esse vel vitellum,
> prehende auriculis, compara labella cum labellis.
> …
> LI. nunc istanc tantisper iube petere atque orare mecum. 686
> …
> PH. mi Libane, ocellus aureus, donum decusque amoris,
> amabo, faciam quod voles, da istuc argentum nobis.
> LI. dic igitur med aneticulam, columbam vel catellum,
> hirundinem, monerulam, passerculum putillum,
> fac proserpentem bestiam me, duplicem ut habeam linguam, 695
> circumda torquem bracchiis, meum collum circumplecte.

> LE. This woman, the one you're going to give this [wallet] to –
> order her to try to get it, and to beg it from me. 662
> …
> PH. Give it, my little eye, my rose, my soul, my pleasure, 665
> Leonida, give the cash to me, don't separate us lovers.
> LE. Then call me your little sparrow, your little chicken, your quail,
> call me your lambie, say I'm your little kid, your little calfie,
> take me by my ears, press my lips with your lips.
> …
> LI. Now order her to try just a bit to get it, and to beg it from me. 686
> …
> PH. My Libanus, my little golden eye, gift and ornament of love,
> please, lovey, I'll do whatever you want, give that cash to us.
> LI. Then call me your duckling, your dove or your puppy,
> your swallow, your jackdaw, your teeny-weeny little sparrow,
> make me the slithering beast, so I'll have a double tongue, 695
> put a necklace on me with your arms, twine your arms around my neck.

Earlier in this scene, Libanus goes out of his way to explain that neither he
nor Leonida wants to substitute for a woman, nor does either desire the
other: "I don't care for *his* embrace, and he shuns mine" (*ego complexum
huius nil moror, meum autem hic aspernatur*, 643). Yet, like Olympio, he is
adept at acting out and voicing the seductive woman, whose *voluptas* (664)
lies in doing "whatever you want" (*quod voles*, 692), and his onstage goal
is a clinch with another man playing a woman. As shown in chapter 4, the

riding scene that ensues reverses the roles of sexual abuser and abused, as
Libanus specifically accuses his owner of having been used for sex as a boy,
while the earlier joke about Libanus' size may suggest that he is himself
smaller, younger. For a male actor, playing the sexy woman re-enacts a role
forced on the (young) male slave (not so young, when an owner starts in
on his *vilicus* at *Cas.* 451–66; see chapter 2). The desire for women voiced
onstage is in fact voiced onstage by males, for males, as the ambiguous
words *mea voluptas* are spoken by male lips through a female mask.

The slippage involved in male slaves' onstage deprivation is enacted,
amidst much else, in the action-packed final party scene in *Persa*. Toxilus
has spent the whole play working to get control of his beloved Lemniselenis,
and, as seen in his verbal duel with the pimp (chapter 3), has paid the pimp
to free her. She appears first at line 763, after Toxilus' speech as victorious
general, and her opening speech invites him to be close to her; a clinch
ensues, and Toxilus tells the audience how it feels: "oh, nothing is sweeter
than this" (*oh, nil hoc magi' dulcest,* 764). Yet all does not go smoothly as
the party progresses; Lemniselenis shows too much concern for her former
owner, the pimp (now her *patronus*), as Toxilus and his allies taunt and,
eventually, beat him. In Toxilus' view, he is himself the *patronus* of the freed
Lemniselenis – a view based on emotional rather than factual justice – and
he upbraids her, playing the owner (835–40):

> ... TO. cave ergo sis malo et sequere me.   835
> te mihi dicto audientem esse addecet, nam hercle apsque me
> foret et meo praesidio, hic faceret te prostibilem propediem.
> sed ita pars libertinorum est: nisi patrono qui advorsatust,
> nec sati' liber sibi videtur nec sati' frugi nec sat honestus,
> ni id effecit, ni ei male dixit, ni grato ingratus repertust.   840

> ... TO. So you watch out for a beating and
>   follow me.   835
> It befits you to be obedient to me, for, by God, without me
> and my rescue, this guy would have made you a street hooker any day now.
> But that's how some freedmen are: unless he's gone up against his *patronus*,
> he doesn't seem free enough to himself, nor prudent enough, nor
>   respectable enough,
> unless he's done the job, unless he's insulted him, unless he's found
>   thankless to the one he ought to thank.   840

Lemniselenis has made a spectacular appearance onstage in this final climactic scene; she is what the spectators have been waiting to see; she has
engaged in a warm embrace; we might expect that the actor playing her
was dressed up accordingly. Yet here, lecturing her, Toxilus slips into a

generic masculine: *advorsatust* (838), *liber, honestus* (839), *ingratus, repertust* (840). The male body of the actor twitches inside the Marilyn costume; this would be cued if 838–40 were played with a nod towards the audience, a metatheatrical gesture towards life offstage. The gender interchangeability of the slave as sex object gets a little push here. "I'm your *patronus*, obviously, because I'm the one who gave this guy the cash for you," insists Toxilus (842); but he isn't her *patronus*, and she isn't a she.[50] Nobody's perfect.

Drag, then, gives a twist to the specularization of the female characters onstage, akin to the "specularization of the grotesque" suggested in chapter 1. The "drooling speeches" of parasites recur in carnal form, spoken by young men, as their beloveds parade before them onstage: how beautiful she is! The grudging slave, and the audience, are asked to collude in admiration, however transparent the gender masquerade was onstage – the more transparent, the funnier this would be, especially since the young men are usually fools. The actors playing them could emphasize the disparity between the pretty-girl character and what the audience saw onstage by making special use of what might be called "deictic receptions." All kinds of characters are routinely heralded onstage by lines like "But look! Here comes Toxilus' slave-boy Paegnium!" (*sed Toxili puerum Paegnium eccum*, *Per.* 271) – *sed*, forms of *video*, and the deictic *eccum/eccam* are part of the shtick.[51] Indeed, with *eccum* and its relatives, the act of hailing itself becomes gendered. In a temporary theater without a rake, as when the *palliata* was produced in a forum with bench seating, not everyone can see; moreover, many deictic receptions tell the audience *how to read* the encased actor who has just appeared (so Pseudolus on the slave Simia: "But here he comes, I see him, it's Mt. Flogmore! How he goes, how he carries himself like a bigshot!" *sed eccum video verberiam statuam: ut it, ut magnifice infert sese!*, 911). As Dutsch says, "onlookers … function as internal spectators modeling spectatorship for the audience" (2015: 18). Female characters are built up at their first entrance by being hailed as gorgeous, as is Erotium in *Menaechmi*: "Look, she's coming out herself! Oh! Can you see how the sun / is darkened next to the brilliance of that body?" (*eapse eccam exit. oh! solem vides / satin ut occaecatust prae huius corporis candoribus?*, *Men.* 179–81). With this kind of help, even the people in the back row can see; deictic receptions create a kind of stage vision.

---

[50] On the obedience expected of a freed sex slave, and the concomitant erasure of the freed slave's volition, also at *Mos.* 204–5, see Marshall 2013: 192–4; above on *voluptas*.

[51] See Marshall 1999 on the entrance shtick *quis hic loquitur*, "Who's that speaking here?"

Not even all the beauties onstage get this kind of welcome, and there are some surprising holes in the lineup, including Philaenium in *Asinaria* and Philocomasium in *Miles*. Many do, however, while another type of welcome is reserved for the unattractive, marked by jokes about their appearance. The vocabulary in the reception of beauty is repetitive; the women are touted, sometimes in a buildup that long precedes their entrance, as *bella, forma eximia* or *expetenda, lepida, liberalis, nitida, pulchra*; they are compared with Venus; and, as with *eccam/eccas*, they are pointed at, by some variation of *haec est*.[52] That's her.

Like Erotium, some women are greeted with elaborate metaphors. As her besotted lover spies on Philematium, he exclaims to the audience that she is the embodiment of the storm of love that featured in his opening song: "Oh, lovely love-goddess, / this is that storm of mine," and so on (*o Venu' venusta, / haec illa est tempestas mea ...*, *Mos.* 161–5). The nasty Diniarchus in *Truculentus* greets the entrance of Phronesium with, "Behold, springtime! / How she is all flowers, how she smells, how shinily she shines!" (*ver vide: / ut tota floret, ut olet, ut nitide nitet!*, 353–4). His evocation of scent adds another element to the imaginary sensorium conveyed from the stage to the benches, an exotic link to the lands of frankincense, and her shine may also emanate from this source, as in the oily base of unguents (see chapter 4). Phaedromus in *Curculio* enlists his slave to admire Planesium: "She's charming." Palinurus is skeptical: "Too charming" (*est lepida. # nimi' lepida*, 167). Stratippocles does the same with his slave Epidicus, after an exchange of demonstratives – *sed quis haec est muliercula* (*Epid.* 620), *haec illa est* (621), *haecine est* (621), *haec est* (622) – then asks Epidicus to give Telestis the once-over, calls her *festivissuma*, and compares her to a painting (622–4). Milphio in *Poenulus* signals the audience that a big entrance is coming up by naming the two sisters and pointing: "But look, Adelphasium is coming out, and Anterastilis!" (*sed Adelphasium eccam exit atque Anterastilis*, 203), explaining which is the prime love-object (*haec est prior*, 204), then calling his owner out to admire the show (*ludos*, 206; *spectare*, 208); Agorastocles fervently agrees (*tam lepidum spectaculum*, 209). Milphio drives the point home (*em amores tuos*,

---

52 *Bella, Bac.* 1171a; *Mil.* 989; *Truc.* 272. *Forma eximia, Mer.* 13, 210, 260; *St.* 381; *forma expetenda, Per.* 521. *Lepida, Bac.* 1169, *Cur.* 167, *Epid.* 43 (*lepida et liberali*), *Mil.* 871, 1003, *Per.* 130 (*lepida et liberali*), *Poen.* 209, *Rud.* 415, 419, *St.* 748. *Liberalis, Epid.* 43, *Per.* 130, 521, 546. *Pulchra, St.* 737. *Nitida, Mil.* 1003, *Truc.* 354. *Haec est, As.* 585, *Epid.* 621–2, *Mos.* 162, *Per.* 464, 545, *Poen.* 1166, *Truc.* 93, cf. *sed quis haec est muliercula, Epid.* 620. Compared with Venus: *Mos.* 161, *Rud.* 420, *St.* 748, cf. *Poen.* 1113 *specie venusta.*

207); Agorastocles is not quick on the uptake. Their exchange emphasizes the theatricality of the girls' appearance.

The longest buildup belongs to the Virgo in *Persa*, described by the slave Toxilus to her father as *forma lepida et liberali* (130), then inspected in her Arab captive disguise (464), then in a (fake) letter (*forma expetenda liberalem virginem*, 521); when she is finally led onstage by her (fake) slave-dealer, the pimp and the slave point her out in a run of deixis: *haecine illast* (545); *specie … liberalist* (546); *sat … concinnast facie* (547), as the long sale scene commences, during which she will be fully examined. Throughout this scene, the actor is costumed as a woman costumed as an exotic woman, so that the talent for double speech s/he performs (above) tallies with his/her appearance.

Indeed, as well as defining beauty, deictic receptions also point to performance elements, the *schema* and voice discussed by Dutsch and Rabinowitz. The two old men about to fall for the Bacchis sisters in *Bacchides* signal their susceptibility by their reception: "Look, here they come, finally, / those snares of sin, those con artistes" (*eunt eccas tandem / probriperlecebrae et persuastrices*, 1166–7); "so charming" (*tam lepidam*, 1169); "although you're pretty" (*quamquam tu bella es*, 1171a); "how sweetly she speaks!" (*ut blandiloquast*, 1174). The two slaves waiting for their shared girlfriend at the end of *Stichus* beseech her to come out of the house with a string of adjectives (*suavis, amabilis, amoena, pulchra, pulcherruma*, 736–7), and, when she speaks, exclaim *lepide* and compare her with Venus (748). The slave Palaestrio comments approvingly to the audience on the appearance of Acroteleutium, a young freed prostitute playing a *matrona*, "But [he's] … / bringing the woman, and she's got quite the shape, too charming! / … How properly dressed she walks along, not like a prostitute at all!" (*sed … mulierem / nimi' lepida forma ducit. … / quam digne ornata incedit, hau meretricie!*, *Mil.* 870–2): *ornata* marks the double costume in this play-within-the-play. When Acroteleutium's slave-woman enters, Palaestrio alerts the soldier (*st tace! aperiuntur fores*, 985), who then eyes her admiringly: "God, this one's really / a pretty little thing" (*edepol haec quidem / bellulast*, 988–89; cf. *nimium lepida nimi'que nitida femina*, 1003). Characters' gait is often pointed out by *ut incedit*, "how s/he walks along"; Palaestrio's reception of Acroteleutium suggests that prostitutes onstage, as well as dressing gaudily, used a particular walk, an indecorous walk, so that the actor playing Acroteleutium playing a *matrona* could have pasted a decorous walk over an indecorous one.[53]

---

[53] See Dutsch 2015: 21–2 on the overlap between Astaphium's *ornatus* (her fake jewelry) and the actor's

Action compounds deixis in scenes where a woman enters and soon goes into a clinch with her lover. As seen above, this happens in *Curculio*, where deictic reception builds into a torrid embrace with side comments from the slave standing by, and in the last act of *Persa*, when Toxilus finally welcomes the long-awaited Lemniselenis (and the audience sees her for the first time). In *Asinaria*, Philaenium and Argyrippus enter already entwined (*Qur me retentas?*, *As.* 591), cued by Libanus: "Is this Philaenium who's coming out of the house and / Argyrippus along with her?" (*Philaenium estne haec quae intus exit atque / una Argyrippus?*, 585–6). This embrace is spun out at length, punctuated and punctured by jokes to the audience by Libanus and Leonida, until they break in at 619 and dissolve the clinch with a joke: "But, this woman you're embracing, what is she, smoke?" (*sed num fumus est haec mulier quam amplexare?*). Argyrippus is forced to play the straight man. An embrace is again played for laughs in the famous pitcher scene in *Rudens*, where Ampelisca enters, seeking water, and the slave Sceparnio exclaims, "Whoa! What good thing do we have here? Yes, by God, it's a woman, and charming to look at!" (*hem! quid hic boni est? eu edepol specie lepida mulierem!*, 415). He calls her *mea lepida, hilara*, and fondles her as she fends him off (419–20); he exclaims that she is the "image of Venus" (*Veneris effigia haec quidem est*, 420); he remarks on her eyes and her body, which he jokes about as "darkish" (*subaquilum*, 421–2), exclaims over her breasts, and then over her kiss (423) – evidently pausing to try her out. When he asks her what she wants and she says that, to a smart person, her *ornatus* (the pitcher) gives the sign of what she wants, he says, "Well, to a smart person, my *ornatus* here gives the sign of what *I* want" (*meu' quoque hic sapienti ornatus quid velim indicium facit*, 429). It seems probable that here he points to his crotch.[54] This comic index of the effects of stage beauty on the admiring male is the soul of deictic reception, the conscious power of *ornatus*.

Both Ampelisca and Sceparnio are low characters, and Ampelisca's role is to be less beautiful than Palaestra. Sceparnio's enthusiasm may be for a *schema* that does not look so enticing to the audience. This is evidently so when Milphio expresses admiration for the Carthaginian

---

ornatus (his "woman" costume), and between Astaphium's painted cheeks and the actor's *imago*. For a prostitute's gait, see Gymnasium's joke at *Cist.* fr. vii–viii, 380 ("tiny steps," *vegrandi gradu*, with a play on *cubituram / cursuram*, "trained more for lying down than for running"), and Dutsch 2015: 33 n. 32.

[54] So de Melo 2012: 447, "*(pointing to his groin).*" Previous English translators going back to Bonnell Thornton (1769: 2.300) refrain from inserting stage directions here and tend to undertranslate, leaving out *ornatus*. For analysis of this scene as an example of "visual obscenity" and embedded stage directions, see Jeppesen 2015: 180–5.

slave nanny Giddenis just before he calls her out to speak to Hanno, her former owner. He describes her as "not very tall, dark body" (*statura hau magna, corpore aquilo, Poen.* 1112) and "lovely to look at, her face and her eyes totally black" (*specie venusta, ore atque oculis pernigris*, 1113). Giddenis is never the object of flirtation, indeed is the butt of jokes, in the scene that follows; Milphio's *venusta* may be part of a sight gag. Other old women are heralded by complaints about how slowly they move: so Euclio says of Staphyla, "Would you look at that, / how she's going" (*illuc sis vide / ut incedit, Aul.* 46–7), comparing her to a turtle (49); so her owner says of Syra in *Mercator*, "and look, here she's coming along, finally. Why don't you move faster?" (*atque eccam incedit tandem. quin is ocius?*, 671). Halisca in *Cistellaria* is recognized by the slave Lampadio (*haec est*, 695; *eccam*, 696), who compares her to a caterpillar (729). The old *lena* in *Curculio* is hailed in a long series of jokes for her capacity to sniff out wine and drink it down; she is compared to a dog (110b), so that when Phaedromus calls her *anus lepida* (120), this is another joke, an oxymoron. The failure of Lysidamus and Olympio at the end of *Casina* to perceive that there is, as Dutsch says, "something visibly wrong with [Chalinus'] *schema*" is a major source of the comedy in this scene, cued for the audience by Olympio's "Oh / delicate little body!" (*o / corpusculum malacum*, 842–3), followed up by "She set her foot down / like an elephant" (*institit plantam / quasi luca bos*, 845–6). This comic indeterminacy will be resolved (911) by something like a cucumber: again, the telltale phallus.[55]

It seems likely, then, that the jokes that greet Alcumena's entrances in *Amphitruo* indicate that there is something funny about how she looks: "Look, here comes the counterfeit Amphitruo out the door / with Alcumena – his wife on a lease" (*Amphitruo subditivos eccum exit foras / cum Alcumena – uxore usuraria*, 497–8); the pregnant-woman jokes at 664–70. In company with lines like these, the second entrance of the sisters in *Poenulus*, when their lover points them out to their long-lost father, suggest that perhaps their first, spectacular entrance was another sight gag (*Poen.* 1166–8):

> AG. sed eccas video ipsas. HA. haecin meae sunt filiae?
> quantae e quantillis iam sunt factae! AG. scin quid est?

---

[55] See Dutsch 2015: 20, 24 on old women onstage as grotesque animals and on *Casina*. For the metatheatrical possibilities of even very minor roles for *ancillae*, see Henderson 1999: 29 on the one-line speech of the *ancilla* at *Poen.* 332 in response to her subordinated greeting by the young man; Klein 2015 on the possibilities for mute characters generally.

†Thraecae sunt: in celonem† sustolli solent.[56]

AG. But look, I see their very selves. HA. Those are my daughters?
What big girls they have grown now, from such little girls! AG. You
    know what?
[They're Thracian women: they like to get up on a stallion.]

Whatever line 1168 originally said, it is clear from the structure of 1167–8
that it was the punchline of a joke about size; if so, Milphio's description of
one sister as *tantilla* (273) would be a sight gag, too. For beauty, hyperbole;
for un-beauty, jokes. The sisters in *Poenulus*, like Planesium, get both. It is
the slave's job to see what is under the mask and costume.

Deictic receptions in general point to the mask/costume markers for
characters onstage and, as seen above, draw attention to the artifice: mask
+ padding + costume + voice + gait = "woman." Dutsch suggests (2015:
20) that Erotium's brilliant body plays off the whiteness of the prostitute's
mask and perhaps body makeup, which itself plays the "lead-white cerussa"
of ancient makeup, which itself plays the ideal color of a woman. Even
the specularization of a character like Astaphium, viewed with grudging
but growing lust by the slave Truculentus, directs the audience to see "the
maid/the actor as a grotesque assemblage" (Dutsch 2015: 22). The joking
lines in particular, I think, suggest an understanding of female characters
as male actors in drag, and the possibility that, at least sometimes, the body
type of the actor did conflict with the body type of the character, a situation that is explicitly staged within the play in the final scene of *Casina*.
That is, sometimes you had RuPaul (glamorous drag queen supermodel),
sometimes Terry Jones (as he played, for example, the cleaning lady in
Monty Python's The Meaning of Life): different jokes. The same conflict
might be exploited with *pueri* as well, who, like women, ceased to be erotic
after a certain age.

In the dressing scene in *Mostellaria*, as Philematium literally specularizes
herself – at one point, she kisses the mirror (265) – her lover simultaneously specularizes her within the diegesis, encouraging the audience to do
the same. Her pretty-girl makeup, however, covers a mask that covers an
actor. What *did* the audience see in the masked kiss, the costumed clinch?
Onstage cues gauge the heat of these clinches, like Toxilus' "nothing

---

[56] I here obelize the dubious portion of Lindsay's text. "Leo's brilliant emendation" (Fraenkel 2007: 29–
30) *tragicae sunt: in calones* is usually adopted (so de Melo 2012: 140), but this depends on a sense of
calones (= *cothurni*) attested otherwise only in a late glossary, nor is it clear to me what *tragicae* would
have meant to a Plautine audience. *Calo* does not appear in the Plautine corpus, but in Horace's
Satires, *calones* are menial slaves (1.2.44, 1.6.103), and elsewhere this is a common term for an army
slave (Welwei 1988: 56–7). See Maurach 1988: 158 for discussion.

sweeter," or Palinurus' line, "Do you see how grimly they're grinding away?" Here envy shows through – or jealousy. Compare Bacall to Bogart in *To Have and Have Not*, as he holds a fainting blonde: "What are you trying to do, guess her weight?" Slavery not only erased an enslaved male's former status but affected his gender, and in many possible ways. Jealousy, rather than envy, might motivate the male slave watching his owner; forced love might still be love, enacted here onstage at the dawn of the bromance.

"I bet you don't weigh eighty pounds yet," says Sophoclidisca to Paegnium, sizing him up (*Per.* 231); *pueri* onstage are specularized, too, however they were played. Conspicuous by its absence from extant New Comedy is any pederastic romance; no *puer* is bought to be set up in an exclusive relationship as is Pasicompsa in *Mercator*; yet *pueri* like Paegnium in *Persa*, or Phaniscus in *Mostellaria*, or Pinacium in *Stichus* can be pert and flirtatious in just the same way as characters like Astaphium. Indeed, Paegnium, whose name means "Plaything," not only flirts with the *ancilla* Sophoclidisca but does a sexy dance[57] in the final scene, aimed at the pimp; his onstage quarrel with the slave Sagaristio could be played as a flirtation (*Per.* 272–300), as could, on a smaller scale, the exchange between Phaniscus and his fellow-slave Pinacium at *Mostellaria* 885–98. Like some *ancillae* and non-speaking female characters (Ballio's prostitute parade in *Pseudolus*; the musicians in *Stichus*), slave-boys onstage could have been played as eye candy, highlighted by sexy costumes and masks; the ugly *puer* who tells the audience his troubles in *Pseudolus* (chapter 4), when he calls attention to his looks (*turpitudinem*, 768), is marking a sight gag for the audience. As seen above, Quintilian reproved Afranius, who wrote half a century after Plautus, for incorporating pederastic themes in his (togate) plays (10.1.100), but in a way they were there onstage all along, behind one mask or another.[58]

Philematium's spectacle is repeated in several plays: the brothel parade in *Pseudolus*, the bathing scene in *Poenulus*, the arrival of two shipwrecked girls dressed in wet rags in *Rudens*. A beauty pageant: it must have been more parody than showgirl tableau, especially if there was an admixture

---

[57] A phrase permanently undercut by Jemaine Clement's mock-funkadelic song "Business Time"; this in turn suggests what could be done with Paegnium's dance – his whole role – by a comedian like Clement. Musical parody: yet another unreachable aspect of the *palliata*.

[58] Welsh 2010 argues that Quintilian meant only that Afranius wrote about love affairs, and in any case had not read Afranius; I think it unlikely, however, that Quintilian's phrase *puerorum foedis amoribus* involves, as Welsh claims, a subjective genitive (2010: 123–5). On this point, compare Plutarch's cryptic comment (*QR* 288b) that Romans going back to early times felt it was not wrong to "love" slave boys of the same age as free boys wearing the *bulla* (hence younger than about fifteen), and that "to this day, their comedies bear witness to this."

of grotesque or otherwise marked costumes and masks. In *Rudens*, it is likely that Ampelisca's dark mask contrasted with Palaestra's light one; in *Pseudolus*, it is possible that Phoenicium's mask was similarly differentiated.[59] Displays of slaves were a familiar sight in the ancient city, staged on the platforms of the slave-dealers in the same public spaces in which the plays were staged (chapter 7). Like the Virgo in *Persa*, slaves in the market were dressed up for sale. Later sources record the efforts expended by slave-dealers to trick out their merchandise so as to appear sexually alluring, particularly to erase the signs of impending manhood from young male slaves.[60] In the *Life of Aesop*, the ugly Aesop is positioned on the platform between an attractively dressed and combed musician and a schoolteacher whose thin legs were hidden by a long robe – two *boupaides*, "boys the size of oxen" (*Vit. Aes.* 20–1). Perhaps this novelistic account reproduces an old comedic sight gag? Comedy gives its audience a conscious reproduction of such a sight, a representation of it, funny (or daring, or sexy, or edgy) because not-it.

The flip side of specularization is monstrification. From the stage, actors dressed as slave-women or freedwomen denounce women as foul and disgusting, the effect of which would have been compounded by characters themselves wearing ugly masks and lumpy costumes, like old Scapha in *Mostellaria* saying that old women use perfume because they smell bad (273–8): Terry Jones speaks here. Her opinion is enthusiastically endorsed by the peeping lover (thereby joining in with Terry Jones), who appeals to the personal experience of men in the audience married to old wives (279–81); the olfactory imagination, then, can be enlisted for stench as well as perfume. Moments like this explicitly activate the reciprocal gaze discussed in chapter 1, but, all along, both primping and ogling are multidirectional, as in the face-out lines seen in chapter 6: looking for an erotic "amen."

As seen above, Anterastilis in *Poenulus* makes a spectacular entrance with her sister, all the more so if they were both masked as Carthaginians. The scenes in *Mostellaria* and *Poenulus* are related, both featuring post-bath primping with kibitzing to one side and substantial overlaps in wording. Anterastilis plays the Scapha role here; in the song she and her sister sing, she compares women to smelly fish (240–5):

---

[59] On the possible placement of dark masks in the *palliata*, see Richlin forthcoming a. The idea that Ampelisca's appearance was somehow differentiated from Palaestra's is an old one, for example Webster 1949: 111.

[60] See Bodel 2005: 184, 186, 193–4, with illustrations; Bradley 1984: 115; Joshel 2010: 98–110.

ANTE. soror, cogita, amabo, item nos perhiberi   240
quam si salsa muriatica esse autumantur,
sine omni lepore et sine suavitate:
nisi multa aqua usque et diu macerantur.
    olent, salsa sunt, tangere ut non velis.
      item nos sumus.   245

ANTE. Sister, think, please, lovey, how they say we   240
are just like salt-pickled fish,
without any charm and without sweetness:
unless they are soaked in a lot of water for a long, long time,
    they stink, they're salty, so you wouldn't want to touch them;
      that's how we are.   245

As Dutsch says, "Dirt and stench are not uncommonly attributed to 'women' in Plautus."[61] Here is Anterastilis, viewed by other players onstage as a desirable woman, a scarce commodity; herself a spectacle at the moment, part of an elaborate song and (possibly) dance number (Moore 2012: 128) – and the voice that comes out of the mouth-hole of her mask sings a verse about how bad women smell. Did the best-friend role belong to Terry Jones, while the soprano roles went to RuPaul? At points like these in the plays, the man inside the woman shows himself to an audience already entertained by his masquerade. For *ancillae* in the audience, though, the drag act was not really about their own experience; what was?

Abusing the *Era*

Oral histories and interviews, as historians have finally gotten around to asking female workers what they think, have made it clear that the view of a female boss from below is often an unflattering one. Testimony ranging from American freed slaves to Bolivian domestic workers to housekeepers in Los Angeles today tells the same story of abuse, overwork, sexual tensions, and unwelcome familiarity with the body and personal habits of the owner or employer. In American slave narratives, "Ole Missy" is the counterpart of "Ole Massa," a byword for hypocrisy, meanness, and physical cruelty. Sandra Joshel (1986) used the example of Sofia in *The Color Purple* to put into perspective the statements about wet-nurses' loyalty by upper-class Roman males during the Principate: in Alice Walker's novel,

---

[61] Dutsch 2008: 158; on self-loathing and self-objectification in this bathing scene, see Dutsch 2008: 42–3, 156–61, and, on Scapha's speech, Dutsch 2015: 29.

the former nurse tells her old nursling that he was, to her, only a job.[62] Literary exposures of the antagonism between female owner and slave-woman long predate modern social realism, and appear in classic form in Ovid (*Amores* 2.7–8, see James 1997) and the satires of Juvenal (6.475–95). Nor does the evidence come only from male observers. Among the very few extant remains of Roman women's writing is a poem in which the elegist Sulpicia expresses sexual jealousy of a woman whom she labels "a whore weighed down / with a wool-basket" (*pressumque quasillo / scortum*, 3.16.3–4), presumably a household slave; yet Jane Stevenson, among others, has argued that an epitaph for a woman named Sulpicia Petale carefully memorializes the freed slave-woman who served as the elegist's "reader" – that is, she read aloud to her owner (2005: 42–4). Whatever the truth in individual cases, it is a fact that, onstage in the *palliata*, *matronae* serve as the butt of a centuries-old tradition of misogynistic jokes.

Within the world onstage, *ancillae* are the special property of the wife; Menaechmus I, railing at his (offstage) wife, complains about all the expensive things he has given her, and slave-women are first on the list (*ancillas*, *Men.* 120). (When the household is evoked, *ancillae* are often plural, and the flamboyant Phronesium has three attending her onstage.) A gendered division of labor within the household is attested throughout the plays, along with in-house textile work (*Cas.* 261, *Men.* 120–1, 796–7, *Mer.* 396–9, 416, 517–20), while *ancillae* tend female owners onstage as they primp (*Mos.* 157–294) or bathe (*Poen.* 332) or, like Phronesium, pretend to be ill (*Truc.* 476–81). This element in the *palliata* is the only evidence we have for what household *ancillae* did in the 200s BCE. If it is realistic, then slave-women in the audience who worked as women's personal servants might have enjoyed the appalling figure cut by *matronae* in the plays, especially in the safely distanced form of men dressed up as old bags. If the *senex* looks bad, his wife looks worse.

Plays in which a *senex* hates his current – or dead – wife, or wives in general, and says so at length and often in the harshest terms, include *Asinaria*, *Aulularia*, *Casina*, *Epidicus* (briefly, 173–80), *Menaechmi*, *Mercator*, *Miles Gloriosus*, *Mostellaria*, and *Trinummus* – almost half the extant plays; Caecilius Statius' *Plocium* certainly belongs to that group (see fr. 158–62, 163 R$_3$ as well as the long fragment above). It is an understatement to say

---

[62] For oral histories and interviews with female slaves and house servants, see for example Gill 1990, Hondagneu-Sotelo 2007, Mellon 1988 (excerpts from the WPA interviews with freed slaves); the short stories of Lucia Berlin (1977, 1981) speak from the writer's lived experience as a cleaning woman. On friction between female owners and slaves in the family of Augustine in the context of domestic violence, with many parallels from the Principate, see Clark 1998.

that *matronae* are rarely specularized onstage.[63] The only plays in which a wife looks at all good are *Amphitruo* (and Alcumena's good points are not unambiguously portrayed) and *Stichus* (where the husbands are reunited onstage with their father-in-law and their *parasitus* but not with their wives, who have been longing to see them). Vengeful wives appear in *Asinaria*, *Casina*, *Menaechmi*, and *Mercator*, spreading terror, ending parties, and threatening to beat their husbands or divorce them. Even the independent Daemones in *Rudens* claims his wife is preventing him from making time with Palaestra and Ampelisca (893–6), and that she will kick him out if he brings home women she considers *paelices* (1045–8). Husbands accuse wives of acquisitiveness, inquisitiveness, garrulity, smelling bad, and living too long; they express fear of their wives; they express disgust at the thought of kissing or having sex with an old wife; they wish for their wives' death or say they rejoiced at the death of a wife. Husbands talk like this to their friends, to their wives' faces, and sometimes to their (male) slaves (especially Demaenetus to Libanus in *Asinaria*, and Lysidamus to Olympio in *Casina*); notably, the slaves chime in. Libanus begins *Asinaria* with an oath that depends on the husband's fear and hatred of his wife (16–22); Olympio calls Cleostrata a bitch (*Cas.* 320). The bewildered Menaechmus II abuses the wife of Menaechmus I, also focusing on her bitchy qualities (*Men.* 714–18, 837). The slave Lampadio in *Cistellaria* insinuates that the *matrona* Phanostrata is drunk (667). Even the occasional casual bystander, like the Cook in *Mercator*, will repeat to a wife some horrible insult (760–1); Chalinus (an unusual example of a male slave in league with a *matrona*) unhesitatingly reports to Cleostrata that her husband would like to see her dead (*Cas.* 354–5); even a divine prologue speaker (Auxilium in *Cistellaria*) will throw in a gratuitous "take my wife" joke: "she passed away, she became dutiful to her husband" (*ea diem suom obiit, facta morigera est viro*, 175). Above all, Sosia in *Amphitruo* takes on an adversarial role in relation to Alcumena, and repeatedly insults her, as seen in chapter 4; interestingly, Mercurius tries to help Jupiter placate her, and she defends him from a beating (540).

Ancillae, however, do not insult their owners as often as male slaves insult theirs, and the only female character who complains at length about *matronae* as a class is the *lena* in *Cistellaria*. Most negative remarks about

---

[63] This curious absence fits in with Parker's demonstration (2007) of a general lack of concern in Roman texts about the possibility that married women are having sex with their slaves; contrast the lurid scenario in Herodas, *Mim.* 5. Still, although the free ex-*virgines* in *Aulularia* and *Truculentus* make no appearance, the Virgo in *Persa* is specularized at length, as seen above, and is chosen precisely for her looks: thinkable because she is poor?

matronae come from prostitutes, or from prostitutes' attendants like Scapha in her excursus on old women's use of perfume. Indeed, *ancillae* sometimes support their owners, most notably in *Casina*, where Pardalisca plays a key role in Cleostrata's plans; as seen above, Bromia defends Alcumena, and Syra in *Mercator*, despite her burdens, speaks on behalf of *matronae*, not of *ancillae*.[64] Milphidippa in *Miles* and Halisca in *Cistellaria* do their best for their freedwoman owners, one at each end of the prostitute's life cycle. As male slaves often do, *ancillae* occasionally help the young owner, in their case a daughter of the house, as do Staphyla in *Aulularia* and the two slave-women in *Truculentus* who smuggle out the unnamed daughter's baby and stand up to the resulting interrogation. But even Pardalisca crowns her gleeful account of the progress of the plot with a gratuitous slam at the gluttony of her owner and the neighbor's wife: "I know those gobblemouth girls" (*novi ego illas ambestrices*, 777–9). As seen in chapter 4, Sophoclidisca complains about Lemniselenis with disgust. And although Astaphium assures Phronesium of her support (*Truc.* 711–18), saying, "You just go on, as you like, in this game of yours," *tu perge ut lubet ludo in istoc*, 718), her expression of comparative loyalty to Phronesium makes it clear that coercion is involved: "Someone's calling me and she has more power over me than you do" (*vocat me quae in me potest plus quam potes*, 755). What did the actors see of their sisters' lives? Maybe to them the abuse of slave-women was beyond a joke. Maybe they kept Casina offstage to protect her. The convention whereby citizen daughters do not appear onstage (resoundingly broken in *Persa*) is often said to reflect Athenian decorum, but this was not Athens, and Menander did not write these plays. Plautus, as the *Casina* prologue explains, broke down the bridge.

"I will still be some mother's daughter"

The one plot element in the plays which might have appealed equally to *ancillae* and *matronae*, to the free poor as well as to slaves and freed slaves, was the occasional reunion of mothers (and sometimes other kin) with their long-lost children (see chapter 7). Such mothers are mentioned, but only briefly, in *Captivi* (389), *Curculio* (642–3), *Menaechmi* (19–21, 28, 1103, 1131), *Poenulus* (1065–8, 1253), and *Rudens* (1163–4, 1174, 1179–81, 1203–5), and the mother's name sometimes plays a part among the recognition signs. The Virgo in *Persa* has no visible mother, and in her made-up Arabian history mentions her mother only in a joke (630–1). The reunion of the

---

[64] On such mutual support, see Feltovich 2011; James 2012 and forthcoming.

Carthaginian *nutrix* Giddenis with her son is staged as a joke, although Giddenis evidently expresses vehement emotion ("loud shouting," *clarus clamor*, 1146), and, uniquely for a *nutrix*, is shown with a child of her own. Both she and her son will remain slaves; their reunion confers no legitimacy; that is part of the joke. But in two plays, mothers of lost children play a major role: in *Cistellaria*, the kind foster mother Melaenis and the birth mother Phanostrata; in *Epidicus*, Philippa, the devoted mother of the war captive Telestis.

Philippa is among those kin in the plays who travel in search of a stolen or captured child. Reunions often occasion a display of strong emotion – respected, as Giddenis' is not: Menaechmus II shouts (*Men.* 1114) and hugs his brother (1124); Hanno weeps both while seeking his grown daughters (*Poen.* 1109) and when he first sees them (1192); Daemones, whose daughter washes up on his doorstep, embraces her (*Rud.* 1175), and her invisible mother is said to fuss over her with much kissing (1203–5). *Epidicus* does not give Philippa the opportunity to fuss, or even to see Telestis onstage; having traveled to Athens from conquered Thebes in search of her daughter, she first confronts Periphanes, the man who raped and deserted her in Epidaurus, then is presented with the freed *fidicina* whom Periphanes thinks is her daughter, much to her dismay – this is when she weeps (601). The actual recognition is usurped by the slave Epidicus (634–54), and Philippa does not appear again in the play. One point about her that is well established is that she was a poor girl when Periphanes raped her (*pauperculam*, 540b; *virgini pauperculae*, 555; *paupertatem*, 556), and is still poor (*pauperem*, 169; *paupertas*, 530); she arrives onstage with no slave to carry her luggage, or any indication she is accompanied.

She is not the only mother in search of a lost daughter. Phanostrata in *Cistellaria*, also raped as a young girl, is trying to find the daughter she had then borne and exposed. This daughter's life was saved by a *meretrix* (now a *lena*, with a *meretrix* daughter of her own, Gymnasium) who saw Phanostrata's father's slave Lampadio expose the baby; the *lena* in turn gave the baby to her friend and fellow *meretrix*, the freedwoman Melaenis. The foster mother has treated the girl Selenium as her own, raised her "well and chastely" (*bene ac pudice*, 173), and allowed her to hope for monogamy, even marriage, with the young man she loves (77, 83–5, 87–8, 98–9). When he breaks his word (101–3, cf. 241, 243), Melaenis confronts him (460–527), standing up to his anger, even his threats to murder them both. She sees the problem in terms of class, as she tells the audience: "So, since it's not allowed for a poor person [to deal] with a rich one on equal terms, / I'll waste my effort rather than lose my daughter" (*postremo, quando aequa*

lege pauperi cum divite / non licet, perdam operam potius quam carebo filia,
532–3). When she overhears Phanostrata and Lampadio identifying her
foundling daughter (549–50), promising respectability and a big dowry for
the daughter (556–63), and giving as their opinion that the foster mother
is a *nutrix* and not a mother (558), she is horrified (551, 576): Phanostrata's
gain will be her loss (573). Phanostrata's search, however belated, is fervent
(670) and determined (759); once the truth is uncovered, Phanostrata and
Lampadio insist that the daughter is hers and not Melaenis' (745–6, 749–
50, 756), and Melaenis' *ancilla* Halisca humbly agrees (762–4). Melaenis,
in contrast, behaves with noble self-sacrifice (626–30; 631–4, in a flurry
of possessive adjectives), and Selenium continues to call her "my mother"
(*mater mea*, 639–40) – almost her last lines in the play. Gymnasium and
the *lena*, unlike other mother-daughter prostitute pairs in the plays, likewise seem to love each other, despite the way the *lena* uses her daughter;
when the *lena* is threatened with losing Gymnasium, Lampadio reports,
"the old woman hugged [Gymnasium's] knees weeping, begging / that she
not desert her" (*anus ei amplexa est genua plorans, opsecrans / ne deserat se,*
567–8). It is clear from the opening scene, indeed from the first two lines
when Selenium greets Gymnasium and her mother as beloved friends, that
Cistellaria concerns mothers and daughters as well as both bonds and divisions between women; as seen above, the *lena* says of *matronae* that they
want women like the *lena* to lack what they have, and that turns out to be
predictive in this play.

The point of this story as well as of Philippa's in *Epidicus* is thus not only
the particular cost to all women of war and of childbirth outside marriage,
but also the heavier cost to slave and freed-slave women. The fantasy of
the rescuing mother does not go so far as to make the free women generalize their benevolence (compare Ampelisca's speech about the priestess of
Venus, above). The irony of the distinction Philippa and Periphanes draw
between their daughter and slave prostitutes (*Epid.* 400–3, 579) is underscored by Epidicus, who retorts to his owner that Acropolistis is certainly
a daughter and indeed the daughter of some mother (*Epid.* 699–700),
echoing Acropolistis' own words: "even if she doesn't want me, I'll still
be [my/a] mother's daughter" (*equidem hac invita tamen ero matris filia,*
585). Still, like the two slave-women in *Truculentus*, all these women know
where slaves come from. For all the lost children and the mothers of lost
children in the audience, the successful search would have been a powerful fantasy. As the Virgo in *Persa* says, "When my father knows / I've been
sold, he'll be here himself and he'll buy me back from you" (*meu' pater, ubi
me sciet / veniisse, ipse aderit et me aps te redimet,* 653–4). Often, the lost,

finally found, address the rescuer "Oh, unhoped-for one" (*o insperate*) and the rescuer responds in kind.

Another fantasy that is played out here is a do-over, the transformation of the almost-family into a legal family, one in which children have a legal claim to parents (what Giddenis and her son lack). Phanostrata's rapist, eighteen years later (755–6), seeks her out to marry her (177–9), and she and her husband want to find and reinstate their lost daughter (180–5); even Periphanes in *Epidicus*, once presented with (what his slave tells him is) his long-lost daughter, not only manumits her (503–9, 564–5) and treats her as virginal (400–3), but wishes vaguely to find and marry her mother (169–72). Their attitudes contrast sharply with that of the *senex* Callicles who tortures the two slave-women: he wants to get his grandson back, but treats his own daughter as damaged goods and tells her rapist to marry her and get her out of his house at once (*Truc.* 839–47). The son-in-law in turn agrees to leave the baby, his own son, on loan with the prostitute Phronesium (878): the seed of a future comedy, another lost child. The 200s BCE were hard on families.

When the Fat Lady Sings

In the *palliata*, she never does; Plautus' sister did not get to Rome, or, if she did, we do not know about it. Behind the masks onstage there might have been a woman passing as a man, as so many women have done in the history of the stage, but their secret has been well kept – do not look for them in John Starks's catalogue of actresses in antiquity. Slave-women in the audience might well have enjoyed characters like Sophoclidisca or Astaphium, or admired the *ancillae* who are interrogated in *Truculentus*, but they must have noticed that the central slave (if the extant plays are typical) is never an *ancilla*, and that the *ancillae* onstage are men wearing dresses. Maybe, for some women in the audience, both slave and freed, this was complicated by the dress itself: the Greek *palla*, worn onstage by slave and free women alike, just as almost everybody onstage has a Greek name. For some, that was their old dress. The plays displace wives' sexual jealousy of *ancillae* onto prostitutes (themselves often slaves or freedwomen), while any fear of wives felt by *ancillae* is left to be expressed by male slave characters. The sexual jeopardy of female household slaves is largely erased from the plays – odd, when the sexual jeopardy of male slaves is so present. This must be an artifact of the maleness of writers and troupe.

Overall, what slave-women want in these plays does not have a lot to do with the desires of the male slaves surveyed in chapter 4, and the audience does not even get a list of anything specific to them: a room somewhere, girls in white dresses with blue satin sashes, a hot dog for my roll. That women like to drink – a very old joke – moves, in the *palliata*, from housewives (as in *Lysistrata* and *Thesmophoriazusae*) to slave-women, usually old ones (Syra's thirst; Leaena's major song in *Curculio*) and other old women (the *lena* in *Cistellaria*). Most of the female characters are seen, as it were, from the outside; *ancillae* very rarely step up and tell the audience how things look from their point of view – Sophoclidisca and Astaphium are exceptional. Syra in *Mercator* speaks up, but for *matronae*, and does so through a crone mask worn by a male actor; Palaestra's lament is undercut by her costume. One major statement about the lot of women in general is made by the unnamed Ancilla in *Truculentus*; the Virgo tells what it feels like to be sold; Acropolistis lays claim to a mother of her own. But, by and large, a lot of the messages we would like to hear from a theater run by slaves are just missing: the ones attesting to the experience and desires of female slaves. Instead, we have, and not too often, a desire common to both male and female members of a slave society: the desire for the restoration of the family. We will see more of this in the memories of freedom in chapter 7, and the fantasies of escape and manumission in chapter 8. First let us turn to a closer examination of how slave characters express what they want when it is dangerous to do so.

CHAPTER 6

Telling Without Saying

The science fiction writer Ursula Le Guin, from the 1990s through the 2000s, was thinking about slavery.[1] In her book *Four Ways to Forgiveness*, she imagines life on a planet that had been owned by corporations and turned into plantations worked by slaves; there has been an uprising, and now the former slaves are in control. An outside observer comes for a visit and is invited to a ceremonial dinner. The after-dinner entertainment begins with a singer (1995: 178–9):

> ... as the table fell silent he sang, but in a whisper.
>
> Instruments of music had been forbidden on most plantations; most Bosses had allowed no singing ... A slave caught wasting Corporation time in singing might have acid poured down his throat. So long as he could work there was no need for him to make noise.
>
> On such plantations the slaves had developed this almost silent music, the touch and brush of palm against palm, a barely voiced, barely varied, long line of melody. The words sung were deliberately broken, distorted, fragmented, so that they seemed meaningless. *Shesh*, the owners had called it, rubbish, and slaves were permitted to "pat hands and sing rubbish" so long as they did it so softly it could not be heard outside the compound walls.

This account must startle any student of Latin literature, where "rubbish" is exactly the term that is used of nonsense, of certain kinds of comic speech – *nugae*. But the slave society Le Guin here imagines is a particularly harsh one, even more harsh than Roman slavery, which, on farms, at least allowed exchanges of insults (chapter 3), and, in the cities, the *palliata*

---

[1] Le Guin's novel *Lavinia* (2008) retells the second half of the *Aeneid* from the perspective of the girl who is silent throughout Vergil's poem. Evidently in preparation for this project, Le Guin published a series of three young adult novels set in a culture that resembles early Italy, especially in its slave system (seen close up in *Voices*, 2006; *Powers*, 2007). She began in the 1990s to write about the brutal plantation culture cited here; with *Four Ways to Forgiveness* (1995), see also the remarkable story "Old Music and the Slave Women," in the collection *The Birthday of the World* (2003: 153–211), and the parable "The Rock that Changed Things" (1994), discussed in chapter 1.

and the hope of manumission.[2] In New World slavery, the brutality gave rise to a major musical tradition. We still live in its aftermath; yet, even with the music, the idea of silenced words, of a need to control vocalization, is hardly unfamiliar to us as a feature of slavery. Among American slave narratives, for example, an ex-slave named Mollie Dawson, speaking to the WPA interviewer, said, "He [the master] threatened to whip him good, if he didn't go and do what he was told ter do, without any backtalk" (in Mellon 1988: 426). Eugene Genovese, in his book about American slave culture, quotes Frederick Douglass on songs sung at slave celebrations:

> The fiddling, dancing, and "jubilee beating" was carried on in all directions. The latter performance was strictly southern. It supplied the place of the violin or other musical instruments and was played so easily that almost every farm had its juba beater. The performer improvised as he beat the instrument, marking the words as he sang so as to have them fall pat with the movement of his hands. Once in a while among a mass of nonsense and wild frolic, a sharp hit was given to the meanness of the slaveholders. Take the following example:

> > We raise de wheat,
> > Dey gib us de corn;
> > We bake de bread,
> > Dey gib us de crust;
> > We sif' de meal,
> > Dey gib us de huss;
> > We peel de meat,
> > Dey gib us de skin;
> > And dat's de way
> > Dey take us in ...

Again, the critique is hidden "among a mass of nonsense." Genovese then remarks, "A few other such songs have survived, along with hints of many others lost. Since the slaves did not sing them in front of whites, the written record remained slim."[3]

---

[2] On Roman work songs, see Horsfall 2003: 43–5; we have evidence of men's songs and a trace of a lullaby used by *nutrices*. See *Commentum Cornuti* 3.15.5–6, on Pers. 3.17–18 (in 18, *mammae lallare* is what nurses do); the commentator observes (Clausen and Zetzel 2004: 73): [*nutrices*] *saepe dicere solent: lalla, lalla, lalla, id est aut dormi aut lacta*. This comment has sometimes been used to reconstruct a line of verse (a phantom, Angelo Mercado tells me, hence not in Mercado 2012), but at least Persius attests to *lallare*. He juxtaposes it to *pappare* ("chew pap") in line 17; cf. the cryptic juxtaposition of *palpas* and *lal(l)as*, or λαλεῖς, at *Poen.* 343. The conjuncture nurse – slave – foreigner – babbler, with the onomatopoeic verb λαλεῖν, resembles the nexus of meanings around *muttio* (below; also below on *etiam muttis?* and its Greek cousin ἔτι λαλεῖς;). See Karanika 2014 for women's work songs in Greek, and Colesanti 2014: 102–6 on Greek lullabies.

[3] Genovese 1976: 581, quoting Frederick Douglass, *The Life and Times of Frederick Douglass*. The song appears in slightly different versions in both of Douglass's extended autobiographies, *My Bondage and*

Anthropological writing about such phenomena goes back at least to Edward and Shirley Ardener in the late 1960s, applying the idea of "muted groups" to the study of women: dominated groups have their own language, one that modifies the dominant language for its own needs. The dominated group understands both languages; the dominant group does not.[4] As with women, so with slaves: Henry Louis Gates, in *The Signifying Monkey* (1988), gives a rhetorical analysis of the African-American speech practice called "signifying," and traces its use of double meanings through the records of observers of slavery from the eighteenth century onwards.[5] The principles of joking speech discussed in chapter 1 are related to the general principles of what ancient rhetoricians called "figured speech," a way of telling without saying, of talking about power in the presence of the powerful; Antonin Obrdlik argued, "if [the oppressors] can afford to ignore it, they are strong" (1942: 716), but it might equally be argued that this kind of speech, in Rome, acted as a warning to the powerful – useful, in a century of power struggles.[6] It is fair to say that, in Roman culture, speaking truth to power in lines with double meaning was an art form from as far back as we have records; in the *palliata*, this works in a way particular to the conditions of slavery in the 200s BCE. The audiences were full of people familiar with these conditions, including slaves and freed slaves. The kinds of speech to be examined in this chapter addressed that experience at two levels, both acting out in scenes onstage the process whereby speech is simultaneously suppressed and expressed, and constituting that process, as slave/actors onstage addressed slaves and freed slaves in the audience. In other words, as is always the case in comedy, some people in the audience "got it" in a way that others could not. Not that the position of the *summus vir* sitting in the audience was a simple one; there were many ways in which he might have enjoyed the performance, even have

---

My Freedom (1855) and *Life and Times* (1881), and can be found in the Gates edition at 1994: 290 and 595. For the problems posed by the historical sources on American slavery, see Genovese 1976: 675–8.

[4] For a chronological review of the Ardeners' evolution of this idea, which became influential in the study of women and language, see S. Ardener 2005. The epistemological dynamics were worked out in feminist standpoint theory by Sandra Harding, Nancy Hartsock, and Dorothy Smith in relation to Hegel's ideas on the master–slave dialectic and their development in Marxism; see essays in Harding 1987. This raises the issue of the priority of sex-based oppression, which, as seen in chapter 5, is hard to get at for this period (addressed by Dutsch 2008).

[5] On the history of slaves' satirical critique, and the ways in which they masked its meaning "as a mode of encoding for self-preservation," see Gates 1988: 66–8; he includes Douglass's discussion and, as here, an excerpt from the song, quoted from *My Bondage and My Freedom*. On "the secret of saying the 'yes' which accomplishes the expressive 'no'" (Ralph Ellison's phrase), see Genovese 1976: 582–3.

[6] On "figured speech" from Aeschylus to the Second Sophistic, see the classic study by Frederick Ahl (1984).

felt that the performance addressed him above all others. As the speakers surveyed in this chapter take pains to emphasize, the meaning of comedy is open: that is the point.

Double Meaning

The much studied lines of the *Amphitruo* prologue in which Mercurius promises a *tragicomoedia* (50–63) incorporate a statement about double meaning (54–5, 59–63):

> eandem hanc, si voltis, faciam \<iam\> ex tragoedia
> comoedia ut sit omnibus isdem vorsibus.   55
> ...
> faciam ut commixta sit; \<sit\> tragicomoedia;
> nam me perpetuo facere ut sit comoedia,   60
> reges quo veniant et di, non par arbitror.
> quid igitur? quoniam hic servos quoque partis habet,
> faciam sit, proinde ut dixi, tragicomoedia.

> This same play, if you want, I'll now make from a tragedy
> into a comedy, with all the very same verses.   55
> ...
> I'll make it be a mixture; let it be a tragicomedy;
> indeed, for me to make it be a comedy all the way through,   60
> where kings and gods come – I don't judge that a match.
> What then? Since a slave also plays a part here,
> I'll make it be, just like I said, a tragicomedy.

That the same lines, or turns – the same *vorsibus* – can be both comic and tragic is what allows slaves on stage to be funny, because, in itself, crucifixion is not funny.[7] Some kinds of comedy rise up out of an underlying social injustice, as a way to ease the pain. Mercurius jokes that this play cannot be entirely a comedy, because *reges* (rich men) and gods are in it, the usual denizens of tragedy – but then slaves also have a part (62): he identifies slaves with the comic. Funny, because in fact it is more fun to be a rich man than it is to be a slave. Just as in the nineteenth-century US and Britain the Great Famine, poverty, emigration, and ensuing structural

---

[7] Except in *Monty Python's Life of Brian*. For discussion of the *Amphitruo* passage, see esp. Bond 1999 (accentuating the tragic) and Moore 1995 (accentuating the comic), both based on performance; also Christenson 2000: 146–50; Gunderson 2015: 77–9, 206–10, 217–26; Lefèvre 1982; Sharrock 2009: 133; Slater 1985: 150–1. Histories of American slavery are full of striking parallels; with *tragicomoedia*, compare again Gates's discussion of Frederick Douglass (1988: 67): "his fellow slaves 'would sing the most pathetic sentiment in the most rapturous tone, and the most rapturous sentiment in the most pathetic tone,' a set of oppositions which led to the song's misreading by non-slaves."

ethnic prejudice made comic Scotsmen and Irishmen, and slavery made the minstrel show (often enacted in the US, as Eric Lott notes, by Irishmen); and just as in the twentieth-century US structural racism made Richard Pryor and ethnic stereotyping made the Marx Brothers and homophobia made Nathan Lane and Harvey Fierstein and misogyny made Lucille Ball and Whoopi Goldberg and Sarah Silverman – so, in the 200s BCE, endemic war and mass enslavement made the comic slave.[8] Mercurius sets up his "tragicomedy" as just what the audience wants, claiming to know this for a fact because he is a god (56–8). The prologue speaker of *Captivi* similarly promises that there will be no tragedy from "us with our comic training" (*comico choragio*, 61–2) – and says so with the two chained men standing onstage. Indeed chains and bonds are common props in the *palliata*. This scene enacts the open secret that also produced its audience: war transforms people by violent changes to their civil status, but everybody pretends slaves are intrinsically slaves. Enslavement is tragic, not comic. This audience gets the joke, which does not need to be spelled out. They are used to telling without saying.

In *Captivi*, as the chained men speak, Tyndarus watches Philocrates fencing with their new owner, Hegio, and comments on his progress, much as Toxilus watches the Virgo fence with the pimp in *Persa*. Both kibitzers are slaves watching a freeborn person masquerade as a slave (in Philocrates' case, a captured slave); both feigned slaves speak to their interlocutors in lines that have two meanings: one true, one meant to throw off the interlocutor, who is an owner or purchaser. "Slavery didn't annoy me much," says Philocrates to Hegio; "it was no different for me than if I were the son of the house" (*non multum fuit molesta servitus, / nec mihi secus erat quam si essem familiaris filius*, 272–3). Just like one of the family. As the audience knows, Philocrates *was* the son of the house. Tyndarus sums up: "How cleverly he tailors his speech to slavery" (*ut facete orationem ad servitutem contulit*, 276). Like Philocrates' line, Tyndarus' has two meanings: (1) Philocrates is doing a good job of sounding like a slave; (2) Philocrates is doing a good job of concealing one meaning inside another, which is how slaves have to speak.

The effectiveness of the joke structure in both shielding and defusing words spoken onstage, and the potential for active misprision by members

---

[8] On the minstrel show and Irish ethnicity, see Lott 1993: 35, 94–6, 136–7; on anti-Irish racism in the nineteenth century, see Curtis 1984; on ethnicity and standup comedy, Daube 2010, A. Davis 2011: 57–60; on misogyny and comedy, Lavin 2004, Lee 2004. Bosher 2013 makes a similar argument about the increasing commonness of slaves on Sicilian vases in the 300s BCE.

of the audience, are spelled out by Gripus at the end of *Rudens*, as he complains about his owner's high-minded appropriation of the suitcase he wants as a ticket to freedom (1249–53):

> spectavi ego pridem comicos ad istunc modum
> sapienter dicta dicere, atque is plaudier,   1250
> quom illos sapientis mores monstrabant poplo:
> sed quom inde suam quisque ibant divorsi domum,
> nullus erat illo pacto ut illi iusserant.

> I've watched comic actors before now, just like this,
> speak wise sayings, and everyone applauds for them,   1250
> when they've pointed out wise ways to the people:
> but when everybody went their separate ways back home from there,
> there was nobody who acted like they'd told them to!

In a previous scene, Gripus, much to his chagrin, had lost possession of the suitcase that (he thinks) holds money; his owner Daemones is the one who decided against him. In this scene, Gripus has come back to try again, offering Daemones a cut, and Daemones has said no. "That's why you're poor," retorts Gripus, "because you're too piously virtuous" (*isto tu pauper es quom nimi' sancte piu's*, 1234). This sets Daemones off into a long, pompous speech about the hazards of appropriating other people's property (1235–48), evidently a speech expected to draw applause (1250).[9] Gripus' reply here, spoken as much to the audience as to Daemones, undercuts Daemones' argument, framing it as just the kind of pious speech that gets made on the comic stage. Nor does this lauded piety, he argues, have any lasting effect on the spectators; his critique, then, is as much of the audience (*poplo*) as it is of the onstage owner, as in other transgressive critiques actors make of the audience (Moore 1998: 8–23, esp. at 15). The reaction is fast: Daemones speaks, some applaud, Gripus picks them up on it. Yet his speech is not unambiguously a critique at all; his words apply, on the one

---

[9] That this speech is a sendup is cued by the lead-in: *O Gripe, Gripe* (1235), picking up the ludicrous address to the bulrush by the pimp: *O scirpe, scirpe* (523). Paratragic: compare perhaps Livius Andronicus, *O Strymon ... <ex> Graio stirpe exo<rti>* (*trag. inc.* 41 Kl = 30 *TrRF*). Or this may have been an Ennian tic: compare *O pater, o patria, o Priami domus* (from *Andromacha*, *trag.* 81 R = 82 Kl = 23.10 *TrRF*); *O terra T<h>r<a>eca* (*trag. inc.* 347–48 R = 347 Kl = 167 *TrRF*); *O Fides alma* (*trag. inc.* 380 R = 380 Kl = 165 *TrRF*). The action of *Rudens* begins with a gesture to the *Alcumena Euripidi* (*Rud.* 86), so perhaps an Ennian version lurks behind the extant version of *Rudens*. Not that there is any reason the parodied line should be extant; paratragedy seems indicated in any case. So also Moore 1998: 80, following Marx *ad loc.* (1959[1928]: 211); Marx compares the use of this figure (epanadiplosis) in Greek tragedy, and several paratragic versions in Aristophanes, positing a sequence Euripides – Diphilus – Plautus. Moore includes this exchange among numerous metatheatrical speeches that set up the plays' moralizing as ironic (67–90); see below on Stasimus' editorial, and on "good slave" speeches.

hand, to speeches like Daemones' and the "good slave" speeches, and on the other hand to the many onstage critiques of slavery (below) – as well as to his own speech: metatheatrical, self-reflexive. As joke structure disclaims hostile content, so Gripus speech defends comedy from the suspicion that it might affect behavior. Like joke structure itself, this defense is disingenuous (chapter 1). Moreover, like Chrysalus, and like Mercurius (chapter 3), Gripus here places himself among those onstage slaves who say they have been to the theater; his comments on the kind of thing that draws applause make a meta-statement about how slaves witness what goes on. In the open-air, broad-daylight setting of Italian theater in the 200s BCE, everyone could see who was there and how they behaved. Gripus words suggest that the spectators were free to do what they wanted to with stage wisdom. Daemones tells Gripus to go in the house and curb his tongue (1254).

As seen in chapter 5, the Virgo in *Persa*, while being sold, produces a string of coded statements that comment on her father's betrayal of her as well as on the experience of enslavement; the pimp is not meant to get the double meaning, but the audience is, and Toxilus comments on her ability to tell the truth in disguise (*nihil scit nisi verum loqui*, 645). His line, too, has one meaning for the pimp, another for the audience, now in collusion with him; aside, he has been expressing delight in her ability to deceive throughout the scene, and, as noted above, the audience gets more than even he does. Many lines from slaves to owners in Plautus have this quality; when the slave Sagaristio, disguised as the slave-dealer from Persia, tells the pimp his name, he (thinly) conceals a declaration of what he has done to the pimp inside the name as he invents it (*Per.* 701–5):

> SAG. ausculta ergo, ut scias:
> Vaniloquidorus Virginesvendonides
> Nugiepiloquides Argentumexterebronides
> Tedigniloquides Nuncaesexpalponides
> Quodsemelarripides Numquameripides. em tibi!   705

> SAG. So listen, you'll know:
> Emptyspeakergift Virginsellerson
> Garbagespeakerson Cashiscrewyououtofson
> Whatyoudeservespeakerson Nowimsqueezingthedoughoutson
> Whatonceistealson Younevergetbackson. There you go!   705

As he responds to the pimp's straight-man question, "What is your name?" (*quid est tibi nomen?*, 700), Sagaristio's lead-in *ausculta* lets the audience know a joke and a lie will be forthcoming, and the name indeed tells the pimp off, telling without saying. The pimp misses the secret message (unlike the audience) and is impressed. This spectacular invented name, a mashup of Greek and Latin, constitutes, unlike the names imposed on slaves, a defiant claim to power; the closing exclamation *em tibi!* often accompanies a slap.

Face-Out Lines

Another sort of speech, associated primarily with slaves, directly addresses the audience with highly charged commentary on slavery as an institution. Unlike the monologues discussed in chapters 2 and 4 in which slaves like Sosia or Sagaristio voice anger towards their owners, these other lines, when read on a page, can just pass as platitudes or generalizing dialogue. In performance, these lines could have been delivered so as to convey a double meaning, letting a dangerous statement be masked as innocuous. The mask itself provides a sort of plausible deniability. Asides, of course, break out of the flow of dialogue to address the audience, with the dialogue and clock then resuming as if nothing had intervened. To deliver an aside, an actor turns his face away from his interlocutor and towards the audience; asides are not marked "aside" in the text, but readers can recognize them by, for instance, a switch from second to third person, or provocative content to which the interlocutor does not react. But some lines, often with gnomic or axiomatic content, arguably address both the interlocutor and the audience, like Gripus' speech about comedy. These, too, might have been indicated by a turn of the speaker's face outwards after the speech, perhaps just a flicker, akin to an unmasked stage wink, and so I have grouped them together as "face-out lines."[10]

A lot of these lines feel dragged in, like non sequiturs, and are marked by the fact that the interlocutor does not pick up on them, as if they were asides. As seen in chapter 4, when the soldier in *Curculio* protests to the banker Lyco that he has no freed slave, Lyco replies, "You act more wisely / than some pimps, who have freedmen and abandon them" (*faci' sapientius/ quam pars lenonum, libertos qui habent et eos deserunt,* 547–8). The soldier comes back with "What now?" (*quid nunc?* 549), and Lyco goes on with an

---

[10] Schechner 2006: 102–3 deals with winks as an example of "metacommunication" – the "I'm joking" cue – but a stage wink, like a wink to a bystander A during conversation with B, enlists A on the side of the speaker. See Moore 1998 on rapport in the Plautus plays, esp. his remarks on class (10–23). For a maneuver comparable to the "face-out" I am suggesting, see Marshall 1999 on the "double aside." Marshall stresses the usefulness and force of sharp head movements in masked acting.

explanation that the deal has been completed. The last two acts of *Curculio* seem to have been drastically condensed (which, following Marshall's model, I take to be an artifact of transcription and/or of a particular performance), but, in the text we have, Lyco's crack at pimps comes out of nowhere and elicits no comeback from the soldier. It constitutes part of the plays' general antagonism towards pimps, with particular appeal to pimps' slaves and freed slaves in the audience, consistent with complaints by such slaves elsewhere (Syncerastus in *Poenulus*, the *puer* in *Pseudolus*) and with the displays of mistreatment of slaves put on by Ballio and, to a lesser extent, by Dordalus in *Persa*. In light of the plays' general dim view of bankers (chapter 3), it is incongruous for Lyco here to speak out on behalf of freed slaves, a break out of character that draws attention to the actor inside the banker costume. As Moore argues, actors in speeches like these express a kind of power over the audience, and I would say that the face-out lines in general constitute a claim to the power of speech for those who, offstage, have none. They turn the whole *palliata* into a kind of *quiritatio*.

A number of face-out lines deal with the pain of slavery and can be generically summed up in the words of the *Captivi* prologue discussed in chapter 3: *haec res agetur nobis, vobis fabula* (52): "This action will be real for us, a play for you." Thus Epidicus replies to his younger owner's threat of a stint in the mill (*Epid.* 146–7),

> facile tu istuc sine periclo et cura, corde libero
> fabulare; novi ego nostros: mihi dolet quom ego vapulo.
>
> You say that easily, without hazard or concern, with a free heart;
> I know how it is with us: I'm the one who hurts when I take a beating.

"I know how it is with us" [wink], or "I know how it is at *our* house" [wink], or "I know how it is with *our* lineage" [wink]: these ambiguous words pull (some people in) the audience into cahoots with the speaker. The meter stresses *novi, nostros, mihi*, while the double *ego* pushes against the meter (the insistent "I" forced into the unstressed position), possibly helped by gestures. The words of Epidicus here recall those of the Ancilla as she stands, bound, on the stage, explaining to her owner that she knows for herself how much it hurts to be beaten (*Truc.* 815; see chapter 5). Similarly, the rude *puer* Phaniscus gives the unrecognized *senex* an answer like Epidicus': "Freedom is a cloak for your back: / for me, unless I fear my owner and take care of him, there's nothing to cover my back with" (*libertas paenulast tergo tuo: / mihi, nisi ut erum metuam et curem, nihil est qui tergum tegam, Mos.* 991–2).

The same reminders of who gets hurt when a slave is beaten pervade the opening dialogue between Agorastocles and his slave Milphio in *Poenulus*, as in this exchange (150–1):

> [AG.] quin si feriri video te, extemplo dolet.
> MI. mihi quidem hercle. AG. immo mihi. MI. istuc mavelim.

> [AG.] Why, if I see you being struck, it hurts me at once.
> MI. Me, in fact, by God. AG. No, me! MI. I'd like that better.

"I'd like that better" [wink]. Milphio repeatedly asks Agorastocles to change places with him, or join him, and see how it feels (142–8, 312). Leonida says to Libanus how miserable a person is when he's in love; Libanus corrects him: "No, by God, really / someone who's strung up for a beating is much more miserable"; and Leonida picks him up: "I know it because I've tried it" (LI. *immo hercle vero / qui pendet multo est miserior*. LE. *scio qui periclum feci, As.* 616–17). [Wink.]

In a full aside, the long-suffering Messenio in *Menaechmi* suggests that ill-usage is what defines him as a slave (249–54):

> MEN II. dictum facessas, datum edis, caveas malo,
> molestus ne sis, non tuo hoc fiet modo. MES. em!   250
> illoc enim verbo esse me servom scio.
> non potuit paucis plura plane proloquei.
> verum tamen nequeo contineri quin loquar.
> audin, Menaechme? ...

> MEN II. Do what you're told, eat what you're given, watch out for a
>   beating,
> don't be annoying, you don't call the shots. MES. Pow!   250
> See, that's the word that let's me know I'm a slave.
> He couldn't say more, more clearly, in just a few words.
> But still I can't be kept from speaking.
> Are you listening to me, Menaechmus? ...

The word *em* in line 250 finishes the progression of thought in Menaechmus II's speech. It often signals a blow, and Moore here translates it "Ouch!" (1998: 42); Messenio, who elsewhere in the play likes to play his own interlocutor (1031–2), takes the *em* of the joke formula in 250–1 and bends it back on itself.[11] Thus *em* is the word that lets Messenio know

---

11 "That one word" is a joke formula, and often picks up on a single, identifiable word: at *Cist.* 248, the slave's *ob istuc unum verbum* refers back to the preceding line, where his owner quotes the words *melillam* and *suavium*; at *St.* 191, *ei ... verbo* picks up *foris* (190), as opposed to *domi* (192; but cf. *haec verba* in 193); at *Rud.* 1076, *verbo illo* picks up *comprimere* in 1075. At *Mos.* 297, Philolaches' *em istuc verbum* picks up Philematium's *mea voluptas*. If Messenio is not picking up his own *em*, to what word does *illoc ... verbo* refer? At *Aul.* 547, *illud ... verbum* stands in apposition with "*quod*

he is a slave (*illoc … verbo*, 251), and that is what he confides to his pals in the audience before telling them he cannot help but try again. Here audible speech is denoted by *loquor* and its compounds; Menaechmus wants Messenio to shut up, Messenio resists being made to hold his speech in (*contineri*). He turns back to his owner with *audin*, "are you listening to me"; "listen," as will be seen below, often means "obey" in the plays, which points again to the inherent power reversal staged when actors command the attention of an audience.

Face-out lines also occasionally tell the audience what is good. When Menaechmus II exclaims that there is no greater joy to sailors than seeing land from the sea, Messenio replies, "A greater one, I'll tell you no lie, / if you see on arrival the land that was once your own" (*maior, non dicam dolo, / [quam] si adveniens terram videas quae fuerit tua*, 228–9). As many people in the audience must have done, he wants to go home. Is that Syracuse, where his owner comes from? His owner has just addressed him by his name (226), a name which places him in Greece (Messene) or Sicily (Messana). Contrast Chrysalus and Sangarinus, returning to Athens: "Greetings, fatherland of my owner" (*Erilis patria, salve, Bac.* 170); "Land and fatherland of my owner, I see you with a right good will" (*terra erilis patria, te video lubens, St.* 650). "Where would we run away to?" says Philocrates; "To your fatherland," replies the *lorarius* (*in patriam, Capt.* 208), and the word *patria* echoes through the play; so Tyndarus says defiantly, to the man he does not know is his own father, that he goes to the quarries proud "that I brought back my owner, captured, out of slavery and the hand of the enemy, / and made him a free man, returned to his fatherland, to his father" (*<me> meum erum captum ex servitute atque hostibus / reducem fecisse liberum in patriam ad patrem*, 685–6). "Where was your *patria*?" the pimp insistently asks the Virgo in *Persa*, but she has given it up.

Freedom is a good repeatedly desired within the plays, and naturalized by axiomatic face-out lines. As seen in chapter 2, Philto says of Stasimus, "he's a person: / he wants to be made free" (*Trin.* 563–4); that all human beings want to be free is also stated as a rule by the *lorarius* in *Captivi* (119–20). He says this in a running dialogue with his owner Hegio, who wants to keep the focus on the personal faults of the *lorarius* (chapter 2), but a face-out on this line would draw audience members into sympathy with the compassion expressed by the *lorarius* for the two bound men. As the

---

nunc habes"; at *Trin.* 439, Stasimus speaks of *nequam illud verbum "bene volt"*; so *verbum* can just mean "thing said." Here, then, Messenio would be summing up his owner's last two lines, which are indeed typical of owners addressing slaves.

play goes on, Hegio is himself brought to the point where he agrees that
one of the captives has a father who wants him back, generalizing: "My son
is dear to me, his own son is dear to every man" (*meu' mihi, suo' quoique
est carus*, 400). A face-out here would address every father in the audience.
Many dialogue exchanges would have pertained to members of the audience as well as to those on stage: so Planesium protests to Curculio, "I was
born a free woman" (*libera ego sum nata*), and he replies (with face-out),
"Like a lot of other people who are slaves now" (*et alii multi qui nunc serviunt*, *Cur.* 607); so Milphio says to his owner, with face-out, "It's an outrage
on your part to let your own fellow countrywomen / be slaves before your
eyes, when they were free at home" (*nam tuom flagitiumst tuas te popularis
pati / servire ante oculos, domi quae fuerint liberae*, *Poen.* 965–6). Hearing
from Ampelisca of how the pimp has stolen Palaestra's proof of free birth,
Trachalio in *Rudens* exclaims, "Oh sluttish deed, / to want a woman to
be a slave who ought to be free!" (*o facinus inpudicum, / quam liberam
esse oporteat servire postulare!*, 393–4). Telestis' line in *Epidicus*, "Even if she
doesn't want me, I'll still be some mother's daughter" (chapter 5), would
have been a highly effective face-out line, addressed to an audience that
included mothers of lost children alongside children lost to their mothers.

More specifically – and astonishingly, in the penumbra of the Second
Punic War – when Agorastocles tells Milphio that he cannot remember
how to speak Punic because he was "lost from Carthage at the age of six"
(*Poen.* 986–7), Hanno overhears them as he walks towards them, observ-
ing, "Very many free boys / were lost from Carthage in that way" (*plurumei
ad illunc modum / periere pueri liberi Carthagine*, *Poen.* 988–9). Hanno's
entrance at 930 is one of the most spectacular in the Plautine corpus, as
he arrives in full Carthaginian costume (975–7) and launches into a prayer
in Punic (930–49), followed by a sort of subtitle in Latin (950–4). This
entrance is cued in the prologue (114–15, 124–5), but his arrival is unantici-
pated by the other characters – a surprise when it happens, a surprise to the
audience. When Hanno responds to Agorastocles at 988–9, he is addressing
the audience, his confidants since he (surprisingly) shifted into Latin at 950
and into conversational mode at 955, but he has been speaking in character.
If he did a double face-out, akin to Marshall's "double aside," he would be
addressing those lost boys, far from home; if not them, then whom?

Captivi is the main locus of such statements; indeed, the whole play
serves as a statement about the (un)naturalness of slavery.[12] True to its

---

[12] On this aspect of *Captivi*, from divergent viewpoints, see Konstan 1983: 57–72; Leigh 2004: 59,
89–97; Moore 1998: 181–201; Stewart 2012: 48–79; Thalmann 1996, with attention to contemporary
philosophical arguments.

opening embodiment of ambiguity in the bodies of the two chained men – which is which? – the play contains many face-out lines concerning equivalence and equality. Tyndarus, pretending to be Philocrates, tells his new owner Hegio about the implications of capture: "Fortune shapes and constrains human affairs as she feels like doing (*lubet*): / she has made me a slave, I who was free – the lowest from the highest" (*fortuna humana fingit artatque ut lubet: / me qui liber fueram servom fecit, e summo infumum*, 304–5). If the actor playing Tyndarus glanced out at the audience as he said this, his eyes would have caught those of people who knew this fortune at first hand, possibly like the actor himself.[13] At the same time, both the audience and the actor know what the character does not: Tyndarus thinks he is lying to Hegio, but in fact – in the world of the play – the words are true, because Tyndarus had in fact been born free. A glance out would put the actor in cahoots with the audience: we all know together how civil status is constructed. Sometimes the point is sharper; Philocrates responds to the information that Hegio's son is also a captive with "So we weren't the only cowards" (*non igitur nos soli ignavi fuimus*, 262). This line, especially with face-out, must have had terrific shock value for an audience populated by many veterans, soldiers' families, captives, and captives' families, and Matthew Leigh has argued that this is "a joke at the expense of the unforgiving public voices … which call for men to fight and frame laws designed to make them choose either victory or death," with reference to Roman state policies in the late 200s that refused the ransom of prisoners of war (2004: 78). But Hegio is not much offended – his next line is the usual straight man's break-off retort in shtick, an order ("get away and come here," *secede huc*, 263) – so he leaves the thought in the air. A response by Tyndarus to interrogation similarly implies that there is no disgrace in capture: "Are you still casting it up to me that I'm a slave, something that happened by enemy force?" (*pergin servom me exprobrare esse, id quod vi hostili optigit?* 591). Again, the contrast is between the capture of a slave and the capture of a free soldier, but the viewer knows that both Tyndarus and his owner were bought from the quaestors (34): how different are they?[14]

---

[13] A move like this is historically attested in a famous story about the equestrian mime-writer Decimus Laberius: forced by Julius Caesar to act in one of his own plays, thereby becoming *infamis*, he is said to have played the slave Syrus and spoken the line *porro, Quirites, libertatem perdimus* (fr. 91 Panayotakis). See chapter 3 on *quiritatio* in Plautus. On Laberius and this story, see Barton 1993: 144, 156–7; Bartsch 1994: 72, 238 n. 21, with many other instances of what she terms "oppositional innuendo"; Panayotakis 2010: 33, 449–82. The story as related by Macrobius also records the audience's reaction and direct interpretation of the line as critique of Caesar.

[14] For further discussion, with consideration of the military issues at stake, see Richlin 2017a: 226–8.

Some explicit complaints are buffered by being stated as axioms – general rules for the interlocutor's consideration, and the audience's as well. As seen in chapter 3, the words *credo* and *fides* and their relatives run through the plays, critiquing the denial of trust to the poor and powerless. Sosia, who spends most of *Amphitruo* not being believed, complains in response to his owner's threat of a beating with unusual directness and in axiomatic terms (590–1):

> Amphitruo, miserruma istaec miseria est servo bono,   590
> apud erum qui vera loquitur, si id vi verum vincitur.

> Amphitruo, this is the most miserable misery for a good slave,   590
> when he tells the truth to his owner, if that truth is conquered by force.

He has previously singled this out as a particular fault of Amphitruo's: "Now you're doing that thing you do, / where you don't count your own people as having *fides*" (*iam tuatim / facis, ut tuis nulla apud te fides sit*, 554–5). That owners, in turn, cannot be trusted by slaves is put much more harshly by Paegnium in the line Finley picked out: everyone knows an owner's *fides* is meretricious (*Per.* 193–4; see chapter 3, and the introduction to Part II). Palinurus, responding to his owner, wishes he had a sane owner (*Cur.* 202); the battered Milphio remarks to the audience, "It's miserable to be a slave to a lover" (*servire amanti miseria est, Poen.* 820); Sosia tells the audience, "the slave of a rich man is more miserable" (*magi' miser est diviti' servos, Am.* 167).[15] Resentment of what they perceive as arrogance is the source of the tension between Agorastocles and the chorus of Advocati in *Poenulus*, seen in chapter 2; as they leave the stage to be replaced by Milphio, they sum up, directly to the audience (809–13):

> iniuriam illic insignite postulat:
> nostro servire nos sibi censet cibo.   810
> verum ita sunt * isti nostri divites:
> si quid bene facias, levior pluma est gratia,
> si quid peccatumst, plumbeas iras gerunt.

> This one demands a markedly insulting injustice:
> he thinks we should be his slave and buy our own lunch.   810
> But that's how those rich men of ours are:
> if you do right by them, their gratitude is lighter than a feather,
> if you cross them, they bear you a grudge made of lead.

---

[15] This formula – "it's miserable to be a slave to a [kind of owner]" – as seen in chapter 1, appears in Greek comedy (e.g. Aristophanes, *Wealth* 1–7), in what Virginia Hunter calls "slave laments"; the focus there tends to remain on the owner.

Like Sosia in his opening song, they expect recognition from the audience of "how those rich men of ours are"; like the Ancilla in *Truculentus*, they point out where injustice lies. Like Trachalio, like Leonida, like Epidicus, like the Ancilla, by invoking *iniuria* they lay claim to honor on behalf of the low against the high, a radical power reversal. A large set of face-out lines gives voice to general resentment of the rich and powerful, often, again, in the context of debt, as in Dinia's line from *Vidularia*, "It's not fitting (*hau decet*) to wear out a needy person with interest payments" (89). The interaction between actors and audience creates a kind of popular morality, a pattern visible to those in need.

Normative Statements and Exploding Cigars

Axiomatic statements bring a deontological element into the plays, cued by words like *decet* and *oportet* – the righteous counterparts to *lubet* (chapter 4).[16] Slaves as well as owners lay claim to the lexicon of virtue. An innocent slave should face up to his owner, says Tyndarus (*Capt.* 665–6):

> decet innocentem servolum atque innoxium   665
> confidentem esse suom apud erum potissumum.

> It's fitting for an innocent little slave, who's done no harm,   665
> to be sure of himself with his own owner most of all.

In this he is echoed by, or echoes, surprisingly, Pseudolus (*Ps.* 460–1):

> decet innocentem qui sit atque innoxium
> servom superbum esse apud erum potissumum.

> It's fitting for a slave who's innocent and who's done no harm
> to be proud with his owner most of all.

Both speeches assert a slave's right to argue when charged, in the face of common assertions by owners of presumption (*confidentia*, never mind *superbia*) as a slave vice: Tyndarus is reacting to Hegio's "How self-assuredly he stood there, opposing me" (*ut confidenter mihi contra astitit, Capt.* 664), Pseudolus to his owner's "Look at the stance on that guy, how kingly" (*statum vide hominis … quam basilicum, Ps.* 458) and his owner's friend's "I see that he's stood himself there, good and sure of himself" (*bene confidenterque astitisse intellego*, 459). Compare Sagaristio's jeer at Paegnium, *confidens* (*Per.* 285), and Paegnium's energetic assent (285) and retort, "I'm

---

[16] On axiomatic speeches, which he groups with some "good-slave" speeches as "performative truisms," see Gunderson 2015: 67–72.

sure I'll be free" (*ego me confido liberum fore*, 286), with discussion in chapters 2 and 3; or Grumio to the audience, reacting to Tranio in their verbal duel, "How self-assuredly he speaks!" (*quam confidenter loquitur*, *Mos.* 38). Conversely, the Mercator's line, "It's not fitting for a slave person to be proud" (*non decet superbum esse hominem servom*, *As.* 470) reacts to Leonida's display of arrogance as he plays the *atriensis*.

Normative statements like these wrestle through the plays, as owners and slaves argue about how things should be in their slave society. As Curculio first runs onstage, he threatens to shove aside the *Graeci palliati* he describes so vividly (288–95), and to step on the "slaves of *scurrae*," whom he warns to stay at home and "avoid some bad luck" (296–8). The clueless Phaedromus thinks this would be a good idea, and – speaking to his onstage slave, Palinurus – generalizes about slaves: "Yes, that's just the way it is today, / that's how the slaves are now: no check can be placed on them at all" (*nam ita nunc mos viget, / ita nunc servitiumst: profecto modus haberi non potest*, 299–300). To him, *Graeci palliati* can only be slaves – ironic, since he, Palinurus, and Curculio are all standing onstage wearing the *pallium*, and *scurrae* and their slaves are their close kin.[17] Phaedromus' line, with face-out, says one thing to the bossy spectator, but something more cheerful to the slave spectator tired of being bossed, for Phaedromus, in the play, is a fool. Or perhaps it is Palinurus who turns and winks. Daemones, after Gripus' speech about comedy, remarks to the audience as Gripus exits, "That's why we have worthless slaves" (*illuc est quod nos nequam servis utimur*, *Rud.* 1258). The placement of the indeclinable adjective *nequam*, "worthless" – a dangling modifier – makes Daemones' dictum wobble between sneer and self-indictment. The *senex* Periplectomenus in *Miles Gloriosus* instructs the slave Sceledrus: "A slave person ought / to keep his eyes and hands and speech under control" (*hominem servom suos / domitos habere oportet oculos et manus/ orationemque*, 563–5); as will be seen below, he later reacts harshly against the idea that slaves might voice complaints. Speeches like this in the mouths of owners make all the more startling the lines of the slave Toxilus to Lemniselenis at the end of *Persa* (835–42), where he complains about thankless freedmen (chapter 5). In the trajectory of each play, speeches like this, then, act like exploding cigars, blowing up in the speaker's face and leaving him with a charcoal coating: nasty, wrong, mean-spirited.

Slave characters also make normative statements on how to get along in the owners' world. Stichus repeatedly uses the wording of Periplectomenus'

---

17 On this point, see Petrone 1983: 170–5.

axiom, *homo servus*, in his maxims for behavior, although his rules focus on the party he is planning. So, jokingly, on seeing his friend arrive (*St.* 442–4):

> servos homo qui nisi temperi ad cenam meat,
> advorsitores pol cum verberibus decet
> dari, uti eum verberabundi adducant domum.

> A slave person who doesn't make his way to dinner on time –
> it's fitting, by God, that greeters be given him with whips,
> so that they can lead him home lashfully.[18]

Stichus here plays on the custom repeatedly shown in the plays whereby slaves were expected to go out to greet and welcome a returning owner (so Chalinus on going to greet his owner, *quom ei advorsum veneram, Cas.* 461; Phaniscus in *Mostellaria*, in his "good slave" song, "Now I'm the only one of these many slaves to go to greet our owner," *solus nunc eo advorsum ero ex plurumis servis*, 880, while bad slaves say, " 'I'm not going, don't be annoying,'" " '*non eo, molestu' ne sis*,'" 877; see chapter 1, and below on this song). Stichus transforms the rules to match the norms of slavery – a bitter joke, in this party context. After his friend announces the humble menu (690–1), Stichus comments, "It's enough for a slave person to make a modest expenditure rather than a lavish one: / his own befits each" (*satiust servo homini modeste facere sumptum quam ampliter, / suom quemque decet*, 692–3). Soon he will happily throw away his *peculium* on sex (751). As seen in chapter 4, he tells the audience not to be surprised to see "little slave persons" (*homines servolos*) having a party, because "in Athens, we're allowed" (*licet haec Athenis nobis*, 446, 448). The balance between Periplectomenus' *oportet* and Stichus' *decet*, on the one hand, and *licet* – better, *lubet* – on the other, is the balance between what is given and what is desired. But the plays put a large thumb on the balance.

Turning Object into Subject

Sosia reproaches Amphitruo for having no faith in "your own people" – *tuis*. A very large class of lines involves the use of possessive adjectives to comment on the effects of ownership. As Fraenkel remarked, "In the terminology of Roman law *meum est* means 'I am the owner'" (1961: 47). When Amphitruo threatens to cut out Sosia's tongue, he replies, "I'm yours, / you can do just as it suits you and whatever you feel like doing"

---

[18] Verses 441–5 are not in P, and are bracketed by de Melo.

(*tuos sum, / proinde ut commodumst et lubet quidque facias*, 557–8, cf. 564).
When Hegio tells the *lorarius* to bind Tyndarus' hands tightly, Tyndarus
replies, "I'm yours, you can just go ahead and order them to be cut off"
(*tuos sum, tu has quidem vel praecidi iube, Capt.* 668). The power relationship involved is worked out in the savage exchange between Saturio and
his daughter in *Persa* as he prepares to sell her (338–41; see chapter 5):

> [VI.] tuin ventris caussa filiam vendas tuam?
> SAT. mirum quin regi' Philippi caussa aut Attali
> te potius vendam quam mea, quae sis mea.   340
> VI. utrum pro ancilla me habes an pro filia?

> [VI.] Are you going to sell your daughter on account of your belly?
> SAT. Strange that I wouldn't sell you on account of King Philip
> or Attalus, rather than on my account, since you're mine.   340
> VI. Do you see me as your slave-woman or your daughter?[19]

The father here sounds like the pimp Ballio addressing his *puer*: "You! –
Since you're mine, now I'm commanding you ..." (*tu, qui meus es, iam
edico tibi ...*, *Ps.* 855). To own is to command. Later in their argument
the Virgo tells her father that he has the power to act wisely rather than
"stupidly" (*stulte*) – that he can choose not to sell her – and he replies, "I
feel like it" (*lubet*, 375). His words, as in Sosia's line to Amphitruo, mark
the basic right of ownership (*quae sis mea*), as well as the basic claim to
free will (see chapter 4 on *lubet*); her reply falls into a tangle of *lubet*
and *licet*, an appeal to what is permitted (376–7), another failed effort
in a losing argument against the man who controls her. At the end, she
gives up and tells him to sell her or do with her "whatever you feel like"
(*quid tibi lubet*, 398). When she is sold onstage, the pimp asks her plainly,
"Do you want to be mine?" (*vin mea esse?*), and she replies in kind (657).
Mea es tu, says the old man to the weeping Pasicompsa – "You're mine"
(*Mer.* 500); then he takes it back, and she asks, *quoia sum?* – "Whose
am I?" (529). Ballio explains how he could sell Phoenicium: *lubuit, mea
fuit* ("I felt like it, she was mine," *Ps.* 348). The transformative power of
manumission appears precisely in the change of possessive adjectives: the
pimp Dordalus frees Lemniselenis, and "so she who was my slave-woman
today, is now *sua*" – "her own" (*ita ancilla mea quae fuit hodie, sua nunc
est, Per.* 472). The use of a second-person possessive with a first-person

---

[19] For the sarcastic *mirum quin* formula and the use of kings as hyperbolic alternatives, see Fraenkel
2007: 12, and chapter 8 on the use of historical kings in the plays.

singular verb – *tuos sum* – points up the exchange of power between a free person and a slave, and the tone is bitter. But power is what is at stake; power creates ownership. Trying to get Sosia to deny his identity as "Amphitruo's slave, Sosia," Mercurius beats him, and asks, "Whose are you *now*?" "Yours," replies Sosia, "for, with your fists, you made me yours by use" ([ME.] *quoius nunc es? SO. tuo', nam pugnis usu fecisti tuom, Am.* 375). *Usucapio* was a legal mode whereby ownership was acquired through possession over time ; here Sosia grounds it in force: just a joke.[20] This was a world in which made objects were commonly inscribed with a *titulus loquens*, like the Cales ware seen in chapter 1, telling the name of their maker or their owner.[21] The definition of a slave as a "talking tool," cited by one of the speakers in Varro's book on agriculture (*instrumenti genus vocale, R.* 1.17.1), exposes the paradox inherent in slave speech: objects are not supposed to be subjects. Possessions are not supposed to have a point of view, or feel pain.

Possessions are not supposed to own anything, either; as seen in chapter 3, this posed serious problems for possessions who were themselves persons. The plays sometimes joke about what slaves have instead of assets. When Calidorus asks his slave Pseudolus to weep for him, Pseudolus at first demurs: "Our kind has always been dry-eyed" (*genu' nostrum semper siccoculum fuit*, 77; see chapter 4 on the claim to family character). Then he agrees, and, like a hired mourner, chimes in with *eheu* at every pause (*Ps.* 79–82). "This is how you're helping me?" says Calidorus. "I give what I have," replies Pseudolus, "for there's an ever-flowing treasury of that at our house" (*do id quod mihi est; / nam is mihi thensaurus iugis in nostra domost*, 83–4). An ever-flowing treasury of *eheu* here replaces the supply of ready money "at home," which is so often at issue, as seen in chapter 3. So Libanus and Leonida joke about their legacy of misery (*As.* 306):

> LI. vae tibi! LE. hoc testamento Servitus legat tibi.
> LI. Woe to you! LE. Slavery's leaving *you* that in her will.

It would be tragic if it were not dressed up as a joke, by speakers who, like Pseudolus, really had something to cry about.

---

[20] On *usucapio* in this period, see Watson 1971: 62–4. The process dates back at least to the XII Tables. For discussion of *usus* and its legal cognates in *Amphitruo*, including this exchange, see Gunderson 2015: 194–7. On "avowal" onstage and as a legal concept, see Dressler 2016: 20.

[21] For a Cales ware *patera* mold that speaks in the first person (*CIL* I².2.2489), see Vine 1993: 134–41; other instances *passim* in Warmington 1940: 196–211, including items from the Esquiline necropolis owned by slaves.

Grumbling

Slaves onstage comment, ironically, on the necessity of limiting their knowledge and speech – of playing the object, although they are manifestly subjects. Philocrates, demonstrating the talent for double speech that begins this chapter, responds to Hegio's command that he not be "false-speaking" (*falsiloquom*) with these two-sided words: "I won't be / as far as I know. If there's something I don't know, I'll tell you what I don't know" (*non ero / quod sciam. si quid nescivi, id nescium tradam tibi, Capt.* 264–5). So Chrysalus, interrogated by his owner: "I don't know. / Nothing is what I ought to know now. I've forgotten everything. / I know I'm a slave" (*nescio. / nil iam me oportet scire. oblitus sum omnia. / scio me esse servom, Bac.* 789–91). He makes use of double meaning to say one thing to his owner, another to the audience: "I know I'm a slave" [= "I know my place"]; "Not-knowing defines being a slave" [and so I'd better keep my mouth shut]. Chrysalus here, as throughout, is in fact the one in charge; immediately after these lines he speaks an aside to the audience about how he has trapped the old man like a bird in a net. But what a slave knows, along with the consciousness of slavery, means that knowledge has to be covered with a disguise, and this is what is acted out onstage, in play after play, for all to see. Chrysalus sounds like his hero Epidicus: "It's better for a slave person to know more than he says; that's wisdom" (*plus scire satiust quam loqui servom hominem. ea sapientia est, Epid.* 60). Later, dealing with the two stupid old men, Epidicus pretends to defer to their wisdom, as seen in chapter 4: "If it'd be fair / for me to be wiser than you" (*si aequom siet / me plus sapere quam vos*, 257–8); "You ought to be first, we ought to speak second, / since you are wiser" (*vos priores esse oportet, nos posterius dicere, / qui plus sapitis*, 261–2). Chrysalus delivers a more general rule for behavior in response to a command by his owner to do as he has been told: "It's right that your slave should slave for you according to your judgment" (*iustumst <ut> tuos tibi servos tuo arbitratu serviat, Bac.* 994). As everyone in the audience knows, not a single one of these maxims is sincere; again, these comments enunciate the need for a kind of doubleness involving speech – a slave must know more than he says. While Periplectomenus instructs Sceledrus that a slave "ought / to keep his eyes and hands and speech under control (*domitos*)" (*Mil.* 564–5), the smart slave Palaestrio, earlier in the play, has lectured his gullible fellow slave: "So, if you're smart, / you'll keep it to a grumble: a slave's supposed to know more than he speaks" (*ergo, si sapis, / mussitabis: plus oportet scire servom quam loqui, Mil.* 476–7).

Palaestrio here recommends to Sceledrus a mode of speech strongly associated with slaves in the plays – once in a while, with other relatively powerless people: muttering under one's breath, semi-audible vocalization, denoted by the verbs *murmuro, mussito, musso,* and *muttio,* and by the noun *muttitio* (connected by Varro with the adjective *mutus* and the onomatopoeic *mu*).[22] I will refer to it here as "grumbling," although it always refers to clandestine speech (like "whispering"), and the sound effect is more like "muttering"; like "grumbling," *muttire* has overtones of unproductive, discounted speech; it is a top-down, class-specific word without an exact English equivalent. Indeed, the translation "grumbling" instantly robs such speech of its claim to validity; readers should take the Latin verbs, as used onstage, as always potentially ironic. The idea that slaves mumble in protest at ill-treatment is shtick already in Aristophanes (*Frogs* 747, in an exchange between two slaves on "slave-like" behavior, cf. *Wasps* 614), and repeatedly appears in complaints by owners in Herodas (*Mim.* 6.7, 7.77, 8.8), where the word for this kind of speech is τονθορύζω; but it is both more common and more self-conscious in Plautus.[23] When words like *muttio* are used in Latin of free people, sometimes even of inanimate objects, they are being likened to slaves.[24] So the praise of a cooperative

---

[22] Varro, *L.* 7.101, *mussare dictum, quod muti non amplius quam* μῦ *dicunt* (cf. Courtney 1993: 21). He gives two instances in Ennius; notably, one of these involves a threat of punishment for speech, the other one involves the fear of speech. Varro, who was proscribed by Antony in 43 BCE, knew what this meant. But the "mute" category of agricultural equipment in Varro's book on agriculture is exemplifed by wagons (*R.* 1.17.1): total muteness, then, a property of inanimate objects. A character in the probably Plautine *Caecus* or *Praedones* responds to another character's *mu* by exclaiming, "God, I'm done for! He's a Carthaginian!" (*perii hercle! Afer est,* fr. 46; cf. *Poen.* 1010–11, where Milphio translates Hanno's *muphursa* into *mures Africanos*), suggesting that interlinguistic unintelligibility was a sort of cultural muteness. Or moo-tness; Nonius takes *mu* to be the sound made by cattle (so, not the letter μ, but a vocalized mooing), calling it "a sound which has no intelligible meaning" (*sonus est proprie qui intellectum non habet*), commenting on lines from Naevius' *Lycurgus* (*ducite / eo cum argutis linguis mutas quadrupedis, trag.* 27–8 R = 46–7 W = 19 *TrRF*) and Accius' *Epinausimache* (*item ac maestitiam mutam infantum quadrupedum,* 315 R = 302 W = 315 Kl). In Greek, the word μῦς ("mouse") seems to have suggested a pun whereby τὸν μῦν means "gag," used in a scene of flogging (Herodas 3.85); or so Headlam conjectured: "a gag, compelling one to close (μύειν) the mouth, unable to do more than μύζειν, that is μῦ μῦ λέγειν," adducing other animal nicknames for instruments of torture (2001[1922]: 156). The Kinsman in *Thesmophoriazusae* exclaims μῦ μῦ as he is depilated, and Euripides replies, τί μύζεις (231). On the association of *muttire* with slaves in Plautus, also Fantham 2005: 223–4. On comic examples in Ennius and Juventius (a string of imperatives enjoining silence), Wright 1974: 67, 75. Wright takes Ennius 393 R (*vocibus concide, fac i<am> mus<s>et obrutus,* quoted at Varro *L.* 7.101; text as in 178 *TrRF*) to be comic, not tragic, and places it in a scene of *flagitatio.* What follows is a complete survey of *muttire* and related verbs in the Plautine corpus, except for *Cas.* 924 *ullum muttit* (fragmentary) and fr. inc. 169 (*quid murmurillas tecum et te discrucias;* speaker unidentified).

[23] See Headlam 2001[1922]: 284–5, 353, where he glosses *mussito,* and ties the need for such speech with the slave's lack of *parrhêsia.*

[24] The exceptions are the father described by his son as publicizing the son's faults, sometimes *summo clamore,* sometimes *mussans* (*Mer.* 49); and, surprisingly, Periplectomenus' self-description, *mecum*

door and hinge (*Cur.* 21, 94); doors, often beaten onstage, are obvious ana-
logues for slaves, and are so hailed (e.g. *As.* 286). So the *Poenulus* prologue
speaker, playing the *imperator*, commands, "Let the *lictor* not grumble a
word – nor his rods" (18, *neu lictor verbum aut virgae muttiant*), thus also
reminding the crowd that the lictors themselves are only servants.

Onstage, keeping your voice down is associated with fear by slave and
free alike.[25] Two centuries later, the philosopher Seneca poses the rhetorical question of whether his slave's semi-audible *murmuratio* really deserves
"flogging and fetters": evidently, for some owners, the answer was "yes."[26]
Seneca's acquaintance, the satirist Persius, with reference to the issue of
free speech in satire, asks (1.119), *me muttire nefas?* "Is it a sin for me to
grumble?" He then likens himself to Midas' barber, the paradigmatic pur-
veyor of secret truths about the high and mighty, and a probable slave (see
chapter 4). The soldier in *Truculentus* disapproves of any soldier "whom the
scurrae praise, while the rank and file always grumble about him" (*quem
scurrae laudant, manipulares mussitant*, 491).[27] This is a form of speech that
is meant to be picked up, but not by those in authority; at times they are
meant to know that the speaker has something critical to say, but not what
it is, in a familiar negotiation with power ("What did I just hear you say?"
"Nothing."). The ostensible intended audience might be other slaves, or
just the speaker's own self; the slave Epidicus talks to himself – that is, to
the audience – throughout his play, turning the hidden transcript inside
out.[28] Grumbling is then a form of controlled speech that is still risky if it
is noticed; if the owner chooses to hear it, it counts as backtalk. The owner

---

mussito (*Mil.* 714), as he contemplates the behavior of his legacy-hunting relatives: the first a hostile
portrait, the second perhaps mock-furtive in a supremely self-satisfied speaker. The tone would have
been determined by the delivery of *Mil.* 715.

[25] So at *Aul.* 131, *Cas.* 665, *Mos.* 401; cf. Naevius *trag. inc.*, *odi <summussos: pro>inde aperte dice <quid
sit quod> times*, 60 R₃ = 60 Kl = 47 *TrRF*.

[26] See discussion in Bradley 2011b: 375.

[27] Note the distinction between the patron-dependent *scurrae* and the *mancipium*-like *manipulares*;
the soldier's juxtaposition of these *scurrae* with the flattering *Homeronida* just above (485) perhaps
evokes the satiric relation between the *palliata* and (Ennian) tragedy seen, for example, in the
Poenulus prologue: epic as *parasitus*. The soldier goes on to reject the flattering *civis argutus*, comparing him to a *praefica* (495–6), the low-status hired lament leader at a Roman funeral (see Richlin
2014a: 267–88). This speech would then directly challenge the top-down models of communal
memory and the warrior aristocracy discussed in chapter 7; its implications do not seem to have
been fully pursued (see, briefly, Corbett 1986: 30–1; Earl 1960: 241; Gruen 1996a: 138). The connection of *Homeronida* with Ennius, an idea of Tenney Frank's grounded in politics, is dismissed by
Enk (1953: 1.117–18); cf. de Melo 2013: 318 n. 25. For discussion in a military context, see Richlin
2017a: 233–4.

[28] Moore 1998: 37–8 sees Epidicus' "shift from self-address to audience address" as part of a growth in
his audience rapport within the play; in the context of *muttitio*, though, surely the audience is with
him all the way.

can also pretend not to hear, and the slave can pretend not to have spoken. Again, the Naevius limit. The power differential between *muttire* on the one hand and the *respondere* that structures verbal dueling (chapter 3) is measured in a line from *Menaechmi*, where a nervous husband placates an angry wife: "The slave-women or the slaves don't talk back to you, do they? Tell me. They'll be punished" (*num ancillae aut servei tibi* / *responsant? eloquere. impune non erit, Men.* 620–1).

Onstage grumbling is then unsurprisingly connected with physical punishment. So Mercurius, in his verbal and physical duel with Sosia, threatens his hapless double (*Am.* 381), "Are you still grumbling?" (*etiam muttis?*), and Sosia replies untruthfully, "Now I'll be quiet" (*iam tacebo*). Later, it is Mercurius' turn; the irritated Jupiter says to him, "What business is this of yours, flogbait, or what's all this grumbling? / You – I should take this stick and …" (*quid tibi hanc curatio est rem, verbero, aut muttitio? / quoii ego iam hoc scipione …* , *Am.* 519–20). Alcumena intercedes – "Oh, don't!" (*ah noli*) – and Jupiter fulminates: "Go on, keep grumbling" (*muttito modo*, 520). As the old miser Euclio comes onstage in *Aulularia*, he is shoving his old slave Staphyla along in front of him, and he hits her (see chapter 2). As she says, stage-inaudibly, that she would rather hang herself than be his slave (50–1), he exclaims, "How that criminal woman grumbles to herself!" (*ut scelesta sola secum murmurat!*, 52) – and threatens to gouge her eyes out and crucify her (53, 59). The audience can hear her loud and clear.[29] In *Bacchides*, as Nicobulus and his *lorarius* bring Chrysalus onstage to tie him up for a beating, Nicobulus orders the *lorarius*, "Punch him one if he grumbles" (*impinge pugnum, si muttiverit*, 800). When Periplectomenus tells Sceledrus that a slave must control his speech, Sceledrus replies, "Me – if after this day / I grumble, even about what I know for sure myself, / you can have me crucified" (*egone si post hunc diem / muttivero, etiam quod egomet certo sciam, / dato excruciandum me, Mil.* 565–7). The owner of Pseudolus demands of him, "Didn't you know that I had a trip to the mill ready for you / when you kept grumbling that stuff?" (*non a me scibas pistrinum in mundo tibi, / quom ea mussitabas?, Ps.* 500–1). The point at issue is why Pseudolus suppressed his speech (*mussitabas*), rather than telling his owner (*si dixem*, 499): he saw that the mill would be the end result,

---

[29] Cf. the similar lines at Menander, *Epitrep.* 1062–75, where the owner enters abusing the old nurse Sophrone, whom he threatens to kill: shtick. Unlike Staphyla, Menander's nurse never gets a word in, although her gestures continue to make her owner angry (1122, 1126–7); hers is evidently a mute part (see Arnott 1979: 521). Contrast Staphyla's stage whisper, followed, after Euclio's exit, by a twelve-line monologue (*Aul.* 67–78); the difference is telling.

either way.[30] When the wife in *Menaechmi* says to Menaechmus II, "Shameless, do you still / dare to grumble a single word or speak to me?" (*etiamne, inpudens, / muttire verbum unum audes aut mecum loqui?*, 710–11), it is part of her treatment of her husband as a slave. This makes it a big shift in power when Toxilus and his fellow slaves beat up the pimp at the end of *Persa* and Sagaristio uses the same line on the pimp: "Are you still grumbling, shameless?" (*etiam muttis, impudens?*, 827). As in Mercurius' line to Sosia (*Am.* 381), the repeated "still" in these formulaic questions implies "even with the threat of force hanging over you?" and "even after I've told you to stop?"[31]

A weak owner accepts grumbling as how slaves express displeasure; Pleusicles explains to his host, Periplectomenus, that he feels he is wearing out his welcome: "Even if the householder is willing to let you, the slaves start grumbling" (*tam etsi dominus non invitus patitur, servi murmurant, Mil.* 744). This elicits a tirade on slave duty from his autocratic host (745–8):

> PE: serviendae servituti ego servos instruxi mihi,   745
> hospes, non qui mi imperarent quibu've ego essem obnoxius:
> si illis aegrest mihi id quod volup est, meo remigio rem gerunt,
> tamen id quod odiost faciundumst cum malo atque ingratiis.

> PE: I've taught my slaves that slavery has to be slaved, my friend –   745
> they're not here to give me orders, or for me to be liable to.
> If my pleasure makes them sick, well, it's my count they're keeping stroke to,
> they still have to do what they hate to do, against their will, and take a beating.

---

[30] Here accepting Ritschl's emendation of *si id faxem* to *si dixem* at *Ps.* 499.

[31] Cf. chapter 3 on the chanted refrain in *Mercator: etiam loquere, larva?* ("are you still talking, you ghost?," 981, 983). This Plautine formula translates a much less well-attested Greek comic formula, ἔτι λαλεῖς: Menander *Sam.* 680, ἔτι λαλεῖς οὗτος (owner strikes slave, splits his lip, slave complains, owner responds, 677–80); *Epitrep.* 249, ἐὰν λαλῇς μεταξὺ (owner threatens to hit Syrus for interrupting Daos, and Syrus accepts this as just, 250); *Epitrep.* 1068–9, οἰμώξει μακρά, / ἂν ἔ[τ]ι λαλῇς (see n. 29). The difference in sense between λαλεῖν "babble" and *muttire* is the difference between the uncomprehended and the half-heard. *Etiam*, however, works generally in the plays as the introduction to indignant rhetorical questions, often with vocative terms of abuse: *carnufex, Am.* 376, *Ba.* 785; *furcifer, As.* 377, *Capt.* 563; *improbe, Am.* 571; *impudens, Men.* 710, *Per.* 827; *sceleste, Am.* 1025, *Au.* 437; *scelus, Per.* 290, *Truc.* 621; *verbero, Am.* 1029, *Cur.* 196, *Mos.* 1132; *verberabilissume, Au.* 633. The mostly second-person verbs in these questions protest speech received as insolent: *audes muttire, Men.* 710, and *audes male loqui, Capt.* 563; *clamas, Am.* 376, and *inclamitor, Epid.* 711; *delusisti, As.* 677; *derides* and *inrides, Men.* 499, *Mos.* 1132; *loquere, Mer.* 981, 983; *male dicis* and *male loquere, Per.* 290, *Trin.* 991; *minitare, Bac.* 785, *Truc.* 621, and *minitatur, Rud.* 711; *negas, Mer.* 763; *pergin, Cur.* 196; *prolectas probris, Bac.* 567; *rogas* and *rogitas, Am.* 571, 1025, 1029, *Aul.* 424, 437, 633, *Bac.* 1196, *Cas.* 997; *vocas, Cur.* 191. Cf. *Rud.* 733–4; many of these lines belong to what might be called "argument shtick."

The harsh emphasis on slavery (*serviendae, servituti, servos*, 745) is the formulation seen in the "good slave speeches" below, and is mocked by the slave Sagaristio in his opening song in *Persa* (chapter 4). The *senex* here insists on the owner's pleasure against the slave's will, threatening, as in the speeches seen above, corporal punishment (747–8). It is Periplectomenus who gives the orders, while a slave must be *obnoxius* (746), a word that has a whole range of connotations associated with slavery: being bound, answerable, accountable, under the domination of; servile, submissive; liable or exposed to harm or danger, or exposed to the elements; subject to punishment; vulnerable. As will be seen, the word is picked up by the fabulist Phaedrus as a label for slavery itself.

Grumbling also serves as a vent, specifically as an alternative to dangerous tattling. Sceledrus' whole problem in *Miles* has to do with an excess of knowledge. Having found out that the woman he is supposed to be guarding has been sneaking out of the house, he says, "Whatever it is, I'll keep grumbling, rather than come to a bad end" (*quidquid est, mussitabo potius quam interream male, Mil.* 311). He is sure his owner will kill him if he tells. The slave Truculentus is not such a coward: "Should I just keep grumbling about this?" No, he decides, "By God, I'll go to the forum right now and tell the old man what's happened" (*egone haec mussitem?/ iam quidem hercle ibo ad forum atque haec facta narrabo seni, Truc.* 312–13). Astaphium likewise tells an importunate customer the unwelcome truth about her owner: "Pay attention to me so I can tell what I want to" (*da mi operam ut narrem quae volo*); "I'm not going to keep grumbling" (*non mussito, Truc.* 722–3) – that is, she will not keep it quiet. Bargaining with his rival Trachalio over the suitcase, Gripus directs him, "You're going to shut up; I'll keep grumbling" (*tu taceto; ego mussitabo, Rud.* 1029) – that is, he will keep his voice down, although, ever competitive, he will make more noise than Trachalio.

Speech, then, has a scale, from various words for "command," to *loquor* "I speak out," down to *narro* "I tell," down to *muttio* "I grumble," and finally to *taceo* "I say nothing." When Messenio suggests that ill-usage is what defines him as a slave (above), he contrasts his owner's ability to speak out (*proloquei, Men.* 252) with his own desire to do so (*nequeo contineri quin loquar*, "I can't be kept from speaking," 253). Audible speech here is denoted by *loquor* and its compounds; Menaechmus wants Messenio to shut up, Messenio resists being made to hold his speech in (*contineri*). He turns back to his owner with *audin* (254), "Are you listening to me?" It is in the context of controlled speech that *(dicto) audiens*, "listening to what's been told (me)," means "obedient, as a slave should be," also used from a relatively powerless person to a relatively powerful one: so the defeated Virgo to her father's command to follow him offstage (*dicto sum audiens*, *Per.* 399), and the prostitute Philaenium responding sadly to her mother the *lena* ("You brought up an obedient daughter, mother," *audientem dicto, mater, produxisti filiam*, *As.* 544). Both women have just lost arguments. So Toxilus lays down the law to the newly freed Lemniselenis (*te mihi dicto audientem esse addecet*, *Per.* 836). One repeated retort in verbal dueling stresses the relationship between ownership and the power to command: "If you want someone to obey you, you have to pay for him," says Paegnium to Sagaristio (*emere oportet, quem tibi oboedire velis*, *Per.* 273); "Better buy a guy to give orders to," says Stasimus to Charmides before he recognizes him as his owner (*emere meliust quoi imperes*, *Trin.* 1061): "You don't own me." Charmides replies, "By god, I did buy him and I paid cash; / but if he doesn't obey me, what do I do?" (*pol ego emi atque argentum dedi; / sed si non dicto audiens est, quid ago?*, *Trin.* 1061–2). "Beat him," replies Stasimus, "unless you're the one who's liable" (*obnoxius*, 1063). Both force and judgment should belong to the owner, although here, as at the end of *Amphitruo*, the owner's power depends on the slave's recognition.

As seen in chapter 2, the verb *comprimo* is used to mean both "silence" and "rape" – combined with an objectifying possessive in Trachalio's line to Daemones about Gripus: "Please stuff him, if he's yours" (*comprime hunc sis, si tuost*, *Rud.* 1073). Slave characters, by deliberate misprision, turn the expression *linguam comprimere*, "stuff your tongue," into a joke about sex with a virgin or *patrona*; so when Mercurius threatens Sosia, "I'll stuff your tongue," Sosia replies, "You can't; / she's kept well and chastely" ([ME.] *comprimam linguam. SO. hau potes: / bene pudiceque adservatur*, *Am.* 348–9). When Libanus overhears Leonida urge himself to order his tongue to be silent (*tacere*), Libanus exclaims to the audience, "God, what an unlucky man, to stuff his *patrona*" (*edepol hominem infelicem, qui patronam comprimat*, *As.* 292). In this exchange from *Casina*, power moves from speaker to speaker along with the insults and the imperative mood (358–62):

> ... CH. adsunt quae imperavisti omnia:
> uxor, sortes, situla atque egomet. OL. te uno adest plus quam ego volo.
> CH. tibi quidem edepol ita videtur; stimulus ego nunc sum tibi,   360
> fodico corculum; adsudascis iam ex metu, mastigia.
> LY. tace, Chaline. CH. comprime istunc. OL. immo istunc qui didicit dare.

> ... CH. Everything's here that you ordered:
> your wife, the lots, the bucket, and me. OL. That's more than I want to be
> here by a factor of *you*.

CH. Oh, sure, by God, that's how it looks to you; now I'm your cattle-
  prod,   360
I'm poking you in your little heart; you're sweating now from fear, you
  whipping-post.
LY. Shut up, Chalinus. CH. Stuff *him*. OL. No, *him*, he's learned to give it.

Olympio wants Chalinus gone (359); Chalinus fashions himself as instrument of torture (360–1); their owner tells Chalinus to be quiet; Chalinus
tells the owner to silence/rape Olympio – *comprime*; Olympio uses the
same verb to tell the owner to rape Chalinus, whom he further insults by
saying he is used to it (362).

The same progression is used in *Rudens*, as Gripus appropriates
Trachalio's *comprime* to insult him for sexual use by his owner (1073–5;
see chapter 2). Yet, although slaves onstage are constantly being told to be
quiet, the fact that this has no effect is an essential part of the work of the
plays. Stasimus' owner in *Trinummus* tells him, "I'll gouge your eye out,
/ if you add one word"; Stasimus replies, "By God, I'll speak nonetheless; / for even if I'm not allowed to speak as I am, I'll speak as a one-eyed
man" (LE. *oculum ego ecfodiam tibi, / si verbum addideris.* ST. *hercle qui
dicam tamen; / nam si sic non licebit, luscus dixero, Trin.* 463–5). The *mum-
mum-mum* sound indicated by the lexicon of muted speech is precisely the
sound that cannot be made by the open mouth of the comic mask, which
thus becomes an emblem of open speech. In the long exchange at the end
of *Rudens*, where Gripus and Trachalio vie for attention from Daemones
(1052–1128), Gripus is repeatedly told to pay attention and be quiet by
both his owner (*animum advorte et tace,* 1062; *audi,* 1063; *tace,* 1084; *cave
malo ac tace tu,* 1089; *advorte animum,* 1102; *non ego te comprimere possum
sine malo?* 1125, *animum advorte ac tace,* 1153) and his rival slave (*ut nequitur
comprimi!,* 1064; *comprime hunc sis,* 1073; *sine me ut occepi loqui,* 1093). He
asks whether he will ever be allowed to speak (1117, 1126) and is threatened with a cracked skull (1118) and a beating (1125). Trachalio, in contrast, is rarely told to be quiet (1108; possibly 1084). The difference between
Trachalio, who indeed is often encouraged to speak in this sequence, and
Gripus, who is not, must also relate to their relative standing as body servant (*Trachalio … calator,* 335) and fisherman. Nevertheless, Gripus, the
low man, continues to insult his interlocutors – to talk back – and, in fact,
although he loses his case, he has the last word in this scene. Again in the
play's final scene, as his owner takes the pimp aside to negotiate for Gripus'
freedom, and although he is once again told to be quiet (1391, 1399, 1401),
Gripus turns the tables: "Conduct your business openly, I don't want any

little grumbling or whispering" (*palam age, nolo ego murmurillum neque susurrum fieri*, 1404).

The imperative mood commonly used in verbs of silencing – *tace, comprime* – is the mood that typifies the owner in scenes where slaves mimic owners' speech (chapter 4). But the mimicry itself undercuts the imperative, both within each scene and in the overall situation of the comic stage, where masked actors tell nasty truths. This is demonstrated at length in the scene in *Persa* where the slaves' slaves Sophoclidisca and Paegnium mock their owners as they act out the behavior of slaves sent with a confidential message. Both have been forbidden to tell anyone what they are doing; in a continuation of their echoic flirtation throughout their long scene together, they mimic their owners' words of instruction (239–42):

> <SO. edictum est mihi>
> ne hoc quoiquam homini dicerem, omnes muti ut loquerentur prius.   240
> PA. edictum est magno opere mihi, ne quoiquam hoc homini crederem,
> omnes muti ut <e>loquerentur prius hoc quam ego.

> SO. But I was told
> not to tell this to any person; the mute should all speak before I did.   240
> PA. I was told, flat out, not to trust this to any person,
> all the mute should speak out before I did.[32]

The message they are carrying is not the message they give each other; what they act onstage has to do with each other and defines them as independent of their owners' commands. The power of speech (*dicerem*) is here linked with the characteristic *edictum* of the one in command; the impossible condition of the oath is the state of muteness, desired by owners in slaves, and famously the condition Aesop leaves behind in the *Life of Aesop*.

Double speech is of course traditionally associated with the fable, a form which has much in common with the *palliata*. The (purported) freedman fabulist Phaedrus, in the autobiographical prologue to book 3 of his collection, offers an explanation of how fables got started that links fables with jokes (*iocis*) as well as with slaves.[33] This origin story has been variously treated as serious (Bradley 1984: 150–3, with discussion of slave-oriented elements in Phaedrus' collection) and viewed as "no more than a rather

---

[32] Text as in de Melo 2011c.

[33] The standard biography of Phaedrus as a freed slave has been dismissed by Edward Champlin as a "complete fantasy" (2005: 99); he argues that the writer known as Phaedrus was a satirist, learned in Roman law, "a member of the Roman élite masquerading as a man of the people" (117). Phaedrus' legal expertise, however, implies nothing about his civil status. For present purposes, the figure this writer adopts for himself is the main thing: his pose relates to a role in cultural circulation.

pretty 'aetiological' invention ... no evidence, then, for a special class of 'slave literature'" (Horsfall 2003: 82).[34] As a model, it seems pertinent to Plautus (Phaedrus 3.pr.33–7):

> Nunc, fabularum cur sit inventum genus,
> brevi docebo. servitus obnoxia,
> quia quae volebat non audebat dicere,   35
> affectus proprios in fabellas transtulit,
> calumniamque fictis elusit iocis.

> Now, how the fable was invented,
> I'll briefly explain. Slaves under constraint,
> since what they wanted to say, they didn't dare,   35
> transposed their real feelings into fables,
> and cheated a charge of slander by fashioning them as jokes.

The last line concisely states the principle in the theory of humor stated in chapter 1: jokes, fashioned out of true feelings by the workman/joker, let the joker evade/trick/outwit (*elusit*) a charge of bringing a false accusation (a bitter word in this context). In a way reminiscent of the Plautine slave/plotmaker, Phaedrus repeatedly uses the verb *fingo* to talk about what he is doing, fashioning himself as fashioner, artisan, artificer on the model of Prometheus.[35]

The fabulous lexicon, in which animals stand for people, is thus well suited to the image-world of the *palliata*. Figures of bird-catching are often used in the plays to talk about trickery (and, as will be seen in chapter 8, to represent human trafficking); so Chrysalus in *Bacchides* lures the old man like a bird into a net (792–3). Chrysalus' fellow trickster Tranio in *Mostellaria* spins this image out into a sort of visual fable. Taking his owner Theopropides to look at the house upon which his scam centers, as the old

---

[34] Scholars differ on the social function of fables and their relation to slaves; see Richlin 2016 for a brief overview, and, for readings that connect fables with folk culture or slave culture, Forsdyke 2012: 9, 59–73; Mann 2015: 36–178, on Aesop and Phaedrus; Rothwell 1995, on Aristophanes (strongly associates fables with slaves and the lower classes; several later discussions are indebted to this one). On Phaedrus, see Hawkins 2014: 128–34 (finds the identity of Phaedrus as an ex-slave plausible based on the poems, and argues that Phaedrus "tends to foster an awareness of ... the bodily plight of the weak and defenseless"); and Henderson 2001, esp. 57–94 (a full reading of 3.pr.). For the opposing view, see Holzberg 2002: 16 (Aesop "definitely does not personify ... the common people's spirit of rebellion against oppressive rule"). All arguments about fables relate to the issue of "figured speech" (Ahl 1984; see above). For later association between "the rustic and uneducated" and fables, see Quint. *Inst.* 5.11.19; on wet-nurses and fables told to children, Quint. *Inst.* 1.9.2, 1.8.19.

[35] Phaedrus 1.pr.7, *fictis ... fabulis* ("made up"); 1.1.15, *fictis causis* ("false"); 2.9.13, *arte fictas ... fabulas* ("fashioned with skill"; a poem on the statue to Aesop set up by the Athenians); 4.15.1, *fictione veretri* (of Prometheus making body parts); 4.16.3, *auctor vulgi fictilis* (of Prometheus); 4.22.5, *a me ... fictum* (on Phaedrus); 5.8.7, *finxere antiqui talem effigiem;* Perotti's Appendix 5/6.9, *callida finxit manu* (of Prometheus).

man who actually owns the house stands by, he teases his owner by asking him to appreciate a wall painting – a painting that exists only in Tranio's words (832–40). He leads off with a setup line: "Do you see the painting there, where one crow makes a fool of two vultures?" (*viden pictum, ubi ludificat una cornix volturios duos?*, *Mos.* 832). Replies his owner, "No, by God, I don't see it" (*non edepol video*). Replies Tranio, "But I see it" (*at ego video*, 833). Twice more he pushes his owner to see what really lies before his eyes; he tells his owner "look towards me" to see the crow (835), and "look towards yourselves" to see the vultures (837), but the owner does not get it; the scene concludes with the words "You can't see it" (*non quis optuerier*, 840). Several things are significant here: the word *ludificat*, shorthand for comedy (compare Tranio's words at 1150, where "your slave made a spectacle out of you," *tuo' te servos ludificaverit*, stands for the comic plot, as seen in chapter 4); the fable-like presentation of the scene onstage in terms of non-human actors; the insistence on the owner's blindness. The owner is made to state his own inability to see, or to recognize who is the crow and who are the vultures in the story/painting; he does not understand double speech. Tranio began his tour by likening the two old men to the doorposts his owner is seriously inspecting, and said they would be fine if coated in pitch (819, 827), as in the punishment with which Tyndarus is threatened in *Captivi* (597). In *Curculio*, the *parasitus*, dicing with the soldier, throws *basilicum* and wins, the soldier throws *vulturios* and loses (357–9), and Theopropides has just lost to Tranio.

Editorials

Phaedrus in the epilogue to book 3 continues his self-defense with reference to a republican text about restricted speech (3.ep.28–35):

> excedit animus quem proposui terminum,
> sed difficulter continetur spiritus,
> integritatis qui sincerae conscius   30
> a noxiorum premitur insolentiis.
> qui sint, requiris? apparebunt tempore.
> ego, quondam legi quam puer sententiam
> "Palam muttire plebeio piaculum est,"
> dum sanitas constabit, pulchre meminero.   35

> My feelings have gone outside the limit I set myself,
> but my spirit is kept in with difficulty,
> because, aware of its pure integrity   30
> it is oppressed by the insults of the guilty.

Who are they, you ask? They'll show themselves in time.
Me, the moral I read once as a boy,
"For a plebeian, to grumble openly is an act demanding atonement" –
as long as I keep my health, I'll remember it well.   35

Line 34 comes from the *Telephus* of Ennius; Phaedrus here displays his own good (and Roman) education in the Latin classics.[36] The line he quotes is plucked from an original context, literary and historical, closer to Plautus' than to his own; Ennius conflates the dangers of outspokenness for plebeians and slaves. As seen in previous chapters, social critique in general in the plays is often put in the mouths of lowly characters, whose lowliness itself serves, like the masks and costumes, to cover the risk. Some of these speeches – monologues – come as a surprise, a bump in the road of the play's development, and have a shaky connection with the character speaking the lines; so most obviously Syra's speech on wives' rights in *Mercator* (chapter 5), but also the opening speech of the *parasitus* Saturio in *Persa*, on *quadruplatores* (bounty-hunting public informers, *Per*. 62–76), and the speech of the mercenary in *Truculentus* mentioned above (*Truc*. 482–96): how can this soldier from Babylonia be making a critique of the Roman army, evidently a critique of the officer class? *Parasiti* work this kind of comment into their routines, like Curculio complaining about *Graeci palliati* as he runs in, or lacing into the banker Lyco with some specific remarks on legal loopholes (*Cur*. 506–11, chapter 3), while Lyco has his own random face-out line on pimps who desert their freed slaves (above). The *parasitus* Ergasilus, as he runs in, delivers up an edict against the street nuisance caused by pig-farming millers, purveyors of smelly fish, and price-gouging butchers whose sheep get in his way (*Capt*. 807–10, 813–22). His speech is explicitly set in the Forum Romanum, as "the smell drives all the guys who hang out next to the *basilica* into the forum" (*odos subbasilicanos omnis abigit in forum*, 815).[37] Or perhaps in any forum (see chapter 7 on the transferability of these speeches).

---

[36] Cf. 3.pr.20, "I was practically born in a school" (*in ipsa paene natus sim schola*), with Champlin 2005: 105–6. On the message, see Fantham (2005: 222–3): "it is difficult not to read this as a protest on behalf of the Roman underlings." The identification of the Ennius quotation (fr. 142 Jocelyn) comes from Pompeius Festus (128L); considering the usage in Plautus, *palam muttire* is an oxymoron, so that Festus' gloss **Muttire** *loqui* can perhaps, then, be seen to be incorrect – possibly an adverb has fallen out before *loqui*. The gloss appears in the same form in Paulus.

[37] For an argument that the Atrium Regium that burned down in the Forum fire of 210 was an early basilica, see Welch 2003, followed by Miles 2008: 87; who hung out in the basilica is specified in the speech of the Choragus in *Curculio* (472–3): rich husbands in debt, male prostitutes and their customers.

Staging as well as status protects these critiques. Ergasilus has a kibitzer, Hegio, who makes sarcastic remarks about his presumption (*confidentiam*, 805), and calls his pronouncements *edictiones aedilicias* (823–4): Ergasilus is no aedile. The long rant of the slave Stasimus in *Trinummus* (1028–58) on the degenerate morals of today is undercut by the fact that he is drunk, and by his eavesdropping owner's pious interjections (1030–1, 1035, 1036, 1045). These monologue speakers mark their speeches as unreal by coming out of them with "silly me" lines that disclaim any right to speak. So Saturio, hinting that those whose job it is to fix things are not doing so: "But aren't I stupid to worry about the state / when there are magistrates who ought to be worrying about it?" (*sed sumne ego stultus qui rem curo publicam / ubi sint magistratus quos curare oporteat? Per.* 75–6). Stasimus echoes him: "But I'm pretty foolish to worry about public affairs" (*sed ego sum insipientior qui rebus curem puplicis, Trin.* 1057). In fact, however, Stasimus starts with the *mos maiorum* his owner points out that he does not have (1030), and continues into a critique of the way corrupt *mos* has usurped the place of *lex*: "the laws are slaves to custom" (*leges mori serviunt*, 1043). Compare Curculio's remarks on the laws passed by the *populus* to try to control bankers (*rogitationes plurumas ... populus scivit, Cur.* 509; *leges*, 511). These speeches, with their direct address to the audience on political issues, occupy a place like that held in Old Comedy by the parabasis, with telling differences. Here in the mid-Republic the playwright stakes no claim to the opinion, protected, as in the editorials of a newspaper, by the fiction of editorial anonymity. Yet, although the speakers are well concealed, the words have been spoken. As on the Plautine stage, so for Ennius and Phaedrus as well, *palam muttire* opens the hidden transcript while pretending to be silent.[38]

"Good Slave" Speeches

Since double speech is so essential to the plays, audiences might well have been suspicious of the axioms on slave behavior that are expanded in a group of "good slave speeches," including some major songs, in which slaves explain why they cooperate with their owners' desires. Unlike Paegnium and Sophoclidisca, they take their orders seriously. These speeches have

---

[38] On Stasimus' speech, cf. Blösel 2000: 29–35; Earl 1960: 237–8. See chapter 1 on debates about Roman "political culture" in the mid-Republic; the basic vocabulary of political critique in Plautus is laid out in Earl 1960. A full lexical study of titles like *aedilis, censor, magistratus, orator, praefectus, praetor, quaestor, tribunus, IIIvir,* and the words *senatus* and *comitium* in the Plautine corpus will show that they often evoke negative emotions.

sometimes been read as straight; in performance, however, their net meaning is not the same as their literal meaning.[39]

The unnamed Slave of Lyconides enters with a monologue explaining how his duty is to help his young owner, just as all slaves act as buoyancy aids to owners in love (*Aul.* 587–602):

> Hoc est servi facinus frugi, facere quod ego persequor,
> ne morae molestiaeque imperium erile habeat sibi.
> nam qui ero ex sententia servire servos postulat,
> in erum matura, in se sera condecet capessere.　　　　　　　590
> sin dormitet, ita dormitet servom sese ut cogitet.
> nam qui amanti ero servitutem servit, quasi ego servio,
> si erum videt superare amorem, hoc servi esse officium reor,
> retinere ad salutem, non enim quo incumbat eo impellere.
> quasi pueri qui nare discunt scirpea induitur ratis,　　　　595
> qui laborent minu', facilius ut nent et moveant manus,
> eodem modo servom ratem esse amanti ero aequom censeo,
> ut <eum> toleret, ne pessum abeat tamquam <catapirateria>.
> eri ille imperium ediscat, ut quod frons velit oculi sciant;
> quod iubeat citis quadrigis citius properet persequi.　　　600
> qui ea curabit apstinebit censione bubula,
> nec sua opera rediget umquam in splendorem compedis.

> This is the deed of a prudent slave, to do what I am setting out to:
> not to consider his owner's command an obstacle or annoyance to himself.
> For a slave who wants to slave to meet his owner's expectations –
> it befits him to watch out early for his owner and late for himself.　590
> Even if he's sleeping, let him sleep so he's aware he's a slave.
> Indeed, one who's slaving in slavery to an owner who's in love, the way I'm slaving,
> if he sees love overcoming his owner, I think this is the slave's duty,

---

[39] As Richard Hunter observed, these speeches, like all comic moralizing, have to be taken in context, as comedy likes to mock the "over-virtuous" (1985: 145–7). Among those who have taken the speeches seriously are Peter Spranger (1961: 24–8), his teacher Joseph Vogt (briefly, 1975: 131) and Jean-Christian Dumont (1987); for a critical overview (much overstating Vogt's notice of the plays), see McKeown 2007: 109–10. I see that these speeches made McKeown, too, think of a pie in the face (cf. below), in an analysis with which I otherwise disagree. Stewart 2012: 132–55 reads Gripus and Messenio as two prime examples of how the plays justify slavery; compare Thalmann 1996 on good slaves and power relations. Moore 1998: 42–3 takes most of the good slave speeches to be ironic, as he takes the plays' moralizing speeches to be (1998: 67–90), but interprets Messenio's as more nuanced (on which, see below); note esp. his remarks on the pomposity of bacchiac meter in association with good-slave speeches (2012: 198–9). On virtuous slaves as a challenge to aristocratic virtue, see Owens 2001. Bradley 1984: 136 takes serious note of the connection between good behavior and fear of the owner that is made in these speeches. Many note that Fraenkel saw these speeches as Plautine; his discussion (2007: 167–9), in passing, ties these speeches in with the old man's entrance speech in *Stichus*, on which see Richlin 2017b: 181–2 and chapter 7 below. The speeches thus exemplify what they profess: channeling the owner.

to hold him back to the safe side, and not to push him the way he's leaning.
Just like boys when they learn to swim are put on a corky float,   595
so they'll struggle less, and swim more easily, and move their hands,
same way – I think it's fair for a slave to be the float for his owner in love,
to bear him up, so he doesn't go to the bottom like a lead sounding line.
Let him learn his owner's command by heart, so his eyes will know what
     his face means,
let him hurry to follow up on what he orders, faster than a fast four-horse
     chariot.   600
One who takes care of these things will avoid the oxhide assessment,
nor will he ever put the shine back on the shackles by his own efforts.

The insistent repetition of *serv-* and its cognates here – eight times in the
first seven lines – again recalls the mockery in Sagaristio's opening speech
in *Persa* and the harshness of Periplectomenus; the speech is full of the
vocabulary of slave virtue and owners' power: *frugi, imperium, ex sententia,
condecet, officium, aequom*. The speaker here advises that a slave should be
conscious he is a slave even while sleeping, that he should anticipate his
owner's orders, that he should even read the owner's facial expressions,
and that by so doing a slave will escape corporal punishment. The serene
conviction of this speech is somewhat undercut by the ludicrous picture
of the owner buoyed up by his slave inner tube; as the play continues, the
Slave jettisons his morals the instant he hears of the pot of gold (618–23),
is beaten by Euclio (632), insults him (637), casts off his owner's orders
(680–1), steals the pot of gold and takes it home with him (701–12), and
fails to persuade his owner to manumit him on the strength of it (808–31) –
no longer serene.

Similar potential credibility problems affect the section of Gripus' long
song in which he extols his own industriousness and sets himself up as a
model (*Rud.* 914–22). Again he uses deontological language (921–2):

> vigilare decet hominem qui volt sua temperi conficere officia,
> non enim illum exspectare <id> oportet, dum eru' se ad suom suscitet
>   officium.

> It's fitting for a person to be wakeful who wants to be on time to do
>   his duties,
> for he shouldn't wait for his owner to get him going on his duty.

As a result of his energy, Gripus sings, "I've found what will let me be lazy
if I want to" (*repperi ut piger si velim siem*, 925) – and the excitement of this
thought causes him to launch into a fantasy of wealth and freedom. Like
the Slave of Lyconides, he is headed from this song into hot water.

Like Gripus and the Slave of Lyconides, the *puer* Phaniscus appears first onstage with a proclamation of his goodness and advice on how to be like him (*Mos.* 858–84); like Gripus, he enters singing and, probably, dancing, in a showy number that continues into his verbal duel with Pinacium.[40] Slaves who fear a beating even when they have not deserved it are useful to owners, he argues; the others are destined for punishment, which Phaniscus does not intend to be. He takes a proprietorial attitude towards his own body (868–72):

> ut adhuc fuit mi, corium esse oportet,
> > sincerum atque uti votem verberari.
> si huic imperabo, probe tectum habebo,   870
> malum quom impluit ceteris, ne impluat mi.
> > nam, ut servi volunt esse erum, ita solet.

> As it's been to me so far, that's the way my hide should stay:
> > intact, and so I can keep it from being flogged.
> If I command *this*, I'll have myself well roofed,   870
> so, when beatings rain down on other people, it doesn't rain on me.
> > Indeed, the way slaves want their owner to be, that's how he
> > usually is.

The lack of a name for what he has to control (*huic*, 870) perhaps implies a gesture here by the actor/dancer. Some translators and commentators take *huic* to refer to his back; Leo notes laconically "huic *mihi*" (a conventional joking self-indication); others imagine *huic* represents the left hand, a joking byword for larceny. Deixis here, as in chapter 5, evokes stage directions, hence Nixon's "If only I could control this article (*surveys his pilfering left hand*)"; the actor might equally lift up his pallium and flash a stage phallus at the audience. Phaniscus' phantasmatic body part points to the millennia of guesswork that separate us from the stage in the Forum: the audience saw the actor, we see the guesswork. Yet the very range of guesses should remind us that the original choreography, the agency, belonged to the actor.[41] Under the mask and costume, he commands his body, in sync with Phaniscus.

---

[40] On Phaniscus as "good slave," see Gunderson 2015: 71–2. The music greatly affected the original meaning: "a very impressive moment of dance" (Timothy Moore, personal communication).

[41] The text of the whole song is vexed; Ritschl (1852) read *huic iam parebo* in line 870 without comment, while Ramsay (1869), based on collation of the MSS, printed *huic imperabo*, the reading of B and D (no comment on *huic* in his notes, unfinished at his death); and indeed *imperabo* had wide circulation in the mashup of the 1679 Delphin edition and Gronovius's 1684 edition printed by Valpy in 1829, with its explicit note, *imperabo meo tergo*. The currency of this reading is suggested by the 1772 Warner translation, "Back, be advis'd by me, keep on thy cloaths." School texts in English opt for "back"; the idea of the left hand is supported by *Per.* 226, *illa … furtifica laeva* (but cf. 227), and by the elliptical thieving body part at *Epid.* 10–12 and *hac mea* at *Ps.* 104–5, where again a

Whatever funny moves he makes, Phaniscus' words are pious, and he complains that his house is full of slaves who are beaten (*plagigeruli*) and "wasteful of their *peculium*" (*peculi … prodigi*, 875); he mimics their contemptuous responses when they are asked to go to greet their owner (877–8), and looks forward to tomorrow, when they will be punished and he will not (880–4). "I care less for their back than mine," he says; he compares his carefully preserved hide to a roof that does not leak, in tune with the play's real estate theme. His metaphor even echoes his owner's friend, the romantic lead: after the verbal duel that opens the play, Philolaches enters singing a song in which he compares people to houses; a *nequam homo* does not maintain the house well and lets in the rain of bad behavior (105–17). Alas, again, as with the Slave of Lyconides, Phaniscus' profession of virtue, such as it is, will be undercut by the scenes that follow: first a verbal duel with his fellow-slave Pinacium (885–98, seen in chapter 2), then a long scene in which the two of them are very rude to the *senex* who, unbeknownst to them, is Philolaches' father (933–92).

The sentiments expressed by the Slave of Lyconides, Gripus, and Phaniscus are developed in the song sung by the soldier's slave Harpax as he makes his second entrance (*Ps.* 1103–15). He begins:

> Malus et nequamst homo qui nihili eri imperium sui servo' facit,
> nihilist autem suom qui officium facere inmemor est nisi est admonitus.
>   nam qui liberos esse ilico se arbitrantur,   1105
>   ex conspectu eri si sui se abdiderunt,
> luxantur, lustrantur, comedunt quod habent, i nomen diu
>   servitutis ferunt.

> He is a bad and worthless person who holds his owner's command to be
>   worth nothing, though he's a slave;
> in fact, he's worth nothing if he can't remember to do his duty unless he's
>   reminded to.
>   Indeed those who think they're free on the spot   1105
>   if they've tucked themselves away from their owner's sight,
> they live it up, they hang out in dives, they eat up what they have, they
>   long bear
>   the name of slavery.

Again the speaker proposes a rule for the *homo servos* (1104): he is to obey his owner's orders without needing to be reminded (see chapter 7 on the lexicon of command). He himself, out of fear, does what he is ordered to do

---

gesture is implied. Leo's tidy idea (1896) is supported by Moore's metrical analysis (2012: 198, 296); Phaniscus' pompous gesture then comes as he launches into pompous bacchiacs. Cf. Halla-aho and Kruschwitz 2010: 143 on the register of self-referential demonstratives, and Moore 2012: 114–19 on gestural dance. Nixon (1924: 378) is followed by others, including de Melo (2011c: 405).

even when his owner is away, just as if the owner were present (1113–15). In other words, a good slave has a sort of internalized owner, seen also above in the songs of Phaniscus and the Slave of Lyconides, and vigorously rejected by Sagaristio in his opening song (note especially *Per.* 9, *ero ... praesenti atque apsenti suo*; chapter 4). Slaves who think they are free when their owner is away engage in pleasurable activities; Harpax wants nothing to do with them (1111–12); like Hegio in *Captivi*, he connects their behavior with a lack of desire to be free. This song is undercut by the fact that the audience knows, as Harpax does not, that he has already unwittingly betrayed the trust placed in him; the song leads into a scene in which Harpax is at first thwarted and taunted by the pimp and the *senex*, including, as seen in chapter 2, suggestions that Harpax allows his owner to use him sexually.

The most evidently sincere of the good slave speeches come from Messenio in *Menaechmi*, who never stops trying to persuade his owner to leave Epidamnus. In reflecting on his failure, he echoes the words used by owners like Periplectomenus (443–4):

> sed ego inscitus qui domino me postulem moderarier:
> dicto me emit audientem, haud imperatorem sibi.

> But I am naive to expect myself to keep a rein on my legal owner:
> He bought me to be obedient, not to be his commander.

This attitude anticipates Messenio's long song (966–85) upon returning from the hotel where he has dutifully checked the luggage and other slaves, "as [the owner] had ordered" (*ut iusserat*, 986). His song repeats the idea that slaves should behave as if the owner were watching at all times (968–9), and repeats almost verbatim four lines on this theme from Phaniscus' song (*Mos.* 858–61 = *Men.* 983a–983b):

Mos. 858–61:

> Servi qui quom culpa carent tamen malum metuont,
> i solent esse eris utibiles.
> nam illi qui nil metuont, postquam sunt malum meriti,   860
> stulta sibi expetunt consilia

> Slaves who, though they lack all blame, still fear a beating –
> these are the ones always useful to their owners.
> For those who fear nothing even after they've earned a beating   860
> get stupid ideas about what they should do

Men. 983a–983b:

> servi qui quom culpa carent metuont, i solent esse eris utibiles.
> nam illi qui nil metuont, postquam malum promeriti, tunc ei metuont.

Slaves who, though they lack all blame, are still afraid – these are the ones
  always useful to their owners.
For those who fear nothing, after they've earned a beating, then they're
  afraid.

The repetition of these lines emphasizes the interchangeability of these
"good slave" sentiments from play to play, which is important to the way
they set up the audience for what is to come.

As in his aside on the word that lets him know he is a slave, Messenio
here explains that his actions are motivated by fear of corporal punishment, and gives a lurid list: "Lashes, fetters, / the mill, weariness, hunger, harsh cold" (*verbera, compedes, / molae, lassitudo, fames, frigu' durum*,
974–5).[42] The parts of the body that suffer punishment are to be accorded
more weight than the parts that give pleasure: "The back ought to be more
important than the gullet, the legs than the stomach" (*tergum quam gulam,
crura quam ventrem oportet / potiora esse*, 970–1). His song puns on *verba*
and *verbera* as punishments (978), and on *molitum* as "something to eat"
and "a trip to the mill" (979). He hints at his hopes of freedom, which he
refers to as the *pretium* his owner will soon pay (984). As his song ends,
he comes upon the besieged Menaechmus I, rescues him (thinking he is
his owner Menaechmus II), asks for manumission as a reward (1023–4),
and receives it, or so he thinks (1025–34, cf. 1058–9; see chapter 8). Being
Messenio, he does not wish to leave his new *patronus*, and tells him he
must continue to command him "no less ... than when I was your slave"
(*ne minus ... quam quom tuos servos fui*); they will always be together
(1033–4). This is the kind of attitude mocked by Palaestrio in his maudlin
farewell scene with the soldier (chapter 8). Messenio's final reward is to be
made the *praeco* for the auction of the goods of Menaechmus I (1155–61) –
an occupation suitable for such an unusually subservient slave. The *praeco*,
as seen in chapter 3, was not a popular figure.

In short, most of the good slave speeches are undercut by subsequent
events; familiarity with plot cues would have caused experienced audience members to have taken these speeches as the equivalent of the spot-
less shirt that awaits the flung pie. On a larger scale, then, these speeches
resemble the "exploding cigars" seen above: the lesson evidently taught by
the speech is the opposite of what it actually teaches. Momentary lapses

---

[42] With the wording in the speeches by Phaniscus and Messenio, cf. *Bac.* fr. ix–x: *quibus ingenium
in animo utibilest, modicum et sine vernilitate* and *vincla, virgae, molae: saevitudo mala.* These lines
are grouped together as part of a "good slave" speech by a *puer*, perhaps the one belonging to the
soldier, upbraided at 578–81.

like Sosia's brief spurt of piety (*Am.* 959–61) or Epidicus' professed interest in obedience (*Epid.* 348) then constitute a non-surprising incongruity with a character elsewhere not at all dutiful or cowed.[43] Sosia tells Jupiter (disguised as Amphitruo) that he will be happy to see Amphitruo and Alcumena reconciled, and preaches that a *servom ... frugi* ought to take his emotions, even his facial expressions, from his owners, but in his previous scene with his owners he has done all he can to mock Alcumena, and Jupiter responds to his speech here with "You're kidding me" (*derides*, 963). Epidicus' line elicits the straight man's "What do you mean?" from his young owner (*nam quid ita*, 349), setting off a run of jokes. All the "good slave" speeches cite the fear of a beating as a chief motivating factor, but the bad slaves who defy the threat of beatings – Sagaristio, Leonida and Libanus – cut a dashing figure in their plays. They are like the "bad" slave who was sometimes the hero of songs and stories in the American South, as in the John stories collected by Roger D. Abrahams and Zora Neale Hurston.[44] In the duel that opens *Mostellaria*, Grumio plays the good slave to Tranio's bad slave, and one of his reproaches has a familiar ring (25–7):

> haecine mandavit tibi, quom peregre hinc it, senex?   25
> hocine modo hic rem curatam offendet suam?
> hoccine boni esse officium servi existumas

> Is this what the old man bid you do, when he left here to go abroad?   25
> Is this the way he's going to find his business taken care of here?
> Is this what you think is the duty of a good slave?

The rhythm and structure of these lines recall Leonida in *Asinaria*, playing the *atriensis* to his fellow slave Libanus (chapter 4); just as this kind of reproach is mocked in *Asinaria*, so in *Mostellaria* it is Tranio who runs the show, while Grumio disappears after this duel.

Telling Without Saying

Like jokes, the plays are able to say forbidden things by using an overall structure that gets the tellers off the hook: they are dressed up as Greek New

---

[43] The pervasiveness of this phenomenon would likewise have prompted the audience to expect the virtuous-woman songs of prostitutes to be followed by, for example, an attempt to extort money (so at *Poen.* 300–7, cf. 340, 346; with which compare *St.* 741–7, cf. 750–1, and *Mos.* 286–92, spoken by the decidedly unvirtuous Scapha). And it might throw further doubt on the straightforwardness of the virtuous-wife songs of Alcumena in *Amphitruo* (633–53, 839–42) and the two sisters in *Stichus* (1–46). On the possibilities for autonomous understandings of virtue by women and slaves, engaging with Parker 1998 on loyal wives and slaves, see Langlands forthcoming.

[44] See Abrahams 1985; Genovese 1976: 625–30; Hurston 1935, 1943, 1981.

Comedy. In addition, as seen in this chapter, a range of smaller structures both talks about and exemplifies the ways in which slavery affects speech and knowledge: double meaning, face-out lines, editorials, self-exploding axioms and routines, turning object into subject, *muttitio*, fables, the good slave speeches headed for trouble. The desire to speak out and speak the truth makes the fabric of the plays. In the next chapter we will turn to another deep desire expressed in the *palliata*: the desire for the homes and families broken by human trafficking.

CHAPTER 7

Remembering the Way Back

The plays of Plautus express meaning not only through what is said onstage but through settings and back stories; the characters onstage have histories and travels behind them. The scenarios of slavery and enslavement require insistent questions: what is your *patria*? Where are you from? What was your name? Who were your parents? A list of locations in the plays shows two things: (1) By far the majority of the plays involve someone going far away and coming back, or just returning, or being taken from one place to another far away (table 7.1); (2) Even if these settings and journeys were lifted by the writers of the *palliata* directly from Greek originals, they were being superimposed on a Mediterranean landscape that, in the course of the 200s BCE, in central Italy, came to mean something much different from what it had meant to Greek writers of previous generations. The perspective has shifted; actors and audience are now living outside the realm of the Diadochoi, and, for some of them, the wars after Alexander have turned that realm into the Old Country. "Setting: Berlin" meant one thing to Brecht in 1923, another to Ernst Lubitsch in 1942. The trafficking, travels, and war zones in Middle and New Comedy, from Antiphanes through Menander's *Aspis, Misoumenos, Sikyonios* and beyond, looked east. Later, far to the west, locations in the *palliata* now start to collide with the Roman wars; hometowns in Italy are now war zones; many stories in the plays involve the slave trade, which went everywhere. The wars created hybrid people with new geographies.

Nicholas Horsfall, in his book on Roman oral culture, emphasizes the relationship between the theater and the life of the Roman plebs. Tertullian, Augustine, and Caesarius of Arles, he points out, all inveigh against workers' habit of singing show tunes they know by heart, and he finds traces of this practice going back at least to Ovid (2003: 13–17). He has in mind the description in the *Fasti* of the festival of Anna Perenna on

Table 7.1 *Travels onstage*

Play	Setting	Travels
Amphitruo	Thebes	Amphitruo and Sosia return from conquering the Teleboi (101).
Asinaria	Athens	The Mercator is from Pella (333).
		The *asini* are Arcadian (333).
		Periphanes, *mercator dives* (fictive), is from Rhodes (499).
Aulularia	Athens	—
Bacchides	Athens	Chrysalus returns from two years in Ephesus (170–1).
		Bacchis' sister has been living on the island of Samos, just across the water from Ephesus (200).
		The sister has been brought from Samos to Athens by the soldier (106, 574).
		The soldier is headed for Elatia, on the island of Zacynthos, and his messenger says the sister must go with him unless she buys herself out of her contract (575–6, 590–1).
Captivi	Aetolia	Philopolemus, an Aetolian, has been captured by the Elians (25–6).
		Philocrates and Tyndarus, Elians, have been captured by the Aetolians (31–4).
		Stalagmus, a *Siculus* (888), escaped from Aetolia twenty years ago, taking Tyndarus with him to Elis and selling him there (8–10, 874–6, 881, 971–4).
		Stalagmus is captured and brought back to Aetolia (874–6).
Casina	Athens	—
Cistellaria	Sicyon	Demipho, a Lemnian *mercator*, went to Sicyon and home again (156–62).
		He has now returned to Sicyon (176–7).
Curculio	Epidaurus	Curculio has been in Caria (67); he returns (275).
		Pretending to be a soldier's freedman, he says he lost his eye in Sicyon (395).
		His fictive journeys with the soldier (437–48): from India to Caria; through Persia, Paphlagonia, Sinope, Arabia, Caria, Crete, Syria, Rhodes, Lycia, Libya, and (doubly fictive) Peredia, Perbibesia, Centauromachia, Classia Unomammia, and Conterebromnia.
Epidicus	Athens	The soldier arrives from Caria (533; no arrival scene).
		The army has returned from Thebes (53).
		The soldier has come from Euboea (153); or from Rhodes (300).

352

		Periphanes raped Philippa in Epidaurus (540a, 541a).
		Philippa took her daughter Telestis to Thebes to raise (636).
		Telestis is brought to Athens from Thebes as *praeda* (43–4).
		Philippa has come to Athens seeking her (532).
Menaechmi	Epidamnus	A *mercator* from Syracuse goes to Tarentum with his son, Menaechmus I, who is kidnapped there by a *mercator* from Epidamnus and taken back to Epidamnus (17–33).
		Menaechmus II and his slave Messenio arrive in Epidamnus, having sailed all around Italy, stopping at Histria, Hispania, Massilia, Illyria (235–8).
Mercator	Athens	The *mercator* Charinus goes to Rhodes; picks up Pasicompsa (93).
		Charinus plans to go wandering (646–7), to: Megara, Eretria, Corinth, Chalcis, Crete, Cyprus, Sicyon, Cnidus, Zacynthus, Lesbos, Boeotia.
Miles Gloriosus	Ephesus	Mad scene (933–47): imaginary trip to Cyprus, to Chalcis, meets a man from Zacynthus, returns to Athens.
		The soldier has fought in: India (25); Cilicia (42); Sardis (44); Macedonia (44); Cappadocia (52); and (doubly fictive) the fields of Curculonia (13) and Scytholatronia (43).
		Pleusicles goes from Athens to Naupactus (100–2).
		The soldier takes Philocomasium from Athens to Ephesus (113).
		Palaestrio sails to Naupactus; captured by pirates; he is taken to Ephesus (115–21).
		Palaestrio sends word to Pleusicles via *mercator* (130–3).
		Pleusicles comes to Ephesus (133–4).
Mostellaria	Athens	The *senex* returns from Egypt (440).
		The (fictive) ghost was a *transmarinus hospes* named Diapontius (497).
Persa	Athens	The pimp moved here from Megara six months ago (137).
		Sagaristio is sent to Eretria (259–60).
		Toxilus' owner's letter (fictive) comes from Persia (498).
		(Fictive) Lucris, stolen from Chrysopolis in Arabia, is brought first to Persia, then to Athens (522).
Poenulus	Calydon	Agorastocles, stolen from Carthage, is brought to Calydon and sold (66, 73).
		Adelphasium and Anterastilis, with their nurse Giddenis, are stolen from Carthage (by a *praedo Siculus*, 897) and taken to Anactorium, where they are sold to a pimp, who brings them to Calydon (84–95).
		Their father Hanno travels the world in search of them (104–11).
		The soldier has fought in (fictive) Penetronica (471).
		The Advocati say the *vilicus* (disguised as a soldier) fought in Sparta (663).

(continued)

353

Table 7.1 (*cont.*)

Play	Setting	Travels
Pseudolus	Athens	The soldier is from Macedonia, has been in Athens, and is now elsewhere (*peregre*, 51). He is paying to have Phoenicium sent to him in Sicyon (995, 1011–12, 1098). Harpax has just arrived (594–5) from Sicyon (1173–6). Simia has just arrived from Carystus in Euboea (730–1).
Rudens	Cyrene	Daemones went from Athens to exile in Cyrene (35). A *praedo* had stolen his daughter and sold her to a pimp (39–40). The pimp brought her to Cyrene (41). A young Athenian in Cyrene fell in love with her (42–4). The pimp's friend is from Agrigentum in Sicily (49–50). The pimp, his friend, and two slave *meretrices* set sail for Sicily (49–63), but are shipwrecked outside Cyrene.
Stichus	Athens	The two husbands have been in Asia (152). They return, ships laden with exotic cargo, including slaves (366–92). They have visitors (fictive?) from Ambracia (491).
Trinummus	Athens	Charmides has been in Seleucia (112). Stasimus fears he will have to leave for Asia or Cilicia (599). The Sycophanta says he has been to: Seleucia, Macedonia, Asia and Arabia (845); Pontus, Arabia, and Jupiter's throne (933).
Truculentus	Athens	The soldier is Babylonian (84). Diniarchus has come back from Lemnos to Athens (91). The soldier has been in Syria (530), Phrygia (536), Arabia (539), Pontus (540).
Vidularia	?	Shipwreck.

For an overview of travels focused on trade, incorporating Terence and providing maps, see (with caution) Callataÿ 2015: 19–23; based on the more comprehensive account in Knapp 1907a and 1907b.

the Ides of March, when the plebs picnics and parties on the banks of the Tiber (*F.* 3.523–42). There the people sing and dance (3.535–8):

> illic et cantant quicquid didicere theatris,   535
>   et iactant faciles ad sua verba manus,
> et ducunt posito duras cratere choreas,
>   cultaque diffusis saltat amica comis.

> There also they sing whatever they've learned at the theater,   535
>   and toss their hands up lightly to the words,
> and, putting their glasses down, they hold a makeshift dance,
>   while someone's dressed-up girlfriend leaps about with
>   streaming hair.

We have no such reports for the 200s BCE, only the remarks by Plautine slave characters on what they have seen at the theater.[1] Still, it is not hard to believe that audience members might have taken some memories home with them, along with, perhaps, a little clay figure of the actor who sang the song: a souvenir, an *aide-mémoire*. For the plays themselves constitute a form of communal remembering, specifically of the time and place before enslavement and loss.

A story is a way of making sense of things, a kind of map or list of way-stations that traces the way here, which is also the way back, and maybe the way forward. Therapists who deal with PTSD see the retelling of traumatic events as essential for survivors, who often obsessively retell their stories in any case (Kaminer 2006). Historians who write on war and trauma see unofficial memory as a means by which damaged groups repair identities; Peter Burke suggests, "It might be useful to think in terms of different 'memory communities' within a given society. It is important to ask the question, who wants whom to remember what, and why?" (1989: 107).[2] The unnamed *lena* in *Cistellaria* tells the audience, "That's how this history went. ... / I want you all to remember it" (*haec sic res gesta est. ... / meminisse ego hanc rem vos volo*, 147–8); as will be seen below, she wants their help in healing an old wound (a stage wound, the finding of the child of a raped mother, a child once abandoned in an alley). The history told by this

---

[1] But compare Theophrastus, *Characters* 27.7, the old man who likes to do youthful things: "At street fairs he sits through three or four shows, trying to learn the songs" (trans. Rusten in Rusten and Cunningham 2002: 131). So this was youthful behavior in Athens in the late 300s, at least.

[2] For an introduction to current theory about PTSD and its possible applications to Roman warfare, I am indebted to Scott Brantner; see Brantner 2014. For discussion of the applicability of the term "PTSD" in antiquity, especially Greek, see Tritle 2014. Many essays in Prentki and Preston 2009 discuss the uses of theater for survivors of trauma; in relation to Greek tragedy, see esp. Rabinowitz 2008, 2013 on Rhodessa Jones's Medea Project. On memory and history, see essays in Olick et al. 2011.

comedy is a low, unofficial one, for an audience who knew this story (an audience for whom abandoned children were real, leaving real wounds).

The survivors' retelling, especially a performative retelling, might then be seen as a kind of communal history-writing. Testimony itself has served as justice, where justice has been a desideratum of the state (Weschler 1998). But justice is always desired, and story-telling makes do when the real thing is unavailable and restitution is not forthcoming. Peter Meineck and others in the project on "Combat Trauma and the Ancient Stage" have argued that Greek tragedy, along with Old and New Comedy, "offered a form of performance-based collective 'catharsis' ... by providing a place where the traumatic experiences faced by the spectators were reflected [in] the gaze of the masked characters performing before them" (2012: 7). The *palliata* dealt with many kinds of traumatic displacement, as enslavement changed names, broke family ties, and opened bodies to physical punishment and sexual abuse; gender displacement was enacted onstage as (possibly) slave actors played slaves both male and female, a displacement emphasized by drag, as in Bromia's joke in *Amphitruo* (chapter 5). The audience decked in victory wreaths, chanting along with insulting refrains (chapter 3), constantly addressed from the stage, asked for help, teased, insulted, praised – they are akin to the "spect-actors" Augusto Boal wanted, and the actors encased in costume and mask give a kind of "engaged performance": by the low, for the low, repurposing borrowed materials. This is not community-based theater in the sense argued by Mary-Kay Gamel for fifth-century Athens, for the actors do not belong to the community, but there is a community of status. When the *grex* at the end of *Cistellaria* says of themselves, *qui deliquit vapulabit, qui non deliquit bibet* (785), they remind the audience of who they are.[3] The Virgo in *Persa* acts out the rupture between who you used to be and who you are now. At the same time, enslaved characters are removed from home, displaced in space. Comedy obsessively jokes about these very sore points, these points of trauma; there was nothing funny about the Truth and Reconciliation Commission, so the degree to which the *palliata* is funny can serve as a measure of the depth to which this hidden transcript is hidden. The Plautine story-lines

---

[3] See Boal 1985: 122 for an anti-Aristotelian model aimed at bringing the spectator into the play's action. On "engaged performance," see Adamitis and Gamel 2013, esp. on classical drama and war veterans, and Gamel 2016 on community-based theater; the differences between the circumstances of production of Attic drama and of the *palliata* suggest how deep a gulf lay between the borrowed material and its original meaning. For the *Cistellaria* line, see chapter 2; note that both its form and content resemble the (undatable) children's rhyme, *rex erit qui recte faciet, qui non faciet, non erit*, much cited in studies of *versus quadratus* and Roman popular culture (e.g. Fraenkel 1927: 365; see chapter 3).

themselves are no joke, as is evident when their bones are removed from the jolly wrappings.

Human Trafficking and the Road Home

Franco Moretti began *Atlas of the European Novel* with the observation that "geography is not an inert container, is not a box where cultural history 'happens', but an active force, that pervades the literary field and shapes it in depth" (1998: 3). Plays are not books – not a "literary field" in the sense Moretti means; yet the *palliata* was a form of cultural cargo conveyed by actors, some of whom were themselves human cargo, and all of whom were performing plays *about* human cargo, to audiences who knew what that meant. Geography was an active force that shaped the entire experience out of which the *palliata* was made.

Traffic

Five common processes by which free people became slaves feature in the plots (table 7.2): exposure of an infant, capture in war, kidnapping, piracy, sale by parents. In addition, some slaves move around through trade, their previous origins being unspecified. Sixteen of the twenty extant plays incorporate enslavement or trafficking somewhere in the back story or onstage action – all but *Asinaria, Aulularia, Mostellaria,* and *Trinummus.* Just as enslavement itself is a drastic movement between statuses, so it constitutes a rupture in the life story of an enslaved character, while trafficking involves long-distance movement around the Mediterranean.

The plays about kidnapped children tell and retell the story of how they were lost. Where age is specified, all the children are taken young: Agorastocles at seven (*Poen.* 66), Menaechmus at seven (*Men.* 24; 1116, just losing his baby teeth), Adelphasium and Anterastilis at five and four (*Poen.* 85), Tyndarus at four (*Capt.* 8, 760, 981–2), Palaestra at three (*Rud.* 744). The pimp describes Planesium as *parvolam* when he bought her (*Cur.* 528). As in the story of Neaira (ps.-Demosthenes *Against Neaira* 59.18, c. 343–340 BCE), training starts in childhood.[4] The festivals

---

[4] On the implications of the capture of children in the aftermath of siege warfare, see Gaca 2010– 11; for the sexual use of children in Roman culture, see Richlin 2015a, and chapter 2. As seen in chapter 4, the *puer* in *Pseudolus* describes himself as too young to have sex: "Alas, how tiny I still am now for that thing" (*eheu, quam illae rei ego etiam nunc sum parvolus,* 783). For an overview of *Against Neaira,* see Robson 2013: 68–9, 186–91; he adduces Metagenes fr. 4 K-A (late 400s), a comic description of barely pubescent girl prostitutes.

Table 7.2 *Processes of natal alienation and enslavement in the plautine corpus*

exposure/ abandonment:	Casina in *Casina*: picked up and made into a household slave-woman Selenium in *Cistellaria*: picked up and given to a prostitute, to be a prostitute baby boy in *Truculentus*: given to a prostitute by an *ancilla*, to be her son
capture in war:	Tyndarus, Philocrates, Aristophontes, Philopolemus in *Captivi*: prisoners, quarries; Elis ↔ Aetolia ? Stalagmus in *Captivi*: household slave-boy, sex slave; Sicily → Aetolia Telestis in *Epidicus*: bought for sex; Thebes → Athens ? "Lucris" in *Persa*: bought by a trader for sale to a pimp; Arabia → Persia Harpax in *Pseudolus*: soldier's slave (origin unspecified) two unnamed Syrian women in *Truculentus*: given to a prostitute to be household slave-women; Syria → Athens
kidnapping:	Tyndarus in *Captivi*: sold to a family as a household slave-boy; Aetolia → Elis Planesium in *Curculio*: sold to a pimp; (unspecified) → Epidaurus Menaechmus I in *Menaechmi*: adopted; Tarentum → Epidamnus Agorastocles in *Poenulus*: sold, then adopted; Carthage → Calydon Adelphasium, Anterastilis, Giddenis in *Poenulus*: sold to a pimp – Adelphasium and Anterastilis, to become prostitutes; Giddenis as a household slave-woman; Carthage → Anactorium → Calydon Palaestra in *Rudens*: sold to a pimp to become a prostitute; Athens → Cyrene
piracy:	Palaestrio in *Miles*: given to a soldier; Athens → ~~Naupactus~~ → Ephesus
sale by parents:	the Virgo in *Persa*: in exchange for a meal ~ Mercurius in *Amphitruo*: becomes his father's body slave (176–8)
trade/trafficking:	Bacchis' sister in *Bacchides*: contracted to a soldier; Samos → Athens [→ Elatia] (a free prostitute) Pasicompsa in *Mercator*: bought for sex; Rhodes → Athens "Lucris" in *Persa*: sold to a pimp to become a prostitute; Persia → Athens Phoenicium in *Pseudolus*: is to be sold to a soldier; Athens → Sicyon Palaestra and Ampelisca in *Rudens*: moved to a better market; Cyrene → Sicily the cargo of music girls and comedians in *Stichus*: Asia → Athens

themselves are risky places for children: Planesium's wet-nurse had taken her to see the Dionysia (*ea me spectatum tulerat per Dionysia, Cur.* 644–5); Menaechmus wanders away from his father at the *ludei*, to which people have come from all over (*Men.* 29–31). The Dionysia and other festivals are also sometimes the scenes of rape, always of girls unmarried (and therefore very young): the young girl in *Aulularia* is raped at night "at the vigil of Ceres" (*noctu, Cereris vigiliis, Aul.* 36); Phanostrata as a young girl was raped at the Dionysia (*Cist.* 156–8), and the daughter born of that rape meets the young man she now loves when "my mother took me to watch the parade at the Dionysia" (*per Dionysia / mater pompam me spectatum duxit, Cist.* 89–90); that is, her adoptive mother, a freed prostitute.[5] Note the presence of a prostitute and her adolescent daughter among the spectators, along with Planesium and her *nutrix*, just as *nutrices* and babies are addressed in the *Poenulus* prologue. It should be emphasized that all the female characters who claim virginity in the plays would have been staged as pubescent; even the freed prostitute Acroteleutium, who is to play the part of a wife, fits the job requirement for a woman who is pretty, sexually experienced and a good earner, "juicy," and "as young as possible": she is presented as a "teenage prostitute" (*forma lepida; quaestuosa, quae alat corpus corpore; consucidam; quamque adulescentem maxume; meretricem adulescentulam, Mil.* 782–9).[6]

The stories of kidnapping tend to involve travel across state lines, often travel by sea (table 7.2).[7] Tyndarus is taken from his father in Aetolia by a household slave, Stalagmus, and sold to a family in Elis (*Capt.* 978–92). Planesium winds up in Epidaurus, her origin (if elsewhere) unspecified, having been snatched from her *nutrix* by a man who sold her to the pimp Cappadox, whose own name is an ethnonym like those typically given to slaves, and one that locates him at a crossroads of the slave trade (*Cur.* 528–30, 644–50).[8] Menaechmus is taken by his father from his home in Syracuse

---

[5] Whatever the relation of these festivals to Attic practice, in the 200s in Rome they would have evoked, for native Romans, the joint worship of Ceres, Liber, and Libera on the Aventine (dating back to the early Republic), and specifically the *ludi Ceriales* organized by the plebeian *aediles Cereris*, which at some point came to feature dramatic performance (see Taylor 1937: 288–9, "probably instituted after the beginning of the Second Punic war," due to the increased demand for drama; Cornell 1995: 263 on the plebeian connections to the cult). On an early (pre-300) start date for dramatic *ludi*, see Richlin 2014b: 214–15. Wiseman (1998: 37–9), in a discussion of Liber, posits dramatic performance at the Liberalia. But the names of these festivals would have meant different things to people from different places.

[6] On the youth of the women who are sex objects in the plays, see Rosivach 1998: 5, 94.

[7] For maps of travels in Plautus and Terence, see Callataÿ 2015: 19–23 (not entirely accurate); for a full listing of travels, esp. as related to trade, see Knapp 1907a and 1907b.

[8] For examples of Cappadocian ethnonyms see Lewis 2011: 109, 111 no. 8, 113 no. 15 (from the Laureum mines); on Cappadocia generally, Scheidel 2011: 304; Thompson 2003: 18.

on a trading voyage to Tarentum, where he is picked up and taken home by a wealthy trader from Epidamnus, who adopts him, makes him his heir, and gives him a well-dowered wife (*Men.* 24–33, 60–6). Agorastocles is stolen from his home in Carthage and brought to Calydon, where he is sold to a *senex* who frees him and then adopts him (*Poen.* 66, 72–7; retold by Milphio, 901–4; and by Agorastocles, 986–7, 1037–8, 1054–5; and by Hanno and Agorastocles together, 1055–65); his two cousins are kidnapped, along with their *nutrix*, from Carthage by a Sicilian *praedo* and brought to Anactorium, where they are sold to a pimp who brings them to Calydon (*Poen.* 84–95; retold by Syncerastus, 894–900; confirmed by Hanno, 1104–5, 1344–6; and by the pimp, 1347–9, 1378–9, 1380–1, 1391–3).[9] Palaestra is stolen by a *praedo* from her home in Athens and sold to a pimp, who brings her to Cyrene, has her trained to be a *fidicina*, and then proposes to bring her to Sicily, where, he is told, the people are *voluptuarii*, so "that's where there's the biggest profit to be made off prostitutes" (*Rud.* 39–43, 49–57, 541–2; *ibi esse quaestum maxumum meretricibus*, 56, cf. 541). So Toxilus coaches Saturio on the tale his daughter is to tell (*fabuletur*): where she was born, who were her parents, where she was stolen, far away from Athens (i.e. far away from "here"), "and that she should weep when she recounts it" (*et ut adfleat quom ea memoret*, *Per.* 149–52). So Milphio coaches Hanno that he is to identify the two prostitutes as his daughters and to claim that they were stolen as "little girls" (*parvolas*) from Carthage (*Poen.* 1100–3), and when Hanno weeps, Milphio congratulates him on the skill and trickiness of his acting (*ut adflet*, 1109).

Similar geographic dislocations mark the stories of captives and exposed infants. In *Epidicus*, the poor girl Philippa who was raped in Epidaurus (540a–b, 554–7) moves to Thebes to bear and raise her daughter Telestis (636), who is then captured in war and winds up in Athens, where Philippa

---

9 The two girls are stolen *a Magaribus* (86), which de Melo renders as "from Magara" and glosses as "a suburb of Carthage" (2012: 27). The root *magar-* or *magal-* is genuine Punic, and the specific naming of a Carthaginian place points to what lies ahead in Act 5, with its torrent of onstage Punic and jokes about unintelligibility and bilingualism (cited in the prologue as a tricky trait in the title character, 112–13). Appian's account of movements by Scipio Aemilianus in 147 BCE (see Mineo 2011: 126 for the source issues) has him attacking Μέγαρα, "a large district in the city abutting the wall" (*Lib.* 117–18); it is described as a "suburb" at least as early as Leo 1896 *ad loc.*, but in Appian's account it is clearly inside the wall, if full of truck gardens. The word *magalia* elsewhere in Latin refers to Carthaginian native dwellings (esp. Vergil *A.* 1.421); Leo rejects *Magalibus* as a correction, with reference to ancient commentary on Vergil. See Moodie 2015 *ad loc.* for further bibliography. The presence of "Megara" on archaeological maps derives from Appian, as in Harden 1939. The dim ghost of a pun making this exotic name into a dramatic festival (- *a Megalensibus*; cf. *Cur.* 644–5) is perhaps visible at *Poen.* 86.

eventually finds her (see chapter 5). Telestis has been bought by a fickle young man, even if not by a pimp, and so reasonably still feels, when she is recognized, that she has escaped ruin: "By the gods' will, I once was lost but now am saved" (*di me ex perdita servatam cupiunt*, *Epid.* 644). The trader who raped the girl in Sicyon in *Cistellaria* runs away to his home in Lemnos afterwards (160–2); years later, he returns to Sicyon, where the two parents search for the now-grown baby girl, Selenium, who had been exposed to die (*ad necem*, 166, 665). Unlike Philippa, this mother had assigned a slave to put her new baby in the street, just as the nameless girl in *Truculentus*, raped by Diniarchus, hands off her baby to the Ancilla to be disposed of. The baby winds up with the prostitute Phronesium, who wants the reward promised her if she bears a child and does not kill it (*si quod peperissem id <non> necarem ac tollerem*, 399). Selenium's story is told from different perspectives: by the *lena* who picked her up and gave her to her foster mother, both of them then prostitutes (*Cist.* 133–48); by the prologue speaker Auxilium (156–87); and by the slave who exposed the baby (616–21). Tyndarus, kidnapped as a child from Aetolia and sold in Elis, as a young man is captured in war with his young owner by the Aetolians and purchased from the spoils by his own father, while his brother is captured at the same time by the Eleans and sold to an associate of the man who had owned Tyndarus (*Capt.* 7–10, 17–34). "Lucris" in *Persa* is supposedly kidnapped or captured from Arabia by the Persians, picked up by a dealer in Persia, and brought by him to Athens to be sold to a pimp (134–6, 506–27). Stalagmus, who as a *puer* belonged to Tyndarus' father Hegio (875–6, 966), came originally from Sicily (888), though no other details are given. The kin of these lost children sometimes travel even more circuitous routes in search of them (below). The only lost child who occasions no wanderings is Casina, who never appears onstage: exposed by a woman and seen by a neighboring slave (like Selenium in reverse), she is taken in by the slave's *era*, who treats her "as if she were her own daughter, not much differently" (*quasi si esset ex se nata, non multo secus*, *Cas.* 46), until, sixteen years later, it is time for her to be married off to one of the household slaves (37–59, 79–82); she is, after all, a fellow slave-woman (*conservam*, 108), actually quite different from a daughter. Whichever slave she is given to, everyone in the play knows she is meant for the sexual use of one of her male owners. After the play's action ends, she will be found to be the neighbor's child and will be married off to the son of the *era* instead, thus giving him the sexual access to her he had been after all along (81–2, 1013–14). Casina is widely believed to be the daughter of the *era*'s friend who unknowingly helps in the scheme; like Hegio, like the mother in *Cistellaria*, she does not know her own child.[10]

Just as Palaestra and her fellow prostitute Ampelisca are being conveyed from Cyrene to Sicily in search of a better market, and "Lucris" is (fictively) brought from Persia to Athens for resale as exotic goods, so the sex trade in itself routinely involves involuntary displacement. The slave prostitute Phoenicium puts it most clearly when, in her letter to her lover, she warns him that the pimp "has sold me abroad" (*peregre ... vendidit*, *Ps.* 51–2), listing the price and the buyer, a mercenary soldier. Phoenicium does not want to go. The same is true, as Anne Feltovich points out, for Bacchis' sister in *Bacchides*; she is free, but under contract to a soldier who has brought her from Samos to Athens, where Bacchis lives, and what motivates the action is her eagerness to get out of the contract so that she will not be moved again, this time to Elatia on Zacynthos (see table 7.1). Adelphasium and her sister in *Poenulus*, on the other hand, are primping to get ready for the *mercatus meretricius* at the temple of Venus, to show themselves off for the *mercatores*, prompting a joke about Adelphasium as *mers*, "goods" (339–42); even if this is all figurative, it accurately suggests the relation between the business model and the shipping trade: the traffic in women. Pasicompsa in *Mercator* (a telling title) is taken home by a trader like a souvenir, and changes hands repeatedly in the course of the play's action; the mute and unnamed music girls in *Stichus* are simply cargo.[11]

The stolen boys in the tales of kidnapping are never sold to pimps (although Tyndarus is enslaved), and the girls are never adopted the way Menaechmus I and Agorastocles are; Selenium is adopted, but into a life of prostitution, although, like all the other girls who will find a husband at the end of a play, she is said to have been raised "well and chastely" (*Cist.* 133–44; *bene ac pudice*, 173). The illegitimate son of Diniarchus is used by Phronesium as her own pretended child, in order to get money out of the soldier by telling him he is the father (*Truc.* 18–19, 198–201, 389–411, 789–809, and Phronesium's cynical song at 448–81); when Diniarchus is forced to marry the child's mother, he tries to ingratiate himself with Phronesium by telling her she can keep the baby for a while, to serve her own ends (872–80). Selenium's adoptive mother is said to have used a plot

---

[10] For Casina's parentage, see chapter 5; on the titillation created by the prologue's reveal of her status, see Marshall 2015: 129 (arguing, however, that the play legitimizes the owner's desire for her).

[11] On the issue of a prostitute's control over her own movements in *Bacchides*, see Feltovich 2015: 134–8, and Marshall 2015: 126–7 on geographic dislocation in both the *palliata* and Menander. James 2010 charts Pasicompsa's exchanges in *Mercator*.

like Phronesium's in order to produce a baby (*Cist.* 133–44), as if she had gotten the idea by going to see *Truculentus*.

Trafficking can expedite the plot, and even minor characters, even names, have back stories. Palaestrio in *Miles*, when his owner's *amica* is carried off from Athens to Ephesus while the owner is in Naupactus, leaves Athens to bring him the news, and on his way is captured by pirates and given as a gift to the soldier who has the *amica*, thus reaching Ephesus himself (*Mil.* 111–20). Harpax in *Pseudolus* proudly tells the pimp that he was not purchased by the soldier, but captured by him in battle, "for I was the top general at home, in my fatherland" (*nam ego eram domi imperator summus in patria mea*, 1170–1); Ballio sneers that this *patria* was the prison (*carcerem*, 1172). The soldier, a Macedonian (*Ps.* 51, 1152), has sent Harpax to Athens from Sicyon to bring back his new purchase, the prostitute Phoenicium (1173). As seen in chapter 2, the soldier in *Truculentus*, arriving in Athens from the East, presents Phronesium with exotic gifts, loot from his campaigns, including two Syrian women to be her *ancillae* (531–2). The presence of ethnic slave names in the plays – most stereotypically *Syra* and *Syrus* – addresses the community's consciousness of the long history of slave-taking in Asia, especially after Alexander, and its long enactment on the comic stage: like "Sambo" on the American stage in the nineteenth century.[12] When Sosia calls himself "son of Davus" (*Am.* 365, 614), he is milking this consciousness for a joke.[13] *Asinaria* has no trafficking, but one of the central slaves is named Libanus, "Frankincense" – exotic cargo; *Bacchides* has no trafficking, but the slave Lydus is marked "Made in Lydia." Hanno in *Poenulus*, searching for his daughters, travels the world, and in each city he rents each prostitute for a night, so he can ask each one (*Poen.* 109–10)

> und' sit, quoiatis, captane an surrupta sit,
> quo genere gnata, qui parentes fuerint.   110

> Where she comes from, from what country, was she captured
>   in war or kidnapped,
> born of what family, who her parents were.   110

---

[12] On Syrian slaves onstage, see Starks 2010; on the geography of the Athenian slave trade, Lewis 2011, and *IG* 1³ 421, l. 33–49, for sixteen slaves listed by ethnic identity in one Athenian household in 414 BCE, including two slaves identified as *Suros*, three as *Thraitta*, a Carian *pais*, and a Carian *paidion*. For slave names in Plautus' plays, see chapter 2, tables 2.1 and 2.2. For "Sambo" on the American stage, see Nathans 2009.

[13] On *Daos* as a Greek slave name, see Tordoff 2013: 25–7 (common onstage, rare in the epigraphic record). It belongs to the class of ethnonyms associated with comic slaves; see chapter 2 above. Knox in Headlam 2001[1922]: 259 comments, *ad* Herodas *Mim.* 5.67–8, another metatheatrical joke: "Phrygian apparently."

Behind every prostitute, an untold story; every one somebody's lost child.[14]

The transformation of war captives into slaves is described in the plays in some detail (see chapter 5 on the sale scene in *Persa*). When Epidicus tells his owner that the troops are back from Thebes and describes the procession of soldiers and their loot (*Epid.* 210–12), he says that "there was a mob along the streets, / everybody went to see their sons" (*fit concursus per vias, / filios suos quisque visunt*). His owner Periphanes – father, as it turns out, of a captive like those displayed in the parade – sends up a cheer: "By God, well done!" (*hercle rem gestam bene!*, 212). Thus there is a certain ambiguity in *filios suos quisque visunt* – the soldiers, yes, but then the captives are also somebody's children. Otherwise the parade is remarkable for the number of prostitutes it draws out to greet the troops (213–18) – again, mingling with the crowd at a spectacle.

Telestis has not actually been captured directly by Periphanes' son; rather, although he is himself a returning soldier, he has bought her from the spoils (43–4).[15] This process appears in *Captivi* as well; Hegio, who is trying to find captives he can trade for his captured son, buys in bulk from the quaestors (*Capt.* 34, 508–9a). A normal purchase, but not a respectable trade: Ergasilus flatly calls this practice *inhonestum*, not proper to Hegio's nature (98–101), and dubs it "a trade belonging to the prison" (*quaestum carcerarium*, 129) – though he says he would let Hegio go into business as a *carnufex* if it would get Philopolemus back (132). For although in theory it is right for soldiers to take captives, who are then sold, in the world of the plays the soldiers who boast of their conquests are ridiculed,

---

[14] That this notion was in wide circulation in the Hellenistic Mediterranean is indicated (e.g.) by Seneca Rhetor, *Controv.* 10.4, about a Fagan-like man who picks up exposed children, cripples them to make them more pitiful, and lives on the proceeds of their begging; the speakers harp on the point that a parent might give alms (or not) to his or her own child. At times the culprit strongly resembles Ballio in the parade scene (10.4.7, 10, 24), but no explicit analogy is drawn, and Seneca emphasizes the popularity of the theme in contemporary Greek declamation (10.4.18–23). Here as always the kinship in plotline among declamation, New Comedy, and the novel is evident; Hanno's plotline animates novels and folk narratives around the Mediterranean, from *The History of Apollonius, King of Tyre* to the *Life of Mary the Harlot* to the story of Beruria, wife of Rabbi Meir. The story appears sentimental/melodramatic due to our consciousness of similar motifs in the Victorian period, from Rossetti's *Found* to the parodic "There Once Was a Poor Young Girl," but melodramatic reunions were formed by the historical circumstances of rural-to-urban migration, while the ancient versions were formed by human trafficking. On *Apollonius*, see Schmeling 1999; on *Mary the Harlot*, see Miller 2003; on Beruria, see Boyarin 1993: 190. See Nochlin 1988: 57–85 on *Found* and the motif of the rescue of the fallen woman in its social context. On the grim background to "Poor Young Girl," written by the blackface vaudeville comedian Charlie Case before 1916, see Cullen 2007: 203–4, Spaeth 1926: 242–3, Stewart 2005: 153; Richlin forthcoming a. I learned it at camp in the 1960s. Content is stable, context makes meaning.

[15] On the documentary evidence for soldiers owning slave-women under the empire, see Phang 2001, an exhaustive survey.

nor is it right to steal children; kidnappers never prosper. The prologue speaker in *Menaechmi* goes out of his way to tell us that the trader who kidnapped little Menaechmus came to a fittingly bad end (63–6). The middleman in *Curculio* is missing, believed dead (529–30); the man who bought Agorastocles is dead (*Poen.* 77 = *Men.* 62). The pimps who buy Planesium, Hanno's daughters, Palaestra, and even the counterfeit Lucris are prosecuted offstage and/or subjected to corporal punishment. When Messenio thinks his owner is being kidnapped in the streets of Epidamnus – "a man who arrived here a free man!" (*qui liber ad vos venerit!*, *Men.* 1006) – he and Menaechmus I lay into the slaves of the *senex* with much eye-gouging and punching (1006–18): *em tibi etiam!* The only kidnapper who is himself a slave, Stalagmus in *Captivi*, is re-enslaved and shackled (1025–8).

The culprits repeatedly avow the same callous attitude, an index of their badness. Like the bankers seen in chapter 3, they will do anything for money. So the pimp Cappadox, reflecting on Planesium's chain of purchase: "What does it matter to me? I've got the cash" (*quid id mea refert? ego argentum habeo, Cur.* 530). So Stalagmus, asked whether the boy he sold is still alive: "I took the cash, I didn't care about the rest" (*argentum accepi, nil curavi ceterum, Capt.* 989). So, more elaborately, the pimp Labrax, responding to Daemones' sad recollection of his stolen daughter (*Rud.* 745–7):

> argentum ego pro istisce ambabus quoiae erant domino dedi;   745
> quid mea refert Athenis natae haec an Thebis sient,
> dum mihi recte servitutem serviant?

> I paid cash for both of those girls to their legal owner, who
>   they belonged to;   745
> what does it matter to me whether they were born at Athens or Thebes,
> just as long as they slave their slavery right for me?

Trachalio, responding indignantly, calls him *feles virginalis* (748); so Saturio calls the pimp Dordalus *scelesta feles virginaria* (*Per.* 751): "criminal virgin-stealing polecat." It is not only *Captivi*, then, that problematizes enslavement, for these plotlines all ask how it can be legitimate for a free person to be enslaved.

To be born into slavery left no route to freedom other than manumission; Trachalio in *Rudens* several times insists that both the shipwrecked girls should by rights be free (649, 714, 736, 1104), but has to admit to the pimp that Ampelisca's right is relative at best: "This other one – what her fatherland might be I really don't know, / except I know that she's a better person than you are, you giant piece of filth" (*huic alterae quae patria sit profecto nescio, / nisi scio probiorem hanc esse quam te, inpuratissime*, 750–1). He does assume that she has a *patria* other than Cyrene, where the play is set. The pimp sneers in reply, "Are those girls yours?" (*tuae istae sunt?*) – emphasizing his ownership (chapter 6); Trachalio then challenges the pimp to compare backs and see who has scars, impugning the pimp's free status (752–8, cf. 737) and implying that he himself is worthy of freedom. Like Ampelisca, he might be said to look *liberalis*. In *Captivi*, goaded by Aristophontes' insistence that he had never been free, Tyndarus snaps back, "How do you know? Or maybe you were my mother's midwife?" (*qui tu scis? an tu fortasse fuisti meae matri obstetrix?*, 629) – a reminder that women know the secrets of birth. Neither of them knows who Tyndarus was before he came to Elis, in the place where he was born.

Even those whose parents are not coming for them, or who are not saving up for manumission, sometimes speak lines that show a sense of slavery as a temporary condition rather than an inborn quality. Pseudolus, pretending to be the trusted slave Syrus, says grandly when Harpax asks if he is slave or free, "For now, I'm still a slave" (*nunc quidem etiam servio*, *Ps.* 610). This is a metatheatrical gesture towards his role-playing (in this scene playing Syrus; as an actor playing a slave), but he also speaks as Pseudolus claiming freedom, and perhaps likewise as a slave actor: a slave playing a slave playing a slave. A typical joke in which the speaker tells a disguised truth to an uncomprehending interlocutor, and Pseudolus' dupe Harpax replies that Pseudolus does not "look worthy to be free" (*non videre dignus qui liber sies*, 611), but Harpax is a fool, and the audience knows better. *Captivi* is full of jokes like this in situations that enact the arbitrary and possibly transitory nature of slave status. The peculiar name "Epidicus" – "Under Litigation" – suggests, like the name "Stamp Paid" in Toni Morrison's *Beloved*, a (self-)consciousness of slaves as traded goods.[16]

Road Maps

The travels laid out in the back stories to the plays belong to a century which saw an explosion in geographical knowledge, alongside the explosion in the slave market – indeed, one went along with the other. The wars of Alexander and of his successors inspired journeys of exploration and funded scholarship like that of the geographer Eratosthenes in Alexandria, born a generation before Plautus and active as a geographer from the 240s

---

[16] On "Epidicus," see Schmidt 1902a: 187–8, with reference to the joke on the name at *Epid.* 25–6 (on which see further Lefèvre 2001: 117–19).

to around 200.[17] It is a good question whether those who were trafficked understood where they were going or what route they had taken, especially across language barriers, especially if they were loaded onto a wagon or ship, as we see at times explicitly in the plays (*St.* 380–1, possibly *Rud.* 930–3), and implicitly in many of the stories seen above. Based on papyri dating to the Principate, Keith Bradley outlines the process of "deracination," demonstrating that sales often moved slaves over long distances, and more specifically that the well-attested sales of individual children would have produced persons with no memory of *patria*, "travelling into the unknown."[18] How audience members envisioned the travels in the plays would have varied according to their level of education and experience, yet the plays arguably constitute a memory map in themselves, as the plotline runs from point to point, and the characters retrace the route taken. Certainly this kind of point-to-point thinking was commonplace in the 200s, when a writer now known as Heraclides Creticus or ps.-Dicaearchus conveyed his advice on how to get around in central Greece. His itinerary goes from town to town, giving distances, condition of the roads, local sights and attractions, advice on customs collectors and the danger of robbers, and estimates of travel time, for example: "From there [Oropus] to Tanagra is 130 stades. The road [goes] through country planted with olive trees and thickly wooded; completely free from the fear of thieves" (1.8).[19] His concern for safety reminds us that travelers and traders were among those most vulnerable to capture.

The acting troupes themselves were experienced travelers, and the landscape of war can be traced through their jokes. Turning a Greek oath into an Italian road trip (*Capt.* 880–3), the parasite Ergasilus swears "By Apollo, by the Maiden" (μὰ τὸν Ἀπόλλω, ναὶ τὰν Κόραν) – and then, punning on *Kora* (Persephone) and *Cora* (the town in Latium), "by Praeneste, by Signia, by Frusino, by Aletrium" (ναὶ τὰν Πραινέστην, ναὶ τὰν Σιγνέαν, ναὶ τὰν Φρουσινῶνα, ναὶ τὸν Ἀλάτριον, *Capt.* 880–3).[20] A map of the via Latina (map 1) shows how this joke depends on familiarity with the valley of the Trerus River (now the Sacco), "the main corridor connecting Latium with Campania" (Wallace-Hadrill 2008: 116); after Cora, over the hills to the west, the towns on the list look across the valley at each other, with

---

[17] For background on Eratosthenes' life, study, and travels, see Roller 2010: 7–15.

[18] Bradley 1984: 52–62, 116, and 1994: 46; cf. Joshel 2010: 93–4.

[19] For English translation and notes, see Austin 1981: 151–4; for the text, German trans., and commentary, see Pfister 1951 (for 1.8, see 76–7, 135, with useful parallels on the "fear of thieves").

[20] This passage has attracted attention mainly due to its dependence on Greek/Latin code-switching (Adams 2003: 21; Shipp 1953: 105–6). See also Dench 1995: 75, with remarks below.

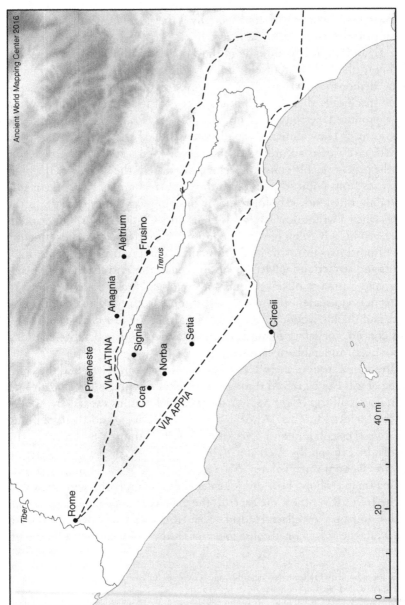

Map 1 The via Latina and the valley of the Trerus River. Map courtesy of the Ancient World Mapping Center, UNC-Chapel Hill.

Rome's powerful ally Praeneste at the head.[21] As it continued southward on the way to Capua, the road passed through Cales. The audience needed to know the road to get the joke, and the troupe knew it as well, because they put the joke into the play – a strong suggestion of life on tour.[22] If so, actors in the time of Naevius, Plautus, and the young Ennius would have been dodging both Carthaginian and Roman troops: Fabius came through Praeneste and down the via Latina in 217 (Livy 22.12.2), and Hannibal came up it in 211 (26.8.10), including Frusino and Anagnia in his trail of destruction (26.9.11), just as Pyrrhus had come up it in 280, getting as far as Anagnia.[23] Both towns reported frightening prodigies from 207 through 202 (27.37.5–6, 30.2.11–12, 30.38.9); the surges of panic described at length for Rome surely also affected the ruins of Latium. Along the via Appia, in the 190s, actors would have found rebels and more soldiers, for the slave uprisings of 198 started at Setia with Carthaginian captives bought from the *praeda* and spread to Norba, even as far as Circeii and Praeneste (32.26.4–18). The rising at Setia, according to Livy, started under cover of the *ludi* going on there (32.26.7). Through this landscape traveled a *grex*, a joke, an audience.

The meaning of roads to both actors and audience cannot be taken for granted.[24] The road network expanded from the late 300s through the 200s BCE as Roman armies moved against towns and peoples in central and northern Italy; even the via Latina belongs to the period in the 330s–320s when colonies were established to ring in the Samnites (Patterson 2006: 608), while the via Appia marks the same process in 312 (Cornell 1995: 354). The roads took the armies where they needed to go, and traders followed behind them, picking up the slaves the armies made (Thompson 2003: 79); the *palliata* spread along with both (see chapter 1). The roads

---

[21] For the status history of the towns on Ergasilus' list, see Salmon 1982: 51–5, 60, 66; Cornell 1995: 300, 357. On the route of the via Latina, see Quilici 1990: 52–6.

[22] On plays as group projects and the problem of who the adapter actually is, see Hutcheon 2006: 79–111. On Plautus' plays as at least partly improvised by the troupe, see Marshall 2006: 273–9, and Richlin 2017b; this joke bears all the earmarks, and would have been easily adaptable to runs in different towns. On touring, see Rawson 1985: 109–10; Taylor 1937: 303–4; Goldberg 2005: 65; Richlin 2014b: 215. Lucilius 1034M does not appear to concern "taking [a] Roman show on the Italian road," as suggested by Habinek 1998: 43, welcome as that would be. See Marx *ad loc.* (1904–1905.2: 331).

[23] Anagnia: Appian *Samn.* 10.3 (*Roman History* 3.10.3), as most conveniently presented in Horace White's 1912 Loeb (reprinted through 1982; the passage is 3.10.10 in the 1962 Teubner, ed. Viereck and Roos). The detail is both late and fragmentary, this part of Appian being preserved only in a Byzantine compilation c. 950, but in any case there is no doubt that Pyrrhus reached central Italy.

[24] For the account of Roman colonization that follows, see Cornell 1995, Hoyos 1976, Dyson 1985, Rosenstein 2012, Salmon 1982; Eckstein 2006a, esp. 133ff., emphasizes that the Celtic tribes constituted a serious threat to Rome. For a model of connectivity around 200 BCE, see Scheidel and Meeks 2012.

bear the names of the *summi viri* who sponsored them, but they were originally built under military supervision by work gangs, either local forced labor or slave labor – sometimes the same thing, for landowners were obliged to take responsibility for maintenance of sections of highway adjacent to their land.[25] Cato lists mending the *via publica* as one of the tasks slaves can be given to occupy them on holidays (*feriae*; *De agr.* 2.4). The massive roads were so well engineered that some of them still exist, incised like the Interstate across the countryside – these roads, in the north, were built over droveways and trails made by the local inhabitants, and brought in the Roman colonists who displaced them; down those roads, in turn, went the former inhabitants, as slaves or just as displaced persons. In 234 BCE, if a young man were to set out for the south from shattered Sarsina, the via Flaminia from Rome to Ariminum would not yet have been built, but it went through in 220, when C. Flaminius was censor; Ray Laurence argues that Flaminius "created the road as a single entity as a public thing to be owned by the Roman state" (2013: 302), and notes how roads like this redefined the local geography, bypassing the pre-existing towns, while the milestones were marked in Latin, "with the distance carefully measured in Roman miles and articulated in Latin numerals" (306).[26] This is the same Flaminius who, as tribune in 232, had sponsored a plan to put Roman settlers on public land in the north, and had then, as consul in 223, led one of the armies that dealt with the concomitant risings of Celtic tribes; a popular hero, until he lost another army at Lake Trasimene in 217. The north in the 200s, as Stephen Dyson describes it (1985), was a frontier, and the Celtic tribes, especially the Boii, were fighting hard to hold onto it. By the time Polybius bore witness in the mid-100s, there were only a few of them left (2.35.4), and he thinks they had believed that the Romans were

---

[25] See esp. Chevallier 1976: 65, 83, 84–5, and 218 n. 59, where he cryptically remarks, "According to records from early excavations, labourers were organised in chain-gangs." I must admit that, in my own experience of archaeological excavations in the early 1970s, the actual trenches were indeed dug by a hired laborer named Paddy, although he was not shackled, while the plans were laid out by the Professor of the Archaeology of the Roman Empire, Sheppard Frere. Thompson (2003) does not deal with road-building directly, and points out the dearth of evidence for the presence of slaves even in provincial quarries, where "the military clearly provided the skilled element," and others did the hard labor; he comments, "The distinction between [slaves] and forced labour gangs is perhaps academic" (137). For condemnation to road-building (*munitiones viarum*) alongside condemnation to the mines or beasts, see Suet. *Cal.* 27.3. On the general question of slaves present with the army as non-combatants, see esp. Welwei 1988: 56–80, with instances of teamsters assigned to build walls and dig trenches, also Kampen 2013, Schumacher 2001: 189–92; except for the Polybius passage discussed in chapter 2, the evidence is all much later, although plentiful in Caesar and Livy.

[26] Laurence separates the via Flaminia from the later roads built in provinces like Macedonia and Gaul as a sign and tool of Roman domination, but surely northern Italy in the 200s was a similar space.

bent on genocide (2.21.9): οὐχ ὑπέρ ἡγεμονίας ἔτι καὶ δυναστείας … ἀλλ' ὑπέρ ὁλοσχεροῦς ἐξαναστάσεως καὶ καταφθορᾶς – an expectation he also attributes to the Romans themselves (2.31.8). An overstatement of the case, as Walbank points out, for Celtic names persist in the area (1957: 211–12); perhaps, however, as Cherokee names persist in North Carolina.

The Boii rose in 238 and were defeated; joined in the Celtic invasion of 225 that got as far as Clusium; were defeated again by Flaminius in 223, who celebrated a triumph *de Galleis* – as later sources report, by popular demand, against the will of the senate. They rose again to join Hannibal as he came down from Spain; Roman troops fought a major battle with them in 216, the year of Cannae, and the Boii went on fighting, for a triumph over them is recorded on the *Fasti Triumphales* for 191 BCE (see Appendix 1). When Ergasilus jokes in *Captivi* about his body as a *provincia* (156), he is setting himself in an active military context, and the roll call of the "army of eating" he wishes for (153) is mustered by Hegio in a series of puns that combines food-words with the names of enemies to Rome and of the Roman colonies that confronted them: *Pistorensibus* (160), "miller people," probably a play on *Pistoriensibus*, "people of Pistoriae"; *Panicis*, "cheap grits people" and (an awful pun) "Carthaginians" (162); *Placentinis*, "cake people" and "people of Placentia" (162); *Turdetanis*, "thrush people" and "the Turdetani" (a Spanish tribe, 163); *Ficedulensibus*, "people of the fig-eaters" (another bird viewed as a delicacy), probably a play on *Ficulensibus* (people of Ficulea, in Latium, 163).[27] Pistoriae – first attested in Latin in Ergasilus' speech, and not again for a century – held a strategic location at the base of the Ligurian mountains, a battleground between Roman armies and the Ligures in the 230s and 190s. Placentia, almost due north of Pistoriae on the other side of the mountains, in the battleground along the Po, was founded as a Latin colony in 218 – an enormous colony, with 6,000 families. Latin colonies served a military purpose not only defensive but offensive, constituting for the local inhabitants, as Nathan Rosenstein remarks, "an armed camp in their midst" (2012: 93), and indeed the Boii attacked Placentia, with its neighbor colony Cremona, soon after the settlers arrived.

On another front, the Turdetani, a highly urbanized tribe, lived on the coast and in the hinterlands behind what is now Gibraltar, west of New Carthage, in an area that had long been under Phoenician and Punic

---

[27] Lindsay glosses *Panicis* as playing on "*panis*, 'a loaf' and *Punici*, 'Carthaginians'" (1921: 79); surely rather from *panicum*, "millet," an animal fodder that could be used in a pinch to make porridge (Dalby 1998: 71). Cf. Garnsey 1988: 52, where millet appears among "famine foods."

influence. Livy deals with them in a succinct addendum to his account of
Roman victories in 214: "and the Turdetani, who had brought war with
the Carthaginians down upon [the Saguntines], they reduced to subjection and sold at auction, and destroyed their city" (*et Turdetanos, qui
contraxerant eis cum Carthaginiensibus bellum, in potestatem redactos sub
corona vendiderunt urbemque eorum deleverunt*, 24.42.11). The Turdetani
still got involved in the uprising in Spain in 195, and it was Cato who, as
consul, headed the army that defeated them. Ficulea was a small town in
Latium, on the way to Tibur but not on the main road, and is evidently
dragged into this militarized zone to finish the joke about the Turdetani.
Captivi is very much a black comedy, and Ergasilus' *provincia* joke here is
a savage one, evoking a landscape on which Roman centuriation and the
great roads were being superimposed – as harsh a transformation as all the
others caused by war.[28] This run of shtick would have been useful onstage
at any point from 218 onward, and jokes about the Boii would have had
an even longer run – as, of course, would jokes about Carthaginians; and
Sicilians.[29]

The ethnic identity of Stalagmus, the slave who had kidnapped
Tyndarus, Hegio's son, as a child, comes out soon after the road-trip joke
discussed above, as Ergasilus earns a meal from Hegio by reporting to him
the good news that Stalagmus has been caught and is being brought back.
Ergasilus turns the standard inquiry about a slave's origin into a grim joke
that combines ethnicity with torture (887–9):

> ER. sed Stalagmus quoius erat tunc nationis, quom hinc abit?
> HE. Siculus. ER. et nunc Siculus non est, Boius est, boiam terit:
> liberorum quaerundorum caussa ei, credo, uxor datast.

---

[28] This reading of the militarization of the Italian landscape is now standard (Patterson 2006: 608–
9, "the establishment of colonies in the ravaged landscape," "a violent and disruptive intervention"; Rosenstein 2012: 90–2, "palpable signs of Rome's dominion"), succeeding a more
Roman-triumphalist, pro-colonialist narrative that, adopting Livy's perspective, had the Boii
"pour[ing] across the central passes," and spoke of "the menace of the Cisalpine Gauls" (Salmon
1982: 76, 77). But the current reading dates back at least to Chevallier (1976: 85). Dyson explicitly
compares the expansion of non-indigenous people into the American West: "The result would be
a dispersed settler frontier. Flaminius was using the frontier as an escape valve in the classic sense
defined by the American historian Frederick Jackson Turner. Like Turner, the Romans forgot that
there were natives on these borders with claims on the land and fears of the new settlers" (Dyson
1985: 28). Horden and Purcell's remark that the point of road-building in the Mediterranean is "the
effect that it achieves through proclaiming and encouraging interaction between microregions" is
unhelpfully nonspecific (2000: 127).

[29] These topographical references have long been noticed, and have sometimes been used in attempts
to pin the play to a specific date; see, for example, Wellesley 1955, with further details of military
history.

ER. But Stalagmus – of what ethnicity was he, when he went away
from here?
HE. Sicilian. ER. And now he's not a Sicilian, he's a Boian, he's
rubbing a *boia*.
She was given to him as a wife to bear him children, I think.

The *boia* was a kind of collar (< Grk. *boeia*, "oxhide"); it appears on
Libanus' list of tortures in *Asinaria* (549–50). In Ergasilus' joke, Stalagmus'
new identity derives from the collar he is "rubbing," or "wearing out," adding a sexual layer to the usual joke whereby slaves are said to "wear out"
shackles or whips or rods; the explanatory line in the joke (889) is there
to nail down the sexual meaning (although perhaps it punningly evokes
the punishment of a runaway who has been given this "wife" *liberorum
quaerundorum causa*, "on account of his lighting out for the free men").
The captured Stalagmus is simultaneously wearing out a collar and having
sex with a Boian woman, which makes him a member of the Boii; here the
word *Boia* approaches the word *scortum* in converting a woman into a hide
to be tanned, pounded, pummeled, and the joke redoes the work of conquest: the violent sexual appropriation of indigenous women. Meanwhile
Stalagmus, in the compression of the joke, is having sex with his collar,
another poke at male slaves' sexual frustration (see chapters 2, 4).[30] Hegio
ignores this joke, keeping up the straight-man role he plays throughout
this scene, but the audience is meant to laugh. Most of them. Many of the
Boii were enslaved after the battles they lost in the north, and they themselves were selling slaves on the market in 230 BCE (*aichmalôtous*, "war captives," by the time the story gets to Zonaras, 8.19); if some in the audience
were afraid of the Boii, were even former slaves of the Boii, others might
have once been Boii themselves – or Celtic neighbors of the Boii.[31] After
all, unlikely as it sounds, Jerome says that Caecilius Statius himself was
an Insubrian Gaul from Mediolanum (a Celtic town, "the central focus

[30] For a more specific idea of how Stalagmus could have sex with his *boia*, see the densely supported
arguments by Allen (1896: 44–5, 55–7), taking the *boia* to be equivalent to the Greek *kloios*: the head
is fastened into the fork in a heavy stick that hangs down in front of the prisoner (in which case, *boia*
must, like *nervos* in Allen's analysis of a more complex bond, refer to the thong that tightened the
bond around the slave's neck). Allen provides a horrific illustration of such bonds in use in contemporary Africa, taken from Livingstone's *Last Journals*, which shows what he has in mind. See further
comments in Thalmann 1996: 135–7, to which I am indebted for the reference to Allen; Thompson
1993 provides a comprehensive illustrated catalogue of extant neck-chains, manacles, and fetters,
with analysis of geographical distribution.
[31] This story about the Boii is repeated by Thompson 2003: 31, and the sale of slaves by the Gauls in
exchange for wine in the 100s BCE (Diod. Sic. 5.26.3) is discussed by Horden and Purcell 2000: 390;
the importation of wine is attested by archaeological evidence, the export of slaves has left no

of Roman campaigns to subdue the Insubres," Dyson 1985: 48–9), and Gellius says he was a freed slave (4.20.13).[32]

Certainly some in the audience would have come from Sicily, and Sicily is not a neutral point of origin for Stalagmus. Although the whole Menaechmus family comes from Syracuse in Sicily (*Siculus sum Syracusanus*, *Men.* 1069), elsewhere in the plays Sicily is the butt of jokes: the pimp's friend Charmides in *Rudens* is a criminal from Agrigentum (*Siculus senex / scelestus, Agrigentinus*, 49–50); Sicily, as seen above, is where pimps can do the best business; good jokes come from Athens (= Rome), inferior ones from Sicily (*Per.* 395); the girls and their nurse in *Poenulus* are stolen by a "Sicilian thug" (*praedone Siculo*, 897). The prologue speaker of *Menaechmi* says that his plot summary "Greekizates, but it doesn't Atticizate, it Sicilicizitates" (*hoc argumentum graecissat, tamen / non atticissat, verum sicilicissitat*, 11–12).[33] In the 200s, there would have been plenty of former Sicilians in the audiences of the *palliata*, slave, freed, and free, to hear jokes like these, somewhat as Ergasilus' jokes about the towns along the via Latina might have been played in those towns, or played before visitors from Praeneste, say, in Rome. Like all jokes based on identity, these jokes interpellated those spectators. Stalagmus meant one thing to former Sicilians, something else to others; the position of any Boian slave present – if so, probably female, probably doing menial labor – points up the problem.[34] Polybius imagines the anger of Sicilians in Rome forced to see the loot from Syracuse (9.10.7–10).[35] Ergasilus' flippant joke here is a mean one, especially in this play, where the first utterances of the *captivi* of the title are groans of pain (200),

---

physical trace. But by all accounts the Gallic tribes regularly fought amongst themselves, ever a productive source of slaves. See esp. Thompson 1993: 81–3 for reliefs illustrating reciprocal trade.

[32] For sources and discussion, see Robson 1938, who argues that it is impossible that Caecilius Statius was a Celt, that "Statius" was not a slave name, whatever Gellius thought, but that, on the basis of his name, he was a Samnite: not much of a step up, around 200. He also suggests that Caecilius might have been a Samnite relocated to the Po valley, at least a useful reminder of the demographic chaos of the period. For Statius as in fact a slave name, and its kinship with other Italic slave names, see Cheesman 2009: 516, 523.

[33] For exegesis of *sicilicissitat*, see Fontaine 2010: 8–11, arguing that this comic nonce formation puns on the Greek *sikilizein* and Latin *sicilicus*, a word for a diacritical mark indicating a double letter, attested as "ancient" by grammarians in the very late empire; the joke is, then, about twins, a theme in this prologue. See chapter 1 on Fontaine's method.

[34] On the particular vulnerability of women and girls to slave-taking in general, see Horden and Purcell 2000: 388–9, with further reference to the excellent overview of medieval slavery by Stuard 1995; see now esp. Gaca 2010–11. Slave names in the plays lead us to look eastward in imagining slave demography in the 200s, but, as Thompson remarks, the wars in Spain and Gaul produced "vast numbers of prisoners" (2003: 20).

[35] On this passage, see Champion 2004: 51 (on the "fear and loathing" instilled in Sicilians by the Roman gutting of Sicily); Richlin 2014b: 205; Richlin 2017a: 220–2 for more on Marcellus's *ovatio* and the spoils of Syracuse.

and where Ergasilus himself has defined his body as a conquered province. Tyndarus' own name perhaps evoked the Sicilian town of Tyndaris, site of a battle in the First Punic War – a battle won by Regulus (Plb. 1.25.1–4), who was a major exemplar of war's reverses.[36] When Tyndarus is first unbound, he tells the audience directly that "It's no inconvenience to have my neck lose its necklace now" (*hau molestumst iam, quod collus collari caret*, 357); soon he will be in chains again.

There is a story about L. Quinctius Flamininus that was often retold by writers after him; the events date to his consulship in Liguria in 192, the story emerges in the historical record in Livy's account of a speech Cato made as censor in 184 (Livy 39.42.8–12; 43.5). The outline of the story remains the same in its retellings: Flamininus had a prostitute with him on his campaign; the prostitute expressed a desire to see a man killed; Flamininus had a man brought into the dining room and killed him on the spot. In some versions, the prostitute is male, in others female; in some versions the man is a prisoner of war, in others a condemned criminal. The geography of Plautus is strongly evoked, however, by Livy's identification of the prisoner as a *Boius* and the prostitute as *Philippum Poenum, carum ac nobile scortum*: "Philip the Carthaginian, an expensive and celebrated whore."[37] This should remind us that among the slaves in Italy, going back to the First Punic War, would have been an admixture of Carthaginians; this Philip has a king name, a Greek slave name, and in the sneering identifier we may be hearing what Cato made of boys like him, the spoils of Carthage.[38] The Carthaginian slaves in the towns near Rome rose up in the early 190s, as seen above. The characters in *Poenulus* want to go home to Carthage; they joke about black faces, they joke in Punic.

---

[36] Schmidt (1902a: 211) notes a few Sicilian examples of related personal names, none elsewhere used for slaves. Thanks to Diana Librandi for Sicilian geography.

[37] For other versions, see Cicero *Sen.* 42, Val. Max. 2.9.3, and esp. Sen. *Controv.* 9.2, where the prostitute is a *meretrix*, the slain man is a condemned criminal, and the speakers wallow in the details of debauchery and beheading. Livy's account of the speech appears in Malcovati (Cato 87); although he does not quote from Cato on the ethnic identifiers, Livy emphasizes that he himself has seen the speech, as the historian Valerius Antias, who makes the prostitute female, has not. The account is taken (in passing) as a true account of what Cato charged by Rosenstein 2012: 253, although he replaces the specific ethnic identifiers with generics: "a Gallic chief," "a young male prostitute." The story is a notorious can of worms; for discussion of the variants and the sexual aspects, see Williams 2010: 46–9, 328–9; on the historical/fictional aspects, Damon 2007: 444. It seems at least probable that the ethnic adjectives and epithets come from Cato's speech.

[38] See Harris 1979: 63 on the scope of plunder and slave-taking in the First Punic War, and Welwei 2000: 65–81 for a thorough overview of the sources; some instances of the taking of African slaves in Thompson 2003: 21–2, and see Appendix 1.

Wolfgang de Melo, in the most thorough and conservative analysis of the long stretches of Punic jokes at the end of *Poenulus*, concludes that not only were the speeches originally in genuine Punic, but they interact with the interlocutors' lines in Latin. The "Aetolian" characters onstage (speaking Latin) are not supposed to understand what is being said – that's the joke; but the Carthaginian Hanno understands what *they* say, and reacts to it. De Melo believes that people in the audience would not have understood the Punic, either, "apart perhaps from some sailors and merchants, who may have had a basic command of the language" (2012: 173). The actors must have understood it, though, in order to make (up) the jokes, and there was in fact another constituency in Italy that had a fluent command of the language – native, or second-generation. If de Melo is right about how the jokes work, the actors must have expected some audience members to get it. Ethnic identity in Italy in this period cannot be understood as monolithic, as Emma Dench demonstrates at length (2005, esp. at 131); this is *a fortiori* more true for slaves and freed slaves and the poor. The rape of slaves made hybrid babies, who (if they stayed with their mothers) grew up bilingual, and slaves, freed slaves, and displaced people could no longer choose a spouse from home.

Hybrid identity among actors and audience would help to explain the blackface masks and ending of *Poenulus*, when all the main characters turn out to be Carthaginian and happily go home to Carthage. The exotic appearance of Hanno (*facies quidem edepol Punicast*, 977) and the dark skin of the *nutrix* Giddenis (*corpore aquilo*, 1112; *ore atque oculis pernigris*, 1113) are marked by Agorastocles and his slave Milphio; in the recognition scene, did Agorastocles change his mask? Did Hanno's daughters change theirs? Or was half the onstage cast *ore pernigro* all along?[39] You would expect it to have come up in the bathing scene, as the two young women are spied on by Agorastocles and Milphio. The soldier who wanted to buy Anterastilis threatens to turn her black by beating her (1289–91):

> iam pol ego illam pugnis totam faciam uti sit merulea,
> ita replebo atritate, atritior multo ut siet   1290
> quam Aegyptini[40] qui cortinam ludis per circum ferunt.

Now, by God, I'll turn her into a blackbird all over with my fists,

---

[39] See Marshall 2006: 130, 148–9 on African masks, although not on this problem in *Poenulus*; Richlin forthcoming a on the color of masks, skin color, and ethnicity.

[40] This word appears elsewhere in Latin only in Paulus Diaconus (26L), where it is simply glossed *Aethiopas*: impossible to know whether the original entry in Verrius Flaccus had been nothing but a gloss on this passage. Elsewhere, as seen in chapter 5, *Aegyptiae* are classed with Syrian women as

I'll fill her so with darkness that she'll be much darker   1290
than the Ethiopians who carry the bucket around at the Circus,
    during the games.

She is onstage as he rants, although he has not yet noticed her and Hanno, so the color-words here must be a sight gag. The soldier is not a sympathetic character; Sceparnio in *Rudens* admires the dark skin of Ampelisca (*corpus quoiusmodi, / ... subaquilum*, "what a body – kind of dusky," 421–2), along with other features, and calls her the "image of Venus" (*Veneris effigia*, 420), just as Milphio describes Giddenis as "attractive" (*specie venusta, Poen.* 1113). Ampelisca will be freed at the end of the play and marry a freed slave. After a century of war and trade between Rome and Carthage, were there dark faces in the audience? Did Philip the Carthaginian attend the show? Did he laugh when the prologue speaker told the *scorta exoleta* to get off the stage? As Hanno says himself in reaction to Agorastocles' story, to the audience, "Very many free boys / were lost from Carthage in that way" (*Poen.* 988–9; see chapter 6). Incidentally, the soldier's joke brings in another slave presence at the *ludi*, for it seems unlikely that carrying the bucket was an elite job.[41]

Curculio complains about a city crowded with Greeks wearing the *pallium*, loaded down with books and handout-baskets, drinking in the *thermopolium*, walking around drunk, and calls them runaway slaves and thieves; he threatens to knock a "polenta fart" out of any one of them he runs into, suggesting that, wherever they come from, they are now eating poor men's food like an Italian peasant (*Cur.* 288–95).[42] The point about these Greeks – *isti Graeci palliati* – is that they do not belong "here"; they are outsiders. Not coincidentally, as seen in chapter 6, they also look like the actors onstage, and Curculio, in his *pallium* and his parasite's mask,

---

ugly enough to be proper slaves for a *matrona*, who also needs an *ancilla* who can take a beating (*Mer.* 415, cf. 397), so possibly here the reference is to Egyptians, after all; in any case the soldier sees the *Aegyptini* as the color of a black eye.

[41] On Punic ethnicity in *Poenulus*, see Starks 2000, esp. at 177, who sees the line about the Aegyptini as "a topical joke about recognizable Ethiopian attendants at games since the Punic Wars," as well as an "allusion to the family from African Carthage across the stage."

[42] Gowers 1993: 53–7 is surely right that the eating of porridge is strongly associated with Italians as *barbari* in Plautus' plays. However, the distinction in the Pliny passage she cites (*HN* 18.19.83–4, between *puls* as Italian and *polenta* as Greek) is not operating as a distinction in this passage in *Curculio*; see above, chapter 2, on *puls* and Nicholas Purcell's observations (2003) on this passage in Pliny (*polenta* is a translation of *alphita*, "barley porridge"). Cato in *De agricultura* lists fine-ground *polenta* as an ingredient in a remedy for colic (156.5), and Libanus talks about the mill as the place "where the worthless persons who grind *polenta* weep" (*As.* 33; picked up by his interlocutor, without surprise, at 37). *Polenta* appears alongside bread, wine, and myrrh-wine in a fragment from the probably Plautine *Acharistio* (fr. 2). See also Dench 2005: 275 on the *Curculio* passage.

attacks his own onstage identity, embodying displacement – all the more effective if, as has been suggested, he runs in through the audience (see Moore 1998: 129). Perhaps a certain fear might have been instilled in outsiders, if the astonishing story is true, by the human sacrifices said to have been carried out in the Forum Boarium, not only in the terrible year 218, but in 228, during the First Illyrian War: two Gauls, two Greeks, in male/female couples, like a reverse Noah's ark, or the Rosenbergs.[43]

A famous postcolonial graffito in England reads, "We are here because you were there"; this sense of "here" as "not home" is present in the plays as produced for the *ludi*.[44] The settings of the plays have long fascinated readers of Roman comedy, and to an extent Adrian Gratwick's dictum that the plays take place in Plautinopolis is true (1982: 113). But they also take place "here," wherever "here" is; as will be seen below, "here" means the special world of the stage and the fantasy worlds beyond it, but in a fundamental sense "here" has a firmly deictic meaning: look around you, we are here. As with all self-conscious theater, "here" is where the performance is being staged today, right now (cf. chapter 1, and Moore 1998: 1–4, 50–66): "your great and pleasing precincts" (*vostris magnis atque amoenis moenibus*, *Truc.* 2). This you/us distinction, as seen in chapter 3, resonates with the marked avoidance in the plays of the words *Roma* and *Romani* and speaks for a troupe with the kind of hybrid makeup postulated in chapter 1. The probably Plautine *Fretum* included a flogging joke about the *ludi magni* at Arretium (fr. 75–6). Thus the plays as we have them are certainly Latin in a cultural sense, but might easily have been tailored for any town, as the troupe toured central Italy. As we have them, they make fun of Lanuvium and especially of Praeneste: "he was bragging so much, I'm sure he comes from Praeneste" (*Praenestinum opino esse, ita erat gloriosus*, *Bac.* fr. xi (viii) in de Melo 2011a); the farm slave Truculentus makes fun of the way people talk there (*Truc.* 691), as does the slave Stasimus in *Trinummus* (609).[45] When the plays were presented out of town, they presumably made fun of Rome. In any case, they make no overt political statements that could

---

43 For sources and discussion, see Várhelyi 2007, who not only believes these sacrifices took place but argues that they were "providing psychological closure to the once-soldiers back in Rome" – that is, addressing popular trauma. Surely also *creating* trauma among the many with hybrid identities in the city. Cf. Eckstein 1982, 2006a: 135–6, who also takes the sacrifices to be real, a sign of Romans' serious fear of the Celts.

44 See Cliff 1985a: 65. This slogan has served as a touchstone for a wide range of debates on colonialism and immigration since the 1980s; see most pertinently *Feminist Review* 100 (2012), a special issue of responses to Avtar Brah's 1999 article "The Scent of Memory."

45 For Lanuvium and Praeneste jokes in Naevius and Plautus, see Wright 1974: 54–5; also discussed in Dench 1995: 74–6, on which see further below.

be pinned down to any one event or person, although there are plenty of speeches that, like Mercurius' on *ambitio* (chapter 3), could be recycled in any year, and could apply to any Italian town in this period, like the "editorials" discussed in chapter 6. That such jokes were part of the entertainer's bag of tricks is strongly suggested by the repertoire of Stratonicus and other funnymen in the late 300s BCE.[46] The freed Advocati in *Poenulus* say piously, "Especially in a time of public peace, with the enemy killed, / it's unseemly to start a riot" (*praesertim in re populi placida atque interfectis hostibus / non decet tumultuari, Poen.* 524–5; cf. *Truc.* 75). They (emphatically, tongue in cheek) know their place; where is it?

The plays as we have them are placed in Rome, identified by a short list of landmarks. Although the word *Roma* does not appear in the corpus, a few locations in the city of Rome do, along with many Roman and Italian institutions and customs, turning the putative Greek locations into a running joke. This often happens in the context of a complaint about urban affairs at a local and humble level. As seen in chapter 2, Ergasilus in *Captivi* says a *parasitus* who cannot stand being punched and having jars broken on his head should go carry bags outside the Porta Trigemina (88–90). Complaining about his former patrons, he says they are all in cahoots, "like the oil-sellers in the Velabrum" (*quasi in Velabro olearii, Capt.* 489). The pimp Cappadox quips that if everybody who was a perjurer wanted to spend the night in the temple of Jupiter, there would not be enough room for them in the Capitolium (*Cur.* 268–9), and one of the old men in *Trinummus,* in an insult involving sacrilege, hooks it to the statue of Jupiter in the Capitolium (*Trin.* 83–5): insert [your local landmark] here.[47] Most famously, the Choragus in *Curculio* stands on the stage and points out where to go in the forum to find various kinds of people, many of them disreputable (461–85). Again, this is the kind of joke that could have played well in any town, with a change of street names; like *extra portam*, where the torturers are (chapter 2), often the word *forum* in a given line is not site-specific; the version we have of *Curculio* was written to be played

---

[46] On Stratonicus, see Gilula 2000; Richlin 2016, on Stratonicus and his peers, whose jokes sometimes caught up with them. The formulaic nature of such jokes is perhaps exemplified in ethnic threats by two *parasiti* running in: at *Cur.* 294–5, against the *Graeci palliati* (*eos ego si offendero, / ex unoquoque eorum crepitum exciam polentarium*), compared with *Capt.* 821–2 (*eum ego si in via Petronem publica conspexero, / et Petronem et dominum reddam mortalis miserrumos*). "Petro" is a Sabellian praenomen, here given to a bellwether as a pet name, like "Bubba"; so de Melo 2011a: 588–9, with which see Weiss 2002: 351–4.

[47] On the old man's speech, see Moore 1998: 82–3. Moreover, as Bispham notes (2000: 175), "*Capitolia* have rightly been identified as key markers of religious and cultural identity in Roman colonies": this was another portable local joke.

in the Forum Romanum. It is sometimes argued that each of these place-names is substituting for Attic place-names in a putative original; better to think of location in the *palliata* as a way for comedians to relate to a local audience.

Remarkably, the Choragus' speech preserves a variant line that includes the name of a person apparently real, a great rarity in the Plautine corpus; perhaps the presence of this line suggests that, for various performances, names could be plugged in. In the Forum, you can "look for rich men and spendthrift husbands by the basilica":

> *dites, damnosos maritos sub basilica quaerito* (472)

Or you can "look for rich men and spendthrift husbands in Leucadia Oppia's house":

> *dites, damnosos maritos apud Leucadiam Oppiam* (485)

If this line is genuine, it performs the welcome task of preserving for history the name of a freed slave-woman whose prices as an expensive prostitute were roasted onstage at the *ludi*.[48]

Similarly, the only instance of the adjective *Romani* in the plays comes with a decidedly low perspective; the soldier in *Poenulus* says that the Carthaginian Hanno is more full of garlic than "Roman rowers," *Romani remiges* (1314; see chapter 3). Actually, the soldier says Hanno is full of two kinds of garlic – regular and African – so perhaps this insult is also a side-swipe at the hybrid nature of the Roman fleet. Built up for the First Punic War in the 260s–240s, the fleet at first used citizens to row, but, in the dire circumstances of the Second Punic War, freedmen, slaves and war captives manned the oars; in any case, citizens who rowed were in the lowest census group.[49] Polybius has Scipio, after the sack of New Carthage in 210 BCE, offer freedom after the war to the enslaved prisoners who are being sent off

---

[48] On the Choragus' speech, see Moore 1991, 1998: 131–9, and Marshall 2006: 40–2. On the variant lines, see Moore 1991: 358, who approves of excising line 485; compare Marshall 2006: 266–72, on textual doublets in the Plautine corpus as evidence of improvisation. On the overtones of "Leucadia" as a slave name, see Manuwald 2014: 592 on the late *palliata* by that title, probably based on one by Menander and involving the story of Sappho and Phaon; Miller 2007: 399–400 on the elegiac beloved of Varro of Atax. If this freedwoman were connected with the C. Oppius who as tribune put forward the sumptuary law of 215 against women's possession of gold, that would amplify the joke, but it was an old *gens*, active throughout Plautus' lifetime (viz. the *tibicen* Marcipor Oppii). See Culham 1982: 793, however, on *Aul.* 477–84 and the Lex Oppia: "Plautus … mainly illustrates the resentment of wealth, displayed through conspicuous consumption."

[49] On the status of rowers, Polybius 6.19.3; Libourel 1973; Rosenstein 2004: 56, 85, 185–6, 2012: 88; Welwei 1988: 28–42. See Leigh 2010: 270–2 on the effects of the catastrophic losses of ships in the First Punic War on the kin of the oarsmen.

to row in the warships (10.17.11–16; cf. Livy 26.47.1–3). The Carthaginian colony there dates back only to 228. After the war, any of these Punic settlers from Spain who survived the navy would have been a long way from home, a home now in ruins. They were *Romani* in the same sense that the backdrop was Epidamnus.

Certainly the plays are not being staged in Greece; metatheatrical comments repeatedly insist that we are in *barbaria*, in a bravura performance of what Michelle Cliff called "claiming an identity they taught me to despise" (chapter 1). "Why do you swear by barbarian cities?" says Hegio to Ergasilus, on hearing his itinerary of places in Latium set in Greek (*quid tu per barbaricas urbis iuras?*, *Capt.* 884). *Barbaria* is *our* country, and the plays are *our* plays: the poet himself, as seen above, is *pultiphagonides*, and what he does with the Greek plays he uses is "turn them barbarian" (*Maccus vortit barbare*, *As.* 11; *Plautus vortit barbare*, *Trin.* 19); Naevius, if that is who is meant, is the sad "barbarian poet" in chains (*os columnatum poetae esse indaudivi barbaro*, *Mil.* 211). Phaedromus in *Curculio* cajoles the bolts of the brothel door as simultaneously slave door-guards and *ludii barbari*, "barbarian festival performers" (*Cur.* 150), marked as such because he wants them to jump – what distinguishes Italian dancing from Greek dancing (compare Ovid on the picnic for Anna Perenna, above).[50] At the same time, *barbaria* is (ironically) despised: drawing attention to the use of stage money – literally "funny money" (*comicum*, *Poen.* 597) – the Advocati comment to the audience, "When this gold is well soaked, oxen in *barbaria* get fat on it" (*macerato hoc pingues fiunt auro in barbaria boves*, 598; see chapter 8). "I've got no use for barbarian spinach," says the fussy Olympio (*nihil moror barbarico blito*, *Cas.* 748); "I've got no use for a barbarian guest for my house," says the rude Sceparnio to the wicked Sicilian (*barbarum hospitem mi in aedis nihil moror*, *Rud.* 583); "indeed, no grits-eating barbarian workman did this work," says the sly Tranio, selling unreal estate (*non enim haec pultiphagus opifex opera fecit barbarus*, *Mos.* 828). Lydus' idiotic young owner and former pupil tells him that he is "a barbarian" (*es barbarus*, *Bac.* 121) and "stupider than a barbarian [something]" (*stultior es barbaro poticio*, 123). "These words force me to learn barbarian ways," complains the starving Gelasimus, about to auction off all his worldly possessions (*haec verba subigunt med ut mores barbaros / discam*, *St.* 193–4, see chapter 3); "now I've made up my mind to go after all my rights under barbarian law," complains Ergasilus, who is likewise having a hard time scrounging a meal (*nunc barbarica lege certumst ius meum omne*

---

[50] So Moore 2012: 120, adducing *Aul.* 626–7 on the *artem ... ludicram*.

persequi, Capt. 492). They will have to go native. That the plays accurately represent both the existence and the tone of this Greek stereotype is suggested by the title of Aristotle's lost work *Nomima barbarika*, cited by Varro in his discussion of the *praefica*, the hired woman who led laments for the dead (*L.* 7.70) – and also by the protests of Cato, who in a letter to his son Marcus says that Greek doctors "habitually call us, too, 'barbarians,' and befoul us more impurely than they do others, by using the epithet *opicoi*" (*nos quoque dictitant barbaros et spurcius nos quam alios opicon appellatione foedant*, in Pliny *HN* 29.14).[51] It is the hybridity (*spurcius*) that disturbs Cato: being mixed up with Oscans, whom the Latin epithet *opici* branded as rustic boors speaking poor Latin.

The potential of *barbaria* that arises out of being simultaneously "here" and "there" is suggested by the fragment of *Faeneratrix* discussed in chapter 1: the speaker places his own defiant words as a quotation from what was said *in barbaria* by a freedman to his *patrona*; *in barbaria* is (later) glossed *in Italia* (fr. 71–3). What happens in *barbaria* stays in *barbaria*. The outspoken freedman was *there*, so he cannot be blamed, but then again the speaker is saying the same thing, and in the barbarian language. The whole project of remaking the *palliata* is defiantly claimed as *not Greek*, made by people Greek high culture despised, in a language Greek despises.[52] Like Curculio's rant, the allegiance to *barbaria* embraces a split identity. Yet the onstage stories push for homecoming.

In search of their enslaved relatives, free characters in the plays engage in Herculean travels. (Indeed, everyone onstage swears by Hercules, and by Castor and Pollux, the sailors' gods; Toxilus in *Persa*, in his opening speech, compares his sufferings with Hercules' labors, resituating the boar in Aetolia; *Amphitruo* sends up the birth of Hercules, and Mercurius, god of trade, twins the comic slave.[53]) Even the pretended slave trader, the title character in *Persa*, says he is also in town to look for his enslaved twin

---

[51] Cato's (reported) code-switch here notably declines Gr. *opikoi* to depend on *appellatione*, claiming an authority he pretends to despise (see Adams 2003: 576–7). His attitude is oddly replicated by scholars who, in dealing with the cultural transmission of Greek drama from Sicily and southern Italy northward, refer to the non-Greek-speaking inhabitants as "natives," and doubt that they could have understood any Greek; see Green 2012: 325–7, and, for a better model of cultural diffusion, Robinson 2004 (and further in Richlin 2017b). Cf. Connors 2004: 202–3 for discussion of Plautine mimicry in the context of colonialism, although, again, set closer to Pydna than to the 260s. My analysis of the meaning of "barbarian" here is at odds with Dench 1995: 74–6, who takes the plays to be expressions of Roman "superiority and centrality"; contrast chapter 3 above, on cheerleading. Dench discusses the Cato fragment at 1995: 44–5 and passim. On the comic meaning of *barbaria*, see Moore 1998: 53–5.

[52] Again, see Gowers 1993: 53–7 on "barbarian spinach" and Plautus' claims to identity.

[53] See Laurence 2013: 303 on Hercules as a god of travelers; Bispham 2000: 162, 164, 169, on Ostia, sets the Castores as gods of sailors in connection with the grain supply (as opposed to the equestrian

brother and set him free (695–6); he has come a long way, from Persia to Athens. Hanno's search for his daughters takes him "everywhere on land and sea" (*mari te<rraque> usquequaque, Poen.* 105). On this model, Charinus in *Mercator* puts on a fake-hallucinatory journey into exile in search of his lost sex slave (931–47) which takes him to Cyprus and Chalcis, where he inquires of a host (*hospes*) from Zacynthos, who sends him back to Athens. Charinus had originally acquired Pasicompsa from a host (*hospes*) on a trading trip to Rhodes (93–106); C. W. Marshall takes this man to be a pimp, and analyzes the travels of Charinus as instances of sex tourism (2013: 185–8; cf. James 2010). Which, as he comments, is what Hanno's journey amounts to as well.

Menaechmus II, his slave complains, has spent more than five years on a tour of the western Mediterranean in search of his twin (*Men.* 235–8):

> Histros, Hispanos, Massiliensis, Hilurios,   235
> mare superum omne Graeciamque exoticam
> orasque Italicas omnis, qua adgreditur mare,
> sumu' circumvecti. ...
>
> The Istrians, the Spaniards, the people of Marseilles, the Illyrians,   235
> the entire upper sea, and Greece abroad,
> the entire seacoast of Italy, wherever the sea touches it –
> that's what we've sailed around.

Like the lost twin, they started out in Syracuse; by a circuitous route, they have come to Epidamnus. It is Messenio's plea that they finally go home that triggers his owner's angry response and Messenio's aside about the mark of slavery (chapter 6). He portrays Epidamnus as a den of iniquity (258–64): travel can be dangerous. Travel by sea, of course, was notoriously dangerous, and the circuitous route Messenio complains of is the feat of a world traveler like the fifth-century Hanno – a *periplous*.[54] Unlike the writer of a *periplous*, however, Messenio bounces back and forth across the breadth of Italy, or makes giant loops around it, from Histria, at the northwest edge of Illyria, to Hispania, then back east along the coast to Massilia, then back to Illyria, then (vaguely) down the Adriatic and bouncing over to Magna Graecia, then all around Italy, to wind up back in Epidamnus at the southeast edge of Illyria – a notably Italocentric journey.

---

connections of Castor and Pollux at Rome) alongside Hercules as god of trade. On the Aetolian boar in *Poenulus*, see Henderson 1999: 34; Richlin 2005: 193.

[54] On classical and Hellenistic *periploi*, see Dilke 1985: 130–7; on the tendency of *periplous* writers to proceed counterclockwise along the coast in keeping with the prevailing currents, see Salway 2004: 52–5. On the dangers of sea travel, see esp. Gabrielsen 2003.

The list of stops certainly springs from the desire for wordplay (*Histros, Hispanos, Hilurios*, and the similarly sibilant *Massiliensis*), but the names are not randomly chosen; they take Messenio through yet more war zones, for the sea-raiders of Histria touched off the Second Illyrian War, the year before the Second Punic War, and inspired the joke in the *Poenulus* prologue where the speaker addresses the audience as their *imperator histricus*, simultaneously their "Histrian general" and their "actor general" (4, 44).[55] The list of stops also affords the actor playing Messenio a shot at extravagant zigzag or looping gestures ending with a complete run around in a circle. It seems unlikely that he just stood still. If he moved in accordance with the actual locations he mentions, he would have been playing off a picture he expected at least some people in his audience to have in their heads.[56] As will be seen in chapter 8, this kind of joke is not so unusual in Plautus' plays, although most commonly found in the fantastic journeys that take characters to Asia and beyond. Gripus, imagining himself as a free man, pictures a life as a wealthy trader when he will board ship and "sail the circuit of the towns" (*oppida circumvectabor, Rud.* 933). The verb *circumvehor* appears elsewhere in the Plautine corpus only once, as the *senex* in *Mostellaria* describes how he felt on arriving home and hearing the bad news about his son. In comparison with his actual voyage to Egypt (*in Aegyptiam ... vectus fui*, 994), he laments, "I have sailed the circuit / to lonely lands and the farthest shores" (*in terras solas orasque ultumas / sum circumvectus*, 995–6). He feels lost.

---

[55] On the Illyrian wars, see Harris 1979: 137, 195–7, 202; for their relation to *Poenulus*, Henderson 1999: 6–7, Richlin 2005: 188, 252. Livy, writing on the year 302/1 BCE, calls the Illyrians, Liburni, and Histrians "wild tribes, and for the most part notorious for piracy" (*gentes ferae et magna ex parte latrociniis maritimis infames*, 10.2.4, with Oakley's note ad loc., 2005: 58) – Messenio is not talking about the Black Sea Istria. See Gabrielsen 2003: 401–3 for the Illyrians and Aetolians among other states that held piracy as a legitimate means of acquiring property. He cites an instance of an exemption issued for the Dionysiac *tekhnitai* (*SIG* 3 399, 507) – another set of troupers passing through a war zone. For a passing Illyrian joke, see Plautus, *Trin.* 852 (*Hilurica facies videtur hominis*, "the guy looks like an Illyrian") – a reaction to the costume and mask of the Sycophanta, on whom see chapter 8. Two Illyrians appear on the list of the slaves of Kephisodoros sold at auction in 414 BCE (*IG* 1.3 421, 1.33–49), along with Thracian men and women, two Syrians, and a Lydian, without other nomenclature: a demonstration of how context changes meaning.

[56] For a similarly loopy journey, cf. Charinus's preliminary list of places where he might go into exile: *Megares, Eretriam, Corinthum, Chalcidem, Cretam, Cyprum, / Sicyonem, Cnidum, Zacynthum, Lesbiam, Boeotiam* (*Mer.* 646–7): bounding around within Greece, then back and forth across the sea and back on land. The list looks as if it might be partly alphabetical, as in a gazetteer (cf. Salway 2012: 200–2), but Plautus likes an alphabetical list, as in the men's names at *As.* 865–6 (see Fraenkel 2007: 302 n. 2 on the list in *Mercator*, pointing out that it is only alliterative in Latin; the same point holds for the list in *Asinaria*). See Schmidt 1902b: 362 on other name lists. These names do fit Charinus's identity as a trader.

If Messenio's itinerary works as I have suggested, it means that the journeys onstage in the *palliata* traced a line in the minds of the spectators, a meaningful trail across a mental map. That such maps existed for "even the highest levels of civil or military authority" in antiquity has been seriously doubted, much less for the mix of people I argue were watching the *palliata*; Romans are held to have thought in lines (itineraries), as in the road trip discussed above, and not in two dimensions (a map). Yet scholars have come to believe that there are clear signs of "Roman map-consciousness" – important, because the way home, for slaves onstage, often lay across the ocean, not only down the road.[57] The *lorarius* in *Captivi* assumes that Tyndarus and Philocrates will of course want to run away to their *patria* (208), never doubting that they know how to get there.[58] The display of maps in public places is sporadically attested in the urban Mediterranean from the mid-280s onward, and the plays themselves are a way of remembering points on the map and the distance between them.[59]

The Choragus – a far cry from his wealthy Athenian cousin – is the magic man responsible for costumes; he controls the location and the identity of characters. If he puts the stage in the Forum Romanum, that is where it is, while he is pointing.[60] He has made the stage come in for a landing next to the audience. Prologues can equally well take the audience far away just by saying the word, so that the stage becomes a form of instantaneous travel. The prologue speaker of *Menaechmi* jokes that

[57] See Talbert 2008, and, among the skeptics he cites, Whittaker 2004, who presents evidence on distorted comparisons of the shapes of places; decisively rebutted by Salway 2012.

[58] On this assumption, see chapter 8, and Bradley 1989: 36: "it is as though Plautus' audience would easily understand that a first-generation Roman slave would ordinarily want to return to his country of origin as a matter of choice"; also 1989: 38, doubting that most would have known how to pull it off, and pointing out that those born into slavery "had no country of origin at all to dominate their thoughts." Tyndarus and Philocrates would have needed to go by ship, and indeed Ergasilus spots Philocrates returning down at the harbor (873–4).

[59] On the display of maps in this period, see Dilke 1985: 30–1 (Athens, c. 286 BCE, a legacy of Theophrastus); 35 (Alexandria, Eratosthenes' map); 148 (Rome, 174 BCE, map of Sardinia); also 39 (Rome, map of Italy described by Varro in 37 BCE); and now Irby 2012: 81–2. The map of Italy Varro places in the Temple of Tellus (*R.* 1.2.1, an ekphrasis) has been taken to date from soon after the temple was built (vowed 268, Florus 1.14); see Holliday 2002: 105–6. Bibliography is listed and dismissed in Roth 2007b: 286–7, holding out for a strictly "odological" understanding of geographical relations even in Varro's day. There is indeed nothing to place the map there so early; the evidence on the temple is thinner even than Roth maintains (cf. esp. Frontinus 12.3). And why Italy? Livy *Per.* 15 states that the year 268 saw the defeat of the Picentes, Umbrians, and Sallentini, the founding of *coloniae* at Ariminum and Beneventum, and the start of silver coinage (see chapter 8); the triumph over Sarsina came two years later; Italy was still a land mass, not a trophy. Cf. Plutarch, *Life of Nicias* 12.1, where "the young men in their wrestling schools and the old men in their workshops and hangouts sat down together and traced out the shape (σχῆμα) of Sicily, and the nature of the sea around it, and the harbors and places where the island faces Africa" (discussed in Vlassopoulos 2007: 41).

[60] The *choragus* handles costumes also at *Per.* 159, *Trin.* 858. On the Athenian *khorêgia*, see Wilson 2000.

he is about to walk to Epidamnus, and asks the audience to pay him to take care of any business they have there (49–55): "Actually I'm going back where I came from and I'm standing still, in one place" (*verum illuc redeo unde abii atque uno asto in loco*, 56). The *Poenulus* prologue speaker makes the same joke (79–82): "I'm going back to Carthage again all over again" (*revortor rusus denuo Carthaginem*, 79). The *Truculentus* prologue speaker, on behalf of Plautus, asks for a little bit of land to "put Athens on without architects" (*Athenas quo sine architectis conferat*, 3), and declares that "I'm moving this stage here from Athens as is, / at least while we're acting this comedy" (*Athenis traveho, ita ut hoc est, proscaenium / tantisper dum transigimus hanc comoediam*, 10–11). The uncertainty about place created by the *scaenae frons*, the backdrop, matches the status uncertainty created by masks. Both are façades with holes in them – as the players metatheatrically remark, the stage can stand for anywhere, and that interchangeability of place is meaningful for an audience peppered with displaced persons. The final lines of the *Menaechmi* prologue make this connection clearly (72–6):

> haec urbs Epidamnus est dum haec agitur fabula:
> quando alia agetur aliud fiet oppidum;
> sicut familiae quoque solent mutarier:
> modo hic habitat leno, modo adulescens, modo senex,   75
> pauper, mendicus, rex, parasitus, hariolus,
> ****

> This city is Epidamnus while this play is being acted,
> when another will be acted, it will become another town;
> just as the *familiae*, too, are often changed:
> now a pimp lives here, now a young man, now an old man,   75
> a poor man, a beggar, a king, a *parasitus*, a soothsayer,
> [? list of slave and/or female characters][61]

Here the stage is the place where everything is always changing: the place, the plot, the people – the *familiae*, those who live behind the doors in the scenery. The *grex* is also a kind of *familia*, also always changing: the mask is the slave's mask, the hungry man's mask, the owner's mask, but who is behind it? Impossible to be sure; a play like *Captivi* or *Amphitruo* or *Poenulus* makes this even more confusing. In real life, the household made up of slave and free changed not only with birth and death but with purchase. "Where was your *patria*?" the pimp asks the girl he is buying;

---

[61] For discussion, see chapter 8 below, esp. on the king in *Men.* 76.

she answers, "What *patria* should I have, unless this one where I am now?" (*Per.* 636; see chapter 5). She could be anywhere; home is not here. "Here," on the stage, characters are transformed from slave to free, and poor men get the better of rich men. Change is possible. Things do not have to be the way they are. You can go home again.

Family Reunion and the Memory of Freedom

In *Captivi*, Aristophontes scoffs at Tyndarus' claims to have been free once: "I suppose you're saying you were born free?" (*tun te<te> gnatum memoras liberum?*, 577). Tyndarus' free birth is precisely what is at issue, though neither speaker knows it; the literal sense of *memoro* lurks behind the speaker's words here, as the free past hides in Tyndarus' memory. As the characters travel through the setting and the plot towards the happy ending, so memory ties them to what they need to know to attain that ending.

In what follows, I will be arguing for a less monolithic form of communal memory than the "cultural memory" advocated by Karl-Joachim Hölkeskamp (2006, 2010), a form much more oriented to the bottom strata of central Italian culture in the 200s BCE, like the oral forms seen in chapter 3. Hölkeskamp's perspective is emphatically that of Scott's "public transcript," especially in its focus on monuments – conspicuous by their absence from the *palliata*, although wished for as something fantastic, out of reach, as will be seen in chapter 8; just as Sosia in *Amphitruo* jokes that a funeral with *imagines* will never include his (chapter 2). If the monuments, and collocations of monuments like the Forum Romanum, signified as sites of memory for elite Romans, this was not the only way a place like the Forum made meaning; the Forum held many more kinds of places than those meaningful to the elite, as amply demonstrated in the speech of the Choragus in *Curculio*. For some people living in Rome, it might have been where they had been sold to their current owner.[62] The temporary stage of the *palliata* was a temporary site of memory, a place where audience and actors made the story together.[63]

---

[62] See Bodel 2005: 186, for Coarelli's argument that there was a "traditional slave market" on the Capitolium. The tour of the Forum in *Curculio* mentions only the sale of sex. Bradley 1984: 116 n. 19 cites the younger Seneca, *De constantia sapientis* 13.4, for dealers near the Temple of Castor: two hundred years later, but in the heart of the Forum. Cf. Joshel 2010: 96–7 for a map.

[63] I say "site of memory" here rather than *lieu de mémoire* so as not to misappropriate the sense intended for this term by Pierre Nora (1989), viz., a locus at which a past is reinvented for present uses; see Gowing 2005: 132–3 for an accurate use of the term to describe how aristocratic

When plays were performed in the Forum, as at least *Curculio* and possibly *Poenulus* and *Trinummus* were, they not only made their own meaning but splashed some paint on the *summi viri*, as is emphatically done by the speech of the Choragus. When plays were performed in front of a temple, as Sander Goldberg has shown they were, they changed the meaning of that ritual space.[64] As all kinds of drama did in this period; but the *palliata* had a particular story to tell, and to be remembered. The miser Euclio, pleading poverty to his affluent future son-in-law, who wants him to dress better, says that expensive display obscures the memory of poverty (*Aul.* 541–2):

> pro re nitorem et gloriam pro copia
> qui habent, meminerint sese unde oriundi sient.
>
> Those who have luster according to their property, and fame
> according to their purse, should remember themselves, where they
> spring from.

An ambiguous speech, surely a face-out line, from this otherwise unsympathetic speaker. Even the rich should remember where they came from and the people they left behind.[65] And/or: the poor have to live within their means.

The map of the Mediterranean in the 200s BCE is a map of broken families, as the newly enslaved became part of *familiae*; *familiae solent mutarier*, as the *Menaechmi* prologue says. Memory is necessary to mend the break; the plays themselves, as suggested above, are a form of communal remembering. This is sometimes made explicit, as when the *lena* in *Cistellaria*, having told the audience the story of the exposure and appropriation of Selenium, further confides that she and the girl's foster mother are the only ones who know – "except *you*, in fact; / ... I want you all to remember this history" (*praeter vos quidem. / ... meminisse ego hanc rem vos volo*, 146, 148). The repeated *vos* enlists the audience in an act of memory.

monuments of the Republic were used during the empire. I am talking about how different classes in the 200s BCE used public space to remember personal histories; see Richlin 2017a: 220–2, and Langlands forthcoming on "sites of exemplarity" and oral story-telling. For Hölkeskamp on the Roman Forum, see 2010: 53–75.

[64] For *Curculio* in the Forum, see Moore 1998: 137–8; for *Trinummus*, Moore 1998: 83; for *Poenulus*, Henderson 1999: 8–9 (in connection with the importation of Venus Erycina from Sicily in 217). On performance in front of the temple of the Magna Mater, see Goldberg 1998, and further in chapter 1 above.

[65] Lindsay and de Melo both read *meminerunt* here, a plain generalization, but *meminerint*, the reading of P, must be right.

Remember Your Orders

In fact the *lena* gives the audience a command, and in a familiar form. The vast majority of memory language in the plays is related to giving and taking orders: the subordinated person says *audio*, the one in command says *moneo* or *facito ut*, and then nails the command down with *ut memineris*; the subordinated person might then confirm with *memini*. A normal sequence is demonstrated as the neighbor *senex* in *Mercator* enters from his house, giving orders to an unnamed slave: "You, go to the *villa* ... / see to it that you put it directly into the hand of [the *vilicus*]. / ... See to it that you tell my wife ... / Go, and remember to say this" (*i tu hinc ad villam ... / facito coram ut tradas in manum. / ... uxori facito ut nunties ... / i, et hoc memento dicere*, 277–82). The slave replies, "Do you want anything more?"; the owner answers, "That's it" (*numquid amplius? # tantumst*, 282–3). In the plays, however, the power differentials involved in the order-giving situation – owner/slave, husband/wife, rich man/poor man, even older sister/younger sister – are constantly reversed. This whole area of onstage action constitutes a more subtle form of "playing the owner," as seen in chapter 4. So Libanus says to his owner as he exits, *meminero* (*As.* 117), but this is after a long back-and-forth that includes a speech in which Libanus says he will be wherever he wants to be, as the owner asks anxiously *audin? ... audin?* (109, 116). The slave Chrysalus says to his owner and dupe, "See to it that you remember to bring the ring" (*anulum ... / facito ut memineris ferre, Bac.* 327–8), and the dupe replies, "I'll remember, and you are right to remind me" (*meminero, et recte mones*, 330). The *senex* Lysidamus says to his neighbor, "See to it that they come" (*facito ut veniant, Cas.* 524), and the neighbor replies, against his better judgment, *meminero* (525). Lysidamus' disgusted wife says to him, "Just get back in the house; I'll remind you, if you have a hard time remembering" (*redi modo huc intro: monebo, si qui meministi minus*, 998). The slave Palaestrio in *Miles* gives a lot of orders: to his owner, PA. "Now you listen to me, Pleusicles." / PL. "I'm obeying you." PA. "See to this ... / that you remember"... / PA. "Enough! Get out of here." / PL. "I'll remember" (PA. *nunc tu ausculta mi, Pleusicles. /* PL. *tibi sum oboediens.* PA. *hoc facito, ... / memineris ... /* PA. *pax! abi. /* PL. *meminero*, 805–9); to the soldier, PA. "Act as if ... / Shout at me ..."/ PY. "I remember, and I'll obey your orders" (PA. *facito ... / inclamato ... /* PY. *memini et praeceptis parebo*, 1034–6); and again to his owner: PA. "Go away right now and put on your costume." PL. "Anything else?" PA. "Remember this" (PA. *abi cito atque orna te.* PL. *numquid aliud?* PA. *haec ut memineris*, 1195).

Analogous contexts of command are pointed up here and there in the plays. The *parasitus* in the opening scene of *Miles* fills his belly by "remembering" the soldier's deeds (16, 37, 42, 48); finally the soldier comments, "God, you have a terrific memory" (*edepol memoria's optima*), and the *parasitus* replies, "The mouthfuls remind me" (*offae monent*, 49). Hunger improves a poor man's memory. The prologue speaker in *Poenulus*, playing the *imperator histricus*, tells the audience that each of them must remember his commands: "By God, it's rightly done that each should remember for himself / these commands made here by authority of the actor general" (*haec imperata quae sunt pro imperio histrico, / bonum hercle factum pro se quisque ut meminerit*, 44–5). He speaks as a mock army general, commanding against the Histrians, but also as an actor who comes onstage saying "I feel like starting the rehearsal of the *Achilles of Aristarchus*" (*Achillem Aristarchi mihi commentari lubet*, 1). Soldiers must remember their officers' commands; like the *lena* in *Cistellaria*, the prologue speaker conscripts the audience.

But actors, too, must memorize their lines, and this is played out at length in the scene between Agorastocles and the Advocati in *Poenulus*, in which Agorastocles desires to rehearse them in the part they must play within the play, and they metatheatrically remind him that they all had to memorize their lines together. "You know the plot," says Agorastocles, about to tell them all over again (*scitis rem*, 547); the Advocati reply (550–4):

> omnia istaec scimus iam nos, si hi spectatores sciant;   550
> horunc hic nunc caussa haec agitur spectatorum fabula:
> hos te satius est docere, ut, quando agas, quod agas sciant.
> nos tu ne curassis: scimus rem omnem, quippe omnes simul
> didicimus tecum una, ut respondere possimus tibi.

> We know all that already, if these spectators know it;   550
> it's for the sake of these spectators now that this play is being acted:
> it's better for you to give *them* instructions, so that, when you're acting,
>   they'll know what you're acting.
> Don't you worry about us: we know the whole plot, since we all
> learned it at the same time as you, so we could respond to your lines.

The Advocati, as seen above, resent Agorastocles for not showing them enough respect; here they remind him that they are all, in fact, actors, and are all on the receiving end of instructions (simultaneously dragging the audience into the same position; compare the prologue speaker in *Captivi*: *iam hoc tenetis?*).[66]

---

[66] On this passage, see Marshall 2006: 29–30, with discussion of what such a rehearsal might have entailed; Moore 1998: 13–14 (arguing that the focus is on the audience).

Agorastocles agrees, but, in character, insists that they repeat it all, "so that I know that you know" (*ut sciam vos scire*, 555); they respond sarcastically, "Really? Is this a test? You think we don't remember … ?" (*itane? temptas an sciamus? non meminisse nos ratu's*, 557). When they come through, Agorastocles says, with relief, "You remember remembrously, you've saved me" (*meministis memoriter, servasti' me*, 562). But when he patronizes them ("you have the thing down," *tenetis rem*, 565), they respond with a small-penis joke ("Just barely, really, God, it's so teeny, just with the tips of our fingers," *vix quidem hercle, ita pauxilla est, digitulis primoribus*, 566).

Like the Advocati, subordinates on the receiving end of orders commonly turn around and say, "Enough, already!" – again, as in chapter 4, the kind of thing spectators might want to be able to say in real life. Showpieces like Sosia's entrance song in *Amphitruo* and particularly Sophoclidisca's entrance song in *Persa* constitute a sort of delayed response, but plenty of subordinates just snap back – repeatedly, like Sophoclidisca, when coming onstage from the house of the one giving orders. Curculio, entering from the young man's house, calls back into the house, "No need for you to remind me when I'm stuffed. I remember and I know" (*nil tu me saturum monueris. memini et scio, Cur.* 384). An unnamed boy in *Miles* enters from the house door, calling back into the house, "Don't you remind me, I remember my duty," and repeats his orders (*ne me moneatis, memini ego officium meum*, 1378). When Palaestrio says to the *meretrix* Philocomasium, "See to it that you remember my orders" (*praecepta facito ut memineris*), she retorts, "It's amazing – so many reminders" (*totiens monere mirumst, Mil.* 354).

The tone rises from expostulation to anger. Pestered for a loan by the slave Toxilus, the *parasitus* Saturio replies, "I remember and I know" (*memini et scio, Per.* 118, picking up on 108–10): he is about to say no. Sophoclidisca complains that her owner thinks she has no training or memory (*indoctae, inmemori, Per.* 168), and protests, "I remember and I know and I've learned it the hard way and I'm keeping it in mind" (*memini et scio et calleo et commemini, Per.* 176; see chapter 4); a few lines later, the boy Paegnium gets impatient with his owner Toxilus face to face. Toxilus nags at him: "Is this clear and plain enough to you? Do you remember this enough and have it down?" (*Satin haec tibi sunt plana et certa? satin haec meministi et tenes?*, 183). Paegnium snaps back, "Better than you, who instructed me"; "God, you can bet me that I don't remember it all and know it" (*melius quam tu qui docuisti*, 184; *da hercle pignus, ni omnia memini et scio*, 186). In their shoving match in *Asinaria*, when the Merchant finally says he is taking Leonida to court (*in ius voco te*); Leonida says he will not go; the Merchant, incredulous, says, "You won't go? *memento*," and Leonida says, *memini* – a move from command/obey to punch/counterpunch (*As.* 480). The slave Simia says to the slave Pseudolus, who is the one giving orders, "Can you shut up? A man who reminds a mindful man of what a mindful man remembers makes the mindful man unmindful. / I've got it down, everything's stored up in my heart, I've rehearsed the plans like a pro" (*potin ut taceas? memorem immemorem facit qui monet quod memor meminit. / teneo, omnia in pectore condita sunt, meditati sunt mihi doli docte, Ps.* 940–1). His speech here echoes Sophoclidisca's song (*potin ut taceas? potin ne moneas?, Per.* 175), along with her multiply emphatic claim to memory (*Per.* 176 – *Ps.* 941); it repeats *teneo* and *docte* as terms indicating an ability to take orders; it gives a nod to Simia's role as actor in Pseudolus' play-within-the-play; and it casts a new light on Sagaristio's opening song (*ne illum edepol multa in pectore suo conlocare oportet / quae ero placere censeat, Per.* 8–9). The slave Sceparnio in *Rudens*, who has been extremely rude to the young man in their opening scene together, facetiously takes the young man's exit line, *valete*, as a command, and replies, "If you didn't remind us, we could remember that ourselves" (*si non moneas, nosmet meminimus, Rud.* 159). A terse *memorem mones* works like "'Nuff said" from the one told to the one telling (Ergasilus to Hegio, *Capt.* 191; brother to brother, *St.* 578).

The boy's line about remembering duty (*officium*) ties his speech in with similar situations in which *officium* is invoked, sometimes in the form of maxims. These situations, like Sagaristio's opening song, share features with the "good slave" speeches discussed in chapter 6. Sosia says to his owner, in response to a command to bring baggage from the ship, "I am both mindful and diligent [in my efforts] to make what you order show up; / I didn't drink away your command along with the wine" (*et memor sum et diligens, ut quae imperes compareant; / non ego cum vino simitu ebibi imperium tuom, Am.* 630–1). This is just what Sophoclidisca says as she enters: "I don't drink up your directions along with [the wine]" (*mandata non consuevi simul bibere una, Per.* 170). These speeches respond to the general idea of knowing your place – being conscious of it – as imposed from above. The wife says to her husband, bossing him around, "By God, it's a wonder that you, in your old age, don't remember / your duty" (*mirum ecastor te senecta aetate officium tuom / non meminisse, Cas.* 259–60; cf. the fragment at *Cist.* 381, *meminere officium suom*). This principle has a particular application to rich and poor, as the bankrupt young man in *Trinummus* says: "This is honor for a person who's not shameless: to remember his duty" (*is est honos homini pudico, meminisse officium suum*, 697). He does not want to give away his sister without a dowry. So the old man grovels at the end of *Mercator* (see chapter 3): "Make this old man – I mean me – your *cliens*; you'll say he's mindful of your goodness" (*hunc senem para me clientem; memorem dices benefici*, 996).

Collectively, these exchanges display a lexicon of command and response in which slavery and acting are hard to tell apart, as in the lines that associate slavery itself with double speech (chapter 6).[67] Like the Advocati (above), actors in onstage plays underscore the slave-like aspects of being an actor; so the Virgo says to her father, as she accepts her role, *docte calleo* (*Per.* 380), *habeo in memoria* (381); and to Toxilus, directing her, *satis est dictum* (615), with subsequent double speech: "although I am a slave-woman, / I know my duty: that I should tell the truth about what I'm asked, as I received it" (*quamquam ego serva sum, / scio ego officium meum, ut quae rogiter vera, ut accepi, eloquar*, 615–16; see chapter 5). For "although" read "because." Not only *teneo* and *docte* but *calleo* recur, and the literal sense of *calleo*, "be toughened," underlies its sense "know by experience"; *docere* means both "rehearse a play" and "give an order." Thus, when Sophoclidisca says *docte calleo*, she is attesting to rehearsal and subordination, to experience and hard treatment. The pimp Dordalus uses *doctos* to mean "taught a lesson" (*Per.* 541). *Callemus probe*, say the Advocati, wrapping up their scene (*Poen.* 574); four lines later, as two slaves enter, one demands of the other, *iam tenes praecepta in corde?* and threatens, *vide sis calleas*: Milphio to the hapless Collybiscus, whom he has been training to act the part of a mercenary (578). Collybiscus replies, "I wouldn't let a boar's tough hide be as toughened [as I am]" (*callum aprugnum callere aeque non sinam*, 579) – Sophoclidisca's line. Eavesdropping on a stream of misogyny from the old woman Scapha, the young man says to the audience, "How well-rehearsedly she's learned it all the hard way!" (*ut perdocte cuncta callet, Mos.* 280) – just before he turns her attack on them. In a display of metatheatrical metatheatricality, the triumphant Phronesium defends her behavior (*Truc.* 931–2):

> venitne in mentem tibi quod verbum in cavea dixit histrio:
> omnes homines ad suom quaestum callent et fastidiunt.

> Doesn't it make you think of the line the actor said in the *cavea*:
> all persons according to their way of making a living get tough or get fussy.

As seen in chapter 4, the verb *fastidio* is associated onstage with arrogance; being fussy is a luxury; the *histrio* who talks about those who learn it the

---

[67] For the metatheatrical reverberations of the exchange between Pseudolus and Simia, see Wright 1975: 413–14.

hard way (*callent*) is (also) talking about himself and the demands of his way of making a living, as Phronesium is talking about herself and the demands of being a prostitute, and, with a face-out, maybe with a voice drop, talking to the audience about the hard life s/he shares with them. She likes this saying (*verbum*), and has said it once before, to defend her use of a borrowed baby (416, *ad suom quemque aequomst esse quaestum callidum*); the *lena* Cleareta says the same in *Asinaria* (186). A dismissive speaker in Cicero's *De natura deorum* draws a direct connection between this kind of knowledge and the banausic body: "I call people *callidi* whose mind has grown tough with use, just as hands do from work" (*appello ... callidos quorum, tamquam manus opere, sic animus usu concalluit, ND* 3.25). Chrysalus and Toxilus use *callidus* to describe their own deeds, and Mercurius uses it of himself imitating Sosia (*Am.* 268; *Bac.* 643; *Per.* 455). Perhaps the word *callidus*, then, in connection with slaves, appropriates *mastigias*, claiming a despised identity, and the *servus callidus* is the slave who has learned the hard way.

The implications for all on the bottom play out in a sequence at the start of *Stichus*. First the two sisters, alone together, discuss what they should do when it seems their husbands have abandoned them, and they end the scene with this exchange (39–47):

PAM. quia pol meo animo omnis sapientis	
suom officium aequom est colere et facere.	40
quam ob rem ego te hoc, soror, tam etsi es maior,	
moneo ut tuom memineris officium:	
etsi illi inprobi sint atque aliter	
nos faciant quam aequomst, tam pol,	
ne quid magi' sit, ***	45
*** omnibus obnixe opibus	45a
nostrum officium meminisse decet.	
PAN. placet: taceo. PAM. at memineris facito.	

Because, God, in my opinion, for all wise people,	
it's fair for them to do their duty, and practice it.	40
For this reason, sister, even though you're older,	
I remind you of this, that you should remember your duty:	
even if they are dishonest and are acting	
otherwise to us than is fair, still, God,	
so nothing more should ...	45
... as hard as we can, with all our resources,	45a
it becomes us to remember our duty.	
PAN. I agree: I'll shut up. PAM. But see to it that you remember.	

This last reminder – *at memineris facito* – recurs in command exchanges, as if an order could be burned into a person's memory by repetition.

The tone of the younger sister's command here is spelled out by the immediate entrance of the sisters' father from the house. We have seen him in chapter 2 as an example of a stingy owner who begrudges food to his slaves; here is his opening speech from the point of entry (58–61):

> Qui manet ut moneatur semper servos homo officium suom
> nec voluntate id facere meminit, servos is habitu hau probust.
> vos meministis quotcalendis petere demensum cibum: 60
> qui minu' meministis quod opus sit facto facere in aedibus?

> A slave person who always hangs around to be reminded of his duty
> and doesn't remember to do it of his own free will, that slave is no good to have around.
> You all remember on the first of the month to look for your
>   food rations: 60
> How come you can't remember to do what needs to be done in the house?

This speech relates directly to the "good slave" speeches seen in chapter 6, and makes it very clear what the problem is: the owner wants the order, even the expectation of the order, to become the slave's *voluntas*. To this owner, the slave's desire to eat – to stay alive – is the wrong kind of memory, superfluous; what really matters is *officium*. He says he will "remind" the slaves of their duty with "oxhide monuments" (*monumentis commonefaciam bubulis*, 63), making explicit the connection between *monumentum*, memory, and power (see chapter 8). The speech is shtick, with a close cousin in Herodas, *Mimiambi* (6.4–8); its Latin vocabulary, however, is deeply rooted in the large-scale response the *palliata* makes to the organization of power in contemporary Latium.[68]

For the format of these exhortations to remember reproduces the format of oaths, promises, and witnessing acted out onstage, where the same power imbalances sometimes come into play. So Pardalisca, administering the mock-oath to the new "bride" (an oath which treats the bride like a conquering army), concludes it with "Please, remember" (*opsecro, memento, Cas.* 824). So Simo swears an oath to Pseudolus: "I give you

---

[68] The speaker in Herodas is a married woman, who, like others in Herodas, is herself both a slut and harsh to slaves; her comic position thus both differs from and resembles that of the *senex* in *Stichus*. For comparison of the two passages, see Headlam 2001[1922]: 282; he adduces *Ps.* 1103–4 (the start of Harpax's good slave song) and *Rudens* 920–1 (from Gripus' self-exhortations). The close verbal resemblance between the Herodas passage and these lines in *Stichus* is of interest as evidence of the circulation of shtick in the 200s BCE; see Richlin 2017b: 181–2. On the joke, see above, chapter 2, on *pulmentum* and *polenta*.

Jupiter as witness / that you will live your life through without punishment" (*do Iovem testem tibi / te aetatem inpune habiturum, Ps.* 514–15),
and Pseudolus replies, "See to it that you remember" (*facito ut memineris,*
515): a reversal of power. So Simo stipulates the deal he has made with the
pimp: "Hey, so remember …" (*heus, memento ergo, Ps.* 1164). Agorastocles
in *Poenulus* nags Hanno to remember he has agreed to betroth his daughter to him: "See to it that you bear in mind that you / betrothed your
older daughter to me" (*facito in memoria habeas tuam maiorem filiam /
mihi te despondisse, Poen.* 1278–9). Hanno replies, "I remember" (*memini*),
and Agorastocles reminds him that he has also promised a dowry (*et dotis
quid promiseris,* 1279). The banker in *Curculio* asks the pimp for a guarantee: "Remember you promised, if anybody should come to make a formal
claim / to free her, that all the money would be returned to me" (*memento
promisisse te, si quisquam hanc liberali / caussa manu adsereret, mihi omne
argentum redditum eiri, Cur.* 490–1). The pimp replies impatiently, "I'll
remember, stay calm about all that" (*meminero, de istoc quietus esto,* 492).
The Advocati, asked to bear witness, reply, "We've seen," "We know," "We
know," "We remember" (*vidimus, scivimus, scivimus, meminimus, Poen.*
723–7), and, when the pimp is caught, and Agorastocles says, "Remember
this, Advocati" (*mementote illuc, Advocati*), they reply, *meminimus* (767).
Again Euclio in *Aulularia* sees this kind of promise and memory as jeop-
ardized by imbalances in power. First he makes a formal promise to betroth
his daughter to his rich neighbor: ME. *sponden ergo?* EU. *spondeo* (256).
Then he gets angry, and says, "See to it that you remember" (*facito ut memineris,* 257) that the daughter comes with no dowry. The neighbor replies,
memini (259). Euclio is not satisfied: "But I know how you guys always
tangle things up. / A deal is no deal, no deal is a deal, if that's what you
feel like doing" (*at scio quo vos soleatis pacto perplexarier. / pactum non pactum est, non pactum pactum est, quod vobis lubet,* 259–60). He sounds like
Paegnium on the untrustworthiness of owners (*scio fide hercle erili ut soleat
inpudicitia opprobrari, Per.* 193). As shouting ruins a reputation (chapter 3),
memory seals the deal, making the fabric of *fides.*

 A special case of such a formula is the promise to manumit. As seen
in chapter 4, Olympio gets into a tangle with his owner Lysidamus, as
Olympio plays the owner and Lysidamus alternately tries to regain command and abases himself. In the midst of this, Olympio cries out, "Am
I not free? / Remember, remember" (*non sum ego liber? / memento, memento,
Cas.* 736–7). Phaedromus promises Planesium he will get her freed in three
days (*quin ego te liberalem liberem, Cur.* 209), and she replies, "See to it that
you remember" (*facito ut memineris,* 210): another reversal. In the scene in

Rudens in which the old man Daemones and the slave Trachalio go back and forth, with first Trachalio responding to all Daemones' lines with *licet* ("okay," 1210–16), and then the reverse, the turning point comes when Trachalio says to Daemones, "But do you know what it is that I want from you? / That you remember what you promised, that I be free today" (*sed scin quid est quod te volo? / quod promisisti ut memineris, hodie ut liber sim,* 1216–17). And Daemones replies, *licet*, and continues to do so for the rest of the scene: a slow-motion reversal.

Another sort of memory in the plays records the mark the powerless hope to make upon those with power over them: a kind of vengeance. Running in, Ergasilus makes a weapon of his body and threatens any man who blocks his path: "I'll see to it that he remembers this day and place, and me, forever" (*faciam ut huius diei locique meique semper meminerit, Capt.* 800). Toxilus says to the pimp, with double meaning, "I'll see to it that you remember me, as long as you live / your life" (*faciam ut mei memineris, dum vitam / vivas, Per.* 494–5). Again with double meaning, Palaestrio says to the soldier, "Please could you remember …" (*quaeso memineris, Mil.* 1362): ostensibly a pathetic request not to forget a former slave, really a foretaste of what Palaestrio has done to him. At the high end of the scale, Tyndarus in *Captivi* lays claim to the inscription in memory that belongs to a noble warrior. Early in the play he states that he has sacrificed his own *caput* for that of his young owner (229–30) – as if he had a *caput* to sacrifice (see chapter 2); when his deceit is exposed, and his owner Hegio is sending him off to the quarries, he says that he has done a deed "that will be remembered of me when I'm dead" (*mi … mortuo memorabile,* 684), and adds, "who dies by *virtus* does not perish" (*qui per virtutem periit, at non interit,* 690), as if he could lay claim to the *honos fama virtusque gloria atque ingenium* of a warrior and noble Roman.[69] "Be famous in hell," says Hegio (*facito ergo ut Accherunti clueas gloria,* 689); "as long as you die, I don't care if they say you're alive" (*dum pereas, nihil interdico aiant vivere,* 694). But he cannot un-say what Tyndarus has said; and the audience knows, as he does not, that he has just wished for the death of his own long-lost son. It is their job to remember.

---

[69] For the virtue list, see *CIL* I².10, the tomb of P. Cornelius Scipio Africanus the *flamen dialis*, who lived c. 211–170 BCE; compare Ennius *Phoenix* 257–60 Kl, esp. *sed virum vera virtute vivere animatum addecet* and *ea libertas est, qui pectus purum et firmum gestitat* (257–60 R²₋₃ = *TrRF* 109), with Leigh 2004: 38–9. Compare the virtue list at *Capt.* 410, where Tyndarus speaks his own eulogy, again ascribing *virtus* to himself. On Tyndarus' appropriation of *caput* in this passage, see also Stewart 2012: 70.

Remember Where You Came from

The usual lexical range of *memini*, then, makes it all the more striking when memory is used, not to remember orders, but to remember the time before enslavement. Most slave characters (if we include the bit-part players, as we should) are not freed within the plays, and, of those that are, many are given no free past to remember. This is pointedly true for the sexually active prostitutes who are freed – Acropolistis and her friend in *Epidicus*, Acroteleutium in *Miles*, Philematium in *Mostellaria*, Lemniselenis in *Persa*, Phoenicium in *Pseudolus*; the discovery of a respectable childhood for them could not undo their history. Hence the insistence on chastity for those who are recovered by their kin, however unlikely it sounds (Tyndarus, *Capt.* 991–2; Casina, *Cas.* 81; Selenium, *Cist.* 173; Planesium, *Cur.* 51, 57, 518, 698; Telestis, *Epid.* 110; Adelphasium and Anterastilis, *Poen.* 98–100, 1096, 1139–40). It usually sounds extremely unlikely and, in *Curculio* and *Poenulus*, triggers jokes that would have been amplified by drag. Still, in the story-line, lost children and their kin sometimes remember a time when things were different.

Above all, memory permeates *Captivi*, where *memini* and its cognates flow through the text.[70] This rises to a torrent particularly in the scenes in which Tyndarus fears that Philocrates, once he is free, will leave him in Aetolia, will (in effect) forget him. In terms of humor, *Captivi* is a black comedy, like the plays of Martin McDonagh, precisely because it deals so closely with the dread of being lost and forgotten, lost for good – a fear that must have been close to home for the audience of the *palliata* in the 200s BCE. As seen in chapter 2, Sosia asks, *si forte oblitus fui* – has he lost his identity with his memory?

Issues of memory arise first in the first scene in which Tyndarus and Philocrates speak. They negotiate with the *lorarius* for some privacy, and, thanking him and the other slaves for their courtesy, they begin to confer about their plan. Philocrates speaks first, giving orders: "come over here," "there has to be," "there has to be," "this has to happen" (*secede*, 219; *opust ... est opus*, 225; *agendum est*, 228). Tyndarus speaks as a good slave: "I'll be however you want me to be" (*ero ut me voles esse*, 228). "I hope so," says Philocrates (true). Then Tyndarus bursts out with a statement of what he is doing for Philocrates (229–30):

---

[70] On *Captivi*, see Leigh 2004: 57–97; Moore 1998: 181–201; and, for a well-argued view opposed to the one here presented, Thalmann 1996, arguing that the play serves to reinforce Roman social hierarchy, with reference to ancient theories of natural slavery.

nam tu nunc vides, pro tuo caro capite
carum offerre <me> meum caput vilitati.

In fact you now see that, in place of your dear *caput*,
I'm offering my dear *caput* for sale, cheap.

He here lays claim to something equivalent to what Philocrates has, and
describes slavery as something beneath him, something low. *Scio*, "I know
it," says Philocrates (not true). Tyndarus returns (231–6),

... at scire memento, quando id quod voles habebis;
nam fere maxuma pars morem hunc homines habent: quod sibi volunt,
     dum id impetrant, boni sunt;
    sed id ubi iam penes sese habent,
   ex bonis pessumi et fraudulentissumi   235
fiunt. ...

... But remember to know it, when you get what you want;
sure, most people have this habit: what they want for themselves,
     while they're going after it, they're good;
    but when they have it safe in their grasp now,
   from good men, they turn very bad   235
and very deceitful. ...

In using the command *scire memento* to his owner, Tyndarus, like other
slaves seen above, is reversing the usual command stream, and vivifying
the formula: *really* know, *really* remember. Philocrates does not reply to
this directly, but tells Tyndarus how he wants him to act; his thoughts keep
returning to his father, for whom he makes Tyndarus an equivalent (*patri*,
237; *patrem*, 238; *patrem* ... *pater*, 239; *patris*, 245). "I'm listening to you,"
says Tyndarus, like a good slave (*audio*, 240). Philocrates voices his anxiety
that Tyndarus, once given the position of owner, will abuse that power
and mistreat him (240–8): "I remind you to remember," he begins (*te uti
memineris moneo*, 240); he ends with a plea "that you not honor me with
honor otherwise than when you were my slave, / and that you remember to
remember who you were and who you now are" (*ne me secus honore honestes
quam quom servibas mihi / atque ut qui fueris et qui nunc sis meminisse ut
memineris*, 247–8). "Who you were": my slave. "Who you now are": standing in for enslaved me, so that I can go home. Tyndarus answers, "I certainly know that I am now you and you are me" (*scio equidem me te esse
nunc et te esse me*, 249). "You are me": see how that feels; know what I do
for you. Philocrates ends their talk by saying there is hope: "watch out –
if you can / remember this remembrously" (*em istuc si potes / memoriter*

meminisse, 249–50). They deal with their situation by taking turns with the terms of command.

At this point each of them is afraid, but not of the same thing. Philocrates wants Tyndarus to remember how the plot is supposed to work, to remember to obey him; Tyndarus wants Philocrates to remember him and what he is doing. "Remember to know it," expressed so as to emphasize its literal meaning, emphasizes the relation between power, knowledge, and altruism that Tyndarus lays out. When it comes time for them to part, in the surge of emotions, the meaning of memory gets tangled up in their switched identities. Their owner Hegio is present, so their speech must be double. Tyndarus gives Philocrates the message he wants him to bear, full of concealed messages about himself as abandoned captive; Philocrates, imitating impatient slaves in other plays (above), tells him he needs no instructions: "no need to lecture me, I've memorized it in my memory, easy" (*istuc ne praecipias, facile memoria memini tamen*, 393). Tyndarus gives a further message; Philocrates tells him not to waste time: "what I've memorized, it's pure delay to be reminded about" (*quae memini, mora mera est monerier*, 396). Tyndarus adds one last reminder; Philocrates answers, "I'll remember" (*meminero*, 398). Asked for further messages, Tyndarus delivers what is in effect an encomium of himself and a plea for manumission as a reward (401–13); now Philocrates answers, "I did do just as you recall, and I'm glad you remember it" (*feci ego ita ut commemoras, et te meminisse id gratum est mihi*, 414). The confusion of identities here does not leave the audience certain about Philocrates' intentions, and this is not helped when he swears he will never be unfaithful – to Philocrates (426–8), just as he previously has proclaimed himself self-serving, having fun with double speech (385–7). Tyndarus makes a last impassioned speech (429–45) reminding Philocrates not to leave him in bondage: "don't you forget me" (*ne tu me ignores*, 434). Philocrates replies, "You've given enough orders" (*mandavisti satis*, 445). He is tired of playing the slave, and impatient with Tyndarus' use of command language to say something real. Philocrates and Hegio go off to get Philocrates on his way; as Tyndarus enters the house, Hegio calls inside and tells the slaves not to let him set foot outside without a guard (456–7).

As it turns out, Philocrates keeps faith with Tyndarus; he does not, however, get back to Aetolia until Tyndarus has been sent to the quarries. Tyndarus returns onstage for his final scene with a vivid comparison of the quarries to hell (998–1004; see chapter 8) and of his return to a birth (1008); the recognition is not consummated, however, until Tyndarus finally, like other found children, remembers his father's name (1022–4):

nunc demum in memoriam redeo, quom mecum recogito,
nunc edepol demum in memoriam regredior audisse me,
quasi per nebulam, Hegionem meum patrem vocarier.

Now at last I return to memory, when I think it over to myself,
now, by God, at last I come back to the memory, that I heard,
as if through a cloud, that my father was named Hegio.

Memory is a place he can now finally go back into, where he knew his
father's name. These are his last words in the play.

They are not, however, the last words spoken by any character; that
speech belongs to Stalagmus, who jokes about his *peculium* as the smith
is summoned to take the shackles off Tyndarus and put them on him
(1028). The punishment of Stalagmus clouds the close of *Captivi*, and,
considering the oddity of his story, this must be significant. He is the
only Plautine kidnapper with a motive: he steals and sells the son of his
own owner, who, as seen in chapter 2, had used Stalagmus for sex when
he was a *puer*. If he was sold out of Sicily to Hegio in Aetolia as a *puer*
under the slave name "Dangle," perhaps the sale of the son as "Paegnium"
constitutes a repayment in kind. Like Tyndarus, Stalagmus is a lost boy,
recognized twenty years later, and is returning, but not to his own home.
When Philocrates is questioning Stalagmus about the sale of the boy
Tyndarus to his father, he asks him, "Why don't I know you?" (*qur ego te
non novi?*) – that is, "Why haven't I recognized you?" Stalagmus replies,
"Because people have the habit of forgetting / and not knowing someone whose goodwill counts for nothing" (*quia mos est oblivisci hominibus
/ neque novisse quoiius nihili sit faciunda gratia*, 985–6). This is much
like what Tyndarus says to Philocrates early in the play; to "know" in
this context is to recognize, to remember. The first time Philocrates saw
Stalagmus, twenty years ago (980), he was himself a child, and Stalagmus
was a runaway *puer*; now both are grown men. Stalagmus, on the other
hand, claims he knows Philocrates' family very well (976). So, although
Stalagmus fills the slot held in other plays by pimps – who are clearly
the butt of the joke, the villain – the ending of *Captivi* is not so clear.
After Stalagmus' final words, the *grex* addresses the audience, claims that
this play is a chaste one because it lacks all the erotic themes common
in plays, and tells the audience to applaud if they want chastity to win
the prize (*qui pudicitiae esse voltis praemium, plausum date*, 1036). This is
a twist and a joke, but it forces, or allows, the audience to applaud (you
don't like chastity?) for a play that questions the basis of slavery, and perhaps also contains a side comment on the story of Stalagmus.

A comparable memory torrent bursts out in another recognition scene, in *Epidicus*, between Philippa, mother of the war captive Telestis, and the girl's father Periphanes, who had raped Philippa long ago in Epidaurus (see chapter 5). They recognize each other gradually as Philippa enters, in a complex split duet; Periphanes quickly comes to a guilty knowledge: "Surely she's the one whom – in Epidaurus – a poor girl – I remember I stuffed her" (*certo east … / quam in Epidauro / pauperculam memini comprimere*, 540–40b). Philippa tells the audience the same thing, from her own perspective, maintaining her dignity (541–41a).[71] Both are wary, and call upon guile to help them negotiate (*astu*, 545; *muliebris … malitia*, 546); it takes some doing for them to remember together, as they break out of song into trochaic conversation (550–54, tr7):

> [PE.] novin ego te? PH. si ego te novi, animum inducam ut tu noveris.   550
> PE. ubi te visitavi? PH. inique iniuriu's. PE. quid iam? PH. quia
> tuae memoriae interpretari me aequom censes. PH. commode
> fabulata's. PH. mira memoras, <Periphane.> PE. em istuc rectius.
> meministin? PH. memini id quod memini. PE. at in Epidauro –

> [PE.] Don't I know you? PH. If I recognize you, I'll be convinced that you
>   did know me.
> PE. Where was it I used to see you? PH. You're unfairly unjust. PE. How
>   so? PH. Because
> you think it's fair for me to channel your memory. PE. You said a mouthful.
> PH. You call strange things to mind, Periphanes. PE. Watch it, that's
>   getting warmer.
> You do remember, then? PH. I remember what I remember. PE. But in
>   Epidaurus –

Here memory bridges both time and space, as the two characters work towards acknowledgment of trauma. Periphanes makes an excuse: "Don't you remember … in Epidaurus … / I lightened your poverty / and your mother's, when you were a poor girl and a virgin?" (*meministin … in Epidauro … / … virgini pauperculae / tuaeque matri me levare paupertatem?*, 554–6). Philippa corrects him: "Aren't you the guy / who sowed me with the seed of a weighty sorrow, for the sake of your pleasure?" (*tun is es / qui per voluptatem tuam in me aerumnam opsevisti gravem?*, 556–7). The raped woman is played (perhaps) by a raped man; the rapist is played (perhaps)

---

[71] On the music, see Moore 2001: 319: "a moment of great musical virtuosity. … [the combination of unusual meters makes it clear that] Plautus was as interested here in presenting enjoyable music as in making his audience feel sorry for Philippa." Maybe both. This is not Maurice Chevalier and Hermione Gingold singing "I Remember It Well." On this scene, see James 2015a: 116–19; also Gunderson 2015: 230–1.

by another raped man. Or by actors who used other actors for sex (see chapter 1). All three subject positions were sitting in the audience. Philippa enters talking of her misery, summed up in the loss of her captured daughter: "Nor do I know now where she might be" (*neque ea nunc ubi sit scio*, 532). The "where" is the problem. When she thinks she is about to be reunited with Telestis, she says, "Now my spirit at last returns home to me" (*remigrat animus nunc demum mihi*, 569). Like Tyndarus, who says *nunc demum in memoriam redeo*, she feels the ruptures of her past as a rupture of her self.

Memory takes the characters back, and takes the audience along with them. Menaechmus I, when asked "What is the farthest back you remember in your fatherland?" (*quid longissume meministi … in patria tua?*, Men. 1111), recalls the trip to Tarentum and running away from his father in the crowd; he knows how old he was and that he was just losing his baby teeth, and he remembers (*memini*, 1118) that he had a twin. A recipe in Pliny's *Natural History* suggests that mothers kept their children's baby teeth (28.41), so this might have been a resonant detail for mothers in the audience. Planesium in *Curculio* announces late in the play that she was born free (607), prompted by the sight of her father's ring (602); Curculio responds, with a wink to the audience, "Like a lot of other people who are slaves today" (*et alii multi qui nunc serviunt, Cur.* 607; see chapter 6). Planesium's skeptical long-lost brother asks her, "If you're recalling the truth, who was your mother?" (*si vera memoras, quae fuit mater tua?*, 642). When – a flashback – she tells how she was kidnapped during a windstorm when the seating for the show blew down (644–50), her now-convinced brother remembers the tumult (*memini*, 651). Agorastocles in *Poenulus* knows his own story and thinks of Carthage as his home town (1053–5); Hanno tests his memory (1061–4):

> dic mihi,
> ecquid meministi tuom parentum nomina,
> patris atque matris? AG. memini. HA. memoradum mihi
> si novi forte aut si sunt cognati mihi.
>
> … [HA.] Tell me,
> do you remember the names of your parents at all,
> your father and mother? AG. I remember. HA. Then recall them for me,
> if maybe I know them or if they're my relatives.

The blackface masks in *Poenulus* push this exchange into the realm of *Captivi*, where "they" are exchanged for "us," and a free man is interchangeable with a slave – especially so here, as Agorastocles announces the startlingly Punic names of his mother and father: Ampsigura and Iahon (1065). Ethnicity here seems as interchangeable as civil status, and memory crosses boundaries – a necessity for those with hybrid identity.

Daemones in *Rudens* drags the memory of his lost daughter into his first meeting with her unwitting lover (106), well before Palaestra appears; when Daemones finally meets her, she reminds him of his daughter, whom he invokes: "Oh my daughter, / when I see this girl, you remind me, lost as you are, of my miseries" (*o filia / mea, quom hanc video, mearum me apsens miseriarum commones*, 742–3). This is a sight gag and a sendup of tragedy, for, as seen in chapters 2 and 5, the actor playing Palaestra is not only in drag, but wet and disheveled; still, as Daemones here apostrophizes his memory, possibly speaking outward, into an audience in which sat parents of actual lost children, he is spoofing a common martyrdom. Palaestra, meanwhile, is conscious of her past from her first appearance onstage, and her lost parents play a major part in her opening song (192, 197a, 216–19); she laments that they are so wretched (*miseri*) as not to know she is wretched (*miseram*, 216–16a). Not knowing, not remembering, make it all worse – for some; others want to forget, just as Primo Levi says at the end of *The Reawakening*.[72] As the Virgo in *Persa* spins her false tale of captivity, Toxilus begs the pimp not to press her too hard: "Stop asking her about that now (don't you see she doesn't want to talk about it?) / Don't lead her back into the memory of her miseries" (*iam de istoc rogare omitte (non vides nolle eloqui?) / ne suarum se miseriarum in memoriam inducas*, 642–3). Pushed to tell her father's name, she replies, "Why should I recall that miserable man, who he once was?" (*quid illum miserum memorem qui fuit?*, 646) – and, as seen in chapter 5, renames her father and herself *Miser* and *Misera*. Chillingly, her memory of freedom (*ut meminit libertatis*) becomes another selling point, which Toxilus predicts will bring in a good income for the pimp (658), for customers will pay more for a girl who was once untouchable, a girl who can feel what she is losing. Both the joke and the frisson are compounded by the male body inside the female mask and costume, as the actors enact the plight of

---

[72] Levi 1986: 221: "Those who refuse to go back, or even to discuss the matter ... or those who would like to forget ... and are tormented by nightmares ... are individuals who ended in the camps through bad luck. ... For them the suffering was traumatic but devoid of meaning .... [For those with political or moral consciousness,] remembering is a duty. They do not want to forget, and above all they do not want the world to forget, because they understand that their experiences were not meaningless" The Virgo's sale scene begins with a long exchange between her and her supposed slave-dealer in which she lists the qualities that make a city morally unsound (*Per.* 549–60; see chapter 1). She ends with *scelus*, which could certainly be played as a description of what has happened to her.

the heroines they are. Flashbacks exacerbate these characters' dire straits, picking up on the displaced person's chief obsession: the moment of loss and the then/now contrast.

One of the strange things about *Epidicus* is that Philippa never meets her daughter Telestis in the extant play. The recognition is left to the slave Epidicus, and here the memory words return (637–40):

> TE. quis tu homo es qui meum parentum nomen memoras et meum?
> EP. non me novisti? TE. quod quidem nunc veniat in mentem mihi.
> EP. non meministi me auream ad te adferre natali die
> lunulam atque anellum aureolum in digitum? TE. memini, mi homo. 640

> TE. Who are you, Mister, who recall the name of my parents? And
> my name?
> EP. You don't know me? TE. But actually it might be coming back to
> mind now.
> EP. You don't remember, I brought you a golden *lunula* on your birthday,
> and a little gold ring for your finger? TE. I remember, Mister. 640

The slave's recognition reconstitutes Telestis, along with the actor who plays her, as a freeborn girl, and her own recollection completes the process. But she is in transition. Speaking now as a slave to a slave, rather than as (former) freeborn girl to her (former) father's possession – a part of Epidicus' back story the audience is left to infer – she interpellates him as an equal person, *mi homo*. Once again here, as in *Truculentus*, it is a slave who knows and remembers the secrets of identity, and for Epidicus this knowledge and memory will unlock his freedom.[73]

In all these scenes, memory (forms of *memini, memoria*) is rooted in misery (*miser/ia*) and the names of parents, and is necessary for recognition (forms of *nosco*). It can also, as here with Telestis, be prompted by the sight, even the memory, of a token. For, as James Tatum points out (1995), material objects evoke memories when displayed to the interpretive community that understands their significance; in performance, the objects appeal to an onstage community and to the audience simultaneously, for the audience members all recognize what they mean.

Tokens trigger recognition in four plays: *Cistellaria, Curculio, Epidicus,* and *Rudens* – all involving lost young women.[74] (A ring also seems to have

---

[73] On this point, see James 2015a: 125 n. 29: "Periphanes's slave knows his daughter better than does Periphanes himself."

[74] On the use of tokens in Greek New Comedy, see Vester 2013, who emphasizes that they evoke wealth and aristocratic standing as well as citizen status, and points out the insecurity caused by the fact that they are detachable.

played a part in *Vidularia*, fr. xiv–xv.) Both the tokens and their effects vary widely, but all the tokens bear a synecdochic relationship to the freedom and bodily integrity of the young women they endorse. For Telestis, the tokens are a golden *lunula* – a moon-shaped pendant, commonly worn by girls – and a gold ring (*anellum aureolum in digitum*, 639–40), both given to her by a slave on her birthday.[75] The tokens are not explicitly stated to be present, although Telestis might underscore her *memini* (640) by touching her hand and throat; the slave Epidicus reminds her of the objects and the giving, and she remembers the giving but does not really recognize Epidicus. The tokens here must constitute a necessary gesture, a concrete place-holder on which to hang memory, recognition, and identity.

In *Cistellaria*, the *cistella* contains the baby amulets (*crepundia*) that will identify Selenium as freeborn and restore her to her birth parents.[76] Their existence comes as news to Selenium (635–7) and is upstaged by her lover's attempted suicide; she takes no further part in the extant play, and the *cistella* becomes the object of a tug-of-war opposing her foster mother's *ancilla* Halisca to her birth mother Phanostrata and Phanostrata's slave Lampadio. The *crepundia* in their container are flourished onstage during this argument (745–52, with repeated *gestitavit*), but the big moment for the *cistella* comes during the initial sparring, as Lampadio asks Halisca what she is looking for (731–3):

> [LA.] quid quaeritas? HA. cistellula hinc mi, adulescens, evolavit.
> LA. in caveam latam oportuit. HA. non edepol praeda magna.
> LA. mirum quin grex venalium in cistella infuerit una.

> [LA.] What are you looking for? HA. A little box flew away from me
> here, young man.

---

[75] For images of these pendants, with discussion, see D'Ambra 2007: 124–5, 127; also K. Olson 2008: 144.

[76] The common translation of *crepundia* as "rattle" cannot be right, despite the charming extant rattles; these are all quite substantial and often made of terracotta, not suitable for hanging around a child's neck (see examples at http://archaeologicalmuseum.jhu.edu/the-collection/object-stories/archaeology-of-daily-life/childhood/terracotta-dog-rattle/). *Crepundia* are vividly identified as dangly pendants by the joke in *Miles Gloriosus* in which the cook, as a punishment for intended adultery, threatens to cut away the soldier's *abdomen* and hang it around his neck "as *crepundia* hang around a child's neck," *quasi puero in collo pendeant crepundia*, 1399; possibly a direct reference to the *fascinum*, the child's apotropaic amulet in the shape of a penis and testicles, otherwise unattested at this date. Certainly castration is the punishment threatened in this scene, just as it forms the basis for adultery-punishment jokes in *Curculio* (30–2) and *Poenulus* (862–3), both in runs of shtick. But *crepundia* is a general term, and the *fascinum* is never explicitly associated with girls. For Roman baby amulets and their use by mothers and nurses, see Richlin 2014a: 264–5.

LA. Should have been put into a cage.[77] HA. By God, it's not big spoils.
LA. Strange if a coffle of slaves wouldn't fit into one little box.

This exchange is marked as complete by the onlooker, Phanostrata (*sine dicat*, 734) – punctuated for emphasis by the straight man, as usual in a run of jokes. The missing box is said to have flown away (like a bird); Lampadio says Halisca should have put it in a cage (like a bird). Halisca replies, as if from the idea of the cage, that the *cistella* is not big *praeda*: spoils of war. A riddle: What kind of spoils are put in a cage? Lampadio's answer suggests the train of thought; using the sarcastic *mirum quin* formula, he says that a *grex venalium*, a group of slaves assembled for sale, would not fit in a box. This joke is kin to the riddling comparison in *Captivi* of captive slaves to wild birds (chapter 2; cf. chapter 8 on birds and cages). The theatrical analogy is underscored by the words *cavea* (seating space) and *grex*; Halisca has already asked the audience to help her find the *cistella* (*mei homines, mei spectatores*, 678), although she teases them by saying she is foolish to ask them, "because they always like to see a woman in trouble" (*qui semper malo muliebri sunt lubentes*, 681) – another campy line. But the *lena*, as seen above, has already enlisted the audience on the woman's side. What is at stake for Selenium in the *cistella* is legitimate parentage (636, 714–15) – just one young woman's life, not a whole *grex*.[78]

Planesium's ring in *Curculio* is recognized by her brother as one which he gave her on her *dies natalis* (653–7), just as she recognizes her father's ring, stolen from her brother by Curculio (601–3; note *gestitavit*, 603). Like the captive Telestis, this freed slave regains a birthday along with her restoration to her family – as seen in chapter 4, something slaves want. Planesium says that, by keeping her father's ring, Curculio is keeping her parents from her (605); Curculio jokingly replies that her parents cannot be in the ring: "Do I have your mother and father tucked away under the gemstone?" (*sub gemmane apstrusos habeo tuam matrem et patrem?*, 606). Although this is a joke, in fact that is just what he has. In the play, the ring has been the key to the price of access to Planesium's body; this is underlined by the review of its history that follows the exchange between Curculio and Planesium (608–15). It then, with the ring she wears, becomes

---

[77] Probably also a pun on *latam*: "should have been *put* (*latam*) into a cage," vs. "should have [gone] into a *big* (*latam*) cage," triggering Halisca's *magnam*; esp. since *praeda* means both "war loot" and "prey."

[78] On the *cistella* in *Cistellaria*, see Telò 2016, who argues that it is a basket, a stand-in for the girl herself, and part of a system of woven, circular images that reflect the play's plot. On various onstage objects as stand-ins for Planesium in *Curculio* "by a kind of transitive property of exchange," see Ketterer 1986a: 201.

the key to her recognition as the sister of the soldier who had been about to buy her (629–39), as Telestis is recognized at the last minute as the half-sister of the man who has just purchased her (*Epid.* 648–50). The rings stave off incest and repair the shattered family.

Palaestra herself says the *cistella* that holds her birth tokens contains her parents (*Rud.* 1144–5):

> … o mei parentes, hic vos conclusos gero,
> huc opesque spesque vostrum cognoscendum condidi.   1145

> Oh my parents, I hold you shut in here,
> here's where I've stored my wealth, my hope of recognizing you.   1145

Again, this earns her mockery, as Gripus chides her for squeezing her parents so (1146–7), but it is still true.

The tokens in *Rudens* are both the most elaborate and the most elaborately staged. Their presence is repeatedly cued before they are seen: Ampelisca explains to Trachalio that the pimp has deliberately taken the *cistella* to keep Palaestra from finding her parents, and packed it inside a suitcase (*vidulus*) that had been on the wrecked ship (389–93); Trachalio identifies the contents as *crepundia* when he claims the *vidulus* for Palaestra (1081–2). Notably, both Ampelisca's first scene with Trachalio here and the quarrel over the ring in *Curculio* trigger face-out lines on the commonness and wrongness of enslavement (chapter 6).

When Daemones shows the *vidulus* to Palaestra, she suggests a test: she will identify what is inside the *cistella* without looking. *Memorato omnia,* Daemones tells her: "Recall them all" (1149). She lists the *crepundia* (1154) as follows: a "little golden sword" (*ensiculus aureolus*), inscribed with the name of her father (1155–6, 1160); a "little double-headed axe" (*securicula ancipes*), also gold, inscribed with the name of her mother (1158–9, 1163–4); then a "little silver dagger" (*siculicula argenteola*), two "little joined hands" (*conexae maniculae*), and a *sucula*, a winch (1169–70); and finally a golden *bulla* which her father gave her on her *dies natalis* (1171). This unique assemblage, and her memory of it, prove her to be Daemones' daughter; the name given here for her mother, Daedalis (1164), both links her with Daemones and plays on the wonder-toy nature of the objects. The *bulla* marks Palaestra as a Roman citizen child – the only girl associated with this quintessential mark, which Plutarch (three hundred years later) says had the particular function of marking off free children from slave children as sexually off limits (*QR* 288a–b). The *sucula*, capping the series *ensiculus, securicula, siculicula, maniculae,* seems to be there only to prompt a coarse joke from Gripus – "Why don't you go get crucified with your 'little sow' and your 'little pigs'" (*quin tu i directa cum sucula et cum porculis*, 1170). This complicated joke plays on the agricultural terms *sucula* and *porculus*, which are parts of a wine-press that look like a sow with a piglet, and in turn probably plays on the slang use of *porcus* for the female genitalia; Varro explains, "Indeed, our women, too, especially *nutrices*, call girls' female genitals their *porcus*, and Greek women call it *choeros*, meaning that the sign is good enough for marriage" (*nam et nostrae mulieres, maxime nutrices, naturam qua feminae sunt in virginibus appellant porcum, et Graecae choeron, significantes esse dignum insigne nuptiarum*, R. 2.4.10).[79] As seen in chapter 2, *Rudens* also has a very dragged-in joke playing on the obscene meaning of *concha* (704), but, again, the identification of the *crepundia* with Palaestra's genitals is correct. The *cistella* inside the *vidulus* contains what will keep her from a life of prostitution, and stands not only for her freedom but for the sexual integrity of her body, a box within a box.

All the tokens in these scenes are objects worn on the body, as is emphasized by the repetition of the verb *gestito* in the *Cistellaria* recognition scene (746, 749, 750, 752). The tokens work like soldiers' dog tags, and reflect the difficulty of affixing labels onto people, a difficulty which must have been strongly felt in the chaos of the 200s BCE. Menander's play *Aspis* centers on the problem of identifying the war dead (James 2014); contracts and runaway slave notices from Hellenistic Egypt identify the participants by birthmarks and other bodily peculiarities. A notice datable to 156 BCE advertises for "Hermôn, also known as Neilos, Syrian by birth, from the city of Bambykê, age about eighteen; medium height, no beard, well-formed legs, cleft in his chin, mark near the left side of his nose, scar above the left corner of his mouth, right wrist tattooed with barbarian letters," along with a fellow runaway, "Biôn, … small in stature, wide-shouldered with thinnish legs, bright-eyed."[80] The aediles' edict is forthright in its list of aspects of slaves' bodies that would have been inspected on sale, including missing fingers and toes (*D.* 21.1), and Alan Watson takes the edict to have existed in some form in the 200s (1971: 134–5, with discussion of slave defects).

---

[79] For discussion of the parts of the wine-press, see Cato, *De agr.* 19.1–2 with Dalby's notes *ad loc.* (1998: 100–3). For the joke form, compare *Cur.* 612 *cum bolis, cum bulbis*. For illustrations of *lunulae* and discussion of girls' amulets, see D'Ambra 2007: 124–5, 127; for a comparable amulet bundle from Renaissance Italy, see Klapisch-Zuber 1985: 149–50.

[80] P. Paris, 10; trans. in Shaw 2001: 56. For this papyrus, see further duBois 2007: 439, D. Thompson 2011: 210, with similar descriptions of a shipment of four boys seven to ten years old in 257 BCE (Thompson 2011: 206–7) and of four runaways c. 250 BCE (209–10). For later instances, which are plentiful, see Shaw 2001: 55–60, and sources listed in Schmeling 2011: 392 *ad* Petronius *Sat.* 97.2 (a *locus classicus*).

Another bodily mark for slaves is attested elsewhere in the Mediterranean as early as Aristophanes, and vividly so in Herodas (270s BCE): tattooing on the face, sometimes with a full statement of a crime committed (Jones 1987). However, and surprisingly, there is little trace of this mark in the *palliata*, despite the omnipresence of other tortures.[81] Nor do we see anything like the welded-on collars with labels extant in the archaeological record ("Adulterous whore. Detain me, because I ran away from Bulla Regia," *Adultera meretrix. tene me quia fugivi de Bulla R(e)g(ia)*, *ILS* 9455, discussed at McGinn 2004: 37). Philocrates' facial features and hair are described when he is identified as a runaway (*Capt.* 646–48). But physical marks almost never appear as signs to be recognized in the plays, except for conventional descriptions of slaves and the scars they bear from being flogged (a sure identifying sign, as Sosia says of Mercurius and himself, *Am.* 446). Libanus describes the supposed *atriensis*, really Leonida (*As.* 400–1); Harpax describes the supposed Syrus, really Pseudolus (*Ps.* 1218–20): both times as part of a scam, in which the dupes have failed to recognize the great comedian ("thick glasses, a big nose, a moustache, and a cigar"). Indeed, descriptions like that of Pseudolus – "a red-headed guy, with a pot belly, thick legs, kind of dark, / with a big head, sharp eyes, a ruddy face, and pretty / big feet" (*rufus quidam, ventriosus, crassis suris, subniger, / magno capite, acutis oculis, ore rubicundo, admodum / magnis pedibus*) – identify only the mask and costume that the actor is wearing (including shoes?). The identifying marks onstage, then, are removable: unreal identities, no use in catching a slave, or recognizing a child.[82] When Milphio describes Giddenis as dark-skinned (*Poen.* 1112–13), it must, again, be a sight gag, part of the running gag about dark-skinned Carthaginians in this play, and a mark that is never brought up by the Carthaginian father who has been searching the Mediterranean for his

---

[81] Jones states with confidence (1987: 148 "certainly," 153 "clearly") that *Cas.* 401 (*si hic litteratus me sinat*) and *Aul.* 325–6 (one cook to another, *tun, trium litterarum homo, / me vituperas? fur*) attest to the practice of tattooing, or possibly (in the case of *Aul.* 325–6) of branding, in Rome in the 200s, but both these jokes seem to me to be justified in the action and context without any reference to marks on the face (with *Casina* line assignments as in MacCary and Willcock 1976); contrast the Herodas scene, in which the owner calls for the tattooist and his needles (*Mim.* 5.65–7, 77–9), a character not present among the torturers' henchmen in the *palliata*. Nor is the punishment listed in the catalogue in *Asinaria* (548–50). But, as noted in chapter 1, the title of Naevius' comedy *Stigmatias* suggests that slaves with facial tattoos had at least circulated into the Italian market, and see chapter 1, n. 22, for another possibility at *Rudens* 478; so taken by Marx *ad loc.*, who adduces also *Rud.* 1159 (one of the recognition tokens; surely not).

[82] On the descriptions as related to costumes, esp. masks, see Marshall 2006: 64, 133–7 (including the Marx Brothers' "masks"), and 149–51 on the way Philocrates' description blurs the line between the stock slave and the stock *adulescens*. On Philocrates, Leigh (2004: 92) observes that his appearance "ought to mark him out as the obvious slave."

lost daughters. The joke about the *boia* in *Captivi* and Tyndarus' remark about the relief of having his *collare* removed suggests that the tokens of freedom are the desired counterpart of the shackles of slavery; for enslaved persons restored to their parents in the *palliata*, the onstage mark of recognition is, not the scars of old beatings, but an object that links the person to the past.

As with gender, so these marks of civil status appear onstage, as it were, in drag: not the thing itself, but a stage prop playing the thing; not a golden ring, but a gold-colored curtain ring. This is seen most obviously in the elaborate stage business in *Poenulus* with the recognition token (*tessera*) that tells Hanno and Agorastocles that they share a guest-friendship (1047–9): a comic *tessera* might well have been made large enough to be visible to the audience, thus larger than life. Mario Telò has argued that props like these, in the plays, are "entities charged with vital energy," with the capacity to serve as "time machines" (2016: 299, 300 n. 5). The family reunion tokens that are held up onstage serve in comedy in place of the tokens that mark a tragic anagnorisis, just as Agorastocles' monkey-bite scar stands in for Odysseus' epic scar (*Poen.* 1072–6).[83] Compare the scene in the *Satyrica* in which Lichas recognizes Encolpius by his penis (105.9–10; note that Encolpius there describes himself as a *fugitivus*); or perhaps, as suggested in chapter 5, the scene where Bromia recognizes Amphitruo. The comic token puts an end to slavery and prostitution, not to a noble tragic exile. Accordingly, comic tokens lead on, not to vengeance, but to happiness.

This association between object and freedom is played out on a large scale in the title scene of *Rudens*. The appearance of the *vidulus* inside the net of the slave fisherman Gripus is what gives this play its title and most memorable scene, as the slave Trachalio tries to get the suitcase away from him. Gripus, who hopes that this suitcase will contain the gold he needs to buy his freedom, argues that what is caught in the sea is fair game (969–85):

TR. non ferat si dominus veniat? GR. dominus huic, ne frustra sis,
nisi ego nemo natust, hunc qui cepi in venatu meo.   970
TR. itane vero? GR. ecquem esse dices in mari piscem meum?
quos quom capio, siquidem cepi, mei sunt; habeo pro meis,
nec manu adseruntur neque illinc partem quisquam postulat.
in foro palam omnis vendo pro meis venalibus.
mare quidem commune certost omnibus. TR. adsentio: 975

---

[83] On this scar and other monkey business in *Poenulus*, see Connors 2004: 193. For a summary of the way props work onstage in the plays, see Ketterer 1986c: 61–6, and cf. chapter 5 above.

qui minus hunc communem quaeso mihi esse oportet vidulum?
in mari inventust communi. GR. esne inpudenter inpudens?
nam si istuc ius sit quod memoras, piscatores perierint.
quippe quom extemplo in macellum pisces prolati sient,
nemo emat, suam quisque partem piscium poscant sibi,   980
dicant in mari communi captos. TR. quid ais, inpudens?
ausu's etiam comparare vidulum cum piscibus?
eadem tandem res videtur? GR. in manu non est mea:
ubi demisi retem atque hamum, quidquid haesit extraho.
meum quod rete atque hami nancti sunt meum potissumumst.   985

TR. If the legal owner comes, wouldn't he take it? GR. The legal owner of
   this baby,
make no mistake, hasn't been born, unless it's me, since I caught it in my
   hunt.   970
TR. Is that true? GR. What fish in the ocean will you admit are mine?
When I catch them, once I've caught them, they're mine; I have them as
   my own,
nor can they be legally claimed, nor can anyone go after any part of them.
In the forum, I sell them all in public, as my objects for sale.
Sure, the ocean's definitely common to everyone. TR. I agree: 975
so then why, I ask you, shouldn't this suitcase be common to me?
It was found in the common ocean. GR. Are you so shamelessly shameless?
If that were law, the way you recall it, fishermen would all die.
Hey, right away, when fish were set out in the market,
nobody would buy them, and everybody would go after his own part of the
   fish,   980
they'd say they were caught in the common ocean. TR. What are you
   saying, shameless?
Do you have the nerve to compare a suitcase with fish?
Does this really seem like the same thing? GR. It's not in my hand [= up
   to me];
when I've thrown out my net and hook, whatever has stuck to it, I pull out.
What my net and hook have found, that's most absolutely mine.   985

David Konstan holds convincingly that the argument here is about property and ownership (1983: 75–80), with a brilliant comparison to the image of Fast-Fish and Loose-Fish from chapter 89 of *Moby-Dick*. Konstan quotes at length, justifiably so; a sample: "What are the sinews and souls of Russian serfs and Republican slaves but Fast-Fish, whereof possession is the whole of the law? … What are the Rights of Man and the Liberties of the World but Loose-Fish?" Gripus, who has already made it clear that his aim is not to abolish slavery but to move himself from the status of slave to that of *rex*, and who intends to buy himself some slaves and ships

(930–1; see chapter 8), upholds a view of property that is fully in keeping with Roman law and justifies the taking of slaves, especially in war. The fish he catches every day, says Gripus, *nec manu adseruntur* (973); they cannot be reclaimed from ownership, and Gripus can sell them openly in the market as his own *venalibus* (974): "things for sale," but often applied to people for sale as slaves (cf. *Cist.* 733, above). Everything in the sea is up for grabs, but once it is taken it belongs to the taker, otherwise the market itself would fail (979–81). What is taken "by the net and hook" is "most absolutely mine" (985); according to Gripus' disingenuous definition of the suitcase as a fish, he has a perfect right to claim it as his by *occupatio*, "the acquisition of ownership of a thing which previously did not have an owner," of which catching fish was a prime example, as were spoils taken from the enemy (Just. *Inst.* 2.1, with an explicit analogy between escaped war captives and wild creatures). Similarly, Roman law defined ownership as originating most absolutely in capture in war. Commenting on the use of the *festuca* (a wand or stick) in the procedure for transfer of property, Gaius says: "Moreover, they used the *festuca*, as it were, in place of a spear, as a kind of sign of rightful ownership, because they considered those things to be most absolutely theirs that they had taken from the enemy" (*festuca autem utebantur quasi hastae loco, signo quodam iusti domini, quod maxime sua esse credebant quae ex hostibus cepissent, Inst.* 4.16). Slavery itself is given a similar etiology under Justinian: "Slaves (*servi*) are so called because military commanders order their captives to be sold, and so are used to preserve them alive (*servare*) instead of killing them. They are also called *mancipia* because they are taken from the enemy by the strong hand (*manu capiuntur*)" (*Servi autem ex eo appellati sunt, quod imperatores captivos vendere iubent ac per hoc servare nec occidere solent: qui etiam mancipia dicti sunt, quod ab hostibus manu capiuntur*, Just. *Inst.* 1.3.3, trans. Lee 1956: 57). *Mancupia* is the word Gripus uses of the slaves he hopes to buy (*Rud.* 930). "Manumit" in Latin is actually a phrase, *manu emittere*, "to release from the hand," so that the hand means ownership, control, power over. Compare the soldier in *Truculentus*: *patriam ego excidi manu*, literally "I hewed down their fatherland with my hand" (532).[84]

Dominus (969) means "legal owner" – valid ownership is *dominium ex iure Quiritium* – and is a more legalistic term than *erus*, the usual word for "slave-owner" in the plays; what Gripus asserts when he claims to be the

---

[84] These ideas about the legal foundations for owning the hunter's and the soldier's catch are incorporated in his overview of law around 200 BCE by Watson 1971: 66 (the definition of *occupatio* is his); see chapter 2 on the wild bird as exemplar of the *res nullius*. Stewart does not deal with *occupatio*

dominus of the suitcase is his incontestable ownership of himself, for by law a slave acquires for his owner. Compare the Advocati in *Poenulus* (519), who insist that it was their own money that was the price of their *caput*: to own the money is to own oneself, as seen in chapter 3. The suitcase contains the price of Gripus' freedom – the end, for him, of hunger and forced manual labor. Unbeknownst to him, it also contains the *cistella* containing the golden tokens that prove the free citizen status of Palaestra. The tug of war staged here acts out the real-life force of war, producer of slaves, along with the competition for survival in the market that war created. As physical humor, the pulling is funny, but the pain this humor builds on is the common dream of leaving lack and becoming a *rex*, no matter the cost to others. Konstan concludes that *Rudens* does not question the moral basis of ownership in the same way Melville does; he believes that the play upholds the "true law of the city" in contrast with the "rule of nature" to which Gripus appeals (Konstan 1983: 80–1). But, for a slave in Italy in the 200s BCE, Gripus law *was* the "law of the city," the law that made slavery possible. Gripus himself is in collusion with the very structure that imprisons him. Like many other slaves in the plays, he is working within the system; as seen above, however, if he succeeds in transforming himself into a trafficker, he will become a really bad man, no longer that comic hero, the bad slave.

The Way Back and the Way Out

Through their geography the plays go back over the terrain of human trafficking; through their use of time and memory in onstage action, and their appeal to the audience's memory, they make whole what has been broken. The *palliata* created temporary sites of memory in the cities of Latium, where audiences could remember together, and make home come closer, or claim their hybrid identity, or embrace family. In a story refracted through the strange compound eye of Diodorus Siculus, the *barbaroi* newly enslaved after the fall of Numantia in 133 BCE, when they were marched away, as they came to the boundaries of their land, flung themselves to the

---

in her discussion of this passage (2012: 137); nor does Konstan, who cites only Roman law on *res communes* (following Marx 1959[1928]: 181), his main concern being with Greek law, in any case (Konstan 1983: 76 n. 7). The actual method used by the army in collecting spoils is described by Polybius (10.16). On Gaius, see Joshel 1992: 29; for discussion of the *vidulus* in *Rudens* in terms of the poetics of property, see Dressler 2016: 28–33. See chapter 8 on manumission in the *palliata*, and on the appearance of the *festuca* at *Mil.* 961.

ground and kissed the earth and took up the dust in their pockets.[85] So memory travels.

As seen in this chapter, performance – play + audience + venue – recognizes persons who, although they are together before the stage, are as diverse and scattered as confetti. Performance honors the experience, the life histories, of those who were now quasi-persons before the law, but who were persons before they got here, or just know themselves to be real. The story-lines in the plays act out the meaning of natal alienation, of sexual redefinition; the place-names in the plays trace the geography of human trafficking and war and the luxury trade that included human beings. The plays evoke the roads whose meaning came from the armies that built them and marched down them, roads that carried troupes of actors along with coffles of slaves, traders' wagons, and refugees; the geography of the stage itself is magically transferable, triggering the spectators' mental maps. By people for whom "here" is not "home," the irony of *barbaria* is deeply felt, as it is for the actors to whom it means the small time, but also the new thing they have made: something to make a tired man laugh and a heart-sore woman sing, something to keep alive the hope of freedom.

The memory of freedom in the plays is complicated by the commonness of the use of the command "remember" to accompany owners' instructions to slaves, repeatedly acted out, as is the stock reply: no need for you to tell me again. Memory is appropriated by slaves who enjoin their owners to remember a promise to manumit; the sore point of the lack of *fides* for slaves and the poor is balanced by challenges to the owner's *fides*, as when Paegnium chides his owner, the slave Toxilus. Slaves also challenge the status quo by laying claim to the moral virtues professed by contemporary aristocrats, as Tyndarus lays claim to *gloria*: the kind of virtue that causes a person to be remembered. It is no accident that the largest concentrations of words connected with memory are found in the two plays that deal most directly with war captives, *Captivi* and *Epidicus*, as well as in the scene of the sale of a fake captive in *Persa*. The recognition scenes and their prop tokens are lifted from tragedy by the actors to make a kind of

---

[85] Diod. Sic. 34/35.4.1. The location of the episode is lost from the fragment, so that it could describe any mass enslavement, anywhere; it is tied to Numantia by its resemblance to the account of the fall of Numantia in Appian (3.96–8): Diodorus tells of some suicides and has the captors be awestruck by the sentiments of even the "beast-like souls of barbarians," while Appian notes the mass suicides and describes the beast-like condition to which the inhabitants had been reduced by the siege – by his time, a well-worn *topos* in the rhetorical schools. But the generic quality itself of Diodorus' dislocated fragment testifies to the common understanding of what enslavement meant. For more on Diodorus Siculus, see chapter 8. On memory and the lament for the fallen city, see Jeppesen 2016, part of a group study of a Mediterranean folk tradition.

shtick that stands in for a ticket home. The suitcase in *Rudens* is the prime example, and perhaps its significance in the play as the container for four slaves' freedom justifies the play's cryptic title: what lies at the end of the fishing line is what they hope for.

Above all, slaves wanted to be free, and in their most fantastical dreams, they escaped, and lit out for the Territory.

CHAPTER 8

Escape

> A keen observer might have detected in our repeated singing of
> "O Canaan, sweet Canaan,
>   I am bound for the land of Canaan,"
> something more than a hope of reaching heaven. We meant to reach
> the *North*, and the North was our Canaan.
>
> Frederick Douglass, *Life and Times*, chapter 19[1]

At least one observer in the 200s BCE remarked on the Romans' odd custom of making citizens of their freed slaves; Philip V, in a letter to the citizens of Larisa in Thessaly dated to 214, lauded the Roman practice as an example of how to make your state stronger.[2] Manumission was a possibility, so that most urban slaves would have known freed slaves – indeed, might have belonged to freed slaves. The gravestones of many *conservi* and *colliberti* from the late Republic onward bear witness to the maintenance of affective relationships within and after slavery, sometimes shared with such former owners. The plays of Plautus bear witness to a set of values shared by people for whom civil status was the first factor that controlled their lives. For these people, freedom was the goal.

Slavery in Plautus has been repeatedly described as steady-state, the tricking of owner by slave a repetitive game to which no end is desired – comedy necessitates continuity. Tranio's attitude at the end of *Mostellaria* has been taken as typical: Why punish me today, when I will just do the same thing tomorrow? (1178–9).[3] In fact, slaves in Plautus wish to escape.

---

[1] In Gates 1994: 607; an instance of what Douglass labels in his Contents, "hymns with a double meaning."

[2] *IG* 9.2.517; for translation with notes, Austin 1981: 118, Burstein 1985: 87–8. Commonly cited, for example by Dench 2003: 294, the start of her essay; Taylor 2013[1960]: 132.

[3] Most influentially by Erich Segal (1968: 159–69), especially at 164: "the clever slave does not even desire manumission." Following Segal, surprisingly, Parker 1989: 241, who quotes this line with approval ("As Segal correctly notes"); again influentially, McCarthy 2000: 212 ("the lack of interest that clever slaves show in manumission underscores their essential collusion in their servitude"); Kurke 2011: 12, following McCarthy ("the clever slave … never achieves freedom (indeed, he does

Like Gripus in *Rudens* (chapter 7), they long to be manumitted, and sometimes are; they fantasize about being rich, about flying away like birds, and
in particular the plays fantasize about travels in the fabulous Orient – not
just going home, as in the travelogues of chapter 7, but going to heaven. All
these fantasies express the desire to be free. The *palliata*, with its song and
dance, snappy dialogue, and happy endings, is well calculated to produce
happy audiences at the plays' end; fantasies of escape are part of this mood,
but not *only* part of this mood. As Frederick Douglass said of songs of
Canaan, their meaning was complex. It is not that these fantasies could not
have produced a smile on the face of free people in the audience; *Aulularia*,
after all, is a whole play about a pot of gold, concealed in a poor man's
hearth, guarded by the Lar familiaris, and revealed by the Lar only for the
sake of the poor man's daughter, who gives the Lar proper worship. She
has been raped by a young man *de summo ... loco* and needs a dowry (*Aul.*
1–36); buried treasure is the quintessential poor people's fantasy.[4] Here,
however, the fantasy is expedited by a god closely associated with slave life,
and in the play the pot of gold is also the price of manumission. Overall,
the content of these fantasies speaks most directly to slaves and freed slaves,
and must be considered in light of what it could have meant to them.

Manumission

There are twenty-six freed slaves (plus a chorus) in the twenty extant plays;
possibly twenty-seven, if de Melo is right about what happens to the Slave
of Lyconides at the end of *Aulularia* (2011a: 251, 352–3), or twenty-eight,
if Soteris in *Vidularia* was recognized as freeborn (Marshall 2015: 125), or
twenty-nine, if Scapha's autobiography means she was at one time freed

---

not even seem to aspire to manumission). At the end of the play, nothing has changed"); duBois
2009: 99 (see chapter 1); Stewart 2012: 189 ("the trickster is not shown as desiring or pursuing release
from slavery for himself"); even Leigh (2004: 85). A prime example of dogmatic drag, even among
those who have read the corpus. This conclusion is reached by limiting the sample to slaves defined
as "clever," necessitating fancy footwork about Epidicus and Tyndarus (see chapter 2 for Segal on
onstage punishment), and excluding female slaves altogether; Segal's dictum, however, seems commonly to be taken to refer to all slaves in the plays. Alison Sharrock argues that the manumissions
do not matter because "successful slaves in comedy are not working for themselves" (2016: 99). This
is true only of a few of the better-known slaves. The structure of the sitcom has been analyzed as a
deliberately endless repetition of the same plotlines, without character development or significant
change (Mintz 1985), but, even though the *palliata* is the remote ancestor of the sitcom, the plays
were, to put it mildly, unlike sitcoms in the circumstances of their production.
4 On *Aulularia* and folk tales, see Konstantakos 2016.

(*Mos.* 194–202).⁵ Of these, some are freed in the course of the action, while four (plus the chorus) have been freed so long before the action of the play that we do not hear much about their stories: the *lena* and Melaenis in *Cistellaria*, Acroteleutium in *Miles*, the unnamed *fidicina* in *Epidicus*, plus the chorus of Advocati in *Poenulus*, who, like the *fidicina*, as we have seen, are proud of their freed status. The *fidicina* makes her status clear: "Nor could anybody buy me, indeed, for any amount of money: / I've been free for more than five years now" (*neque me quidem emere quisquam ulla pecunia / potuit: plus iam sum libera quinquennium*, *Epid.* 497–8). Another nine are, like her, female sex workers: Planesium in *Curculio*, the *fidicina* Acropolistis in *Epidicus*, the *tibicina* Philematium in *Mostellaria*, Lemniselenis in *Persa*, Adelphasium and Anterastilis in *Poenulus*, Phoenicium in *Pseudolus*, Palaestra and Ampelisca in *Rudens* (Ampelisca's freedom is negotiated at 1405–9). Acroteleutium had belonged to the *senex* Periplectomenus and is still doing sex work under his patronage (*Mil.* 782–9, 915); Philematium's former owner is not mentioned; the rest are purchased from pimps, although several turn out to have been provably free all along and the money is refunded. Acropolistis, although purchased (*Epid.* 47–8, 367–8) and then freed (503–9), is dismissed into the house of the *senex*, now her *patronus*, and is casually promised to the son of her *patronus* as "something for you to love" (*quod ames*, 653).⁶ Telestis in *Epidicus* is purchased as a captive and released from slavery once Epidicus recognizes her; Casina is recognized as free, having been raised as a slave. Hegio's freed slave Cordalus in *Captivi*, although he does not appear onstage, is available *extra portam* to help his owner with the punishment of Tyndarus (735–6).

Six male slaves are manumitted in the plays: Tyndarus in *Captivi* (he is given as a gift to his previous owner Philocrates "that he might be free," *ut sit liber*, 947–8), Epidicus in *Epidicus*, Messenio in *Menaechmi*, Palaestrio in *Miles* (not seen but promised), Trachalio and Gripus in *Rudens* (1266,

---

⁵ It is unclear who, if anybody, owns Scapha, who is threatened with a beating by Philematium (240) and with various tortures by Philematium's lover (193, 203, 212, 218–19, 223, 238), in whose house they are both living.
⁶ On redemption of the freeborn from slavery, see Watson 1971: 44, 51, Scafuro 1997: 400–5 on Greek law, 405–9 on Roman law, and 409–24 on *Persa* and *Rudens* in relation to their reconstructed Greek originals; there is, however, no evidence for Roman practice in the 200s outside the plays. Watson takes the plays of Plautus as witness to the state of contemporary law: "when he employs an elaborate scene we can be reasonably sure his point was understandable by his not over-educated audience" (1971: 3). Philematium is identified as a *tibicina* at *Mos.* 971; on the status of Acropolistis, see chapter 5 (Marshall 2015 holds that she is still a slave). For freed slaves onstage, see Rawson 1993, who takes them to reflect the presence of freed slaves in the audience.

1410–11, arranged). The most surprising example, and the most easily over-
looked, is Agorastocles in *Poenulus*, who is clearly stated to have been kidnapped and then sold to a "wealthy owner" (*domino … diviti*, 73); this old
man, having unknowingly (*imprudens*) bought the son of an old guest-
friend (75), adopts him as a *puer* in the place of a son and makes him his
heir (75–7). The manumission of this *puer* is elided, and the old man's
death removes his *patronus*, but he is a freed slave nonetheless, a subtext
that informs the play, although not the scenes with the Advocati. The two
war captives Philocrates and Philopolemus in *Captivi* round out the tally;
the unknowing of kinship ties explicitly informs their play (*nec scit pater*,
21; *nescit*, 29; *imprudens*, 44; generalized, 44–5; *inscientes*, 46; *ignorans*, 50).
The Virgo in *Persa* makes it twenty-six (at least): not really an Arabian
captive, but still a girl sold to a pimp for real money, a girl whose father
reclaims her.

Every slave and freed slave sitting in the audience would have known
to a penny the exact amount of money the owner wanted for manumission, recognizing the unreality of a plot in which a man pays the very high
price asked for a prostitute and then manumits her: enviable, as portrayed
in *Epidicus* (243–4).[7] Elaine Fantham (1975: 51) attributed such an action
to "infatuation," adducing the real-life case of Neaira, who persuaded her
former and present lovers to chip in with her to buy her freedom. What
such freedom meant from the woman's point of view is spelled out by
Scapha in *Mostellaria*, who says to Philematium, "You're free now. / Now
you have what you were looking for" (*libera es iam. / tu iam quod quaerebas
habes*, 209–10). The former music girl, she argues, need no longer try to
please the man who bought her out of slavery. It is clear, however, both
in *Mostellaria* and in *Persa*, that there are strings attached for the freedwoman, as was true in Roman law for any freed slave, or so we hear from
later jurists.[8] That the freedwoman's predicament had a particular meaning

---

[7] "A common enough practice in Athens," says Adele Scafuro (1997: 414). For a thorough review of the
Greek evidence, see Glazebrook 2014, who points out that such a purchase was viewed as extravagant
(67–71) and deals briefly with *Mostellaria* as a comparandum, closer to Greek than to Roman law.

[8] On freed slaves' *obsequium* (deferential attitude) and *operae* (work owed to the patron as a condition
of manumission), see Bradley 1984: 33, 36, 81, and esp. 39 (on Plautus); Joshel 1992: 34; Treggiari
1969: 68–78. The opinion of the jurist Callistratus (fl. 200 CE) that a slave-woman prostitute's *operae*,
after manumission, cannot consist in prostitution, McGinn argues, means only that such labor does
not count as her *operae*, and may in fact have discouraged owners from manumitting such women
(1998: 305, 330–1). In *Miles Gloriosus* Acroteleutium's job is a matter of course, and Watson notes
that "there is no indication of how developed the law [on *operae*] was in our time" (1971: 55 n. 4). On
the restrictive covenant on the sale of a female slave that she should not be prostituted, see McGinn
1998: 288–319 (not that restrictive). That a freedman's duty (*officium*) to his owner involved sexual
favors was the subject of a joke recalled by the elder Seneca (Richlin 1992b[1983]: 225, 258–9 n. 11 on

for male slaves is suggested by Toxilus' insistence that he, not the pimp, is Lemniselenis' *patronus* (842), although the pimp has addressed her as *liberta* (798) and she addresses the pimp as *patrone* (849). Toxilus wants something more, as he sang when the party began: "This wished-for day / has been granted me today by the gods, since it is permitted for me to put my arms around you, a free woman" (*optatus hic mi / dies datus hodiest ab dis, quia te licet liberam med amplecti*, 773a–74; cf. chapter 4). The desire for an exclusive, freely chosen sexual relationship structures many of the plays (*Asinaria, Bacchides, Casina, Cistellaria, Curculio, Mercator, Miles Gloriosus, Mostellaria, Persa, Poenulus, Pseudolus, Rudens, Truculentus*), seen most clearly in *Cistellaria* and from the woman's point of view; for Planesium in *Curculio*, however, getting free seems to be the main goal, the young man being a means to that end, just as Scapha advises Philematium. The pimp Ballio jeers at Phoenicium for repeatedly declaring she will have the money to pay for her freedom (*iam iamque semper, Ps.* 225): she wants it.[9] For Toxilus, the freeing of Lemniselenis means the chance at a sort of control usually unavailable to slaves; the buying of *contubernales* is well attested in epigraphy, and Toxilus' motives are echoed over two hundred years later by Hermeros' words in the *Satyrica*, "I bought my *contubernalis*, so that nobody could wipe his hands on her <front>" (*Sat.* 57.6, *contubernalem meam redemi, ne quis in <sinu> illius manus tergeret*).[10] In the late Republic, the epitaph of a real (Aurelia) Philematium commemorates her long relationship with her husband, her fellow freed slave, Lucius Aurelius Hermia, from the time she was seven years old – a problem for historians.[11]

The manumissions of Acropolistis, Epidicus, and Messenio are acted out or discussed in detail. Epidicus in his messenger speech to the *senex* Periphanes claims to have overheard two women talking about how lucky

---

[9] *Controv.* 4.pr.10), and indeed the use of slaves by owners left a permanent stigma (Richlin 1993: 533, 535–6, 563).

[9] Compare the plain statement by Habrotonon in Menander's *Epitrepontes* that she wants freedom more than anything (538–49, esp. 548, ἐλευθέρα μόνον γενοίμην, ὦ θεοί): unique in the extant corpus.

[10] The inserted *sinu* comes from Nicolaas Heinsius the Elder; Pieter Burman is credited with the *capillis* now accepted by Smith, Mueller, and Schmeling *ad loc.*, who take Hermeros here to be referring to the same action performed by Trimalchio at 27.6. But that action is presented as part of Trimalchio's outrageous introductory appearance, nor does it appear elsewhere in Latin, and *capillis* is something of a stretch, whereas *sinu* is an easy haplography. In fact Burman in his 1709 edition mooted various possibilities without coming down in favor of any of them; whatever the text originally said, it seems unlikely to have been *capillis*.

[11] *CIL* 1.1221 = 6.9499; British Museum 1867,0508.55. See Treggiari 1981, 1993: 53–4, 124, 232 (the funerary relief is the cover illustration for this authoritative book on Roman marriage). On the relief, see in general Koortbojian 2006; as he points out, Philematium is not an uncommon name in inscriptions. For the intergenerational relationship, cf. Menander *Sikyonios.*

his son's *mulier* is to be freed by him (*Epid.* 236–54). This is a fiction, but the story of how Acropolistis was freed is told again by the unnamed *fidicina*, who claims to know her well (503–9). These episodes, along with Epidicus' (fictive) description of Stratippocles' beloved at the parade accompanied by four *tibicinae*, and the peculiar review of women's dress styles it inspires (217–35), produce the impression of a network of women's friendships in which slave-women and freedwomen cheer each other on, like the friendship among freedwomen enacted and expounded at the start of *Cistellaria*.[12] The freeing of Epidicus has been discussed above (chapter 4); his owner speaks the words *liber esto* right there on the stage (730), and the *grex* approves and asks the audience to applaud (732–33). Messenio is freed onstage twice; the first to do so is Menaechmus I, who cannot legally free him, hence this exchange (*Men.* 1029–32):

> MEN I. mea quidem hercle caussa liber esto atque ito quo voles.
> MES. nemp' iubes? MEN I. iubeo hercle, si quid imperi est in te
> mihi.   1030
> MES. salve, mi patrone. "quom tu liber es, Messenio,
> gaudeo." credo hercle vobis. ...

> MEN I. Sure, as far as I'm concerned, by God, be thou free, and go
> thou where you want to.
> MES. Of course that's your command? MEN I. By God, I command
> it, if I have any right to command you.   1030
> MES. Be well, my *patronus*. "Since you are free, Messenio,
> I rejoice." By God, I believe you. ...

Messenio is holding out for the proper wording. Although Menaechmus I has it partly right – compare Periphanes' *liber esto*, and his sarcastic line to Epidicus, *quom tu es liber gaudeo* (*Epid.* 711) – it is important that the owner use the verb *iubere* and greet the former slave formally by name as a freedman, in order for the process to work.[13] Compare the sarcastic question

---

[12] On women's friendships generally, see Feltovich 2011, James forthcoming *passim*. For a real-life example (two women brickyard workers), see Richlin 2014a: 1–2; and above, chapter 4, on slave friendships onstage. With Acropolistis' doubted manumission, compare the similar chain of comments on the freeing of Phoenicium in *Pseudolus* (225 desire, 419–20 gossip, 1311 *libera*), which perhaps confirms the sequence in *Epidicus*.

[13] There is no trace in any of these scenes of the *festuca*, the rod with which the lictor touched the slave being freed, mentioned with some disdain by the soldier at *Mil.* 961 (*ingenuan an festuca facta e serva liberast?* – freeborn is better); see Nisbet 1918 (highly speculative, but makes an interesting connection between striking the slave, listening, and memory). Nisbet wished for a trace of stage business in onstage manumissions, but no owner says *em tibi, liber esto*. Indeed the whole process was supposed to take place before the praetor, but in the plays this happens only once, when the pimp Dordalus frees Lemniselenis, offstage (*Per.* 483–8); it is wished for by Pseudolus (*Ps.* 358) and Gripus (*Rud.* 927, reading *praetor*); otherwise it is the wrongful owners who are dragged off to see the praetor, or not (*Cur.* 721–3, *Per.* 745–50, *Poen.* 1338–66, 1391–2, 1403). See Watson 1971: 48–9,

put by the fake *atriensis* to the slave Libanus, seen in chapter 4: "Did I hail you as Libanus the freedman today? Are you manumitted now?" (*hodie salvere iussi / Libanum libertum? iam manu emissu'?, As.* 410–11). The formal greeting *iubeo salvere* normally works like an Althusserian interpellation: an act of recognition, with respect, often using the person's name or station. So young Callidamates, aiming to impress his friend's recently arrived father: "I hail you, Theopropides, and that you have returned safely / I rejoice" (*iubeo te salvere et salvos quom advenis, Theopropides, / … gaudeo, Mos.* 1128–9, in combination with the formulaic returned-traveler greeting); or the two prostitutes greeting the priestess they hope will shelter them: "We hail you, mother" (*iubemus te salvere, mater, Rud.* 263); or the old man Philto to his son's bankrupt friend and his slave, "Philto heartily hails owner and slave, / Lesbonicus and Stasimus" (*erum atque servom plurimum Philto iubet / salvere, Lesbonicum et Stasimum, Trin.* 435–6). Onstage the greeting is sometimes used for people the speaker is trying to propitiate; so the guilty Lysimachus greets his wife: "Her husband hails his wife" (*iubet salvere suo' vir uxorem suam, Mer.* 713); so Tranio to the moneylender: "I hail you truly, Misargyrides" (*salvere iubeo te, Misargyrides, bene, Mos.* 568); so the slave Cyamus to the prostitute he has just insulted (*Truc.* 577).[14] Hence the ironic greeting of Cleostrata to her very guilty husband: "I hail you, lover" (*iubeo te salvere, amator, Cas.* 969). Thus when Libanus hails Leonida at the top of his voice (*iubeo te salvere voce summa, As.* 296), he is being mock-polite, picking up on Leonida's use of *iubeo* in a command, five lines previously, and Leonida responds with, "Greetings, workout gym for the whip" (297; chapter 3). At times, the literal sense of *iubere* stirs within the idiom, and this is certainly so in the formula for manumission. Hence Menaechmus I's joke at *Men.* 1030, *iubeo … si quid imperi est in te mihi.* Command belongs to the owner.[15]

At the end of the play, the twins free Messenio together, at his prompting, although he is still dissatisfied with the wording (1148–50):

> MEN II. liber esto. MEN I. quom tu es liber, gaudeo, Messenio.
> MES. sed meliorest opus auspicio, ut liber perpetuo siem.   1149–50

---

where the formulae *liber esto* and *liberum esse iubeo* are associated with testamentary manumission, based on later legal sources without reference to Plautus.

[14] On *Mer.* 713, see de Melo 2010: 97.

[15] For a brief discussion of *iubeo salvere* as a greeting formula, see Poccetti 2010: 126, who treats it as polite but does not comment on its interpellative function or its relation to manumission formulae. He adduces a possible Faliscan parallel, which, with the discussion of *salve* (124–5), "demonstrates that a number of Plautine greeting and politeness formulae date back to a very early period and were shared by other Italic languages."

MEN II. Be thou free. MEN I. Since you are free, I rejoice, Messenio.
MES. But we need a better omen: that I should be *permanently*
    free.   1149–50

He has learned from experience.

Wording is important. The correct formula for recognition in a reunion
scene is outlined by Periphanes in his instructions to Acropolistis: "You
should see your mother, / go up to her, and, as she comes towards you,
give her a greeting and a kiss" (*matrem tuam / videas, adeas, advenienti des
salutem atque osculum, Epid.* 570–1). The kiss, or embrace, and especially
the greeting seem to be key elements in a transition from lost to found,
slave to free, as *salve* means both "hello" and "be well"; it is a command,
like *liber esto*. So long-lost relations greet each other: "Be well, my much-
hoped-for son" (*salve, exoptate gnate mi, Capt.* 1006); "My brother, be well"
(*frater mi, salve, Cur.* 641, 658); "Be well, my sister" (*salve, mea soror, Cur.*
657); "Be well, brother" (*salve, frater, Epid.* 649); "My own twin brother, be
well" (*mi germane, gemine frater, salve, Men.* 1125); "Oh, be well, unhoped-
for one" (*o salve, insperate, Men.* 1132); "Be very well, my father" / "Be well,
my daughter" (*salve multum, mi pater / salve, mea gnata, Per.* 739–40); "My
uncle, be well" (*mi patrue, salve, Poen.* 1076); "Be well, father we could
not / hope for" *salve, insperate nobis / pater, Poen.* 1259–60); "Hoped-for
one, be well" (*sperate, salve, Poen.* 1268); "Be well, my unhoped-for father"
(*salve, mi pater insperate, Rud.* 1175). This is the joke at *Rudens* 1360, when
the pimp greets his long-lost suitcase: *salve, vidule.* And this is the joke at
Poenulus 1141–4, where two lines of Punic draw the explanation, "He greets
his mother, and she greets him as her son" (*matrem hic salutat suam, haec
autem hunc filium,* 1144). Both characters remain enslaved – a passing gesture to the fact that slaves have parents.[16] The formal greeting to the freed
slave, then, evokes this kind of reunion: *hodie salvere iussi / Libanum libertum?* The abstract deity Salus is frequently appealed to in the plays, sometimes in tandem with Fortuna or Spes or Victoria, gods of the fortunes of
war: timely.[17] As in the freedman's meta-greeting *Salve, libertas* (chapter 1),
the greeting marks a rebirth into legal personhood.

The possibility of manumission inspires many more slaves throughout
the plays; those without hope also look to escape, sometimes by more
drastic measures. Slaves in impossible positions think about hanging

---

[16] On the Punic, see de Melo 2012: 219–20.

[17] *As.* 713, 718, 727; *Bac.* 879; *Capt.* 529, 864; *Cist.* 644, 742; *Mer.* 867; *Mos.* 351; *Poen.* 128. Fraenkel
    (2007) points out that Spes, Salus, and Victoria "had long enjoyed a cult in Rome by Plautus' time"
    (155), and argues that a joint cult of Spes and Salus may date back to the Republic (350 n. 22). See
    Clark 2007: 49–69 on the rise of abstract deities in the 200s in connection with social upheavals.

themselves, as does Staphyla (*Aul.* 50–1), who jokes grimly (77–8) that she will make herself into an elongated letter (*litteram / longam*); or the deeply frustrated Chalinus (*Cas.* 111–12, 424–7, 447–8).[18] Others joke about running away (Sceledrus, if only temporarily, *Mil.* 582) or both hanging themselves and running away (Gripus, *Rud.* 1189, 1288); Milphio jokes that running away is more his job than Agorastocles' (*Poen.* 427). Running away is, of course, the central action of *Captivi*, discussed throughout the play, and practiced by Stalagmus as well as Philocrates. *Fugax* is an insult (*Per.* 421), and Curculio calls the Greeks he despises *drapetae* (*Cur.* 290), but the desire to be elsewhere is made fully understandable.[19] Hope of manumission underlies both Leonida's unreal wish ("I'd be willing to be a slave all my life, if I could just find Libanus," *aetatem velim servire, Libanum ut conveniam modo, As.* 274) and Libanus' tacit endorsement of it (275), along with Pseudolus' ironic bet ("Take me away to be your slave, if I don't get this done," *servitum tibi me abducito, ni fecero, Ps.* 520), and also underlies Chrysalus' sarcastic prediction about his own manumission (chapter 3). The malicious wish that a person might be a slave forever appears repeatedly in threats and insults: "that she should be a slave until the day she dies" (*usque ad mortem ut serviat, Epid.* 269); "It's a sure thing / that I'll be made a slave myself rather than ever manumit you" (*certissumumst / mepte potius fieri servom quam te umquam emittam manu, Men.* 1058–9); "you permanent slave" (*perenniserve, Per.* 421). When Palaestrio says he would rather be the soldier's slave than another man's *libertus* (*Mil.* 1356–7), when Epidicus pretends not to want to be manumitted, this is self-evidently false.

Indeed, many slaves voice their hope that they will be freed. Sosia sees a chance of it in his loss of identity, hoping that his owner will not recognize him (*Am.* 461–2):

nisi etiam is quoque me ignorabit: quod ille faxit Iuppiter,
ut ego hodie raso capite calvos capiam pilleum.

Unless he, too, won't recognize me – Jupiter should only make that happen,
so that I'll get my head shaved today and, once I'm bald, put on a *pilleus*.

Here the bodily transformation that marks the transition between slave and free is a mark to be desired. Someone in the probably Plautine

---

[18] "An elongated letter" (reading with de Melo): cf. *Poen.* 838, *cubitum longis litteris* (labels on wine jars); *Rud.* 1294, *cubitum … longis litteris* (a public notice). Hanging will stretch her out and make her message readable.

[19] On suicide, see Bradley 2011b: 377–8; on running away, 367–73.

Cornicula begs another Lydus, calling him "my *pilleus*, my companion, my Healthfulness" (*pilleum meum, mi sodalis, mea Salubritas*, fr. 67–8) – *Salubritas* here, then, a variant on *Salus*. Paegnium is working towards his freedom (*Per.* 286); an entire process of work, savings, and payoff underlies the evaluative term *frugi* and the mentions of being freed "for free" (*gratiis*, *Capt.* 408) or "for a penny" (*Cas.* 316). (Paegnium, as all can see, is being *frugi* by prostituting himself, a painful process, as the *puer* in *Pseudolus* remarks.) Syncerastus wishes not to be the pimp's slave any more (*Poen.* 909). Pseudolus, as seen in chapter 7, when impersonating the trusted Syrus implies that he will be free in future, and this becomes the basis for an exchange of insults (*Ps.* 610–12). He has already, as himself, hinted casually to his young owner that manumission is something desirable: how eager is he to insult the pimp? "I'd never run that fast to the praetor to get myself manumitted" (*numquam ad praetorem aeque cursim curram, ut emittar manu*, *Ps.* 358). Only a figure of speech, since nobody in this play thinks of freedom for Pseudolus, despite his displays of power and the large bag of cash he gets at the end of the play.

One of the cooks in *Aulularia* jokes with Strobilus about the stingy Euclio (309–10):

> censen talentum magnum exorari pote
> ab istoc sene, ut det qui fiamus liberi?   310

> Do you think a thousand bucks could be wheedled
> from that old man, so he'd give it to us so we could become free?   310

Answer: he wouldn't lend you his hunger if you asked for it (311). Sagaristio, pretending to be a Persian slave-dealer, while he is at it pretends to be his own twin brother, on his way to free himself (*Per.* 695–6). Stasimus uses the wish to be free as an example of an impossible desire (*Trin.* 440–1):

> ego quoque volo esse liber: nequiquam volo;   440
> hic postulet frugi esse: nugas postulet.

> I also want to be free; I want it in vain;   440
> this guy might wish he were prudent: he'd be wishing for nonsense.

(Here, speaking to the audience, the slave also insults his owner in terms usually reserved for slaves.) Later in the scene Philto says of Stasimus, as seen in chapter 2, "He's a person; he wants to become free" (*homost: / volt fieri liber*, 563–4). Not only here, and in the wish of the two cooks, but in the deceptive farewell speech of Palaestrio in *Miles*, the change from slave to free is expressed as a process of becoming (*si forte liber fieri occeperim*, *Mil.* 1362).

For all these slaves, their wishes are in the optative mood; but when Trachalio repeatedly reminds Daemones to help him gain his freedom from Plesidippus (*Rud.* 1216–20), his wish will come true (if *liberte* at 1266 can be taken literally; but Gripus' envy seems to confirm it, 1291). And Tyndarus in *Captivi*, who has made his wish for manumission very clear (401–13), presents a serious argument to Hegio about how a slave can earn the right to be manumitted (711–14):

> nam cogitato, siquis hoc gnato tuo
> tuo' servos faxit, qualem haberes gratiam?
> emitteresne necne eum servom manu?
> essetne apud te is servos acceptissumus?

> Just think it over: if any slave of yours should do this
> for your son, what would you think you owed him?
> Would you or wouldn't you manumit that slave?
> Would he not be your very favorite slave?

Hegio, who has been on the verge of having him killed, is partly won over by this argument and has him sent to the quarries instead (715, 721–6; see further below). The play's ending demonstrates that he should have listened harder.

Slaves who have done their owners a signal service, or who have found enough money to buy their freedom, push their hopes and enter into negotiations for their freedom onstage. The problem for the Slave of Lyconides and for Gripus, whose claim to ownership of the suitcase is discussed above (chapter 7), is that neither of them actually owns the money he has found. The Slave of Lyconides announces he will ask for manumission, and then does so: "I'll beg that he manumit me"; "now I want myself to be manumitted" (*orabo ut manu me emittat, Aul.* 817; *nunc volo me emitti manu*, 823). His owner reacts badly: "I should manumit you, / you giant heap of crime?" (*egone emittam manu, / scelerum cumulatissume?*, 824–5). The Slave backs off: just kidding (827), but his final extant line is "Go ahead and kill me, by God, you'll never take [the gold] away from me" (*vel hercle enica, numquam hinc feres a me*, 831).[20] The end of the play is gone, but de Melo believes that the request for some *hallec* to go with the vegetables (fr. v) is the Slave's request to have some extras thrown in with his manumission, like the request Epidicus makes (de Melo 2011a: 351). Gripus, in the long-drawn-out reaches of *Rudens*, negotiates for the *vidulus* twice (1065–1128,

---

[20] Sharrock (2016: 122–5) argues that the Slave at first gives no indication of "what he wants the money *for*," and concludes that in the end he "self-deprecatingly ironised his position, remaining forever subordinate to his master." This is hard to reconcile with line 831.

1227–57) and then tries for a reward for its recovery (1288–1423); throughout the recognition scene he sees Palaestra's success as his own ruin (1161,
1164, 1165–8), and is taunted by Trachalio (1178–9). The *vidulus* has immediately meant manumission to him (925–36a), and he originally plans he
will make a deal for his freedom without explaining where the money
comes from: "I'll go to my owner well rehearsed and trickily. / Bit by bit
I'll promise him the cash for my *caput*, that I should be free" (*ad erum
veniam docte atque astu. / pauxillatim pollicitabor pro capite argentum ut
sim liber*, 928–9; see chapter 2 on *caput*). In the final negotiations, even
after Daemones has said that the reward the pimp has promised the slave
belongs to Daemones as owner (1384–5), Gripus still hopes to get the
money and hand it over "so that he'll manumit me" (*me ut hic emittat
manu*, 1388), and sees *libertas* on the horizon as the pimp weakens (1394).
In the end, Daemones never relinquishes the money, but he does finally
use it to manumit Gripus (1410), possibly signifying that Gripus is free by
inviting him to dinner in the play's last line (1423); in dire straits at the
end of *Mostellaria*, Tranio perhaps has this in mind as he tries for a dinner
invitation (1131–3).[21] It is thought-provoking that the character Cacistus in
Vidularia makes a speech almost identical to one of Gripus' disappointed
cries in *Rudens* (*Rud.* 1167–8 = *Vid.* 63–4); his name, "Worst," suggests that
the role "finder of someone else's treasure" is not unproblematically sympathetic. Or possibly Cacistus is just one of the bad slaves who are heroized
onstage (chapter 6), here, for once, clearly labeled. This would make three
plays featuring treasure as somebody's freedom. Certainly Gripus presents
his claim to the suitcase as a right, and his loss of it as a wrong done to
him. In a long sight gag towards the end of *Rudens*, he comes onstage with
a rusty spit (*verum*) which he proceeds to scour, with much comment, all
building up to the punchline: Pimp: "What's up?" Gripus: *verum exterge-
tur* – "The spit is being scoured," but also "the truth is being wiped" (1304,
initiating a run of shtick).[22]

Messenio, who saves Menaechmus I from being carried off and reu-
nites the twins, has less trouble parlaying rescue into payoff, although
he, too, has to be persistent. Despite his good slave song and his (as it
turns out) continued devotion to his owner, he immediately responds
to Menaechmus I's expression of gratitude with a formal request for

---

[21] Manumission via dinner invitation was not a legal form until the late empire (Lee 1956: 51), but
Daemones' action seems marked, if only in the carnivalesque sense – the pimp, after all, is also invited.
[22] For sight gags in burlesque that, like this one, involve visual puns, see Davis 2011: 99–100.

manumission: "So, by God, if you wanted to do right, owner, you'd manumit me" (*ergo edepol, si recte facias, ere, med emittas manu, Men.* 1023). He continues to insist (1024, "I saved you," *te servavi*; 1028, 1030), until, as seen above, he hears the right words. Unfortunately he has the wrong owner, and, although he repeats his claim to freedom (*te servavi*, 1055), his real owner Menaechmus II denies it. During the recognition scene, Menaechmus II promises manumission conditionally ("Be thou free, if ..." *liber esto, si* ... , 1093); some lines later, Messenio is able to repeat his request again (1146), this time successfully. "It's very fair" (*aequissimum*), says Menaechmus I (1147).

Even more slaves receive at least the promise of freedom onstage; some get it, some do not. Acanthio in *Mercator* (152–3) and Milphio in *Poenulus* (133–4, 420, 429, with garbled oath) are both promised their freedom; both take this skeptically, and indeed Acanthio disappears after line 224. Milphio calls Agorastocles' promise *blanditiae*, "sweet talk," and *gerrae germanae*, "true baloney" (136–7), especially in light of the previous day's flogging (138–9); he continues promoting his owner's plans all the way up the last act and then disappears after line 1154, still a slave, threatening Hanno's slaves with punishment. Moreover, he has himself promised liberty to the pimp's slave Syncerastus in return for his help (910) – a liberty for which Syncerastus has expressed his fervent desire, and which Milphio, despite his success as a plotter, has no power to give. Libanus and Leonida extort groveling babble about manumission from their owner (*As.* 650–3, 689–90) shortly before Libanus climbs on the owner's back and makes him beg, but nothing comes of it, and nothing is just what Leonida expected: "I certainly, by God, have lost no [*patronus*], because I never had one" (*equidem hercle nullum [patronum] perdidi, ideo quia numquam ullum habui*, 622). Compare Milphio on Agorastocles' plea "by your freedom" (*per ... tuam leibertatem*): "Watch it, now you're pleading by nothing" (*em nunc nihil opsecras, Poen.* 420). Some prostitutes are promised freedom only at the price of their sexual industriousness or compliance – "Lucris" (*Per.* 656), Pasicompsa (*Mer.* 531–32); Ballio announces he will be tallying up his prostitutes' take for the day to see who is working hard towards her freedom and who will be sold (*Ps.* 174–6).

Philematium reminds Scapha that she wheedled her freedom out of Philolaches (*Mos.* 221), and he in turn reminds Philematium of how much he paid for her and in what ways she is worth it to him (297–307); in their rapid exchange of ledger shtick, Philematium cracks her mask for a wink, showing the audience that her identification of her own desire with her patron's is an act (297–8):

[PHILEM.] mea voluptas. PHILOL. em istuc verbum vile est viginti minis. PHILEM. cedo, amabo, decem: bene emptum tibi dare hoc verbum volo.

[PHILEM.] … my pleasure. PHILOL. Whoa, that word is cheap at twenty minae.
PHILEM. Just give me ten, lovey: I want to give you that word / cheat you – cheap.

Her riff on the shtick *em istuc verbum* turns it into the *verba dare* that marks the skills of slaves like Tranio (*Mos.* 925, 1073, 1108).[23] The same emphasis is placed on cost when Phaniscus breaks the news of this action to Philolaches' father (970–5), with a specification of the legal process ("he manumitted her," *eam manu emisisse*, 975). The audience sees the wheedling process acted out onstage in *Curculio* and *Poenulus*, where Adelphasium pouts and refuses to let Agorastocles touch her, simultaneously pressing him to pay for her freedom (*Poen.* 350–1, 359–63, 404–5), while Planesium in *Curculio* (between clinches) specifically asks Phaedromus when he is going to pay for her. Planesium's closing words in her first scene put it bluntly: "If you love me, buy me, don't keep asking, and see to it that you make the winning bid" (*si amas, eme, ne rogites, facito ut pretio pervincas tuo*, 213). Using the owner's command seen in chapter 7, she tells Phaedromus not to forget ("see to it that you remember," *facito ut memineris*, 210); she asks him how long she will have to wait (*quo usque* … , 204) and expresses impatience ("too long," *nimium … diu*, 207). In return, Phaedromus promises her he will purchase her and free her, and tells her when (208–9):

ita me Venus amet, ut ego te hoc triduom numquam sinam
in domo esse istac, quin ego te liberalem liberem.

So help me Venus, I'll never let you stay in that house
another three days, before I set you free, you fit-to-be-free girl.

Adelphasium makes a speech to Agorastocles (*Poen.* 359–63) about how often he has promised her freedom, without effect; she is frank about it: "You swore to free me, not once but a hundred times / … / … and so I'm a slave now nonetheless" (*liberare iuravisti me hau semel sed centiens / … / … ita nunc servio nihilo minus*, 361, 363). Milphio then promises

---

[23] For the pickup *istuc verbum* as a joke formula, see chapter 6 above; indeed Philolaches has used it earlier, at 174 and 252. On the meretricious identification of a prostitute's own pleasure with her client's, see chapter 4. On this scene, see James forthcoming; also Gunderson 2015: 130–9 on duty, desire, and money.

(speaking for Agorastocles), "He'll make you an Athenian citizen and also a free woman" (*te faciet ut sies civis Attica atque libera*, 372); this is a continuity error, since the play is set in Calydon, but is also thereby a powerful instance of the use of "Athens" to mean "Rome" in comedy. Adelphasium calls him "a con artist like your owner" (*sycophanta par ero*, 376). In the buildup to the recognition scene, she tells her own father that he can have both her and her sister if he buys their freedom – a double entendre in which only the non-innocent sense is available to her (1218).

Interestingly, Palaestrio in *Miles* is promised his freedom by his owner in much the same words as Planesium is promised hers by Phaedromus. Palaestrio, instructing the witless Pleusicles that they will all embark together for Athens, is told, "And when you get there, / I'll never let you be a slave for three days, without your being free" (*atque ubi illo veneris, / triduom servire numquam te quin liber sis sinam, Mil.* 1193–4). Pleusicles no longer actually owns him – he has been given to his present owner, the soldier, by the *latro* who captured him at sea, and the soldier has given Palaestrio to Philocomasium as a gift (1205) – but the soldier also promises him liberty, somewhat unconvincingly: "Also I'll set you free"; "I'll give you freedom and riches" (*idem ego te liberabo*, 1207; *libertatem tibi ego et divitias dabo*, 1213). In the action of the play, we do not even hear that Palaestrio has boarded the ship, much less been freed; instead, we see him pretend he cannot bear to leave the soldier: "How can I live without you?", "I'm crying because we're being parted" (*quo modo ego vivam sine te?*, 1206; *lacrumo quia diiungimur*, 1328, cf. 1342–3). Many of his parting lines have a double meaning (1354–7, 1358–9, 1362–5, 1366–7); when Palaestrio begs the soldier, "Please remember, if maybe I become free / ... not to desert me" (*quaeso memineris, si forte liber fieri occeperim / ... ne me deseras*), he is planning to be unforgettable, and in a bad way: "Today you will really know the truth" (*verum .... hodie maxume / scies*, 1366–7).[24] He does not think much of either of his owners, preferring the mean and selfish *senex*, over whom he rhapsodizes (649–50, 657–68, 669, 716–17, 725–35, 757, 763), and he has throughout also shown contempt for his fellow slaves in the soldier's house: "This old man has ordered my fellow-slaves' ankles to be broken, / but he's left me out of it; I don't care what he does with those others" (*hic senex talos elidi iussit conservis meis. / sed me excepit: nihili facio quid illis faciat ceteris*, 167–8); (to his fellow slave Sceledrus), "You jump / alone" (*tu sali / solus*, 279–80). This kind of attitude appears elsewhere mainly in the soon-to-be-punctured good slave speeches seen in chapter 6. Sceledrus,

---

[24] See chapter 4 on the freed slave's need for support from the former owner.

as seen in chapter 2, envies Palaestrio's favored position in the household
(348–51), and complains that Palaestrio acts "as if he weren't slaving his
slavery" (*quasi non servitutem serviat*, 482). Palaestrio's pious farewell to the
Lar familiaris and his fellow slaves, then, is particularly hypocritical (1339–
41), and his progress towards freedom is unusually selfish.

The case of Olympio and Chalinus in *Casina* shows the promise of manumission as a tease by a greedy and cruel owner. Olympio, after Lysidamus
treats him as a practice bride, still tries to make his owner slow down;
Lysidamus then uses a promise of manumission to bully Olympio, after
Olympio protests that his owner cannot usurp Olympio's access to Casina
on his very wedding day: "It can happen, / if you think you can be manumitted tomorrow" (*potest, / siquidem cras censes te posse emitti manu*, 473–
4). Earlier, Lysidamus had tried to bribe his son's slave Chalinus with a
similar promise (283–94):

> [LY.] probum et frugi hominem iam pridem esse arbitror. CH. intellego.
> quin, si ita arbitrare, emittis me manu? LY. quin id volo.   284–85
> sed nihil est me cupere factum, nisi tu factis adiuvas.
> CH. quid velis modo id velim me scire. LY. ausculta, ego loquar.
> Casinam ego uxorem promisi vilico nostro dare.
> CH. at tua uxor filiusque promiserunt mihi. LY. scio.
> sed utrum nunc tu caelibem te esse mavis liberum   290
> an maritum servom aetatem degere et gnatos tuos?
> optio haec tua est: utram harum vis condicionem accipe.
> CH. liber si sim, meo periclo vivam; nunc vivo tuo.
> de Casina certum est concedere homini nato nemini.

> LY. I've long thought you were a good and prudent person. CH. That's my
>   understanding.
> If that's what you think, why don't you manumit me? LY. Why not? I'd
>   like to.   284–85
> but there's no point in my wanting it done, unless you help out by deeds.
> CH. What you'd like, that's just what I'd like to know. LY. Listen, I'll
>   tell you.
> I've promised to give Casina as a wife to our *vilicus*.
> CH. But your wife and your son promised her to me. LY. I know.
> But would you rather be a free man and single   290
> or get married and spend your life as a slave – you and your children?
> It's your choice: take whichever option you like.
> CH. If I were free, I'd live at my own risk; now I live at the risk of you.
> About Casina, it's a sure thing that I'll yield to no person born.

Chalinus reacts to his (ultimate) owner's attribution to him of a major
slave virtue (*frugi*) with a direct request for manumission; the *frugi* slave,

as seen in chapters 3 and 6, is the one who saves up to buy his freedom. It all depends on his owner's will (*volo*; *velis*), but the slave still has his own will (*velim*), doomed though it is. His owner in turn reacts with a double threat: no wife plus freedom; wife, plus lifelong slavery for Chalinus and his children (see chapter 4). He gives this to Chalinus as a choice. That Chalinus desires Casina has been established in the opening scene (107–8). Olympio has already taunted him by threatening to have sex with Casina while Chalinus is forced to listen (132–40; chapter 5). Chalinus, then, replies to his owner here with a double message: on the surface, that he prefers to have Lysidamus feed him ([*periclo*] *tuo*); below the surface, that, if free, he would control his own life (*meo periclo*), but that as long as he is a slave, he is under Lysidamus' control. He does not trust Lysidamus, and, once he has found out Lysidamus's plan, he says he could not be hired for three manumissions not to make trouble for Lysidamus and Olympio (*tribu' non conduci possum libertatibus*, 504). He is wise not to trust Lysidamus, who has no intention of freeing anyone; the less perceptive Olympio tells Cleostrata that he can "be made free for a penny," even if she and her son are against it (314–16; *una libella liber possum fieri*, 316). When he gets carried away and acts the owner with Lysidamus, he asks pathetically, "Am I not free? / Remember, remember" (*non sum ego liber? / memento, memento*, 737–8). Indeed, it is precisely the impossibility for a slave of enforcing the promise to manumit that elicits the urgings to "remember" seen in chapter 7. It is the ambiguous promise/threat *te peculiabo* that elicits Paegnium's response that an owner's *fides* is meretricious (*Per.* 192–4), and cynicism about such promises that prompts Chrysalus' sarcastic prediction in *Bacchides* (828–9), as seen in chapter 3. Angling for his dinner invitation, Tranio urges his owner: *promitte* (*Mos.* 1131).

The most poignant promise of manumission in the plays is made by Tyndarus to himself. Speaking to Philocrates while pretending to be Philocrates, Tyndarus promises that Philocrates' father will free Tyndarus (*Capt.* 406–8):

> haec pater quando sciet,
> Tyndare, ut fueris animatus erga suom gnatum atque se,
> numquam erit tam avaru' quin te gratiis emittat manu

> When my father knows this,
> Tyndarus – how you were minded towards his son and him –
> he'll never be so stingy that he won't manumit you for free.

Again note the understanding, in *gratiis*, that manumission normally had to be paid for by the slave. Philocrates never picks up on this promise during their farewell; when he returns, he says he wishes to have Tyndarus back so he can reward him (938–40), but it is Hegio who says he will give Tyndarus to Philocrates "free of charge, that he might be free" (*gratiis … ut sit liber*, 948). The wish for manumission is expressed by the character Tyndarus and then fulfilled by the action of the play itself. The story belongs much more to him than to any of the war captives who were free when captured.

Not all the plays of Plautus work in this way, by any means. All the plays but *Persa* have a free people's story-line as well as a slave story-line, and in *Aulularia, Cistellaria, Menaechmi, Mercator, Trinummus*, and *Truculentus*, the play works mainly to fulfill the desires of free people. Yet even in these plays there are some major statements of the wish to be free: by the Slave of Lyconides in *Aulularia*, by Messenio (freed onstage) in *Menaechmi*. *Cistellaria* deals with freed prostitutes, *Trinummus* cuts to the perspective of the slave Stasimus, and *Truculentus* includes the onstage interrogation of the two *ancillae*. As we go on to look at more fantastical modes of escape, we must continue to ask, whose fantasy is this?

Kings

The slave Gripus sings that he will be called "a king among kings," *apud reges rex* (*Rud.* 931), and his wish makes use of a poignant sense of *rex* as "rich man," although *rex* also evokes the kings of history – or of legend.[25] The plays of Plautus incorporate some historic kings by name: Agathocles of Sicily (*Men.* 409–10, *Mos.* 775, *Ps.* 532), and his line (*Men.* 409–12); Alexander the Great (*Mil.* 777, *Mos.* 775); Antiochus (*Poen.* 694); Attalus (*Per.* 339, *Poen.* 664); Darius (*Aul.* 86); Demetrius (*Cornicula*, fr. 63); Jason (*Ps.* 193); Philip (*Aul.* 86, 704, *Per.* 339); and Seleucus (the founder of Antiochus's dynasty, and also the name of his son; *Mil.* 75, 948–51). Indeed, most of these king names could denote any member of a dynasty, and to an audience in central Italy in the 200s BCE these names would call to mind, among other things, the kings currently in the news: possibly Demetrius II of Macedon (ruled 239–229); Philip V of Macedon, with whom the Romans were at war both during the Second Punic War and immediately afterwards (214–205, 200–196); Attalus I, who ruled from the 230s to 197; Antiochus the Great, who reigned from 223–186, and whose outrageous life is the centerpiece of John Ma's essay on Hellenistic kings

---

[25] The passages reviewed in this section on *rex* (also *regina*) were discussed by Fraenkel (2007: 127–33), whose main conclusion was that they are Roman and not Greek.

(2003). Moreover, these king names are associated with places exotic to a native of central Italy and simultaneously familiar to a substantial number of slaves in this period: the Near East, Macedon, and Sicily. Even if the king references derive from some original Greek text (and Fraenkel did not think they did), the meaning of these kings and their locations would have been considerably different for an audience and players in third-century BCE Italy, as the *palliata* developed. The Near East stands for a particular range of meanings in the plays, associated with trade, conquest, and escape from slavery or poverty. The king names have similar associations. They belong not to comedy or to fable but to the circulation of biographical anecdotes into "popular knowledge," as in the stories dealt with by Rebecca Langlands (chapter 1); the historical mishmosh of kings onstage most closely resembles the kings in the *Life of Aesop* and in the tales of comedians and kings in the *Chreiai* of Machon (Alexandria, mid-200s). In the *palliata*, the named kings belong to the far away.[26]

Speakers in the plays sometimes appear not to have a datable king in mind; rather, each name means "proverbially powerful king." The unnamed Slave of Lyconides in *Aulularia*, clutching Euclio's pot of gold, shows how kings' gold stands for the jackpot, the winning lottery ticket, the ticket out of here (701–4):

> picis divitiis, qui aureos montis colunt,
> ego solus supero. nam istos reges ceteros
> memorare nolo, hominum mendicabula:
> ego sum ille rex Philippus. o lepidum diem!
>
> I alone surpass in wealth the griffins
> who live in the Golden Mountains. Those other kings –
> I don't even want to name them, that bunch of beggarmen:
> I am King Philip himself. Oh charming day!

His words epitomize the associations of kings in the *palliata*: wealth; the exotic East; and the transformation of slave into king – from the very bottom to the very top. Moreover, as in the *Menaechmi* prologue, the Slave here juxtaposes kings and beggars. The "King Philip" he means is Philip II, whose gold coinage clinks through the plays, but Philip's reality here is on the same plane as that of the griffins and the "Golden Mountains": Latin *pix* comes from a variant form of the Greek word "sphinx," here mutated

---

[26] See Richlin 2016, and compare Hägg 2012: 99–147 on "open biography." So, on the *Life of Aesop*, Winkler 1985: 280: "Popular narrative gives famous names to its characters with no thought for chronology and changes them according to the fluctuations of what is currently famous among those with minimal education."

into the gold-guarding griffins located by Herodotus in the land of the one-eyed Arimaspeans. They evoke not only the mythological but the exotic, the Far East – in this case, very far east indeed, between Kazakhstan and China, or at least as far away as Persia, where another character locates the mountains of gold (*St.* 24–5).[27] In this company, the Slave feels he has now become, not just any king, but the king identical with money, and he takes the gold home (712, 823) and tries to use it to gain manumission (816–31). As we have seen (chapter 4, chapter 7), the money for manumission is portrayed in Plautus as identical with the freedom itself: to be a rich man is to be a free man.

Fraenkel pointed to the way in which speeches like the Slave's mix history with myth (2007: 11–12):

> Whether the parallel is taken from myth or history makes no difference to Plautus, as the passage just quoted from *Aulularia* shows, putting both [myth and history] next to each other. … It must further be said that Philip of Macedon, too, is mentioned in Plautus in only very stereotyped expressions. … There is a strong impression that for Plautus he was not the actual king of Macedon, the father of Alexander, but merely the eponym of the *Philippum aurum* … which was familiar to the Romans at an early date, as prosody demonstrates.

He argues here that such seemingly topical references were part of what he calls "Mediterranean lore of the Hellenistic period." Surely a joke like this about Philip II does not belong to those hurt most by Chaeronea (338 BCE), still within living memory as the *palliata* took shape in the early 200s. This joke comes from lower down and far away. It was clear to

---

[27] The griffins are strongly associated with the Scythians, who appear along with the Arimaspeans in the *locus classicus*, Herodotus 3.116 and 4.13–27. For an overview including some ancient sources, see Mayor 2011: 15–53; she locates the home of the griffins amid the gold-bearing sands of the western Gobi Desert "between the Tien Shan and the Altai Mountains" (22), "along the old trade routes from China to the West, from the western Gobi Desert to the Dzungarian Gate" (27). With her sketch maps at 2011: 24 and 28, compare the more detailed map in Narain 1989: 390, and his account of the Greeks of Bactria and India in this period. Fraenkel discusses this passage among instances of the use of "mythological material," also as typically Plautine in its double dose of legend (2007: 55–6); the Arimaspeans and their gold show up in Ennius' satires (see Courtney 1993: 21). Mayor rightly argues that the griffins belong to folklore rather than to mythology; evidently this folklore circulated with trade into Ionia and spread from there. See Roselaar 2012 on Italian traders in Ionia in this period, and, among many mentions of exotic trade in Plautus, the arrival of the ship at *Stichus* 376–89, with its mixed cargo of silver, gold, cloth, purple dye, *lecti* with ivory and gold trim, Babylonian tapestries, slave-women, perfumes, and comedians. For the confusion between griffins and sphinxes in this passage, see Nonius Marcellus 222L; Festus 226L, "*Picati* is the name given to certain <couches?> whose feet are formed to look like sphinxes, because the Dorians call sphinxes φῖκας" (Picati *appellantur quidam <lecti>, quorum pedes formati sunt in speciem sphingum, quod eas* φῖκας *Dori vocant*). Evidently the word for "griffin" (γρύψ) has fallen off its context and has been replaced by something close enough.

Fraenkel that stories circulated not only with the trade in decorated objects from the south to central Italy, but with the trade in human beings: "one must not forget that the numerous Greek slaves and freedmen in Rome had brought with them the wondrous tales of their people and undoubtedly found eager listeners." The tales changed focus and meaning as they traveled (Fraenkel 2007: 66–7). Later cultural commentators complained that upper-class children's minds were warped by the tales told them by their slave caregivers, and, as we have seen, *nutrices* are not only represented within plays as taking their charges to the theater, but also are addressed directly from the stage, in the *Poenulus* prologue, along with the babies they are nursing.[28] "What every child knows" is the basic ingredient of every culture; "the words that by custom / are said to the pimp in comedies, even children know them," as Ballio puts it (*Ps.* 1081–2).

The king names recur in a significantly limited range of contexts. At their most abstract, they show up in the sarcastic *mirum quin* formula as an impossible model, like the King of Sweden in "Minnie the Moocher," or the King of Spain in the nursery rhyme. "Strange that I wouldn't sell you on account of King Philip / or Attalus," says Saturio in response to his daughter's protest at being sold (*Per.* 339–40; see chapter 6); "Strange that Jupiter wouldn't turn me into King Philip / or Dareus on account of you, triple-witch," says the miser Euclio, responding to his slave-woman's protest that they have nothing in the house for her to guard (*mirum quin tua me caussa faciat Iuppiter / Philippum regem aut Dareum, trivenefica, Aul.* 85–6). These kings are fantasy figures and appear here as part of common parlance. In both cases, a relatively recent name is paired with a legendary name: Philip (which one?) with the imposing figure of the king who sent the Magna Mater to Rome in 204 BCE (Livy 29.11, 14); Philip (which one?) with the antique figure of Darius (so also Fraenkel 2007: 12). Each is there to point a sharp contrast with the lowly speaker – a *parasitus*, a poor man; a man selling his daughter for the price of a meal, a man with nothing in his house worth guarding. Kings exemplify what they are not.

Indeed, these kings are directly comparable to the King of Sweden in "Minnie the Moocher" and to Cleopatra, the Sultan of Turkey, and the

---

[28] Complaints about story-telling: Quintilian, *Inst.* 1.8.19, 1.9.2; Tacitus *Dialogus* 29, *at nunc natus infans delegatur Graeculae alicui ancillae, cui adiungitur unus aut alter ex omnibus servis, plerumque vilissimus nec cuiquam serio ministerio adcommodatus. Horum fabulis et erroribus teneri statim et rudes animi imbuuntur*, "But now the newborn child is handed over to some little Greek slave-woman, along with one or the other of the whole group of slaves, often the cheapest one, unsuited for any serious job. With their tales and false beliefs these tender and unformed minds are imbued from the start."

Queen of Sheba in "Willie the Weeper," and the history of these songs illustrates how popular material moves from oral circulation to performance record, from small-time to big-time performers, from adult entertainment to children's, and back again. The Queen gives Willie "a fancy automobile, / with a diamond headlight and a golden wheel"; in some versions she is the Queen of Belgium. In other versions he goes to the "island of Siam" and shoots dice with the King. He had

> a million cattle and a million sheep.
> He had a million vessels on the ocean deep.
> He had a million dollars, all in nickels and dimes;
> well, he knew it 'cause he'd counted them a million times.

The King of Sweden, in Cab Calloway's version of "Minnie the Moocher," buys Minnie "a house of gold and steel, / a diamond car with platinum wheels";

> He gave her his town house and his racing horses,
> each meal she ate was a dozen courses.
> She had a million dollars worth of nickels and dimes,
> she sat around and counted them a million times.

Cattle, ships, coins, and a feast: all would be at home in the *palliata*.

Both songs are about opium addicts and their dreams, and come from African-American jazz culture in the 1920s–1930s, taking on new force with the Depression. "Minnie the Moocher" is well known today from its crossover into the mainstream by way of a Betty Boop cartoon (1932) that was revived in the 1950s for children's television and again in the 1970s when those children grew up and rediscovered drugs; hence the re-use of the song in *The Blues Brothers* (1980). Hugh Laurie sings it in the first episode of *Jeeves and Wooster* (1990), as Stephen Fry chimes in with "ho-de-ho-de ho, sir": spoofing upper-class appropriation, a kind of musical slumming. Cab Calloway's description of how he wrote the song (1976: 111) replicates the way in which the *palliata* recycled old material: he needed a theme song in 1931, he was using "St. James Infirmary" ("In the early twenties Louis Armstrong and Kid Ory made it famous, but nobody knows who wrote it"), he wanted something in the same vein, so he wrote a similar melody and refashioned "Willie the Weeper" ("a song going around at that time … I don't know who wrote it, but it was pretty popular").[29] But both

---

[29] In fact the song was recorded by numerous artists between 1923 and 1927, including Louis Armstrong and Frankie "Half Pint" Jaxon, well attested as a vaudeville singer, comedian, and female impersonator (died in the Los Angeles VA hospital, 1944; see www.redhotjazz.com/jaxon.html).

songs form part of a folk tradition of fantasies about wealth (see further below). As with those fantasies, these have a dark side; similarly, the lines from *Aulularia* and *Persa* about Darius, Philip, Attalus connect directly to hunger and the sale of a daughter into prostitution. They belong to people with no money. At the Cotton Club, which had a "racial policy" that restricted guest admission to whites, while all the performers and staff were black, Minnie's story for the celebrity-filled audience was just another form of slumming; for the chorus girls, paid $35 a week, or the waiters, paid $1 a night, closer to home.[30] So in the *cavea*, where poor and rich sat side by side, jokes about hunger played differently to the hungry.

Onstage, the gold coinage of Philip II is known as *nummi Philippi*, or just *Philippi*, so that "Philips" *are* coins – both coveted and respected. Money, as seen in chapter 3, is constantly coming up in the plays, in a neutral mix of Latin words (*aes*, *argentum*, *libella*) with Latinized Greek (*mina*, *talentum magnum*, *triobolum*) and the generic *nummus*, a Greek word adopted into Latium and evidently circulated back to south Italy and Sicily, from νόμιμος to *nummus* to νοῦμμος: the edges wearing off the word just as coins and people circulated north and south. Rome only began minting its own silver and bronze coins around 300; until 211, even silver and bronze coinage was limited in issue, and even the silver coinage was limited in importance. Meanwhile, southern Italian mints until c. 250 were producing smaller denomination silver and bronze coinage, and thereafter, "from Umbria to Lucania," bronze coinage in large amounts; this must be the economy behind lines like those of the *lena* in *Asinaria* who explains how shopping works: *si aes habent, dant mercem* (*As*. 201), or the prologue

Carl Sandburg included the song in his 1927 collection of American folk songs, with reference to the collecting practice of the great musicologist Robert Winslow Gordon, founder of the Archive of American Folk Song at the Library of Congress ("thirty versions … about one hundred verses different") and to a performer at the University of Alabama; notably, something resembling the scat singing Calloway claims to have invented at the Cotton Club (1976: 113) is already present in Sandburg's score (1927: xi, 204–5).

[30] Pay at the Cotton Club: Harry Sobol, quoted in Calloway 1976: 98. Calloway on décor at the Cotton Club (1976: 88): "The bandstand was a replica of a southern mansion, with large white columns and a backdrop painted with weeping willows and slave quarters. The band played on the veranda of the mansion, and in front of the veranda, down a few steps, was the dance floor, which was also used for the shows. The waiters were dressed in red tuxedos, like butlers in a southern mansion … the whole set was like the sleepy-time-down-South during slavery. Even the name, Cotton Club, was supposed to convey the southern feeling. I suppose the idea was to make whites who came to the club feel like they were being catered to and entertained by black slaves." Calloway on the "racial policy" (1976: 90): "Of course, ordinary folks in Harlem never did get to see the inside of the Cotton Club or the famous Cotton Club revues. … It was wrong. But on the other hand, I doubt that jazz would have survived if musicians hadn't gone along with such racial practices there and elsewhere."

speaker who advises slaves, *aes pro capite dent* (*Poen.* 24). Money was crucial, but the coins themselves came from out of town. Rome rarely struck gold coinage – almost none from the end of the Second Punic War to the time of Sulla – making Philip's coinage doubly exotic.[31] *Philippi* connect the speaker with the big wars and the realm of the golden Orient. The necessary bait for the scam in *Poenulus*, "three hundred golden Philips," is invoked eight times in the play: *aurei trecenti nummi Philippi* (165–6); *trecentos Philippos* (415, 558, 771, 1363); *trecentos nummos Philippos* (670); *aurei / trecenti nummi qui vocantur Philippei* (713–14); *trecentos Philippeos* (781). The Advocati show it to the audience, and explain that this is "comedy gold" (*aurum ... comicum*), used to fatten cattle "in barbarian-land" (*in barbaria*). Funny money, prop money, gold-painted cattle chow, *playing* what is itself a symbol of value.[32] And so the Advocati emphasize: "it's Philip's gold: that's what we'll be pretending" (*Philippum est: ita nos adsimulabimus*, 597–9). Again here, self-location in *barbaria* cues the claim to a despised identity.

With this money the *vilicus* will be able to pretend he is a mercenary soldier (*latro*) just in from Sparta (663–4), where he fought for King Attalus; now he is able to order up for himself the best the pimp has to offer. For, typically, soldiers have *Philippi* (confirming the bona fides of this pretended mercenary): the soldier's *parasitus* in *Bacchides* demands the return of his "two hundred golden Philips" (*ducentos Philippos ... aureos*, 590); the soldier in *Miles* claims to have "more than a thousand bushels of Philip's gold" (*plus ... auri mille ... modiorum Philippi*, 1064), which Palaestrio augments into mountains of silver bigger than Mt. Aetna (1065),

---

[31] On the development of coinage in the 200s BCE, see esp. Burnett 2012 (308 quoted on the range of Italian bronze coinage); Kay 2014: 11, 14, 15–16, 23–4, 44 (tied to "inflows of booty and war indemnities"), 88, 327–8; Mattingly and Robinson 1935 (on *nummus*); Pobjoy 2006: 64–72; also Callataÿ 2015: 24–8, who, however, argues that all coinage in the *palliata* is Attic. Kay (2014: 93) argues that the plays "reveal an urban environment that is highly monetized," but he dates them to the late third/early second centuries. Perhaps the saturation of the Plautine corpus with coin terms suggests monetization earlier, due to the presence in Latium of non-Roman coinage (*argentum*, four pages in Lodge 1926; *nummus*, over a page); cf. *argentum mutuum* in Naevius *Triphallus* (*com.* 96–8 R₃), along with the discussion of debt in chapter 3. Hence the smell of silver on Philematium's hand (*Mos.* 268–9). The relatively few uses of *aes* include *aes alienum* ("debt"), not only at *Cas.* 23 but at *Cur.* 372, *St.* 203; *aera usuraria*, *Truc.* 72. On the word *nummus* see Ernout-Meillet s.v., adducing Varro *L.* 5.173 *ab Siculis*, Festus 178L *nummus ex Graeco nomismate dicitur*.

[32] Cattle chow: possibly fenugreek (*fenum graecum*, "Greek hay"), recommended as cattle feed by Cato (*De agr.* 27), with its golden seeds that, bagged, could pass for gold coins; see Allen 1959 on beans (*faba*) and lupines as stage money. See chapter 2 on beans as poor men's food and the play on *fabuli/ fabulae* in *Poenulus*; stage business in this scene might have included one of the Advocati "eating" some of the "money" (a suggestion I owe to Hans Bork). On symbols of exchange onstage, see Dressler 2016: 18 and Ketterer 1986a: 201, 1986c: 66; cf. chapters 5 and 7 above on props.

evoking Sicily; so Chrysalus aptly brags, in the middle of his big Trojan-War-themed solo, of the "four hundred golden Philips" (*quadringentis Philippis aureis*) and the "two hundred bucks in Philips" (*ducentos / nummos Philippos*) he has inveigled (*Bac.* 934, 969–69a).[33] Earlier, he has said of himself, "This man is worth his weight in gold, this man ought to have a golden statue put up to him" (*hunc hominem decet auro expendi, huic decet statuam statui ex auro*, 640). Curculio, masquerading as a soldier's freedman, says the soldier, on his way back from India, has stopped in Caria to arrange for a seven-foot statue of himself made "out of Philip's gold" (*ex auro Philippo*), a perfect monument to his fantastic conquests (*factis monumentum suis; Cur.* 437–41).[34] The idea of a "golden statue" is proverbial, as when Phaedromus promises the drunken old *lena* a vineyard "instead of a golden statue" (*pro aurea statua*) as a *monumentum* to her gullet (*Cur.* 139–40). The soldier's statue is in the East, like the Golden Mountains in *Aulularia*, or the Arabian City of Gold in *Persa* (*Chrysopolim Persae cepere urbem in Arabia, Per.* 506), or the Persian mountains of gold in *Stichus* (*Persarum / montis, qui esse aurei perhibentur, St.* 24–5).

For a slave, famous kings are a byword for luxury; the disguised *vilicus* in *Poenulus* says he wants to go "where I can be taken care of more delicately / than the eyes of King Antiochus are taken care of" (*ubi ego curer mollius / quam regi Antiocho oculi curari solent*, 693–4). Wealth is similarly associated by slave characters with fantastic accessories. As Chrysalus spins his tale of Theotimus of Ephesus, his owner asks, "Is he rich?" "Can you ask?" says Chrysalus; "a man who's had soles nailed onto his *socci* with gold?" (*qui habeat auro soccis subpactum solum?, Bac.* 332; see chapter 3). Like the rich girl who had diamonds on the soles of her shoes, Theotimus is so rich that he walks on wealth; yet his shoes are the shoes of slaves and comic actors.[35] Masquerading as a slave, Philocrates makes up a

---

[33] Callataÿ remarks on the association between mercenaries and the circulation of gold, but claims that monetized gold disappeared by 270 BCE, along with the *alazon* himself (2015: 28–30); surely not, as the eastern wars rolled on, and the Mercenary War flared up in Carthage (241–237; see below). Five hundred Italian traders were caught there and were brought home by the Roman government (Plb. 1.83.78; Kay 2014: 13 for the significance of their presence).

[34] On honorific statues in this period, see Ma 2013 on "golden" statues (actually gilded), 116–17 ("shiny = valuable," just as "high = mighty"), 253–4; and esp. 55–62, on the meaning of statues in combination with their inscriptions. As noted in chapter 7, the elite monuments Hölkeskamp takes to constitute Rome as a community make no appearance in the *palliata* under the name of those commemorated; instead, the plays project cartoons of them. See below on the "statue on the strait" in the Polla stone, and on the *columna rostrata* of C. Duilius, both of which commemorate the taking of slaves as part of office-holding.

[35] The song "Diamonds on the Soles of Her Shoes" (Shabalala and Simon 1986), on Paul Simon's *Graceland* album, was co-written by Joseph Shabalala, founder of Ladysmith Black Mambazo; although Simon wrote the light-hearted nonsense words in English to go along with the Zulu lyric,

name for his own father (*Capt.* 285): "Treasure-gold-victory, son of gold" (*Thensaurochrysonicochrysides*). Hegio's reply marks him as the straight man, easily gulled: "Obviously he got this name because of his wealth" (*videlicet propter divitias inditum id nomen quasi est*, 286).

Like slaves, *parasiti* associate the *rex* with wealth – in their case, the *rex* is the patron who feeds them, and *rex* takes on the sense of "rich man."[36] Gelasimus in *Stichus* is happy that his patron is finally back home from his trading voyage, and says to the audience, "I've looked over my jokebooks; I'm pretty sure / I can hang onto my king with my funny stories" (*libros inspexi; tam confido quam potis / me meum optenturum regem ridiculis logis*, *St.* 454–5; chapter 3). So the *parasitus* in *Asinaria* fears that, if he does not arrange a timeshare in the prostitute Philaenium for the young man he serves, he will have lost his *rex* (918–19); Philopolemus to Ergasilus is *meu' rex* (*Capt.* 92). As Timothy Moore notes, at the end of the *Menaechmi* prologue, in the list of the characters of comedy who might live behind the onstage door, the *rex* unexpectedly appears; he is sandwiched between *pauper, mendicus, parasitus* – poor man, beggar man, parasite (*Men.* 76; see chapter 7).[37] The missing line that follows should add some mix of slaves and female characters to the list.[38] As seen in Peniculus' speech (chapter 2), the relation of such a *rex* to his dependents is compared onstage to that of owner and slave by the dependents themselves. That the usage belongs to a view from below is suggested by the way it is picked up in later elite texts, especially by Persius in his second *Satire*, where he ventriloquizes a *nutrix*, who prays on behalf of the baby she tends that a *rex* and *regina* may pick him for their son-in-law someday (2.37). The satire speaker views this prayer with contempt; this is her terminology, not one he endorses.

this song, like the rest of Shabalala's catalogue, comes out of the experience of apartheid and poverty, a useful comparative corpus for the *palliata*. Underneath both images lies the fact that mining was the work of slaves in antiquity, and is the work of indigenous men in South Africa. In turn, ancient mines and slave labor produced the raw material for coinage; it was the wars of the late 200s BCE that gave control of mining areas to Rome (Thompson 2003: 156–81; Kay 2014: 43–58).

[36] See Richlin 2016: 72–4 for discussion of the oddity of this usage, with reference to Fraenkel's discussion (2007: 130, 343 n. 101) and to Wright's discussion of *rex* in Naevius' *Tarentilla* (1974: 45–6).

[37] See Moore 1998: 281 n. 28. The pair "beggar/king" is so strong an association that it enables a joke; *Epid.* 223 turns the *regilla tunica* ("straight-woven tunic," Festus 364L) into the "princess dress," opposed to the (joke) *mendiculam* ("beggar dress"). This is what put Telephus on both the comic and tragic stage, as in Aristophanes *Acharnians*; cf. Ennius *Telephus* (chapter 6). For more on the king/beggar opposition, see chapter 2.

[38] Adrian Gratwick attempted to resolve the textual problem outlined by Lindsay in the OCT (1993: 134) by repositioning lines 72–6 after line 10 of the prologue; he is followed by de Melo (2011b: 428), but the suggestion is rightly rejected by Moore 1998: 56, 211 n. 27. The repositioning does not deal with the oddly foreshortened cast of characters in line 76.

The best-known context in which king names appear is in boasting, usually by a central slave, usually making a favorable comparison between his own achievements and those of some Eastern monarch (see chapter 4). Chrysalus in his great rap solo (*Bac.* 925–77, a mix of tr8 and ia8) compares himself to Agamemnon and Ulysses (940, 946, 949–52, 962–5) – not here called *reges*, but perhaps, especially for Agamemnon, the association is felt. Tranio claims his own "immortal deeds" (*facinora immortalia*) will outdo those of "Alexander the Great" and Agathocles (*Mos.* 775–7). As Fraenkel observes, slave characters in these speeches typically express themselves in comparative terms – better, bigger (2007: 5–16, 166). The Slave of Lyconides does the same thing. The distance between slave and king is precipitous; Simo says to Pseudolus that, if Pseudolus brings off his coup, he will outdo King Agathocles in *virtus*, but that, if he fails, there is no reason why Simo, his owner, should not send him to the mill (*Ps.* 531–4).

Next to these grand claims of vying with named kings are the recurring claims to be acting like a king. The Greek/Latin hybrid adverb *basilice* is used repeatedly to denote actions by slaves that escape from the usual bounds: so Toxilus to Sagaristio, "I'm celebrating the Freedom Festival like a king" (*basilice agito eleutheria*, *Per.* 29).[39] This is a joke, and one that goes by really fast: the most famous Eleutheria was the celebration at Plataea of the victory over the Persians, a celebration at which neither kings nor slaves were welcome; to this slave, *eleutheria* means a different kind of freedom, a personal freedom, and *basilice* is how he wants to be. So he says to Sagaristio, "You'll be welcomed with a kingly dinner" (*basilico accipiere victu*, 31); and again, seeing Sagaristio in disguise, "You're costumed like a king" (*exornatus basilice*, 462). Toxilus says to his own slave Paegnium, who is tormenting the pimp, "You brought that off like a king, and in style" (*basilice te intulisti et facete*, 806). Sounding like Toxilus, Agorastocles in *Poenulus* says of his *vilicus* disguised as a mercenary, "He's walking along, costumed like a king" (*basilice exornatus cedit*, 577). Sceparnio in *Rudens*, pushing his luck with Ampelisca, tells her that, if she wants water, she will have to beg, because his labor in digging the well has made him royal: "But I'm like a king: ... / we dug that well at our own risk and with our own tools" (*at ego basilicus sum:* ... / *nostro illum puteum periclo et ferramentis fodimus*, *Rud.* 431–2). A major appropriation of labor as the slave's own; not, however, met with any success here. Chrysalus expresses his power by boasting that he has given his young owner "royal and golden support"

---

[39] See Fraenkel 2007: 130–1, 411 *ad* 131, for thoughts on the development of *basilice* in central Italy as a Plautine, or local, coinage; "in every case ... used with reference to the slave" (131).

(*regias copias aureasque*, *Bac.* 647); the *puer* Pinacium says that even a *rex* will have to get out of his way as he runs in (*St.* 287). In contrast, Simo says disapprovingly of Pseudolus' stance, "How kingly!" (*quam basilicum!*, *Ps.* 458); his attitude here goes along with the critique of the slave as overly self-assured (see chapters 2, 3 on *confidenter*).

Not all the characters who call themselves "king" when successful are slaves. The association for free speakers – most of them lower class – is still the same as that for slaves: wealth, success. Ballio, anticipating great returns of grain from the efforts of his prostitute Hedylium with her customers among the grain merchants, says people will call him "King Jason" (*regem Iasonem*, *Ps.* 193). His wish conflates an actual king of (grain-rich) Thessaly in the generation before Philip II with the Iasion of mythology, recalling Fraenkel's concept of "Mediterranean lore."[40] Ballio is hoping to entertain the *summi viri* and be recognized by them as their equal: "I want to welcome the men at the top like a bigshot, so they'll think I have substance" (*magnifice volo me viros summos accipere, ut mihi rem esse reantur*, *Ps.* 167). More simply, the pimp Lycus, anticipating a big profit on the supposed Spartan mercenary, says, "I am the king" (*rex sum*, *Poen.* 671). *Parasiti* have similar aspirations: so Gelasimus in *Stichus*, hearing of the exotic party goods just landed in his patrons' ship, exclaims, "I'll be reclining like a king!" (*accubabo regie!*, 377). The *parasitus* Ergasilus, anticipating a big reward from Hegio, says, "Now I'm not a *parasitus* but a kinglier king of kings" (*non ego nunc parasitus sum sed regum rex regalior*, *Capt.* 825), and Hegio, listening in, calls his edicts *basilicas* (811), full of *confidentia* (812). The best throw in dice, with which Curculio wins the soldier's ring that means access to Planesium, is the king's throw (*iacto basilicum*, *Cur.* 359). All these instances look to a hoped-for future, different from the present.

Fueling this hope, however, is a certain anger from below. The distance between "kings" on the one hand and slaves and prostitutes on the other is measured by Milphio, jeering at Adelphasium from the sidelines for despising prostitutes who have sex with slaves (*Poen.* 271–4):

> i in malam crucem! tun audes etiam servos spernere,
> propudium? quasi bella sit, quasi eampse reges ductitent,
> monstrum mulieris, tantilla tanta verba funditat,
> quoius ego nebulai cyatho septem noctes non emam.

---

[40] Fraenkel, however, took this King Jason to be "a slip" (2007: 23), an error pasted in as part of an effort to "elevate" the style of Ballio's song; "rich Iasion" comes out of "a rich complex of legends from Hellas" (44). For Jason of Pherae, king of Thessaly in the 370s, see Xenophon *Hellenika* 6.1.5–16: boasting that his country has so much food that he can export grain, 6.1.11; cf. 6.4.29, a donation of a thousand cattle for sacrifice. For this King Jason in political context, see Butler 2010.

[at Adelphasium] Go to hell! You actually dare to scorn slaves,
you shameful thing? [to the audience] As if she were pretty, as if kings
    liked to take her home,
monster woman, she's so little and she's pouring out such big words,
    when I wouldn't buy seven nights with her for a bottle of nothing.

Milphio, however, has no chance of buying any nights with Adelphasium; his attitude towards her contrasts sharply with that of his owner, who immediately bursts into raptures of adoration. The pose of all three is in any case complicated by the presence of the male actor under the female mask, and by the indeterminate status of the actors playing Milphio and his owner. But Milphio's lines identify with the not-kings and expect some in the audience to do the same.[41]

Like Pinacium elbowing *reges* aside as he runs onstage, Milphio is pushing upwards. That this onstage thrust represented real resistance is perhaps suggested by the presence of the runaway slave Spendios as a leader in the Mercenary War (241–237 BCE; see chapter 1), a forerunner of the leaders of the Sicilian slave revolts a century later. As told by Diodorus Siculus, the Syrian slave Eunus in 132 not only proclaimed himself king but took the name Antiochus, in the rising known as the First Slave War; echoing this, the slave leader Salvius in 104 took the name Tryphon, the name taken by a Seleucid usurper in the 140s, while the bankrupt *eques* Titus Minutius, in Capua before 104, costumed himself as a king (Diodorus 34/35.2.24, 36.7.1, 36.2.4). Eunus issued his own coinage, showing his own face, stamped with the words "of King Antiochus" (Shaw 2001: 84); Salvius' name "Tryphon" is probably confirmed by its appearance on one of the sling bullets found in southeastern Sicily (Shaw 2001: 128).

Diodorus had his own agenda, as a Greek intellectual in Augustan Rome, and Liv Yarrow classes his treatment of the Slave Wars among what she calls "Anti-Romes" in his writing; on the repeated presence of lictors and consular trappings amidst the slave-kings' props of Hellenistic kingship, she remarks, "The adoption of Roman symbols of power by those rebelling against Roman authority raises serious questions regarding the identity of the subjected, or at least the historian's understanding of that identity" (2006: 224). An important qualifier; coming from a different angle, Peter Morton (2013) argues that Diodorus' characterization of

---

[41] The idea of catering for an elite clientele perhaps also underlies the prostitute Erotium's recognition of Menaechmus in terms of the genealogy of the kings of Sicily (*Men.* 407–12), and the complacent acceptance of this royalty-by-association by Menaechmus II and the subservient Messenio (412–15). On this passage, see further Richlin 2016: 76.

Eunus as a charlatan wonder-worker and dinner entertainer is part of an overall negative take by an historian who disapproves of *terateia*. Yet in fact Diodorus, no matter how he tsk-tsks, loves *terateia*; the slave uprisings float among the choice gobbets that remain of these books – atrocities and freaks from all over the Mediterranean, savored by the Byzantine excerptor.[42] Side by side we find the tale of Ptolemy Physcon, who (copying Medea) killed his own son, mutilated his body, packed the body in a chest, and shipped it to his sister for her birthday (131 BCE; 34/35.14.1); the tale of the rise and murder of Gaius Gracchus (34/35.24–27, 28a–30); the tale of Antiochus Cyzicenus, King of Syria in 113, who loved *thaumatopoioi* and *mimoi* and learned to manipulate giant animal puppets covered with silver and gold foil (34/35.34.1); and Slave Wars. These war stories, after all, belong to Sicily, Diodorus' homeland, the great entrepôt in the circulation of slaves and comedy.

His attitude does not mean these risings did not happen, and indeed they are well attested in Roman histories and speeches and inscriptions; the very roads were marked with proud commemorations of slave risings crushed. Moreover, accounts of the Slave Wars by others as well as by Diodorus repeatedly say they inspired outbreaks of rebellion elsewhere, as word spread.[43] At the time of the First Slave War, there were risings in Rome, Attica, Delos, and "many other places" (Diod. Sic. 34/35.2.19), also "throughout Asia" (Diod. Sic. 34/35.2.26) and, under another Sicilian leader, a slave from Cilicia, in Acragas (34/35.2.43); specifically in the mines at Athens, at Delos, and, in Italy, at Minturnae, where 450 slaves were crucified, and Sinuessa, where "up to 4,000" slaves rose (Orosius, *Contra Paganos* 5.9.4–5; "the contagion spread," as Augustine's student puts

---

[42] Yarrow provides a trenchant analysis of the social placement of Greek intellectuals in late Republican Rome, especially of those who were commodified through enslavement (2006: 37–44; see also Gowing 2010), and Morton 2013 is very fully documented; neither, however, deals with the part played by the fantastical in Diodorus' writing overall. Despite his main argument, Morton makes thought-provoking connections between the language Diodorus uses of Eunus as wonder-worker, and the vocabulary associated, within Greek historiography, with what is known as "tragic history," the melodramatic, sensationalist history-writing characteristic of the Hellenistic period, and critiqued as such by Polybius (Morton 2013: 245, 247); is Eunus, like Pseudolus, the slave as author?

[43] Roads marked: see the discussion of the Polla stone, with illustration, in Pobjoy 2006: 56–8 (also, briefly, Laurence 2013: 298–9). This stone measures the miles on the road from Nuceria through Capua, to "the statue on the strait," to Rhegium – a road built by a Roman magistrate, who adds: "And when I was praetor in Sicily, I hunted down and returned 917 runaway slaves belonging to *Italici*. And I was the first to see to it that on public land shepherds gave way to plowmen" (Pobjoy's translation). Following arguments by Brennan and Wiseman, Pobjoy connects the stone with the slave risings from c. 135, and takes the ex-praetor to be addressing "an audience of property-owners," and the statue to be of himself. But both were visible to slaves as well as owners; subject to an oppositional gaze. On slave revolts in general, see Bradley 2011b: 364–7.

it). After the death of Attalus III in 133, a pretender, Aristonicus, headed an uprising and called his slave and free poor followers "Heliopolitai" – "Citizens of the City of the Sun" – promising freedom.[44] Leading up to the Second Slave War in 104, small risings took place at Nuceria (thirty slaves) and Capua (two hundred slaves) (Diod. Sic. 36.2.1, 36.2a), while Diodorus delivers a full-blown account of the romantic rising led by Titus Minutius (Diod. Sic. 36.2.2–6, at Capua) or Titus Vettius (36.2a, location unspecified), a rising spurred by the well-born leader's infatuation with a slave-woman and subsequent bankruptcy (he paid seven talents for her): a weird conflation of New Comedy with a Slave War tale. The Second Slave War, too, is said to have set off a rising at the mines at Sounion (Athenaeus, *Deip.* 6.272d–f). As the timeline shows (Appendix 1), slave uprisings took place all over Italy in the 300s and 200s, continuing into the 190s and 180s, when there was a great slave uprising in Apulia (Shaw 2001: 69–78). Word spread: testimony to traffic. Moreover, if it is true, as Diodorus relates, that not only Minutius but Salvius/Tryphon adopted lictors as part of their kingly guise, this is indeed a marked instance of mimetic violence, exported violence; already in the *palliata*, lictors stand for the violence of the state against the slave. Diodorus also says that Eunus' troops staged a mime in which "the slaves acted out their rebellion against their individual masters, casting blame upon them for their arrogance and the way their wanton violence had crossed the line and brought about their own ruin" (34/35.2.46): Herodas turned upside down. Of the First Slave War, Diodorus remarks that the "common crowd" (δημοτικὸς ὄχλος) was happy to see the rich men and their estates fall to the slave armies, the envy caused by their "unequal lot" finally assuaged (ἀνίσου τύχης, 34/35.2.48). In short, his account mixes a period taste for the lurid, indeed dramatic, with the brutal realities that moved thousands of people to a hopeless fight; we may doubt the story of Titus Minutius, but no one doubts what went on in the mines of Laurium. This is the context in which the real Eunus chose to become King Antiochus. *Haec res agetur nobis, vobis fabula.*

Onstage, back in the 200s, the wars are themselves fantastic, and inhabit Alexander's empire. Soldiers in the plays add another perspective to the roster of kings onstage, routinely claiming to have defeated kings in battle. This is seen as a running gag in *Amphitruo*, where Amphitruo is repeatedly said to have killed "King Pterela" (*Pterela rex*) and taken his "golden [ceremonial dish]" (*patera aurea*) as a prize (260–1, 413, 415, 419, 534–5, 746, 760, 769–92); the conjunction of Pterelaos, obscure progenitor of the Teleboans,

---

[44] On Aristonicus and the meaning of a "City of Slaves," see discussion in duBois 2007: 439–44.

with this Roman vessel is evidently there for the sake of the tongue-twister (*Pterela rex qui potitare solitus est patera aurea*, 419).[45] As Stefan Weinstock made clear (1957), the Roman cult of Victoria starting soon after 300 BCE was firmly grounded in the iconography of Alexander and his successors. The soldier in *Curculio* says he has made kings obey him (555–6); the soldier in *Epidicus*, recognizing with awe a famous retired soldier in the *senex* Periphanes, asks if he is the same Periphanes who, in his youth, won "great wealth among the kings" (*apud reges … divitias magnas*, 450–1). The soldier in *Truculentus*, as seen above, has brought back a couple of "queens" (*reginae*) as loot, having laid waste their *patria* (531–2): shades of Alexander. Soldiers lay claim to royal prerogatives in other ways as well; the *parasitus* Artotrogus describes the soldier in *Miles* as "kingly in beauty" (*forma regia*, 10), victor over a general with golden armor (15–16), and his slave Palaestrio says of the soldier that he claims that he surpasses the beauty of Alexander (777). Again, here, the line blurs between the mythic past of Homer (is this Paris?) and the already-legendary past of Greek conquest (is this Alexander the Great?). The king as the measure of relative power relates to the tendency of central slaves to describe themselves as conquering generals (*Bac.* 709–11; *Mos.* 1047–8; *Per.* 753–7; *Ps.* 574–91; cf. Fraenkel 2007: 159–65). Thus when Simia rehearses his impersonation of the soldier's slave Harpax, it is arrogance that he enacts, saying to Pseudolus, "How should I not look down on you, / I, who am famous as a military man?" (*quippe ego te ni contemnam, / stratioticus homo qui cluear?*, 917–18). Pseudolus admires his style: "How he goes, how he carries himself like a bigshot!" (*ut it, ut magnifice infert sese!*, 911). Simia is a slave himself (727–8, 737, 744).

Soldiers also work for kings. The soldier in *Miles* claims to be recruiting mercenaries as a favor to King Seleucus (75–7, 948–50). Someone in the probably Plautine *Cornicula* worked as a mercenary for Demetrius for ten years (fr. 63). The Advocati in *Poenulus* (set in Calydon) make up the story that the *vilicus* has been a mercenary in Sparta, working for King Attalus (663–4); the real Attalus I was active as Rome's ally against Philip V in both the First and Second Macedonian Wars. The Sicyonians, who had already set up a colossal statue to Attalus in their agora, subsequently voted him a golden statue – the kind of thing that inspired the fantasy of the soldier's statue in *Curculio*.[46]

---

[45] See chapter 3, n. 12, on Holliday 2002: 186–8.

[46] Plb. 22.8.10, Livy 26.24.8–11 (helping Rome, 211 BCE); Livy 31.25.1, 31.33.2, 31.44.1–47.3, 32.8.9–16 (helping Rome, 200–198); Plb. 18.16 (the statues at Sicyon). On the first statue, which Polybius says was 10 cubits high (about 15 feet), see Ma 2013: 119. On golden statues, see n. 34 above.

One meaning of these itineraries for slaves and army veterans in the audience is suggested by two speeches of the slave Stasimus in *Trinummus*. He fears what will happen if his owner loses his last field (595–9):

> sed id si alienatur, actumst de collo meo,   595
> gestandust peregre clupeus, galea, sarcina:
> ecfugiet ex urbe, ...
> ibit istac, aliquo, in maxumam malam crucem,
> latrocinatum, aut in Asiam aut in Ciliciam.

> But if this one is sold, it's going to come out of my neck,   595
> I'll have to carry abroad his shield, his helmet, his pack:
> he'll run away from the city, ...
> He'll go there, somewhere, to hell and back,
> to be a mercenary, either to Asia or to Cilicia.

He repeats this fear when all seems lost (718–26):

>   quid ego nunc agam,
> nisi uti sarcinam constringam et clupeum ad dorsum accommodem,
> fulmentas iubeam suppingi soccis? non sisti potest.   720
> video caculam militarem me futurum hau longius:
> at aliquem ad regem in saginam erus sese coniciet meus,
> credo ad summos bellatores acrem – fugitorem fore,
> et capturum spolia ibi illum qui – meo ero advorsus venerit.
> egomet autem quom extemplo arcum [mihi] et pharetram et sagittas
>   sumpsero,   725
> cassidem in caput – dormibo placide in tabernaculo.

>   What will I do now,
> unless I can tie up a pack, fit a shield to my back,
> and have stiffeners fastened to my *socci*? It can't be stopped.   720
> I see I'm going to be a soldier's slave in the near future;
> but my owner's going to throw himself into some king's feed lot;
> I believe that, compared with the top warriors, he'll be a fierce – runaway,
> and that man will seize the spoils – the one who comes to meet my owner.
> But me – as soon as I've picked up my bow and quiver and arrows,   725
> and the helm for my head, I'll be sound asleep in the tent.

This story of exile into a non-Roman army fighting in the Near East would sound both familiar and strange to an audience in the Forum, especially since the armor and pack here could just as well belong to a Roman soldier as to a mercenary. The army on the audience's mind was close to home, and, as seen in chapter 2, normally included slaves, perhaps as body servants, but there are also traces of Italian mercenaries in the East from this period, and there may have been Greek-speaking Italians among the soldiers who turned against Carthage in the Mercenary War.[47] A threat to leave town to take up the life of a mercenary is old shtick from Greek comedy; the young man in Menander's *Samia* decides to pretend he is leaving for Bactria or Caria, contemporary hotspots (627–36). Menander's *Aspis* opens with the return of the slave Daos from a raid in Lycia in which he served alongside his young owner, killed (he thinks) in battle; this is not funny, and Daos is a competent soldier (52–82). In the *palliata*, slaves make a joke of battle. Stasimus will have to fasten "stiffeners" to his *socci* (that is, he will make his comedian's soft shoes into the sturdy boots of a soldier, immortalized for their gouging qualities by Juvenal, 3.248).[48] He will become a soldier's slave, like Harpax in *Pseudolus*, an armor-bearer like Thesprio in *Epidicus* or Chalinus in *Casina*; he expects his owner to sign up with "some king" (*aliquem ... regem*, 722), and lose his battles. He himself, though armed, will be a coward, like Sosia in *Amphitruo* (199–200, 427–32). This stands in contrast to the boasting scenes in which slaves portray themselves as generals and epic heroes; the "coward" speeches are less figurative, though still much more figurative than the soldiering in *Aspis*. The connection between going for a soldier and the loss of land is significant, as will be seen.

Mercurius in the *Amphitruo* prologue describes comedy as the wrong place for kings and gods (61). Certainly characters in Plautine comedy think of kings as what they desire to be, something apart from them and above them. Jupiter, "commander of gods and men" (*imperator divom atque hominum*), commands the star Arcturus (*Rud.* 9); in *Amphitruo*,

---

[47] Elsewhere, the *clipeus* shows up alongside the *machaera*, a sword with Greek associations, as part of the personal kit of soldiers in *Curculio* (574) and *Miles Gloriosus* (1–5), as well as on the tall-tale wish list of the putative baby son of the soldier in *Truculentus* (506). For Italian mercenaries in this period, see Rawlings 2011: 49–50, and Hoyos 2007: 6–8 on the makeup of the forces at Carthage. For the possibility of Roman legionaries with slave body servants in the mid-Republic, see Welwei 1988: 69–74, esp. discussion of the *cacula militaris* in comedy, incl. *Trin.* 721, at 73–4. On soldiers' slaves onstage, class in the army, and the association of *clueo* with military arrogance, see Richlin 2017a.

[48] De Melo takes *fulmentas* at 720 to refer to a change from the flat comic *soccus* to the tragic high soles (2013: 193). *Fulmenta* (f.) appears in Plautus only here, and elsewhere in Latin only at Lucilius 160M, which refers to the feet on a *lectus* in their capacity to raise it up (usually *fulmentum*). But Stasimus is talking about army gear. Compare the use of *praefulcio* at *Per.* 12, *Ps.* 772; elsewhere, *fulcio* means "stiffen, fasten, secure, sustain, uphold." Elizabeth Greene, based on experience with the large amounts of footwear extant from Roman forts in northern Europe, identifies the *soccus* as "a loose ankle-height shoe without much support," laced, rather than slip-on. It had hobnails, as all shoes did but the *carbatina* ("a soleless house shoe"), but was much flimsier than soldiers' boots, which were reinforced (personal communication). See Driel-Murray 1993: 31–7, 2010 for lists of shoe-types. To what extent, however, shoe-types remained stable over the three hundred years that separate Plautus from Vindolanda is a good question; could his *socci* have been soleless, like moccasins, so that the *fulmenta* are soles?

Jupiter describes himself as living "on the top floor" (*in superiore … cenaculo*, 863). The kings of comedy are not the Tarquins, not the cruel tyrants who raped Lucretia and so caused the Republic to be born. They are kings as in the children's game attested by Porphyrio centuries after Plautus: *rex erit qui recte faciet, qui non faciet non erit*.[49] They are rich men as seen by poor men. Expressing your wishes in terms of being king is in this period essentially a non-senatorial attitude: these are not Cato's fantasies.[50] The fantasy of being king is a fantasy of escape upward and outward, an idea which is played out in terms that go beyond the human in Plautus' most fantastical thoughts of escape.

Birds and Cages

Running away had its own verb in Latin; just as *muttio* commonly means "speak under your breath, as slaves do," so *fugio* commonly means "run away from slavery." Hence the joke at *Poen.* 427: Owner: "I'm running away." Slave: "That's more my job than yours" (*fugio. # meum est istuc magis officium quam tuom*). In the joking exchange between two slaves that starts *Epidicus*, a slave says his owner's weapons "ran away" (*transfugerunt*) to the enemy, and then that they "flew away," like magic weapons (*travolaverunt*, *Epid.* 30–5): desertion and escape, both forms of flight. Running away thus has its own imagery, and one that recurs in the traditions of modern slavery. While Frederick Douglass's song used the metaphor of Canaan to represent the state of freedom, slaves in the Middle Passage also used the metaphor of flying to express their longing to go home to freedom, as in Michelle Cliff's autobiographical novel *Abeng*:

> Before the slaves came to Jamaica, the old women and men believed, before they had to eat salt during their sweated labor in the canefields, Africans could fly. They were the only people on this earth to whom God had given this power. Those who refused to become slaves and did not eat salt flew back to Africa; those who did these things, who were slaves and ate salt to replenish their sweat, had lost the power, because the salt made them heavy, weighted down.[51]

---

[49] Porphyrio *ad* Horace *Epist.* 1.1.59; see Horsfall 2003: 46. So Fraenkel 2007: 127. For Jupiter upstairs and gods as "high" onstage, see Slater 2014: 121–2.

[50] Arthur Eckstein, personal communication. The theme of kings as predators is strikingly absent from the *palliata*; contrast the situation in fables, Aesopic as well as Phaedrian, shown in Henderson 2001, and see Richlin 2016: 90–1.

[51] Cliff 1990: 63–4.

The same metaphor appears sometimes in the *palliata*, expressed most vividly in the scene in *Captivi* in which the *lorarius* talks about slavery with
his owner, Hegio: "I'll make myself just like a wild bird" (*Capt.* 123; above,
chapter 2). The oddity of this exchange is better understood in the context
of the other *lorarii* in the plays, so before we consider flying, a look at those
whose job it was to prevent it.

Lorarii onstage do not usually have much in the way of speaking roles,
and are commonly on the receiving end of commands in the imperative
mood.[52] They are comic muscle, like Mr. T, and, like other bit-part players
onstage for extended periods without speaking, they constitute a visual
joke, just as mute prostitutes, *ancillae*, and *pueri* are eye candy (chapter 5).
Turbalio and Sparax, the pair who belong to Daemones in *Rudens* (657),
are in their first scene given a single line, a thick-headed response to the
pimp's search for fire with which to force the two girls off the altar of
Venus: "We have no fire, we live on dried figs" (*nullum habemus ignem, ficis
victitamus aridis*, 764). They are initially summoned to drag the pimp out
of the temple of Venus (*ite ... foras*, 656; *sequimini hac*, 658; *proripite*, 660);
the sound of a fight is reported (661–2); onstage again, they are ordered to
punch the pimp in the face (*pugnum in os impinge*, 710), beat the pimp's
eyes out, or else be beaten themselves (*ni ei caput exoculassitis*, 731), and
fetch some clubs (*i dum, Turbalio, curriculo, affert<o domo> / duas clavas;
propera*, 798–9), and finally are given an elaborate set of instructions for
guarding the girls and the pimp, this time threatened with death if they
do a poor job (807–16). They are ordered to stand one on each side of
the pimp, as if in a scene of *flagitatio*, and indeed with similar phraseol-
ogy (*alter istinc, alter hinc assistite. / assistite ambo sic*, 808–9); if the pimp
addresses the girls, they are to answer (*respondetote*, 814). Accordingly, once
their owner exits, they come to life, with a brisk series of threats and commands of their own (826–36), although the pimp describes them as statues
of Hercules who have somehow come to give orders "like human beings"
(822–3, 829 *ut homines*). Their orders include some of the most common
commands given to slaves: *cave sis infortunio* ("Watch out for bad luck,"
828) and *illic astato ilico* ("Stand right over there," 836). By the end of the

---

[52] On the question of whether *lorarii* existed as a named category in Plautus, see Prescott 1936: 100–3.
The overview here suggests that the slaves labeled *lorarii* in the scene superscripts did have a differentiated function and character type, even though the word *lorarius* does not appear in the text. See
Gellius 10.3.19, where he refers to those *in scaenicis fabulis qui dicebantur "lorarii*," in the course of
explicating a passage in Cato's speech *De falsis pugnis*; he dates the quasi-servile "floggers" assigned
to accompany magistrates in their provinces to the period after the Second Punic War, with a story
about the collusion of the Bruttii. This might at least indicate an antiquarian tradition on the association between this function and co-optation in the middle Republic.

next scene, they are giving advice (*equidem suadeo*) on the girls' safekeeping (879–80), and telling Plesidippus to take the pimp and go (*rape*, 881). Then they vanish inside the house.

The *lorarii* in *Miles Gloriosus* are ordered to drag the soldier in, to string him up and split him if he resists, to beat him with clubs, and to spread-eagle him (*ducite, rapite, facite, discindite*, 1394–5; *verberetur fustibus*, 1401; *feri*, 1403; *dispennite, distendite*, 1407); one of them asks for further directions: "Am I still beating him, or are you letting him off now?" (*verberon etiam, an iam mittis?*), setting up for a pun from the soldier (*mitis sum equidem fustibus*, 1424). They are ordered to release him (*solvite*, 1425). The *lorarii* in *Mostellaria* are ordered to stand behind the door and wait to handcuff Tranio (*astate, manicas ... conectite*, 1064–5). The *senex* Callicles in *Truculentus*, while interrogating the two *ancillae*, is evidently accompanied by *lorarii*, since he commands someone to unbind the women during the scene (*solvite istas*, 838); Sophie Klein (2015: 55) points out the menace of their mute presence onstage from around lines 770–2. Nicobulus in *Bacchides* brings with him the *lorarius* Artamo, and orders him to bind Chrysalus' hands (*constringe ... manus*, 799) and punch him if he says a word (*impinge pugnum, si muttiverit*, 800); exasperated with Chrysalus, Nicobulus orders Artamo, evidently with a silent fellow slave, to take him away and tie him to a column (*abducite, astringite*, 822–3); by the end of the interrogation, Chrysalus is giving orders not only to Artamo (*aperi; ne crepa*, 833) but to Nicobulus (*sequere*, 831; *accede huc tu*, 834), and it is here that he makes the sarcastic remark about his manumission seen in chapter 3 (*Bac.* 828–9). The *lorarii* Colaphus, Cordalio, and Corax in *Captivi* are commanded to bring out the straps (*ite istinc, ecferte lora*) – at which Colaphus asks if they are being sent to gather wood (*num lignatum mittimur*, 658) – and then to handcuff Tyndarus (*inicite huic manicas*, 659), tie his hands tightly (*astringite ... manus*, 667), and take him away to be shackled and led to the quarries (*ducite*, 721; *abducite, iubete, facite deductus siet, dicite*, 733–7; *abducite*, 746), eventually with threats against their own lives (*periistis, nisi ... abducitis*, 749).[53] Presumably they are the ones ordered to bring him back (*ite, ... arcessite*, 950), and presumably they mutely accompany Tyndarus in the final scene. Two of their names, like that of Hegio's freedman Cordalus (735), pun on the floggable hide (*corium*) that marks the slave; *Colaphus* just

---

[53] The connection between leather straps and "wood" perhaps ties in with Allen's theories on the structure of the *nervos* as a wooden collar tightened by straps; see Allen 1896: 62 and *Poen.* 1365 *lignea in custodia*. In that case, this is a joke, not just another dumb-*lorarius* line. But see *Aul.* 413–14 for a joke on firewood and clubs.

means "Punch." In short, *lorarii* display the owner's power onstage, as both its instruments and its objects. When they speak at all, they often say something stupid that underscores their own brute powerlessness, making a joke of a real-life terror. It is a surprise when they speak.

This being so, the two scenes featuring *lorarii* early in *Captivi* are strikingly odd. They enter with Hegio as he instructs one of them on how to rechain the two bound men (110–15): *advorte, indito, demito, sinito*. As seen in chapter 2, the exchange between Hegio and the unnamed chief *lorarius* (116–24) establishes their opposing points of view with regard to slaves' desire for freedom. When the *lorarius* picks up Hegio's simile of the wild bird and claims it as his own (123), Hegio replies that he will then put the *lorarius* into a cage (*caveam*, 124). Later, the captives' first speech will be to the *lorarius* who is guarding them and giving them kind advice on how to survive; he thinks they are planning escape, and says flat out that he will not discourage them if they get the chance (209). When they ask him for privacy in which to speak to each other, he complies, and Tyndarus thanks him and his fellow slaves for giving them that power: "We have the resources for what we want; / you all are putting us in possession" (*quae volumus nos / copia est*; *ea facitis nos compotes*, 217–18). This articulate *lorarius* sets up the message of *Captivi* about the unnaturalness of slavery, and is opposed to Hegio, the Commander, the quintessential owner.

The simile of the wild bird in *Captivi* resonates with other lines in the plays where flight means freedom. Among the jolly tales of massacre told by soldiers is one in *Poenulus*, where the soldier Antamoenides tells the pimp Lycus about how he killed 60,000 flying men in a single day with his own hands (470–87). The pimp is skeptical (475–6):

> LY. an, opsecro, usquam sunt homines volatici?   475
> ANTA. fuere. verum ego interfeci. ...
>
> LY. Excuse me, are there flying men anywhere?   475
> ANTA. There *were*. But I killed them. ...

This battle takes place off the map altogether, in "Pentetronica." The method of killing is both fantastical and ridiculous – slings filled with "great globs of birdlime" (*visci ... grandiculos globos*, 481); the soldier orders the flying men to be "exterminated"; they fall to earth "like pears"; and, as each one falls, the soldier stabs him through the head with one of his own feathers, "like a dove" (*quasi turturem*, 487).[54] The mercenaries in Plautus

---

[54] For resemblances in structure and content between this tall tale and one in Antiphanes' *Stratiôtês* (fr. 200 = Ath. 6.257d–f), see Richlin 2017b: 185. In Antiphanes, the joke is about a king fanned by pigeons as a luxury.

are all unsympathetic characters, and the wholesale slaughter in which they take pride is not admired. Here, not even the pimp Lycus is impressed. This scene of fantastic carnage echoes the real carnage in the spectators' lives, the real destruction of whole populations, the real soldiers dealing with pimps, the real slaves, made so by soldiers, who (male) have nothing to give a pimp, and who (female) belong to a pimp. As for the men who could fly: *fuere*, echoing the line of the Virgo in *Persa*: "I count for nothing everything that was, since it is past" (*omne ego pro nihilo esse duco quod fuit, quando fuit*, 637).

The joke in the soldier's tale here was echoed by P. G. Wodehouse, a great channeler of Plautus, in his story "The Ordeal of Osbert Mulliner" (1928). Here the feckless hero is confronted by a rival in the form of a famous empire-builder:

> Bashford Braddock laughed a short, metallic laugh.
> "Did you ever hear what I did to the King of Mgumbo-Mgumbo?"
> "I didn't even know there was a King of Mgumbo-Mgumbo."
> "There isn't – now," said Bashford Braddock.

Same joke; the speaker intends it to terrify, the recipient is intimidated, the reader laughs at such a blowhard.[55] The postcolonial reader cannot but reflect on the implication of comedy in empire, and the relation of this joke to real exterminations in places with funny names; yet scenes like this attest to a third layer of meaning, as empire produces epic/adventure, and epic produces comedy. So Wodehouse's African explorer is to Allan Quatermain as the comic mercenaries are to, say, the hero of the *Achilles* of Aristarchus, target of the sendup in the *Poenulus* prologue, or to the character of M. Claudius Marcellus in Naevius' lost *Clastidium*, based on the victory of 222 BCE over the Gauls of the Po Valley. Jokes travel. Clastidium is not far from Placentia, founded as a military *colonia* in 218, a joke name

---

[55] The story was first published in Dec. 1928, in *The Strand*; here cited from Wodehouse 2000 [1928]: 196. The obvious parallels between Wodehouse and Plautus are many. Wodehouse denied having read Plautus or Terence in a 1969 letter to the scholar of ancient comedy Peter G. McC. Brown: mentioned, with reservations, in Brown 1986: 72, and quoted in McCrum 2004: 29–30 (identifying Brown only as "a young Oxford don"). The influence on Wodehouse's writing might certainly have been indirect, through the long reception of the *palliata*; in fact, however, during the years when Wodehouse (b. 1881) was a student there (1894–1900), the curriculum of Dulwich College for the forms in which he was enrolled included Plautus *Miles Gloriosus* (Summer 1896), *Rudens* (Michaelmas 1896), and *Menaechmi* ("part," Michaelmas 1897), along with Aristophanes *Peace* and *Knights* in 1899 and 1900. The school was reading Plautus regularly in the upper forms, and Wodehouse might have heard his older brother discussing *Trinummus, Captivi,* and *Mostellaria*. Not *Curculio*; but it is the same joke nonetheless. Wodehouse played a frog in Aristophanes' *Frogs* in 1898, while his brother played the piano (*The Alleynian* 26.188 (July 1898): 186–8). Many thanks to Mrs. Soraya Cerio, Archivist of Dulwich College, for making this information available, and to Peter Brown for the story behind the letter.

in Ergasilus' army of eating in chapter 7. In Rome and in *coloniae*, around 200, the audience included the colonizers and the colonized, who might well have wished they could fly.[56]

When Syncerastus in *Poenulus* wants to escape from the pimp, he complains to Milphio, "It's not easy to fly without feathers; my wings don't have feathers" (*sine pinnis volare hau facilest: meae alae pinnas non habent*, 871). He evidently flaps his arms, and Milphio turns this into a joke about hair in his armpits (*alae*), but the connection between escape and flying is assumed, as in the speech of the *lorarius* in *Captivi*. Flight is challenged by cages: so in *Cistellaria*, the slave-woman Halisca says the *cistella* has flown away (*evolavit*), and the slave Lampadio says she should have put it in a cage (*caveam*, 731–2), leading to the joke about *praeda* and the *grex venalium* discussed in chapter 7. So in *Rudens* the wicked Sicilian tells the audience the pimp will soon be imprisoned and bound, playing on the words for "pigeon," "pigeon-box," and "slave collar" (887–9):

> illic in columbum, credo, leno vortitur,
> nam in columbari collus hau multo post erit;
> in nervom ille hodie nidamenta congeret.

> This pimp, I believe, is being turned into a pigeon,
> since his neck will be in a "pigeon-box" pretty soon;
> he'll be carrying his nest-making kit today into his neck-lock.

Like the *cavea*, the *columbare* is a form of restraint; both are joking names for unfunny objects, like "bracelets" for "handcuffs," and both play on the perception of a prisoner as someone given to flight.[57]

The banker in *Curculio*, faced with Curculio's tale of how he and the soldier conquered fifteen nations and half the world, envisions this conquest, too, in terms of birds and cages (449–51):

---

[56] On *Clastidium*, see Boyle 2006: 50–5; Manuwald 2011: 141; and chapter 4 above on the *praetexta*. With Wodehouse's Bashford Braddock, cf. Groucho Marx as Captain Spaulding in *Animal Crackers* (1930); note the complicating factors of Marx's ethnic identity and of the position of the black actors who carry him in, with his guns – one bearer speaks a line in a mock-African language. (The film remakes the Broadway musical of 1928, book by George S. Kaufman and Morrie Ryskind; down the street, Wodehouse was working on *Rosalie*.)

[57] On this passage, see Allen 1896: 49; for his arguments that, in Plautus' time, *nervos* specifically denoted "a wooden instrument confining the neck," see 1896: 46–52, 60–4. See above, chapter 3, n. 41, chapter 6, n. 22, on animal nicknames for instruments of confinement. In a familiar transfer, *columbare* itself turns into a term of abuse in the possibly Plautine fr. inc. 146, *non ego te novi, navalis scriba, columbare impudens?* ("Don't I know you, you petty officer, you shameless *columbare*?"). Festus explains that the *navalis scriba* was looked down on even among *scribae*, due to the dangers his service was subject to (168L).

    ... quia enim in cavea si forent
conclusi, itidem ut pulli gallinacei,
ita non potuere uno anno circumirier.

    ... Why, even if they were shut up
in a cage, like poultry chicks,
you still couldn't make a round trip around them in a single year.

Here the idea of the imprisonment of war captives is conflated with the image of the supposedly conquered territories as vast tracts of land on an itinerary: map as enclosure.

    Metaphors of hunting and bird-catching are common in ancient literature; when the Advocati call the *vilicus* a pigeon (*palumbem*) they have brought to the wolfish pimp (*Poen.* 676–7), or Adelphasium calls herself Agorastocles' "chick" (*pullus*), threatened by the soldier as "kite" (*milvus, Poen.* 1292–3), or the *lena* Cleareta compares prostitution to bird-catching (*As.* 215–26), they are using stock images of predation that go back to Homer and to Hesiod's fable of the Hawk and the Nightingale. But the image of escape from slavery as flight is not so inanimate a metaphor, and the associated image of the birdcage as prison, as slavery itself, raises questions about the use of *cavea* to mean "audience seating space." Chicken coops both ancient and modern have what one expert refers to as "chicken bleachers": did the term *cavea* refer to the benches on which the audience perched? Was there some kind of lattice-work enclosure around the seating area?[58] Who is in that space, and in what sense are they caged? What had they survived? What would it mean to them to fly away? As seen above, North American slaves told stories of when the people could fly, of flying home to Africa, and metaphors of birds and cages recur in songs and poems of slavery. The wish for wings is a fantasy of the body. In the plays it keeps company with fantasies of place.

---

[58] Thanks to Thomas Vogler (his real name), who also contributes this: Q: Why does a henhouse have just one door? A: Because if it had two, it'd be a coupe. For the *cavea*, cf. Varro, *R.* 3.9.6: "If you want to raise two hundred [chickens], you must give them an enclosed space, in which two big coops joined together should be set up ... there should be a broad window in either one ... made of laths widely spaced so that they give a lot of light, but not so widely spaced that anything can get through them that likes to do damage to chickens. ... In the coops let perches be set close together, so that they can carry all the hens" (*Si ducentos alere velis, locus saeptus adtribuendus, in quo duae caveae coniunctae magnae constituendae. ... in utraque fenestra lata ... e viminibus factae raris, ita ut lumen praebeant multum, neque per eas quicquam ire intro possit, quae nocere solent gallinis. ... in caveis crebrae perticae traiectae sint, ut omnes sustinere possint gallinas*). See Richlin 2011: 86 and 105 n. 40; so also Goldberg 2012, Wiseman 2015: 50–9.

Getting Off the Grid

In Horace's sixteenth *Epode*, the speaker urges his compatriots to join him in an escape from civil breakdown, a voyage to a paradise where crops grow of their own accord (41–56, 61–2):

> nos manet Oceanus circumvagus; arva beata
>   petamus, arva divites et insulas,
> reddit ubi Cererem tellus inarata quotannis
>   et imputata floret usque vinea,
> germinat et numquam fallentis termes olivae   45
>   suamque pulla ficus ornat arborem,
> mella cava manant ex ilice, montibus altis
>   levis crepante lympha desilit pede.
> illic iniussae veniunt ad mulctra capellae
>   refertque tenta grex amicus ubera,   50
> nec vespertinus circumgemit ursus ovile,
>   nec intumescit alta viperis humus.
> pluraque felices mirabimur, ut neque largis
>   aquosus Eurus arva radat imbribus
> pinguia nec siccis urantur semina glaebis,   55
>   utrumque rege temperante caelitum.
> ...
> nulla nocent pecori contagia, nullius astri   61
>   gregem aestuosa torret impotentia.

> The Ocean awaits us, wandering round: let us seek
>   the blessed fields, the fields and the wealthy isles,
> where the unplowed earth returns the grain each year
>   and the unpruned vines bloom on and on,
> and the bough of the unfailing olive buds out,   45
>   and the young fig decks its tree,
> honey drips from the hollow oak, on the high mountains
>   the light creek leaps with rattling foot.
> There the she-goats come unbidden to the milk-pail
>   and the friendly flock brings home its swollen udders,   50
> nor does the bear growl round the pens at evening,
>   nor does the deep earth swell with snakes.
> We'll wonder at more things, happy: that neither the watery
>   southeast wind scours the fields with rain,
> nor are the fat seeds burned in the dry earth,   55
>   because the king of the sky-dwellers moderates both.
> ...
> No blights beset the herd, the summer craziness   61
>   of no star parches the flock.

These lines have been connected by David Mankin (1995) with the renegade general Sertorius, who amid the chaotic wars in the time of Marius and Sulla heard tales of the "Isles of the Blest" from some sailors in Spain and wished to go there himself, to be safe from tyranny and the ceaseless wars – or so Plutarch says (*Sertorius* 8–9).[59] Related wishes structure the story of the runaway slave king Drimakos of Chios, recounted in the *Periplous* of Nymphodorus of Syracuse as "a story that the Chians tell," preserved by Athenaeus in the 200s CE but dating to the late 300s BCE. In this tale, set "a little before our own time," the runaway slaves of Chios formed a community in the mountains, choosing Drimakos as their king for his bravery.[60] He ruled them with scrupulous fairness, striking a treaty with the people of Chios and even measuring what he stole with his own set of weights and measures, and taking only a fair amount. He died by a romantic act of self-sacrifice, benefiting his young *erômenos* who took the reward money and "left Chios to settle back in his homeland." After his death the Chians made a hero shrine to him, where runaway slaves would bring offerings from what they stole; he would appear to Chians in their dreams to warn them against slave plots. This is the legend of a legend, an example of what Emilio Gabba called "false history," a favorite narrative form in the Hellenistic period, with elements of paradoxography and a distinct appeal to what Gabba calls "levels of society other than the élite of the classical *polis*" (1981: 53). Gabba remarks further (1981: 58):

> That period, indeed, saw a proliferation of utopias, in which primitivist longings, already present in fourth century history writing, are combined with philosophical theories and egalitarian leanings. It seems reasonable to argue that they arise in response to social crises of the period; and they offer an account of a Golden Age, located on distant islands, dressed up to suit contemporary tastes.

---

[59] Mankin 1995: 261–2, with further remarks on the Golden Age and the history of utopias before Horace, 262–72. Mankin is here perhaps following Gabba 1981: 59, where Sertorius and Horace's *Epod.* 16 are juxtaposed, although connected only by the context of each in civil wars. See also García Moreno 1992: 143–8 on the relation between the story of Sertorius and the Isles of the Blest in Plutarch and Sallust, and Cynic-Stoic traditions of ideal government.

[60] The story of Drimakos has attracted much attention from historians of slavery (so Finley 1998[1980]: 181–2, in a brief discussion of outlawry and maroon colonies); the story appears in translation in Shaw 2001: 64–6 (Athenaeus 6.265d–66d), and is discussed by Bradley 1989: 38–41, who comments on the location of maroon colonies in hinterlands, an important principle for this chapter. Drimakos is the centerpiece of Forsdyke's discussion of "the culture of subordinate groups in ancient Greece" (2012: 37–89); see also duBois 2003: 26.

Among the utopias Gabba cites are several collected by Diodorus Siculus, alongside his other wonder tales.[61] One was set by Euhemerus on an island in the Indian Ocean (early 200s BCE; no private property); one was set by Iambulus in the far southern ocean (mid-200s; egalitarian); and two were set by Dionysius Skytobrachion (mid-100s) in the far west of Libya (Amazons) and in the Far East (Dionysus hid there). The story of Iambulus in particular is a tale of enslavement that turns out well: on a trading venture to the "spice-bearing part" of Arabia, the well-educated narrator and his men are captured by robbers and made to be herdsmen, then captured by the Ethiopians, and sent off to sea, finally reaching an island paradise where they are warmly welcomed. On each island, a bountiful nature provides easy sustenance.

These faint traces of fantasies of escape from misery into plenty, from injustice to justice, from danger to peace, all contemporary with the *palliata*, are closely comparable with songs and stories found throughout Europe from the Middle Ages through the Depression of the 1930s, like the songs about Minnie the Moocher seen above. When they show up in the record, they are necessarily inflected by the purposes at hand, but they are inherently, as A. L. Morton (1952) said, visions of the "Poor Man's Heaven."[62] Moreover, some of them are connected with actual movement of populations. Jews hoping to escape the poverty, pogroms, and conscriptions of Tsarist Russia spoke of America as the *goldene medina*, the "golden land"; Chinese immigrants to California in the late nineteenth and early twentieth centuries called it *jīn shān*, the Gold Mountain. Drimakos and Sertorius are only dimly visible now, but once, like the mass enslavements and colony foundations of the 200s, they were immediate, inspiring dreams more or less desperate. Fantasies like this were parodied in a satirical song written by the Norwegian journalist Ditmar Meidell in 1853, mocking the failure of the Norwegian colony founded in Pennsylvania by Ole Bull (trans. Blegen and Ruud 1936: 192–8, sel.):

[61] Diod. Sic. 2.55–60 (Iambulus); 6.1, 41–6 (Euhemerus); 3.53.4–6, 3.68.5–69.4 (Dionysius Skytobrachium). The first six volumes of the Loeb translation of Diodorus Siculus (1933–54) were the work of Charles Oldfather, on whom see chapter 1. On Greek folk utopias, see Forsdyke 2012: 55–9 (but cf. duBois 2003: 110, pointing out that some of these utopias still had slaves); and esp. Reckford 1987 on Old Comedy.

[62] Morton 1952: 11–34; discussed in Rammel 1990: 2–3. The Marxist historian A. L. Morton was the author of *A People's History of England* (1938); in *The English Utopia*, he concludes that heaven on earth has been realized in "the Stalin Plans which are now changing the face and the climate of the U.S.S.R." (1952: 213). Morton, who in turn follows his friend, the great English folklorist and folksinger A. L. Lloyd, in a discussion of Oleana (30–1), credits Lloyd for the suggestion that Ibsen took the idea of Gyntiana in *Peer Gynt* from Oleana; see below for the slave Gripus' plan to found a city and name it after himself.

In Oleana, that's where I'd like to be, and not drag the chains of slavery in
Norway.
In Oleana, they give you land for nothing, and the grain just pops out of
the ground. Golly, that's easy.
The grain threshes itself in the granary while I stretch out at ease in
my bunk.
Münchener beer, as sweet as Ytteborg's, runs in the creeks for the poor
man's delectation.
And the salmon, they leap like mad in the rivers, and hop into the kettles,
and cry out for a cover.
Little roasted piggies rush about the streets, politely inquiring if you wish
for ham.
And we all stalk about in velvet suits with silver buttons, smoking
meerschaum pipes which the old woman fills for us.
And she has to sweat and toil and struggle; and if she doesn't do it, she gives
herself a beating.
Aye, go to Oleana, there you'll begin to live! The poorest wretch in Norway
is a count over there.

The violinist Ole Bull in 1852 bought 120,000 acres in Pennsylvania and
persuaded emigrants to move there from Norway, a sample of the mil-
lions who came to the New World as a real-life place outside the grid they
knew. Norway in the mid-nineteenth century was in the grip of a labor
crisis augmented by emigration, the emigrants being mainly poor farmers
(*bønder*); Bull's colony got a big push from the labor movement newspaper
Arbeider-Foreningernes Blad, which predicted that hundreds of thousands
would leave Norway for Oleana. The image of gold recurs in songs from
the period, boosted by the actual gold rush that started in California in
1848, so that the sentiments Bull aroused were expressed in a poem titled
"Bedre End Guld" ("Better Than Gold") and in the song "Amerika, Ole
Bull og det Nye Norge," which begins, "Across the Western Ocean lies a
land rich in gold and virgin forests." So Meidell's satire is reacting to an
already-in-play song tradition, and, ironically, his song became "the most
famous of all the 'America songs'." It was reprinted in 1870 with the following preface: "Let us reprint one of these ballads, which became folk songs
to the extent that young and old, *bønder* and civil servants, workers and
sailors, from one end of the country to the other, sang them."[63]

---

[63] Account of Oleana and its historical context from Blegen and Ruud 1936: 170–241; on Oleana itself,
pp. 176–98, and see Rammel 1990: 20–1, among examples of "fabulous promotion," also based on
Blegen and Ruud. The publication of Blegen and Ruud's book itself reflects the Midwestern pride
in regional roots given voice during the Depression (see chapter 1); Blegen (1891–1969), the son of
Norwegian emigrants, was a leader in Norwegian-American history in Minnesota, and President
of the Organization of American Historians in 1943. On the Norwegian labor movement and

Meidell's satire uses traditional images in a hostile, not a hopeful way – these people are fools – but the motives for their voyage were real; similarly, Horace's sixteenth *Epode* is balanced, but not undercut, by the second *Epode* in his poetry book, with its golden-age view of country life turned to tin by its surprise ending. The moneylender Alfius who turns out to be the speaker (*faenerator Alfius*, 67) cannot testify to the goodness of country life; still, there was nothing imaginary about the wars Horace lived through, and a wish to escape them was based in real misery. In an essay published in a book honoring Herbert Marcuse, Finley dismissed the fantasies of Iambulus and Euhemerus as not true utopias (1967: 6–10): "the traditional dream-fantasies of the oppressed," that is, without a practical political agenda, and Blegen and Ruud (1936) differentiated emigration from the labor movement in that "it was not organized. It had no genius at its head to guide its progress." But they continue, "Nevertheless, it did produce a literature of songs" (1936: 5); and they estimate that three-quarters of a million people left Norway, "a number almost equal to the population of Norway at the beginning of the nineteenth century" (4). Paul Shaner Dunkin saw the Hellenistic visions as "a horde of proletarian Utopias" (1946: 17–18; see chapter 1).

Meidell's satire suggests that the emigrants' egalitarian dreams did not include women's rights ("she gives herself a beating"), although they were certainly in the air in the 1850s: not everybody's paradise. As seen throughout this book, dreams do not escape all the conditions of the dreamer, nor the successive conditions of historical circulation. When Harry McClintock, former hobo and member of the IWW, recorded "The Big Rock Candy Mountain" in 1928, he claimed he wrote it in 1895 and took the images from ideas in circulation among hoboes in the early 1890s – that is, the heyday of the Populist Party, the depths of the rural depression that put the rural poor on the road. Bryan gave his "Cross of Gold" speech in 1896 (see chapter 1). McClintock said in an interview that the version he wrote was a "cleaned up" version of the one he had heard, in which the visions of "cigarette trees" were used by a hobo to seduce a "punk" – a teenaged boy – who rejects the vision in a final stanza, no longer willing "to be buggered sore, like a hobo's whore."[64] The song as McClintock knew

emigration, see Blegen and Ruud's introduction, which describes the social inequities that motivated so many to leave their homes. The translated song was recorded by Pete Seeger in the 1950s and became a children's song, which is how I learned it.

[64] On McClintock and the song, see DePastino 2003: 88–9, Rammel 1990: 10, 26–7, who gives several parallel examples, including one from an ex-slave; on hobo sexuality in general, DePastino 2003: 85–94. For a comparison between "The Big Rock Candy Mountain" and ancient Greek popular fantasy, see Forsdyke 2012: 53–9; she prints the cleaned-up lyrics, without context. The song after

it was a cynical one, rooted in the real circumstances of men on the road; the fantasy, too, belongs to their desires, and a more innocent version of the song may well have circulated alongside the obscene one, as is so often the case, from the dirty blues to children's parodies.

As Frederick Douglass says in the epigraph to this chapter, when he sang about Canaan, he was thinking of the North. The formal similarities of the modern fantasies are obvious; what should be emphasized is that they all come from poor people who want to escape from oppressive conditions: poverty, starvation, homelessness, hard labor, forced labor or conscription, slavery. Significant elements of content recur: no more hard work, cold, rags; good food is so available that it asks you to take it; a poor man could become noble, like the Plautine *rex*; no fear of police or prison; gold. McClintock's story serves as a reminder that desperate circumstances inflect desire: the hobo and the punk belong to destitution. At the time Plautus was writing, Italy was full of slaves and refugees from the places Rome had conquered, some from within Italy, some from Spain, Greece, Illyria, Macedonia, and Carthage; nor were Roman conquests the only source of slaves. The presence of Italian traders in the entrepôts of the eastern Mediterranean from the early 200s onwards implies a flow of slaves between East and West, for slaves were not a segregated cargo.[65] As we will see, fantastic journeys in Plautus take place in the East, which, for all of his listeners, meant "away from here," and for some of them meant "towards home." They brought with them, as Fraenkel said, "the wondrous tales of their people." Moreover, at the time Plautus was writing, the Roman army was not entirely an occupying army, and there were still large areas of the Mediterranean outside of what would become the Roman empire as an administrative entity. There were still territories to light out for.

It is, of course, a great difference between Roman slavery and the slavery Douglass knew, that there was no "North" in the ancient Mediterranean – no line a person could hope to cross, on the other side of which slavery was illegal. Many historians of ancient slavery have held that slavery as a structural element in society was an export of Greeks and Romans as they pushed into other parts of the Mediterranean, where indigenous

McClintock, further cleaned up, was marketed by Little Golden Records in 1949 as a record for children – part of the American folk revival – which is how I learned it.

[65] This presence long predates the Third Macedonian War (172–168 BCE) and the subsequent boom at Delos that caused the Rhodians to complain and Cato to speak on their behalf; see Roselaar 2012: 152–3 ("The examples are endless, attesting to the wide spread of Italians from an Oscan or southern Italian background, all over the Eastern Mediterranean, from the early third century onwards"). See Richlin 2016 on the circulation of comedy alongside goods, including slaves.

cultures did not depend on chattel slavery, but there was no such place, even among, as a reader of Kipling might say, the lesser breeds without the Law.[66] Still, how far across the Tiber did a Roman title run? Finley cites the case of Cicero's runaway slave Dionysius, who "managed to disappear in Dalmatia, not yet under Roman rule and at the moment under invasion by the Romans," noting, however, that not all slaves would have had his resources (1998[1980]: 180). Keith Bradley is surely right to speculate that many slaves who ran away hoped to find freedom "by submerging themselves in the communities in which they had formerly been slaves"; all the more so, surely, in a major urban center like Rome.[67] At the same time, as he says, maroon colonies existed, here and there; in the hinterlands.

The Isles of the Blest and the Isles of the Damned

The utopian societies listed by Emilio Gabba are all set on islands, like the "island of Siam" in "Willie the Weeper." Drimakos' maroon colony is said to have been on the island of Chios, Horace's crew seeks the "wealthy isles," and the big slave wars are on the big island of Sicily. Did islands have a special meaning for slaves? They figure significantly in Plautus' plays. Gabba states that the view of an island as "something apart, untouched by corruption" made it the natural location for utopian fantasies: "It is not surprising that strange phenomena, whether natural or human, tended to be located on islands, distant, inaccessible, apart. The island is the characteristic element in paradoxographical literature" (1981: 57).

A joke in *Trinummus* about the Isles of the Blest (549) suggests an association between islands and fantasy. The slave Stasimus, who fears they will starve without his owner's one remaining field (514), tries to convince the *senex* Philto not to accept it as the dowry for his owner's sister, and turns it into a dystopic tall tale, structured like the hyperbolic descriptions of utopian landscapes, only in reverse:

---

[66] This debate occupies a surprisingly central place in the discussion of ancient slavery, due to a sort of reverse exceptionalism for Greece and Rome as two of the five known "slave societies" in world history – as David Lewis puts it (2017: 48), a "strange mantra," and one that Patterson vigorously countered. The position was strongly maintained by Finley 1998[1980]; often cited, with further discussion by Shaw 1998: 20; D. Thompson 2011 (not an indigenous Egyptian institution). For a well-documented argument that in fact slavery was important throughout the Near East, see Lewis 2011, who points out that sales of Greek slaves northward and eastward into Persian territory were brisk from the 400s BCE onward; also Lewis 2017, in progress (including Carthage).

[67] Bradley 1989: 38; cf. Bradley 2011b: 372 on the point that there was no Roman equivalent to Douglass's "North."

terra quom proscinditur,
in quincto quoque sulco moriuntur boves.   (523–4)
               Accheruntis ostium in nostrost agro.
tum vinum priu' quam coctumst pendet putidum.   (525–6)
             frumenti quam alibi messis maxumast,
tribu' tantis illi minu' redit quam opseveris.   (529–30)
neque umquam quisquamst quoius illic ager fuit
quin pessume ei res vorterit: quoium fuit,
alii exsulatum abierunt, alii emortui,
alii se suspendere.   (533–6)
      fulguritae sunt alternae arbores;
sues moriuntur angina acerrume;
oves scabrae sunt, tam glabrae, em, quam haecst manus.
tum autem Surorum, genu' quod patientissumumst
hominum, nemo exstat qui ibi sex menses vixerit:
ita cuncti solstitiali morbo decidunt.   (539–44)

        When the ground is plowed,
in every fifth furrow the oxen die. (523–4)
       The gateway to Hell is in our field.
Then, before the grapes are ripe, they're hanging rotten. (525–6)
       When the harvest is greatest elsewhere,
this field returns three times less than you've sown. (529–30)
       There never was anyone, ever, who owned this field,
who didn't have things turn out terribly for him; whoever had it,
some went into exile, some died,
some hanged themselves … (533–6)
       Every second tree's been struck by lightning,
the pigs die of quinsy, something terrible,
the sheep are mangy, as smooth as this hand here, look at it!
Then even Syrians, the kind most able to take it,
of all people – there's none of them left who's lived there more than six
      months,
the way they've all died of the midsummer fever. (539–44)

Fields in Horace's sixteenth *Epode* bear bountifully without plowing; the flocks are protected from disease and harsh weather; living is easy. Stasimus' field holds the gateway to hell. Accheruns appears in the Plautine corpus more than once as a hell of torment, especially in Tyndarus' comparison of the quarries to hell. He says he has often seen the tortures of the damned in paintings (*Capt.* 998–1001):

vidi ego multa saepe picta quae Accherunti fierent
cruciamenta: verum enimvero nulla adaequest Accheruns

atque ubi ego fui, in lapicidinis. illic ibi demumst locus   1000
ubi labore lassitudost exigunda ex corpore.

I've seen many times, in paintings, the torments that happen
in Accheruns: but it's the plain truth that there's no Accheruns equal
to the place where I've been, in the quarries. That's the place, right
      there,   1000
where weariness has to be driven out of the body by work.

It is a hell of labor. Tyndarus then makes a bitter joke contrasting the
upupa he was issued in the quarries with the pet birds given to "aristocratic boys" (*patriciis pueris*, 1002–4): birds in cages, birds of torment. Hell
is for the lowly.[68] This concept in turn spawns the kind of joke in which
a slave is called "cudgel hell" (*ulmorum Accheruns, Am.* 1029), the slave's
body being the place where cudgels go to die. It is a good question where
Plautus' audience might have seen "often painted" scenes of the torments
of hell; Fraenkel remarked that "images of the realm of the dead and its
terrors generally occupy a large part of the Roman imagination at the
time of Plautus," and attributed this to Etruscan influence, also taking the
Etruscan tomb paintings as a comparandum for the paintings that Plautus
and his audience might have seen (Fraenkel 2007: 120–1). The 200s BCE
certainly gave the inhabitants of central Italy reason to think about death
and hell; this must, then, have been expressed in public art, as the Dance
of Death decorated churches during the Black Death.

Stasimus' field, moreover, ruins those who work it, sending them to
exile, death, or suicide by hanging – as seen above, a way out for the desperate slave. It is accursed and tainted land – every other tree struck by
lightning, the pigs and sheep diseased; even the tough slaves who work it
can last no more than six months without succumbing to illness. Again, the
slaves are Syrians, suited, as seen above, for hard labor, and too ugly to be
used as personal servants. Stasimus' use of them to mark the utmost ability
to take punishment (*patientissumumst*, 542) is picked up on by Philto to
make a joke in passing on the effeminacy (*patientia*) of Campanians: "But
the Campanian kind / now much outdoes the Syrian kind in taking it" (*sed
Campans genus / multo Surorum iam antidit patientia*, 545–6): a boomerang
joke that arcs back to mark the sexual use of slaves as well. The joke is overdetermined, and, like other ethnic jokes (chapter 7), would resonate differently at different times: Capua was a byword for effete luxury (*Ps.* 146, *Rud.*

---

[68] The translation of *upupa* ("hoopoe") as "pickaxe" goes back at least to John Florio in 1598 (Florio 2013[1598]: 755), but there is no contemporary attestation, nor does *upupa* appear in Cato or Varro; possibly, then, an instrument of restraint? See above on animal nicknames for bonds.

631), but (so Livy says) after the Romans took the city in 210, anti-Roman Capuans were condemned to be sold, with their families, at Rome (*libera corpora quae venum dari placuerat Romam mitti ac Romae venire*, 26.34.11). They would learn what "taking it" meant.

Philto moves on from this rimshot to reinterpret Stasimus' field (547–52),

> sed istest ager profecto, ut te audivi loqui,
> malos in quem omnis publice mitti decet,
> sicut fortunatorum memorant insulas,
> quo cuncti qui aetatem egerint caste suam   550
> conveniant; contra istoc detrudi maleficos
> aequom videtur. ...

> But that field of yours is the one, for sure, as I've listened to you tell it,
> to which it's fit that all the bad men be sent by the state,
> just like the Fortunate Isles they tell about,
> where all the people who've led their lives chastely   550
> get together; contrariwise, it seems fair that evildoers
> be cast out in this field of yours. ...

He interprets the field first as a place where the state should fittingly (*decet*) punish "bad men" (*malos*, 548; *maleficos*, 551), then as an analogue to the mythical Isles of the Blest. The field, then, is a dystopia, the anti-type of a recognized utopia, here probably evoking moral philosophy. Fraenkel took this joke to be a Plautine addition to Philemon's original description of the field, dragged in, a typically vague connection of ideas (2007: 87–8). But the idea of sending men to work the land as a form of punishment permeates the *palliata*; Philto's suggestion is based in the plays' own system and the role of the harsh owner. The exchange balances the country as the place of punishment on earth against the Fortunate Isles where goodness was rewarded after death. And, ironically, for Stasimus, the field represents his hope of staying home rather than having to go to war.[69]

Compare the beginning of *Asinaria* (31–43), where the slave Libanus makes a similarly riddling speech to his owner Demaenetus:

> LI. num me illuc ducis ubi lapis lapidem terit?
> DE. quid istuc est? aut ubi istuc est terrarum loci?
> LI. ubi flent nequam homines qui polentam pinsitant,
> apud fustitudinas, ferricrepinas insulas,
> ubi vivos homines mortui incursant boves.   35

---

[69] Cf. Moore 1998: 85 for these passages as part of a pattern in *Trinummus* that ties its moralizing to a Roman context and undercuts it with comedy and metatheater.

DE. modo pol percepi, Libane, quid istuc sit loci:
ubi fit polenta, te fortasse dicere. LI. ah,
neque hercle ego istuc dico nec dictum volo,
teque opsecro hercle ut quae locutu's despuas.
DE. fiat, geratur mos tibi. LI. age age, usque exscrea.   40
DE. etiamne? LI. age quaesso hercle usque ex penitis faucibus.
etiam amplius. DE. nam quo usque? LI. usque ad mortem volo.
DE. cave sis malam rem. LI. uxoris dico, non tuam.

LI. You're not taking me where stone rubs stone, are you?
DE. What's that? Or where on earth is that?
LI. Where weep the worthless men who grind up grits,
in the cattleproddian, shackleclankian islands,
where dead oxen hit living men.   35
DE. Jeeze, now I get it, Libanus, what place that is –
where grits happen, maybe you're saying. LI. Oh,
God, I don't say that, and I don't want it said,
and, God, I beg you to spit out what you said.
DE. So be it, I'll do my duty to you. LI. Come on, come on, really hock it
    out.   40
DE. Again? LI. Yes, please, God, do it, right from the bottom of your
    throat.
Again, bigger. DE. How long already? LI. Long enough to kill you, I want.
DE. Better watch out – something bad could happen to you. LI. I mean
    your wife, not you.

Again here this elaborate fantastic geography, set as a riddle, forms part of a joking interchange: Q: What are these hellish islands? A: The mill. Then apotropaic spitting by the fantastically obliging owner (*geratur mos*) turns into stage spitting; the slave wishes for the owner to die; the owner threatens the slave; the slave converts the curse to one against the owner's wife. But the weird beauty of the riddling image of the mill, like Philto's "field where all the bad men should be sent," sets it up as a parodic balance for the Isles of the Blest and all the other places where you could, as will be seen, reach Jupiter's throne and visit with Rhadamanthus. And the *polenta* the men are grinding in the mill, here translated "grits," is what the *Graeci palliati* in *Curculio* are eating (295), along with Plautus *Pultiphagonides* (*Poen.* 54): poor people's food. The mill is a place to go, and not a good place. Plautus' *ferricrepinas insulas* echo Naevius' *molae crepitum*, where the shackles jingle (*tintinnabant compedes*, *Com. inc.* 114 R₃), and Ennius' *Caupuncula* chimes in with *molarum strepitum* (4 R₃): loud. Pseudolus' owner Simo plans to make Pseudolus "enroll his name in the *colonia* of Molae" (*ut det nomen ad Molas coloniam*, 1100): how is a move to a military *colonia* like penal servitude? The mill is also likened to military service itself: Sagaristio says, "For a little over a year, / in the mill, I've been the iron-man sergeant in charge of getting beat up," *plusculum annum / fui praeferratus apud molas tribunus vapularis,* to which Toxilus replies, "That's an old tour of duty for you," *vetu' iam istaec militiast tua, Per.* 21–3. Compare Grumio's threat to send Tranio to the *pistrinum*: "You'll fill out the country contingent, the iron-clad kind" (*augebis ruri numerum, genu' ferratile, Mos.* 19).[70] The riddling format again implies an equivalence: how is the army like forced labor?

Conquest

These dystopias have a more numerous counterpart in tales of trade and conquest. As seen in chapter 7, wealthy characters in Plautus engage in strenuous travel around the Mediterranean on the track of lost kin and lovers. Slaves and *parasiti,* on the other hand, tell tales of fantastic voyages off the map, tales which recall the speech of the Slave of Lyconides and the griffins that dwell in the Gold Mountains.

Artotrogus in *Miles Gloriosus,* as he racks up the improbable arithmetic of his soldier's kills, says plainly, "My stomach is making up all these labors" (*venter creat omnis hasce aerumnas,* 33). A battle against "Bumbomachides Clutomestoridysarchides," grandson of Neptune, with his golden armor, in the fields of Curculonia ("Weevillia"), where the soldier also saved the life of Mars (13–16); an elephant wounded in India (25–30); the tally of those slain in a single day, 150 in Cilicia, 100 in Scytholatronia ("Thuggistan"), thirty Sardinians, sixty Macedonians (42–5), absurdly totaling seven thousand (46–7); five hundred in one blow (almost) in Cappadocia (52); and all the women love him (58–9) – these fantasies put food in Artotrogus' mouth. The soldier depends on Artotrogus to remember for him (16, 42,

---

[70] These mill jokes have a long pedigree, appearing in Aristophanes, *Babylonians* (fr. 71 K-A) as well as in Menander (*Aspis* 242–5, the Thracian waiter boasts to the Phrygian Daos that his countrymen, the Getai, are real men, and so fill the mills; *Her.* 1–3, the slave Getas asks Daos if he looks sad because he expects to be sent to the mill in irons, in an opening scene closely resembling the opening of *Persa*; *Pk.* 277–8, Daos and his owner joke about Daos becoming a miller). See Jones 1987: 148, 149, Konstan 2013: 157, for the scene in *Heros,* and esp. duBois 2003: 103–9, V. Hunter 1994: 165–84 on slave punishments in Greek comedy and oratory. Hunter (1994: 171–2, 244 n. 32) discusses the mill as "a kind of jail (*desmôtêrion*) or house of correction (*kolastêrion*) for slaves," comparing it with purpose-built torture-houses in Rome and Brazil. The mills in the *palliata* seem to be conceived rather as places where work of a servile nature is done by slaves condemned to it – perhaps too fine a distinction. See chapter 1 on the different part played by violence against slaves in various forms of Greek and Roman comedy.

48); like those of the soldier in *Poenulus*, his tales demand a very high body count. Like both of them, the soldier in *Truculentus* has conquered widely, picking up exotic loot (clothing, purple, frankincense, balsam, as well as the two Syrian queens) in Syria, Phrygia, Arabia, and Pontus (530–40); he himself is based in Babylonia (84).[71]

The same sorts of fantasies pop out of the mouth of Curculio himself, who has recently run all the way from Caria to Epidaurus, arriving understandably famished (*genua inedia succidunt*, *Cur.* 309), and has been rewarded with food for his brilliant scheme (369). Masquerading as the one-eyed freed slave Summanus (413; he says he has lost his eye in Sicyon, 395), he obliges the banker with an account of where he has been with the soldier he is pretending he serves (437–48):

> [LY.] ubi ipsus? qur non venit? CU. ego dicam tibi:
> quia nudiusquartus venimus in Cariam
> ex India; ibi nunc statuam volt dare auream
> solidam faciundam ex auro Philippo, quae siet   440
> septempedalis, factis monumentum suis.
> LY. quam ob rem istuc? CU. dicam. quia enim Persas, Paphlagonas,
> Sinopas, Arabes, Caras, Cretanos, Syros,
> Rhodiam atque Lyciam, Perediam et Perbibesiam,
> Centauromachiam et Classiam Unomammiam,   445
> Libyamque oram <omnem>, omnem Conterebromniam,
> dimidiam partem nationum usque omnium
> subegit solus intra viginti dies.

> [LY.] But where's the man himself? Why isn't he here? CU. I'll tell you;
> because three days ago we got to Caria
> from India; he wants to donate a solid gold statue there now,
> to be made of gold Philips, and it's to be   440
> seven feet high – as a monument to his deeds.
> LY. And why do that? CU. I'll tell you. Because he beat the Persians, the
>   Paphlagonians,
> the Sinopians, Arabs, Carians, Cretans, Syrians,
> Rhodes and Lycia, Chowdownistan, Getdrunkistan,
> Centaurwarland and Tribal Onetittistan,   445
> the whole coast of Libya, and Igonnascrewyoubad –
> yea, even unto the half part of all nations –
> single-handed, in less than twenty days.

---

[71] Not, in this period, in the city of Babylon. Within Syria (much larger than in the present day), the region of Babylonia, with Seleucia at its center, was in the 200s engulfed in the general chaos of Seleucid rule; the soldier, if at all true to life, will have been imagined as a Macedonian. See Walbank 1981: 123–35, with map on p. 260.

An itinerary by now familiar: he has traveled all over the East, from Caria to India, also taking in two islands in the eastern Mediterranean, the coast of North Africa, and several places not on the map, places full of eating and drinking, mythic battles and epic trickery; the soldier has subjugated all these places in twenty days, which justifies a *monumentum* seven feet high; and, as seen above, the Orient is full of gold, here again the gold coins named after King Philip. Curculio's repeated *dicam* marks the banker as the straight man and the *parasitus* as the funny man; this question-and-answer always sets up for a big lie, and the joke names, much like Sagaristio's pseudo-Persian names (chapter 6), tell the audience and the oblivious banker what Curculio is up to: geography as put-down, geography as power.[72] Conquest lists, like the cult of Victory, belong to the legacy of Alexander; Seleucus in 301 BCE, for example, is said to have taken "Mesopotamia, Armenia, Cappadocia, the Persians, the Parthians, the Bactrians, the Arabs, the Tapyri, Sogdiana, Arachosia, and Hyrcania," pushing his kingdom all the way to the Indus, the most of anyone after Alexander (Appian *Syr.* 11.55). Such lists have a material existence outside the pages of the historians in victory monuments, most pertinently for the *palliata* in something like the *columna rostrata* of C. Duilius: standing in the Forum, it commemorated Duilius' victory as consul in the naval battle of Mylae in 260, and concludes a list of ships sunk, generals humiliated, towns taken, and money captured with the line, "he led [many] [freebo]rn Carthaginians," probably "in his triumph." Reminders of conquest were part of the public transcript all around the temporary stages of the *palliata*; comic conquest lists make them look silly. But more than this: like the actor who played Messenio, the actor who played Curculio/Summanus might have encouraged his audience to use their mental maps by acting out great swoops across the world, away from here, and, this time, out of the world altogether.[73] The East is not just code for "what Rome conquered" in the *palliata*, but a real place where unreal things could happen.

---

[72] For funny man cues, see Richlin 2017b: 187.

[73] The inscription on the *columna rostrata* (sense conjectural due to its fragmentary state): *CIL* I².25 = 6.1300, [*multosque*] *Cartacinie*[*ns*]*is* [*ince*]*nuos d*[*uxit ante*] / [*curum 3*] *eis capt*[. The extant inscription is an Augustan reproduction. For lists as senatorial boasting, see Rosenstein 2006: 370; for comic conquest lists as sendups of senatorial boasting, see Gruen 1996b: 137–40; Hanson 1965: 57–8, 61: "If originally [the *miles gloriosus*] reflected the early Hellenistic mercenary captain, his traits as we meet him in Plautine comedy have become thoroughly congruent with the native Roman general turned world conqueror in Plautus' own time." Rather, shtick evolving in the Hellenistic world took on Roman form and local meaning in Rome, where Alexander's legacy was copied in all seriousness. See Richlin 2016, 2017a, 2017b.

Sagaristio is dressed up as the Persian slave trader when he makes the pimp look stupid. With a similar straight-man/funny-man setup, he launches into his list of names, then explains to the amazed pimp, "That's how the Persians are, we have long names, / very combobulous" (*ita sunt Persarum mores, longa nomina, / contortiplicata habemus, Per.* 707–8). Sagaristio's freedom in the play lies in his costume as a Persian; he is the title character, and, when the play is staged, he often holds the spotlight. His Persian names lay claim to a status he desires for himself, as he exits to carry out his business: as he has told the company, to set his twin brother free (695–6).

To set up the scam, earlier in the play, Toxilus cooks up a letter from his absent owner, puts him in Persia, and imagines what could come from there (*Per.* 503–9, 520–3):

> ego valeo recte et rem gero et facio lucrum
> neque istoc redire his octo possum mensibus,
> itaque hic est quod me detinet negotium.   505
> Chrysopolim Persae cepere urbem in Arabia,
> plenam bonarum rerum atque antiquom oppidum:
> ea comportatur praeda, ut fiat auctio
> publicitus; ea res me domo expertem facit.
> ...
> ist' qui tabellas adfert adduxit simul   520
> forma expetenda liberalem virginem,
> furtivam, abductam ex Arabia penitissuma;
> eam te volo curare ut istic veneat.

> I'm feeling well, I'm doing business, I'm making a profit,
> and I can't get back to town for another eight months or so,
> such is the business that's detaining me here.   505
> The Persians have seized the City of Gold
> in Arabia, an ancient town, full of luxury goods:
> these spoils are being collected for an auction,
> a public one, and that's what's keeping me away from home.
> ...
> The guy who brings this letter has brought with him   520
> a free-type girl – a virgin with a very choice body –
> stolen – she was carried off from deepest Arabia.
> I want you to see to it that she gets sold here.

Every line of this letter expresses a fantasy: "away" means "making a profit" (*lucrum*); the owner will not return for eight months; there is a "City of Gold" in Arabia, "full of good things"; the owner is in on the loot; he is sending some loot to Toxilus to sell; the loot includes "a free-type virgin, with a choice body," stolen from "deepest Arabia" (a place impossibly remote, cf. *Per.* 541, where Toxilus assures the pimp that no one would follow the girl all that way). Compare the American slave story where the owner has gone to "Philanewyork and he won't be back til next Javember."[74] This fantasy, within the play, represents, not Toxilus' freedom, but that of the prostitute Lemniselenis; the dress-up act of Sagaristio and the Virgo, their impersonation of the exotic, will serve to get Toxilus what he wants. The Virgo knows what the bottom line is when she names herself "Lucris."

We never see, in the plays, the dream of a world without slavery. But we do see slaves dreaming of escape into the wide world, where they may turn the tables and rise to be *reges* – rich men – themselves. Gripus, in *Rudens*, in his song about what the suitcase could mean to him, falls into a fantasy of what he would do if he were free (930–37a):

> iam ubi liber ero, igitur demum instruam agrum atque aedis,
>   mancupia,   930
> navibu' magnis mercaturam faciam, apud reges rex perhibebor.
> post animi caussa mihi navem faciam atque imitabor Stratonicum,
> oppida circumvectabor.
> ubi nobilitas mea erit clara,
> > oppidum magnum communibo;
> > ei ego urbi Gripo indam nomen,
> > monumentum meae famae et factis,   935
> > ibi qui regnum magnum instituam.
> > magnas res hic agito in mentem
> > instruere. hunc nunc vidulum condam.
> > sed hic rex cum aceto pransurust
> > et sale sine bono pulmento.

> Now when I get free, then finally I'll organize a field and a house, and
>   slaves,   930
> I'll carry on trade in big ships, I'll be called a king among kings.
> Then, because I want to, I'll have me a ship built and I'll imitate
>   Stratonicus,
> > I'll cruise around the towns.
> > When my reputation gets famous,
> > I'll fortify a big town;
> > I'll give this city the name "Gripus,"
> > a monument to my fame and deeds,   935
> > there I'll set up my big kingdom.
> > I'm working up big things in my mind
> > to organize. Now I'll bury this suitcase.

---

[74] See Abrahams 1985: 291–2; Hurston 1981: 82–3.

> But this king's going to eat a lunch with vinegar
> and salt, without any good meaty bits.

Gripus' plan, like the exploits of onstage mercenary soldiers, emulates Alexander's *epigonoi*; the Stratonicus he takes as his model is certainly the famous musician and comic from the late 300s, but his name means "military victory."[75] Whereas the soldier in *Curculio* (as his pretended freedman pretends) put up a golden monument to himself, Gripus will build a whole town and name it after himself as a *monumentum*: like Alexandria, or Seleucia, or Antioch. More prosaically, he will engage in trade, like Toxilus' owner, or the brothers in *Stichus*, or the title character in *Mercator*, or many of the *senes* in the plays; implicitly, this trade will involve slaves, for, although *Captivi* reproaches Hegio for engaging in an occupation that is not *honestum*, the soldiers and traders often do trade in slaves. Gripus here uses the term *mancupia*, evoking the basic meaning of a slave as something "taken by the strong hand" in war (chapter 7). His travels, like those of Menaechmus II and the fictional soldier in *Curculio*, involve a round trip, a loop, a *periplous*: *circumvectabor* (933). But for now, he is still hungry – a *rex* limited to a poor man's condiments, lacking the *pulmentum* always instanced, as seen in chapter 2, as the special treat desired by hungry slaves and poor men.[76]

Heaven

Not all travel involves conquest and colonization. The unnamed Sycophanta in *Trinummus*, driven by poverty (*egestas*, 847) to a life of lying, bumps into an old man and tells him a story about where he has been with

---

[75] Stratonicus: this cithara-player/poet exemplifies that enduring folk figure, the wandering wise guy; he is the hero of a long string of anecdotes at Athenaeus 8.347f–348a, 348c–352d, mostly excerpted from the *Chreiai* of Machon (Alexandria, mid-200s BCE). The stories place him as a dinner entertainer, performing from Alexandria to Thessaly and as far west as the coast of Aetolia, known as much for his wisecracks as for his playing; see full discussion in Richlin 2016: 85–92. Cf. Anderson 1986, who takes it as a given that neither Plautus nor his audience knew who Stratonicus was, and that Plautus took this unknown name from Diphilus, inferring from the name's meaning "that the man was perhaps one of the great Hellenistic generals" (562): "obvious to all Plautine scholars." Moore rightly observes on this point, "Plautus seems to have been able to take for granted his audience's knowledge of the most famous musicians of the Greek world" (2012: III n. 14), following up on Fraenkel's argument on Italian familiarity with Greek song and dance (2007: 381–2; Moore cites also Benz 2001: 239). Indeed the circulation of performers in this period was contemporaneous with the circulation of audience members, and Stratonicus as popular hero ties the comedian in the slave costume to the slave who sings of sailing away. See Langlands forthcoming on the characteristics of knowledge about exemplary characters.

[76] On the resemblance of this element in Gripus' song to a *parasitos* speech attributed to Epicharmus (Ath. 6.236b), see Richlin 2016: 87.

Charmides. Unfortunately the old man *is* Charmides, and, in cahoots with the audience, he makes the gag play out. The Sycophanta complains that he has come "from Seleucia, Macedonia, Asia and Arabia" (845) – that is, from a city near the Tigris, to the land of Philip, back to Asia again, and down to Arabia; Charmides, however, has actually been in Seleucia (112), and knows the way back, as the Sycophanta does not (937). When fed the straight line "Tell me your name" (883), the Sycophanta says his name is so long it would take a day's journey to get through it (884–6), but the everyday version is *Pax* – "Enough already!" (889). Then he launches into his travelogue, once again replying to the straight man's questions with cues that mark the joke and the lie (928, 931–5, 939–45):

> [CH.] sed ipse ubi est? SY. pol illum reliqui ad Rhadamantem in Cecropio
> [insula].[77]
>
> …
>
> [CH.] quos locos adiisti? SY. nimium mirimodis mirabilis.
> CH. lubet audire nisi molestumst. SY. quin discupio dicere.
> omnium primum in Pontum advecti ad Arabiam terram sumus.
> CH. eho an etiam Arabiast in Ponto? SY. est: non illa ubi tus gignitur,
> sed ubi apsinthium fit ac cunila gallinacea.   935
>
> …
>
> [CH.] sed quid ais? quo inde isti porro? SY. si animum advortes, eloquar.
> ad caput amnis, quod de caelo exoritur sub solio Iovis.   940
> CH. sub solio Iovis? SY. ita dico. CH. e caelo? SY. atque medio quidem.
> CH. eho an etiam in caelum escendisti? SY. immo horiola advecti sumus
> usque aqua advorsa per amnem. CH. eho an tu etiam vidisti Iovem?
> SY. alii di isse ad villam aiebant servis depromptum cibum.
> deinde porro – CH. deinde porro nolo quicquam praedices.   945
>
> [CH.] But he himself, where is he? SY. By God, I left him with
> Rhadamanthus in [the island of] Cecrops.
>
> …
>
> [CH.] What places did you visit? SY. Extremely amazing, amazingly so.
> CH. I'd like to hear about it, if it's no trouble. SY. No, I'm longing to
> tell you.
> First of all we sailed to Pontus, to the land of Arabia.
> CH. Whoa, is there also an Arabia in Pontus? SY. Yes, there is; not the one
> where the incense comes from,
> but where the wormwood comes from, and the chicken oregano.   935
>
> …

---

[77] De Melo accepts Guyet's conjecture *Cercopio*, "Monkeyland." The Cercopes were monkey-like creatures that belong to the stories about Hercules; see Connors 2004: 185–6, and 197–8 on *Trinummus*, where "monkey business is part of the creation of a fictional parallel reality."

[CH.] But what are you saying? Then where did you go? SY. If you'll pay
attention, I'll explain.
We went to the head of the river that rises out of the sky, under the throne
of Jupiter.   940
CH. Under the throne of Jupiter? SY. What I'm saying. CH. Out of the
sky? SY. Right smack in the middle of it.
CH. Whoa, and did you even climb up into the sky? CH. No, we sailed
there in a dinghy,
upstream all the way on the river. CH. Whoa, and did you even see Jupiter?
SY. The other gods were saying he'd gone to the *villa*, to deliver food to the
slaves.
And then after that – CH. Then after that I don't want you to tell any
more.   945

The Orient, for the Sycophanta, is not only full of good things; not only
can you find the just judge Rhadamanthus there; it is the jumping-off point
where you can take a sailboat and sail right up to Jupiter's throne. And the
Jupiter you will find there is envisioned as a slave-owner, but a kindly one,
who has gone down to the *villa* to bring food to the slaves, reversing the
usual flow of goods. This image of Jupiter as a kindly, openhanded owner
is the direct opposite of the picture of the owner as stingy to the slaves,
seen particularly in the opening speech of the *senex* in *Stichus*, and fully
embodied in the character of Euclio in *Aulularia*. The Sycophanta has been
to heaven; which still has slaves.

Over Jordan

Albert Raboteau sums up in *Slave Religion*: "It does not always follow that
belief in a future state of happiness leads to acceptance of suffering in this
world," arguing that, "in the midst of slavery, religion was for slaves a
space of meaning, freedom, and transcendence" (1978: 317–18). The *palliata*, with its dreams of freedom, might have provided a similar space for
slaves in central Italy in the 200s. Eugene Genovese in *Roll, Jordan, Roll*
(1976) moved from a discussion of slave holidays to the scant fragments
of slave satires against owners (see chapter 6). With reservations echoing
those of Frederick Douglass on the "safety valve" nature of such cultural
critique, he marks a transition to a chapter on slave rebellions with this
conclusion (Genovese 1976: 584):

> Oppressed peoples who can laugh at their oppressors contain within them-
> selves a politically dangerous potential … Their more dangerous content
> remains latent so long as the general conditions of life do not generate a
> crisis that heightens their critical thrust and points it to political terrain – a

crisis that upsets the balance within the bitter-sweet laughter and liberates the anger behind the laughter.

This is essentially the argument developed at length by James C. Scott: the hidden transcript, even as it dodges into the public view, is the precondition to rebellion, not (only) a safety valve. "Perhaps the theater is not revolutionary in itself, but it is surely a rehearsal for the revolution": so Augusto Boal. So slaves in the *palliata* mocked their owners; so Eunus staged his mime. As we know, slave uprisings went on throughout the 200s and continued into the 190s. Plautus did not live to see them, but by the 130s, as the "general conditions of life" changed, as Rome's hegemony grew complete and the wealth of the upper classes skyrocketed, and Sicily turned into a vast labor camp, the uprisings turned into wars, and real slave leaders claimed the names of kings. As in the wars that enslaved so many in the first place, thousands of people died, and no one got to go home; nor was slavery abolished. In 71, the road from Capua to Rome was lined with 6,000 crucified slaves.[78] And gradually the *palliata* fades from view.

[78] So Finley 1998[1980]: 166–7: "the need of teaching the slave population as a whole an unforgettable lesson." On a smaller scale, Hegio says, as he sends his son off to the quarries, "I'll teach those other prisoners a lesson: / that none of them should try a deed like that" (*ego illis captivis aliis documentum dabo, / ne tale quisquam facinus incipere audeat, Capt.* 752–3). The play, however, is not teaching the lesson Hegio thinks he is teaching. See Boal 1985: 122. As Page duBois says, alongside the question of empire, "the silences, silences revealed in the invisibility of failed utopian efforts in the historical record must be interrogated as well" (2007: 443).

Conclusion
From Stage to Rebellion

It has been the contention of this book that slaves, not just in Rome but all over central Italy, went to the theater, and that their experiences shaped the early *palliata*, which primarily addressed slaves, freed slaves, and the poor. That the theater itself served as a magical place where slaves had unusual rights is explicitly stated at several points in the plays. The prologue speaker in *Casina* remarks on slave marriage; the love of Toxilus stands at the center of *Persa*; Stichus adjures the audience not to be surprised that *homines servoli* can have a good time. The chief claim of the *servolus* in the plays is to be a *homo*, a person. The places where slaves can have pleasure are like the *loci liberi* seen in chapter 4, and the theater is chief among them.

Fraenkel saw that the *palliata* changed Greek New Comedy by enlarging the roles of slaves. But, circulating to Italy along with the shtick that was their stock in trade, slave and low-class actors made the *palliata*, and the slave characters they made (probably from before Livius Andronicus, and at least through the death of Plautus) do not just take center stage. They joke about their most painful experiences, and, along with poor men, they joke about the hardship of poverty and the fear of debt, using folk forms like *flagitatio* and verbal dueling. They act out the fulfillment of their most forbidden desires, chastising their owners and, at least for male slaves, sometimes gaining access to sex. They both act out the particular horrors of slavery for women and, as actors under the mask, joke about what slavery did to masculinity, at the same time carving out a space for the unspoken expression of male slaves' desires for other male slaves, even for male owners. How much of what was unspoken was plainly conveyed by voice and body language, we can only guess from hints in the wording. Slave characters share with their audience the communal memory of the losses entailed by war and slavery; they share the memory of the way back down the road and across the sea. They act out and sing about the dream of liberty, both through manumission and through fantastical escape. They speak truth to power, so that the whole *palliata* becomes an act of *quiritatio*: fellow countrymen, stand by us!

They were playing to an audience that had a lot to be angry about, an audience that had suffered greatly, just as the actors had who walked with their cart full of props and gear through the ravaged landscape of Italy in the 200s. And then things changed; the plays of Terence in the 160s bear eloquent testimony to the kind of change it was, for the *palliata* is now a Menandrian revival, and the language is suddenly subdued, and the slave is upstaged.

Let us return to the curious story of an incident that took place in the First Sicilian Slave War in 132, fifty years after Plautus' death, that shows slaves using comedy as open critique. According to Diodorus Siculus – something of a dramatist himself, as seen in chapter 8 – Eunus, the leader of the uprising, drew up his troops near the walls of a town and staged a performance (Diod. Sic. 34/35.2.46):

> Ὅτι ὁ Εὔνους ἐκτὸς βέλους ἐπιστήσας τὴν δύναμιν ἐβλασφήμει τοὺς Ῥωμαίους, ἀποφαινόμενος οὐχ ἑαυτοὺς ἀλλ' ἐκείνους εἶναι δραπέτας τῶν κινδύνων. μίμους δὲ ἐξ ἀποστάσεως τοῖς ἔνδον ἐπεδείκνυτο, δι' ὧν οἱ δοῦλοι τὰς ἀπὸ τῶν ἰδίων κυρίων ἀποστασίας ἐξεθεάτριζον, ὀνειδίζοντες αὐτῶν τὴν ὑπερηφανίαν καὶ τὴν ὑπερβολὴν τῆς εἰς τὸν ὄλεθρον προαγούσης ὕβρεως.

> Eunus, having drawn up his forces out of range of missiles, was reviling the Romans, declaring that not his own men but the Romans were runaways from danger. Then he put on mime-shows visible from that distance to those in the city, in which the slaves acted out their rebellion against their individual masters, casting blame upon them for their arrogance and the way their wanton violence had crossed the line and brought about their own ruin.

At this point, the hidden transcript has broken out into plain sight; but the content of this mime bears an important resemblance to the content of the *palliata*. If the story is not true, it is telling.

Columella's vice list for urban slaves claims that slaves liked to see shows (*Rust.* 1.8.2). The *Poenulus* prologue says as much, while joking that some of them were not supposed to be there. Maybe some of them, like Stichus, had asked for and received a day off, or part of a day. Maybe, like Stichus, they were ready to pay out money from their hoarded *peculium*, in order to buy something to eat while they sat (or stood) and watched the show; maybe, like Chrysalus, they had seen the same shows more than once, and had favorite actors. Not only Chrysalus in his famous speech in *Bacchides*, but also Sceparnio and Gripus in *Rudens*, and Mercurius in *Amphitruo*, speak as slaves who have not just gone to the theater but have opinions about it. After all, "the theater," in the 200s in central Italy, was just a temporary enclosure with some benches and a collapsible stage, a birdcage, a space in a forum full of other attractions on a festival day; or, maybe, in a small town on a market day, or out in the country in a field, as Juvenal depicts a performance three hundred years later. Most slaves in Italy were working the land, with little access to a day out at the theater, and they were the ones who rose up. Still, the slaves who could have watched the plays of Plautus could have seen a lot, as this book has argued, to make them laugh. And they needed a laugh. All comedy starts with anger.

Timeline: War and Comedy in the 200s BCE

This chart maps the *fasti triumphales* (Degrassi 1954) against the lifespans of the major comic poets and information on their productions, along with reports of wars, major incidents of mass enslavement, and public violence. All information derived from texts is italicized to emphasize its uncertain status; the poets' lifelines are also, to varying degrees, dubious. The *fasti* appear in roman type in their capacity as what T. J. Cornell calls "a hard core of authentic data" (1995: 18); but cf. Bruce Frier's comments (1999: viii–ix). Years for which the *fasti* are lacking are marked "[tr.?]." For comprehensive information on mass enslavements, see Volkmann 1990 and Welwei 2000.

Year	Comic Poets			Fasti Triumphales	Wars	Events of Note
	Philemon (born 368/60)	Diphilus	Menander		**Second Samnite War** (starts 326)	
321						*Menander's first play* Orgê (Anger)
320	Ph	D	M		2SW	
319	Ph	D	M	tr. de Samnitibus	2SW	
318	Ph	D	M		2SW	
317	Ph	D	M		2SW	
316	Ph	D	M		2SW	*Demetrius of Phalerum rules Athens; Menander's Dyskolos*
315	Ph	D	M		2SW	*DPh*
314	Ph	D	M	tr. de Samnitibus	2SW	*DPh*
313	Ph	D	M		2SW	*DPh*
312	Ph	D	M	tr. de Samnitibus Soraneisq(ue)	2SW	*DPh*
311	Ph	D	M	tr. de Samnitibus; de Errusceis	2SW	*DPh*
310	Ph	D	M		2SW	*DPh*
309	Ph	D	M	tr. de Samnitibus; de Errusceis	2SW	*DPh*
308	Ph	D	M		2SW	*DPh*
307	Ph	D	M		2SW	*Demetrius Poliorcetes rules Athens.*
306	Ph	D	M	tr. de Anagnineis Herniceisq(ue)	2SW	*DP*
305	Ph	D	M	tr. de Samnitibus	2SW	*DP*
304	Ph	D	M	tr. de Aequeis; de Samnitibus	2SW	*DP*
303	Ph	D	M			*DP*

Year						
302	Ph	D	M	tr. de Aequeis		*DP. Romans intervene in popular uprising in Arretium.* *DP*
301	Ph	D	M	tr. [de] Errusceis et [Ma]rseis		
300	Ph	*D dies*	M	tr. de Samnitibus		
299	Ph		M	Nequinatibusque		
298	Ph		M	tr. de Samnitibus Errusceisque	**Third Samnite War**	*Scipio Barbatus cos.; later tomb inscription states that he took Samnium and Lucania and "brought away hostages".*
297	Ph		M		**3SW**	*Romans intervene in popular uprising in Lucania.*
296	Ph		M		**3SW**	
295	Ph		M	tr. de Samnitibus et Errusceis, Galleis	**3SW**	*Battle of Sentinum: Romans defeat Samnite/Gaul coalition.*
294	Ph		M	tr. de Samnitib(us) et Errusceis; de Volsonibus et Samnitib(us)	**3SW**	
293	Ph		M	tr. de Samnitibus (twice)	**3SW**	
292	Ph		M?		**3SW**	
291	Ph		*Menander dies*	tr. [de Samnitibus?]	**3SW**	
290	Ph			[tr.?]	**3SW**	
289	Ph			[tr.?]	**3SW**	

(*continued*)

Year	Comic Poets	Fasti Triumphales	Wars	Events of Note
288	Ph	[tr.?]		
287	Ph	[tr.?]		
286	Ph	[tr.?]		
285	Ph	[tr.?]		
284	Ph *Livius Andronicus born*	[tr.?]		
283	Ph *L*	[tr.?]		
282	Ph *L*	tr. [de Samnitibus, Lucaneis, Brutti]eisque		
281	Ph *L*	tr. de Etrusceis		
280	Ph *L*	tr. de Tarentineis, Samnitibus et Sallentineis	**War against Pyrrhus**	
279	Ph *L*		Py	
278	Ph *L*	tr. de Lucaneis, Bruttieis, Tarentin(eis), Samnitibus	Py	
277	Ph *L*	tr. de Lucaneis et Bruttieis	Py	
276	Ph *L*	tr. de Samnitibus, Lucaneis, Bruttieis Quirinalib(us)	Py	
275	Ph *L*	tr. [de Sa]mnitib(us) et rege Pyrrho; de Samnitibus et [Lucaneis]	Py	

Year				Triumphs	First Punic War	Events
274	Ph	L				
273	Ph	L		tr. [de Luca]neis, Samnitibus [Bruttieisque]		
272	Ph	L		tr. [de Samnitib(us), Lucaneis, Bruttieis] Tarentin[eis]que		*Siege of Tarentum*
271	Ph	L		tr. de Regi[neis]		
270	Ph	L				
269	Ph	L				
268	Ph	L		tr. de Peicentibus ... (twice)		
267	*Philemon dies*	L		tr. de Sallentineis (twice)		
266		L	N?	tr. de Sassinatibus (twice); tr. de Sallentineis Messapieisque		
265		L	N?			
264		L	N?	tr. de Vulsiniensibus	**First Punic War** **1PW**	*Romans put down slave uprising at Volsinii.*
263		L	N?	tr. de Poenis et rege Siculor(um) Hierone	**1PW**	
262		L	N?		**1PW**	*Romans destroy Agrigentum. Hamilcar attacks the Italian coast.*
261	*Naevius born?*	L				
260	N	L		tr. navalem de Siculeis et classe Poenica	**1PW**	*Duilius's columna rostrata*

(continued)

Year	Comic Poets			Fasti Triumphales	Wars	Events of Note
259	L	N		tr. de Poeneis et Sardin(ia), Corsica	1PW	
258	L	N		tr. de Poeneis; tr. de Poeneis et Sardeis	1PW	
257	L	N		tr. de Poeneis; tr. de Poeneis navalem	1PW	
256	L	N		tr. de Poeneis navalem	1PW	*Romans besiege Aspis, enslave 20,000.*
255	L	N			1PW	
254	L	N	*Plautus born?*	tr. de Cossurensibus et Poeneis navalem (twice)	1PW	
253	L	N	P	tr. de Poeneis (twice)	1PW	
252	L	N	P	tr. de Poeneis et Siculeis	1PW	
251	L	N	P		1PW	
250	L	N	P	tr. de Poeneis	1PW	
249	L	N	P		1PW	
248	L	N	P		1PW	
247	L	N	P		1PW	
246	L	N	P		1PW	
245	L	N	P		1PW	
244	L	N	P		1PW	
243	L	N	P		1PW	
242	L	N	P		1PW	
241	L	N	P	tr. de Poeneis ex Sicilia naval(em), twice; tr. de Falisceis	1PW	*Rebellion at Falerii put down; uprising of runaway slaves. Mercenary War in Carthage.*

Year	Event	Triumph	C	P	N	L	E	Note
240				P	N	L		*Report of first performance of a Latin play at the ludi (Livius Andronicus).*
239	*Ennius born*			P	N	L	*E*	
238				P	N	L	E	
237		tr. de Liguribus		P	N	L	E	
236		tr. de Sardeis		P	N	L	E	
235				P	N	L	E	*Report of first play by Naevius at the ludi.*
234		tr. de Sardeis		P	N	L	E	*Cato born*
233		tr. de Liguribus; tr. de Sardeis		P	N	L	E	
232				P	N	L	E	
231				P	N	L	E	
230	*Caecilius Statius born?*	tr. de Corseis		P	N	L	E	
229	**First Illyrian War**		C	P	N	L	E	
228		tr. ex Illurieis naval(em)	C	P	N	L	E	
227			C	P	N	L	E	
226			C	P	N	L	E	
225		tr. de Galleis	C	P	N	L	E	
224			C	P	N	L	E	
223		tr. de Galleis; tr. de Galleis et Liguribus	C	P	N	L	E	
222		tr. de Galleis Insubribus et Germ[an(eis)]	C	P	N	L	E	*Sack of Mantinea*
221		[tr.?]	C	P	N	L	E	*Clastidium. Marcellus wins the spolia opima.*

(continued)

Year	Comic Poets					Fasti Triumphales	Wars	Events of Note
220	E	L	N	P	C	[tr.?]	Second Punic War	
219	E	L	N	P	C	[tr.?]	2PW	*Hannibal sacks Saguntum*
218	E	L	N	P	C	[tr.?]	2PW	*Convivium publicum.*
217	E	L	N	P	C	[tr.?]	2PW	*Lake Trasimene. Roman POWs in chains. Fabius dictator. Freed slaves enlisted.*
216	E	L	N	P	C	[tr.?]	2PW	*Cannae. Battle with Boii. Hannibal sacks Nuceria. Roman POWs not ransomed; volones enlisted. 25 slaves crucified for conspiracy.*
215	E	L	N	P	C	[tr.?]	2PW	*Romans win in Sardinia, take 3,700 prisoners. 3-day funeral games.*
214	E	L	N	P	C	[tr.?]	2PW **First Macedonian War**	*Romans take seven Italian towns, capture or kill 25,000; 370 Roman deserters beaten with rods in the Comitium, thrown from Tarpeian Rock. Romans sack Megara, Henna. Volones freed after Beneventum. Four days of scaenici at the ludi.*

Year	E	L	N	P	C	[tr.?]	2PW	1MW	Events
213	E	L	N	P	C	[tr.?]	2PW	1MW	*Romans enslave the Turdetani.*
212	E	L	N	P	C	[tr.?]	2PW	1MW	*Hostages from Tarentum and Thurii thrown off the Tarpeian Rock. Romans take Hanno's camp: 7,000 prisoners. Sack of Syracuse.*
211	E	L	N	P	C	[tr.?]	2PW	1MW	*Hannibal reaches the gates of Rome, marching up the via Latina.*
210	E	L	N	P	C	[tr.?]	2PW	1MW	*Romans take Agrigentum, sell citizens. Romans take New Carthage, mass enslavement. Capuan citizens sold at Rome.*
209	E	L	N	P	C	[tr.?]	2PW	1MW	*Romans take Tarentum; 30,000 slaves taken among the spoils.*
208	E	L	N	P	C	[tr.?]	2PW	1MW	
207	E	L	N	P	C	[tr.?]	2PW	1MW	*Battle of the Metaurus; 5,400 Carthaginian POWs*
206	E	L	N	P	C	[tr.?]	2PW	1MW	*Romans take Iliturgi and Astapa; mass suicides.*
205	E	L *Livius Andronicus dies*	N?	P	C	[tr.?]	2PW	1MW	
204	E	L	N?	P	C	[tr.?]	2PW	1MW	*Locrians protest Pleminius's war crimes.*
203	E		N?	P	C	[tr.?]	2PW		

(continued)

Year	Comic Poets			Fasti Triumphales	Wars	Events of Note
202	E	*N?*	P C	[tr.?]	**2PW**	*Romans defeat Hannibal in Africa.*
201	E	*Naevius dies?*	P C	[tr.?]		*Roman deserters punished (beheaded/crucified)*
200	E		P C	[tr.?]	**Second Macedonian War**	*Stichus produced at the Ludi Plebeii*
199	E		P C	[tr.?]	**2MW**	
198	E		P C	[tr.?]	**2MW**	*Romans sack Dyme and enslave the inhabitants. Revolt of Carthaginian slaves at Setia, Norba, Circeii, spreading to Praeneste.*
197	E		P C	tr. de G[alleis Liguribusque]	**2MW**	*Cynoscephalae*
196	E		P C	tr. de Gal[leis Ins]ubrib(us); ovans [de Celtibereis]		*Slave revolt in Etruria*
195	E	*Terence born*	P C	[ovans de Celtibereis]; tr. [ex Hispania ulteriore]		
194	E	T	P C	tr. ex Hi[spania citeriore]; tr. [ex Macedonia et rege] Philippo		*Censors order aediles to begin segregating senatorial seating at the ludi. Flamininus negotiates the return of 1,200 enslaved Roman soldiers.*

Year	E	T	P	C	Triumphi	War against the Aetolians and Antiochus III of Syria	Events
193	E	T	P	C			
192	E	T	P	C			
191	E	T	P	C	ov[ans ex Hispania ulteriore]; [tr. de Galleis Boicis]	AetW	*Pseudolus performed at the Ludi Megalenses*
190	E	T	P	C		AetW	*Slave revolt in Bruttium and Apulia, through 184*
189	E	T	P	C	tr. ex Asia de [reg(e) Antiocho naval(em)]; tr. ex Asia de r[ege Antiocho]	AetW	
188	E	T	P	C	tr. ex Asia de rege Antioch[o navalem]		
187	E	T	P	C	tr. [de] Aetoleis et Ceph[allenia]; tr. [ex Asia de Galleis]; tr. [de Celtib]ereis Hispaneisq(ue)		
186	E	T	P	C			
185	E	T	*Plautus dies*	C			
184	E	T	P	C			*Cato is censor*

Brief Plot Summaries of the Extant Plays Attributed to Plautus, with Titles of Early Comedies for which Fragments are Extant

The twenty mostly complete plays extant, with the fragments of a twenty-first, are usually taken to be the canonical list of twenty-one plays, then generally held to be genuine and endorsed as such, along with some others, by the antiquarian M. Terentius Varro in the first century BCE (see Gell. 3.3). The twenty-first play, *Vidularia*, exists now as about five pages of fragments; it is printed in the OCT before the fragments from the non-canonical plays. Translating the plays is notoriously difficult; the recent Loeb translation by Wolfgang de Melo is literal, and can be recommended to those new to Plautus for its inclusion of all the fragments, with translations and notes (de Melo 2013). The thumbnail plot summaries here are intended for those who have not yet read all the plays.

Extant Plays Attributed to Plautus

Amphitruo: Jupiter and Mercurius disguise themselves as Amphitruo and his slave Sosia; Jupiter has sex with Amphitruo's wife, while Mercurius beats up Sosia. Amphitruo comes home and accuses his wife of adultery. The play ends with the birth of Hercules.

Asinaria: The slaves Libanus and Leonida help their younger owner gain access to the free prostitute Philaenium. Leonida rides the younger owner like a horse. Demaenetus, the older owner, tries to have sex with Philaenium, and his wife catches him.

Aulularia: The miser Euclio finds a buried treasure; the Slave of Lyconides finds and takes it, and is probably freed (the end of the play is missing), while Euclio's daughter now has a dowry and can marry: a good thing, since she has already given birth.

Bacchides: The slave Chrysalus tricks two old men out of the money needed by their sons to purchase access to two free prostitutes, both named Bacchis. In the end, all four owners have a party with the prostitutes.

Captivi: Philocrates and his slave Tyndarus are taken as war captives; both wind up freed, and Tyndarus is reunited with his family, while his childhood kidnapper, the slave Stalagmus, is punished. The *parasitus* Ergasilus gets fed.

Casina: A young slave-woman, Casina, is fought over by her younger and older owner, who use their male slaves Olympio and Chalinus as proxies. After the play ends, she will be found to be freeborn and will marry the younger owner (neither of them appears in the play). Chalinus and the older owner's wife unite to trick her husband and Olympio by dressing up Chalinus as Casina.

Cistellaria: Selenium, a young free prostitute, wishes to marry her lover; she is found to be freeborn, taken from her foster mother Melaenis, and reclaimed by her birth family.

Curculio: The *parasitus* Curculio helps his patron Phaedromus get access to Planesium, a slave prostitute, and foil the pimp Cappadox; she is found to be freeborn and is reunited with her brother, and she and Phaedromus end the play engaged to be married.

Epidicus: The slave Epidicus helps his younger owner get the money to pay for the war captive Telestis, having already arranged for his previous love object, the slave musician Acropolistis, to be freed. Telestis is found to be not only freeborn but the young man's half-sister. Epidicus is freed onstage at the end of the play.

Menaechmi: Twin brothers, separated when one of them was kidnapped as a child, are reunited; identity problems involve both with the same free prostitute. The slave Messenio, who helps them find each other, is freed onstage at the end of the play. The *parasitus* Peniculus does not get fed.

Mercator: Charinus, a young trader, brings back a sex slave, Pasicompsa; his father tries to acquire her, scandalizing his neighbor's wife Dorippa and her slave Syra.

Miles Gloriosus: The slave Palaestrio helps his previous owner get access to a free prostitute now the *concubina* of his present owner, a soldier. Palaestrio is promised his freedom.

Mostellaria: The slave Tranio helps his younger owner keep his father from finding out that he has spent all his father's money on parties with his freedwoman, Philematium.

Persa: The slave Toxilus purchases the freedom of the slave prostitute Lemniselenis, with the help of his friend, the slave Sagaristio, and of the *parasitus* Saturio and Saturio's daughter (who is sold onstage to the pimp Dordalus, as the captive Lucris). Dordalus is foiled.

Poenulus: The slave Milphio helps his owner Agorastocles retain access to the slave prostitute Adelphasium. Her father, Hanno, arrives from Carthage, and it turns out that she and her sister are freeborn, that she and Agorastocles are cousins, and that most of the characters in the play are Carthaginian. The pimp Lycus is foiled.

Pseudolus: The slave Pseudolus helps his younger owner retain access to the slave prostitute Phoenicium, who is freed during the play. The extant *didascaliae* indicate that this play was performed in 191 BCE at the Megalesian Games.

Rudens: Two slave prostitutes, Palaestra and Ampelisca, are shipwrecked on the coast of Cyrene with their pimp, Labrax. The slave Gripus finds the tokens that prove Palaestra is freeborn, and she is reunited with her family. Labrax is foiled. Gripus, Ampelisca, and the slave Trachalio are promised their freedom.

Stichus: The slave Stichus returns from a trading trip with his owner. The *parasitus* Gelasimus does not get fed. Stichus and his friend Sangarinus end the play with a party; both plan to have sex with the slave-woman Stephanium. The extant *didascaliae* indicate that this play was performed in 200 BCE at the Plebeian Games.

Trinummus: The slave Stasimus and his younger owner are saved from having to sell the family farm by the arrival of the young man's father.

Truculentus: The free prostitute Phronesium tricks one of her customers, a soldier, into thinking she has given birth to his son, using the baby born from the rape of a young woman by one of her other customers, Diniarchus. Two slave-women identify Diniarchus as the rapist, and he is forced to marry the young woman. Meanwhile, Phronesium's slave-woman Astaphium flirts with and thwarts the slave Truculentus.

Vidularia: A young man is shipwrecked and tries to get work as a farm laborer. The slave Cacistus finds the tokens that prove a young woman is freeborn. Most of this play is lost.

Titles of Early Roman Comedies for Which Fragments are Extant

All titles come from de Melo 2013 and Ribbeck 1962.

Titles of Comedies by Livius Andronicus for Which Fragments Remain (3)

Gladiolus, Ludius, Verpus

Titles of Comedies by Naevius for Which Fragments Remain (33)

Acontizomenos, Agitatoria, Agrypnuntes, Appella, Ariolus, Astiologa, Carbonaria, Clamidaria, Colax, Commotria, Corollaria, Dementes, Demetrius, Dolus, Figulus, Glaucoma, Guminasticus, Lampadio, Nagido, Nautae, Nervolaria, Paelex, Personata, Proiectus, Quadrigemini, Stalagmus, Stigmatias, Tarentilla, Technicus, Testicularia, Tribacelus, Triphallus, Tunicularia

Titles of Comedies by Plautus for Which Fragments Remain (32)

Acharistio, Addictus, Agroecus, Artemo, Astraba, Bacaria, Boeotia, Caecus or *Praedones, Carbonaria, †Cesistio†, Colax, Commorientes, Condalium, Cophinus, Cornicula, Dyscolus, Faeneratrix, Fretum, Frivolaria, Fugitivi, Gemini Lenones, Hortulus, Lipargus, Nervolaria, Parasitus Medicus, Parasitus Piger, Phago, Plocinus, Saturio, Schematicus, Sitellitergus, Trigemini*

Titles of Comedies by Ennius for Which Fragments Remain (2)

Caupuncula, Pancratiastes

Titles of Comedies by Caecilius Statius for Which Fragments Remain (42)

Aetherio, Andria, Androgynos, Asotus, Chalcia, Chrysion, Dardanus, Davos, Demandati, Ephesio, Epicleros, Epistathmos, Epistula, Exhautuhestos, Exul, Fallacia, Gamos, Harpazomene, Hymnis, Hypobolimaeus or *Subditivos, Hypobolimaeus Chaerestratus, Hypobolimaeus Rastraria, Hypobolimaeus Aeschinus, Imbrii, Karine, Meretrix, Nauclerus, Nothus Nicasio, Obolostates* or *Faenerator, Pausimachus, Philumena, Plocium, Polumeni, Portitor, Progamos, Pugil, Symbolum, Synaristosae, Synephebi, Syracusii, Titthe, Triumphus*

Bibliography

ABBREVIATIONS

BDNAC = Briggs, Ward W., Jr., ed. 1994. *Biographical Dictionary of North American Classicists*. Westport, CT: Greenwood Press.

Ernout-Meillet = Ernout, A., and A. Meillet. 1959. *Dictionnaire étymologique de la langue latine*. 4th ed. Paris: Klincksieck.

K-A = Kassel, R., and C. Austin, eds. 1983–2001. *Poetae Comici Graeci*. 8 vols. Berlin: Walter de Gruyter.

TrRF = *Tragicorum Romanorum Fragmenta*. 2012–. 4 vols. Göttingen: Vandenhoeck & Ruprecht.

Abrahams, Roger D., ed. 1985. *Afro-American Folktales: Stories from Black Traditions in the New World*. New York, NY: Pantheon.

Adamitis, Jana, and Mary-Kay Gamel. 2013. "Theaters of War." In *Roman Literature, Gender and Reception: Domina Illustris*, eds Donald Lateiner, Barbara K. Gold, and Judith Perkins: 284–302. New York, NY: Routledge.

Adams, Colin. 2012. "Transport." In *The Cambridge Companion to the Roman Economy*, ed. Walter Scheidel: 218–40. Cambridge University Press.

Adams, J. N. 1982. *The Latin Sexual Vocabulary*. Baltimore, MD: Johns Hopkins University Press.

1983. "Words for 'Prostitute' in Latin." *Rheinisches Museum* 126: 321–58.

2003. *Bilingualism and the Latin Language*. Cambridge University Press.

Ade, George. 1899. *Fables in Slang*. Illustr. Clyde J. Newman. Chicago, MI: Herbert S. Stone and Co.

Ahl, Frederick. 1984. "The Art of Safe Criticism in Greece and Rome." *AJPh* 105: 174–208.

Aldrete, Gregory S. 1999. *Gestures and Acclamations in Ancient Rome*. Baltimore, MD: Johns Hopkins University Press.

Allen, Frederic D. 1896. "On '*Os Columnatum*' (Plaut. M. G. 211) and Ancient Instruments of Confinement." *Harvard Studies in Classical Philology* 7: 37–64.

Allen, Walter, Jr. 1959. "Stage Money (*fabam mimum*: Cic. *Att.* 1.16.13)." *TAPA* 90: 1–8.

Althusser, Louis. 1971. "Ideology and Ideological State Apparatuses (Notes towards an Investigation)." In *Lenin and Philosophy and Other Essays*, trans. Ben Brewster: 127–86. New York, NY: Monthly Review Press.

Anderson, William S. 1986. "Gripus and Stratonicus: Plautus, *Rudens* 930–936." *AJPh* 107.4: 560–3.

Andreau, Jean. 1999. *Banking and Business in the Roman World*, trans. Janet Lloyd. Cambridge University Press.

2002. "Markets, Fairs and Monetary Loans: Cultural History and Economic History in Roman Italy and Hellenistic Greece." In *Money, Labour and Land: Approaches to the Economies of Ancient Greece*, eds Paul Cartledge, Edward E. Cohen, and Lin Foxhall: 113–29. London: Routledge.

Andreussi, M. 1993. "Aventinus Mons." In *Lexicon Topographicum Urbis Romae*, ed. Eva Margareta Steinby: 1. 147–50. Rome: Edizioni Quasar.

Ardener, Shirley. 2005. "Ardener's 'Muted Groups': The Genesis of an Idea and its Praxis." *Women and Language* 28.2: 50–4.

Armstrong, Michael. 1993. "A German Scholar and Socialist in Illinois: The Career of William Abbott Oldfather." *CJ* 88.3: 235–53.

1994. "Oldfather, William Abbott." *BDNAC*: 459–61.

Arnott, W. G., ed. and trans. 1979. *Menander*. Vol. 1. Cambridge, MA: Harvard University Press.

ed. and trans. 1996a. *Menander*. Vol. 2. Cambridge, MA: Harvard University Press.

1996b. Review of Wallochny 1992. *Gnomon* 68.1: 66–8.

2003. "Diphilus' Κληρούμενοι and Plautus' *Casina*." In *Lecturae Plautinae Sarsinates VI*, Casina, eds Renato Raffaelli and Alba Tontini: 23–44. Urbino: QuattroVenti.

Astin, Alan E. 1978. *Cato the Censor*. Oxford: Clarendon Press.

Austin, M. M., ed. 1981. *The Hellenistic World from Alexander to the Roman Conquest: A Selection of Ancient Sources in Translation*. Cambridge University Press.

Barker, Naomi J. 2013. "*Charivari* and Popular Ritual in 17th-Century Italy: A Source and Context for Improvised Performance?" *Early Music* 41.3: 447–59.

Barton, Carlin A. 1993. *The Sorrows of the Ancient Romans: The Gladiator and the Monster*. Princeton University Press.

2001. *Roman Honor: The Fire in the Bones*. Berkeley, CA: University of California Press.

Bartsch, Shadi. 1994. *Actors in the Audience: Theatricality and Doublespeak from Nero to Hadrian*. Cambridge, MA: Harvard University Press.

Bassi, Karen. 1995. "Male Nudity and Disguise in the Discourse of Greek Histrionics." *Helios* 22: 3–22.

Beard, Mary. 2003. "The Triumph of the Absurd: Roman Street Theatre." In *Rome the Cosmopolis*, eds Catharine Edwards and Greg Woolf: 21–43. Cambridge University Press.

2007. *The Roman Triumph*. Cambridge, MA: Harvard University Press.

2014. *Laughter in Ancient Rome: On Joking, Tickling, and Cracking Up*. Berkeley, CA: University of California Press.

Beare, W. 1964. *The Roman Stage: A Short History of Latin Drama in the Time of the Republic*. 3rd edn. London: Methuen.

Bennett, Judith M. 2000. "'Lesbian-Like' and the Social History of Lesbianisms." *Journal of the History of Sexuality* 9.1/2: 1–24.

Benz, Lore. 1995. "Die römisch-italische Stegreifspieltradition zur Zeit der Palliata." In *Plautus und die Tradition des Stegreifspiels: Festgabe für Eckard Lefèvre zum 60. Geburtstag*, eds Lore Benz, Ekkehard Stärk, and Gregor Vogt-Spira: 139–54. Tübingen: Gunter Narr.

    2001. "*Mimica convivia* und das Sklavenbankett im plautinischen *Persa*." In *Studien zu Plautus' Persa*, ed. Stefan Faller: 209–53. Tübingen: Gunter Narr.

Benz, Lore, Ekkehard Stärk, and Gregor Vogt-Spira, eds. 1995. *Plautus und die Tradition des Stegreifspiels: Festgabe für Eckard Lefèvre zum 60. Geburtstag*. Tübingen: Gunter Narr.

Berger, John. 1972. *Ways of Seeing*. London: British Broadcasting Corporation; Harmondsworth: Penguin.

Berlin, Lucia. 1977. *A Manual for Cleaning Ladies*. Washington, DC: Zephyrus Image.

    1981. *Angels Laundromat: Short Stories*. Berkeley, CA: Turtle Island Foundation.

Bernabò Brea, Luigi. 1992/93. "Masks and Characters of the Greek Theatre in the Terracottas of Ancient Lipara." Trans. C. Coen and J.-P. Descœudres. *Mediterranean Archaeology* 5/6: 23–31.

    2001. *Maschere e personaggi del teatro greco nelle terracotte liparesi*. Rome: "L'Erma" di Bretschneider.

Bernstein, Frank. 2007. "Complex Rituals: Games and Processions in Republican Rome." In *A Companion to Roman Religion*, ed. Jörg Rüpke: 222–34. Oxford: Blackwell.

Beta, Simone. 2014. "*Libera lingua loquemur ludis Liberalibus*: Gnaeus Naevius as a Latin Aristophanes?" In *Ancient Comedy and Reception: Essays in Honor of Jeffrey Henderson*, ed. S. Douglas Olson: 203–22. Berlin: Walter de Gruyter.

Bettini, Maurizio. 1982. "A proposito dei versi sotadei greci e romani: Con alcuni capitoli di 'analisi metrica lineare'." *Materiali e Discussioni* 9: 59–105.

    1995. "*Amphitruo* 168–172: *Numeri innumeri* und metrische Folklore." In *Plautus und die Tradition des Stegreifspiels: Festgabe für Eckard Lefèvre zum 60. Geburtstag*: 89–96. Tübingen: Gunter Narr.

    2012. *Vertere: Un'antropologia della traduzione nella cultura antica*. Turin: Einaudi.

Bianco, Maurizio Massimo. 2007. *Interdum vocem comoedia tollit: Paratragedia "al femminile" nella commedia plautina*. Bologna: Pàtron.

Bieber, Margarete. 1961. *The History of the Greek and Roman Theater*. 2nd edn. Princeton University Press.

Binsfeld, Andrea. 2009. "Imagens da escravidão na Antiguidade como meios de auto-representação." *Varia Historia* 25.41: 27–42.

Bispham, Edward. 2000. "Mimic? A Case Study in Early Roman Colonisation." In *The Emergence of State Identities in Italy in the First Millennium BC*, eds Edward Herring and Kathryn Lomas: 157–86. London: Accordia Research Institute, University of London.

Blegen, Theodore C., and Martin B. Ruud. 1936. *Norwegian Emigrant Songs and Ballads*. Minneapolis, MN: University of Minnesota Press.

Bleisch, Pamela R. 1997. "Plautine Travesties of Gender and Genre: Transvestism and Tragicomedy in *Amphitruo*." *Didaskalia* 4.1. http://didaskalia.net/issues/vol4no1/bleisch.html.

Blösel, Wolfgang. 2000. "Die Geschichte des Begriffes *mos maiorum* von den Anfängen bis zu Cicero." In *Mos Maiorum: Untersuchungen zu den Formen der Identitätsstiftung und Stabilisierung in der Römischen Republik*, ed. Bernhard Linke and Michael Stemmler: 25–97. *Historia* Einzelschriften 141. Stuttgart: Franz Steiner.

Bloomer, W. Martin. 1997. "Schooling in Persona: Imagination and Subordination in Roman Education." *Classical Antiquity* 16.1: 57–78.

Boal, Augusto. 1985. *Theatre of the Oppressed*. Trans. Charles A. and Maria-Odilia Leal McBride. New York, NY: Theatre Communications Group.

Bodel, John. 1994. *Graveyards and Groves: A Study of the Lex Lucerina*. *AJAH* 11: 1–133. Cambridge, MA: Gorgias Press.

———. 1999. "Death on Display: Looking at Roman Funerals." In *The Art of Ancient Spectacle*, ed. Bettina Bergmann and Christine Kondoleon: 259–81. New Haven, CT: Yale University Press.

———. 2000. "Dealing with the Dead: Undertakers, Executioners, and Potter's Fields in Ancient Rome." In *Death and Disease in the Ancient City*, ed. Valerie M. Hope and Eireann Marshall: 128–51. London: Routledge.

———. 2005. "*Caveat Emptor*: Towards a Study of Roman Slave-Traders." *Journal of Roman Archaeology* 18: 181–95.

———. 2017. "Death and Social Death." In *On Human Bondage: After Slavery and Social Death*, ed. John Bodel and Walter Scheidel: 81–108. Chichester: John Wiley & Sons.

Bond, R. P. 1999. "Plautus' *Amphitryo* as Tragi-Comedy." *Greece and Rome*, 2nd series 46.2: 203–20.

Boone, Joseph Allen. 2014. *The Homoerotics of Orientalism*. New York, NY: Columbia University Press.

Bosher, Kathryn, ed. 2012. *Theater Outside Athens: Drama in Greek Sicily and South Italy*. Cambridge University Press.

———. 2013. "'*Phlyax*' Slaves: From Vase to Stage?" In *Slaves and Slavery in Ancient Greek Comic Drama*, ed. Ben Akrigg and Rob Tordoff: 197–208. Cambridge: Cambridge University Press.

Boyarin, Daniel. 1993. *Carnal Israel: Reading Sex in Talmudic Culture*. Berkeley, CA: University of California Press.

Boyle, A. J. 2006. *An Introduction to Roman Tragedy*. London: Routledge.

Bradley, Adam. 2009. *Book of Rhymes: The Poetics of Hip Hop*. New York, NY: Basic Civitas Books.

Bradley, Keith. 1984. *Slaves and Masters in the Roman Empire: A Study in Social Control*. New York, NY: Oxford University Press.

———. 1989. *Slavery and Rebellion in the Roman World, 140 B.C.–70 B.C.* Bloomington, IN: Indiana University Press.

1994. *Slavery and Society at Rome.* Cambridge University Press.

2000. "Animalizing the Slave: The Truth of Fiction." *JRS* 90: 110–25.

2011a. "Slavery in the Roman Republic." In *The Cambridge World History of Slavery,* vol. 1: *The Ancient Mediterranean World,* ed. Keith Bradley and Paul Cartledge: 241–64. Cambridge University Press.

2011b. "Resisting Slavery at Rome." In *The Cambridge World History of Slavery,* vol. 1: *The Ancient Mediterranean World,* eds Keith Bradley and Paul Cartledge: 362–84. Cambridge University Press.

2015. "The Bitter Chain of Slavery." *Dialogues d'histoire ancienne* 41/1: 149–76.

Brah, Avtar. 1999. "The Scent of Memory: Strangers, Our Own and Others." *Feminist Review* 61: 4–26.

Brantner, Scott. 2014. "*Imaginibus, non mente falluntur:* PostTraumatic Stress in Roman Medicine and Literature, 100 BCE–100 CE." MA thesis, California State University, Northridge.

Bridenthal, Renate, and Claudia Koonz, eds. 1977. *Becoming Visible: Women in European History.* Boston, MA: Houghton Mifflin.

Briscoe, John. 2010. "The Fragments of Cato's *Origines.*" In *Colloquial and Literary Latin,* eds Eleanor Dickey and Anna Chahoud: 154–60. Cambridge University Press.

Bronner, Stephen Eric. 2012. *Modernism at the Barricades: Aesthetics, Politics, Utopia.* New York, NY: Columbia University Press.

Brooten, Bernadette J. 1996. *Love between Women: Early Christian Responses to Female Homoeroticism.* University of Chicago Press.

Brown, Mary Ellen. 2011. *Child's Unfinished Masterpiece: The English and Scottish Popular Ballads.* Urbana, IL: University of Illinois Press.

Brown, Peter G. McC. 1986. "The First Roman Literature." In *The Oxford Illustrated History of the Roman World,* ed. John Boardman, Jasper Griffin, and Oswyn Murray: 60–75. Oxford University Press.

1990. "Plots and Prostitutes in Greek New Comedy." *Papers of the Leeds International Latin Seminar* 6: 241–66.

2002. "Actors and Actor-Managers at Rome in the Time of Plautus and Terence." In *Greek and Roman Actors: Aspects of an Ancient Profession,* ed. Pat Easterling and Edith Hall: 225–37. Cambridge University Press.

2004. "Soldiers in New Comedy: Insiders and Outsiders." *Leeds International Classical Studies* 3.08. www.leeds.ac.uk/classics/lics.

2013. "The Audiences of Roman Comedy." Paper delivered at the Popular Comedy Conference, Glasgow.

Brunt, P. A. 1966. "The Roman Mob." *Past and Present* 35: 3–27.

1971a. *Italian Manpower 225 B.C.–A.D. 14.* Oxford: Clarendon Press.

1971b. *Social Conflicts in the Roman Republic.* London: Chatto & Windus.

1980. "Free Labour and Public Works at Rome." *JRS* 70: 81–100.

Buckland, W. W. 1908. *The Roman Law of Slavery: The Condition of the Slave in Private Law from Augustus to Justinian.* Cambridge University Press.

Burke, Carol. 1989. "Marching to Vietnam." *Journal of American Folklore* 102: 424–41.

Burke, Peter. 1989. "History as Social Memory." In *Memory: History, Culture and the Mind*, ed. Thomas Butler: 97–113. Oxford: Blackwell.

Burman, Pieter, ed. and comm. 1709. *Titi Petronii Arbitri Satyricôn quae Supersunt.* Vol. 1. Utrecht: Willem van de Water.

Burnett, Andrew. 2012. "Early Roman Coinage and Its Italian Context." In *The Oxford Handbook of Greek and Roman Coinage*, ed. William E. Metcalf: 297–314. Oxford University Press.

Burstein, Stanley M., ed. and trans. 1985. *The Hellenistic Age from the Battle of Ipsos to the Death of Kleopatra VII*. Cambridge University Press.

Burton, Paul J. 2011. *Friendship and Empire: Roman Diplomacy and Imperialism in the Middle Republic (353–146 BC)*. Cambridge University Press.

Butler, Margaret E. 2010. "The Logic of Opportunity: Philip II, Demosthenes, and the Charismatic Imagination." *Syllecta Classica* 21: 1–33.

Byatt, A. S. 2009. *The Children's Book*. New York, NY: Alfred A. Knopf.

Calder, William M., III. 1994. "Classical Scholarship in the United States: An Introductory Essay." *BDNAC*: xix–xxxix.

Callataÿ, François de. 2015. "Comedies of Plautus and Terence: An Unusual Opportunity to Look into the Use of Money in Hellenistic Time." *Revue Belge de Numismatique* 161: 17–53.

Callier, Reina Erin. 2014. "Men in Drag Are Funny: Metatheatricality and Gendered Humor in Aristophanes." *Didaskalia* 10: 13. ADIP II. http://didaskalia.net/issues/10/13.

Calloway, Cab, and Bryant Rollins. 1976. *Of Minnie the Moocher and Me*. New York, NY: Crowell.

Cameron, Alan. 1995. *Callimachus and His Critics*. Princeton University Press.

Carabelli, Giancarlo. 1996. *In the Image of Priapus*. London: Duckworth.

Carr, E. H. 1961. *What Is History?* New York, NY: Vintage.

Case, Sue-Ellen. 1985. "Classic Drag: The Greek Creation of Female Parts." *Theatre Journal* 37.3: 317–27.

Castagnetti, Sergio. 2012. *Le leges libitinariae flegree: Edizione e commento.* Pubblicazioni del Dipartimento di diritto romano, storia e teoria del diritto F. De Martino dell'Università degli studi di Napoli Federico II, 34. Naples: Satura editrice.

Caught Looking. 1988. *Caught Looking: Feminism, Pornography and Censorship.* 2nd edn. Seattle, WA: Real Comet Press.

Certeau, Michel de. 1984. *The Practice of Everyday Life*, trans. S. Rendall. Berkeley, CA: University of California Press.

Chalmers, Walter R. 1965. "Plautus and his Audience." In *Roman Drama*, eds T. A. Dorey and Donald R. Dudley: 21–50. New York, NY: Basic Books.

Champion, Craige B. 2004. *Cultural Politics in Polybius's Histories*. Berkeley, CA: University of California Press.

Champlin, Edward. 2005. "Phaedrus the Fabulous." *JRS* 95: 97–123.

Cheesman, Clive. 2009. "Names in *-por* and Slave Naming in Republican Rome." *CQ* 59.2: 511–31.

Chevallier, Raymond. 1976. *Roman Roads*, trans. N. H. Field. Berkeley, CA: University of California Press.

Christenson, David M., ed. and comm. 2000. *Plautus: Amphitruo*. Cambridge University Press.

Ciaghi, Silvia. 1993. *Le Terrecotte Figurate da Cales del Museo Nazionale di Napoli: Sacro – Stile – Committenza*. Rome: "L'Erma" di Bretschneider.

Clark, Anna. 2007. *Divine Qualities: Cult and Community in Republican Rome*. Oxford University Press.

Clark, Konnor. 2015. *"Morigerus*: The Masculine, Servile, and Homoerotic Prevalence of 'Wifely' Behavior." MA thesis, SUNY Buffalo.

Clark, Patricia. 1998. "Women, Slaves, and the Hierarchies of Domestic Violence: The Family of St. Augustine." In *Women and Slaves in Greco-Roman Culture: Differential Equations*, eds Sandra R. Joshel and Sheila Murnaghan: 109–29. London: Routledge.

Clarke, John R. 1998. *Looking at Lovemaking: Constructions of Sexuality in Roman Art, 100 B.C.–A.D. 250*. Berkeley, CA: University of California Press.

Clausen, Wendell V., and James E. G. Zetzel, eds. 2004. *Commentum Cornuti in Persium*. Munich: K. G. Saur.

Cliff, Michelle. 1982. "Object into Subject: Some Thoughts on the Work of Black Women Artists." *Heresies* 4.3: 34–40.

　　1985a. "If I Could Write This in Fire, I Would Write This in Fire." In *The Land of Look Behind*: 57–76. Ithaca, NY: Firebrand Books.

　　1985b. "Claiming an Identity They Taught Me to Despise." In *The Land of Look Behind*: 40–7. Ithaca, NY: Firebrand Books.

　　1990. *Abeng*. New York, NY: Dutton.

Coarelli, F. 1996a. "Murus Servii Tullii; mura repubblicane: Porta Esquilina." In *Lexicon Topographicum Urbis Romae*, ed. Eva Margareta Steinby: 3. 326–7. Rome: Edizioni Quasar.

　　1996b. "Murus Servii Tullii; mura repubblicane: Porta Trigemina." In *Lexicon Topographicum Urbis Romae*, ed. Eva Margareta Steinby: 3. 332–3. Rome: Edizioni Quasar.

Colesanti, Giulio. 2014. "Two Cases of Submerged Monodic Lyric: Sympotic Poetry and Lullabies." In *Submerged Literature in Ancient Greek Culture: An Introduction*, eds Giulio Colesanti and Manuela Giordano: 90–106. Berlin: Walter de Gruyter.

Coltman, Viccy. 2009. *Classical Sculpture and the Culture of Collecting in Britain Since 1760*. Oxford University Press.

Combahee River Collective. 1983. "The Combahee River Collective Statement." In *Home Girls: A Black Feminist Anthology*, ed. Barbara Smith: 272–82. New York, NY: Kitchen Table: Women of Color Press.

Conington, John, trans. and comm. 1872. *The Satires of A. Persius Flaccus*. Oxford: Clarendon Press.

Connors, Catherine. 2004. "Monkey Business: Imitation, Authenticity, and Identity from Pithekoussai to Plautus." *Classical Antiquity* 23.2: 179–207.

Corbeill, Anthony. 2004. *Nature Embodied: Gesture in Ancient Rome*. Princeton University Press.

Corbett, Philip. 1986. *The Scurra*. Edinburgh: Scottish Academic Press.

Cornell, T. J. 1995. *The Beginnings of Rome: Italy and Rome from the Bronze Age to the Punic Wars (c. 1000–264 B.C.)*. London: Routledge.

Courtney, Edward, ed. and comm. 1993. *The Fragmentary Latin Poets*. Oxford: Clarendon Press.

Cox, Cheryl. 2013. "Coping with Punishment: The Social Networking of Slaves in Menander." In *Slaves and Slavery in Ancient Greek Comic Drama*, ed. Ben Akrigg and Rob Tordoff: 159–72. Cambridge University Press.

Crawford, Michael. 2011. "Reconstructing What Roman Republic?" Review of Hölkeskamp 2011. *BICS* 54.2: 105–14.

Csapo, Eric. 1999, "Performance and Iconographic Tradition in the Illustrations of Menander." *Syllecta Classica* 10: 154–88.

2014. "Performing Comedy in the Fifth through Early Third Centuries." In *The Oxford Handbook of Greek and Roman Comedy*, ed. Michael Fontaine and Adele C. Scafuro: 50–69. Oxford University Press.

Csapo, Eric, and William J. Slater, eds. 1994. *The Context of Ancient Drama*. Ann Arbor, MI: University of Michigan Press.

Cucchiarelli, Andrea. 2001. *La satira e il poeta: Orazio tra Epodi e Sermones*. Pisa: Giardini.

2002. "*Iter satiricum:* Le voyage à Brindes et la satire d'Horace." *Latomus* 61.4: 842–51.

Culham, Phyllis. 1982. "The Lex Oppia." *Latomus* 41.4: 786–93.

Cullen, Frank. 2007. *Vaudeville, Old and New: An Encyclopedia of Variety Performers in America*. 2 vols. New York, NY: Routledge.

Curtis, Liz. 1984. *Nothing But the Same Old Story: The Roots of Anti-Irish Racism*. London: Greater London Council (Information on Ireland).

Dalby, Andrew, ed. and trans. 1998. *Cato On Farming*. Totnes, Devon: Prospect Books.

D'Ambra, Eve. 2007. *Roman Women*. Cambridge University Press.

Damon, Cynthia. 1997. *The Mask of the Parasite: A Pathology of Roman Patronage*. Ann Arbor, MI: University of Michigan Press.

2007. "Rhetoric and Historiography." In *A Companion to Roman Rhetoric*, eds William Dominik and Jon Hall: 439–50. Malden, MA: Blackwell.

Darnton, Robert. 1984. "Peasants Tell Tales: The Meaning of Mother Goose." In *The Great Cat Massacre and Other Episodes in French Cultural History*: 8–72. New York, NY: Basic Books.

Daube, Matthew. 2010. "Laughter in Revolt: Race, Ethnicity, and Identity in the Construction of Stand-Up Comedy." Diss. Stanford University.

Davidson, James. 2000. "*Gnesippus Paigniagraphos*: The Comic Poets and the Erotic Mime." In *The Rivals of Aristophanes: Studies in Athenian Old Comedy*, ed. David Harvey and John Wilkins: 41–64. London: Duckworth.

Davis, Andrew. 2011. *Baggy Pants Comedy: Burlesque and the Oral Tradition*. New York, NY: Palgrave Macmillan.

Davis, Natalie Zemon. 1971. "The Reasons of Misrule: Youth Groups and Charivaris in Sixteenth-Century France." *Past and Present* 50: 41–75.

——— 1975. "Women on Top." In *Society and Culture in Early Modern France*: 124–51. Stanford University Press.

Degrassi, Attilio. 1954. *Fasti Capitolini*. Turin: G. B. Paravia.

de Melo, Wolfgang. 2010. "Possessive Pronouns in Plautus." In *Colloquial and Literary Latin*, eds Eleanor Dickey and Anna Chahoud: 71–99. Cambridge University Press.

——— ed. and trans. 2011a. *Plautus: Amphitryon, The Comedy of Asses, The Pot of Gold, The Two Bacchises, The Captives*. Cambridge, MA: Harvard University Press.

——— ed. and trans. 2011b. *Plautus: Casina, The Casket Comedy, Curculio, Epidicus, The Two Menaechmuses*. Cambridge, MA: Harvard University Press.

——— ed. and trans. 2011c. *Plautus: The Merchant, The Braggart Soldier, The Ghost, The Persian*. Cambridge, MA: Harvard University Press.

——— ed. and trans. 2012. *Plautus: The Little Carthaginian, Pseudolus, The Rope*. Cambridge, MA: Harvard University Press.

——— ed. and trans. 2013. *Plautus: Stichus, Three-Dollar Day, Truculentus, The Tale of a Traveling-Bag, Fragments*. Cambridge, MA: Harvard University Press.

Dench, Emma. 1995. *From Barbarians to New Men: Greek, Roman, and Modern Perceptions of Peoples of the Central Apennines*. Oxford: Clarendon Press.

——— 2003. "Beyond Greeks and Barbarians: Italy and Sicily in the Hellenistic Age." In *A Companion to the Hellenistic World*, ed. Andrew Erskine: 294–310. Oxford: Blackwell.

——— 2005. *Romulus' Asylum: Roman Identities from the Age of Alexander to the Age of Hadrian*. Oxford University Press.

DePastino, Todd. 2003. *Citizen Hobo: How a Century of Homelessness Shaped America*. University of Chicago Press.

Dickey, Eleanor. 2002. *Latin Forms of Address: From Plautus to Apuleius*. Oxford University Press.

Dilke, O. A. W. 1985. *Greek and Roman Maps*. London: Thames & Hudson.

Dolansky, Fanny. 2011. "Reconsidering the Matronalia and Women's Rites." *Classical World* 104.2: 191–209.

Donahue, John F. 2003. "Toward a Typology of Roman Public Feasting." *AJPh* 124: 423–41.

Dressler, Alex. 2016. "Plautus and the Poetics of Property: Reification, Recognition, and Utopia." *MD* 77: 9–56.

Driel-Murray, C. van. 1993. "The Leatherwork." In *Vindolanda Reseach Reports*, vol. 3: *The Early Wooden Forts: Preliminary Reports on the Leather, Textiles, Environmental Evidence and Dendrochronology*, eds Carol van Driel-Murray et al.: 1–75. Hexham: The Vindolanda Trust.

——— 2007. "Footwear in the North-Western Provinces of the Roman Empire." In *Stepping through Time: Archaeological Footwear from Prehistoric Times until 1800*, eds O. Goubitz, C. van Driel-Murray, and W. Groenman-van Waateringe: 336–76. Zwolle: Stichting Promotie Archeologie.

duBois, Page. 1991. *Torture and Truth*. New York, NY: Routledge.

2003. *Slaves and Other Objects*. University of Chicago Press.

2007. "The Coarsest Demand: Utopia and the Fear of Slaves." In *Fear of Slaves – Fear of Enslavement in the Ancient Mediterranean. . . . Actes du XXIXe Colloque international du . . . GIREA*, ed. Anastasia Serghidou: 435–44. Besançon: Presses universitaires de Franche-Comté.

2009. *Slavery: Antiquity and its Legacy*. Oxford University Press.

2010. *Out of Athens: The New Ancient Greeks*. Cambridge, MA: Harvard University Press.

Duckworth, George E. 1938. "The Unnamed Characters in the Plays of Plautus." *CP* 33.3: 267–82.

1952. *The Nature of Roman Comedy: A Study in Popular Entertainment*. Princeton University Press.

Dumont, Jean-Christian. 1987. *Servus: Rome et l'esclavage sous la République*. Rome: École française de Rome.

Dunbabin, Katherine M. D. 1999. *Mosaics of the Greek and Roman World*. Cambridge University Press.

Duncan, Anne. 2006. *Performance and Identity in the Classical World*. Cambridge University Press.

Dunkin, Paul Shaner. 1946. *Post-Aristophanic Comedy: Studies in the Social Outlook of Middle and New Comedy at Both Athens and Rome*. = Illinois Studies in Language and Literature 31.3–4. Urbana, IL: University of Illinois Press.

Dunsch, Boris. 2014. "*Lege dura vivont mulieres*: Syra's Complaint about the Sexual Double Standard (Plautus *Merc.* 817–29)." In *Ancient Comedy and Reception: Essays in Honor of Jeffrey Henderson*, ed. S. Douglas Olson: 235–58. Berlin: Walter de Gruyter.

Dutsch, Dorota M. 2004. "Female Furniture: A Reading of Plautus' *Poenulus* 1141–6." *Classical Quarterly* 54.2: 625–9.

2008. *Feminine Discourse in Roman Comedy: On Echoes and Voices*. Oxford University Press.

2015. "Feats of Flesh: The Female Body on the Plautine Stage." In *Women in Roman Republican Drama*, eds Dorota Dutsch, Sharon L. James, and David Konstan: 17–36. Madison, WI: University of Wisconsin Press.

Forthcoming. "On 'Mothers' and 'Whores.'" In *The Cambridge Companion to Roman Comedy*, ed. Martin Dinter. Cambridge University Press.

Dyck, Andrew R. 1996. *A Commentary on Cicero, De Officiis*. Ann Arbor, MI: University of Michigan Press.

Dyson, Stephen L. 1985. *The Creation of the Roman Frontier*. Princeton University Press.

Earl, D. C. 1960. "Political Terminology in Plautus." *Historia* 9.2: 235–43.

Eckstein, Arthur M. 1982. "Human Sacrifice and Fear of Military Disaster in Republican Rome." *AJAH* 7: 69–95.

2006a. *Mediterranean Anarchy, Interstate War, and the Rise of Rome*. Berkeley, CA: University of California Press.

2006b. "Conceptualizing Roman Imperial Expansion under the Republic: An Introduction." In *A Companion to the Roman Republic*, ed. Nathan Rosenstein and Robert Morstein-Marx: 567–89. Malden, MA: Blackwell.

Edwards, Catharine. 1997. "Unspeakable Professions: Public Performance and Prostitution in Ancient Rome." In *Roman Sexualities*, eds Judith P. Hallett and Marilyn B. Skinner: 66–95. Princeton University Press.

Ellis, Robinson, ed. and comm. 1889. *A Commentary on Catullus*. Oxford: Clarendon Press.

Enk, P. J., ed. and comm. 1953. *Plauti Truculentus cum Prolegomenis, Notis Criticis, Commentario Exegetico*. 2 vols. Leiden: A. W. Sijthoff.

Erasmo, Mario. 2001. "Staging Brutus: Roman Legend and the Death of Caesar." In *Essays in Honor of Gordon Williams: Twenty-Five Years at Yale*, eds Elizabeth Tylawsky and Charles Weiss: 101–14. New Haven, CT: Henry R. Schwab.

Erdkamp, Paul. 1998. *Hunger and the Sword: Warfare and Food Supply in Roman Republican Wars (264–30 B.C.)*. Amsterdam: J. C. Gieben.

Fantham, Elaine. 1975. "Sex, Status, and Survival in Hellenistic Athens: A Study of Women in New Comedy." *Phoenix* 29.1: 44–74.

2005. "Liberty and the People in Republican Rome." *TAPA* 135.2: 209–29.

2011. "Women of the Demi-Monde and Sisterly Solidarity in the *Cistellaria*." In *Roman Readings: Roman Response to Greek Literature from Plautus to Statius and Quintilian*: 157–75. Berlin: Walter de Gruyter.

2015. "Women in Control." In *Women in Roman Republican Drama*, eds Dorota Dutsch, Sharon L. James, and David Konstan: 91–107. Madison, WI: University of Wisconsin Press.

Feeney, Denis. 2010. "Crediting Pseudolus: Trust, Belief, and the Credit Crunch in Plautus' *Pseudolus*." *CP* 105.3: 281–300.

2016. *Beyond Greek: The Beginnings of Latin Literature*. Cambridge, MA: Harvard University Press.

Feldherr, Andrew. 1998. *Spectacle and Society in Livy's History*. Berkeley, CA: University of California Press.

Feltovich, Anne. 2011. "Women's Social Bonds in Greek and Roman Comedy." Diss. University of Cincinnati.

2015. "The Many Shapes of Sisterhood in Roman Comedy." In *Women in Roman Republican Drama*, eds Dorota Dutsch, Sharon L. James, and David Konstan: 128–54. Madison, WI: University of Wisconsin Press.

Ferriss-Hill, Jennifer L. 2015. *Roman Satire and the Old Comic Tradition*. New York, NY: Cambridge University Press.

Feuvrier-Prévotat, Claire. 2005. "Travail et travailleurs dans le théâtre de Plaute." *Dialogues d'histoire ancienne suppl. 1, Hommage à Pierre Lévêque*: 91–111.

Finley, Moses I. 1967. "Utopianism Ancient and Modern." In *The Critical Spirit: Essays in Honor of Herbert Marcuse*, eds Kurt H. Wolff and Barrington Moore, Jr.: 3–20. Boston, MA: Beacon Press.

1998[1980]. *Ancient Slavery and Modern Ideology*. Expanded edition, ed. Brent D. Shaw. Princeton, MJ: Markus Wiener.

Fitzgerald, William. 1995. *Catullan Provocations: Lyric Poetry and the Drama of Position.* Berkeley, CA: University of California Press.

2000. *Slavery and the Roman Literary Imagination.* Cambridge University Press.

Florio, John. 2013[1598]. *A Worlde of Wordes: A Critical Edition*, ed. Hermann W. Haller. University of Toronto Press.

Flower, Harriet I. 1996. *Ancestor Masks and Aristocratic Power in Roman Culture.* Oxford: Clarendon Press.

Foerst, Gabriele. 1978. *Die Gravierungen der Pränestinischen Cisten.* Rome: Giorgio Bretschneider.

Fontaine, Michael. 2010. *Funny Words in Plautine Comedy.* Oxford University Press.

Forehand, Walter E. 1973. "Plautus' *Casina*: An Explication." *Arethusa* 6.2: 233–56.

Forsdyke, Sara. 2012. *Slaves Tell Tales and Other Episodes in the Politics of Popular Culture in Ancient Greece.* Princeton University Press.

Fountoulakis, Andreas. 2007. "Punishing the Lecherous Slave: Desire and Power in Herondas 5." In *Fear of Slaves – Fear of Enslavement in the Ancient Mediterranean. ... Actes du XXIXe Colloque international du ... GIREA*, ed. Anastasia Serghidou: 251–64. Besançon: Presses universitaires de Franche-Comté.

Fraenkel, Eduard. 1916. "Zur Geschichte des Wortes *Fides*." *RhM* 71: 187–99.

1927. "Die Vorgeschichte des Versus Quadratus." *Hermes* 62.3: 357–70.

1942. "The Stars in the Prologue of the *Rudens*." *CQ* 36.1–2: 10–14.

1961. "Two Poems of Catullus." *JRS* 51: 46–53.

1964 [1920]. "*Cevere* im Plautustext." In his *Kleine Beiträge zur klassischen Philologie*: 2.45–52. Rome: Edizioni di Storia e Letteratura.

2007. *Plautine Elements in Plautus*, trans. Tomas Drevikovsky and Frances Muecke. Oxford University Press.

Franchi De Bellis, Annalisa. 2005. *Iscrizioni prenestine su specchi e ciste.* Alessandria: Edizioni dell'Orso.

Fredrick, David. 2002. "Mapping Penetrability in Late Republican and Early Imperial Rome." In *The Roman Gaze: Vision, Power, and the Body*, ed. David Fredrick: 236–64. Baltimore, MD: Johns Hopkins University Press.

Freud, Sigmund. 1960. *Jokes and their Relation to the Unconscious*, trans. James Strachey. Standard ed., vol. 8. New York, NY: W. W. Norton.

2001[1927]. "Humour." In *The Future of an Illusion, Civilization and its Discontents, and Other Works*, trans. James Strachey. Standard ed., vol. 21: 159–66. London: Vintage.

Friedlander, Saul, ed. 1992. *Probing the Limits of Representation: Nazism and the "Final Solution."* Cambridge, MA: Harvard University Press.

Frier, Bruce W. 1989. *A Casebook on the Roman Law of Delict.* Atlanta, GA: Scholars Press.

1999. *Libri Annales Pontificum Maximorum: The Origins of the Annalistic Tradition.* 2nd ed. Ann Arbor, MI: University of Michigan Press.

Gabba, Emilio. 1981. "True History and False History in Classical Antiquity." *JRS* 71: 50–62.

Gabrielsen, Vincent. 2003. "Piracy and the Slave-Trade." In *A Companion to the Hellenistic World*, ed. Andrew Erskine: 389–404. Oxford: Blackwell.

Gaca, Kathy L. 2010. "The Andrapodizing of War Captives in Greek Historical Memory." *TAPA* 140.1: 117–61.

2010–11. "Telling the Girls from the Boys and Children: Interpreting Παῖδες in the Sexual Violence of Populace-Ravaging Ancient Warfare." *ICS* 35/36: 85–109.

2011. "Girls, Women, and the Significance of Sexual Violence in Ancient Warfare." In *Sexual Violence in Conflict Zones: From the Ancient World to the Era of Human Rights*, ed. Elizabeth D. Heineman: 73–88. Philadelphia: University of Pennsylvania Press.

2014. "Martial Rape, Pulsating Fear, and the Sexual Maltreatment of Girls (παῖδες), Virgins (παρθένοι), and Women (γυναῖκες) in Antiquity." *AJPh* 135.3: 303–57.

2015. "Ancient Warfare and the Ravaging Martial Rape of Girls and Women: Evidence from Homeric Epic and Greek Drama." In *Sex in Antiquity: Exploring Gender and Sexuality in the Ancient World*, eds Mark Masterson, Nancy Sorkin Rabinowitz, and James Robson: 278–97. London: Routledge.

Gamel, Mary-Kay. 1999. "Staging Ancient Drama: The Difference Women Make." *Syllecta Classica* 10: 22–42.

2016. "The Festival of Dionysos: A Community Theatre." In *Close Relations: Spaces of Greek and Roman Theatre*, eds Paul Monaghan and Jane Montgomery Griffiths: 91–117. Newcastle on Tyne: Cambridge Scholars Publishing.

Gamman, Lorraine, and Margaret Marshment. 1988. *The Female Gaze: Women as Viewers of Popular Culture*. London: Women's Press.

García Moreno, Luis A. 1992. "Paradoxography and Political Ideals in Plutarch's *Life of Sertorius*." In *Plutarch and the Historical Tradition*, ed. Philip A. Stadter: 132–58. London: Routledge.

Garnsey, Peter. 1988. *Famine and Food Supply in the Graeco-Roman World: Responses to Risk and Crisis*. Cambridge University Press.

1998. *Cities, Peasants and Food in Classical Antiquity: Essays in Social and Economic History*. Cambridge: Cambridge University Press.

1999. *Food and Society in Classical Antiquity*. Cambridge University Press.

Garton, Charles. 1972. *Personal Aspects of the Roman Theatre*. Toronto: Hakkert.

Gates, Henry Louis, Jr. 1988. *The Signifying Monkey: A Theory of African-American Literary Criticism*. New York, NY: Oxford University Press.

ed. 1994. *Frederick Douglass: Autobiographies*. New York, NY: Library of America.

Genovese, Eugene D. 1976. *Roll, Jordan, Roll: The World the Slaves Made*. New York, NY: Vintage.

Gerick, Thomas. 1996. *Der versus quadratus bei Plautus und seine volkstümliche Tradition*. Tübingen: Gunter Narr.

Gill, Lesley. 1990. "Painted Faces: Conflict and Ambiguity in Domestic Servant-Employer Relations in La Paz, 1930–1988." *Latin American Research Review* 25.1: 119–36.

Gilula, Dwora. 2000. "Stratonicus, the Witty Harpist." In *Athenaeus and his World: Reading Greek Culture in the Roman Empire*, eds David Braund and John Wilkins: 423–33. University of Exeter Press.

Glazebrook, Allison. 2014. "The Erotics of Manumission: Prostitutes and the πρᾶσις ἐπ᾽ ἐλευθερίᾳ." *EuGeStA* 4: 53–80.

Gold, Barbara K. 1998. "'Vested Interests' in Plautus' *Casina*: Cross-Dressing in Roman Comedy." *Helios* 25.1: 17–29.

Goldberg, Sander M. 1998. "Plautus on the Palatine." *JRS* 88: 1–20.

2005. *Constructing Literature in the Roman Republic: Poetry and its Reception.* Cambridge University Press.

2012. "Seeing Plays the Roman Way." Webster Lecture, Oct. 31, University of London.

Golden, Mark. 1985. "*Pais*, 'Child' and 'Slave.'" *L'Antiquité Classique* 54: 91–104.

Gossen, Gary H. 1976. "Verbal Dueling in Chamula." In *Speech Play: Research and Resources for Studying Linguistic Creativity*, eds Barbara Kirshenblatt-Gimblett: 121–46. Philadelphia: University of Pennsylvania Press.

Gossett, Hattie. 1984. "Is it True What They Say about Colored Pussy?" In *Pleasure and Danger: Exploring Female Sexuality*, ed. Carole S. Vance: 411–12. Boston, MA: Routledge & Kegan Paul.

Gowers, Emily. 1993. *The Loaded Table: Representations of Food in Roman Literature.* Oxford: Clarendon Press.

1994. "Horace, *Satires* 1.5: An Inconsequential Journey." *PCPhS* 39: 48–66.

ed. and comm. 2012. *Horace: Satires Book I.* Cambridge University Press.

Gowing, Alain M. 2005. *Empire and Memory: The Representation of the Roman Republic in Imperial Culture.* Cambridge University Press.

2010. "From Polybius to Dionysius: The Decline and Fall of Hellenistic Historiography." In *A Companion to Hellenistic Literature*, eds James J. Clauss and Martine Cuypers: 384–94. Chichester: Wiley-Blackwell.

Gratwick, A. S. 1973. "'Titus Maccius Plautus.'" *CQ* 23.1: 78–84.

1982. "Drama." In *The Cambridge History of Classical Literature*, vol. 2, part 1, *The Early Republic*, ed. E. J. Kenney: 77–137. Cambridge University Press.

ed. and comm. 1993. *Plautus: Menaechmi.* Cambridge University Press.

Green, F. Mira. 2015. "Witnesses and Participants in the Shadows: The Sexual Lives of Enslaved Women and Boys." *Helios* 42.1: 143–62.

Green, J. R. 2012. "Comic Vases in South Italy: Continuity and Innovation in the Development of a Figurative Language." In *Theater Outside Athens: Drama in Greek Sicily and South Italy*, eds Kathryn Bosher: 289–342. Cambridge University Press.

Griffith, Mark. 1990. "Contest and Contradiction in Early Greek Poetry." In *Cabinet of the Muses: Essays on Classical and Comparative Literature in Honor of Thomas G. Rosenmeyer*, eds Mark Griffith and Donald J. Mastronarde: 185–207. Atlanta, GA: Scholars Press.

Griffiths, Suzanne N. 1978–9. "Doctoral Dissertations Completed at the University of Illinois under William Abbott Oldfather." *CJ* 74.2: 149–53.

[Gronovius, J. F.] 1829. *M. Accii Plauti Comoediae ex editione J. F. Gronovii … in usum Delphini.* Vol. 2. London: A. J. Valpy.

Gruen, Erich S. 1996a. "Plautus and the Public Stage." In *Studies in Greek Culture and Roman Policy:* 124–57. Berkeley, CA: University of California Press.

1996b. "Poetry and Politics: The Beginnings of Latin Literature." In *Studies in Greek Culture and Roman Policy:* 79–123. Berkeley, CA: University of California Press.

2014. "Roman Comedy and the Social Scene." In *The Oxford Handbook of Greek and Roman Comedy*, eds Michael Fontaine and Adele C. Scafuro: 601–14. Oxford University Press.

Gunderson, Erik. 2000. *Staging Masculinity: The Rhetoric of Performance in the Roman World.* Ann Arbor: University of Michigan Press.

2005. "The Libidinal Rhetoric of Satire." In *The Cambridge Companion to Roman Satire*, eds Kirk Freudenburg: 224–40. Cambridge University Press.

2015. *Laughing Awry: Plautus and Tragicomedy.* Oxford University Press.

Gutzwiller, Kathryn, and Ömer Çelik. 2012. "New Menander Mosaics from Antioch." *AJA* 116.4: 573–623.

Habinek, Thomas N. 1998. *The Politics of Latin Literature: Writing, Identity, and Empire in Ancient Rome.* Princeton University Press.

2005. *The World of Roman Song: From Ritualized Speech to Social Order.* Baltimore, MD: Johns Hopkins University Press.

Hägg, Tomas. 2012. *The Art of Biography in Antiquity.* Cambridge University Press.

Halla-aho, Hilla, and Peter Kruschwitz. 2010. "Colloquial and Literary Language in Early Roman Tragedy." In *Colloquial and Literary Latin*, eds Eleanor Dickey and Anna Chahoud: 127–53. Cambridge University Press.

Hallett, Judith P. 2011. "Ballio's Brothel, Phoenicium's Letter, and the Literary Education of Greco-Roman Prostitutes: The Evidence of Plautus's *Pseudolus.*" In *Greek Prostitutes in the Ancient Mediterranean, 800 BCE–200 CE*, ed. Allison Glazebrook and Madeleine M. Henry: 172–96. Madison, WI: University of Wisconsin Press.

Hancock, Ange-Marie. 2016. *Intersectionality: An Intellectual History.* Oxford University Press.

Hanson, John Arthur. 1965. "The Glorious Military." In *Roman Drama*, eds T. A. Dorey and Donald R. Dudley: 51–85. New York, NY: Basic Books.

Harden, D. B. 1939. "The Topography of Punic Carthage." *Greece and Rome* 9.25: 1–12.

Harding, Sandra, ed. 1987. *Feminism and Methodology.* Bloomington, IN: Indiana University Press.

Harper, Kyle. 2011. *Slavery in the Late Roman World, AD 275–425.* Cambridge University Press.

Harris, William V. 1979. *War and Imperialism in Republican Rome 327–70 BC.* Oxford: Clarendon Press.

ed. 2013. *Moses Finley and Politics.* Leiden: Brill.

Hawkins, Tom. 2014. *Iambic Poetics in the Roman Empire.* Cambridge University Press.

Headlam, Walter. 2001[1922]. *Herodas: The Mimes and Fragments*, ed. A. D. Knox. London: Bristol Classical Press.

Heinze, Richard. 1929. "*Fides.*" *Hermes* 64: 140–66.

Henderson, Jeffrey. 1975. *The Maculate Muse: Obscene Language in Attic Comedy.* New Haven, CT: Yale University Press.

ed. and trans. 2002. *Aristophanes: Frogs, Assemblywomen, Wealth.* Cambridge, MA: Harvard University Press.

Henderson, John. 1999. "Hanno's Punic Heirs: Der *Poenulus*-Neid des Plautus." In *Writing down Rome: Satire, Comedy, and Other Offences in Latin Poetry*: 3–37. Oxford: Clarendon Press.

2001. *Telling Tales on Caesar: Roman Stories from Phaedrus.* Oxford University Press.

trans. and comm. 2006. *Asinaria: The One about the Asses.* Madison, WI: University of Wisconsin Press.

Henry, Madeleine M. 1992. "The Edible Woman: Athenaeus's Concept of the Pornographic." In *Pornography and Representation in Greece and Rome*, ed. Amy Richlin: 250–68. Oxford University Press.

2000. "Athenaeus the Ur-Pornographer." In *Athenaeus and his World: Reading Greek Culture in the Roman Empire*, ed. David Braund and John Wilkins: 503–13. Exeter: University of Exeter Press.

Hickey, Doralyn J. 1975. "Paul Shaner Dunkin, 28 September 1905–25 August 1975: An Appreciation." *Library Resources and Technical Services* 19.4: 293.

1993. "Dunkin, Paul S." In *World Encyclopedia of Library and Information Services*, 3rd ed., edn., Robert Wedgeworth: 258–60. Chicago, MI: American Library Association.

Highet, Gilbert. 1973. "*Libertino Patre Natus.*" *AJPh* 94.3: 268–81.

Hinard, François, and Jean-Christian Dumont, eds. 2003. *Libitina: Pompes funèbres et supplices en Campanie à l'époque d'Auguste. Édition, traduction et commentaire de la Lex Libitinae Puteolana.* Paris: De Boccard.

Hölkeskamp, Karl-J. 2006. "History and Collective Memory in the Middle Republic." In *A Companion to the Roman Republic*, eds Nathan Rosenstein and Robert Morstein-Marx: 478–95. Malden, MA: Blackwell.

2010. *Reconstructing the Roman Republic: An Ancient Political Culture and Modern Research*, trans. Henry Heitmann-Gordon. Princeton University Press.

2014. "In Defense of Concepts, Categories, and Other Abstractions: Remarks on a Theory of Memory (in the Making)." In *Memoria Romana: Memory in Rome and Rome in Memory*, ed. Karl Galinsky: 63–70. Ann Arbor, MI: University of Michigan Press.

Holliday, Peter J. 2002. *The Origins of Roman Historical Commemoration in the Visual Arts.* Cambridge University Press.

Holzberg, Niklas. 2002. *The Ancient Fable: An Introduction*, trans. Christine Jackson-Holzberg. Bloomington, IN: Indiana University Press.

Hondagneu-Sotelo, Pierrette. 2007. *Doméstica: Immigrant Workers Cleaning and Caring in the Shadows of Affluence.* Rev. edn. Berkeley, CA: University of California Press.

hooks, bell. 1992. "The Oppositional Gaze." In *Black Looks: Race and Representation*: 115–32. Boston, MA: South End Press.

Hopkins, Keith. 1993. "Novel Evidence for Roman Slavery." *Past and Present* 138: 3–27.

Horden, Peregrine, and Nicholas Purcell. 2000. *The Corrupting Sea: A Study of Mediterranean History*. Oxford: Blackwell.

Horsfall, Nicholas. 2003. *The Culture of the Roman Plebs*. London: Duckworth.

Hough, John N. 1934. "The Use of Greek Words by Plautus." *AJPh* 55.4: 346–64.

Hoyos, B. D. 1976. "Roman Strategy in the Cisalpina, 224–222 and 203–191 B.C." *Antichthon* 10: 44–55.

2007. *Truceless War: Carthage's Fight for Survival, 241 to 237 BC*. Leiden: Brill.

Hunter, Richard L. 1985. *The New Comedy of Greece and Rome*. Cambridge University Press.

1995. "Plautus and Herodas." In *Plautus und die Tradition des Stegreifspiels: Festgabe für Eckard Lefèvre zum 60. Geburtstag*, eds Lore Benz, Ekkehard Stärk, and Gregor Vogt-Spira: 155–69. Tübingen: Gunter Narr.

Hunter, Virginia J. 1994. *Policing Athens: Social Control in the Attic Lawsuits, 420–320 B.C.* Princeton: Princeton University Press.

Hurston, Zora Neale. 1935. *Mules and Men*. Philadelphia, PA: J. B. Lippincott.

1943. "High John de Conquer." *The American Mercury*, Oct.: 450–8.

1981. *The Sanctified Church*. Berkeley, CA: Turtle Island.

Hutcheon, Linda. 2006. *A Theory of Adaptation*. New York, NY: Routledge.

Idle, Eric. 2000. *The Road to Mars: A Post-Modern Novel*. New York, NY: Vintage.

Irby, Georgia L. 2012. "Mapping the World: Greek Initiatives from Homer to Eratosthenes." In *Ancient Perspectives: Maps and Their Place in Mesopotamia, Egypt, Greece and Rome*, ed. Richard J. A. Talbert: 81–107. University of Chicago Press.

James, Sharon L. 1997. "Slave-Rape and Female Silence in Ovid's Love Poetry." *Helios* 24.1: 60–76.

2010. "Trafficking Pasicompsa: A Courtesan's Travels and Travails in Plautus' *Mercator*." *NECJ* 37: 39–50.

2012. "Domestic Female Slaves in Roman Comedy." In *A Companion to Women in the Ancient World*, eds Sharon L. James and Sheila Dillon: 235–7. Chichester: Blackwell.

2014. "The Battered Shield: Survivor Guilt and Family Trauma in Menander's *Aspis*." In *Combat Trauma and the Ancient Greeks*, eds Peter Meineck and David Konstan: 237–60. New York, NY: Palgrave Macmillan.

2015a. "*Mater, Oratio, Filia*: Listening to Mothers in Roman Comedy." In *Women in Roman Republican Drama*, eds Dorota Dutsch, Sharon L. James, and David Konstan: 108–27. Madison, WI: University of Wisconsin Press.

2015b. Review of Valentini 2012. *JRS* 105: 349–50.

Forthcoming. *Women in New Comedy*. Oxford University Press.

Jefferson, Eleanor. 2012. "Problems and Audience in Cato's *Origines*." In *Processes of Integration and Identity Formation in the Roman Republic*, ed. S. T. Roselaar: 311–26. Leiden: Brill.

Jeppesen, Seth A. 2015. "Obscenity and Performance on the Plautine Stage." In *Ancient Obscenities: Their Nature and Use in the Ancient Greek and Roman Worlds*, eds Dorota Dutsch and Ann Suter: 175–98. Ann Arbor, MI: University of Michigan Press.

    2016. "Lament for Fallen Cities in Early Roman Drama: Naevius, Ennius, and Plautus." In *The Fall of Cities in the Mediterranean: Commemoration in Literature, Folk-Song, and Liturgy*, eds Mary R. Bachvarova, Dorota Dutsch, and Ann Suter: 127–55. Cambridge University Press.

Johanson, Christopher. Forthcoming. *Funerary Spectacle: Aristocratic Display in the Roman Forum*. Berkeley, CA: California Classical Studies.

Johnson, Merri Lisa, ed. 2002. *Jane Sexes It Up: True Confessions of Feminist Desire*. New York, NY: Four Walls Eight Windows.

Jones, C. P. 1987. "*Stigma*: Tattooing and Branding in Graeco-Roman Antiquity." *JRS* 77: 139–55.

Jones, Gregory S. 2014. "Voice of the People: Popular Symposia and the Non-Elite Origins of the Attic *Skolia*." *TAPA* 144.2: 229–62.

Jones, LeRoi. 1999. *Blues People: Negro Music in White America*. 2nd ed. New York, NY: William Morrow.

Joshel, Sandra R. 1986. "Nurturing the Master's Child: Slavery and the Roman Child-Nurse." *Signs* 12.1: 3–22.

    1992. *Work, Identity, and Legal Status at Rome: A Study of the Occupational Inscriptions*. Norman, OK: University of Oklahoma Press.

    2010. *Slavery in the Roman World*. Cambridge University Press.

Joshel, Sandra R. and Sheila Murnaghan, eds. 1998. *Women and Slaves in Greco-Roman Culture: Differential Equations*. London: Routledge.

Joshel, Sandra R. and Lauren Hackworth Petersen. 2014. *The Material Life of Roman Slaves*. Cambridge University Press.

Kajava, Mika. 1998. "*Visceratio*." *Arctos* 32: 109–31.

Kaminer, Debra. 2006. "Healing Processes in Trauma Narratives: A Review." *South African Journal of Psychology* 36.3: 481–99.

Kampen, Natalie Boymel. 2013. "Slaves and *Liberti* in the Roman Army." In *Roman Slavery and Roman Material Culture*, ed. Michele George: 180–97. University of Toronto Press.

Karanika, Andromache. 2014. *Voices at Work: Women, Performance, and Labor in Ancient Greece*. Baltimore, MD: Johns Hopkins University Press.

Kaster, Robert A., ed. and comm. 1995. *C. Suetonius Tranquillus De Grammaticis et Rhetoribus*. Oxford: Clarendon Press.

Kay, Philip. 2014. *Rome's Economic Revolution*. Oxford University Press.

Kelly, J. M. 1966. *Roman Litigation*. Oxford: Clarendon Press.

Kent, Sarah, and Jacqueline Morreau, eds. 1985. *Women's Images of Men*. London: Writers and Readers Publishing.

Ketterer, Robert C. 1986a. "Stage Properties in Plautine Comedy I." *Semiotica* 58.3/4: 193–217.

    1986b. "Stage Properties in Plautine Comedy II." *Semiotica* 59.1/2: 93–135.

    1986c. "Stage Properties in Plautine Comedy III." *Semiotica* 60.1/2: 29–72.

Klapisch-Zuber, Christiane. 1985. *Women, Family, and Ritual in Renaissance Italy,* trans. Lydia G. Cochrane. University of Chicago Press.

Klein, Sophie. 2015. "When Actions Speak Louder than Words: Mute Characters in Roman Comedy." *CJ* III.1: 53–66.

Knapp, Charles. 1907a. "Travel in Ancient Times as Seen in Plautus and Terence. I." *CP* 2.1: 1–24.

1907b. "Travel in Ancient Times as Seen in Plautus and Terence. II." *CP* 2.3: 281–304.

Konstan, David. 1983. *Roman Comedy.* Ithaca, NY: Cornell University Press.

2013. "Menander's Slaves: The Banality of Violence." In *Slaves and Slavery in Ancient Greek Comic Drama,* eds Ben Akrigg and Rob Tordoff: 144–58. Cambridge University Press.

Konstantakos, Ioannis M. 2016. "Plautus' *Aulularia* and Popular Narrative Tradition." In *Roman Drama and Its Contexts,* eds Stavros Frangoulidis, Stephen J. Harrison, and Gesine Manuwald: 143–66. Trends in Classics – Supplementary Volumes 34. Berlin: Walter de Gruyter.

Koortbojian, Michael. 2002. "A Painted *Exemplum* at Rome's Temple of Liberty." *JRS* 92: 33–48.

2006. "The Freedman's Voice: The Funerary Monument of Aurelius Hermia and Aurelia Philematio." In *The Art of Citizens, Soldiers and Freedmen in the Roman World,* eds Eve D'Ambra and Guy P. R. Métreaux: 91–9. Oxford: BAR International.

Kruschwitz, Peter. 2013. *"Populi sensus maxime theatro et spectaculis perspectus est."* Paper delivered at the Popular Comedy Conference, Glasgow. PDF available at http://reading.academia.edu/PeterKruschwitz/Talks.

Kurke, Leslie. 2002. "Gender, Politics and Subversion in the *Chreiai* of Machon." *PCPhS* 48: 20–65.

2011. *Aesopic Conversations: Popular Tradition, Cultural Dialogue, and the Invention of Greek Prose.* Princeton University Press.

Lada-Richards, Ismene. 2007. *Silent Eloquence: Lucian and Pantomime Dancing.* London: Duckworth.

Langlands, Rebecca. 2006. *Sexual Morality in Ancient Rome.* Cambridge University Press.

2016. "Extratextuality: Literary Interactions with Oral Culture and Exemplary Ethics." In *Literary Interactions under Nerva, Trajan, and Hadrian,* eds A. König and C. L. Whitton: 68–80. Cambridge University Press.

Forthcoming. *Exemplary Ethics in Ancient Rome.* Cambridge University Press.

Langslow, David. 2012. "Integration, Identity, and Language Shift: Strengths and Weaknesses of the 'Linguistic' Evidence." In *Processes of Integration and Identity Formation in the Roman Republic,* ed. S. T. Roselaar: 289–309. Leiden: Brill.

Lape, Susan. 2004. *Reproducing Athens: Menander's Comedy, Democratic Culture, and the Hellenistic City.* Princeton University Press.

La Penna, Antonio. 1979. "Cassio Parmense nella storia del teatro latino." In *Fra teatro, poesia e politica romana ...* : 143–51. Turin: Einaudi.

Laurence, Ray. 2013. "Roads and Bridges." In *A Companion to the Archaeology of the Roman Republic*, ed. Jane DeRose Evans: 296–308. Chichester: Wiley-Blackwell.

Lavin, Suzanne. 2004. *Women and Comedy in Solo Performance: Phyllis Diller, Lily Tomlin, and Roseanne.* New York, NY: Routledge.

Lee, Rachel C. 2004. "'Where's My Parade?': Margaret Cho and the Asian American Body in Space." *Drama Review* 48.2: 108–32.

Lee, R. W. 1956. *The Elements of Roman Law.* 4th edn. London: Sweet & Maxwell.

Lefèvre, Eckard. 1982. *Maccus vortit barbare: Vom tragischen Amphitryon zum tragikomischen Amphitruo.* Wiesbaden: Franz Steiner.

1999. "Plautus' *Amphitruo* zwischen Tragödie und Stegreifspiel." In *Studien zu Plautus' Amphitruo,* ed. Thomas Baier: 11–50. Tübingen: Gunter Narr.

2001. "*nimium familiariter* – plautinische Sklaven unter sich: *Epidicus* I 1 (mit einem Blick auf das Original)." In *Studien zu Plautus' Epidicus,* ed. Ulrike Auhagen: 105–29. Tübingen: Gunter Narr.

2014. "Plautus und die Techniken des Improvisationstheaters." In *Ancient Comedy and Reception: Essays in Honor of Jeffrey Henderson,* ed. S. Douglas Olson: 223–34. Berlin: Walter de Gruyter.

Lefkowitz, Mary R., and Maureen B. Fant, eds. 2016. *Women's Life in Greece and Rome: A Source Book in Translation.* 4th edn. Baltimore, MD: Johns Hopkins University Press.

Le Guen, Brigitte. 2001. *Les Associations de Technites dionysiaques à l'époque hellénistique.* 2 vols. Nancy: Association pour la diffusion de la recherche sur l'antiquité.

2014. "The Diffusion of Comedy from the Age of Alexander to the Beginning of the Roman Empire." Trans. Christopher Welser. In *The Oxford Handbook of Greek and Roman Comedy,* eds Michael Fontaine and Adele C. Scafuro: 359–77. Oxford University Press.

Le Guin, Ursula K. 1994. "The Rock that Changed Things." In *A Fisherman of the Inland Sea*: 57–67. New York, NY: HarperPrism.

1995. *Four Ways to Forgiveness.* New York, NY: HarperPrism.

2003. "Old Music and the Slave Women." In *The Birthday of the World*: 153–211. New York, NY: Perennial.

2006. *Voices.* Orlando, FL: Harcourt.

2007. *Powers.* Orlando, FL: Harcourt.

2008. *Lavinia.* Orlando, FL: Harcourt.

Leigh, Matthew. 2004. *Comedy and the Rise of Rome.* Oxford University Press.

2010. "Early Roman Epic and the Maritime Moment." *CP* 105.3: 265–80.

2013. *From Polypragmon to Curiosus: Ancient Concepts of Curious and Meddlesome Behaviour.* Oxford University Press.

Lejay, Paul, ed. 1911. *Satires.* Paris: Hachette.

Leo, Friedrich, ed. 1896. *Plauti Comoediae.* Vol. 2. Berlin: Weidmann.

1912. *Plautinische Forschungen: Zur Kritik und Geschichte der Komödie.* Berlin: Weidmann.

Levi, Primo. 1986. *The Reawakening.* 2nd edn. Trans. Stuart Woolf and Ruth Feldman ("Afterword"). New York, NY: Collier Books.

Levin-Richardson, Sarah. 2013. *"Fututa Sum Hic:* Female Subjectivity and Agency in Pompeian Sexual Graffiti." *CJ* 108.3: 319–45.

Lewis, David M. 2011. "Near Eastern Slaves in Classical Attica and the Slave Trade with Persian Territories." *CQ* 61.1: 91–113.

2017. "Orlando Patterson, Property, and Ancient Slavery: The Definitional Problem Revisited." In *On Human Bondage: After Slavery and Social Death,* eds John Bodel and Walter Scheidel: 31–54. Chichester: John Wiley & Sons.

In progress. *Greek Slave Systems and their Eastern Neighbours: A Comparative Study.*

Lewis, Sian. 1995. "Barbers' Shops and Perfume Shops: 'Symposia without Wine.'" In *The Greek World,* ed. Anton Powell: 432–41. London: Routledge.

Libourel, Jan M. 1973. "Galley Slaves in the Second Punic War." *CP* 68.2: 116–19.

Lindsay, W. M., ed. and comm. 1921. *T. Macci Plauti Captivi.* Rev. edn. Oxford: Clarendon Press.

Lintott, Andrew. 1999. *Violence in Republican Rome.* 2nd edn. Oxford University Press.

Lodge, Gonzalez. 1926. *Lexicon Plautinum.* 2 vols. Leipzig: Teubner.

Lott, Eric. 1993. *Love and Theft: Blackface Minstrelsy and the American Working Class.* New York, NY: Oxford University Press.

Lowe, J. C. B. 1989. "Plautus' Parasites and the Atellana." In *Studien zur vorliterarischen Periode im frühen Rom,* ed. Gregor Vogt-Spira: 161–9. Tübingen: Gunter Narr.

Luce, T. James. 1994. "Duckworth, George Eckel." *BDNAC:* 146–7.

Ma, John. 2003. "Kings." In *A Companion to the Hellenistic World,* ed. Andrew Erskine: 177–95. Oxford: Blackwell.

2013. *Statues and Cities: Honorific Portraits and Civic Identity in the Hellenistic World.* Oxford University Press.

McCarthy, Kathleen. 2000. *Slaves, Masters, and the Art of Authority in Plautine Comedy.* Princeton University Press.

MacCary, W. Thomas, and M. M. Willcock, eds. and comm. 1976. *Plautus: Casina.* Cambridge University Press.

McClure, Laura K. 2003. *Courtesans at Table: Gender and Greek Literary Culture in Athenaeus.* New York, NY: Routledge.

McCrum, Robert. 2004. *Wodehouse: A Life.* New York, NY: W. W. Norton.

McElduff, Siobhán. 2013. *Roman Theories of Translation: Surpassing the Source.* New York, NY: Routledge.

McGinn, Thomas A. J. 1998. *Prostitution, Sexuality, and the Law in Ancient Rome.* New York, NY: Oxford University Press.

2004. *The Economy of Prostitution in the Roman World: A Study of Social History and the Brothel.* Ann Arbor, MI: University of Michigan Press.

McKeown, Niall. 2007. *The Invention of Ancient Slavery?* London: Duckworth.

Mankin, David, ed. and comm. 1995. *Horace: Epodes.* Cambridge University Press.

Mann, Kristin. 2015. "The Fabulist in the Fable Book." Diss. UCLA.

Manuwald, Gesine. 2011. *Roman Republican Theatre*. Cambridge University Press.
  2014. "Tragedy, Paratragedy, and Roman Comedy." In *The Oxford Handbook of Greek and Roman Comedy*, eds Michael Fontaine and Adele C. Scafuro: 580–98. Oxford University Press.
  2015. "*Haut facul … femina una invenitur bona?*: Representations of Women in Republican Tragedy." In *Women in Roman Republican Drama*, eds Dorota Dutsch, Sharon L. James, and David Konstan: 171–91. Madison, WI: University of Wisconsin Press.
Marchand, Suzanne L. 1996. *Down from Olympus: Archaeology and Philhellenism in Germany, 1750–1970*. Princeton University Press.
Marshall, C. W. 1997. "Shattered Mirrors and Breaking Class: Saturio's Daughter in Plautus' *Persa*." *Text and Presentation* 18: 100–9.
  1999. "*Quis Hic Loquitur?* Plautine Delivery and the 'Double Aside.'" In *Crossing the Stages: The Production, Performance, and Reception of Ancient Theater*, eds John Porter, Eric Csapo, C. W. Marshall, and Robert C. Ketterer: 105–29 (= *Syllecta Classica* 10: 105–29).
  2006. *The Stagecraft and Performance of Roman Comedy*. Cambridge University Press.
  2013. "Sex Slaves in New Comedy." In *Slaves and Slavery in Ancient Greek Comic Drama*, eds Ben Akrigg and Rob Tordoff: 173–96. Cambridge University Press.
  2015. "Domestic Sexual Labor in Plautus." *Helios* 42.1: 123–41.
Marx, Friedrich, ed. and comm. 1904–5. *C. Lucilii Carminum Reliquiae*. 2 vols. Leipzig: Teubner.
  ed. and comm. 1959[1928]. *Plautus: Rudens*. Amsterdam: Hakkert.
Mattingly, Harold, and E. S. G. Robinson. 1935. "Nummus." *AJPh* 56.3: 225–31.
Maurach, Gregor, ed. and comm. 1988. *Der Poenulus des Plautus*. Heidelberg: Carl Winter.
Mavrogenes, Nancy A. 1994. "Lodge, Gonzalez." *BDNAC*: 366–7.
Mayor, Adrienne. 2011. *The First Fossil Hunters: Dinosaurs, Mammoths, and Myth in Greek and Roman Times*. Rev. edn. Princeton: Princeton University Press.
Mayor, John E. B., ed. and comm. 1872. *Thirteen Satires of Juvenal: The Latin Text of Otto Jahn. Edited, with English notes …* 2nd edn. London: Macmillan.
Meineck, Peter. 2012. "Combat Trauma and the Tragic Stage: 'Restoration' by Cultural Catharsis." *Intertexts* 16.1: 7–24.
Mellon, James, ed. 1988. *Bullwhip Days: The Slaves Remember*. New York, NY: Weidenfeld & Nicolson.
Memmi, Albert. 1991[1957]. *The Colonizer and the Colonized*. Expanded ed., trans. Howard Greenfeld. Boston, MA: Beacon Press.
  1992[1955]. *The Pillar of Salt*, trans. Édouard Roditi. Boston, MA: Beacon Press.
Mercado, Angelo. 2012. *Italic Verse: A Study of the Poetic Remains of Old Latin, Faliscan, and Sabellic*. Innsbrucker Beiträge zur Sprachwissenschaft 145. Innsbruck: Institut für Sprachen und Literaturen der Universität Innsbruck.
Meyer, Moe. 2010. *An Archaeology of Posing: Essays on Camp, Drag, and Sexuality*. Madison, WI: Macater Press.

Michels, Agnes Kirsopp. 1967. *The Calendar of the Roman Republic*. Princeton University Press.

Miles, Margaret. 2008. *Art as Plunder: The Ancient Origins of Debate about Cultural Property*. New York, NY: Cambridge University Press.

Millar, Fergus. 1989. "Political Power in Mid-Republican Rome: Curia or Comitium?" *JRS* 79: 138–50.

Miller, Patricia Cox. 2003. "Is There a Harlot in This Text? Hagiography and the Grotesque." *Journal of Medieval and Early Modern Studies* 33.3: 419–35.

Miller, Paul Allen. 2007. "Catullus and Roman Love Elegy." In *A Companion to Catullus*, ed. Marilyn B. Skinner: 399–417. Malden, MA: Blackwell.

Millett, Paul. 1991. *Lending and Borrowing in Ancient Athens*. Cambridge University Press.

Millis, Benjamin. 2014. "Post-Menandrian Comic Poets: An Overview of the Evidence and a Checklist." In *The Oxford Handbook of Greek and Roman Comedy*, eds Michael Fontaine and Adele C. Scafuro: 871–84. Oxford University Press.

Mineo, Bernard. 2011. "Principal Literary Sources for the Punic Wars (Apart from Polybius)." In *A Companion to the Punic Wars*, ed. Dexter Hoyos: 111–28. Oxford: Wiley-Blackwell.

Mintz, Lawrence E. 1985. "Situation Comedy." In *TV Genres: A Handbook and Reference Guide*, ed. Brian G. Rose: 107–29. Westport, CT: Greenwood Press.

Momigliano, Arnaldo. 2012[1959]. "Athens in the Third Century B.C. and the Discovery of Rome in the Histories of Timaeus of Tauromenium." In *Essays in Ancient and Modern Historiography*: 37–66. University of Chicago Press.

Monda, Salvator, ed. 2004. *Titus Maccius Plautus: Vidularia et deperditarum fabularum fragmenta*. Sarsina: QuattroVenti.

Moodie, Erin K., comm. 2015. *Plautus' Poenulus: A Student Commentary*. Ann Arbor, MI: University of Michigan Press.

Moore, Allan. 2013. "Conclusion: A Hermeneutics of Protest Music." In *The Routledge History of Social Protest in Popular Music*, ed. Jonathan C. Friedman: 387–99. New York, NY: Routledge.

Moore, Timothy J. 1991. "*Palliata Togata*: Plautus, *Curculio* 462–86." *AJPh* 112.3: 343–62.

1994/95. "Seats and Social Status in the Plautine Theatre." *CJ* 90.2: 113–23.

1995. "Tragicomedy as a Running Joke: Plautus' *Amphitruo* in Performance." *Didaskalia* supplement 1, vol. 1.6. www.didaskalia.net/issues/vol1no6/contents.html.

1998. *The Theater of Plautus: Playing to the Audience*. Austin, TX: University of Texas Press.

2001. "Music in *Epidicus*." In *Studien zu Plautus' Epidicus*, ed. Ulrike Auhagen: 313–34. Tübingen: Gunter Narr.

2012. *Music in Roman Comedy*. Cambridge University Press.

2015. "Music and Gender in Terence's *Hecyra*." In *Women in Roman Republican Drama*, eds Dorota Dutsch, Sharon L. James, and David Konstan: 68–87. Madison, WI: University of Wisconsin Press.

Morel, Jean-Paul. 1989. "The Transformation of Italy, 300–133 B.C.: The Evidence of Archaeology." In *The Cambridge Ancient History.* 2nd edn. 8. 477–516. Cambridge University Press.

2009. "Céramiques à vernis noir et histoire." *Journal of Roman Archaeology* 22: 477–88.

Moretti, Franco. 1998. *Atlas of the European Novel 1800–1900.* London: Verso.

Morris, Edward P., ed. and comm. 1909. *Horace: The Satires.* New York, NY: American Book Co.

Morton, A. L. 1952. *The English Utopia.* London: Lawrence & Wishart.

Morton, Peter. 2013. "Eunus: The Cowardly King." *CQ* 63.1: 237–52.

Naiden, F. S. 2014. "Finley's War Years." *AJPh* 135.2: 243–66.

Narain, A. K. 1989. "The Greeks of Bactria and India." In *The Cambridge Ancient History.* 2nd edn: 8. 388–421. Cambridge University Press.

Nathans, Heather S. 2009. *Slavery and Sentiment on the American Stage, 1787–1861: Lifting the Veil of Black.* Cambridge University Press.

Neff, Ali Colleen. 2009. *Let the World Listen Right: The Mississippi Delta Hip-Hop Story.* Jackson, MS: University Press of Mississippi.

Nelsestuen, G. 2011. "Polishing Scrofa's Agronomical *Eloquentia*: Representation and Revision in Varro's *De Re Rustica*." *Phoenix* 65: 315–51.

Nervegna, Sebastiana. 2014. "Graphic Comedy: Menandrian Mosaics and Terentian Miniatures." In *The Oxford Handbook of Greek and Roman Comedy,* eds Michael Fontaine and Adele C. Scafuro: 717–34. Oxford University Press.

Newton, Esther. 1979[1972]. *Mother Camp: Female Impersonators in America.* University of Chicago Press.

Nisbet, R. G. 1918. "The *Festuca* and the *Alapa* of Manumission." *JRS* 8: 1–14.

Nixon, Paul, ed. and trans. 1924. *Plautus.* Vol. 3. London: Heinemann.

Nochlin, Linda. 1988. *Women, Art, and Power and Other Essays.* New York, NY: Harper & Row.

Nora, Pierre. 1989. "Between Memory and History: *Les Lieux de Mémoire*." Trans. Marc Roudebush. *Representations* 26: 7–24, with Note on p. 25.

Novick, Peter. 1988. *That Noble Dream: The "Objectivity Question" and the American Historical Profession.* Cambridge University Press.

Nussbaum, Alan J. 2014. "The PIE Proprietor and His Goods." In *Munus amicitiae: Norbert Oettinger a collegis et amicis dicatum,* eds H. Craig Melchert, Elisabeth Ricken, and Thomas Steer: 228–54. Ann Arbor, MI: Beech Stave Press.

Nussbaum, Martha C. 1995. "Objectification." *Philosophy and Public Affairs* 24.4: 249–91.

Oakley, S. P. 1998. *A Commentary on Livy, Books VI–X,* vol. 2: *Books VII–VIII.* Oxford: Clarendon Press.

2005. *A Commentary on Livy, Books VI–X,* vol. 4: *Book X.* Oxford: Clarendon Press.

Obrdlik, Antonin J. 1942. "'Gallows Humor' – A Sociological Phenomenon." *American Journal of Sociology* 47.5: 709–16.

Olick, Jeffrey K., Vered Vinitzky-Seroussi, and Daniel Levy, eds. 2011. *The Collective Memory Reader.* Oxford University Press.

Olson, Kelly. 2008. "The Appearance of the Young Roman Girl." In *Roman Dress and the Fabrics of Roman Culture*, eds Jonathan Edmondson and Alison Keith: 139–57. University of Toronto Press.

Olson, S. Douglas, ed. and trans. 2008. *Athenaeus: The Learned Banqueters, Books VI–VII*. Cambridge, MA: Harvard University Press.

Opie, Iona, and Peter Opie. 1969. *Children's Games in Street and Playground: Chasing, Catching, Seeking, Hunting, Racing, Duelling, Exerting, Daring, Guessing, Acting, Pretending*. Oxford: Clarendon Press.

Otto, A. 1965 [1890]. *Die Sprichwörter und Sprichwörtlichen Redensarten der Römer*. Hildesheim: Georg Olms.

Owens, William. 1994. "The Third Deception in *Bacchides*: *Fides* and Plautus' Originality." *AJPh* 115.3: 381–407.

2001. "Plautus' Satire of Roman Ideals in *Rudens*, *Amphitruo*, and *Mostellaria*." In *Essays in Honor of Gordon Williams: Twenty-Five Years at Yale*, eds Elizabeth Tylawsky and Charles Weiss: 213–27. New Haven, CT: Henry R. Schwab.

Padilla Peralta, Dan-el. 2014. "Divine Institutions: Religious Practice, Economic Development, and Social Transformation in Mid-Republican Rome." Diss. Stanford University.

In progress. "Pottery and Pilgrims: The Mid-Republican *Pocola* in Religious Context."

Pagliai, Valentina. 2009. "The Art of Dueling with Words: Toward a New Understanding of Verbal Duels across the World." *Oral Tradition* 24.1: 61–88.

2010. "Conflict, Cooperation, and Facework in *Contrasto* Verbal Duels." *Journal of Linguistic Anthropology* 20.1: 87–100.

Palmisciano, Riccardo. 2014. "Submerged Literature in an Oral Culture." In *Submerged Literature in Ancient Greek Culture: An Introduction*, eds Giulio Colesanti and Manuela Giordano: 19–32. Berlin: Walter de Gruyter.

Panayotakis, Costas, ed. and comm. 2010. *Decimus Laberius: The Fragments*. Cambridge University Press.

2014. "Hellenistic Mime and its Reception in Rome." In *The Oxford Handbook of Greek and Roman Comedy*, eds Michael Fontaine and Adele C. Scafuro: 378–96. Oxford University Press.

Pansiéri, Claude. 1997. *Plaute et Rome, ou, les ambiguïtés d'un marginal*. Brussels: Latomus.

Parker, Holt N. 1989. "Crucially Funny or Tranio on the Couch: The *Servus Callidus* and Jokes about Torture." *TAPA* 119: 233–46.

1996. "Plautus vs. Terence: Audience and Popularity Re-Examined." *AJPh* 117.4: 585–617.

1998. "Loyal Slaves and Loyal Wives: The Crisis of the Outsider-Within and Roman *Exemplum* Literature." In *Women and Slaves in Greco-Roman Culture: Differential Equations*, eds Sandra R. Joshel and Sheila Murnaghan: 152–73. London: Routledge.

2000. "Flaccus." *CQ* 50.2: 455–62.

2007. "Free Women and Male Slaves, or Mandingo Meets the Roman Empire." In *Fear of Slaves – Fear of Enslavement in the Ancient Mediterranean. ...*

Actes du XXIXe Colloque du ... GIREA, ed. Anastasia Serghidou: 281–98. Besançon: Presses universitaires de Franche-Comté.

2011. "Toward a Definition of Popular Culture." *History and Theory* 50.2: 147–70.

Patterson, John R. 2006. "Rome and Italy." In *A Companion to the Roman Republic*, eds Nathan Rosenstein and Robert Morstein-Marx: 606–24. Malden, MA: Blackwell.

Patterson, Orlando. 1982. *Slavery and Social Death: A Comparative Study.* Cambridge, MA: Harvard University Press.

Perdrizet, Paul F. 1898. "The Game of Morra." *JHS* 18: 129–32.

Peretti, Burton W. 2013. "Signifying Freedom: Protest in Nineteenth-Century African American Music." In *The Routledge History of Social Protest in Popular Music*, ed. Jonathan C. Friedman: 3–18. New York, NY: Routledge.

Perry, Jonathan S. 2014. "From Frankfurt to Westermann: Forced Labor and the Early Development of Finley's Thought." *AJPh* 135.2: 221–41.

Perry, Matthew J. 2014. *Gender, Manumission, and the Roman Freedwoman.* Cambridge University Press.

Petrides, Antonis K. 2014. "Plautus between Greek Comedy and Atellan Farce: Assessments and Reassessments." In *The Oxford Handbook of Greek and Roman Comedy*, ed. Michael Fontaine and Adele C. Scafuro: 424–43. Oxford University Press.

Petrone, Gianna. 1983. *Teatro Antico e Inganno: Finzioni Plautine.* Palermo: Palumbo.

Pfister, Friedrich, ed. and trans. 1951. *Die Reisebilder des Herakleides.* Österreichische Akademie der Wissenschaften, Philosophisch-Historische Klasse, Sitzungsberichte 227.2. Vienna: Rudolf M. Rohrer.

Phang, Sara Elise. 2001. *The Marriage of Roman Soldiers (13 B.C.–A.D. 235): Law and Family in the Imperial Army.* Leiden: Brill.

Philippides, Katerina. 2011. "Tyndarus' Past: The Name Paegnium in Plautus' *Captivi*." *Classica et Mediaevalia* 62: 99–112.

Pobjoy, Mark. 2006. "Epigraphy and Numismatics." In *A Companion to the Roman Republic*, eds Nathan Rosenstein and Robert Morstein-Marx: 51–80. Malden, MA: Blackwell.

Poccetti, Paolo. 2010. "Greeting and Farewell Expressions as Evidence for Colloquial Language: Between Literary and Epigraphical Texts." In *Colloquial and Literary Latin*, eds Eleanor Dickey and Anna Chahoud: 100–26. Cambridge University Press.

Prentki, Tim, and Sheila Preston, eds. 2009. *The Applied Theatre Reader.* Abingdon: Routledge.

Prescott, Henry W. 1936. "Silent Rôles in Roman Comedy." *CP* 31.2: 97–119.

1937. "Silent Rôles in Roman Comedy." *CP* 32.3: 193–209.

Purcell, Nicholas. 1983. "The *Apparitores*: A Study in Social Mobility." *PBSR* 51: 125–73.

2003. "The Way We Used to Eat: Diet, Community, and History at Rome." *AJPh* 124.3: 329–58.

Quilici, Lorenzo. 1990. *Le strade: Viabilità tra Roma e Lazio.* Rome: Quasar.

Raaflaub, Kurt A. 2014. "War and the City: The Brutality of War and its Impact on the Community." In *Combat Trauma and the Ancient Greeks*, ed. Peter Meineck and David Konstan: 15–46. New York, NY: Palgrave Macmillan.

Rabinowitz, Nancy Sorkin. 1998. "Embodying Tragedy: The Sex of the Actor." *Intertexts* 2.1: 3–25.

2008. "The Medea Project for Incarcerated Women: Liberating Medea." *Syllecta Classica* 19: 237–54.

2013. "Ancient Myth and Feminist Politics: The Medea Project and San Francisco Women's Prisons." In *Roman Literature, Gender and Reception: Domina Illustris*, ed. Donald Lateiner, Barbara K. Gold, and Judith Perkins: 267–83. New York, NY: Routledge.

Raboteau, Albert J. 1978. *Slave Religion: The "Invisible Institution" in the Antebellum South*. Oxford University Press.

Rammel, Hal. 1990. *Nowhere in America: The Big Rock Candy Mountain and Other Comic Utopias*. Urbana, IL: University of Illinois Press.

Ramsay, William, ed. and comm. 1869. *The Mostellaria of Plautus …*, ed. George G. Ramsay. London: Macmillan.

Rawlings, Louis. 2011. "Army and Battle During the Conquest of Italy (350–264 BC)." In *A Companion to the Roman Army*, ed. Paul Erdkamp: 45–62. Oxford: Wiley-Blackwell.

Rawson, Elizabeth. 1985. "Theatrical Life in Republican Rome and Italy." *PBSR* 53: 97–113.

1993. "Freedmen in Roman Comedy." In *Theater and Society in the Classical World*, ed. Ruth Scodel: 215–33. Ann Arbor, MI: University of Michigan Press.

Reckford, Kenneth J. 1987. *Aristophanes' Old-and-New Comedy, vol. 1: Six Essays in Perspective*. Chapel Hill, NC: University of North Carolina Press.

Rei, Annalisa. 1998. "Villains, Wives, and Slaves in the Comedies of Plautus." In *Women and Slaves in Greco-Roman Culture: Differential Equations*, ed. Sandra R. Joshel and Sheila Murnaghan: 92–108. London: Routledge.

Reinhold, Meyer. 1994a. "Finley, Moses Isaac." *BDNAC*: 178–80.

1994b. "Westermann, William Linn." *BDNAC*: 684–5.

Revermann, Martin. 2006. *Comic Business: Theatricality, Dramatic Technique, and Performance Contexts of Aristophanic Comedy*. Oxford University Press.

Ribbeck, Otto, ed. 1962. *Comicorum Romanorum praeter Plautum et Terentium Fragmenta*. Hildesheim: Georg Olms.

Rich, Adrienne. 1980. "Compulsory Heterosexuality and Lesbian Existence." *Signs* 5.4: 631–60.

Richlin, Amy, ed. 1992a. *Pornography and Representation in Greece and Rome*. New York, NY: Oxford University Press.

1992b[1983]. *The Garden of Priapus: Sexuality and Aggression in Roman Humor*. Rev. edn. Oxford University Press. (Originally New Haven, CT: Yale University Press.)

1993a. "The Ethnographer's Dilemma and the Dream of a Lost Golden Age." In *Feminist Theory and the Classics*, ed. Nancy Sorkin Rabinowitz and Amy Richlin: 272–303. New York, NY: Routledge.

1993b. "Not Before Homosexuality: The Materiality of the *Cinaedus* and the Roman Law Against Love between Men." *Journal of the History of Sexuality* 3.4: 523–73.

1997a. "Gender and Rhetoric: Producing Manhood in the Schools." In *Roman Eloquence: Rhetoric in Society and Literature*, ed. William J. Dominik: 90–110. London: Routledge.

1997b. "Towards a History of Body History." In *Inventing Ancient Culture: Historicism, Periodization, and the Ancient World*, eds Mark Golden and Peter Toohey: 16–35. London: Routledge.

1999. "Cicero's Head." In *Constructions of the Classical Body*, ed. James I. Porter: 190–211. Ann Arbor, MI: University of Michigan Press.

trans. 2005. *Rome and the Mysterious Orient: Three Plays by Plautus*. Berkeley, CA: University of California Press.

2011. "Talking to Slaves in the Plautine Audience." Seminar paper for "The Audience of Roman Comedy," American Philological Association meeting, San Antonio.

2013a. "Role-Playing in Roman Civilization and Roman Comedy Courses: How to Imagine a Complex Society." *CJ* 108.3: 347–61.

2013b. "Sexuality and History." In *The SAGE Handbook of Historical Theory*, ed. Nancy Partner and Sarah Foot: 294–310. London: SAGE Publications.

2014a. *Arguments with Silence: Writing the History of Roman Women*. Ann Arbor, MI: University of Michigan Press.

2014b. "Talking to Slaves in the Plautine Audience." *CA* 33.1: 174–226.

2015a. "Reading Boy-Love and Child-Love in the Greco-Roman World." In *Sex in Antiquity: Exploring Gender and Sexuality in the Ancient World*, eds Mark Masterson, Nancy Sorkin Rabinowitz, and James Robson: 352–73. London: Routledge.

2015b. "Slave-Woman Drag." In *Women in Roman Republican Drama*, eds Dorota Dutsch, Sharon L. James, and David Konstan: 37–67. Madison, WI: University of Wisconsin Press.

2016. "The Kings of Comedy." In *Roman Drama and its Contexts*, ed. Stavros Frangoulidis, Stephen J. Harrison, and Gesine Manuwald: 67–95. Trends in Classics – Supplementary Volumes 34. Berlin: Walter de Gruyter.

2017a. "The Ones Who Paid the Butcher's Bill: Soldiers and War Captives in Roman Comedy." In *Brill's Companion to Loss and Defeat in the Ancient World*, eds Jessica M. Clark and Brian Turner: 213–39. Leiden: Brill.

2017b. "The Traffic in Shtick." In *Rome, Empire of Plunder: The Dynamics of Cultural Appropriation*, eds Matthew P. Loar, Carolyn MacDonald, and Dan-el Padilla Peralta: 169–93. Cambridge University Press.

Forthcoming a. "Blackface and Drag in the *Palliata*." In *Complex Inferiorities: The Poetics of the Weaker Voice in Latin Literature*, eds Stephen J. Harrison and Sebastian Matzner. Oxford University Press.

Forthcoming b. "The Stage at the Fair: Trade and Human Trafficking in the *Palliata*." In *Travel and Geography in Latin Poetry*, eds Erika Damer and Micah Myers.

Riggsby, Andrew M. 1997. "'Public' and 'Private' in Roman Culture: The Case of the *Cubiculum*." *Journal of Roman Archaeology* 10: 36–56.

Ritschl, Friedrich, ed. 1852. *T. Macci Plauti* Mostellaria. *Plautus: Comoediae*, vol. 7. Bonn: H. B. Koenig.

Robinson, David M. 2006. *Closeted Writing and Lesbian and Gay Literature: Classical, Early Modern, Eighteenth-Century*. Aldershot: Ashgate.

Robinson, E. G. D. 2004. "Reception of Comic Theatre amongst the Indigenous South Italians." *Mediterranean Archaeology* 17: 193–214.

Robson, D. O. 1938. "The Nationality of the Poet Caecilius Statius." *AJPh* 59.3: 301–8.

Robson, James. 2013. *Sex and Sexuality in Classical Athens*. Edinburgh University Press.

Roller, Duane W. 2010. *Eratosthenes' Geography*. Princeton University Press.

Rose, Peter W. 2012. *Class in Archaic Greece*. Cambridge University Press.

Roselaar, Saskia T. 2012. "Mediterranean Trade as a Mechanism of Integration between Romans and Italians." In *Processes of Integration and Identity Formation in the Roman Republic*, eds S. T. Roselaar: 141–58. Leiden: Brill.

Roselli, David Kawalko. 2011. *Theater of the People: Spectators and Society in Ancient Athens*. Austin, TX: University of Texas Press.

Rosen, Ralph M., and Donald R. Marks. 1999. "Comedies of Transgression in Gangsta Rap and Ancient Classical Poetry." *New Literary History* 30.4: 897–928.

Rosenman, Ellen Bayuk. 1995. *A Room of One's Own: Women Writers and the Politics of Creativity*. New York, NY: Twayne.

Rosenstein, Nathan. 2004. *Rome at War: Farms, Families, and Death in the Middle Republic*. Chapel Hill, NC: University of North Carolina Press.

　　2006. "Aristocratic Values." In *A Companion to the Roman Republic*, eds Nathan Rosenstein and Robert Morstein-Marx: 365–82. Malden, MA: Blackwell.

　　2012. *Rome and the Mediterranean 290 to 146 BC: The Imperial Republic*. Edinburgh University Press.

Rosivach, Vincent J. 1998. *When a Young Man Falls in Love: The Sexual Exploitation of Women in New Comedy*. London: Routledge.

Roth, Roman. 2007a. *Styling Romanisation: Pottery and Society in Central Italy*. Cambridge University Press.

　　2007b. "Varro's *picta Italia* (*RR* I.ii.1) and the Odology of Roman Italy." *Hermes* 135.3: 286–300.

　　2013. "Before Sigillata: Black-Gloss Pottery and its Cultural Dimensions." In *A Companion to the Archaeology of the Roman Republic*, ed. Jane DeRose Evans: 81–96. Chichester: Wiley-Blackwell.

Rothwell, Kenneth S., Jr. 1995. "Aristophanes' *Wasps* and the Sociopolitics of Aesop's Fables." *CJ* 90.3: 233–54.

Russell, D. A. 1983. *Greek Declamation*. Cambridge University Press.

Rusten, Jeffrey, and I. C. Cunningham, eds. and trans. 2002. *Theophrastus Characters, Herodas Mimes, Sophron and Other Mime Fragments*. Cambridge, MA: Harvard University Press.

Saadoun, Haim. 2003. "Tunisia." In *The Jews of the Middle East and North Africa in Modern Times*, eds Reeva Spector Simon, Michael Menachem Laskier, and Sara Reguer: 444–57. New York, NY: Columbia University Press.

Ste. Croix, G. E. M. de. 1981. *The Class Struggle in the Ancient Greek World.* London: Duckworth.

Saller, Richard P. 1994. *Patriarchy, Property and Death in the Roman Family.* Cambridge University Press.

1998. "Symbols of Gender and Status Hierarchies in the Roman Household." In *Women and Slaves in Greco-Roman Culture: Differential Equations*, eds Sandra R. Joshel and Sheila Murnaghan: 85–91. London: Routledge.

Salmon, E. T. 1982. *The Making of Roman Italy.* London: Thames & Hudson.

Salway, Benet. 2004. "Sea and River Travel in the Roman Itinerary Literature." In *Space in the Roman World: Its Perception and Presentation*, eds Richard Talbert and Kai Brodersen: 43–96. Münster: Lit Verlag.

2012. "Putting the World in Order: Mapping in Roman Texts." In *Ancient Perspectives: Maps and Their Place in Mesopotamia, Egypt, Greece, and Rome*, ed. Richard J. A. Talbert: 193–234. University of Chicago Press.

Sandburg, Carl. 1927. *The American Songbag.* New York, NY: Harcourt, Brace & Co.

1936. *The People, Yes.* New York, NY: Harcourt, Brace.

Scafuro, Adele C. 1997. *The Forensic Stage: Settling Disputes in Graeco-Roman New Comedy.* Cambridge University Press.

2014. "Comedy in the Late Fourth and Early Third Centuries BCE." In *The Oxford Handbook of Greek and Roman Comedy*, eds Michael Fontaine and Adele C. Scafuro: 199–217. Oxford University Press.

Schechner, Richard. 2006. *Performance Studies: An Introduction.* 2nd edn. New York, NY: Routledge.

Scheidel, Walter. 2011. "The Roman Slave Supply." In *The Cambridge World History of Slavery*, vol. 1: *The Ancient Mediterranean World*, eds Keith Bradley and Paul Cartledge: 287–310. Cambridge University Press.

Scheidel, Walter. and Elijah Meeks. 2012. *ORBIS: The Stanford Geospatial Network Model of the Roman World.* orbis.stanford.edu.

Schmeling, Gareth. 1999. "The History of Apollonius King of Tyre." In *Latin Fiction: The Latin Novel in Context*, ed. Heinz Hofmann: 141–52. London: Routledge.

2011. *A Commentary on the Satyrica of Petronius.* Oxford University Press.

Schmidt, Karl. 1902a. "Die griechischen Personennamen bei Plautus I." *Hermes* 37: 173–211.

1902b. "Die griechischen Personennamen bei Plautus II." *Hermes* 37: 353–90.

1902c. "Die griechischen Personennamen bei Plautus III." *Hermes* 37: 608–26.

Schrecker, Ellen. 2013. "Moses Finley and the Academic Red Scare." In *Moses Finley and Politics*, ed. W. V. Harris: 61–78. Leiden: Brill.

Schultz, Celia E. 2007. "*Sanctissima Femina*: Social Categorization and Women's Religious Experience in the Roman Republic." In *Finding Persephone: Women's Rituals in the Ancient Mediterranean*, eds Maryline Parca and Angeliki Tzanetou: 92–113. Bloomington, IN: Indiana University Press.

2013. Review of Valentini 2012. *BMCR* 2013.12.39.

Schumacher, Leonhard. 2001. *Sklaverei in der Antike: Alltag und Schicksal der Unfreien*. Munich: Beck.

Schwarzmaier, Agnes. 2012. *Die Masken aus der Nekropole von Lipari, Palilia 21*. Wiesbaden: Ludwig Reichert.

Scott, James C. 1990. *Domination and the Arts of Resistance: Hidden Transcripts*. New Haven, CT: Yale University Press.

Sedgwick, Eve Kosofsky. 1992. *Between Men: English Literature and Male Homosocial Desire*. 2nd ed. New York, NY: Columbia University Press.

Segal, Erich. 1968. *Roman Laughter: The Comedy of Plautus*. Cambridge, MA: Harvard University Press.

Severy-Hoven, Beth. 2012. "Master Narratives and the Wall Painting of the House of the Vettii, Pompeii." *Gender and History* 24.3: 540–80.

Shabalala, Joseph, and Paul Simon. 1986. "Diamonds on the Soles of Her Shoes." *Graceland*. © Warner Bros. Records.

Shackleton Bailey, D. R., ed. and trans. 1965. *Cicero's Letters to Atticus*. Vol. 2. Cambridge University Press.

Sharrock, Alison. 2009. *Reading Roman Comedy: Poetics and Playfulness in Plautus and Terence*. Cambridge University Press.

2016. "Genre and Social Class, or Comedy and the Rhetoric of Self-aggrandisement and Self-deprecation." In *Roman Drama and its Contexts*, eds Stavros Frangoulidis, Stephen J. Harrison, and Gesine Manuwald: 97–126. Trends in Classics – Supplementary Volumes 34. Berlin: Walter de Gruyter.

Shaw, Brent D. 1998. "'A Wolf by the Ears': M. I. Finley's *Ancient Slavery and Modern Ideology* in Historical Context." In Finley 1998[1980]: 3–74. Princeton: Markus Wiener.

ed. and trans. 2001. *Spartacus and the Slave Wars: A Brief History with Documents*. Boston, MA: Bedford/St Martin's.

Shipp, G. B. 1953. "Greek in Plautus." *WS* 66: 105–12.

Slater, Niall W. 1985. *Plautus in Performance: The Theatre of the Mind*. Princeton University Press.

1990. "*Amphitruo, Bacchae*, and Metatheatre." *Lexis* 5/6: 101–25.

1992. "Plautine Negotiations: The *Poenulus* Prologue Unpacked." *YCS* 29: 131–46.

2001. "Appearance, Reality, and the Spectre of Incest in *Epidicus*." In *Studien zu Plautus' Epidicus*, ed. Ulrike Auhagen: 191–203. Tübingen: Gunter Narr.

2014. "Gods on High, Gods Down Low: Romanizing Epiphany." In *Plautine Trends: Studies in Plautine Comedy and its Reception*, eds Ioannis N. Perysinakis and Evangelis Karakasis: 105–26. Trends in Classics – Supplementary Volumes 29. Berlin: Walter de Gruyter.

Spaeth, Sigmund. 1926. *Read 'Em and Weep: The Songs You Forgot to Remember*. Garden City, NY: Doubleday, Page.

Spranger, Peter P. 1961. *Historische Untersuchungen zu den Sklavenfiguren des Plautus und Terenz*. Akademie der Wissenschaften und der Literatur,

Abhandlungen der Geistes- und Sozialwissenschaftlichen Klasse, Jahrgang 1960, nr. 8. Wiesbaden: Franz Steiner.

Stärk, Ekkehard. 1990. "Plautus' *uxores dotatae* im Spannungsfeld literarischer Fiktion und gesellschaftlicher Realität." In *Theater und Gesellschaft im Imperium Romanum*, ed. Jürgen Blänsdorf: 69–79. Tübingen: Francke.

    1995. "'*Durum equidem judicium*': Rettungen des Plautus vor Horaz." In *Plautus und die Tradition des Stegreifspiels: Festgabe für Eckard Lefèvre zum 60. Geburtstag*, eds Lore Benz, Ekkehard Stärk, and Gregor Vogt-Spira: 241–54. Tübingen: Gunter Narr.

Starks, John H., Jr. 2000. "*Nullus Me Est Hodie Poenus Poenior*: Balanced Ethnic Humor in Plautus' *Poenulus*." *Helios* 27.2: 163–86.

    2010. "*Servitus, sudor, sitis*: Syra and Syrian Slave Stereotyping in Plautus' *Mercator*." *NECJ* 37.1: 51–64.

Steinberg, David. 2008. "Takes One to Know One." *Los Angeles Times Magazine*, Nov. 30: 34, 36.

Stevenson, Jane. 2005. *Women Latin Poets: Language, Gender, and Authority from Antiquity to the Eighteenth Century*. Oxford University Press.

Stewart, D. Travis [Trav S.D.]. 2005. *No Applause – Just Throw Money, or, The Book That Made Vaudeville Famous: A High-Class, Refined Entertainment*. New York, NY: Faber & Faber.

Stewart, Roberta. 2012. *Plautus and Roman Slavery*. Chichester: Wiley-Blackwell.

Strong, Anise K. 2012. "Working Girls: Mother–Daughter Bonds among Ancient Prostitutes." In *Mothering and Motherhood in Ancient Greece and Rome*, eds Lauren Hackworth Petersen and Patricia Salzman-Mitchell: 121–40. Austin, TX: University of Texas Press.

Stuard, Susan Mosher. 1995. "Ancillary Evidence for the Decline of Medieval Slavery." *Past and Present* 149: 3–28.

Taaffe, Lauren K. 1993. *Aristophanes and Women*. London: Routledge.

Talbert, Richard. 2008. "Greek and Roman Mapping: Twenty-First Century Perspectives." In *Cartography in Antiquity and the Middle Ages: Fresh Perspectives, New Methods*, eds Richard J. A. Talbert and Richard W. Unger: 9–27. Leiden: Brill.

Tatum, James. 1995. "Aunt Elvie's Quilt on the Bed of Odysseus: The Role of Artifacts in Natural Memory." *Helios* 22.2: 167–77.

Taylor, Lily Ross. 1937. "The Opportunities for Dramatic Performances in the Time of Plautus and Terence." *TAPA* 68: 284–304.

    2013[1960]. *The Voting Districts of the Roman Republic*. PMAAR 34. 2nd edn., with material by Jerzy Linderski. Ann Arbor, MI: University of Michigan Press.

Telò, Mario. 2016. "Basket Case: Material Girl and Animate Object in Plautus's *Cistellaria*." In *Roman Drama and Its Contexts*, eds Stavros Frangoulidis, Stephen J. Harrison, and Gesine Manuwald: 299–316. Trends in Classics – Supplementary Volumes 34. Berlin: Walter de Gruyter.

Terrenato, Nicola. 1998. "The Romanization of Italy: Global Acculturation or Cultural *Bricolage*?" In *TRAC 97: Proceedings of the Seventh Annual Theoretical*

Roman Archaeology Conference, eds Colin Forcey, John Hawthorne, and Robert Witcher: 20–7. Oxford: Oxbow Books.

Thalmann, William G. 1996. "Versions of Slavery in the *Captivi* of Plautus." *Ramus* 25: 112–45.

Thompson, Dorothy J. 2011. "Slavery in the Hellenistic World." In *The Cambridge World History of Slavery*, vol. 1: *The Ancient Mediterranean World*, eds Keith Bradley and Paul Cartledge: 194–213. Cambridge University Press.

Thompson, E. P. 1966. *The Making of the English Working Class*. New York, NY: Vintage.

1992. "Rough Music Reconsidered." *Folklore* 103.1: 3–26.

Thompson, F. Hugh. 1993. "Iron Age and Roman Slave-Shackles." *Archaeological Journal* 150.1: 57–168.

2003. *The Archaeology of Greek and Roman Slavery*. London: Duckworth.

Thornton, Bonnell, trans. 1769. *Comedies of Plautus, Translated into Familiar Blank Verse*, vols. 1–2. 2nd edn. London: T. Becket and P. A. de Hondt.

Tompkins, Daniel P. 2014. "No Poetry from the Past: The Archaeology of Moses Finley's *Ancestral Constitution*." *AJPh* 135.2: 205–19.

Tordoff, Rob. 2013. "Introduction: Slaves and Slavery in Ancient Greek Comedy." In *Slaves and Slavery in Ancient Greek Comic Drama*, eds Ben Akrigg and Rob Tordoff: 1–62. Cambridge University Press.

Toynbee, J. M. C. 1971. *Death and Burial in the Roman World*. Ithaca, NY: Cornell University Press.

Trager, Oliver. 2002. *Dig Infinity! The Life and Art of Lord Buckley*. New York, NY: Welcome Rain Publishers.

Treggiari, Susan. 1969. *Roman Freedmen during the Late Republic*. Oxford: Clarendon Press.

1981. "*Contubernales* in *CIL* 6." *Phoenix* 35.1: 42–69.

1993. *Roman Marriage: Iusti Coniuges from the Time of Cicero to the Time of Ulpian*. Oxford: Clarendon Press.

Trinh, T. Minh-ha. 1989. *Woman, Native, Other: Writing Postcoloniality and Feminism*. Bloomington, IN: Indiana University Press.

Tritle, Lawrence A. 2014. "'Ravished Minds' in the Ancient World." In *Combat Trauma and the Ancient Greeks*, ed. Peter Meineck and David Konstan: 87–103. New York, NY: Palgrave Macmillan.

Tucci, Pier Luigi. 2011/12. "The Pons Sublicius: A Reinvestigation." *MAAR* 56/57: 177–212.

Turner, Graeme. 1996. *British Cultural Studies: An Introduction*. 2nd edn. London: Routledge.

Tylawsky, Elizabeth Ivory. 2002. *Saturio's Inheritance: The Greek Ancestry of the Roman Comic Parasite*. New York, NY: Peter Lang.

Untermeyer, Louis, ed. 1946. *A Treasury of Laughter*. New York, NY: Simon & Schuster.

Usener, H. 1901. "Italische Volksjustiz." *RhM* 56: 1–28.

Valentini, Alessandra. 2012. *Matronae tra novitas e mos maiorum: Spazi e modalità dell'azione pubblica femminile nella Roma medio repubblicana. Memorie*.

Classe di scienze morali, lettere ed arti, 138. Venice: Istituto Veneto di Scienze, Lettere, ed Arti.

Várhelyi, Zsuzsanna. 2007. "The Specters of Roman Imperialism: The Live Burials of Gauls and Greeks at Rome." *CA* 26.2: 277–304.

Vélissaropoulos-Karakostas, Julie. 2002. "Merchants, Prostitutes and the 'New Poor': Forms of Contract and Social Status." Trans. Lin Foxhall and Paul Cartledge. In *Money, Labour and Land: Approaches to the Economies of Ancient Greece*, eds Paul Cartledge, Edward E. Cohen, and Lin Foxhall: 130–9. London: Routledge.

Vester, Christina. 2013. "Tokens of Identity in Menander's *Epitrepontes*: Slaves, Citizens and In-Betweens." In *Slaves and Slavery in Ancient Greek Comic Drama*, eds Ben Akrigg and Rob Tordoff: 209–27. Cambridge University Press.

Viereck, P., and A. G. Roos, eds. 1962–. *Appianus: Historia Romana*. Leipzig: Teubner.

Vine, Brent. 1993. *Studies in Archaic Latin Inscriptions*. Innsbrucker Beiträge zur Sprachwissenschaft 75. Innsbruck: Institut für Sprachwissenschaft der Universität Innsbruck.

Vlassopoulos, Kostas. 2007. "Free Spaces: Identity, Experience and Democracy in Classical Athens." *CQ* 57.1: 33–52.

2010. "Athenian Slave Names and Athenian Social History." *ZPE* 175: 113–44.

2011. "Greek Slavery: From Domination to Property and Back Again." *JHS* 131: 115–30.

2016. "Finley's Slavery." In *M. I. Finley: An Ancient Historian and His Impact*, eds Daniel Jew, Robin Osborne, and Michael Scott: 76–99. Cambridge University Press.

Vogt, Joseph. 1975. *Ancient Slavery and the Ideal of Man*, trans. Thomas Wiedemann. Cambridge, MA: Harvard University Press.

Vogt-Spira, Gregor. 2001. "Traditions of Theatrical Improvisation in Plautus: Some Considerations." Trans. Leofranc Holford-Strevens. In *Oxford Readings in Menander, Plautus, and Terence*, ed. Erich Segal: 95–106. Oxford University Press.

Volkmann, Hans. 1990. *Die Massenversklavungen der Einwohner eroberter Städte in der hellenistisch-römischen Zeit*. 2nd ed. Stuttgart: Franz Steiner.

Wachter, Rudolf. 1987. *Altlateinische Inschriften: Sprachliche und epigraphische Untersuchungen zu den Dokumenten bis etwa 150 v. Chr.* Bern: Peter Lang.

Walbank, F. W. 1957. *A Historical Commentary on Polybius*. Vol. 1. Oxford: Clarendon Press.

1981. *The Hellenistic World*. Cambridge, MA: Harvard University Press.

Wald, Elijah. 2012. *The Dozens: A History of Rap's Mama*. Oxford University Press.

Wallace-Hadrill, Andrew. 2008. *Rome's Cultural Revolution*. Cambridge University Press.

Wallochny, Beatrix. 1992. *Streitszenen in der griechischen und römischen Komödie*. Tübingen: Gunter Narr.

Walters, Jonathan. 1997. "Invading the Roman Body: Manliness and Impenetrability in Roman Thought." In *Roman Sexualities*, eds Judith P. Hallett and Marilyn B. Skinner: 29–43. Princeton University Press.

Warmington, E. H., ed. and trans. 1938. *Remains of Old Latin*. Vol. 3. Cambridge, MA: Harvard University Press.

ed. and trans. 1940. *Remains of Old Latin*. Vol. 4. Cambridge, MA: Harvard University Press.

Warner, Richard, trans. 1772. *Comedies of Plautus, Translated into Familiar Blank Verse*. Vol. 3. London: T. Becket and P. A. de Hondt. [Continuation of the Bonnell Thornton translation.]

Watling, E. F., trans. 1964. *Plautus: The Rope and Other Plays*. Harmondsworth: Penguin.

trans. 1965. *Plautus: The Pot of Gold and Other Plays*. Harmondsworth: Penguin.

Watson, Alan. 1971. *Roman Private Law around 200 BC*. Edinburgh University Press.

1975. *Rome of the XII Tables: Persons and Property*. Princeton University Press.

Webster, T. B. L. 1949. "The Masks of Greek Comedy." *Bulletin of the John Rylands Library* 32.1: 97–133.

1995. *Monuments Illustrating New Comedy*. 3rd edn. rev. and enlarged by J. R. Green and A. Seeberg. 2 vols. *BICS* Supplement 50. London: Institute for Classical Studies.

Weinstock, Stefan. 1957. "Victor and Invictus." *Harvard Theological Review* 50.3: 211–47.

Weiss, Michael. 2002. "Observations on the South Picene Inscription TE1 (S. Omero)." In *Indo-European Perspectives*, ed. Mark R. V. Southern: 351–66. Journal of Indo-European Studies Monograph Series 43. Washington, DC: Institute for the Study of Man.

Welch, Katherine. 2003. "A New View of the Origins of the Basilica: The Atrium Regium, Graecostasis, and Roman Diplomacy." *Journal of Roman Archaeology* 16: 5–34.

Wellesley, K. 1955. "The Production Date of Plautus' *Captivi*." *AJPh* 76.3: 298–305.

Welsh, Jarrett T. 2010. "Quintilian's Judgement of Afranius." *CQ* 60.1: 118–26.

Welwei, Karl-Wilhelm. 1974. *Unfreie im antiken Kriegsdienst*. Vol. 1. Forschungen zur Antiken Sklaverei 5. Wiesbaden: Franz Steiner.

1988. *Unfreie im antiken Kriegsdienst*. Vol. 3. Forschungen zur Antiken Sklaverei 21. Stuttgart: Franz Steiner.

2000. *Sub Corona Vendere: Quellenkritische Studien zu Kriegsgefangenschaft und Sklaverei in Rom bis zum Ende des Hannibalkrieges*. Forschungen zur Antiken Sklaverei 34. Stuttgart: Franz Steiner.

Weschler, Lawrence. 1998. *A Miracle, a Universe: Settling Accounts with Torturers*. University of Chicago Press.

West, M. L. 2011. *The Making of the Iliad: Disquisition and Analytical Commentary*. Oxford: Oxford University Press.

Westermann, William L. 1955. *The Slave Systems of Greek and Roman Antiquity*. Philadelphia: American Philosophical Society.

White, Horace, ed. and trans. 1912. *Appian's Roman History*. Vol. 1. London: Heinemann.

Whittaker, C. R. 2004. "Mental Maps and Frontiers: Seeing Like a Roman." In *Rome and its Frontiers: The Dynamics of Empire*, 63–87. Abingdon: Routledge.

Wiles, David. 1991. *The Masks of Menander: Sign and Meaning in Greek and Roman Performance*. Cambridge University Press.

Wilkins, John. 2000. *The Boastful Chef: The Discourse of Food in Ancient Greek Comedy*. Oxford University Press.

Williams, Craig A. 2010. *Roman Homosexuality*. 2nd edn. Oxford University Press.

2012. *Reading Roman Friendship*. Cambridge University Press.

Williams, Gordon. 1958. "Some Aspects of Roman Marriage Ceremonies and Ideals." *JRS* 48: 16–29.

1982. "Phases in Political Patronage of Literature in Rome." In *Literary and Artistic Patronage in Ancient Rome*, ed. Barbara K. Gold: 3–27. Austin, TX: University of Texas Press.

1995. "*Libertino Patre Natus:* True or False?" In *Homage to Horace: A Bimillenary Celebration*, ed. S. J. Harrison: 296–313. Oxford: Clarendon Press.

Williamson, George S. 2004. *The Longing for Myth in Germany: Religion and Aesthetic Culture from Romanticism to Nietzsche*. University of Chicago Press.

Willis, Paul E. 1981. *Learning to Labor: How Working Class Kids Get Working Class Jobs*. New York, NY: Columbia University Press.

Wilson, Peter. 2000. *The Athenian Institution of the Khoregia: The Chorus, the City and the Stage*. Cambridge University Press.

Winkler, John J. 1985. *Auctor & Actor: A Narratological Reading of Apuleius's Golden Ass*. Berkeley, CA: University of California Press.

Wiseman, T. P. 1998. *Roman Drama and Roman History*. University of Exeter Press.

2014. "Popular Memory." In *Memoria Romana: Memory in Rome and Rome in Memory*, ed. Karl Galinsky: 43–62. Ann Arbor, MI: University of Michigan Press.

2015. *The Roman Audience: Classical Literature as Social History*. Oxford University Press.

Wittig, Monique. 1969. *Les Guérillères*. Paris: Les Éditions de Minuit.

Witzke, Serena S. 2015. "Harlots, Tarts, and Hussies? A Problem of Terminology for Sex Labor in Roman Comedy." *Helios* 42.1: 7–27.

Wodehouse, P. G. 2000 [1928]. "The Ordeal of Osbert Mulliner." In *The Most of P. G. Wodehouse*: 193–210. New York, NY: Simon & Schuster.

Woolf, Virginia. 1929. *A Room of One's Own*. New York, NY: Harcourt, Brace & Co.

1992. *Women and Fiction: The Manuscript Versions of A Room of One's Own*. Transcribed and ed. S. P. Rosenbaum. Oxford: Blackwell.

Woytek, Erich, ed. and comm. 1982. *T. Maccius Plautus: Persa*. Österreichische Akademie der Wissenschaften, Philosophisch-Historische Klasse, Sitzungsberichte 385. Vienna: Verlag der Österreichischen Akademie der Wissenschaften.

Wrenhaven, Kelly. 2013. "A Comedy of Errors: The Comic Slave in Greek Art." In *Slaves and Slavery in Ancient Greek Comic Drama*, eds Ben Akrigg and Rob Tordoff: 124–43. Cambridge University Press.

Wright, John. 1974. *Dancing in Chains: The Stylistic Unity of the Comoedia Palliata*. PMAAR 25. Rome: American Academy in Rome.

——— 1975. "The Transformations of Pseudolus." *TAPA* 105: 403–16.

Yarrow, Liv Mariah. 2006. *Historiography at the End of the Republic: Provincial Perspectives on Roman Rule*. Oxford University Press.

Zeitlin, Froma I. 1985. "Playing the Other: Theater, Theatricality, and the Feminine in Greek Drama." *Representations* 11: 63–94.

Zelnick-Abramovitz, R. 2005. *Not Wholly Free: The Concept of Manumission and the Status of Manumitted Slaves in the Ancient Greek World*. Leiden: Brill.

Zhang, Benzi. 2011. "The Cultural Politics of Gender Performance: An Inquiry into Fe/male Impersonation." *Cultural Studies* 25.3: 294–312.

Zweig, Bella. 1992. "The Mute Nude Female Characters in Aristophanes' Plays." In *Pornography and Representation in Greece and Rome*, ed. Amy Richlin: 73–89. Oxford University Press.

General Index

abolition, 2, 54, 473, 476–77
acting, as slavery, 393
actors
  and drag, 112
  and experience of rape, 402
  and *infamia*, 16, 281n. 30
  and military service, 17n. 31, 142
  as agents, 24, 47, 160, 345
  as folk heroes, 225
  as outsiders, 139, 142, 149, 378
  beaten, 103, 146
  circulation of, 20, 162n. 34, 357
  class of, 20, 146, 185
  commodified, 55
  critique audience, 49, 124, 145, 316
  ethnicity of, 3, 376
  gender of, 14, 252, 309
  grex (troupe), 3, 3n. 3, 4n. 5, 41, 48, 54, 124,
    220, 367, 422
  mute, as eye candy, 288
  not at funerals, 73n. 3
  sexual ambiguity of, 281
  sisters of, 306
  skill set, 11, 56, 139, 157–58, 160, 287, 289
  speak from experience, 124, 140, 160
  status of, 3, 13, 16, 56, 71, 97, 103, 137, 140,
    146, 236, 323, 356, 407
  T. Publilius Pellio, 13, 224
  tekhnitai, 5n. 6, 11, 384n. 55
  used for sex, 4, 56, 104, 109, 119, 282, 287
Aesop
  and muteness, 338
  and Phaedrus, 339n. 34
  in the market, 263, 302
Afranius, pederastic themes in, 112, 301n. 58
Alcumena, comic or tragic?, 289n. 45
Aldrete, Gregory, 150n. 21
anger, 4, 26, 42, 45–46, 57, 66, 124, 194, 214,
    278, 290, 307, 318, 374, 391, 444,
    477, 479

Antiphanes
  and Plautus, 11
  on comedy vs. tragedy, 138n. 1
  tall tale in, 454n. 54
Ardener, Edward and Shirley, 313
Aristophanes
  and fables, 339n. 34
  parabases, 144
  verbal dueling in, 162n. 34
army, Roman
  and class, 37, 103, 142
  and debt, 186n. 61
  and spoils, 414n. 84
  critique of, 43, 223, 341
  gear, 449
  punishment in, 103, 129n. 69
  recruitment, 145n. 13, 182n. 57
  slaves in, 142n. 9, 370n. 25
Arnott, W. G., 46
auctions
  and bankruptcy, 134, 189
  slave, 114, 135, 372, 472
audience
  "narrative" and "authorial", 287
  after the show, 221
  and class, 213
  and debt, 184, 197
  and empathy with slaves, 26, 39, 49, 71, 86,
    91, 105, 110–11, 119, 137, 140, 144, 203,
    207, 212, 214, 223, 229–30, 232, 260n. 15,
    260–61, 264–65, 321, 340, 391, 445
  and experience of rape, 403
  and experience of war, 27, 39, 125, 137, 141n.
    7, 145, 148
  and sense of geography, 367, 384–85
  as participants in performance, 3, 47, 49n.
    78, 70, 155, 164, 172, 174, 181, 356, 387,
    390, 397
  claques in, 145
  ethnicity of, 374

Index Locorum

Index Verborum

Made in the USA
Coppell, TX
20 January 2023

11402317R00321